# Spring Boot Persistence Best Practices

## Optimize Java Persistence Performance in Spring Boot Applications

Anghel Leonard

Apress®

*Spring Boot Persistence Best Practices: Optimize Java Persistence Performance in Spring Boot Applications*

Anghel Leonard
Banesti, Romania

ISBN-13 (pbk): 978-1-4842-5625-1
https://doi.org/10.1007/978-1-4842-5626-8

ISBN-13 (electronic): 978-1-4842-5626-8

Managing Director, Apress Media LLC: Welmoed Spahr
Acquisitions Editor: Steve Anglin
Development Editor: Matthew Moodie
Coordinating Editor: Mark Powers

Cover designed by eStudioCalamar

Cover image designed by Freepik (www.freepik.com)

Distributed to the book trade worldwide by Apress Media, LLC, 1 New York Plaza, New York, NY 10004, U.S.A. Phone 1-800-SPRINGER, fax (201) 348-4505, e-mail orders-ny@springer-sbm.com, or visit www.springeronline.com. Apress Media, LLC is a California LLC and the sole member (owner) is Springer Science + Business Media Finance Inc (SSBM Finance Inc). SSBM Finance Inc is a **Delaware** corporation.

For information on translations, please e-mail editorial@apress.com; for reprint, paperback, or audio rights, please email bookpermissions@springernature.com.

Apress titles may be purchased in bulk for academic, corporate, or promotional use. eBook versions and licenses are also available for most titles. For more information, reference our Print and eBook Bulk Sales web page at http://www.apress.com/bulk-sales.

Any source code or other supplementary material referenced by the author in this book is available to readers on GitHub via the book's product page, located at www.apress.com/9781484256251. For more detailed information, please visit http://www.apress.com/source-code.

Printed on acid-free paper

*This book is dedicated to my dear wife, Octavia.*

# Table of Contents

# About the Author

 **Anghel Leonard** is a Chief Technology Strategist and independent consultant with 20+ years of experience in the Java ecosystem. In his daily work, he focuses on architecting and developing Java distributed applications that empower robust architectures, clean code, and high-performance. Anghel is also passionate about coaching, mentoring, and technical leadership. He is the author of several books, videos, and dozens of articles related to Java technologies.

# About the Technical Reviewer

**Manuel Jordan Elera** is an autodidactic developer and researcher who enjoys learning new technologies for his own experiments and creating new integrations. Manuel won the Springy Award – Community Champion and Spring Champion 2013. In his little free time, he reads the Bible and composes music on his guitar. Manuel is known as dr_pompeii. He has tech reviewed numerous books for Apress, including *Pro Spring Boot 2* (2019), *Rapid Java Persistence and Microservices* (2019), *Java Language Features* (2018), *Spring Boot 2 Recipes* (2018), and *Java APIs, Extensions and Libraries* (2018). Read his 13 detailed tutorials about many Spring technologies, contact him through his blog at `http://www.manueljordanelera.blogspot.com`, and follow him on his Twitter account, `@dr_pompeii`.

# Introduction

In a nutshell, this book is a collection of best practices for Java persistence performance in Spring Boot applications. These practices have been exposed via 120+ items, and they can be grouped into three categories:

- First, we discuss the best practices for defining entities, mapping relationships, writing queries, fetching data, choosing identifiers generators, and so on. Mainly, we cover the areas where Spring Boot cannot help you with built-in artifacts and where you can avoid important performance penalties that are hard to fix and may require significant changes in your domain model.

- Second, we address best practices for using Spring Boot support (more precisely, Spring Data). As you will see, relying on built-in support as a silver bullet can come with performance penalties. For example, using the Open Session in View, offset pagination, post-commits hooks, or misunderstanding `@Transactional` are just a few of the covered topics. I'm pretty sure that you are ready and impatient to jump into this category of items.

- Third, we deep dive into several Hibernate goodies that can sustain the performance of your applications. By default, Spring Data relies on Hibernate as its persistence provider, therefore you can exploit Hibernate via Spring Data, and you can exploit underlying Hibernate goodies as well. Goodies such as populating a child-side parent association via a Hibernate proxy, using Dirty Tracking, delaying connection acquisition, lazy loading attributes, and using natural keys are just a few of the covered items.

The prerequisites of this book are pretty intuitive. You'll need an IDE (e.g., NetBeans, Eclipse, IntelliJ IDEA, Visual Studio, etc.), MySQL, and PostgreSQL. Optionally, you may install or use other database vendors as well (e.g., Oracle, SQL Server, etc.).

As you will see, I prefer to add @Repository annotation at repository interface level. Is well-known that @Repository is useful for translating the unchecked SQL specific exception to Spring exceptions. This way, we have to handle only DataAccessException (and its subclasses).

Nevertheless, this is a valid statement in general when we use Spring, but Spring Data repositories are already backed by a Spring proxy. In other words, using @Repository doesn't make any difference. I prefer to use it for avoiding any confusions and simpy highlight the repository interfaces, but if you consider this too verbose or just noise then feel free to remove it.

In an overwhelming percentage the examples used in this book uses Hibernate JPA. In other words, we boostrap Hibernate as the JPA provider which is the most common use case in Spring Boot applications that uses Spring Data JPA. If your Sping Boot (Spring) application boostraps Hibernate nativelly (e.g., via SessionFactoryBuilder, BootstrapServiceRegistryBuilder, SessionRegistry, Configuration, HibernateTransactionManager, etc.) then, depending on the case/scenario, you may notice different behaviors.

In this book, when you encounter "*Hibernate-specific*" or "*Hibernate ORM*" then I refer to something that doesn't exist in JPA (exist only in Hibernate) and it might not be that obvious in the corresponding context.

For brevity's sake and in order to avoid cluttering the climax of topics you will see several shortcomings in code that should be avoided in production as follows:

- hard-coded identifiers (primary keys) or other data that is a good candidate for being arguments of metods

- usage of `orElseThrow()` for unwrapping `Optional` objects (I prefer this approach because it quicky signals if is something wrong with finding/loading the requested data)

- maybe something else that I forgot to mention here

# Main performance penalties

Use eager fetching

- Items: 1-5, 7, 8, 9, 23, 24

Don't prevent/fix N+1 issues

- Items: 6-9, 23, 24, 39-41, 43, 56, 66, 67, 81, 108

Fetch more data than needed

- Items: 10, 12, 21, 23-38, 42, 43, 45, 56, 57, 97, 98, 105, 128

Update/deletes huge lists of elements one-by-one

- Items: 6, 51-53, 59, 109, 126, 129

Use entities for read-only operations

- Items: 16, 22, 25-38, 42, 43, 56, 57, 95, 96

Implement low-performing batching

- Items: 46-55

Implement low-performing associations

- Items: 1-5, 11, 12, 14, 75, 76, 80

Use Open Session in View

- Items: 23, 110

Use low-performing identifiers

- Items: 55, 65-76

Use low-performing pagination

- Items: 44, 94-102

INTRODUCTION

Avoid using @Transactional for read-only queries

- Items: 61, 64

Don't use @Transactional in an optimal way

- Items: 61-64

Don't delay connection acquisition

- Items: 60, 64

Don't use the most efficient queries (avoid window functions, CTE and native queries)

- Items: 10, 28-30, 34, 39, 41-45, 56, 59, 103, 105, 107, 108, 119-129

Don't use *smart* entities

- Items: 13, 15-17, 19

Don't exploit Hibernate goodies

- Items: 10, 16, 18, 23, 35, 36, 37, 48, 60, 66, 67, 69-71, 77-80, 89-91, 103, 109, 111, 115, 124, 126, 132, 143-147

Use low-performing events and callbacks

- Items: 20, 104, 106

Don't monitor and audit

- Items: 81-85, 88-91

Don't exploit database capabilities

- Items: 112, 114, 116-120, 130

Perform faulty or low-performing settings

- Items: 86, 87, 92, 93

Avoid optimistic locking

- Items: 131-137

Use low-performing inheritance

- Items: 138-142

Lack of skills in fundamental JPA, SQL, flush, transactions, indexes, Second Level Cache

- Appendices: A-K

# CHAPTER 1

# Associations

## Item 1: How to Effectively Shape the @OneToMany Association

The bidirectional @OneToMany association is probably the most encountered association in our Domain Model. Based on this statement, this book takes advantage of this association in a significant number of examples.

*For a supersonic guide to association efficiency, check out* **Appendix B**.

Consider two entities, Author and Book, involved in a bidirectional lazy @OneToMany association. In Figure 1-1, you can see the corresponding @OneToMany table relationship.

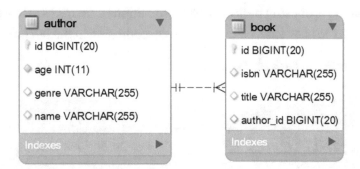

***Figure 1-1.*** *The @OneToMany table relationship*

So, the author table has a @OneToMany relationship with the book table. An author row can be referenced by multiple book rows. The author_id column maps this relationship via a foreign key that references the primary key of the author table. A book cannot exist without an author, therefore, the author is the parent-side (@OneToMany) while the book is the child-side (@ManyToOne). The @ManyToOne association is responsible for synchronizing the foreign key column with the Persistence Context (the First Level Cache).

© Anghel Leonard 2020
A. Leonard, *Spring Boot Persistence Best Practices*, https://doi.org/10.1007/978-1-4842-5626-8_1

For a super-fast, but meaningful, guide to JPA fundamentals, see **Appendix A**.

> As a rule of thumb, use bidirectional @OneToMany associations instead of unidirectional ones. As you will see soon, **Item 2** tackles the performance penalties of unidirectional @OneToMany and explains why it should be avoided.

The best way to code a bidirectional @OneToMany association is discussed in the following sections.

## Always Cascade from Parent-Side to Child-Side

Cascading from child-side to parent-side is a code smell and bad practice and it is a clear signal that it is time to review your Domain Model and application design. Think how improper or illogical it is for a child to cascade the creation of its parent! On one hand, a child cannot exist without a parent, while on the other hand, the child cascades the creation of his parent. This is not logical, right? So, as a rule of thumb, always cascade from parent-side to child-side, as in the following example (this is one of the most important advantages of using bidirectional associations). In this case, we cascade from the Author side to the Book side, so we add the cascade type in the Author entity:

@OneToMany(**cascade = CascadeType.ALL**)

> In this context, never use CascadeType.* on @ManyToOne since entity state transitions should be propagated from parent-side entities to child-side ones.

## Don't Forget to Set mappedBy on the Parent-Side

The mappedBy attribute characterizes a bidirectional association and must be set on the parent-side. In other words, for a bidirectional @OneToMany association, set mappedBy to @OneToMany on the parent-side and add @ManyToOne on the child-side referenced by mappedBy. Via mappedBy, the bidirectional @OneToMany association signals that it mirrors the @ManyToOne child-side mapping. In this case, we add in Author entity to the following:

```
@OneToMany(cascade = CascadeType.ALL,
            mappedBy = "author")
```

## Set orphanRemoval on the Parent-Side

Setting orphanRemoval on the parent-side guarantees the removal of children without references. In other words, orphanRemoval is good for cleaning up dependent objects that should not exist without a reference from an owner object. In this case, we add orphanRemoval to the Author entity:

```
@OneToMany(cascade = CascadeType.ALL,
            mappedBy = "author",
            orphanRemoval = true)
```

## Keep Both Sides of the Association in Sync

You can easily keep both sides of the association in sync via helper methods added to the parent-side. Commonly, the addChild(), removeChild(), and removeChildren() methods will do the job pretty well. While this may represent the "survival kit," more helper methods can be added as well. Just identify the operations that are used and involve synchronization and extract them as helper methods. If you don't strive to keep both sides of the association in sync, then the entity state transitions may lead to unexpected behaviors. In this case, we add the Author entity to the following helpers:

```
public void addBook(Book book) {
    this.books.add(book);
    book.setAuthor(this);
}

public void removeBook(Book book) {
    book.setAuthor(null);
    this.books.remove(book);
}
```

```java
public void removeBooks() {
    Iterator<Book> iterator = this.books.iterator();

    while (iterator.hasNext()) {
        Book book = iterator.next();

        book.setAuthor(null);
        iterator.remove();
    }
}
```

# Override equals() and hashCode()

By properly overriding equals() and hashCode() methods, the application obtains the same results across all entity state transitions (this aspect is dissected in **Item 68**). For @OneToMany associations, these methods should be overridden on the child-side. In this case, we use the auto-generated database identifier to override these two methods. Overriding equals() and hashCode() based on auto-generated database identifier is a special case that is detailed in **Item 68**. The most important aspect to keep in mind is that, for auto-generated database identifiers, the equals() method should perform a null check of the identifier before performing the equality check, and the hashCode() method should return a constant value. Since the Book entity is on the child-side, we highlight these two aspects as follows:

```java
@Override
public boolean equals(Object obj) {
    ...
    return id != null && id.equals(((Book) obj).id);
}

@Override
public int hashCode() {
    return 2021;
}
```

# Use Lazy Fetching on Both Sides of the Association

By default, fetching a parent-side entity will not fetch the children entities. This means that @OneToMany is set to lazy. On the other hand, fetching a child entity will eagerly fetch its parent-side entity by default. It is advisable to explicitly set @ManyToOne to lazy and rely on eager fetching only on a query-basis. Further details are available in **Chapter** 3. In this case, the Book entity explicitly maps the @ManyToOne as LAZY:

```
@ManyToOne(fetch = FetchType.LAZY)
```

# Pay Attention to How toString() Is Overridden

If toString() needs to be overridden, then be sure to involve only the basic attributes fetched when the entity is loaded from the database. Involving lazy attributes or associations will trigger separate SQL statements that fetch the corresponding data or throw LazyInitializationException. For example, if we implement the toString() method for Author entity then we don't mention the books collection, we mention only the basic attributes (id, name, age and genre):

```java
@Override
public String toString() {
    return "Author{" + "id=" + id + ", name=" + name
        + ", genre=" + genre + ", age=" + age + '}';
}
```

# Use @JoinColumn to Specify the Join Column Name

The join column defined by the owner entity (Book) stores the ID value and has a foreign key to the Author entity. It is advisable to specify the desired name for this column. This way, you avoid potential confusions/mistakes when referring to it (e.g., in native queries). In this case, we add @JoinColumn to the Book entity as follows:

```
@JoinColumn(name = "author_id")
```

# Author and Book Samples

Gluing these previous instructions together and expressing them in code will result in the following Author and Book samples:

```java
@Entity
public class Author implements Serializable {

    private static final long serialVersionUID = 1L;

    @Id
    @GeneratedValue(strategy = GenerationType.IDENTITY)
    private Long id;

    private String name;
    private String genre;
    private int age;

    @OneToMany(cascade = CascadeType.ALL,
            mappedBy = "author", orphanRemoval = true)
    private List<Book> books = new ArrayList<>();

    public void addBook(Book book) {
        this.books.add(book);
        book.setAuthor(this);
    }

    public void removeBook(Book book) {
        book.setAuthor(null);
        this.books.remove(book);
    }

    public void removeBooks() {
        Iterator<Book> iterator = this.books.iterator();
        while (iterator.hasNext()) {
            Book book = iterator.next();
            book.setAuthor(null);
            iterator.remove();
        }
    }
```

```java
    // getters and setters omitted for brevity

    @Override
    public String toString() {
        return "Author{" + "id=" + id + ", name=" + name
                        + ", genre=" + genre + ", age=" + age + '}';
    }
}

@Entity
public class Book implements Serializable {

    private static final long serialVersionUID = 1L;

    @Id
    @GeneratedValue(strategy = GenerationType.IDENTITY)
    private Long id;

    private String title;
    private String isbn;

    @ManyToOne(fetch = FetchType.LAZY)
    @JoinColumn(name = "author_id")
    private Author author;

    // getters and setters omitted for brevity

    @Override
    public boolean equals(Object obj) {

        if(obj == null) {
            return false;
        }

        if (this == obj) {
            return true;
        }

        if (getClass() != obj.getClass()) {
            return false;
        }
```

```
        return id != null && id.equals(((Book) obj).id);
    }

    @Override
    public int hashCode() {
        return 2021;
    }

    @Override
     public String toString() {
        return "Book{" + "id=" + id + ", title=" + title
                               + ", isbn=" + isbn + '}';
    }
}
```

The source code is available on GitHub[1].

> Pay attention to remove entities operations, especially child entities operations. While `CascadeType.REMOVE` and `orphanRemoval=true` will do their jobs, they may produce too many SQL statements. Relying on *bulk* operations is typically the best way to delete a significant amount of entities. To delete in batches, consider **Item 52** and **Item 53**, while to see the best practices for deleting child entities, consider **Item 6**.

# Item 2: Why You Should Avoid the Unidirectional @OneToMany Association

Consider the Author and Book entities involved in a bidirectional lazy @OneToMany association (an author has written several books and each book has a single author). Trying to insert a child entity, a Book, will result in one SQL INSERT statement triggered against the book table (one child-row will be added). Trying to delete a child entity will result in one SQL DELETE statement triggered against the book table (one child-row is deleted).

---

[1]HibernateSpringBootOneToManyBidirectional

Now, let's assume that the same `Author` and `Book` entities are involved in a unidirectional `@OneToMany` association mapped, as follows:

```
@OneToMany(cascade = CascadeType.ALL, orphanRemoval = true)
private List<Book> books = new ArrayList<>();
```

The missing `@ManyToOne` association leads to a separate junction table (`author_books`) meant to manage the parent-child association, as shown in Figure 1-2.

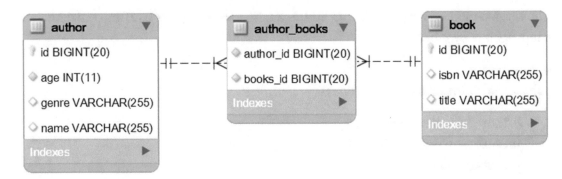

***Figure 1-2.*** *The @OneToMany table relationship*

The junction table holds two foreign keys, so indexing consumes more memory than in the case of bidirectional `@OneToMany`. Moreover, having three tables affects the query operations as well. Reading data may require three joins instead of two, as in the case of bidirectional `@OneToMany` association. Additionally, let's see how `INSERT` and `DELETE` act in a unidirectional `@OneToMany` association.

Let's assume that there is an author named *Joana Nimar* who has written three books. The data snapshot looks like Figure 1-3.

| author | | | | | author_books | | | book | | |
|---|---|---|---|---|---|---|---|---|---|---|
| id | age | genre | name | | author_id | books_id | | id | isbn | title |
| 1 | 34 | History | Joana Nimar | | 1 | 1 | | 1 | 001-JN | A History of Ancient Prague |
| | | | | | 1 | 2 | | 2 | 002-JN | A People's History |
| | | | | | 1 | 3 | | 3 | 003-JN | World History |

***Figure 1-3.*** *Data snapshot (unidirectional @OneToMany)*

# Regular Unidirectional @OneToMany

The following subsections tackle the INSERT and REMOVE operations in a regular unidirectional @OneToMany association.

Notice that each scenario starts from the data snapshot shown in Figure 1-3.

## Persisting an Author and Their Books

The service-method for persisting an author and the associated books from the data snapshot is shown here:

```
@Transactional
public void insertAuthorWithBooks() {

    Author jn = new Author();
    jn.setName("Joana Nimar");
    jn.setAge(34);
    jn.setGenre("History");

    Book jn01 = new Book();
    jn01.setIsbn("001-JN");
    jn01.setTitle("A History of Ancient Prague");

    Book jn02 = new Book();
    jn02.setIsbn("002-JN");
    jn02.setTitle("A People's History");

    Book jn03 = new Book();
    jn03.setIsbn("003-JN");
    jn03.setTitle("World History");

    jn.addBook(jn01);
    jn.addBook(jn02);
    jn.addBook(jn03);

    authorRepository.save(jn);
}
```

Inspecting the generated SQL INSERT statements reveals that, in comparison to the bidirectional @OneToMany association, there are three additional INSERTs in the junction table (for *n* books, there are *n* additional INSERTs):

```
INSERT INTO author (age, genre, name)
  VALUES (?, ?, ?)
Binding:[34, History, Joana Nimar]
```

```
INSERT INTO book (isbn, title)
  VALUES (?, ?)
Binding:[001-JN, A History of Ancient Prague]
```

```
INSERT INTO book (isbn, title)
  VALUES (?, ?)
Binding:[002-JN, A People's History]
```

```
INSERT INTO book (isbn, title)
  VALUES (?, ?)
Binding:[003-JN, World History]
```

```
-- additional inserts that are not needed for bidirectional @OneToMany
INSERT INTO author_books (author_id, books_id)
  VALUES (?, ?)
Binding:[1, 1]
```

```
INSERT INTO author_books (author_id, books_id)
  VALUES (?, ?)
Binding:[1, 2]
```

```
INSERT INTO author_books (author_id, books_id)
  VALUES (?, ?)
Binding:[1, 3]
```

So, in this context, the unidirectional @OneToMany association is less efficient than the bidirectional @OneToMany association. Each of the next scenarios uses this data snapshot as the starting point.

# Persisting a New Book of an Existing Author

Since *Joana Nimar* has just published a new book, we have to add it to the book table. This time, the service-method looks as follows:

```
@Transactional
public void insertNewBook() {

    Author author = authorRepository.fetchByName("Joana Nimar");

    Book book = new Book();
    book.setIsbn("004-JN");
    book.setTitle("History Details");

    author.addBook(book); // use addBook() helper

    authorRepository.save(author);
}
```

Calling this method and focusing on SQL INSERT statements results in the following output:

```
INSERT INTO book (isbn, title)
  VALUES (?, ?)
Binding:[004-JN, History Details]

-- the following DML statements don't appear in bidirectional @OneToMany
DELETE FROM author_books
WHERE author_id = ?
Binding:[1]

INSERT INTO author_books (author_id, books_id)
  VALUES (?, ?)
Binding:[1, 1]

INSERT INTO author_books (author_id, books_id)
  VALUES (?, ?)
Binding:[1, 2]

INSERT INTO author_books (author_id, books_id)
  VALUES (?, ?)
```

```
Binding:[1, 3]
```

```
INSERT INTO author_books (author_id, books_id)
  VALUES (?, ?)
Binding:[1, 4]
```

So, in order to insert a new book, the JPA persistence provider (Hibernate) deletes all associated books from the junction table. Next, it adds the new book in-memory and persists the result back again. This is far from being efficient and the potential performance penalty is quite obvious.

## Deleting the Last book

Deleting the last book involves fetching the associated List<Book> of an author and deleting the last book from this list, as follows:

```
@Transactional
public void deleteLastBook() {

    Author author = authorRepository.fetchByName("Joana Nimar");
    List<Book> books = author.getBooks();

    // use removeBook() helper
    author.removeBook(books.get(books.size() - 1));
}
```

Calling deleteLastBook() reveals the following relevant SQL statements:

```
DELETE FROM author_books
WHERE author_id = ?
Binding:[1]
```

```
INSERT INTO author_books (author_id, books_id)
  VALUES (?, ?)
Binding:[1, 1]
```

```
INSERT INTO author_books (author_id, books_id)
  VALUES (?, ?)
Binding:[1, 2]
```

```
-- for bidirectional @OneToMany this is the only needed DML
```

```
DELETE FROM book
WHERE id = ?
Binding:[3]
```

So, in order to delete the last book, the JPA persistence provider (Hibernate) deletes all associated books from the junction table, removes in-memory the last book, and persists the remaining books back again. So, in comparison to the bidirectional @OneToMany association, there are several additional DML statements representing a performance penalty. The more associated books there are, the larger the performance penalty.

## Deleting the First Book

Deleting the first book involves fetching the associated List<Book> of an author and deleting the first book from this list, as follows:

```
@Transactional
public void deleteFirstBook() {

    Author author = authorRepository.fetchByName("Joana Nimar");
    List<Book> books = author.getBooks();

    author.removeBook(books.get(0));
}
```

Calling deleteFirstBook() reveals the following relevant SQL statements:

```
DELETE FROM author_books
WHERE author_id = ?
Binding:[1]

INSERT INTO author_books (author_id, books_id)
  VALUES (?, ?)
Binding:[1, 2]

INSERT INTO author_books (author_id, books_id)
  VALUES (?, ?)
Binding:[1, 3]

-- for bidirectional @OneToMany this is the only needed DML
```

```
DELETE FROM book
WHERE id = ?
Binding:[1]
```

So, deleting the first book acts exactly as deleting the last book.

> Besides the performance penalties caused by the dynamic number of additional SQL statements, we also face the performance penalties caused by the deletion and reinsertion of the index entries associated with the foreign key column of the junction table (most databases use indexes for foreign key columns). When the database deletes all the table rows associated with the parent entity from the junction table, it also deletes the corresponding index entries. When the database inserts back in the junction table, it inserts the index entries as well.

> So far, the conclusion is clear. Unidirectional @OneToMany association is less efficient than bidirectional @OneToMany association for reading, writing, and deleting data.

# Using @OrderColumn

By adding the @OrderColumn annotation, the unidirectional @OneToMany association becomes ordered. In other words, @OrderColumn instructs Hibernate to materialize the element index (index of every collection element) into a separate database column of the junction table so that the collection is sorted using an ORDER BY clause. In this case, the index of every collection element is going to be stored in the books_order column of the junction table. In code:

```
@OneToMany(cascade = CascadeType.ALL, orphanRemoval = true)
@OrderColumn(name = "books_order")
private List<Book> books = new ArrayList<>();
```

Further, let's see how the association works with @OrderColumn.

# Persist the Author and Books

Persisting the author and the associated books from the snapshot via the `insertAuthorWithBooks()` service-method triggers the following relevant SQL statements:

```
INSERT INTO author (age, genre, name)
  VALUES (?, ?, ?)
Binding:[34, History, Joana Nimar]
```

```
INSERT INTO book (isbn, title)
  VALUES (?, ?)
Binding:[001-JN, A History of Ancient Prague]
```

```
INSERT INTO book (isbn, title)
  VALUES (?, ?)
Binding:[002-JN, A People's History]
```

```
INSERT INTO book (isbn, title)
  VALUES (?, ?)
Binding:[003-JN, World History]
```

```
-- additional inserts not needed for bidirectional @OneToMany
INSERT INTO author_books (author_id, books_order, books_id)
  VALUES (?, ?, ?)
Binding:[1, 0, 1]
```

```
INSERT INTO author_books (author_id, books_order, books_id)
  VALUES (?, ?, ?)
Binding:[1, 1, 2]
```

```
INSERT INTO author
_books (author_id, books_order, books_id)
  VALUES (?, ?, ?)
Binding:[1, 2, 3]
```

Looks like @OrderColumn doesn't bring any benefit. The three additional INSERT statements are still triggered.

## Persist a New Book of an Existing Author

Persisting a new book via the insertNewBook() service-method triggers the following relevant SQL statements:

```
INSERT INTO book (isbn, title)
  VALUES (?, ?)
Binding:[004-JN, History Details]

-- this is not needed for bidirectional @OneToMany
INSERT INTO author_books (author_id, books_order, books_id)
  VALUES (?, ?, ?)
Binding:[1, 3, 4]
```

There is good news and bad news!

The good news is that, this time, Hibernate doesn't delete the associated books to add them back from memory.

The bad news is that, in comparison to bidirectional @OneToMany association, there is still an additional INSERT statement in the junction table. So, in this context, @OrderColumn brought some benefit.

## Delete the Last Book

Deleting the last book via deleteLastBook() triggers the following relevant SQL statements:

```
DELETE FROM author_books
WHERE author_id = ?
  AND books_order = ?
Binding:[1, 2]

-- for bidirectional @OneToMany this is the only needed DML
DELETE FROM book
WHERE id = ?
Binding:[3]
```

Looks like @OrderColumn brought some benefit in the case of removing the last book. The JPA persistence provider (Hibernate) did not delete all the associated books to add the remaining back from memory.

But, in comparison to the bidirectional @OneToMany association, there is still an additional DELETE triggered against the junction table.

## Delete the First Book

Deleting the first book via deleteFirstBook() triggers the following relevant SQL statements:

```
DELETE FROM author_books
WHERE author_id = ?
  AND books_order = ?
Binding:[1, 2]
```

```
UPDATE author_books
SET books_id = ?
WHERE author_id = ?
AND books_order = ?
Binding:[3, 1, 1]
```

```
UPDATE author_books
SET books_id = ?
WHERE author_id = ?
AND books_order = ?
Binding:[2, 1, 0]
```

```
-- for bidirectional @OneToMany this is the only needed DML
DELETE FROM book
WHERE id = ?
Binding:[1]
```

The more you move away from the end of the collection, the smaller the benefit of using @OrderColumn. Deleting the first book results in a DELETE from the junction table followed by a bunch of UPDATE statements meant to preserve the in-memory order of the collection in the database. Again, this is not efficient.

Adding @OrderColumn can bring some benefits for removal operations.
Nevertheless, the closer an element to be removed is to the head of the fetched
list, the more UPDATE statements are needed. This causes performance penalties.
Even in the best-case scenario (removing an element from the tail of the
collection), this approach is not better than bidirectional @OneToMany association.

## Using @JoinColumn

Now, let's see if adding @JoinColumn will bring any benefit:

```
@OneToMany(cascade = CascadeType.ALL, orphanRemoval = true)
@JoinColumn(name = "author_id")
private List<Book> books = new ArrayList<>();
```

Adding @JoinColumn instructs Hibernate that the @OneToMany association is capable of
controlling the child-table foreign key. In other words, the junction table is eliminated
and the number of tables is reduced from three to two, as shown in Figure 1-4.

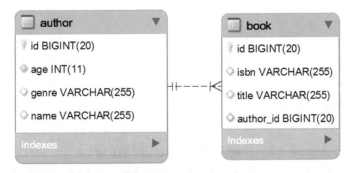

***Figure 1-4.*** *Adding @JoinColumn eliminates the junction table*

## Persist the Author and Books

Persisting the author and the associated books via the insertAuthorWithBooks()
service-method triggers the following relevant SQL statements:

```
INSERT INTO author (age, genre, name)
  VALUES (?, ?, ?)
Binding:[34, History, Joana Nimar]
```

```
INSERT INTO book (isbn, title)
  VALUES (?, ?)
Binding:[001-JN, A History of Ancient Prague]

INSERT INTO book (isbn, title)
  VALUES (?, ?)
Binding:[002-JN, A People's History]

INSERT INTO book (isbn, title)
  VALUES (?, ?)
Binding:[003-JN, World History]

-- additional DML that are not needed in bidirectional @OneToMany
UPDATE book
SET author_id = ?
WHERE id = ?
Binding:[1, 1]

UPDATE book
SET author_id = ?
WHERE id = ?
Binding:[1, 2]

UPDATE book
SET author_id = ?
WHERE id = ?
Binding:[1, 3]
```

So, for each inserted book, Hibernate triggers an UPDATE to set the author_id value. Obviously, this adds a performance penalty in comparison to the bidirectional @OneToMany association.

## Persist a New Book of an Existing Author

Persisting a new book via the insertNewBook() service-method triggers the following relevant SQL statements:

```
INSERT INTO book (isbn, title)
  VALUES (?, ?)
Binding:[004-JN, History Details]
```

```
-- additional DML that is not needed in bidirectional @OneToMany
UPDATE book
SET author_id = ?
WHERE id = ?
Binding:[1, 4]
```

This is not as bad as a regular unidirectional @OneToMany association, but it still requires an UPDATE statement that is not needed in bidirectional @OneToMany associations.

## Delete the Last Book

Deleting the last book via deleteLastBook() triggers the following relevant SQL statements:

```
UPDATE book
SET author_id = NULL
WHERE author_id = ?
AND id = ?
Binding:[1, 3]
```

```
-- for bidirectional @OneToMany this is the only needed DML
DELETE FROM book
WHERE id = ?
Binding:[3]
```

The JPA persistence provider (Hibernate) dissociates the book from its author by setting author_id to null.

Next, the disassociated book is deleted, thanks to orhpanRemoval=true. Nevertheless, this additional UPDATE is not necessary with bidirectional @OneToMany association.

## Delete the First Book

Deleting the first book via deleteFirstBook() triggers the following relevant SQL statements (these are the same SQL statements as in the previous subsection):

```
UPDATE book
SET author_id = NULL
WHERE author_id = ?
AND id = ?
Binding:[1, 1]
```

```
-- for bidirectional @OneToMany this is the only needed DML
DELETE FROM book
WHERE id = ?
Binding:[1]
```

The UPDATE is still there! Once again, the bidirectional @OneToMany association wins this game.

> Adding @JoinColumn can provide benefits over the regular unidirectional @OneToMany, but is not better than a bidirectional @OneToMany association. The additional UPDATE statements still cause a performance degradation.

> Adding @JoinColumn and @OrderColumn at the same time is still not better than bidirectional @OneToMany. Moreover, using Set instead of List or bidirectional @OneToMany with @JoinColumn (e.g., @ManyToOne @JoinColumn(name = "author_id", updatable = false, insertable = false)) still performs worse than a bidirectional @OneToMany association.

> As a rule of thumb, a unidirectional @OneToMany association is less efficient than a bidirectional @OneToMany or unidirectional @ManyToOne associations.

The complete code is available on GitHub[2].

# Item 3: How Efficient Is the Unidirectional @ManyToOne

As **Item 2** has highlighted, the unidirectional @OneToMany association is not efficient, and bidirectional @OneToMany association is better. But, how efficient is the unidirectional @ManyToOne association? Let's assume that Author and Book are involved in a unidirectional lazy @ManyToOne association. The @ManyToOne association maps exactly to the one-to-many table relationship, as shown in Figure 1-5.

---

[2]HibernateSpringBootOneToManyUnidirectional

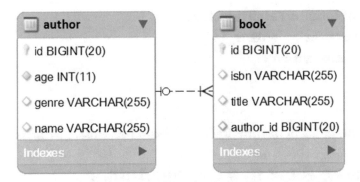

**Figure 1-5.** *The one-to-many table relationship*

As you can see, the underlying foreign key is under child-side control. This is the same for a unidirectional or bidirectional relationship.

In code, the Author and Book entities are as follows:

```
@Entity
public class Author implements Serializable {

    private static final long serialVersionUID = 1L;

    @Id
    @GeneratedValue(strategy = GenerationType.IDENTITY)
    private Long id;

    private String name;
    private String genre;
    private int age;
    ...
}

@Entity
public class Book implements Serializable {

    private static final long serialVersionUID = 1L;

    @Id
    @GeneratedValue(strategy = GenerationType.IDENTITY)
    private Long id;

    private String title;
    private String isbn;
```

```
@ManyToOne(fetch = FetchType.LAZY)
@JoinColumn(name = "author_id")
private Author author;

...
}
```

Now, let's see how efficient the unidirectional @ManyToOne association is.

## Adding a New Book to a Certain Author

The most efficient way to add a new book to a certain author is shown in the following example (for brevity, we simply hardcode the author id to 4):

```
@Transactional
public void insertNewBook() {
    Author author = authorRepository.getOne(4L);

    Book book = new Book();
    book.setIsbn("003-JN");
    book.setTitle("History Of Present");
    book.setAuthor(author);

    bookRepository.save(book);
}
```

This method will trigger a single INSERT SQL statement. The author_id column will be populated with the identifier of the associated Author entity:

```
INSERT INTO book (author_id, isbn, title)
  VALUES (?, ?, ?)
Binding:[4, 003-JN, History Of Present]
```

> Notice that we used the getOne() method, which returns an Author reference via EntityManager.getReference() (more details are found in **Item 14**). The reference state may be lazily fetched, but you don't need it in this context. Therefore, you avoid an unneeded SELECT statement. Of course, relying on findById() is also possible and desirable if you need to actually load the Author instance in the Persistence Context. Obviously, this will happen via a SELECT statement.

The Hibernate Dirty Checking mechanism works as expected (if you are not familiar with Hibernate Dirty Checking then consider **Item 18**). In other words, updating the book will result in UPDATE statements triggered on your behalf. Check out the following code:

```
@Transactional
public void insertNewBook() {
    Author author = authorRepository.getOne(4L);

    Book book = new Book();
    book.setIsbn("003-JN");
    book.setTitle("History Of Present");
    book.setAuthor(author);

    bookRepository.save(book);

    book.setIsbn("not available");
}
```

This time, calling insertNewBook() will trigger an INSERT and an UPDATE:

```
INSERT INTO book (author_id, isbn, title)
  VALUES (?, ?, ?)

UPDATE book
SET author_id = ?,
    isbn = ?,
    title = ?
WHERE id = ?
```

> Since Hibernate populates the author_id column with the identifier of the associated Author entity, adding a new book to a certain author is efficient.

# Fetching All Books of an Author

You can fetch all the books written by an author via a JPQL query as follows:

```
@Transactional(readOnly = true)
@Query("SELECT b FROM Book b WHERE b.author.id = :id")
List<Book> fetchBooksOfAuthorById(Long id);
```

Calling `fetchBooksOfAuthorById()` from a service-method is quite simple:

```
public void fetchBooksOfAuthorById() {
    List<Book> books = bookRepository.fetchBooksOfAuthorById(4L);
}
```

The triggered SELECT is shown here:

```
SELECT
  book0_.id AS id1_1_,
  book0_.author_id AS author_i4_1_,
  book0_.isbn AS isbn2_1_,
  book0_.title AS title3_1_
FROM book book0_
WHERE book0_.author_id = ?
```

Modifying a book will take advantage of the Dirty Checking mechanism. In other words, updating a book from this collection will result in a UPDATE statement triggered on your behalf. Check out the following code:

```
@Transactional
public void fetchBooksOfAuthorById() {
    List<Book> books = bookRepository.fetchBooksOfAuthorById(4L);

    books.get(0).setIsbn("not available");
}
```

This time, calling `fetchBooksOfAuthorById()` will trigger a SELECT and an UPDATE:

```
SELECT
  book0_.id AS id1_1_,
  book0_.author_id AS author_i4_1_,
  book0_.isbn AS isbn2_1_,
```

```
    book0_.title AS title3_1_
FROM book book0_
WHERE book0_.author_id = ?

UPDATE book
SET author_id = ?,
    isbn = ?,
    title = ?
WHERE id = ?
```

> Fetching all books of an author requires a single SELECT; therefore, this operation is efficient. The fetched collection is not managed by Hibernate but adding/removing books is quite efficient and easy to accomplish. This topic is covered soon.

## Paging the Books of an Author

Fetching all books work fine as long as the number of child records is rather small. Generally speaking, fetching large collections is definitely a bad practice that leads to important performance penalties. Pagination comes to the rescue as follows (just add a Pageable argument to produce a classical Spring Data offset pagination):

```
@Transactional(readOnly = true)
@Query("SELECT b FROM Book b WHERE b.author.id = :id")
Page<Book> fetchPageBooksOfAuthorById(Long id, Pageable pageable);
```

You can call fetchPageBooksOfAuthorById()from a service-method, as in the following example (of course, in reality, you will not use hardcoded values as shown here):

```
public void fetchPageBooksOfAuthorById() {
    Page<Book> books = bookRepository.fetchPageBooksOfAuthorById(4L,
        PageRequest.of(0, 2, Sort.by(Sort.Direction.ASC, "title")));

    books.get().forEach(System.out::println);
}
```

This method triggers two SELECT statements:

```
SELECT
    book0_.id AS id1_1_,
    book0_.author_id AS author_i4_1_,
    book0_.isbn AS isbn2_1_,
    book0_.title AS title3_1_
FROM book book0_
WHERE book0_.author_id = ?
ORDER BY book0_.title ASC LIMIT ?

SELECT
    COUNT(book0_.id) AS col_0_0_
FROM book book0_
WHERE book0_.author_id = ?
```

> Optimizing offset pagination can be done as in **Item 95** and **Item 96**.

Exactly as in the previous section, the fetched collection is not managed by Hibernate, but modifying a book will take advantage of the Dirty Checking mechanism.

# Fetching All Books of an Author and Adding a New Book

The section "Fetching All Books of an Author" already covered half of this topic while the section "Adding a New Book to a Certain Author" covered the other half. Joining these sections results in the following code:

```
@Transactional
public void fetchBooksOfAuthorByIdAndAddNewBook() {
    List<Book> books = bookRepository.fetchBooksOfAuthorById(4L);

    Book book = new Book();
    book.setIsbn("004-JN");
    book.setTitle("History Facts");
    book.setAuthor(books.get(0).getAuthor());

    books.add(bookRepository.save(book));
}
```

The triggered SQL statements are:

```
SELECT
  book0_.id AS id1_1_,
  book0_.author_id AS author_i4_1_,
  book0_.isbn AS isbn2_1_,
  book0_.title AS title3_1_
FROM book book0_
WHERE book0_.author_id = ?

INSERT INTO book (author_id, isbn, title)
  VALUES (?, ?, ?)
```

> Since fetching all the books of an author requires a single SELECT and adding a new book into the fetched collection requires a single INSERT, this operation is efficient.

## Fetching all Books of an Author and Deleting a Book

The following code fetches all books of an author and deletes the first book:

```
@Transactional
public void fetchBooksOfAuthorByIdAndDeleteFirstBook() {
    List<Book> books = bookRepository.fetchBooksOfAuthorById(4L);

    bookRepository.delete(books.remove(0));
}
```

Besides the well known SELECT needed to fetch all books of the author, deletion takes place in a single DELETE statement, as follows:

```
DELETE FROM book
WHERE id = ?
```

> Since fetching all books of an author requires a single SELECT and removing a book from the fetched collection requires a single DELETE, this operation is efficient.

It looks like unidirectional @ManyToOne association is quite efficient and it can be used whenever a bidirectional @OneToMany association is not needed. Again, try to avoid the unidirectional @OneToMany association (see **Item 2**).

The complete application is available on GitHub[3].

# Item 4: How to Effectively Shape the @ManyToMany Association

This time, the well-known Author and Book entities are involved in a bidirectional lazy @ManyToMany association (an author has written more books and a book was written by several authors). See Figure 1-6.

***Figure 1-6.*** *The @ManyToMany table relationship*

The bidirectional @ManyToMany association can be navigated from both sides, therefore, both sides can be parents (parent-side). Since both are parents, none of them will hold a foreign key. In this association, there are two foreign keys that are stored in a separate table, known as the junction or join table. The junction table is *hidden* and it plays the child-side role.

The best way to code a bidirectional @ManyToMany association is described in the following sections.

---

[3]HibernateSpringBootJustManyToOne

## Choose the Owner of the Relationship

Using the default @ManyToMany mapping requires the developer to choose an owner of the relationship and a mappedBy side (aka, the inverse side). Only one side can be the owner and the changes are only propagated to the database from this particular side. For example, Author can be the owner, while Book adds a mappedBy side.

```
@ManyToMany(mappedBy = "books")
private Set<Author> authors = new HashSet<>();
```

## Always Use Set not List

Especially if remove operations are involved, it is advisable to rely on Set and avoid List. As **Item 5** highlights, Set performs much better than List.

```
private Set<Book> books = new HashSet<>();        // in Author
private Set<Author> authors = new HashSet<>(); // in Book
```

## Keep Both Sides of the Association in Sync

You can easily keep both sides of the association in sync via helper methods added on the side that you are more likely to interact with. For example, if the business logic is more interested in manipulating Author than Book then the developer can add Author to least these three helpers: addBook(), removeBook() and removeBooks().

## Avoid CascadeType.ALL and CascadeType.REMOVE

In most of the cases, cascading removals are bad ideas. For example, removing an Author entity should not trigger a Book removal because the Book can be referenced by other authors as well (a book can be written by several authors). So, avoid CascadeType.ALL and CascadeType.REMOVE and rely on explicit CascadeType.PERSIST and CascadeType.MERGE:

```
@ManyToMany(cascade = {CascadeType.PERSIST, CascadeType.MERGE})
private Set<Book> books = new HashSet<>();
```

> The orphan removal (orphanRemoval) option is defined on @OneToOne and @OneToMany relationship annotations, but on neither of the @ManyToOne or @ManyToMany annotations.

# Setting Up the Join Table

Explicitly setting up the join table name and the columns names allows the developer to reference them without confusion. This can be done via @JoinTable as in the following example:

```
@JoinTable(name = "author_book",
        joinColumns = @JoinColumn(name = "author_id"),
        inverseJoinColumns = @JoinColumn(name = "book_id")
)
```

# Using Lazy Fetching on Both Sides of the Association

By default, the @ManyToMany association is lazy. Keep it this way! Don't do this:

```
@ManyToMany(fetch=FetchType.EAGER)
```

# Override equals() and hashCode()

By properly overriding the equals() and hashCode() methods, the application obtains the same results across all entity state transitions. This aspect is dissected in **Item 68**. For bidirectional @ManyToMany associations, these methods should be overridden on both sides.

# Pay Attention to How toString() Is Overridden

If toString() needs to be overridden, involve only the basic attributes fetched when the entity is loaded from the database. Involving lazy attributes or associations will trigger separate SQL statements for fetching the corresponding data.

# Author and Book Samples

Gluing these instructions together and expressing them in code will result in the following Author and Book samples:

```
@Entity
public class Author implements Serializable {

    private static final long serialVersionUID = 1L;
```

```java
@Id
@GeneratedValue(strategy = GenerationType.IDENTITY)
private Long id;

private String name;
private String genre;
private int age;

@ManyToMany(cascade = {CascadeType.PERSIST, CascadeType.MERGE})
@JoinTable(name = "author_book",
        joinColumns = @JoinColumn(name = "author_id"),
        inverseJoinColumns = @JoinColumn(name = "book_id")
)
private Set<Book> books = new HashSet<>();

public void addBook(Book book) {
    this.books.add(book);
    book.getAuthors().add(this);
}

public void removeBook(Book book) {
    this.books.remove(book);
    book.getAuthors().remove(this);
}

public void removeBooks() {
    Iterator<Book> iterator = this.books.iterator();

    while (iterator.hasNext()) {
        Book book = iterator.next();

        book.getAuthors().remove(this);
        iterator.remove();
    }
}

// getters and setters omitted for brevity

@Override
public boolean equals(Object obj) {
```

```java
        if(obj == null) {
            return false;
        }
        if (this == obj) {
            return true;
        }

        if (getClass() != obj.getClass()) {
            return false;
        }

        return id != null && id.equals(((Author) obj).id);
    }

    @Override
    public int hashCode() {
        return 2021;
    }

    @Override
    public String toString() {
        return "Author{" + "id=" + id + ", name=" + name
                    + ", genre=" + genre + ", age=" + age + '}';
    }
}

@Entity
public class Book implements Serializable {

    private static final long serialVersionUID = 1L;

    @Id
    @GeneratedValue(strategy = GenerationType.IDENTITY)
    private Long id;

    private String title;
    private String isbn;

    @ManyToMany(mappedBy = "books")
    private Set<Author> authors = new HashSet<>();
```

```java
    // getters and setter omitted for brevity

    @Override
    public boolean equals(Object obj) {

        if(obj == null) {
            return false;
        }

        if (this == obj) {
            return true;
        }

        if (getClass() != obj.getClass()) {
            return false;
        }

        return id != null && id.equals(((Book) obj).id);
    }

    @Override
    public int hashCode() {
        return 2021;
    }

    @Override
    public String toString() {
        return "Book{" + "id=" + id + ", title=" + title
                              + ", isbn=" + isbn + '}';
    }
}
```

The source code is available on GitHub[4].

---

[4]HibernateSpringBootManyToManyBidirectional

> Alternatively, @ManyToMany can be replaced with two bidirectional @OneToMany associations. In other words, the junction table can be mapped to an entity. This comes with several advantages, discussed in this article[5].

# Item 5: Why Set Is Better than List in @ManyToMany

First of all, keep in mind that Hibernate deals with @ManyToMany relationships as two unidirectional @OneToMany associations. The owner-side and the child-side (the junction table) represents one unidirectional @OneToMany association. On the other hand, the non-owner-side and the child-side (the junction table) represent another unidirectional @OneToMany association. Each association relies on a foreign key stored in the junction table.

In the context of this statement, the entity removal (or reordering) results in deleting all junction entries from the junction table and reinserts them to reflect the memory content (the current Persistence Context content).

## Using List

Let's assume that Author and Book involved in a bidirectional lazy @ManyToMany association are mapped via java.util.List, as shown here (only the relevant code is listed):

```
@Entity
public class AuthorList implements Serializable {
    ...
    @ManyToMany(cascade = {CascadeType.PERSIST, CascadeType.MERGE})
    @JoinTable(name = "author_book_list",
            joinColumns = @JoinColumn(name = "author_id"),
            inverseJoinColumns = @JoinColumn(name = "book_id")
    )
    private List<BookList> books = new ArrayList<>();
    ...
}
```

---

[5]https://vladmihalcea.com/the-best-way-to-map-a-many-to-many-association-with-extra-columns-when-using-jpa-and-hibernate

```
@Entity
public class BookList implements Serializable {

    ...

    @ManyToMany(mappedBy = "books")
    private List<AuthorList> authors = new ArrayList<>();

    ...

}
```

Further, consider the data snapshot shown in Figure 1-7.

**Figure 1-7.**  *Data snapshot (bidirectional @ManyToMany)*

The goal is to remove the book called *One Day* (the book with ID of *2*) written by the author, *Alicia Tom* (the author with ID *1*). Considering that the entity representing this author is stored via a variable named alicia, and the book is stored via a variable named oneDay, the deletion can be done via removeBook() as follows:

```
alicia.removeBook(oneDay);
```

The SQL statements triggered by this deletion are:

```
DELETE FROM author_book_list
WHERE author_id = ?
Binding: [1]

INSERT INTO author_book_list (author_id, book_id)
    VALUES (?, ?)
Binding: [1, 1]

INSERT INTO author_book_list (author_id, book_id)
    VALUES (?, ?)
Binding: [1, 3]
```

So, the removal didn't materialized in a single SQL statement. Actually, it started by deleting all junction entries of `alicia` from the junction table. Further, the junction entries that were not the subject of removal were reinserted to reflect the in-memory content (Persistence Context). The more junction entries reinserted, the longer the database transaction.

# Using Set

Consider switching from `List` to `Set` as follows:

```
@Entity
public class AuthorSet implements Serializable {
    ...
    @ManyToMany(cascade = {CascadeType.PERSIST, CascadeType.MERGE})
    @JoinTable(name = "author_book_set",
            joinColumns = @JoinColumn(name = "author_id"),
            inverseJoinColumns = @JoinColumn(name = "book_id")
    )
    private Set<BookSet> books = new HashSet<>();
    ...
}

@Entity
public class BookSet implements Serializable {
    ...
    @ManyToMany(mappedBy = "books")
    private Set<AuthorSet> authors = new HashSet<>();
    ...
}
```

This time, calling `alicia.removeBook(oneDay)` will trigger the following SQL DELETE statement:

```
DELETE FROM author_book_set
WHERE author_id = ?
  AND book_id = ?
Binding: [1, 2]
```

The source code is available on GitHub[6]. This is much better since a single DELETE statement is needed to accomplish the job.

> When using the @ManyToMany annotation, always use a `java.util.Set`. Do not use the `java.util.List`. In the case of other associations, use the one that best fits your case. If you go with `List`, do not forget to be aware of the HHH-5855[7] issue that was fixed starting with Hibernate 5.0.8.

## Preserving the Order of the Result Set

It's a well-known fact that `java.util.ArrayList` preserves the order of inserted elements (it has precise control over where in the list each element is inserted), while `java.util.HashSet` doesn't. In other words, `java.util.ArrayList` has a predefined entry order of elements, while `java.util.HashSet` is, by default, unordered.

There are at least two ways to order the result set by the given columns defined by JPA specification:

- Use @OrderBy to ask the database to order the fetched data by the given columns (appends the ORDER BY clause in the generated SQL query to retrieve the entities in a specific order) and Hibernate to preserve this order.

- Use @OrderColumn to permanently order this via an extra column (in this case, stored in the junction table).

> This annotation (@OrderBy) can be used with @OneToMany/@ManyToMany associations and @ElementCollection. Adding @OrderBy without an explicit column will result in ordering the entities ascending by their primary key (ORDER BY author1_.id ASC). Ordering by multiple columns is possible as well (e.g., order descending by age and ascending by name, @OrderBy("age DESC, name ASC"). Obviously, @OrderBy can be used with `java.util.List` as well.

---

[6]HibernateSpringBootManyToManyBidirectionalListVsSet
[7]https://hibernate.atlassian.net/browse/HHH-5855

# Using @OrderBy

Consider the data snapshot in Figure 1-8.

**author list**

| id | age | genre | name |
|----|-----|-------|------|
| 1 | 23 | Anthology | Mark Janel |
| 2 | 51 | Anthology | Quartis Young |
| 3 | 38 | Anthology | Alicia Tom |
| 4 | 56 | Anthology | Katy Loin |
| 5 | 38 | Anthology | Martin Leon |
| 6 | 56 | Anthology | Qart Pinkil |

**author_book_list**

| author_id | book_id |
|-----------|---------|
| 1 | 1 |
| 2 | 1 |
| 3 | 1 |
| 4 | 1 |
| 5 | 1 |
| 6 | 1 |

**book_list**

| id | isbn | title |
|----|------|-------|
| 1 | 001-all | Encyclopedia |

***Figure 1-8.*** *Data snapshot (many-to-many Set and @OrderBy)*

There is a book written by six authors. The goal is to fetch the authors in descending order by name via Book#getAuthors(). This can be done by adding @OrderBy in Book, as shown here:

```
@ManyToMany(mappedBy = "books")
@OrderBy("name DESC")
private Set<Author> authors = new HashSet<>();
```

When getAuthors() is called, the @OrderBy will:

- Attach the corresponding ORDER BY clause to the triggered SQL. This will instruct the database to order the fetched data.

- Signal to Hibernate to preserve the order. Behind the scenes, Hibernate will preserve the order via a LinkedHashSet.

So, calling getAuthors() will result in a Set of authors conforming to the @OrderBy information. The triggered SQL is the following SELECT containing the ORDER BY clause:

```
SELECT
    authors0_.book_id AS book_id2_1_0_,
    authors0_.author_id AS author_i1_1_0_,
    author1_.id AS id1_0_1_,
    author1_.age AS age2_0_1_,
    author1_.genre AS genre3_0_1_,
    author1_.name AS name4_0_1_
```

```
FROM author_book authors0_
INNER JOIN author author1_
  ON authors0_.author_id = author1_.id
WHERE authors0_.book_id = ?
ORDER BY author1_.name DESC
```

Displaying Set will output the following (via Author#toString()):

```
Author{id=2, name=Quartis Young, genre=Anthology, age=51},
Author{id=6, name=Qart Pinkil, genre=Anthology, age=56},
Author{id=5, name=Martin Leon, genre=Anthology, age=38},
Author{id=1, name=Mark Janel, genre=Anthology, age=23},
Author{id=4, name=Katy Loin, genre=Anthology, age=56},
Author{id=3, name=Alicia Tom, genre=Anthology, age=38}
```

The source code is available on GitHub[8].

> Using @OrderBy with HashSet will preserve the order of the loaded/fetched
> Set, but this is not consistent across the transient state. If this is an issue, to
> get consistency across the transient state as well, consider explicitly using
> LinkedHashSet instead of HashSet. So, for full consistency, use:
>
> ```
> @ManyToMany(mappedBy = "books")
> @OrderBy("name DESC")
> private Set<Author> authors = new LinkedHashSet<>();
> ```

# Item 6: Why and When to Avoid Removing Child Entities with CascadeType.Remove and orphanRemoval=true

First of all, let's quickly highlight the differences between CascadeType.REMOVE and
orphanRemoval=true. Let's use the Author and Book entities involved in a bidirectional
lazy @OneToMany association, written as follows:

```
// in Author.java
@OneToMany(cascade = CascadeType.ALL,
         mappedBy = "author", orphanRemoval = true)
```

---

[8]HibernateSpringBootManyToManySetAndOrderBy

```java
private List<Book> books = new ArrayList<>();

// in Book.java
@ManyToOne(fetch = FetchType.LAZY)
@JoinColumn(name = "author_id")
private Author author;
```

Removing an Author entity is automatically cascaded to the associated Book entities. This is happening as long as CascadeType.REMOVE or orphanRemoval=true is present. In other words, from this perspective, the presence of both is redundant.

Then how are they different? Well, consider the following helper-method used to disconnect (or disassociate) a Book from its Author:

```java
public void removeBook(Book book) {
    book.setAuthor(null);
    this.books.remove(book);
}
```

Or, to disconnect all Books from their Authors:

```java
public void removeBooks() {
Iterator<Book> iterator = this.books.iterator();

    while (iterator.hasNext()) {
        Book book = iterator.next();

        book.setAuthor(null);
        iterator.remove();
    }
}
```

Calling the removeBook() method in the presence of orphanRemoval=true will result in automatically removing the book via a DELETE statement. Calling it in the presence of orphanRemoval=false will trigger an UPDATE statement. Since disconnecting a Book is not a remove operation, the presence of CascadeType.REMOVE doesn't matter. So, orphanRemoval=true is useful for cleaning up entities (remove dangling references) that should not exist without a reference from an owner entity (Author).

But how efficient are these settings? The short answer is: not very efficient if they must affect a significant number of entities. The long answer starts by deleting an author in the following service-method (this author has three associated books):

```
@Transactional
public void deleteViaCascadeRemove() {
    Author author = authorRepository.findByName("Joana Nimar");

    authorRepository.delete(author);
}
```

Deleting an author will cascade the deletion to the associated books. This is the effect of CascadeType.ALL, which includes CascadeType.REMOVE. But, before deleting the associated books, they are loaded in the Persistence Context via a SELECT. If they are already in the Persistence Context then they are not loaded. If the books are not present in the Persistence Context then CascadeType.REMOVE will not take effect. Further, there are four DELETE statements, one for deleting the author and three for deleting the associated books:

```
DELETE
FROM book
WHERE id=?
Binding:[1]
```

```
DELETE
FROM book
WHERE id=?
Binding:[2]
```

```
DELETE
FROM book
WHERE id=?
Binding:[4]
```

```
DELETE
FROM author
WHERE id=?
Binding:[4]
```

For each book there is a separate DELETE statement. The more books there are to delete, the more DELETE statements you have and the larger the performance penalty.

Now let's write a service-method that deletes based on the orphanRemoval=true. For the sake of variation, this time, we load the author and the associated books in the same SELECT:

```
@Transactional
public void deleteViaOrphanRemoval() {
    Author author = authorRepository.findByNameWithBooks("Joana Nimar");

    author.removeBooks();
    authorRepository.delete(author);
}
```

Unfortunately, this approach will trigger the exact same DELETE statements as in the case of cascading the deletes, so it's prone to the same performance penalties.

If your application triggers sporadic deletes, you can rely on CascadeType.REMOVE and/or orphanRemoval=true. This is useful especially if you delete managed entities, so you need Hibernate to manage the entities state transitions. Moreover, via this approach, you benefit from the automatic Optimistic Locking mechanism (e.g., @Version) for parents and children. But, if you are just looking for approaches that delete more efficiently (in fewer DML statements), we will consider a few of them. Of course, each approach has its own trade-offs.

The following four approaches delete the authors and the associated books via *bulk* operations. This way, you can optimize and control the number of triggered DELETE statements. These operations are very fast, but they have three main shortcomings:

- They ignore the automatic Optimistic Locking mechanism (for example, you cannot rely on @Version anymore)

- The Persistence Context is not synchronized to reflect the modifications performed by the *bulk* operations, which may lead to an outdated context

- They don't take advantage of cascading removals (CascadeType. REMOVE) or orphanRemoval

If these shortcomings matter to you, you have two options: avoid *bulk* operations or explicitly deal with the problem. The most difficult part is to emulate the job of the automatic Optimistic Locking mechanism for children that are not loaded in the Persistence Context. The following examples assume that there is no automatic Optimistic Locking mechanism enabled. However, they manage the Persistence Context synchronization issues via flushAutomatically = true and clearAutomatically = true. Do not conclude that these two settings are always needed. Their usage depends on what you want to achieve.

## Deleting Authors that Are Already Loaded in the Persistence Context

Let's tackle the case when, in the Persistence Context, there is only one Author loaded and the case when there are more Authors loaded, but not all of them. The associated books (which are or aren't already loaded in the Persistence Context) have to be deleted as well.

## One Author Has Already Been Loaded in the Persistence Context

Let's assume that the Author that should be deleted was loaded earlier in the Persistence Context without their associated Book. To delete this Author and the associated books, you can use the author identifier (author.getId()). First, delete all the author's associated books:

```
// add this method in BookRepository
@Transactional
@Modifying(flushAutomatically = true, clearAutomatically = true)
@Query("DELETE FROM Book b WHERE b.author.id = ?1")
public int deleteByAuthorIdentifier(Long id);
```

Then, let's delete the author by his identifier:

```
// add this method in AuthorRepository
@Transactional
@Modifying(flushAutomatically = true, clearAutomatically = true)
@Query("DELETE FROM Author a WHERE a.id = ?1")
public int deleteByIdentifier(Long id);
```

The presence of flushAutomatically = true, clearAutomatically = true is explained a little bit later. For now, the service-method responsible for triggering the deletion is:

```
@Transactional
public void deleteViaIdentifiers() {
    Author author = authorRepository.findByName("Joana Nimar");

    bookRepository.deleteByAuthorIdentifier(author.getId());
    authorRepository.deleteByIdentifier(author.getId());
}
```

Calling deleteViaIdentifiers() triggers the following queries:

```
DELETE FROM book
WHERE author_id = ?

DELETE FROM author
WHERE id = ?
```

Notice that the associated books are not loaded in the Persistence Context and there are only two DELETE statements triggered. The number of books doesn't affect the number of DELETE statements.

The author can be deleted via the built-in deleteInBatch(Iterable<T> entities) as well:

```
authorRepository.deleteInBatch(List.of(author));
```

# More Authors Have Been Loaded in the Persistence Context

Let's assume that the Persistence Context contains more Authors that should be deleted. For example, let's delete all Authors of age *34* fetched as a List<Author> (let's assume that there are two authors of age *34*). Trying to delete by author identifier (as in the previous case) will result in a separate DELETE for each author. Moreover, there will be a separate DELETE for the associated books of each author. So this is not efficient.

This time, let's rely on two *bulk* operations. One defined by you via the IN operator (which allows you to specify multiple values in a WHERE clause) and the built-in deleteInBatch(Iterable<T> entities):

```
// add this method in BookRepository
@Transactional
@Modifying(flushAutomatically = true, clearAutomatically = true)
@Query("DELETE FROM Book b WHERE b.author IN ?1")
public int deleteBulkByAuthors(List<Author> authors);
```

The service-methods to delete a List<Author> and the associated Book are as follows:

```
@Transactional
public void deleteViaBulkIn() {
    List<Author> authors = authorRepository.findByAge(34);

    bookRepository.deleteBulkByAuthors(authors);
    authorRepository.deleteInBatch(authors);
}
```

Calling deleteViaBulkIn() triggers the following queries:

```
DELETE FROM book
WHERE author_id IN (?, ?)

DELETE FROM author
WHERE id = ?
  OR id = ?
```

Notice that the associated books are not loaded in the Persistence Context and there are only two DELETE statements triggered. The number of authors and books doesn't affect the number of DELETE statements.

# One Author and His Associated Books Have Been Loaded in the Persistence Context

Assume that the Author (the one that should be deleted) and his associated Books are already loaded in the Persistence Context. This time there is no need to define *bulk* operations since the built-in deleteInBatch(Iterable<T> entities) can do the job for you:

```
@Transactional
public void deleteViaDeleteInBatch() {
    Author author = authorRepository.findByNameWithBooks("Joana Nimar");

    bookRepository.deleteInBatch(author.getBooks());
    authorRepository.deleteInBatch(List.of(author));
}
```

The main shortcoming here is the default behavior of the built-in deleteInBatch(Iterable<T> entities), which, by default, don't flush or clear the Persistence Context. This may leave the Persistence Context in an outdated state.

Of course, in the previous methods, there is nothing to flush before deletions and no need to clear the Persistence Context because, after the delete operations, the transaction commits. Therefore the Persistence Context is closed. But, flush and clear (not necessarily both of them) are needed in certain cases. Commonly, the clear operation is needed much more often than the flush operation. For example, the following method doesn't need a flush prior to any deletions, but it needs a clear after any deletions. Otherwise it will cause an exception:

```
@Transactional
public void deleteViaDeleteInBatch() {
    Author author = authorRepository.findByNameWithBooks("Joana Nimar");

    bookRepository.deleteInBatch(author.getBooks());
    authorRepository.deleteInBatch(List.of(author));

    ...

    // later on, we forgot that this author was deleted
    author.setGenre("Anthology");
}
```

The highlighted code will cause an exception of type:

```
org.springframework.orm.ObjectOptimisticLockingFailureException: Object of
class [com.bookstore.entity.Author] with identifier [4]: Optimistic Locking
failed; nested exception is org.hibernate.StaleObjectStateException: Row
was updated or deleted by another transaction (or unsaved-value mapping was
incorrect) : [com.bookstore.entity.Author#4]
```

Practically, the modification (the call of setGenre()) changes the Author entity contained in the Persistence Context, but this context is outdated since the author was deleted from the database. In other words, after deleting the author and the associated books from the database, they will continue to exist in the current Persistence Context. The Persistence Context is not aware of the deletions performed via deleteInBatch(Iterable<T> entities). To make sure that the Persistence Context is cleared after the deletions, you can override the deleteInBatch(Iterable<T> entities) to add @Modifying(clearAutomatically = true). This way, the Persistence Context is automatically cleared after the deletions. If you are in a use case that requires a prior flush as well, then use @Modifying(flushAutomatically = true, clearAutomatically = true) or call the flush() method. Or, even better, you can reuse the deleteViaIdentifiers() method, as shown here (we've already annotated this method with @Modifying(flushAutomatically = true, clearAutomatically = true)):

```
@Transactional
public void deleteViaIdentifiers() {
    Author author = authorRepository.findByNameWithBooks("Joana Nimar");

    bookRepository.deleteByAuthorIdentifier(author.getId());
    authorRepository.deleteByIdentifier(author.getId());
}
```

Calling deleteViaIdentifiers() triggers the following queries:

```
DELETE FROM book
WHERE author_id = ?

DELETE FROM author
WHERE id = ?
```

The number of books doesn't affect the number of DELETE statements.

> If the Persistence Context manages several Authors and the associated Books that should be deleted then rely on the `deleteViaBulkIn()`.

## Deleting When the Author and Books that Should Be Deleted Are Not Loaded in the Persistence Context

If the author that should be deleted and his associated books are not loaded in the Persistence Context then you can hardcode the author identifier (if you know it), as in the following service-method:

```
@Transactional
public void deleteViaHardCodedIdentifiers() {
    bookRepository.deleteByAuthorIdentifier(4L);
    authorRepository.deleteByIdentifier(4L);
}
```

The `deleteByAuthorIdentifier()` and `deleteByIdentifier()` methods are the same from "One Author Have Been Already Loaded in the Persistence Context" section. The triggered queries are quite obvious:

```
DELETE FROM book
WHERE author_id = ?
```

```
DELETE FROM author
WHERE id = ?
```

If there are more authors, you can use bulk operations to delete them:

```
// add this method in BookRepository
@Transactional
@Modifying(flushAutomatically = true, clearAutomatically = true)
@Query("DELETE FROM Book b WHERE b.author.id IN ?1")
public int deleteBulkByAuthorIdentifier(List<Long> id);

// add this method in AuthorRepository
@Transactional
@Modifying(flushAutomatically = true, clearAutomatically = true)
```

```
@Query("DELETE FROM Author a WHERE a.id IN ?1")
public int deleteBulkByIdentifier(List<Long> id);
```

Now, let's delete two authors and their associated books:

```
@Transactional
public void deleteViaBulkHardCodedIdentifiers() {
    List<Long> authorsIds = Arrays.asList(1L, 4L);

    bookRepository.deleteBulkByAuthorIdentifier(authorsIds);
    authorRepository.deleteBulkByIdentifier(authorsIds);
}
```

The triggered SQL statements are as follows:

```
DELETE FROM book
WHERE author_id IN (?, ?)
```

```
DELETE FROM author
WHERE id IN (?, ?)
```

The number of authors and books doesn't affect the number of DELETE statements. Since we don't load anything in the Persistence Context, flushAutomatically = true, clearAutomatically = true has no effect.

> In order to avoid outdated entities in the Persistence Context, do not forget to flush the EntityManager before the query is executed (flushAutomatically = true) and clear it after the query is executed (clearAutomatically = true). If you don't want/need to flush and/or clear then pay attention to how you manage to avoid outdated entities in Persistence Context. **As long as you know what you are doing, it's not problematic to not flush and/or clear the Persistence Context. Ideally isolate *bulk* operations in dedicated transactional service-methods. This way, there is no need to explicitly flush and clear the Persistence Context. Issues may arise when you interleave *bulk* operations with managed entity operations.**
>
> If you need a refresher on how flush works, read **Appendix H**.

> The most efficient way to delete all entities is via the built-in
> `deleteAllInBatch()`, which trigger a *bulk* operation.

The complete application is available on GitHub[9].

# Item 7: How to Fetch Associations via JPA Entity Graphs

> **Item 39** and **Item 41** describe how to fetch the association in the same `SELECT`
> query with its parent via `(LEFT) JOIN FETCH`. This is quite useful in scenarios
> involving lazy associations that should be fetched eagerly on a query-basis to
> avoid lazy loading exceptions and N+1 issues. While `(LEFT) JOIN FETCH` lives
> inside the query, entity graphs are independent of the query. Therefore, the query
> and entity graphs can be reused (e.g., a query can be used with or without an
> entity graph, while an entity graph can be used with different queries).

Now, in a nutshell, entity graphs (aka, fetch plans) were introduced in JPA 2.1 and they
help you improve the performance of loading entities by solving lazy loading exceptions
and N+1 issues. The developer specifies the entity's related associations and basic fields
that should be loaded in a single `SELECT` statement. The developer can define multiple
entity graphs for the same entity and can chain any number of entities, and even use
sub-graphs to create complex fetch plans. Entity graphs are global and reusable across
the entities (Domain Model). To override the current `FetchType` semantics, there are two
properties that you can set:

- *Fetch graph*: This is the default fetching type represented by the
  `javax.persistence.fetchgraph` property. The attributes present
  in `attributeNodes` are treated as `FetchType.EAGER`. The remaining
  attributes are treated as `FetchType.LAZY`, regardless of the default/
  explicit `FetchType`.

---

[9]HibernateSpringBootCascadeChildRemoval

- *Load graph*: This fetching type can be employed via the javax.
  persistence.loadgraph property. The attributes present in
  attributeNodes are treated as FetchType.EAGER. The remaining
  attributes are treated according to their specified or default FetchType.

An entity graph can be defined via annotations (e.g., @NamedEntityGraph), via
attributePaths (ad hoc entity graphs), and via the EntityManager API by calling the
getEntityGraph() or createEntityGraph() methods.

Assume the Author and Book entities involved in a bidirectional lazy @OneToMany
association. The entity graph (a fetch graph) should load all Authors and the associated
Books in the same SELECT. The same thing can be obtained via JOIN FETCH, but this time
let's do it via entity graphs.

# Defining an Entity Graph via @NamedEntityGraph

The @NamedEntityGraph annotation occurs at entity-level. Via its elements, the
developer can specify a unique name for this entity graph (via the name element) and the
attributes to include when fetching the entity graph (via the attributeNodes element,
which contains a list of @NamedAttributeNode annotations separated by commas; each
@NamedAttributeNode from this list corresponds to a field/association that should be
fetched). The attributes can be basic fields and associations.

Let's put the entity graph in code in the Author entity:

```
@Entity
@NamedEntityGraph(
    name = "author-books-graph",
    attributeNodes = {
        @NamedAttributeNode("books")
    }
)
public class Author implements Serializable {

    private static final long serialVersionUID = 1L;

    @Id
    @GeneratedValue(strategy = GenerationType.IDENTITY)
    private Long id;
```

```
    private String name;
    private String genre;
    private int age;

    @OneToMany(cascade = CascadeType.ALL,
              mappedBy = "author", orphanRemoval = true)
      private List<Book> books = new ArrayList<>();

    // getters and setters omitted for brevity
}
```

Next, focus on the repository of the Author entity, AuthorRepository.

The AuthorRepository is the place where the entity graph should be specified. Spring Data provides support for entity graphs via the @EntityGraph annotation (the class of this annotation is org.springframework.data.jpa.repository.EntityGraph).

## Overriding a Query Method

For example, the code to use the entity graph (author-books-graph) to find all Authors, including the associated Book, is as follows (EntityGraph.EntityGraphType.FETCH is the default and indicates a fetch graph; EntityGraph.EntityGraphType.LOAD can be specified for a load graph):

```
@Repository
@Transactional(readOnly = true)
public interface AuthorRepository extends JpaRepository<Author, Long> {

    @Override
    @EntityGraph(value = "author-books-graph",
                type = EntityGraph.EntityGraphType.FETCH)
    public List<Author> findAll();
}
```

Calling the findAll() method will result in the following SQL SELECT statement:

```
SELECT
  author0_.id AS id1_0_0_,
  books1_.id AS id1_1_1_,
  author0_.age AS age2_0_0_,
  author0_.genre AS genre3_0_0_,
```

```
    author0_.name AS name4_0_0_,
    books1_.author_id AS author_i4_1_1_,
    books1_.isbn AS isbn2_1_1_,
    books1_.title AS title3_1_1_,
    books1_.author_id AS author_i4_1_0__,
    books1_.id AS id1_1_0__
FROM author author0_
LEFT OUTER JOIN book books1_
    ON author0_.id = books1_.author_id
```

Notice that the generated query took into account the entity graph specified via
@EntityGraph.

## Using the Query Builder Mechanism

Overriding findAll() is a convenient way to fetch all entities. But, use the Spring Data
Query Builder mechanism to filter the fetched data via the WHERE clause. For example,
you can fetch the entity graph for authors younger than the given age and in descending
order by name as follows:

```
@Repository
@Transactional(readOnly = true)
public interface AuthorRepository extends JpaRepository<Author, Long> {

    @EntityGraph(value = "author-books-graph",
                type = EntityGraph.EntityGraphType.FETCH)
    public List<Author> findByAgeLessThanOrderByNameDesc(int age);
}
```

The generated SQL SELECT statement is shown here:

```
SELECT
    ...
FROM author author0_
LEFT OUTER JOIN book books1_
    ON author0_.id = books1_.author_id
WHERE author0_.age < ?
ORDER BY author0_.name DESC
```

## Using Specification

Using Specification is also supported. For example, let's assume the following classical Specification for generating WHERE age > 45:

```
public class AuthorSpecs {
    private static final int AGE = 45;

    public static Specification<Author> isAgeGt45() {
        return (Root<Author> root,
            CriteriaQuery<?> query, CriteriaBuilder builder)
                -> builder.greaterThan(root.get("age"), AGE);
    }
}
```

Let's use this Specification:

```
@Repository
@Transactional(readOnly = true)
public interface AuthorRepository extends JpaRepository<Author, Long>,
    JpaSpecificationExecutor<Author> {

    @Override
    @EntityGraph(value = "author-books-graph",
                 type = EntityGraph.EntityGraphType.FETCH)
    public List<Author> findAll(Specification spec);
}
```

```
List<Author> authors = authorRepository.findAll(isAgeGt45());
```

The generated SQL SELECT statement is as follows:

```
SELECT
  ...
FROM author author0_
LEFT OUTER JOIN book books1_
  ON author0_.id = books1_.author_id
WHERE author0_.age > 45
```

# Using @Query and JPQL

Finally, using @Query and JPQL is also possible.

> Pay attention to queries that are used with entity graphs that specify join fetching. In such cases, it's mandatory to have the owner of the fetched association present in the SELECT list.

Check out the following explicit JPQL query:

```
@Repository
@Transactional(readOnly = true)
public interface AuthorRepository extends JpaRepository<Author, Long> {

    @EntityGraph(value = "author-books-graph",
                 type = EntityGraph.EntityGraphType.FETCH)
    @Query(value="SELECT a FROM Author a WHERE a.age > 20 AND a.age < 40")
    public List<Author> fetchAllAgeBetween20And40();
}
```

The SQL SELECT statement is as follows:

```
SELECT
    ...
FROM author author0_
LEFT OUTER JOIN book books1_
  ON author0_.id = books1_.author_id
WHERE author0_.age > 20 AND author0_.age < 40
```

> Pay attention to using entity graphs that attempt multiple eager fetching (e.g., Author has two @OneToMany associations declared LAZY and mapped to List, and both of them appear in the entity graph). Triggering a SELECT with multiple left outer joins will eagerly fetch more than one Hibernate-specific Bag (an unordered collection with duplicates that is not meant to

removed duplicates), and this will lead to `MultipleBagFetchException`. In other words, when you trigger a query using the entity graph hint, Hibernate will respond with a `MultipleBagFetchException` if you attempt a multiple eager fetch.

But, do not assume that `MultipleBagFetchException` is something specific to entity graphs, because this is a wrong assumption. It appears whenever you try to trigger a query that attempts multiple eager fetching. This kind of exception is often encountered in the case of fetching multiple levels deep in entities hierarchies, such as *Book* has *Chapter* that has *Section* that has *Page*.

The most popular solution to this problem is to switch from `Set` to `List`. While this will work as expected, it is *far away* from being an efficient solution because the Cartesian product that results from merging the intermediate results sets will be huge. Generally speaking, assume that you want to fetch some A entities along with their B and C associations. And you have 25 A rows associated with 10 B rows and 20 C rows. The Cartesian product for fetching the final result will have 25 x 10 x 20 rows = 5000 rows! This is really bad from a performance perspective! The best solution is to fetch at most one association at a time. Even if this means more than one query it avoids this huge Cartesian product. For a complete example, check out this awesome article[10] by Vlad Mihalcea.

Trying to use a native query with entity graphs will result in a Hibernate exception of type: `A native SQL query cannot use EntityGraphs`.

Pay attention to using pagination (`Pageable`) when the entity graph is translated into an SQL `JOIN` that fetches associated collection. In such cases, the pagination takes place in-memory, which can lead to performance penalties.

---

[10]https://vladmihalcea.com/hibernate-multiplebagfetchexception/

Native queries cannot be used with entity graphs. Relying on window functions (**Item 95**) is not an option as well. Next to writing sub-queries outside of WHERE and HAVING clauses,  performing set operations (e.g., UNION, INTERSECT, EXCEPT), using database specific hints, and writing recursive queries, using window functions in JPQL represents the top five limitations of JPQL.

On the other hand, if the entity graph fetches only basic (@Basic) attributes and/or associations that are not collections, then pagination (Pageable) will be done by the database via LIMIT or counterparts.

The complete application is available on GitHub[11].

There is one very important aspect to notice here. The entity graph (fetch graph) explicitly specifies via @NamedAttributeNode to load only the books association. For fetch graphs, the remaining attributes should be treated as FetchType.LAZY regardless of the default/explicit FetchType. Then why does the previous query contain the basic attributes of Author as well? The answer and solution to this question is available in **Item 9**. See **Item 9** for fetching only the needed basic attributes via an entity graph (fetch and load graph). For now, let's continue with the ad hoc entity graphs.

## Ad Hoc Entity Graphs

An ad hoc entity graph can be defined via the attributePaths element of the @EntityGraph annotation. The entity's related associations and basic fields that should be loaded in a single SELECT are specified as a list separated by comma of type, @EntityGraph(attributePaths = {"attr1", "attr2", ...}. Obviously, this time, there is no need to use @NamedEntityGraph. For example, the entity graph from the previous section can be written as follows:

```
@Repository
@Transactional(readOnly = true)
public interface AuthorRepository extends JpaRepository<Author, Long> {
```

---

[11]HibernateSpringBootNamedEntityGraph

```
    @Override
    @EntityGraph(attributePaths = {"books"},
                type = EntityGraph.EntityGraphType.FETCH)
    public List<Author> findAll();
}
```

Calling findAll() triggers the same SQL SELECT statement as @NamedEntityGraph:

```
SELECT
    author0_.id AS id1_0_0_,
    books1_.id AS id1_1_1_,
    author0_.age AS age2_0_0_,
    author0_.genre AS genre3_0_0_,
    author0_.name AS name4_0_0_,
    books1_.author_id AS author_i4_1_1_,
    books1_.isbn AS isbn2_1_1_,
    books1_.title AS title3_1_1_,
    books1_.author_id AS author_i4_1_0__,
    books1_.id AS id1_1_0__
FROM author author0_
LEFT OUTER JOIN book books1_
    ON author0_.id = books1_.author_id
```

Reiterating the examples of using @EntityGraph with the Query Builder mechanism, Specification, and JPQL will result in the following repository:

```
@Repository
@Transactional(readOnly = true)
public interface AuthorRepository extends JpaRepository<Author, Long>,
        JpaSpecificationExecutor<Author> {

    @Override
    @EntityGraph(attributePaths = {"books"},
        type = EntityGraph.EntityGraphType.FETCH)
    public List<Author> findAll();
```

```
@EntityGraph(attributePaths = {"books"},
    type = EntityGraph.EntityGraphType.FETCH)
public List<Author> findByAgeLessThanOrderByNameDesc(int age);

@Override
@EntityGraph(attributePaths = {"books"},
    type = EntityGraph.EntityGraphType.FETCH)
public List<Author> findAll(Specification spec);

@EntityGraph(attributePaths = {"books"},
    type = EntityGraph.EntityGraphType.FETCH)
@Query(value="SELECT a FROM Author a WHERE a.age > 20 AND a.age<40")
public List<Author> fetchAllAgeBetween20And40();
}
```

The complete application is available on GitHub[12].

> Ad hoc entity graphs are a convenient way to keep the entity graph definition at the repository-level and not alter the entities with @NamedEntityGraph.

## Defining an Entity Graph via EntityManager

To get an entity graph directly via EntityManager, you call the getEntityGraph(String entityGraphName) method. Next, pass the return of this method to the overloaded find() method, as in the following snippet of code:

```
EntityGraph entityGraph = entityManager
                .getEntityGraph("author-books-graph");

Map<String, Object> properties = new HashMap<>();
properties.put("javax.persistence.fetchgraph", entityGraph);
Author author = entityManager.find(Author.class, id, properties);
```

---

[12]HibernateSpringBootEntityGraphAttributePaths

JPQL and EntityManager can be used as well:

```
EntityGraph entityGraph = entityManager
                .getEntityGraph("author-books-graph");
```

```
Author author = entityManager.createQuery(
     "SELECT a FROM Author a WHERE a.id = :id", Author.class)
  .setParameter("id", id)
  .setHint("javax.persistence.fetchgraph", entityGraph)
  .getSingleResult();
```

Or via CriteriaBuilder and EntityManager:

```
EntityGraph entityGraph = entityManager
                .getEntityGraph("author-books-graph");
```

```
CriteriaBuilder criteriaBuilder = entityManager.getCriteriaBuilder();
CriteriaQuery<Author> criteriaQuery
   = criteriaBuilder.createQuery(Author.class);
```

```
Root<Author> author = criteriaQuery.from(Author.class);
criteriaQuery.where(criteriaBuilder.equal(root.<Long>get("id"), id));
```

```
TypedQuery<Author> typedQuery = entityManager.createQuery(criteriaQuery);
typedQuery.setHint("javax.persistence.loadgraph", entityGraph);
```

```
Author author = typedQuery.getSingleResult();
```

You can create an entity graph via the EntityManager#createEntityGraph() method. For more details, read the documentation.

# Item 8: How to Fetch Associations via Entity Sub-Graphs

If you are not familiar with entity graphs, read **Item 7** before this one.

Entity graphs are prone to performance penalties as well. Creating  big trees of entities (e.g., sub-graphs that have sub-graphs) or loading associations (and/or fields) that are not needed will cause performance penalties. Think about how easy it is to create Cartesian products of type m x n x p x..., which grow to huge values very fast.

Sub-graphs allow you to build complex entity graphs. Mainly, a sub-graph is an entity graph that is embedded into another entity graph or entity sub-graph. Let's look at three entities—Author, Book, and Publisher. The Author and Book entities are involved in a bidirectional lazy @OneToMany association. The Publisher and Book entities are also involved in a bidirectional lazy @OneToMany association. Between Author and Publisher there is no association. Figure 1-9 shows the involved tables (author, book, and publisher).

**Figure 1-9.**  *Table relationships*

The goal of this entity graph is to fetch all authors with associated books, and further, the publishers associated with these books. For this, let's use the entity sub-graphs.

## Using @NamedEntityGraph and @NamedSubgraph

In the Author entity use the @NamedEntityGraph to define the entity graph to eagerly load the authors and the associated books and @NamedSubgraph to define the entity sub-graph for loading the publishers associated with the loaded books:

```
@Entity
@NamedEntityGraph(
    name = "author-books-publisher-graph",
    attributeNodes = {
        @NamedAttributeNode(value = "books", subgraph = "publisher-subgraph")
    },
    subgraphs = {
        @NamedSubgraph(
            name = "publisher-subgraph",
            attributeNodes = {
                @NamedAttributeNode("publisher")
            }
        )
    }
)
public class Author implements Serializable {

    private static final long serialVersionUID = 1L;

    @Id
    @GeneratedValue(strategy = GenerationType.IDENTITY)
    private Long id;

    private String name;
    private String genre;
    private int age;

    @OneToMany(cascade = CascadeType.ALL,
                mappedBy = "author", orphanRemoval = true)
    private List<Book> books = new ArrayList<>();

    // getters and setters omitted for brevity
}
```

And the relevant part from Book is listed here:

```
@Entity
public class Book implements Serializable {
    ...
    @ManyToOne(fetch = FetchType.LAZY)
    @JoinColumn(name = "publisher_id")
    private Publisher publisher;
    ...
}
```

Further, let's use the entity graph in AuthorRepository:

```
@Repository
@Transactional(readOnly = true)
public interface AuthorRepository extends JpaRepository<Author, Long> {

    @Override
    @EntityGraph(value = "author-books-publisher-graph",
                 type = EntityGraph.EntityGraphType.FETCH)
    public List<Author> findAll();
}
```

Calling findAll() triggers the following SQL SELECT statement:

```
SELECT
    author0_.id AS id1_0_0_,
    books1_.id AS id1_1_1_,
    publisher2_.id AS id1_2_2_,
    author0_.age AS age2_0_0_,
    author0_.genre AS genre3_0_0_,
    author0_.name AS name4_0_0_,
    books1_.author_id AS author_i4_1_1_,
    books1_.isbn AS isbn2_1_1_,
    books1_.publisher_id AS publishe5_1_1_,
    books1_.title AS title3_1_1_,
    books1_.author_id AS author_i4_1_0__,
    books1_.id AS id1_1_0__,
    publisher2_.company AS company2_2_2_
```

```
FROM author author0_
LEFT OUTER JOIN book books1_
  ON author0_.id = books1_.author_id
LEFT OUTER JOIN publisher publisher2_
  ON books1_.publisher_id = publisher2_.id
```

Although it's quite obvious, let's mention that sub-graphs can be used with the Query Builder mechanism, Specification, and JPQL. For example, here's the sub-graph used with JPQL:

```
@Repository
@Transactional(readOnly = true)
public interface AuthorRepository extends JpaRepository<Author, Long> {

    @EntityGraph(value = "author-books-publisher-graph",
                 type = EntityGraph.EntityGraphType.FETCH)
    @Query(value="SELECT a FROM Author a WHERE a.age > 20 AND a.age<40")
    public List<Author> fetchAllAgeBetween20And40();
}
```

Calling fetchAllAgeBetween20And40() triggers the following SQL SELECT statement (notice how the query was enriched to respect the entity graph):

```
SELECT
  author0_.id AS id1_0_0_,
  books1_.id AS id1_1_1_,
  publisher2_.id AS id1_2_2_,
  author0_.age AS age2_0_0_,
  author0_.genre AS genre3_0_0_,
  author0_.name AS name4_0_0_,
  books1_.author_id AS author_i4_1_1_,
  books1_.isbn AS isbn2_1_1_,
  books1_.publisher_id AS publishe5_1_1_,
  books1_.title AS title3_1_1_,
  books1_.author_id AS author_i4_1_0__,
  books1_.id AS id1_1_0__,
  publisher2_.company AS company2_2_2_
FROM author author0_
```

```
LEFT OUTER JOIN book books1_
  ON author0_.id = books1_.author_id
LEFT OUTER JOIN publisher publisher2_
  ON books1_.publisher_id = publisher2_.id
WHERE author0_.age > 20
AND author0_.age < 40
```

> Pay attention to JPQL queries used with entity graphs that specify join fetching. In such JPQL queries, it's mandatory to have the owner of the fetched association present in the SELECT list.

## Using the Dot Notation (.) in Ad Hoc Entity Graphs

Sub-graphs can be used in ad hoc entity graphs as well. Remember that ad hoc entity graphs allows you to keep the entity graph definition at repository-level and not alter the entities with @NamedEntityGraph.

To use sub-graphs, you just chain the needed associations using the dot notation (.), as shown in the following example:

```
@Repository
@Transactional(readOnly = true)
public interface AuthorRepository extends JpaRepository<Author, Long> {

    @Override
    @EntityGraph(attributePaths = {"books.publisher"},
                type = EntityGraph.EntityGraphType.FETCH)
    public List<Author> findAll();
}
```

So, you can fetch the publishers associated with the books via the books.publisher path. The triggered SELECT is the same as when using @NamedEntityGraph and @NamedSubgraph.

Let's look at another example, just to get familiar with this idea. Let's define an ad hoc entity graph to fetch all publishers and associated books, and further, the authors associated with these books. This time, the entity graph is defined in PublisherRepository as follows:

```
@Repository
@Transactional(readOnly = true)
public interface PublisherRepository
    extends JpaRepository<Publisher, Long> {

    @Override
    @EntityGraph(attributePaths = "books.author"},
                 type = EntityGraph.EntityGraphType.FETCH)
    public List<Publisher> findAll();
}
```

The SQL SELECT statement triggered this time is listed here:

```
SELECT
  publisher0_.id AS id1_2_0_,
  books1_.id AS id1_1_1_,
  author2_.id AS id1_0_2_,
  publisher0_.company AS company2_2_0_,
  books1_.author_id AS author_i4_1_1_,
  books1_.isbn AS isbn2_1_1_,
  books1_.publisher_id AS publishe5_1_1_,
  books1_.title AS title3_1_1_,
  books1_.publisher_id AS publishe5_1_0__,
  books1_.id AS id1_1_0__,
  author2_.age AS age2_0_2_,
  author2_.genre AS genre3_0_2_,
  author2_.name AS name4_0_2_
FROM publisher publisher0_
LEFT OUTER JOIN book books1_
  ON publisher0_.id = books1_.publisher_id
LEFT OUTER JOIN author author2_
  ON books1_.author_id = author2_.id
```

Ad hoc sub-graphs can be used with the Spring Data Query Builder mechanism, Specification, and JPQL. For example, here it is the above ad hoc sub-graph used with JPQL:

```
@Repository
@Transactional(readOnly = true)
public interface PublisherRepository
    extends JpaRepository<Publisher, Long> {

    @EntityGraph(attributePaths = {"books.author"},
                 type = EntityGraph.EntityGraphType.FETCH)
    @Query("SELECT p FROM Publisher p WHERE p.id > 1 AND p.id < 3")
    public List<Publisher> fetchAllIdBetween1And3();
}
```

Calling fetchAllIdBetween1And3() triggers the following SQL SELECT statement (notice how the query was enriched to respect the entity graph):

```
SELECT
  publisher0_.id AS id1_2_0_,
  books1_.id AS id1_1_1_,
  author2_.id AS id1_0_2_,
  publisher0_.company AS company2_2_0_,
  books1_.author_id AS author_i4_1_1_,
  books1_.isbn AS isbn2_1_1_,
  books1_.publisher_id AS publishe5_1_1_,
  books1_.title AS title3_1_1_,
  books1_.publisher_id AS publishe5_1_0__,
  books1_.id AS id1_1_0__,
  author2_.age AS age2_0_2_,
  author2_.genre AS genre3_0_2_,
  author2_.name AS name4_0_2_
FROM publisher publisher0_
LEFT OUTER JOIN book books1_
  ON publisher0_.id = books1_.publisher_id
LEFT OUTER JOIN author author2_
```

```
  ON books1_.author_id = author2_.id
WHERE publisher0_.id > 1
AND publisher0_.id < 3
```

The complete application is available on GitHub[13].

## Defining an Entity Sub-Graph via EntityManager

You can build an entity sub-graph directly via `EntityManager` and the `EntityGraph.addSubgraph(String attributeName)` method, as shown in the following snippet of code:

```
EntityGraph<Author> entityGraph = entityManager
    .createEntityGraph(Author.class);
```

```
Subgraph<Book> bookGraph = entityGraph.addSubgraph("books");
bookGraph.addAttributeNodes("publisher");
```

```
Map<String, Object> properties = new HashMap<>();
properties.put("javax.persistence.fetchgraph", entityGraph);
Author author = entityManager.find(Author.class, id, properties);
```

# Item 9: How to Handle
# Entity Graphs and Basic Attributes

When Hibernate JPA is around, using entity graphs to fetch only some basic attributes of an entity (not all) requires a compromise solution based on:

- Enabling Hibernate Bytecode Enhancement

- Annotating the basic attributes that should not be part of the entity graph with `@Basic(fetch = FetchType.LAZY)`

The main drawback consists of the fact that these basic attributes are fetched lazy by all other queries (e.g. `findById()`) and not only by the queries using the entity graph, and most probably, you will not want this behavior. So use it carefully!

---

[13]HibernateSpringBootNamedSubgraph

Conforming to JPA specifications, entity graphs can override the current FetchType semantics via two properties—javax.persistence.fetchgraph and javax.persistence.loadgraph. Depending on the used property, the entity graph can be a *fetch graph* or a *load graph*. In the case of a fetch graph, the attributes present in attributeNodes are treated as FetchType.EAGER. The remaining attributes are treated as FetchType.LAZY regardless of the default/explicit FetchType. In the case of load graph, the attributes present in attributeNodes are treated as FetchType.EAGER. The remaining attributes are treated according to their specified or default FetchType.

That being said, let's assume that the Author and Book entities are involved in a bidirectional lazy @OneToMany association. Moreover, in the Author entity, let's define an entity graph to load the names of the authors and the associated books. There is no need to load the ages and genres of authors, so the age and genre basic fields are not specified in the entity graph:

```
@Entity
@NamedEntityGraph(
    name = "author-books-graph",
    attributeNodes = {
        @NamedAttributeNode("name"),
        @NamedAttributeNode("books")
    }
)
public class Author implements Serializable {

    private static final long serialVersionUID = 1L;

    @Id
    @GeneratedValue(strategy = GenerationType.IDENTITY)
    private Long id;

    private String name;
    private String genre;
    private int age;

    @OneToMany(cascade = CascadeType.ALL,
                mappedBy = "author", orphanRemoval = true)
    private List<Book> books = new ArrayList<>();

    // getters and setters omitted for brevity
}
```

Let's use this entity graph in `AuthorRepository`. To have both in the same repository, you can use two methods via the Query Builder mechanism. It produces almost identical SQL statements named `findByAgeGreaterThanAndGenre()` and `findByGenreAndAgeGreaterThan()`:

```
@Repository
@Transactional(readOnly = true)
public interface AuthorRepository extends JpaRepository<Author, Long> {

    @EntityGraph(value = "author-books-graph",
                type = EntityGraph.EntityGraphType.FETCH)
    public List<Author> findByAgeGreaterThanAndGenre(int age, String genre);

    @EntityGraph(value = "author-books-graph",
                type = EntityGraph.EntityGraphType.LOAD)
    public List<Author> findByGenreAndAgeGreaterThan(String genre, int age);
}
```

Calling the `findByAgeGreaterThanAndGenre()` triggers the following SQL SELECT statement (this is the fetch graph):

```
SELECT
  author0_.id AS id1_0_0_,
  books1_.id AS id1_1_1_,
  author0_.age AS age2_0_0_,
  author0_.genre AS genre3_0_0_,
  author0_.name AS name4_0_0_,
  books1_.author_id AS author_i4_1_1_,
  books1_.isbn AS isbn2_1_1_,
  books1_.title AS title3_1_1_,
  books1_.author_id AS author_i4_1_0__,
  books1_.id AS id1_1_0__
FROM author author0_
LEFT OUTER JOIN book books1_
  ON author0_.id = books1_.author_id
WHERE author0_.age > ?
AND author0_.genre = ?
```

Notice that, even if age and genre are not part of the fetch graph, they have been fetched in the query. Let's try the load graph via findByGenreAndAgeGreaterThan():

```
SELECT
  author0_.id AS id1_0_0_,
  books1_.id AS id1_1_1_,
  author0_.age AS age2_0_0_,
  author0_.genre AS genre3_0_0_,
  author0_.name AS name4_0_0_,
  books1_.author_id AS author_i4_1_1_,
  books1_.isbn AS isbn2_1_1_,
  books1_.title AS title3_1_1_,
  books1_.author_id AS author_i4_1_0__,
  books1_.id AS id1_1_0__
FROM author author0_
LEFT OUTER JOIN book books1_
  ON author0_.id = books1_.author_id
WHERE author0_.genre = ?
AND author0_.age > ?
```

This time the presence of age and genre is normal. But these attributes (age and genre) are also loaded in the case of the fetch graph even if they are not explicitly specified via @NamedAttributeNode.

By default, attributes are annotated with @Basic, which relies on the default fetch policy. The default fetch policy is FetchType.EAGER. Based on this statement, a compromise solution consists of annotating the basic attributes that should not be fetched in the fetch graph with @Basic(fetch = FetchType.LAZY) as here:

```
...
@Basic(fetch = FetchType.LAZY)
private String genre;
@Basic(fetch = FetchType.LAZY)
private int age;
...
```

But executing the fetch and load graph again reveals the exactly same queries. This means that the JPA specifications don't apply to Hibernate with the basic (@Basic) attributes. Both the fetch graph and the load graph will ignore these settings as long as Bytecode Enhancement is not enabled. In Maven, add the following plug-in:

```xml
<plugin>
    <groupId>org.hibernate.orm.tooling</groupId>
    <artifactId>hibernate-enhance-maven-plugin</artifactId>
    <version>${hibernate.version}</version>
    <executions>
        <execution>
            <configuration>
                <failOnError>true</failOnError>
                <enableLazyInitialization>true</enableLazyInitialization>
            </configuration>
            <goals>
                <goal>enhance</goal>
            </goals>
        </execution>
    </executions>
</plugin>
```

Finally, executing the fetch graph will reveal the expected SELECT:

```sql
SELECT
    author0_.id AS id1_0_0_,
    books1_.id AS id1_1_1_,
    author0_.name AS name4_0_0_,
    books1_.author_id AS author_i4_1_1_,
    books1_.isbn AS isbn2_1_1_,
    books1_.title AS title3_1_1_,
    books1_.author_id AS author_i4_1_0__,
    books1_.id AS id1_1_0__
FROM author author0_
```

```
LEFT OUTER JOIN book books1_
  ON author0_.id = books1_.author_id
WHERE author0_.age > ?
AND author0_.genre = ?
```

Executing the load graph will reveal the expected SELECT as well:

```
SELECT
  author0_.id AS id1_0_0_,
  books1_.id AS id1_1_1_,
  author0_.name AS name4_0_0_,
  books1_.author_id AS author_i4_1_1_,
  books1_.isbn AS isbn2_1_1_,
  books1_.title AS title3_1_1_,
  books1_.author_id AS author_i4_1_0__,
  books1_.id AS id1_1_0__
FROM author author0_
LEFT OUTER JOIN book books1_
  ON author0_.id = books1_.author_id
WHERE author0_.genre = ?
AND author0_.age > ?
```

The complete application is available on GitHub[14].

# Item 10: How to Filter Associations via a Hibernate-Specific @Where Annotation

Rely on the @Where approach only if JOIN FETCH WHERE (**Item 39**) or @NamedEntityGraph (**Item 7** and **Item 8**) is not suitable for your case.

[14]HibernateSpringBootNamedEntityGraphBasicAttrs

The @Where annotation is simple to use and can be useful for filtering the fetched association by appending a WHERE clause to the query.

Let's use the Author and Book entities involved in a bidirectional lazy @OneToMany association. The goal is to lazy fetch the following:

- All books

- All books cheaper than $20

- All books more expensive than $20

To filter the cheaper/more expensive books, the Author entity relies on @Where as follows:

```
@Entity
public class Author implements Serializable {

    private static final long serialVersionUID = 1L;

    @Id
    @GeneratedValue(strategy = GenerationType.IDENTITY)
    private Long id;

    private String name;
    private String genre;
    private int age;

    @OneToMany(cascade = CascadeType.ALL,
            mappedBy = "author", orphanRemoval = true)
    private List<Book> books = new ArrayList<>();

    @OneToMany(cascade = CascadeType.ALL,
            mappedBy = "author", orphanRemoval = true)
    @Where(clause = "price <= 20")
    private List<Book> cheapBooks = new ArrayList<>();

    @OneToMany(cascade = CascadeType.ALL,
            mappedBy = "author", orphanRemoval = true)
    @Where(clause = "price > 20")
    private List<Book> restOfBooks = new ArrayList<>();
    ...
}
```

Further, let's write three service-methods that will trigger the three queries:

```
@Transactional(readOnly = true)
public void fetchAuthorWithAllBooks() {

    Author author = authorRepository.findById(1L).orElseThrow();
    List<Book> books = author.getBooks();

    System.out.println(books);
}

@Transactional(readOnly = true)
public void fetchAuthorWithCheapBooks() {

    Author author = authorRepository.findById(1L).orElseThrow();
    List<Book> books = author.getCheapBooks();

    System.out.println(books);
}

@Transactional(readOnly = true)
public void fetchAuthorWithRestOfBooks() {

    Author author = authorRepository.findById(1L).orElseThrow();
    List<Book> books = author.getRestOfBooks();

    System.out.println(books);
}
```

Calling fetchAuthorWithCheapBooks() triggers the following SQL statement, which fetches the books cheaper than $20:

```
SELECT
    cheapbooks0_.author_id AS author_i5_1_0_,
    cheapbooks0_.id AS id1_1_0_,
    cheapbooks0_.id AS id1_1_1_,
    cheapbooks0_.author_id AS author_i5_1_1_,
    cheapbooks0_.isbn AS isbn2_1_1_,
    cheapbooks0_.price AS price3_1_1_,
    cheapbooks0_.title AS title4_1_1_
```

```
FROM book cheapbooks0_
WHERE (cheapbooks0_.price <= 20)
AND cheapbooks0_.author_id = ?
```

Hibernate has appended the WHERE clause to instruct the database to filter the books by price <= 20.

Calling fetchAuthorWithRestOfBooks() will append the WHERE clause to filter the books by price > 20:

```
SELECT
    restofbook0_.author_id AS author_i5_1_0_,
    restofbook0_.id AS id1_1_0_,
    restofbook0_.id AS id1_1_1_,
    restofbook0_.author_id AS author_i5_1_1_,
    restofbook0_.isbn AS isbn2_1_1_,
    restofbook0_.price AS price3_1_1_,
    restofbook0_.title AS title4_1_1_
FROM book restofbook0_
WHERE (restofbook0_.price > 20)
AND restofbook0_.author_id = ?
```

The complete application is available on GitHub[15].

Notice that these queries fetch the books in a lazy fashion. In other words, these are additional SELECT queries triggered after fetching the author in a separate SELECT. This is okay as long as you don't want to fetch the author and the associated books in the same SELECT. In such cases, switching from LAZY to EAGER should be avoided. Therefore, relying on JOIN FETCH WHERE is much better at least from two aspects:

- It fetches the associated books in the same SELECT with author

- It allows us to pass the given price as a query binding parameter

Nevertheless, @Where can be useful in several situations. For example, it can be used in a soft deletes implementation (**Item 109**).

---

[15]HibernateSpringBootFilterAssociation

# Item 11: How to Optimize Unidirectional/ Bidirectional @OneToOne via @MapsId

Let's use the Author and Book entities involved in a @OneToOne association. In Figure 1-10 there is the corresponding one-to-one table relationship.

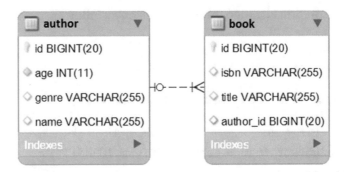

***Figure 1-10.***  *The one-to-one table relationship*

In relational databases (RDBMS), the one-to-one association involves a parent-side and a child-side that are "linked" via a unique foreign key. In JPA, this association is mapped via the @OneToOne annotation, and the association can be either unidirectional or bidirectional.

In this context, why is @MapsId so important in unidirectional and bidirectional @OneToOne associations? Well, let's use a regular mapping and highlight the drawbacks from a performance perspective. Therefore, we focus on the unidirectional @OneToOne association.

## Regular Unidirectional @OneToOne

The Author is the parent-side and the Book is the child-side of the one-to-one association. The Author entity is listed here:

```
@Entity
public class Author implements Serializable {

    private static final long serialVersionUID = 1L;

    @Id
    @GeneratedValue(strategy = GenerationType.IDENTITY)
    private Long id;
```

```
    private String name;
    private String genre;
    private int age;

    // getters and setters omitted for brevity
}
```

The @OneToOne annotation is added on the child-side as follows:

```
@Entity
public class Book implements Serializable {

    private static final long serialVersionUID = 1L;

    @Id
    @GeneratedValue(strategy = GenerationType.IDENTITY)
    private Long id;

    private String title;
    private String isbn;

    @OneToOne(fetch = FetchType.LAZY)
    @JoinColumn(name = "author_id")
    private Author author;

    // getters and setters omitted for brevity
}
```

> The @JoinColumn annotation is used to customize the name of the foreign key column.

The unidirectional @OneToOne controls the associated foreign key. In other words, the owning side of the relationship controls the foreign key. You call setAuthor() from a service-method as follows (do not use orElseThrow() in production; here it is used just for quickly unwrapping the Author from the returned Optional):

```
@Transactional
public void newBookOfAuthor() {

    Author author = authorRepository.findById(1L).orElseThrow();
```

```
Book book = new Book();
book.setTitle("A History of Ancient Prague");
book.setIsbn("001-JN");
book.setAuthor(author);

bookRepository.save(book);
}
```

Calling newBookOfAuthor() will produce the following INSERT statement in the book table:

```
INSERT INTO book (author_id, isbn, title)
    VALUES (?, ?, ?)
Binding:[1, 001-JN, A History of Ancient Prague]
```

So, the JPA persistence provider (Hibernate) has populated the foreign key column (author_id) value with the author identifier.

Everything looks fine so far! However, when the parent-side of such an association needs to fetch the associated child, it needs to trigger a JPQL query because the child entity identifier is unknown. Check out the following JPQL query:

```
@Repository
public interface BookRepository extends JpaRepository<Book, Long> {

    @Query("SELECT b FROM Book b WHERE b.author = ?1")
    public Book fetchBookByAuthor(Author author);
}
```

And, the service-method is as follows:

```
@Transactional(readOnly = true)
public Book fetchBookByAuthor() {
    Author author = authorRepository.findById(1L).orElseThrow();

    return bookRepository.fetchBookByAuthor(author);
}
```

Calling fetchBookByAuthor() will produce the following SQL statement:

```
SELECT
    book0_.id AS id1_1_,
    book0_.author_id AS author_i4_1_,
```

```
    book0_.isbn AS isbn2_1_,
    book0_.title AS title3_1_
FROM book book0_
WHERE book0_.author_id = ?
Binding:[1] Extracted:[1, 1, 001-JN, A History of Ancient Prague]
```

If the parent-side constantly/always needs the child-side as well, then triggering a new query can be a performance penalty.

---

The performance penalty highlighted gets worse if the application uses the Second Level Cache for storing Authors and Books. While the Authors and Books are stored in the Second Level Cache, fetching the associated child will still require a database round trip via the JPQL query listed here. Assuming that the parent knows the identifier of the child, it can take advantage of the Second Level Cache as follows (don't give your attention to orElseThrow(); it's just for quickly solving the returned Optional):

```
Author author = authorRepository.findById(1L).orElseThrow();
```

```
Book book = bookRepository.findById(author.getId()).orElseThrow();
```

But, since the child identifier is unknown, this code cannot be used.

Other (not better) workarounds are to rely on query cache or @NaturalId.

---

## Regular Bidirectional @OneToOne

Let's use the Author and Book entities involved in a bidirectional @OneToOne association. In other words, the parent-side relies on mappedBy as follows (the child-side remains the same):

```
@Entity
public class Author implements Serializable {

    private static final long serialVersionUID = 1L;
```

```
@Id
@GeneratedValue(strategy = GenerationType.IDENTITY)
private Long id;

private String name;
private String genre;
private int age;

@OneToOne(mappedBy = "author", cascade = CascadeType.ALL,
        fetch = FetchType.LAZY)
private Book book;

// getters and setters omitted for brevity
}
```

The main drawback of the bidirectional @OneToOne can be observed by fetching the parent (Author) as follows:

```
Author author = authorRepository.findById(1L).orElseThrow();
```

Even if this is a LAZY association, fetching the Author will trigger the following SELECT statements:

```
SELECT
  author0_.id AS id1_0_0_,
  author0_.age AS age2_0_0_,
  author0_.genre AS genre3_0_0_,
  author0_.name AS name4_0_0_
FROM author author0_
WHERE author0_.id = ?

SELECT
  book0_.id AS id1_1_0_,
  book0_.author_id AS author_i4_1_0_,
  book0_.isbn AS isbn2_1_0_,
  book0_.title AS title3_1_0_
FROM book book0_
WHERE book0_.author_id = ?
```

Next to the parent entity, Hibernate fetched the child entity as well. Obviously, if the application needs only the parent then fetching the child is just a waste of resources, which is a performance penalty.

> The secondary query is caused by a parent-side dilemma. Without fetching the child entity, the JPA persistent provider (Hibernate) cannot know if it should assign the child reference to `null` or to an `Object` (concrete object or proxy object). Adding non-nullability awareness via the `optional=false` element to @OneToOne doesn't help in this case.
>
> A workaround consists of relying on Bytecode Enhancement and `@LazyToOne(LazyToOneOption.NO_PROXY)` on the parent-side. Or, even better, rely on unidirectional @OneToOne and @MapsId.

## @MapsId to the Rescue of @OneToOne

The `@MapsId` is a JPA 2.0 annotation that can be applied to @ManyToOne and unidirectional (or bidirectional) @OneToOne associations. Via this annotation, the book table's primary key can also be a foreign key referencing the author's table primary key. The author and book tables share primary keys (the child shares the primary key with the parent table), as shown in Figure 1-11.

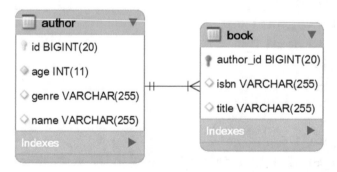

***Figure 1-11.***  *@MapsId and @OneToOne shared key*

You add @MapsId to the child entity, as shown here:

```
@Entity
public class Book implements Serializable {

    private static final long serialVersionUID = 1L;

    @Id
    private Long id;

    private String title;
    private String isbn;

    @MapsId
    @OneToOne(fetch = FetchType.LAZY)
    @JoinColumn(name = "author_id")
    private Author author;

    // getters and setters omitted for brevity
}
```

Check out the identifier of the Book entity. There is no need for it to be generated (@GeneratedValue is not present) since this identifier is exactly the identifier of the author association. The Book identifier is set by Hibernate on your behalf.

The @JoinColumn annotation is used to customize the name of the primary key column.

The parent entity is quite simple because there is no need to have a bidirectional @OneToOne (if this is what you initially had). The Author is as follows:

```
@Entity
public class Author implements Serializable {

    private static final long serialVersionUID = 1L;
```

```
    @Id
    @GeneratedValue(strategy = GenerationType.IDENTITY)
    private Long id;

    private String name;
    private String genre;
    private int age;

    // getters and setters omitted for brevity
}
```

Now, you can persist a Book via a service-method as follows (consider the highlighted comment):

```
@Transactional
public void newBookOfAuthor() {
    Author author = authorRepository.findById(1L).orElseThrow();

    Book book = new Book();
    book.setTitle("A History of Ancient Prague");
    book.setIsbn("001-JN");

    // this will set the id of the book as the id of the author
    book.setAuthor(author);

    bookRepository.save(book);
}
```

Calling newBookOfAuthor() reveals the following INSERT statement (this is the effect of calling the save() method):

```
INSERT INTO book (isbn, title, author_id)
  VALUES (?, ?, ?)
Binding:[001-JN, A History of Ancient Prague, 1]
```

Notice that author_id was set to the author identifier. This means that the parent and the child tables share the same primary key.

Further, the developer can fetch the Book via the Author identifier, as follows (since the identifier is shared between Author and Book, the developer can rely on author.getId() to specify the Book identifier):

```
@Transactional(readOnly = true)
public Book fetchBookByAuthorId() {
    Author author = authorRepository.findById(1L).orElseThrow();

    return bookRepository.findById(author.getId()).orElseThrow();
}
```

There are a bunch of advantages of using @MapsId, as follows:

- If Book is present in the Second Level Cache it will be fetched accordingly (no extra database round trip is needed). This is the main drawback of a regular unidirectional @OneToOne.

- Fetching the Author doesn't automatically trigger an unnecessary additional query for fetching the Book as well. This is the main drawback of a regular bidirectional @OneToOne.

- Sharing the primary key reduces memory footprint (no need to index both the primary key and the foreign key).

The complete code is available on GitHub[16].

# Item 12: How to Validate that Only One Association Is Non-Null

Consider the Review entity. It defines three @ManyToOne relationships to Book, Article, and Magazine:

```
@Entity
public class Review implements Serializable {

    private static final long serialVersionUID = 1L;
```

---

[16]HibernateSpringBootOneToOneMapsId

```
    @Id
    @GeneratedValue(strategy = GenerationType.IDENTITY)
    private Long id;

    private String content;

    @ManyToOne(fetch = FetchType.LAZY)
    private Book book;

    @ManyToOne(fetch = FetchType.LAZY)
    private Article article;

    @ManyToOne(fetch = FetchType.LAZY)
    private Magazine magazine;

    // getters and setters omitted for brevity
}
```

In this context, a review can be associated with a book, a magazine, or an article. Implementing this constraint at application-level can be achieved via Bean Validation[17]. Start by defining an annotation that will be added at class-level to the Review entity:

```
@Target({ElementType.TYPE})
@Retention(RetentionPolicy.RUNTIME)
@Constraint(validatedBy = {JustOneOfManyValidator.class})
public @interface JustOneOfMany {

    String message() default "A review can be associated with either
                              a book, a magazine or an article";
    Class<?>[] groups() default {};
    Class<? extends Payload>[] payload() default {};
}
```

Following the Bean Validation documentation, the @JustOneOfMany annotation is empowered by the following validation:

```
public class JustOneOfManyValidator
        implements ConstraintValidator<JustOneOfMany, Review> {
```

---

[17]https://beanvalidation.org/

```
@Override
public boolean isValid(Review review, ConstraintValidatorContext ctx) {

    return Stream.of(
            review.getBook(), review.getArticle(), review.getMagazine())
        .filter(Objects::nonNull)
        .count() == 1;
}
}
```

Finally, just add the @JustOneOfMany annotation at the class-level to the Review entity:

```
@Entity
@JustOneOfMany
public class Review implements Serializable {
    ...
}
```

# Testing Time

The database already contains a Book, an Article, and a Magazine. The following service-method will successfully save a Review of a Book:

```
@Transactional
public void persistReviewOk() {

    Review review = new Review();
    review.setContent("This is a book review ...");
    review.setBook(bookRepository.findById(1L).get());

    reviewRepository.save(review);
}
```

On the other hand, the following service-method will not succeed to persist a Review. It will fail the validation specified via @JustOneOfMany since the code tries to set this review to an Article and to a Magazine:

```
@Transactional
public void persistReviewWrong() {
```

```
Review review = new Review();
review.setContent("This is an article and magazine review ...");
review.setArticle(articleRepository.findById(1L).get());
```

**// this will fail validation**
**review.setMagazine(magazineRepository.findById(1L).get());**

```
reviewRepository.save(review);
}
```

Nevertheless, note that native queries can bypass this application-level validation. If you know that such a scenario is possible, you have to add this validation at the database-level as well. In MySQL, this can be done via a TRIGGER, as follows:

```
CREATE TRIGGER Just_One_Of_Many
    BEFORE INSERT ON review
    FOR EACH ROW
    BEGIN
        IF (NEW.article_id IS NOT NULL AND NEW.magazine_id IS NOT NULL)
            OR (NEW.article_id IS NOT NULL AND NEW.book_id IS NOT NULL)
            OR (NEW.book_id IS NOT NULL AND NEW.magazine_id IS NOT NULL) THEN
                SIGNAL SQLSTATE '45000'
                SET MESSAGE_TEXT='A review can be associated with either
                                    a book, a magazine or an article';
        END IF;
END;
```

The complete application is available on GitHub[18].

---

[18]HibernateSpringBootChooseOnlyOneAssociation

# CHAPTER 2

# Entities

## Item 13: How to Adopt a Fluent API Style in Entities

Consider the Author and Book entities, which are involved in a bidirectional lazy @OneToMany association, as shown in Figure 2-1.

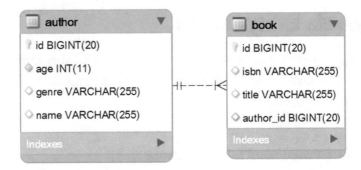

***Figure 2-1.*** *The @OneToMany table relationship*

Usually, you can create an Author with Books as follows (e.g., one author with two books):

```
Author author = new Author();
author.setName("Joana Nimar");
author.setAge(34);
author.setGenre("History");

Book book1 = new Book();
book1.setTitle("A History of Ancient Prague");
book1.setIsbn("001-JN");
```

91

© Anghel Leonard 2020
A. Leonard, *Spring Boot Persistence Best Practices*, https://doi.org/10.1007/978-1-4842-5626-8_2

```
Book book2 = new Book();
book2.setTitle("A People's History");
book2.setIsbn("002-JN");

// addBook() is a helper method defined in Author class
author.addBook(book1);
author.addBook(book2);
```

You can also write this snippet in fluent-style in at least two ways.

Fluent-style is primarily designed to be readable and to create a code-flowing sensation.

## Fluent-Style via Entity Setters

Let's employee fluent-style via the entity setters. Typically, an entity setter method returns void. You can alter the entity setters to return this instead of void as follows (this should be done for the helper methods as well):

```
@Entity
public class Author implements Serializable {

    private static final long serialVersionUID = 1L;

    @Id
    @GeneratedValue(strategy = GenerationType.IDENTITY)
    private Long id;

    private String name;
    private String genre;
    private int age;

    @OneToMany(cascade = CascadeType.ALL,
                mappedBy = "author", orphanRemoval = true)
    private List<Book> books = new ArrayList<>();
```

```java
    public Author addBook(Book book) {
        this.books.add(book);
        book.setAuthor(this);
        return this;
    }

    public Author removeBook(Book book) {
        book.setAuthor(null);
        this.books.remove(book);
        return this;
    }

    public Author setId(Long id) {
        this.id = id;
        return this;
    }

    public Author setName(String name) {
        this.name = name;
        return this;
    }

    public Author setGenre(String genre) {
        this.genre = genre;
        return this;
    }
    public Author setAge(int age) {
        this.age = age;
        return this;
    }

    public Author setBooks(List<Book> books) {
        this.books = books;
        return this;
    }

    // getters omitted for brevity
}
```

```java
@Entity
public class Book implements Serializable {

    private static final long serialVersionUID = 1L;

    @Id
    @GeneratedValue(strategy = GenerationType.IDENTITY)
    private Long id;

    private String title;
    private String isbn;

    @ManyToOne(fetch = FetchType.LAZY)
    @JoinColumn(name = "author_id")
    private Author author;

    public Book setId(Long id) {
        this.id = id;
        return this;
    }

    public Book setTitle(String title) {
        this.title = title;
        return this;
    }

    public Book setIsbn(String isbn) {
        this.isbn = isbn;
        return this;
    }

    public Book setAuthor(Author author) {
        this.author = author;
        return this;
    }

    // getters omitted for brevity
}
```

The setters return this instead of void, so they can be chained in a fluent-style as follows:

```
Author author = new Author()
    .setName("Joana Nimar")
    .setAge(34)
    .setGenre("History")
    .addBook(new Book()
        .setTitle("A History of Ancient Prague")
        .setIsbn("001-JN"))
    .addBook(new Book()
        .setTitle("A People's History")
        .setIsbn("002-JN"));
```

The source code is available on GitHub[1].

## Fluent-Style via Additional Methods

You can also implement a fluent-style approach via other methods, instead of altering the entity setters, as follows:

```
@Entity
public class Author implements Serializable {

    private static final long serialVersionUID = 1L;

    @Id
    @GeneratedValue(strategy = GenerationType.IDENTITY)
    private Long id;

    private String name;
    private String genre;
    private int age;

    @OneToMany(cascade = CascadeType.ALL,
               mappedBy = "author", orphanRemoval = true)
    private List<Book> books = new ArrayList<>();
```

---

[1]HibernateSpringBootFluentApiOnSetters

```java
    public Author addBook(Book book) {
        this.books.add(book);
        book.setAuthor(this);
        return this;
    }

    public Author removeBook(Book book) {
        book.setAuthor(null);
        this.books.remove(book);
        return this;
    }

    public Author id(Long id) {
        this.id = id;
        return this;
    }

    public Author name(String name) {
        this.name = name;
        return this;
    }

    public Author genre(String genre) {
        this.genre = genre;
        return this;
    }

    public Author age(int age) {
        this.age = age;
        return this;
    }

    public Author books(List<Book> books) {
        this.books = books;
        return this;
    }

    // getters and setters omitted for brevity
}
```

```java
@Entity
public class Book implements Serializable {

    private static final long serialVersionUID = 1L;

    @Id
    @GeneratedValue(strategy = GenerationType.IDENTITY)
    private Long id;

    private String title;
    private String isbn;

    @ManyToOne(fetch = FetchType.LAZY)
    @JoinColumn(name = "author_id")
    private Author author;

    public Book id(Long id) {
        this.id = id;
        return this;
    }

    public Book title(String title) {
        this.title = title;
        return this;
    }

    public Book isbn(String isbn) {
        this.isbn = isbn;
        return this;
    }

    public Book author(Author author) {
        this.author = author;
        return this;
    }

    // getters and setters omitted for brevity
}
```

This time, these additional methods can be used in a fluent-style approach, as shown in the following snippet of code:

```
Author author = new Author()
    .name("Joana Nimar")
    .age(34)
    .genre("History")
    .addBook(new Book()
        .title("A History of Ancient Prague")
        .isbn("001-JN"))
    .addBook(new Book()
        .title("A People's History")
        .isbn("002-JN"));
```

The source code is available on GitHub[2].

# Item 14: How to Populate a Child-Side Parent Association via a Hibernate-Specific Proxy

You can fetch an entity by identifier via the Spring built-in query methods, findById() or getOne(). Behind the findById() method, Spring uses EntityManager#find(), and behind the getOne() method, Spring uses EntityManager#getReference().

Calling findById() returns the entity from the Persistence Context, the Second Level Cache, or the database (this is the strict order of attempting to find the indicated entity). Therefore, the returned entity is the same type as the declared entity mapping.

On the other hand, calling getOne() will return a Hibernate-specific proxy object. This is not the actual entity type. A Hibernate-specific proxy can be useful when a child entity can be persisted with a reference to its parent (@ManyToOne or @OneToOne lazy association). In such cases, fetching the parent entity from the database (executing the corresponding SELECT statement) is a performance penalty and merely a pointless action, because Hibernate can set the underlying foreign key value for an uninitialized proxy.

Let's put this statement in practice via the @ManyToOne association. This association is a common JPA association, and it maps exactly to the one-to-many table relationship.

---

[2]HibernateSpringBootFluentApiAdditionalMethods

Therefore, consider that the Author and Book entities are involved in an unidirectional lazy @ManyToOne association. In the following example, the Author entity represents the parent-side, while the Book is the child-side. The author and book tables involved in this relationship are shown in Figure 2-2.

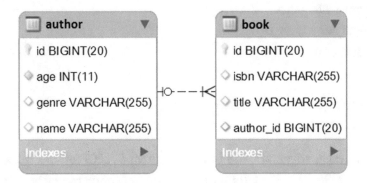

***Figure 2-2.***  *The one-to-many table relationship*

Consider that, in the author table, there is one author with an ID of 1. Now, let's create a Book for this entry.

## Using findById()

Relying on findById() may result in the following code (of course, don't use orElseThrow() in production; here, orElseThrow() is just a quick shortcut to extract the value from the returned Optional):

```
@Transactional
public void addBookToAuthor() {

    Author author = authorRepository.findById(1L).orElseThrow();

    Book book = new Book();
    book.setIsbn("001-MJ");
    book.setTitle("The Canterbury Anthology");
    book.setAuthor(author);

    bookRepository.save(book);
}
```

Calling addBookToAuthor() triggers the following SQL statements:

```
SELECT
  author0_.id AS id1_0_0_,
  author0_.age AS age2_0_0_,
  author0_.genre AS genre3_0_0_,
  author0_.name AS name4_0_0_
FROM author author0_
WHERE author0_.id = ?

INSERT INTO book (author_id, isbn, title)
  VALUES (?, ?, ?)
```

First, a SELECT query is triggered via findById(). This SELECT fetches the author from the database. Next, the INSERT statement saves the new book by setting the foreign key, author_id.

# Using getOne()

Relying on getOne() may result in the following code:

```
@Transactional
public void addBookToAuthor() {
    Author proxy = authorRepository.getOne(1L);

    Book book = new Book();
    book.setIsbn("001-MJ");
    book.setTitle("The Canterbury Anthology");
    book.setAuthor(proxy);

    bookRepository.save(book);
}
```

Since Hibernate can set the underlying foreign key value of an uninitialized proxy, this code triggers a single INSERT statement:

```
INSERT INTO book (author_id, isbn, title)
  VALUES (?, ?, ?)
```

Obviously, this is better than using `findById()`.

The complete code is available on GitHub[3].

# Item 15: How to Use Java 8 Optional in Persistence Layer

The goal of this item is to identify the best practices for using Java 8 Optional API in the persistence layer. To show these practices in examples, we use the well-known `Author` and `Book` entities that are involved in a bidirectional lazy `@OneToMany` association.

The golden rule in coding says that the best way to use things is to exploit them for the purpose of what they were created and tested. Java 8 `Optional` is not an exception to this rule. The purpose of Java 8 `Optional` is clearly defined by Brian Goetz, Java's language architect:

> *Optional is intended to provide a limited mechanism for library method return types where there needed to be a clear way to represent "no result," and using null for such was overwhelmingly likely to cause errors.*

Having this statement in mind, let's apply it to the persistence layer.

## Optional in Entities

`Optional` can be used in entities. More precisely, `Optional` should be used in certain getters of an entity (e.g., getters that are prone to return `null`). In the case of the `Author` entity, `Optional` can be used for the getters corresponding to `name` and `genre`, while for the `Book` entity, `Optional` can be used for `title`, `isbn`, and `author`, as follows:

```
@Entity
public class Author implements Serializable {
```

---

[3]HibernateSpringBootPopulatingChildViaProxy

```
    ...
    public Optional<String> getName() {
        return Optional.ofNullable(name);
    }

    public Optional<String> getGenre() {
        return Optional.ofNullable(genre);
    }
    ...
}

@Entity
public class Book implements Serializable {
    ...
    public Optional<String> getTitle() {
        return Optional.ofNullable(title);
    }

    public Optional<String> getIsbn() {
        return Optional.ofNullable(isbn);
    }

    public Optional<Author> getAuthor() {
        return Optional.ofNullable(author);
    }
    ...
}
```

Do not use Optional for:

- Entity fields (Optional is not Serializable)

- Constructor and setter arguments

- Getters that return primitive types and collections

- Getters specific to the primary key

# Optional in Repositories

Optional can be used in repositories. More precisely, Optional can be used to wrap the result set of a query. Spring already comes with built-in methods that return Optional, such as findById() and findOne(). The following snippet of code uses the findById() method:

```
Optional<Author> author = authorRepository.findById(1L);
```

In addition, you can write queries that return Optional, as in the following two examples:

```
@Repository
@Transactional(readOnly = true)
public interface AuthorRepository extends JpaRepository<Author, Long> {

    Optional<Author> findByName(String name);
}

@Repository
@Transactional(readOnly = true)
public interface BookRepository extends JpaRepository<Book, Long> {

    Optional<Book> findByTitle(String title);
}
```

Do not assume that Optional works only in conjunction with the Query Builder mechanism. It works with JPQL and native queries as well. The following queries are perfectly okay:

```
@Query("SELECT a FROM Author a WHERE a.name=?1")
Optional<Author> fetchByName(String name);

@Query("SELECT a.genre FROM Author a WHERE a.name=?1")
Optional<String> fetchGenreByName(String name);

@Query(value="SELECT a.genre FROM author a WHERE a.name=?1",
        nativeQuery=true)
Optional<String> fetchGenreByNameNative(String name);
```

The source code is available on GitHub[4].

---

[4]HibernateSpringBootOptional

# Item 16: How to Write Immutable Entities

An immutable entity must respect the following contract:

- It must be annotated with @Immutable(org.hibernate.annotations.Immutable)

- It must not contain any kind of association (@ElementCollection, @OneToOne, @OneToMany, @ManyToOne, or @ManyToMany)

- The hibernate.cache.use_reference_entries configuration property must be set to true

> An immutable entity is stored in the Second Level Cache as an entity reference instead as a *disassembled state*. This will prevent the performance penalty of reconstructing an entity from its *disassembled state* (create a new entity instance and populate it with the *disassembled state*).

Here an immutable entity will be stored in the Second Level Cache:

```
@Entity
@Immutable
@Cache(usage = CacheConcurrencyStrategy.READ_ONLY, region = "Author")
public class Author implements Serializable {

    private static final long serialVersionUID = 1L;

    @Id
    private Long id;

    private String name;
    private String genre;
    private int age;

    // getters and setters omitted for brevity
}
```

The code bundled with this book comes with a complete solution that relies on the EhCache implementation of the Second Level Cache.

Now, let's apply the CRUD operations to this entity:

- Creating a new Author: The following method creates a new Author and persists it in the database. Moreover, this Author will be stored in the Second Level Cache via the *write-through* strategy (for more details about the Second Level Cache, see **Appendix I**):

```
public void newAuthor() {

    Author author = new Author();

    author.setId(1L);
    author.setName("Joana Nimar");
    author.setGenre("History");
    author.setAge(34);

    authorRepository.save(author);
}
```

- Fetching the created Author: The next method fetches the created Author from the Second Level Cache, without hitting the database:

```
public void fetchAuthor() {
    Author author = authorRepository.findById(1L).orElseThrow();
    System.out.println(author);
}
```

- Updating Author: This operation will not work since the Author is immutable (it cannot be modified). This will not cause any errors, it will just be silently ignored:

```
@Transactional
public void updateAuthor() {
    Author author = authorRepository.findById(1L).orElseThrow();
    author.setAge(45);
}
```

- Deleting Author: This operation will fetch the entity from the Second Level Cache and will delete it from both places (the Second Level Cache and the database):

```
public void deleteAuthor() {
    authorRepository.deleteById(1L);
}
```

Entities of immutable classes are automatically loaded as *read-only* entities.

The complete code is available on GitHub[5].

# Item 17: How to Clone Entities

Cloning entities is not a daily task but sometimes it can be the easiest way to avoid having to create entities from scratch. There are many well-known cloning techniques, such as manual cloning, cloning via clone(), cloning via a copy-constructor, using the Cloning library, cloning via serialization, and cloning via JSON.

In the case of entities, you'll rarely need to use deep cloning, but if this is what you need, then the Cloning[6] library can be really useful. Most of the time, you'll need to copy only a subset of the properties. In such cases, a copy-constructor provides full control over what is cloned.

Let's use the Author and Book entities involved in a bidirectional lazy @ManyToMany association for the example. For brevity, let's use the slim data snapshot from Figure 2-3 (an author with two books).

---

[5]HibernateSpringBootImmutableEntity
[6]https://github.com/kostaskougios/cloning

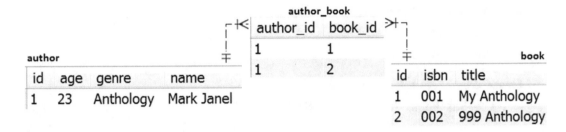

**Figure 2-3.**  *Data snapshot*

# Cloning the Parent and Associating the Books

Let's assume that *Mark Janel* is not the only author of these two books (*My Anthology* and *999 Anthology*). Therefore, you need to add the co-author. The co-author has the same genre and books as *Mark Janel,* but has a different age and name. One solution is to clone the *Mark Janel* entity and use the clone (new entity) to create the co-author.

Assuming that the co-author's name is *Farell Tliop* and he is *54,* you can expect to obtain the data snapshot from Figure 2-4.

**Figure 2-4.**  *Cloning the parent and associate the books*

To accomplish this task, you need to focus on the Author entity. Here, you add the following two constructors:

```
@Entity
public class Author implements Serializable {

    private static final long serialVersionUID = 1L;

    @Id
    @GeneratedValue(strategy = GenerationType.IDENTITY)
    private Long id;
```

```
    private String name;
    private String genre;
    private int age;

    @ManyToMany(...)
    private Set<Book> books = new HashSet<>();

    private Author() {
    }

    public Author(Author author) {
        this.genre = author.getGenre();

        // associate books
        books.addAll(author.getBooks());
    }
    ...
}
```

The private constructor is needed internally by Hibernate. The public copy-constructor is what you need to clone an Author. More precisely, you clone the genre property only. Further, all the Book entities that were referenced by the initial Author entity (*Mark Janel*) are going to be associated with the new co-author entity (*Farell Tliop*).

A service-method can create the co-author entity (*Farell Tliop*) via the initial Author entity (*Mark Janel*) as follows:

```
@Transactional
public void cloneAuthor() {
    Author author = authorRepository.fetchByName("Mark Janel");

    Author authorClone = new Author(author);
    authorClone.setAge(54);
    authorClone.setName("Farell Tliop");

    authorRepository.save(authorClone);
}
```

The triggered SQL statements—except for the SELECT JOIN FETCH triggered via fetchByName()—for fetching *Mark Janel* and the associated books are the expected INSERT statements:

```
INSERT INTO author (age, genre, name)
  VALUES (?, ?, ?)
Binding: [54, Anthology, Farell Tliop]
```

```
INSERT INTO author_book (author_id, book_id)
  VALUES (?, ?)
Binding: [2, 1]
```

```
INSERT INTO author_book (author_id, book_id)
  VALUES (?, ?)
Binding: [2, 2]
```

Notice that this example uses the Set#addAll() method and not the classical addBook() helper. This is done to avoid the additional SELECT statements triggered by book.getAuthors().add(this):

```
public void addBook(Book book) {
    this.books.add(book);
    book.getAuthors().add(this);
}
```

For example, if you replace books.addAll(author.getBooks()) with:

```
for (Book book : author.getBooks()) {
    addBook((book));
}
```

Then, for each book, there is an additional SELECT. In other words, both sides of the association between the co-author and books are synchronized. For example, if you run the following snippet of code in the service-method before saving the co-author:

```
authorClone.getBooks().forEach(
    b -> System.out.println(b.getAuthors()));
```

You would get:

```
[

    Author{id=1, name=Mark Janel, genre=Anthology, age=23},
    Author{id=null, name=Farell Tliop, genre=Anthology, age=54}
]

[

    Author{id=1, name=Mark Janel, genre=Anthology, age=23},
    Author{id=null, name=Farell Tliop, genre=Anthology, age=54}
]
```

You can see that the author and the co-author IDs are null since they were not saved in the database and you are using the IDENTITY generator. On the other hand, if you run the same snippet of code, relying on Set#addAll(), you would obtain this:

```
[

    Author{id=1, name=Mark Janel, genre=Anthology, age=23}
]

[

    Author{id=1, name=Mark Janel, genre=Anthology, age=23}
]
```

This time, the co-author is not visible since you didn't set it on the books (you didn't synchronized this side of the association). Since Set#addAll() helps you avoid additional SELECT statements, and after cloning an entity, you will likely immediately save it in the database, this should not be an issue.

## Cloning the Parent and the Books

This time, assume that you want to clone the Author (*Mark Janel*) and the associated books. Therefore, you should expect something like Figure 2-5.

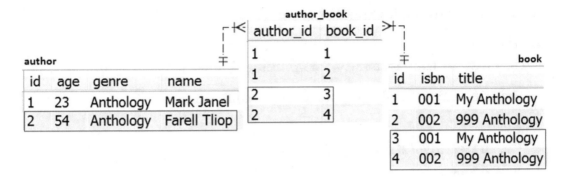

***Figure 2-5.*** *Cloning the parent and the books*

To clone the Book, you need to add the proper constructors in the Book entity, as follows:

```
@Entity
public class Book implements Serializable {

    private static final long serialVersionUID = 1L;

    @Id
    @GeneratedValue(strategy = GenerationType.IDENTITY)
    private Long id;

    private String title;
    private String isbn;

    private Book() {
    }

    public Book(Book book) {
        this.title = book.getTitle();
        this.isbn = book.getIsbn();
    }
    ...
}
```

The private constructor is needed internally by Hibernate. The public copy-constructor clones the Book. This example clones all properties of the Book.

Further, you would provide the Author constructors:

```
@Entity
public class Author implements Serializable {

    private static final long serialVersionUID = 1L;

    @Id
    @GeneratedValue(strategy = GenerationType.IDENTITY)
    private Long id;

    private String name;
    private String genre;
    private int age;

    @ManyToMany(...)
    private Set<Book> books = new HashSet<>();

    private Author() {
    }

    public Author(Author author) {
        this.genre = author.getGenre();

        // clone books
        for (Book book : author.getBooks()) {
            addBook(new Book(book));
        }
    }

    public void addBook(Book book) {
        this.books.add(book);
        book.getAuthors().add(this);
    }
    ...
}
```

The service-method remains the same:

```
@Transactional
public void cloneAuthor() {
    Author author = authorRepository.fetchByName("Mark Janel");
```

```
    Author authorClone = new Author(author);
    authorClone.setAge(54);
    authorClone.setName("Farell Tliop");

    authorRepository.save(authorClone);
}
```

The triggered SQL statements—except the SELECT JOIN FETCH triggered via fetchByName()—for fetching *Mark Janel* and the associated books are the expected INSERT statements:

```
INSERT INTO author (age, genre, name)
  VALUES (?, ?, ?)
Binding: [54, Anthology, Farell Tliop]

INSERT INTO book (isbn, title)
  VALUES (?, ?)
Binding: [001, My Anthology]

INSERT INTO book (isbn, title)
  VALUES (?, ?)
Binding: [002, 999 Anthology]

INSERT INTO author_book (author_id, book_id)
  VALUES (?, ?)
Binding: [2, 1]

INSERT INTO author_book (author_id, book_id)
  VALUES (?, ?)
Binding: [2, 2]
```

## Joining These Cases

You can easily decide between these two cases (cloning the parent and associating the books or cloning the parent and the books) from the service-method by using a boolean argument to reshape the copy-constructor of Author, as shown here:

```
public Author(Author author, boolean cloneChildren) {
    this.genre = author.getGenre();
```

```
    if (!cloneChildren) {
        // associate books
        books.addAll(author.getBooks());
    } else {
        // clone each book
        for (Book book : author.getBooks()) {
            addBook(new Book(book));
        }
    }
}
```

The complete application is available in GitHub[7].

# Item 18: Why and How to Activate Dirty Tracking

> *Dirty Checking* is a Hibernate mechanism dedicated to detecting, at flush time, the managed entities that have been modified since they were loaded in the current Persistence Context. It then fires the corresponding SQL UPDATE statements on behalf of the application (the data access layer). **Note that Hibernate scans all managed entities even if only one property of a managed entity has changed.**

Prior to Hibernate 5, the Dirty Checking mechanism relies on the Java Reflection API to check every property of every managed entity. From a performance perspective, this approach is "harmless" as long as the number of entities is relatively small. For a large number of managed entities, this approach may cause performance penalties.

Starting with Hibernate 5, the Dirty Checking mechanism relies on the *Dirty Tracking* mechanism, which is the capability of an entity to track its own attributes' changes. The Dirty Tracking mechanism results in better performance and its benefits are noticeable,

---

[7]HibernateSpringBootCloneEntity

especially when the number of entities is quite big. In order to work, the Dirty Tracking mechanism needs the Hibernate *Bytecode Enhancement* process to be added to the application. Moreover, the developer must enable the Dirty Tracking mechanism via a specific flag-configuration:

```
<plugin>
    <groupId>org.hibernate.orm.tooling</groupId>
    <artifactId>hibernate-enhance-maven-plugin</artifactId>
    <version>${hibernate.version}</version>
    <executions>
        <execution>
            <configuration>
                <failOnError>true</failOnError>
                <enableDirtyTracking>true</enableDirtyTracking>
            </configuration>
            <goals>
                <goal>enhance</goal>
            </goals>
        </execution>
    </executions>
</plugin>
```

Generally speaking, Bytecode Enhancement is the process of instrumenting the bytecode of a Java class for certain purposes. Hibernate Bytecode Enhancement is a process that commonly takes place at build-time; therefore, it doesn't affect the runtime of the application (there is no runtime performance penalty, but of course there will be an overhead during the build-time). However, it can be set to take place at runtime or deploy-time.

You can add Bytecode Enhancement to your application by adding the corresponding Maven or Gradle plug-in (Ant is also supported).

Once the Bytecode Enhancement plugin is added, the bytecode of all the entity classes is instrumented. This process is known as *instrumention*, and it consists of adding to the code a set of instructions needed to serve the chosen

> configurations (e.g., you need the entity's code to be instrumented for Dirty Tracking; via this instrumentation, an entity is capable of tracking which of its attributes has changed). At flush time, Hibernate will require each entity to report any changes, rather than relying on state-diff computations.
>
> You enable Dirty Tracking via the `enableDirtyTracking` configuration.
>
> **Nevertheless, having a thin Persistence Context is still recommended. The *hydrated state* (entity snapshot) is still saved in the Persistence Context.**

To check if Dirty Tracking was activated, simply decompile the source code of an entity class and search for the following code:

```
@Transient
private transient DirtyTracker $$_hibernate_tracker;
```

`$$_hibernate_tracker` is used to register the entity modifications. During flushing, Hibernate calls a method named `$$_hibernate_hasDirtyAttributes()`. This method returns the dirty properties as a `String[]`.

Or, just check the logs for messages, as shown here:

```
INFO: Enhancing [com.bookstore.entity.Author] as Entity
Successfully enhanced class [D:\...\com\bookstore\entity\Author.class]
```

Hibernate Bytecode Enhancement serves three main mechanisms (for each mechanism, Hibernate will push in the bytecode the proper instrumentation instructions):

- Dirty Tracking (covered in this item): `enableDirtyTracking`

- Attribute lazy initialization (**Item 23**): `enableLazyInitialization`

- Association management (automatic sides synchronization in the case of bidirectional associations): `enableAssociationManagement`

The complete code is available on GitHub[8].

---

[8]HibernateSpringBootEnableDirtyTracking

# Item 19: How to Map a Boolean to a Yes/No

Consider a legacy database that has a table author with the following Data Definition Language (DDL):

```
CREATE TABLE author (
  id bigint(20) NOT NULL AUTO_INCREMENT,
  age int(11) NOT NULL,
  best_selling varchar(3) NOT NULL,
  genre varchar(255) DEFAULT NULL,
  name varchar(255) DEFAULT NULL,
  PRIMARY KEY (id)
);
```

Notice the best_selling column. This column stores two possible values, *Yes* or *No*, indicating if the author is a best-selling author or not. Further, let's assume that this schema cannot be modified (e.g., it's a legacy and you can't modify it) and the best_selling column should be mapped to a Boolean value.

Obviously, declaring the corresponding entity property as Boolean is necessary but not sufficient:

```
@Entity
public class Author implements Serializable {

    ...
    @NotNull
    private Boolean bestSelling;
    ...

    public Boolean isBestSelling() {
        return bestSelling;
    }

    public void setBestSelling(Boolean bestSelling) {
        this.bestSelling = bestSelling;
    }
}
```

At this point, Hibernate will attempt to map this Boolean as shown in the following table:

| Java Type | <- Hibernate Type -> | JDBC Type |
|---|---|---|
| boolean/Boolean | BooleanType | BIT |
| boolean/Boolean | NumericBooleanType | INTEGER (e.g, 0 or 1) |
| boolean/Boolean | YesNoType | CHAR (e.g., N/n or Y/y) |
| boolean/Boolean | TrueFalseType | CHAR (e.g., F/f or T/t) |

So, none of these mappings matches VARCHAR(3). An elegant solution consists of writing a custom converter that Hibernate will apply to all CRUD operations. This can be done by implementing the AttributeConverter interface and overriding its two methods:

```
@Converter(autoApply = true)
public class BooleanConverter
        implements AttributeConverter<Boolean, String> {

    @Override
    public String convertToDatabaseColumn(Boolean attr) {

        return attr == null ? "No" : "Yes";
    }

    @Override
    public Boolean convertToEntityAttribute(String dbData) {

        return !"No".equals(dbData);
    }
}
```

The convertToDatabaseColumn() converts from Boolean to String while convertToEntityAttribute() converts from String to Boolean.

This converter is annotated with @Converter(autoApply = true), which means that this converter will be used for all attributes of the converted type (Boolean). To nominate the attributes, simply remove autoApply or set it to false and add @Converter at the attribute-level, as shown here:

```
@Convert(converter = BooleanConverter.class)
private Boolean bestSelling;
```

Notice that AttributeConverter cannot be applied to attributes annotated with @Enumerated.

The complete application is available on GitHub[9].

# Item 20: The Best Way to Publish Domain Events from Aggregate Roots

Entities managed by Spring repositories are known as aggregate roots. In a Domain Driven Design (DDD), the aggregate roots can publish events or domain events. Starting with the Spring Data Ingalls release, publishing such events by aggregate roots (entities) became much easier.

Spring Data comes with a @DomainEvents annotation that can be used on a method of the aggregate root to make that publication as easy as possible. A method annotated with @DomainEvents is recognized by Spring Data and is automatically invoked whenever an entity is saved using the proper repository. Moreover, besides the @DomainEvents annotation, Spring Data provides the @AfterDomainEventsPublication annotation to indicate the method that should be automatically called to clear events after publication. In code, this commonly looks as follows:

---

[9]HibernateSpringBootMapBooleanToYesNo

```
class MyAggregateRoot {

    @DomainEvents
    Collection<Object> domainEvents() {
        // return events you want to get published here
    }

    @AfterDomainEventsPublication
    void callbackMethod() {
        // potentially clean up domain events list
    }
}
```

But Spring Data Commons comes with a convenient template base class
(AbstractAggregateRoot) that helps register domain events and uses the publication
mechanism implied by @DomainEvents and @AfterDomainEventsPublication. The
events are registered by calling the AbstractAggregateRoot#registerEvent() method.
The registered domain events are published if you call one of the *save* methods of the
Spring Data repository (e.g., save()) and clear it after publication.

Let's look at a sample application that relies on AbstractAggregateRoot and its
registerEvent() method. There are two entities—Book and BookReview—involved in
a bidirectional lazy @OneToMany association. A new book review is saved to the database
in CHECK status and a CheckReviewEvent is published. This event is responsible for
checking the review grammar, content, etc., and for switching the review status from
CHECK to ACCEPT or REJECT. It then propagates the new status in the database. So, this
event is registered before saving the book review in CHECK status and is published
automatically after you call the BookReviewRepository.save() method. After
publication, the event is cleared.

Let's start with the aggregator root, BookReview:

```
@Entity
public class BookReview extends AbstractAggregateRoot<BookReview>
            implements Serializable {

    @Id
    @GeneratedValue(strategy = GenerationType.IDENTITY)
    private Long id;
```

```
private String content;
private String email;

@Enumerated(EnumType.STRING)
private ReviewStatus status;

@ManyToOne(fetch = FetchType.LAZY)
@JoinColumn(name = "book_id")
private Book book;

public void registerReviewEvent() {
    registerEvent(new CheckReviewEvent(this));
}

// getters, setters, etc omitted for brevity
}
```

BookReview extends AbstractAggregateRoot and exposes the registerReviewEvent() method to register domain events via AbstractAggregateRoot#registerEvent(). The registerReviewEvent() method is called to register the event (CheckReviewEvent) before saving a book review:

```
@Service
public class BookstoreService {

    private final static String RESPONSE
        = "We will check your review and get back to you with an email
        ASAP :)";

    private final BookRepository bookRepository;
    private final BookReviewRepository bookReviewRepository;
    ...

    @Transactional
    public String postReview(BookReview bookReview) {

        Book book = bookRepository.getOne(1L);
        bookReview.setBook(book);

        bookReview.registerReviewEvent();
```

```
    bookReviewRepository.save(bookReview);

        return RESPONSE;
    }
}
```

After the save() method is called and the transaction commits, the event is published. The CheckReviewEvent is listed here (it passes the bookReview instance, but you can pass only the needed properties as well by writing the proper constructor):

```
public class CheckReviewEvent {

    private final BookReview bookReview;

    public CheckReviewEvent(BookReview bookReview) {
        this.bookReview = bookReview;
    }

    public BookReview getBookReview() {
        return bookReview;
    }
}
```

Finally, you need the event handler, which is implemented as follows:

```
@Service
public class CheckReviewEventHandler {

    public final BookReviewRepository bookReviewRepository;
    ...

    @TransactionalEventListener
    public void handleCheckReviewEvent(CheckReviewEvent event) {

        BookReview bookReview = event.getBookReview();

        logger.info(() -> "Starting checking of review: "
            + bookReview.getId());

        try {
            // simulate a check out of review grammar, content, acceptance
            // policies, reviewer email, etc via artificial delay of 40s for
```

```
        // demonstration purposes
        String content = bookReview.getContent(); // check content
        String email = bookReview.getEmail(); // validate email

        Thread.sleep(40000);
    } catch (InterruptedException ex) {
        Thread.currentThread().interrupt();
        // log exception
    }

    if (new Random().nextBoolean()) {
        bookReview.setStatus(ReviewStatus.ACCEPT);
        logger.info(() -> "Book review " + bookReview.getId()
            + " was accepted ...");
    } else {
        bookReview.setStatus(ReviewStatus.REJECT);
        logger.info(() -> "Book review " + bookReview.getId()
            + " was rejected ...");
    }

    bookReviewRepository.save(bookReview);

    logger.info(() -> "Checking review " + bookReview.getId() + " done!");
    }
}
```

We simulate a check of the review grammar, content, acceptance policies, reviewer email, etc. via an artificial delay of 40s (`Thread.sleep(40000);`) for demonstration purposes. After the review check completes, the review status is updated in the database.

## Synchronous Execution

The event handler is annotated with @TransactionalEventListener. The event handler can be explicitly bound to a phase of the transaction that published the event via the phase element. Commonly, events are handled after the transaction completes successfully (TransactionPhase.AFTER_COMMIT). While AFTER_COMMIT is the default

setting for @TransactionalEventListener, it can be further customized as BEFORE_
COMMIT or AFTER_COMPLETION (transaction has completed regardless of its success) or
AFTER_ROLLBACK (transaction has rolled back). AFTER_COMMIT and AFTER_ROLLBACK are
specializations of AFTER_COMPLETION.

> If no transaction is running, the method annotated with @Transactional
> EventListener won't be executed unless there is a parameter called
> fallbackExecution set to true.

Since we rely on AFTER_COMMIT and there is no explicit transactional-context specified
for handleCheckReviewEvent(), we may expect that the review check (simulated via
Thread.sleep()) will run outside a transaction. Further, we expect an UPDATE caused by
the call of save() method (bookReviewRepository.save(bookReview);). This UPDATE
should be wrapped in a new transaction. But if you analyze the application log, you'll see
that this is far from reality (this is just the relevant part of the output):

Creating new transaction with name [...**BookstoreService.postReview**]:
PROPAGATION_REQUIRED,ISOLATION_DEFAULT

Opened new EntityManager [SessionImpl(719882002<open>)] for JPA transaction

**begin**

**insert into book_review (book_id, content, email, status) values (?, ?, ?, ?)**

Committing JPA transaction on EntityManager [SessionImpl(719882002<open>)]

**committing**

**// The application flow entered in handleCheckReviewEvent()**

**Starting checking of review: 1**

HikariPool-1 - Pool stats (total=10, active=1, idle=9, waiting=0)

**Found thread-bound EntityManager [SessionImpl(719882002<open>)] for JPA
transaction**

**Participating in existing transaction**

**Checking review 1 done!**

**Closing JPA EntityManager [SessionImpl(719882002<open>)] after transaction**

Several things to note here. First, the transaction started when it called postReview() and is committed before running the code of the handleCheckReviewEvent() event handler. This is normal, since you instruct Spring to execute handleCheckReviewEvent() after the transaction commits (AFTER_COMMIT). But committing the transaction doesn't mean that the transactional resources have been released. The transactional resources are still accessible. As you can see, the connection was not returned in the connection pool (HikariCP reports an active connection, active=1) and the associated Persistence Context is still open. For example, triggering a bookReviewRepository.findById(*book_reivew_id*) will fetch the BookReview from the current Persistence Context!

Second, there is no UPDATE statement executed! The book review status was not propagated to the database. This is happening because the transaction has already been committed. At this point, a data access code will still participate in the original transaction, but there will be no commits (no write operations will be propagated to the database). This is exactly what will happen to this code, bookReviewRepository.save(bookReview);.

You can easily conclude that we are in a very unpleasant situation. There is a long-running transaction (because of the long process simulated via Thread.sleep()) and, in the end, the book review status is not updated. You might think that switching to AFTER_COMPLETION (or AFTER_ROLLBACK) will return the connection in the connection pool before executing handleCheckReviewEvent(), and adding @Transactional at the handleCheckReviewEvent() level will trigger the expected UPDATE statement. But none of the following would help. The result will be exactly the same:

```
@TransactionalEventListener(phase = TransactionPhase.AFTER_COMPLETION)
public void handleCheckReviewEvent(CheckReviewEvent event) {
    ...
}

@Transactional
public void handleCheckReviewEvent(CheckReviewEvent event) {
    ...
}
```

```
@Transactional
@TransactionalEventListener(phase = TransactionPhase.AFTER_COMPLETION)
public void handleCheckReviewEvent(CheckReviewEvent event) {
    ...
}
```

To fix this situation, you have to explicitly require a new transaction for handleCheck ReviewEvent() via Propagation.REQUIRES_NEW, as follows:

```
@TransactionalEventListener
@Transactional(propagation = Propagation.REQUIRES_NEW)
public void handleCheckReviewEvent(CheckReviewEvent event) {
    ...
}
```

> Propagating changes (write operations) to the database in the event handler (the method annotated with @TransactionalEventListener) requires an explicit new transaction (Propagation.REQUIRES_NEW). But be sure to read the following discussion, because this is not cost-free from a performance perspective.

Let's check the application log again:

```
Creating new transaction with name [...BookstoreService.postReview]:
PROPAGATION_REQUIRED,ISOLATION_DEFAULT

Opened new EntityManager [SessionImpl(514524928<open>)] for JPA transaction

begin

insert into book_review (book_id, content, email, status) values (?, ?, ?, ?)

Committing JPA transaction on EntityManager [SessionImpl(514524928<open>)]

committing

// The application flow entered in handleCheckReviewEvent()

Suspending current transaction, creating new transaction with name [com.
bookstore.event.CheckReviewEventHandler.handleCheckReviewEvent]
```

Opened new EntityManager [SessionImpl(**1879180026**<open>)] for JPA transaction

**begin**

HikariPool-1 - Pool stats (total=10, **active=2**, idle=8, waiting=0)

Found thread-bound EntityManager [SessionImpl(**1879180026**<open>)] for JPA transaction

**Participating in existing transaction**

**select bookreview0_.id as id1_1_0_, ... where bookreview0_.id=?**

Committing JPA transaction on EntityManager [SessionImpl(**1879180026**<open>)]

**committing**

**update book_review set book_id=?, content=?, email=?, status=? where id=?**

Closing JPA EntityManager [SessionImpl(**1879180026**<open>)] after transaction

**Resuming suspended transaction after completion of inner transaction**

Closing JPA EntityManager [SessionImpl(**514524928**<open>)] after transaction

This time, the transaction started when you called postReview() and is suspended when the application flow hits handleCheckReviewEvent(). A new transaction and a new Persistence Context are created and used further. The expected UPDATE is triggered and the book review status is updated in the database. **During this time, two database connections are active (one for the suspended transaction and one for the current transaction).** This transaction commits and the attached database connection is returned to the connection pool. Further, the suspended transaction is resumed and closed. Finally, the connection that is opened when you called postReview() is returned to the connection pool. Obviously, the only benefit here is that the UPDATE was triggered, but the performance penalty is significant. **This holds two database connections active for a long time. So, two long-running transactions!** To fix this situation, you can switch to BEFORE_COMMIT and remove @Transactional:

```
@TransactionalEventListener(phase = TransactionPhase.BEFORE_COMMIT)
public void handleCheckReviewEvent(CheckReviewEvent event) {
    ...
}
```

This time, the transaction started when you called postReview() and is committed at the end of running the event handler (handleCheckReviewEvent()). So, the UPDATE of the book review status is triggered in this transactional-context. Now, you have a single long running-transaction and the UPDATE is executed against the database. The database connection is opened when you call postReview() and is closed at the end of executing handleCheckReviewEvent(). Besides the performance penalty represented by this long-running transaction, you also have to keep in mind that using BEFORE_COMMIT doesn't always accommodate the scenario. If you really need to commit the transaction before continuing, this is not an option.

Alternatively, you could still rely on AFTER_COMMIT and delay the connection acquisition for the transaction required via Propagation.REQUIRES_NEW. This can be done as in **Item 60**. So, in application.properties, you need to disable auto-commit:

```
spring.datasource.hikari.auto-commit=false
spring.jpa.properties.hibernate.connection.provider_disables_
autocommit=true
```

```
@TransactionalEventListener
@Transactional(propagation = Propagation.REQUIRES_NEW)
public void handleCheckReviewEvent(CheckReviewEvent event) {
    ...
}
```

Let's check out the application log:

**// The application flow entered in handleCheckReviewEvent()**

**Suspending current transaction, creating new transaction with name [com.bookstore.event.CheckReviewEventHandler.handleCheckReviewEvent]**

Opened new EntityManager [SessionImpl(**1879180026**<open>)] for JPA transaction

**begin**

HikariPool-1 - Pool stats (total=10, **active=1**, idle=9, waiting=0)

Found thread-bound EntityManager [SessionImpl(**1879180026**<open>)] for JPA transaction

**Participating in existing transaction**

**select bookreview0_.id as id1_1_0_, ... where bookreview0_.id=?**

Committing JPA transaction on EntityManager [SessionImpl(**1879180026**<open>)]

**committing**

**update book_review set book_id=?, content=?, email=?, status=? where id=?**

Closing JPA EntityManager [SessionImpl(**1879180026**<open>)] after transaction

**Resuming suspended transaction after completion of inner transaction**

Closing JPA EntityManager [SessionImpl(**514524928**<open>)] after transaction

This time, the transaction required via Propagation.REQUIRES_NEW is delayed until you call bookReviewRepository.save(bookReview);. This means that the long process of checking the book review will hold open a single database connection instead of two. This is a little bit better, but still not acceptable.

## Asynchronous Execution

So far, we cannot say that the involved performance penalties can be ignored. This means that we need to strive to optimize this code further. Since the book review checking process is time-consuming, there is no need to block the reviewer until this process ends. As you can see in the postReview() method, after saving the book review and registering the event, we return a string-response as, We will check your review and get back to you with an email ASAP :). The implementation relies on a synchronous execution, so you need to send this string-response after the event handler finishes execution. Obviously, the response is late since the reviewer was blocked during the book review check process.

It will be much better to return the string-response immediately, before the event-handler starts its execution, while an email with the decision can be sent later. By default, the event handler is executed in the caller thread. It is therefore time to empower the asynchronous execution to allocate a different thread to the event handler execution. In Spring Boot, you enable asynchronous capabilities via @EnableAsync. Next, you annotate the event handler with @Async:

**@Async**
```
@TransactionalEventListener
@Transactional(propagation = Propagation.REQUIRES_NEW)
public void handleCheckReviewEvent(CheckReviewEvent event) {
    ...
}
```

It's time to check out the application log again:

Creating new transaction with name [**...BookstoreService.postReview**]:
PROPAGATION_REQUIRED,ISOLATION_DEFAULT

Opened new EntityManager [SessionImpl(1691206416<open>)] for JPA
transaction

**begin**

insert into book_review (book_id, content, email, status) values (?, ?, ?, ?)

Committing JPA transaction on EntityManager [SessionImpl(1691206416<open>)]
...
**Closing JPA EntityManager [SessionImpl(1691206416<open>)] after transaction**

Creating new transaction with name [**...CheckReviewEventHandler.
handleCheckReviewEvent**]: PROPAGATION_REQUIRES_NEW,ISOLATION_DEFAULT

Opened new EntityManager [SessionImpl(1272552918<open>)] for JPA
transaction

**// since the execution is asynchronous the exact moment in time when the
// string response is sent may slightly vary
Response: We will check your review and get back to you with an email ASAP :)**

**begin**

**Starting checking of review: 1**

**HikariPool-1 - Pool stats (total=10, active=0, idle=10, waiting=0)**

Found thread-bound EntityManager [SessionImpl(1272552918<open>)] for JPA
transaction

```
Participating in existing transaction
select bookreview0_.id as id1_1_0_, ... where bookreview0_.id=?
```

**Checking review 1 done!**

**Committing JPA transaction on EntityManager [SessionImpl(1272552918<open>)]**
**...**

This time, the application log reveals that you've eliminated the long-running transactions. The transaction started when the postReview() call was committed and closed (the attached database connection is returned in the connection pool) and the string-response is sent to the reviewer immediately. The event handler execution is asynchronous and requires a new thread and a new transaction. The database connection acquisition is delayed until it's really needed (when the book review status should be updated). Therefore, the book review check doesn't hold any database connection active/busy for free.

> Generally speaking, most applications rely on connection pooling to reuse physical database connections and a database server can serve a limited number of such connections. This means that performing long-running transactions will hold connections busy for long periods of time and this will affect scalability. This is not in adherence with MVCC (Multi-Version Concurrency Control). In order to have a happy connection pool and database server, it's better to have short database transactions. In the context of domain events, you should pay attention to at least the following bullets to avoid major performance penalties.
>
> **During asynchronous execution:**
>
> - Use an asynchronous event handler with AFTER_COMPLETION (or its specializations) if you need to execute any tasks that fit well with async execution.
>
> - If these tasks don't involve database operations (read/write), then don't use @Transactional at the event handler method level (don't start a new transaction).

- If these tasks involve database read and/or write operations, then use `Propagation.REQUIRES_NEW` and delay the database connection acquisition until it is needed (after the database connection is open, avoid time-consuming tasks).

- If these tasks involve only database read operations, then annotate the event handler method with `@Transactional` (`readOnly=true, Propagation.REQUIRES_NEW`).

- If these tasks involve database write operations, then annotate the event handler method with `@Transactional(Propagation.REQUIRES_NEW)`.

- Avoid performing async tasks in the `BEFORE_COMMIT` phase, as you won't have a guarantee that these tasks will complete before the producer's transaction is committed.

- Depending on your scenario, you may need to intercept the completion of the event handler thread.

**During synchronous execution:**

- Consider asynchronous execution (including its specific drawbacks).

- Use `BEFORE_COMMIT` only if the event handler is not time-consuming and database write operations are needed (and, of course, if it fits your scenario to execute the event handler code before commit). Obviously, you can still read the current Persistence Context (which is open) and trigger read-only database operations.

- Use `AFTER_COMPLETION` (or its specializations) only if the event handler is not time-consuming and database write operations are not needed (strive to avoid using `Propagation.REQUIRES_NEW` in synchronous execution). Nevertheless, you can still read the current Persistence Context (which is open) and trigger read-only database operations.

- In the case of using `BEFORE_COMMIT`, a failure of a database operation executed in the event handler will roll back the entire transaction (depending on your scenario, this can be okay or not).

Spring domain events are useful for simplifying event infrastructure, but pay attention to the following caveats:

- Domain events work only with Spring Data repositories.

- Domain events are published as expected only if we explicitly call a *save* method (e.g., `save()`).

- If an exception occurs while events are published then the listeners (event handlers) will not be notified. Therefore, the events will be lost.

Before employing domain events in your applications, it is advisable to evaluate if using JPA callbacks (**Item 104**), the Observer design pattern, Hibernate-specific `@Formula` (**Item 77**), or another approach won't also work well.

The complete application is available on GitHub[10].

---

[10]HibernateSpringBootDomainEvents

# CHAPTER 3

# Fetching

## Item 21: How to Use Direct Fetching

*Direct fetching* or fetching by ID is the preferable way to fetch an entity when its identifier is known and its lazy associations will not be navigated in the current Persistence Context.

By default, direct fetching will load the entity according to the default or specified FetchType. It's important to keep in mind that, by default, the JPA @OneToMany and @ManyToMany associations are considered LAZY, while the @OneToOne and @ManyToOne associations are considered EAGER.

So, fetching an entity by ID that has an EAGER association will load that association in the Persistence Context even if is not needed, and this causes performance penalties. On the other hand, fetching an entity that has a LAZY association and accessing this association in the current Persistence Context will cause extra queries for loading it as well—also leading to performance penalties.

> The best approach is to keep all the associations LAZY and rely on manual fetching strategy (see **Item 39**, **Item 41**, and **Item 43**) to load these associations. Rely on direct fetching only if you don't plan to access the LAZY associations in the current Persistence Context.

Now, let's look at several approaches for fetching an entity by ID. Consider the following Author entity:

```
@Entity
public class Author implements Serializable {

    private static final long serialVersionUID = 1L;
```

135

© Anghel Leonard 2020
A. Leonard, *Spring Boot Persistence Best Practices*, https://doi.org/10.1007/978-1-4842-5626-8_3

```
    @Id
    @GeneratedValue(strategy = GenerationType.IDENTITY)
    private Long id;

    private int age;
    private String name;
    private String genre;

    // getters and setters omitted for brevity
}
```

The purpose of the following three examples is to use direct fetching to load the entity with an ID of *1*.

## Direct Fetching via Spring Data

You can do direct fetching in Spring Data via the built-in findById() method. This method gets as argument the ID and returns an Optional that wraps the corresponding entity. In code, findById() is used as follows:

```
@Repository
public interface AuthorRepository extends JpaRepository<Author, Long> {}
```

**Optional<Author> author = authorRepository.findById(1L);**

The SQL SELECT statement that loads this Author is:

```
SELECT
  author0_.id AS id1_0_0_,
  author0_.age AS age2_0_0_,
  author0_.genre AS genre3_0_0_,
  author0_.name AS name4_0_0_
FROM author author0_
WHERE author0_.id = ?
```

> Behind the scenes, findById() uses the EntityManager.find() method.

# Fetching via EntityManager

You can inject the EntityManager via @PersistenceContext. Having the EntityManager in your hands, the rest is just about calling the find() method. This method follows Spring Data style and returns an Optional:

```
@PersistenceContext
private EntityManager entityManager;

@Override
public Optional<T> find(Class<T> clazz, ID id) {
    if (id == null) {
        throw new IllegalArgumentException("ID cannot be null");
    }

    return Optional.ofNullable(entityManager.find(clazz, id));
}
```

The SQL SELECT statement that loads this Author is the same as with findById():

```
SELECT
   author0_.id AS id1_0_0_,
   author0_.age AS age2_0_0_,
   author0_.genre AS genre3_0_0_,
   author0_.name AS name4_0_0_
FROM author author0_
WHERE author0_.id = ?
```

# Fetching via Hibernate-Specific Session

To fetch by ID using the Hibernate-specific Session.get() method, you need to unwrap the Session from EntityManager. The following method performs this unwrap and returns an Optional:

```
@PersistenceContext
private EntityManager entityManager;

@Override
public Optional<T> findViaSession(Class<T> clazz, ID id) {
```

```
    if (id == null) {
        throw new IllegalArgumentException("ID cannot be null");
    }

    Session session = entityManager.unwrap(Session.class);

    return Optional.ofNullable(session.get(clazz, id));
}
```

The SQL SELECT statement that loads this Author is the same as in the case of findById() and EntityManager:

**SELECT**
  author0_.id **AS** id1_0_0_,
  author0_.age **AS** age2_0_0_,
  author0_.genre **AS** genre3_0_0_,
  author0_.name **AS** name4_0_0_
**FROM** author author0_
**WHERE** author0_.id = ?

The complete application is available on GitHub[1].

---

The JPA persistence provider (Hibernate) fetches the entity with the given ID via findById(), find(), and get(), by searching it in this order:

- The current Persistence Context (if it's not found, go to the next step)

- The Second Level Cache (if it's not found, go to the next step)

- The database

The order of searching is strict.

---

[1]HibernateSpringBootDirectFetching

# Direct Fetching and Session-Level Repeatable-Reads

This section expands on the first bullet (searching in the current Persistence Context). Why does Hibernate check the Persistence Context first to find the entity with the given ID? The answer is that Hibernate guarantees *session-level repeatable reads.* This means that the entity fetched the first time is cached in the Persistence Context (the First Level Cache). Subsequent fetches of the same entity (via direct fetching or explicit entity query (JPQL/HQL)) are done from the Persistence Context. In other words, *session-level repeatable reads* prevent *lost updates* in concurrent writes cases.

Check out the following example, which groups these three direct fetching techniques under a transactional service-method:

```
@Transactional(readOnly=true)
public void directFetching() {
    // direct fetching via Spring Data
    Optional<Author> resultSD = authorRepository.findById(1L);
    System.out.println("Direct fetching via Spring Data: "
        + resultSD.get());

    // direct fetching via EntityManager
    Optional<Author> resultEM = dao.find(Author.class, 1L);
    System.out.println("Direct fetching via EntityManager: "
        + resultEM.get());

    // direct fetching via Session
    Optional<Author> resultHS = dao.findViaSession(Author.class, 1L);
    System.out.println("Direct fetching via Session: "
        + resultHS.get());
}
```

How many SELECT statements will be executed? If you answered one, you are right! There is a single SELECT caused by the authorRepository.findById(1L) call. The returned author is cached in the Persistence Context. The subsequent calls—dao.find(Author.class, 1L) and dao.findViaSession(Author.class, 1L)—fetch the same author instance from the Persistence Context without hitting the underlying database.

Now, let's assume that we use explicit JPQL queries, as in the following example. First, we write the explicit JPQL that fetches an author by ID (we use Optional just to maintain the trend, but it's not relevant for this topic):

```
@Repository
@Transactional(readOnly = true)
public interface AuthorRepository extends JpaRepository<Author, Long> {

    @Query("SELECT a FROM Author a WHERE a.id = ?1")
    public Optional<Author> fetchById(long id);
}
```

Next, let's look at the following service-method:

```
@Transactional(readOnly=true)
public void directFetching() {
    // direct fetching via Spring Data
    Optional<Author> resultSD = authorRepository.findById(1L);
    System.out.println("Direct fetching via Spring Data: "
        + resultSD.get());

    // direct fetching via EntityManager
    Optional<Author> resultJPQL = authorRepository.fetchById(1L);
    System.out.println("Explicit JPQL: "
        + resultJPQL.get());
}
```

How many SELECT statements will be executed? If you answered two, you are right:

```
-- triggered by authorRepository.findById(1L)
-- the returned author is loaded in the Persistence Context
SELECT
  author0_.id AS id1_0_0_,
  author0_.age AS age2_0_0_,
  author0_.genre AS genre3_0_0_,
  author0_.name AS name4_0_0_
FROM author author0_
WHERE author0_.id = ?
```

```
-- identical SELECT triggered by authorRepository.fetchById(1L)
-- the returned data snapshot is ignored and
-- the returned author is from Persistence Context
SELECT
  author0_.id AS id1_0_,
  author0_.age AS age2_0_,
  author0_.genre AS genre3_0_,
  author0_.name AS name4_0_
FROM author author0_
WHERE author0_.id = ?
```

The first SELECT is caused by the authorRepository.findById(1L) call, when the Persistence Context is empty. The second SELECT hits the database because, unless we use the Second Level Cache, any explicit query will be executed against the database. Therefore, our explicit SELECT is not an exception to this rule. The author returned as the result of calling authorRepository.fetchById(1L) is the one from the current loaded database snapshot or is the author from the Persistence Context that was loaded when we called authorRepository.findById(1L)? Since the Persistence Context guarantees session-level repeatable-reads, Hibernate ignores the database snapshot loaded via our JPQL and returns the author that already exists in the Persistence Context.

> From a performance perspective, it is advisable to use findById(), find(), or get() instead of an explicit JPQL/SQL to fetch an entity by ID. That way, if the entity is present in the current Persistence Context, there is no SELECT triggered against the database and no data snapshot to be ignored.

While, at first glance, this behavior may not be that obvious, we can reveal it via a simple test using two concurrent transactions shaped via the Spring TransactionTemplate API. Consider the following author:

```
INSERT INTO author (age, name, genre, id)
  VALUES (23, "Mark Janel", "Anthology", 1);
```

And the following service-method:

```
private final AuthorRepository authorRepository;
private final TransactionTemplate template;
...
public void process() {

    template.setPropagationBehavior(
        TransactionDefinition.PROPAGATION_REQUIRES_NEW);
    template.setIsolationLevel(Isolation.READ_COMMITTED.value());

    // Transaction A
    template.execute(new TransactionCallbackWithoutResult() {
        @Override
        protected void doInTransactionWithoutResult(
                          TransactionStatus status) {

            Author authorA1 = authorRepository.findById(1L).orElseThrow();
            System.out.println("Author A1: " + authorA1.getName() + "\n");

            // Transaction B
            template.execute(new TransactionCallbackWithoutResult() {
                @Override
                protected void doInTransactionWithoutResult(
                                  TransactionStatus status) {

                    Author authorB = authorRepository
                        .findById(1L).orElseThrow();
                    authorB.setName("Alicia Tom");

                    System.out.println("Author B: "
                        + authorB.getName() + "\n");
                }
            });

            // Direct fetching via findById(), find() and get()
            // doesn't trigger a SELECT
            // It loads the author directly from Persistence Context
            Author authorA2 = authorRepository.findById(1L).orElseThrow();
```

```
System.out.println("\nAuthor A2: " + authorA2.getName() + "\n");

// JPQL entity queries take advantage of
// session-level repeatable reads
// The data snapshot returned by the triggered SELECT is ignored
Author authorViaJpql = authorRepository.fetchByIdJpql(1L);
System.out.println("Author via JPQL: "
    + authorViaJpql.getName() + "\n");

// SQL entity queries take advantage of
// session-level repeatable reads
// The data snapshot returned by the triggered SELECT is ignored
Author authorViaSql = authorRepository.fetchByIdSql(1L);
System.out.println("Author via SQL: "
    + authorViaSql.getName() + "\n");

// JPQL query projections always load the latest database state
String nameViaJpql = authorRepository.fetchNameByIdJpql(1L);
System.out.println("Author name via JPQL: " + nameViaJpql + "\n");

// SQL query projections always load the latest database state
String nameViaSql = authorRepository.fetchNameByIdSql(1L);
System.out.println("Author name via SQL: " + nameViaSql + "\n");
    }
});
}
```

There is a lot of code but it's pretty simple. First of all, we run this code against MySQL, which relies on REPEATABLE_READ as the default isolation level (more details about Spring transaction isolation levels are available in **Appendix F**). We need to switch to the READ_COMMITTED isolation level in order to highlight how the Hibernate session-level repeatable reads work without interleaving the REPEATABLE_READ isolation level. We also ensure that the second transaction (Transaction B) doesn't participate in the context of Transaction A by setting PROPAGATION_REQUIRES_NEW (more details about Spring transaction propagations are available in **Appendix G**).

Further, we start Transaction A (and Persistence Context A). In this transaction context, we call findById() to fetch the author with an ID of 1. So, this author is loaded in the Persistence Context A via the proper SELECT query.

Next, we leave Transaction A as it is and start Transaction B (and Persistence Context B). In Transaction B context, we load the author with an ID of *1* via the proper SELECT and perform an update of the name (*Mark Janel* becomes *Alicia Tom*). The corresponding UPDATE is executed against the database at flush time, right before Transaction B commits. So now, in the underlying database, the author with an ID of *1* has the name *Alicia Tom*.

Now, we come back to Transaction A (and Persistence Context A) and trigger a succession of queries, as follows:

- First, we call findById() to fetch the author with an ID of *1*. The author is returned directly from Persistence Context A (without any SELECT) and the name is *Mark Janel*. Therefore, the session-level repeatable reads work as expected.

- Second, we execute the following explicit JPQL query (fetchByIdJpql()):

```
@Query("SELECT a FROM Author a WHERE a.id = ?1")
public Author fetchByIdJpql(long id);
```

  The data snapshot returned by the triggered SELECT is ignored and the returned author is the one from Persistence Context A (*Mark Janel*). Again, the session-level repeatable reads work as expected.

- Next, we execute the following explicit native SQL query (fetchByIdSql()):

```
@Query(value = "SELECT * FROM author WHERE id = ?1",
        nativeQuery = true)
public Author fetchByIdSql(long id);
```

  Again, the data snapshot returned by the triggered SELECT is ignored and the returned author is the one from Persistence Context A (*Mark Janel*). The session-level repeatable reads work as expected.

> So far, we can conclude that the Hibernate session-level repeatable reads work as expected for entity queries expressed via JPQL or native SQL. Next, let's see how this works with SQL query projections.

- We execute the following JPQL query projection
  (fetchNameByIdJpql()):

```
@Query("SELECT a.name FROM Author a WHERE a.id = ?1")
public String fetchNameByIdJpql(long id);
```

This time, the data snapshot returned by the triggered SELECT is not ignored. The returned author has the name *Alicia Tom*. Therefore, the session-level repeatable reads didn't work in this case.

- Finally, we execute the following native SQL query projection
  (fetchNameByIdSql()):

```
@Query(value = "SELECT name FROM author WHERE id = ?1",
    nativeQuery = true)
public String fetchNameByIdSql(long id);
```

Again, the data snapshot returned by the triggered SELECT is not ignored. The returned author has the name *Alicia Tom*. Therefore, the session-level repeatable reads didn't work.

> So far, we can conclude that Hibernate session-level repeatable reads don't work for SQL query projections expressed via JPQL or as native SQL. These kinds of queries always load the latest database state.
>
> Nevertheless, if we switch the transaction isolation level back to REPEATABLE_READ then SQL query projection will return the author *Mark Janel.* This is happening because, as the name suggests, the REPEATABLE_READ isolation level states that a transaction reads the same result across multiple reads. In other words, the REPEATABLE_READ isolation level prevents the SQL non-repeatable reads anomaly (**Appendix E**). For example, a transaction that reads one record from the database multiple times obtains the same result at each read (**Appendix F**).
>
> Do not confuse Hibernate session-level repeatable reads with the REPEATABLE_READ transaction isolation level.

Okay, two more aspects to consider:

> Hibernate provides session-level repeatable reads out-of-the-box. But sometimes you'll want to load the latest state from the database. In such cases, you can call the `EntityManager#refresh()` method (since Spring Data doesn't expose this method, you can extend the `JpaRepository` to add it).

> Do not confuse Hibernate session-level repeatable reads with *application-level repeatable reads,* which are commonly employed when the conversation spans over multiple requests (**Item 134**). Hibernate guarantees session-level repeatable reads and offers support for application-level repeatable reads. More precisely, the Persistence Context guarantees session-level repeatable reads and you can shape application-level repeatable reads via detached entities or the Extended Persistence Context. Application-level repeatable reads should receive the help of an application-level concurrency control strategy such as Optimistic Locking in order to avoid lost updates (see **Appendix E**).

The complete application is available on GitHub[2].

# Direct Fetching Multiple Entities by ID

Sometimes you'll need to load more than one entity by ID. In such cases, the quickest approach to loading the entities by ID will rely on a query that uses the IN operator. Spring Data provides out-of-the-box the `findAllById()` method. It takes as argument an `Iterable` of the IDs and returns a `List` of entities (Book is the entity and BookRepository is a classic Spring repository for this entity):

```
List<Book> books = bookRepository.findAllById(List.of(1L, 2L, 5L));
```

The same result (the same triggered SQL) can be obtained via JPQL as follows:

```
@Query("SELECT b FROM Book b WHERE b.id IN ?1")
List<Book> fetchByMultipleIds(List<Long> ids);
```

---

[2]HibernateSpringBootSessionRepeatableReads

Using the IN clause in combination with a database that supports Execution Plan Cache can be further optimized as in **Item 122**.

Using Specification is also an option. Check out the following example:

```
List<Book> books = bookRepository.findAll(
    new InIdsSpecification(List.of(1L, 2L, 5L)));
```

Where InIdsSpecification is:

```
public class InIdsSpecification implements Specification<Book> {

    private final List<Long> ids;

    public InIdsSpecification(List<Long> ids) {
        this.ids = ids;
    }

    @Override
    public Predicate toPredicate(Root<Book> root,
        CriteriaQuery<?> cquery, CriteriaBuilder cbuilder) {

        return root.in(ids);

        // or
        // Expression<String> expression = root.get("id");
        // return expression.in(ids);
    }
}
```

All three of these approaches trigger the same SQL SELECT and benefit from session-level repeatable reads. The complete application is available on GitHub[3].

Another approach is to rely on the Hibernate-specific MultiIdentifierLoadAccess interface. Among its advantages, this interface allows you to load multiple entities by ID in batches (withBatchSize()) and to specify if the Persistence Context should be inspected or not before executing the database query (by default it's not inspected but this can be enabled via enableSessionCheck()). Since MultiIdentifierLoadAccess is a Hibernate-specific API, we need to shape it in Spring Boot style. A complete application is available on GitHub[4].

---

[3]HibernateSpringBootLoadMultipleIdsSpecification
[4]HibernateSpringBootLoadMultipleIds

# Item 22: Why Use Read-Only Entities Whenever You Plan to Propagate Changes to the Database in a Future Persistence Context

Consider the Author entity that shapes an author profile via several properties as id, name, age, and genre. The scenario requires you to load an Author profile, edit the profile (e.g., modify the age), and save it back in the database. You don't do this in a single transaction (Persistence Context). You do it in two different transactions, as follows.

## Load Author in Read-Write Mode

Since the Author entity should be modified, you may think that it should be loaded in read-write mode as follows:

```
@Transactional
public Author fetchAuthorReadWriteMode() {

    Author author = authorRepository.findByName("Joana Nimar");

    return author;
}
```

Note that the fetched author is not modified in the method (transaction). It is fetched and returned, so the current Persistence Context is closed before any modifications and the returned author is detached. Let's see what do we have in the Persistence Context.

Persistence Context after fetching the read-write entity:

```
Total number of managed entities: 1
Total number of collection entries: 0

EntityKey[com.bookstore.entity.Author#4]:
    Author{id=4, age=34, name=Joana Nimar, genre=History}
Entity name: com.bookstore.entity.Author
Status: MANAGED
State: [34, History, Joana Nimar]
```

Notice the highlighted content. The status of the entity is MANAGED and the hydrated state is present as well. In other words, this approach has at least two drawbacks:

- Hibernate is ready to propagate entity changes to the database (even if we have no modifications in the current Persistence Context), so it keeps the hydrated state in memory.

- At flush time, Hibernate will scan this entity for modifications and this scan will include this entity as well.

The performance penalties are reflected in memory and CPU. Storing the unneeded hydrated state consumes memory, while scanning the entity at flush time and collecting it by the Garbage Collector consumes CPU resources. It will be better to avoid these drawbacks by fetching the entity in read-only mode.

## Load Author in Read-Only Mode

Since the Author entity is not modified in the current Persistence Context, it can be loaded in read-only mode as follows:

```
@Transactional(readOnly = true)
public Author fetchAuthorReadOnlyMode() {

    Author author = authorRepository.findByName("Joana Nimar");

    return author;
}
```

The entity loaded by this method (transaction) is a read-only entity. Do not confuse read-only entities with DTO (projections). A read-only entity is meant to be modified only so the modifications will be propagated to the database in a future Persistence Context. A DTO (projection) is never loaded in the Persistence Context and is suitable for data that will never be modified.

Let's see the Persistence Context content in this case.

Persistence Context after fetching a read-only entity:

```
Total number of managed entities: 1
Total number of collection entries: 0

EntityKey[com.bookstore.entity.Author#4]:
    Author{id=4, age=34, name=Joana Nimar, genre=History}
Entity name: com.bookstore.entity.Author
Status: READ_ONLY
State: null
```

This time the status is READ_ONLY and the hydrated state was discarded. Moreover, there is no automatic flush time and no Dirty Checking is applied. This is much better than fetching the entity in read-write mode. We don't consume memory for storing the hydrated state and we don't burn CPU with unneeded actions.

## Update the Author

After fetching and returning the entity (in read-write or read-only mode) it becomes detached. Further, we can modify it and merge it:

```
// modify the read-only entity in detached state
Author authorRO = bookstoreService.fetchAuthorReadOnlyMode();
authorRO.setAge(authorRO.getAge() + 1);
bookstoreService.updateAuthor(authorRO);

// merge the entity
@Transactional
public void updateAuthor(Author author) {

    // behind the scene it calls EntityManager#merge()
    authorRepository.save(author);
}
```

The author is not the current Persistence Context and this is a merge operation. Therefore, this action is materialized in a SELECT and an UPDATE.

Further, the merged entity is managed by Hibernate. The complete code is available on GitHub[5].

> Notice that the case presented here uses the Persistence Context-per-request idiom. The Persistence Context is bound to the lifecycle of a single physical database transaction and a single logical @Transactional. If you choose to go with the Extended Persistence Context, then the implementation is governed by other rules. Nevertheless, using Extended Persistence Context in Spring is quite challenging. If you aren't completely sure you understand it, it's better to avoid it.

The scenario presented in this item is commonly encountered in web applications and is known as a *HTTP long conversation*. Commonly, in a web application, this kind of scenario requires two or more HTTP requests. Particularly in this case, the first request will load the author profile, while the second request pushes the profile changes. Between the HTTP requests is the author thinking time. This is detailed in **Item 134**.

# Item 23: How to Lazy Load the Entity Attributes via Hibernate Bytecode Enhancement

Assume that the application contains the following Author entity. This entity maps an author profile:

```
@Entity
public class Author implements Serializable {

    private static final long serialVersionUID = 1L;

    @Id
    private Long id;
```

---

[5]HibernateSpringBootReadOnlyQueries

```
@Lob
private byte[] avatar;

private int age;
private String name;
private String genre;
...

// getters and setters omitted for brevity
}
```

# Enabling Lazy Loading of Attributes

Attributes such as the entity identifier (id), name, age, or genre are to be fetched eagerly on every entity load. But the avatar should be fetched lazily, only when it's being accessed by the application code. So, the avatar column shouldn't be present in the SQL triggered to fetch an Author.

In Figure 3-1, you can see the avatar column of the author table.

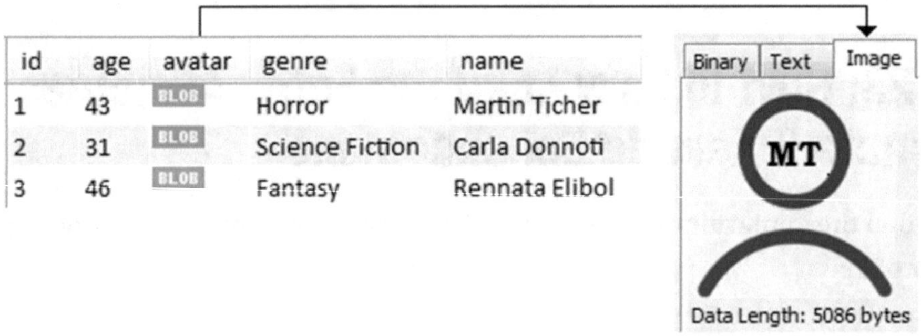

*Figure 3-1.*  *The avatar should be loaded lazy*

By default, the attributes of an entity are loaded eagerly (all at once, in the same query), so avatar will be loaded even if it is not needed/required by the application.

The avatar represents a picture; therefore, it's a potential large amount of byte data (e.g., in Figure 3-1, the avatar takes up 5086 bytes). Loading the avatar on every entity load without using it is a performance penalty that should be eliminated.

A solution to this problem relies on *attributes lazy loading*.

> Attributes lazy loading is useful for column types that store large amounts of data—CLOB, BLOB, VARBINARY, etc.—or for *details* that should be loaded on demand.

To employ attributes lazy loading, you need to follow some steps. The first step is to add Hibernate Bytecode Enhancement plug-in for Maven. Next, you instruct Hibernate to instrument the entity classes' bytecode with the proper instructions by enabling lazy initialization via the enableLazyInitialization configuration (if you are curious to see the added instructions, then simply decompile an instrumented entity class). For Maven, add pom.xml to the Bytecode Enhancement plug-in in the <plugins> section, as shown here:

```
<plugin>
    <groupId>org.hibernate.orm.tooling</groupId>
    <artifactId>hibernate-enhance-maven-plugin</artifactId>
    <version>${hibernate.version}</version>
    <executions>
        <execution>
            <configuration>
                <failOnError>true</failOnError>
                <enableLazyInitialization>true</enableLazyInitialization>
            </configuration>
            <goals>
                <goal>enhance</goal>
            </goals>
        </execution>
    </executions>
</plugin>
```

> Hibernate Bytecode Enhancement takes place at build-time; therefore, it doesn't add overhead to runtime. Without adding Bytecode Enhancement as shown here, the attribute lazy loading will not work.

The second step consists of annotating the entity attributes that should be loaded lazy with @Basic(fetch = FetchType.LAZY). For the Author entity, annotate the avatar attribute as follows:

```
@Lob
@Basic(fetch = FetchType.LAZY)
private byte[] avatar;
```

> By default, the attributes are annotated with @Basic, which relies on the default fetch policy. The default fetch policy is FetchType.EAGER.

Further, a classical Spring repository for the Author entity can be written. Eventually, just for fun, add a query to fetch all authors older than or equal to the given age:

```
@Repository
public interface AuthorRepository extends JpaRepository<Author, Long> {

    @Transactional(readOnly=true)
    List<Author> findByAgeGreaterThanEqual(int age);
}
```

The following service-method will load all authors older than the given age. The avatar attribute will not be loaded:

```
public List<Author> fetchAuthorsByAgeGreaterThanEqual(int age) {
    List<Author> authors = authorRepository.findByAgeGreaterThanEqual(age);

    return authors;
}
```

Calling this method will reveal an SQL that fetches only id, name, age, and genre:

```
SELECT
  author0_.id AS id1_0_,
  author0_.age AS age2_0_,
  author0_.genre AS genre4_0_,
  author0_.name AS name5_0_
FROM author author0_
WHERE author0_.age >= ?
```

Picking up an author id from the returned list of authors and passing it to the following method will fetch the avatar attribute as well. The explicit call of the getAvatar() method will trigger a secondary SQL meant to load the avatar's bytes:

```
@Transactional(readOnly = true)
public byte[] fetchAuthorAvatarViaId(long id) {

    Author author = authorRepository.findById(id).orElseThrow();
    return author.getAvatar(); // lazy loading of 'avatar'
}
```

Fetching the author with the given id is accomplished in two SELECT statements. The first SELECT fetches the id, age, name, and genre, while the second SELECT fetches the avatar:

```
SELECT
    author0_.id AS id1_0_0_,
    author0_.age AS age2_0_0_,
    author0_.genre AS genre4_0_0_,
    author0_.name AS name5_0_0_
FROM author author0_
WHERE author0_.id = ?

SELECT
    author_.avatar AS avatar3_0_
FROM author author_
WHERE author_.id = ?
```

> Trying to fetch the lazy attributes (e.g., avatar) outside the context of a session (outside a Persistence Context) will cause a LazyInitializationException.

## Attribute Lazy Loading and N+1

The N+1 represents a performance penalty caused by triggering more SQL statements (queries) than needed/expected. In other words, performing more database round trips than necessary consumes resources such as CPU, RAM memory, database connections,

155

etc. Most of the time, N+1 remains undetected until you are inspecting (counting/asserting) the number of triggered SQL statements.

> The more additional and unnecessary SQL statements you have, the slower the application will get.

Consider the following method:

```
@Transactional(readOnly = true)
public List<Author> fetchAuthorsDetailsByAgeGreaterThanEqual(int age) {

    List<Author> authors = authorRepository.findByAgeGreaterThanEqual(age);

    // don't do this since this is a N+1 case
    authors.forEach(a -> {
        a.getAvatar();
    });

    return authors;
}
```

The query triggered by calling findByAgeGreaterThanEqual() fetches a list of authors older than the given age (this is the 1 from N+1). Looping the list of authors and calling getAvatar() for each author leads to a number of additional queries equal to the number of authors. In other words, since the avatar is fetched lazily, calling getAvatar() will trigger an SQL SELECT for each author (this is the N from N+1). For two authors, we have the following three SQL statements (the last two queries are the additional queries needed to fetch the avatars):

```
SELECT
    author0_.id AS id1_0_,
    author0_.age AS age2_0_,
    author0_.genre AS genre4_0_,
    author0_.name AS name5_0_
FROM author author0_
WHERE author0_.age >= ?
```

**SELECT**
    author_.avatar **AS** avatar3_0_
**FROM** author author_
**WHERE** author_.id = ?

**SELECT**
    author_.avatar **AS** avatar3_0_
**FROM** author author_
**WHERE** author_.id = ?

You can avoid N+1 performance penalties by employing the subentities technique (see **Item 24**) or by triggering an SQL SELECT that explicitly loads the lazy fetched attributes in a DTO. For example, the following query will trigger a single SELECT to fetch the names and avatars of authors older than the given age as a DTO (Spring projection):

```
public interface AuthorDto {

    public String getName();
    public byte[] getAvatar();
}

@Transactional(readOnly = true)
@Query("SELECT a.name AS name, a.avatar AS avatar
        FROM Author a WHERE a.age >= ?1")
List<AuthorDto> findDtoByAgeGreaterThanEqual(int age);
```

The source code is available on GitHub[6].

## Attribute Lazy Loading and Lazy Initialization Exceptions

Enabling attributes lazy loading in a Spring Boot application will eventually lead to lazy initialization exceptions that are specific to this context. Commonly, this happens when the developer disables Open Session in View (which is enabled by default in Spring Boot). Let's tackle a typical scenario.

---

[6]HibernateSpringBootAttributeLazyLoadingBasic

By default, Open Session in View forces the current Persistence Context to remain open, while Jackson forces initialization of lazy loaded attributes (generally speaking, the View layer triggers the proxy initialization). For example, if Open Session in View is enabled, and the application returns a `List<Author>` from a REST controller endpoint, the View (Jackson serializes the JSON response) will force the initialization of the `avatar` attribute as well. OSIV will supply the current active `Session`, so no lazy initialization issues will occur.

> Even if this is another topic, consider the following question: is it wise to expose entities via a REST API? I suggest you read this article[7] by Thorben Janssen for a good perspective.

Obviously, this is against the application's goal. The solution consists of disabling OSIV by setting the following in `application.properties`:

`spring.jpa.open-in-view=false`

But this leads to an exception. This time, when Jackson tries to serialize the `List<Author>` to JSON (this is the data received by the client of the application via a controller endpoint), there will be no active `Session` available.

Most probably, the exception is as follows:

```
Could not write JSON: Unable to perform requested lazy initialization [com.
bookstore.entity.Author.avatar] - no session and settings disallow loading
outside the Session;
```

So, Jackson forces the initialization of lazy loaded attributes without being in a Hibernate session, and this causes a lazy initialization exception. On the other hand, there is nothing wrong with not having an active Hibernate session at this point.

There are at least two ways to fix this issue and still take advantage of attributes lazy loading.

---

[7]https://thoughts-on-java.org/dont-expose-entities-in-api/

## Setting Explicit Default Values for Lazy Loaded Attributes

A quick approach consists of explicitly setting default values for lazy loaded attributes. If Jackson sees that the lazy loaded attributes have been initialized with values, then it will not attempt to initialize them. Consider the following method:

```
@Transactional(readOnly = true)
public Author fetchAuthor(long id) {

    Author author = authorRepository.findById(id).orElseThrow();

    if (author.getAge() < 40) {
        author.getAvatar();
    } else {
        author.setAvatar(null);
    }

    return author;
}
```

The method fetches an author by id, and, if the fetched author is younger than 40, it loads the avatar via a secondary query. Otherwise, the avatar attribute is initialized with null. This time, Jackson serialization doesn't cause any problems, but the JSON received by the client may be as follows:

```
{
  "id": 1,
  "avatar": null,
  "age": 43,
  "name": "Martin Ticher",
  "genre": "Horror"
}
```

Now, depending on the implemented feature, you may want to serialize the avatar as null or instruct Jackson not to serialize the attributes that have default values (e.g., null in the case of objects, 0 in the case of primitive integers, etc.). Most commonly, the application should avoid the serialization of avatar; therefore, setting @JsonInclude(Include.NON_DEFAULT) is the setting needed at entity-level. In the presence of this setting, Jackson will skip the serialization of any attribute having a default value (depending on your case, other values of Include can be used as well, such as Include.NON_EMPTY):

```
import com.fasterxml.jackson.annotation.JsonInclude;
import com.fasterxml.jackson.annotation.JsonInclude.Include;
...
@Entity
@JsonInclude(Include.NON_DEFAULT)
public class Author implements Serializable {
    ...
}
```

This time, the resulting JSON doesn't contain the avatar:

```
{
  "id": 1,
  "age": 43,
  "name": "Martin Ticher",
  "genre": "Horror"
}
```

Setting explicit default values for lazy loaded attributes keeps the View from triggering the lazy loading of them. From this angle, it doesn't matter if OSIV is enabled or disabled since the Session will not be used. However, the Session is still open and consumes resources, so it is advisable to disable OSIV.

The source code is available on GitHub[8].

## Providing a Custom Jackson Filter

Alternatively, Jackson can be informed via a custom filter about what should be serialized and what not. In this case, Jackson should serialize id, age, name, and genre, and not serialize avatar.

---

[8]HibernateSpringBootAttributeLazyLoadingDefaultValues

Assume the following service-method, which simply fetches the authors older than the given age without their avatars:

```
public List<Author> fetchAuthorsByAgeGreaterThanEqual(int age) {

    List<Author> authors = authorRepository.findByAgeGreaterThanEqual(age);

    return authors;
}
```

There are several approaches for writing and configuring Jackson's filters.

One approach starts by annotating the entity with @JsonFilter as follows (the text between quotes acts as an identifier of this filter used for referencing it later):

```
@Entity
@JsonFilter("AuthorId")
public class Author implements Serializable {

    ...
}
```

The filter identified via AuthorId is implemented in the BookstoreController, as follows (the important part was highlighted; notice the list of attributes that should be serialized passed to the filterOutAllExcept() method):

```
@Controller
public class BookstoreController {

    private final SimpleFilterProvider filterProvider;
    private final BookstoreService bookstoreService;

    public BookstoreController(BookstoreService bookstoreService) {
        this.bookstoreService = bookstoreService;

        filterProvider = new SimpleFilterProvider().addFilter("AuthorId",
        SimpleBeanPropertyFilter.filterOutAllExcept(
            "id", "name", "age", "genre"));
        filterProvider.setFailOnUnknownId(false);
    }
    ...
}
```

The filter is used in the REST endpoint as follows:

```
@GetMapping("/authors/{age}")
public MappingJacksonValue fetchAuthorsByAgeGreaterThanEqual(
          @PathVariable int age) throws JsonProcessingException {

    List<Author> authors = bookstoreService.
        fetchAuthorsByAgeGreaterThanEqual(age);

    MappingJacksonValue wrapper = new MappingJacksonValue(authors);
    wrapper.setFilters(filterProvider);

    return wrapper;
}
```

The returned MappingJacksonValue can be serialized as shown in the following JSON:

```
{
  "id": 1,
  "age": 43,
  "name": "Martin Ticher",
  "genre": "Horror"
}
```

This looks good, but the application must also cover the case when the avatar attribute was fetched. Otherwise, Jackson will throw an exception of type, Cannot resolve PropertyFilter with id 'AuthorId'. When the avatar is fetched, it should be serialized as well. Therefore, the filter should serialize all the attributes. Being the default behavior, the filter can be configured globally (at the application-level) to be used for serializing all attributes of the Author entity:

```
@Configuration
public class WebConfig extends WebMvcConfigurationSupport {

    @Override
    protected void extendMessageConverters(
                List<HttpMessageConverter<?>> converters) {

        for(HttpMessageConverter<?> converter: converters) {
            if(converter instanceof MappingJackson2HttpMessageConverter) {
```

```
        ObjectMapper mapper = ((MappingJackson2HttpMessageConverter)
            converter).getObjectMapper();
        mapper.setFilterProvider(
            new SimpleFilterProvider().addFilter("AuthorId",
                SimpleBeanPropertyFilter.serializeAll()));
        }
      }
    }
}
```

A REST endpoint that will return a List<Author> will rely on this filter that serializes all attributes of Author, including avatar.

> Jackson has an add-on module for the JSON processor, which handles Hibernate data types and specifically aspects of lazy-loading (**Item 110**). This module is identified by the artifact id, jackson-datatype-hibernate5. Unfortunately, so far, this module doesn't have an effect on lazy loaded attributes. It takes care of lazy loaded associations.

The source code is available on GitHub[9].

# Item 24: How to Lazy Load the Entity Attributes via Subentities

Assume that the application contains the following Author entity. This entity maps an author profile:

```
@Entity
public class Author implements Serializable {

    private static final long serialVersionUID = 1L;
```

---

[9]HibernateSpringBootAttributeLazyLoadingJacksonSerialization

```
    @Id
    private Long id;

    @Lob
    private byte[] avatar;

    private int age;
    private String name;
    private String genre;
    ...
    // getters and setters omitted for brevity
}
```

This item shows an alternative to **Item 23**; therefore, the goal is to load id, age, name, and genre eagerly, and to leads avatar lazily (only on demand). This approach is based on splitting the Author entity into subentities, as shown in Figure 3-2.

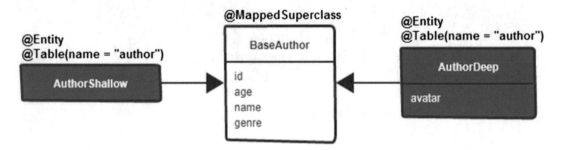

***Figure 3-2.*** *Attributes lazy loading via subentities*

The class from the center of Figure 3-2 is the base class (this is not an entity and doesn't have a table in the database), BaseAuthor, and is annotated with @MappedSuperclass. This annotation marks a class whose mapping information is applied to the entities that inherit from it. So, BaseAuthor should host the attributes that are loaded eagerly (id, age, name, and genre). Each subclass of BaseAuthor is an entity that inherits these attributes; therefore, loading a subclass will load these attributes as well:

```
@MappedSuperclass
public class BaseAuthor implements Serializable {

    private static final long serialVersionUID = 1L;

    @Id
```

```
    private Long id;

    private int age;
    private String name;
    private String genre;

    // getters and setters omitted for brevity
}
```

The AuthorShallow is a subentity of BaseAuthor. This subentity inherits the attributes from the superclass. Therefore, all the attributes should be loaded eagerly. It's important to explicitly map this subentity to the author table via the @Table annotation:

```
@Entity
@Table(name = "author")
public class AuthorShallow extends BaseAuthor {
}
```

The AuthorDeep is also a subentity of BaseAuthor. This subentity inherits the attributes from the superclass and defines the avatar as well. The avatar lands in the author table as well by explicitly mapping this subentity via @Table, as follows:

```
@Entity
@Table(name = "author")
public class AuthorDeep extends BaseAuthor {

    @Lob
    private byte[] avatar;

    public byte[] getAvatar() {
        return avatar;
    }

    public void setAvatar(byte[] avatar) {
        this.avatar = avatar;
    }
}
```

If subentities are not explicitly mapped to the same table via @Table, then the attributes will land in different tables. Moreover, the inherited attributes will land in different tables. For example, without @Table(name = "author"), id, name, age, and genre will land in a table named author_shallow and in a table named author_deep. On the other hand, the avatar will land only in the author_deep table. Obviously, this is not good.

At this point, AuthorShallow allows fetching the id, age, name, and genre eagerly, while the AuthorDeep allows fetching these four attributes plus the avatar. In conclusion, the avatar can be loaded on demand.

The next step is quite simple. Just provide the classical Spring repositories for these two subentities as follows:

```
@Repository
public interface AuthorShallowRepository
        extends JpaRepository<AuthorShallow, Long> {
}

@Repository
public interface AuthorDeepRepository
        extends JpaRepository<AuthorDeep, Long> {
}
```

Calling findAll() from AuthorShallowRepository will trigger the following SQL (notice that the avatar is not loaded):

```
SELECT
  authorshal0_.id AS id1_0_,
  authorshal0_.age AS age2_0_,
  authorshal0_.genre AS genre3_0_,
  authorshal0_.name AS name4_0_
FROM author authorshal0_
```

Calling findAll() from AuthorDeepRepository will trigger the following SQL (notice that the avatar is loaded):

**SELECT**
    authordeep0_.id **AS** id1_0_,
    authordeep0_.age **AS** age2_0_,
    authordeep0_.genre **AS** genre3_0_,
    authordeep0_.name **AS** name4_0_,
    authordeep0_.avatar **AS** avatar5_0_
**FROM** author authordeep0_

> At this point, a conclusion starts to take shape. Hibernate supports attributes to be lazily loaded (see **Item 23**), but this requires Bytecode Enhancement and needs to deal with the Open Session in View and Jackson serialization issues. On the other hand, using subentities might be a better alternative, since it doesn't require Bytecode Enhancement and doesn't encounter these issues.

The source code is available on GitHub[10].

# Item 25: How to Fetch DTO via Spring Projections

> Fetching data from the database results in a copy of that data in memory (usually referred to as the *result set* or *JDBC result set*). This zone of memory that holds the fetched result set is known and referred to as the Persistence Context or the First Level Cache or simply the Cache. By default, Hibernate operates in read-write mode. This means that the fetched result set is stored in the Persistence Context as Object[] (more precisely, as Hibernate-specific EntityEntry instances), and is known in Hibernate terminology as the *hydrated state*, and

---

[10]HibernateSpringBootSubentities

as entities built from this hydrated state. The hydrated state serves the Dirty Checking mechanism (at flush time, Hibernate compares the entities against the hydrated state to discover the potential changes/modifications and triggers UPDATE statements on your behalf), the Versionless Optimistic Locking mechanism (for building the WHERE clause), and the Second Level Cache (the cached entries are built from the disassembled hydrated state, or more precisely, from Hibernate-specific CacheEntry instances built from the hydrated state that was first disassembled).

In other words, after the fetching operation, the fetched result set lives outside the database, in memory. The application accesses/manages this data via entities (so, via Java objects), and, to facilitate this context, Hibernate applies several specific techniques that transform the fetched *raw* data (JDBC result set) into the hydrated state (this process is known as *hydration*) and further into the manageable representation (entities).

**This is a good reason for NOT fetching data as entities in read-write mode if there is no plan to modify them.** In such a scenario, the read-write data will consume memory and CPU resources for nothing. This adds serious performance penalties to the application. Alternatively, if you need read-only entities then switch to read-only mode (e.g., in Spring, use readOnly element, @Transactional(readOnly=true)). This will instruct Hibernate to discard the hydrated state from memory. Moreover, there will be no automatic flush time and no Dirty Checking. Only entities remain in the Persistence Context. As a consequence, this will save memory and CPU resources (e.g., CPU cycles). Read-only entities still mean that you plan to modify them at some point in the near future as well (e.g., you don't plan to modify them in the current Persistence Context, but they will be modified in the detached state and merged later in another Persistence Context). **This is a good reason for NOT fetching data as entities in read-only mode if you never plan to modify them.** However, as an exception here, you can consider read-only entities as an alternative to DTOs that mirror the entity (contains all columns).

As a rule of thumb, if all you need is read-only data that it will not be modified then use Data Transfer Object (DTO) to represent read-only data as Java objects. Most of the time, DTOs contain only a subset of entity attributes and this way you avoid fetching more data (columns) than needed. Don't forget that, besides skipping the unneeded columns, you should consider limiting the number of fetched rows via LIMIT or its counterparts.

For a variety of reasons, some voices will tell you to fetch entities only to use a converter/mapper to create DTOs. Before deciding, consider reading the Vlad Mihalcea's tweet[11] that also argues against this anti-pattern. Vlad says: "Don't fetch entities, only to use a mapper to create DTOs. That's very inefficient, yet I keep on seeing this anti-pattern being promoted."

DTO and Spring projections have essentially the same purpose. Martin Folwer defines a DTO as "an object that carries data between processes in order to reduce the number of method calls". At the implementation level, DTO and Spring projections are not the same. DTO relies on classes with constructor and getters/setters, while Spring projections rely on interfaces and automatically generated proxies. However, Spring can rely on classes as well and the result is known as *DTO projection.*

Assume that we have the following Author entity. This entity maps an author profile:

```
@Entity
public class Author implements Serializable {

    private static final long serialVersionUID = 1L;

    @Id
    @GeneratedValue(strategy = GenerationType.IDENTITY)
    private Long id;
```

---

[11]https://twitter.com/vlad_mihalcea/status/1207887006883340288

```
    private int age;
    private String name;
    private String genre;

    // getters and setters omitted for brevity
}
```

The goal is to fetch only the name and age of the two authors having the same genre. This time, the application relies on Spring projections.

A Spring projection may debut with a Java interface that contains getters only for the columns that should be fetched from the database (e.g., name and age).

This type of Spring projection is known as an *interface-based closed projection* (methods defined in this kind of projection exactly match the names of the entity properties):

```
public interface AuthorNameAge {

    String getName();
    int getAge();
}
```

Behind the scenes, Spring generates a proxy instance of the projection interface for each entity object. Further, the calls to the proxy are automatically forwarded to that object.

The projection interface can be declared as an inner interface of the repository interface as well. It can be declared static or non-static, as in the following example:

```
@Repository
public interface AuthorRepository extends JpaRepository<Author, Long>
{

    @Transactional(readOnly = true)
    List<AuthorNameAge> findFirst2ByGenre(String genre);
```

```
    public static interface AuthorNameAge {

        String getName();
        int getAge();
    }
}
```

The complete application is available on GitHub[12].

The proper query for fetching only two authors in this projection is (take advantage of the Spring Data Query Builder mechanism or rely on JPQL or native SQL):

```
@Repository
@Transactional(readOnly = true)
public interface AuthorRepository extends JpaRepository<Author, Long> {

    List<AuthorNameAge> findFirst2ByGenre(String genre);
}
```

Notice that this query returns a List<AuthorNameAge> not a List<Author>.

Calling this method for the given genre will trigger the following SQL:

```
SELECT
  author0_.name AS col_0_0_,
  author0_.age AS col_1_0_
FROM author author0_
WHERE author0_.genre=?
LIMIT ?
```

The fetched data can be manipulated via the projection getters, as in this simple example:

```
List<AuthorNameAge> authors = ...;
for (AuthorNameAge author : authors) {
```

---

[12]HibernateSpringBootDtoViaProjectionsIntefaceInRepo

```
System.out.println("Author name: " + author.getName()
                             + " | Age: " + author.getAge());
}
```

The source code is available on GitHub[13].

> Using projections is not limited to using the Query Builder mechanism built
> into the Spring Data repository infrastructure. Fetching projections via JPQL or
> native SQL queries is an option as well. For example, the previous query can
> be written via a native SQL query as follows:
>
> ```
> @Query(value = "SELECT a.name, a.age FROM author a
>                 WHERE a.genre=?1 LIMIT 2", nativeQuery=true)
> ```
>
> When the names of the columns doesn't correspond to the name of the
> entity's attributes then simply rely on the SQL AS keyword to define the
> corresponding aliases. For example, if the name attribute is mapped to the
> author_name column and the age attribute is mapped to the author_age
> column then a native SQL query will be as follows:
>
> ```
> @Query(value = "SELECT a.author_name AS name, a.author_age AS age
>                 FROM author a WHERE a.genre=?1 LIMIT 2",
>                 nativeQuery=true)
> ```
>
> If there is no need to use LIMIT then just rely on JPQL. On GitHub[14], there is
> an example that uses JPQL and Spring projections.

# JPA Named (Native) Queries
# Can Be Combined with Spring Projections

If you are not familiar with using named (native) queries in Spring Boot applications,
then I suggest you postpone this section until you read **Item 127**.

---

[13]HibernateSpringBootDtoViaProjections

[14]HibernateSpringBootDtoViaProjectionsAndJpql

Say you have a bunch of named queries in your project and you want to take advantage of Spring Projection. Here is a sample of accomplishing this task. First, you define two named queries and their native counterparts using the @NamedQuery and @NamedNativeQuery annotations. The first query, Author.fetchName, represents a scalar mapping to List<String>, while the second query, Author.fetchNameAndAge, represents a Spring projection mapping to List<AuthorNameAge>:

```
@NamedQuery(
    name = "Author.fetchName",
    query = "SELECT a.name FROM Author a"
)

@NamedQuery(
    name = "Author.fetchNameAndAge",
    query = "SELECT a.age AS age, a.name AS name FROM Author a"
)
@Entity
public class Author implements Serializable {

    ...

}

@NamedNativeQuery(
    name = "Author.fetchName",
    query = "SELECT name FROM author"
)

@NamedNativeQuery(
    name = "Author.fetchNameAndAge",
    query = "SELECT age, name FROM author"
)
@Entity
public class Author implements Serializable {

    ...

}
```

Or, you could define the same queries via a `jpa-named-queries.properties` file (this is the recommended way for taking advantage of dynamic sort (`Sort`) in named queries that are not native) and `Sort` in `Pageable` (in both, named queries and named native queries):

```
# Find the names of authors
Author.fetchName=SELECT a.name FROM Author a

# Find the names and ages of authors
Author.fetchNameAndAge=SELECT a.age AS age, a.name AS name FROM Author a
```

And their native counterparts:

```
# Find the names of authors
Author.fetchName=SELECT name FROM author

# Find the names and ages of authors
Author.fetchNameAndAge=SELECT age, name FROM author
```

Or, you can define the same queries via the `orm.xml` file (notice that this approach has the same shortcomings as using @NamedQuery and @NamedNativeQuery):

```
<!-- Find the names of authors -->
<named-query name="Author.fetchName">
    <query>SELECT a.name FROM Author a</query>
</named-query>

<!-- Find the names and ages of authors -->
<named-query name="Author.fetchNameAndAge">
    <query>SELECT a.age AS age, a.name AS name FROM Author a</query>
</named-query>
```

And their native counterparts:

```
<!-- Find the names of authors -->
<named-native-query name="Author.fetchName">
    <query>SELECT name FROM author</query>
</named-native-query>

<!-- Find the names and ages of authors -->
<named-native-query name="Author.fetchNameAndAge">
    <query>SELECT age, name FROM author</query>
</named-native-query>
```

174

Independent of which approach you prefer, the AuthorRepository is the same:

```
@Repository
@Transactional(readOnly = true)
public interface AuthorRepository extends JpaRepository<Author, Long> {

    // Scalar Mapping
    List<String> fetchName();

    // Spring projection
    List<AuthorNameAge> fetchNameAndAge();
}
```

Or the native counterpart:

```
@Repository
@Transactional(readOnly = true)
public interface AuthorRepository extends JpaRepository<Author, Long> {

    // Scalar Mapping
    @Query(nativeQuery = true)
    List<String> fetchName();

    // Spring projection
    @Query(nativeQuery = true)
    List<AuthorNameAge> fetchNameAndAge();
}
```

That's all! Spring Boot will automatically do the rest for you. Depending on how the named (native) queries are provided, you can choose from the following applications:

- How to use JPA named queries via @NamedQuery and Spring projection[15]

- How to use JPA named native queries via @NamedNativeQuery and Spring projection[16]

---

[15]HibernateSpringBootDtoSpringProjectionAnnotatedNamedQuery
[16]HibernateSpringBootDtoSpringProjectionAnnotatedNamedNativeQuery

- How to use JPA named queries via a properties file and Spring projection[17]

- How to use JPA named native queries via a properties file and Spring projection[18]

- How to use JPA named queries via the `orm.xml` file and Spring projection[19]

- How to use JPA named native queries via the `orm.xml` file and Spring projection[20]

# Class-Based Projections

Besides interface-based projections, Spring supports *class-based* projections. This time, instead of an interface, you write a class. For example, the AuthorNameAge interface becomes the AuthorNameAge class from the following:

```
public class AuthorNameAge {

    private String name;
    private int age;

    public AuthorNameAge(String name, int age) {
        this.name = name;
        this.age = age;
    }

    // getters, setters, equals() and hashCode() omitted for brevity
}
```

As you can see, the names of the constructor's arguments must match the entity properties.

---

[17]HibernateSpringBootDtoSpringProjectionPropertiesNamedQuery
[18]HibernateSpringBootDtoSpringProjectionPropertiesNamedNativeQuery
[19]HibernateSpringBootDtoSpringProjectionOrmXmlNamedQuery
[20]HibernateSpringBootDtoSpringProjectionOrmXmlNamedNativeQuery

Notice that interface-based projections can be nested, while class-based projections cannot.

The complete application is available on GitHub[21].

# How to Reuse a Spring Projection

This time, consider that we've enriched the Author entity to contain the following attributes: id, name, genre, age, email, address, and rating. Or, generally speaking, an entity with a large number of attributes. When an entity has a significant number of attributes, we potentially need a bunch of read-only queries to fetch different subsets of attributes. For example, a read-only query may need to fetch the age, name, genre, email, and address, while another query may need to fetch the age name and genre, and yet another query may need to fetch only the name and email.

To satisfy these three queries, we may define three interface-based Spring closed projections. This is not quite practical. For example, later, we may need one more read-only query that fetches the name and address. Following this logic, we need to define one more Spring projection as well. It will be more practical to define a single Spring projection that works for all read-only queries executed against the authors.

To accomplish this task, we define a Spring projection that contains getters to satisfy the heaviest query (in this case, the query that fetches the age, name, genre, email, and address):

```
@JsonInclude(JsonInclude.Include.NON_DEFAULT)
public interface AuthorDto {

    public Integer getAge();
    public String getName();
    public String getGenre();
    public String getEmail();
    public String getAddress();
}
```

---

[21]HibernateSpringBootDtoViaClassBasedProjections

The projection was annotated with @JsonInclude(JsonInclude.Include.NON_ DEFAULT). This is needed to avoid serializing null values (values that haven't been fetched in the current query). This will instruct the Jackson serialization mechanism to skip null values from the resulted JSON.

Now, we can rely on Spring Data Query Builder mechanism to generate the query for fetching the age, name, genre, email, and address as follows:

```
List<AuthorDto> findBy();
```

Or, you can write a JPQL as follows:

```
@Query("SELECT a.age AS age, a.name AS name, a.genre AS genre, "
    + "a.email AS email, a.address AS address FROM Author a")
List<AuthorDto> fetchAll();
```

Calling fetchAll() and representing the result as JSON will produce the following:

```
[
   {
     "genre":"Anthology",
     "age":23,
     "email":"markj@gmail.com",
     "name":"Mark Janel",
     "address":"mark's address"
   },
   ...
]
```

Further, you can reuse the AuthorDto projection for a query that fetches only the age, name, and genre:

```
@Query("SELECT a.age AS age, a.name AS name, a.genre AS genre FROM Author a")
List<AuthorDto> fetchAgeNameGenre();
```

Calling fetchAgeNameGenre() and representing the result as JSON will produce something as follows:

```
[
   {
      "genre":"Anthology",
      "age":23,
      "name":"Mark Janel"
   },
   ...
]
```

Or, you can reuse the AuthorDto projection for a query that fetches only the name and email:

```
@Query("SELECT a.name AS name, a.email AS email FROM Author a")
List<AuthorDto> fetchNameEmail();
```

Calling fetchNameEmail() and representing the result as JSON will produce something as follows:

```
[
   {
      "email":"markj@gmail.com",
      "name":"Mark Janel"
   },
   ...
]
```

The complete application is available on GitHub[22].

## How to Use Dynamic Spring Projections

Consider the Author entity from the previous section, which has the following attributes: id, name, genre, age, email, address, and rating. Moreover, consider two Spring projections for this entity, defined as follows:

```
public interface AuthorGenreDto {

    public String getGenre();
}
```

---

[22]HibernateSpringBootReuseProjection

```
public interface AuthorNameEmailDto {

    public String getName();
    public String getEmail();
}
```

You can fetch the entity type, `AuthorGenreDto` type, and `AuthorNameEmailDto` type via the same query-method by writing three queries, as shown here:

```
Author findByName(String name);
```

```
AuthorGenreDto findByName(String name);
```

```
AuthorNameEmailDto findByName(String name);
```

You essentially write the same query-method to return different types. This is somehow cumbersome, and Spring tackles such cases via *dynamic* projections. You can apply dynamic projections just by declaring a query-method with a `Class` parameter, as follows:

```
<T> T findByName(String name, Class<T> type);
```

Here are two more examples:

```
<T> List<T> findByGenre(String genre, Class<T> type);
```

```
@Query("SELECT a FROM Author a WHERE a.name=?1 AND a.age=?2")
<T> T findByNameAndAge(String name, int age, Class<T> type);
```

This time, depending on the type that you expect to be returned, you can call `findByName()` as follows:

```
Author author = authorRepository.findByName(
    "Joana Nimar", Author.class);
```

```
AuthorGenreDto author = authorRepository.findByName(
    "Joana Nimar", AuthorGenreDto.class);
```

```
AuthorNameEmailDto author = authorRepository.findByName(
    "Joana Nimar", AuthorNameEmailDto.class);
```

The complete application is available on GitHub[23].

---

[23]HibernateSpringBootDynamicProjection

# Item 26: How to Add an Entity in a Spring Projection

If you are not familiar with Spring projections, then consider reading the previous item before continuing.

Typically, a Spring projection (DTO) is used to fetch read-only data. But there might be cases when the application needs to fetch an entity inside the Spring Projection. For such cases, the steps that need to be followed are highlighted in this example.

## Materialized Association

Consider the Author and Book entities involved in a bidirectional lazy @OneToMany association.

The Spring projection should map the Author entity and, from the Book entity, only the title attribute. Based on the previous item, the Spring projection interface can be written as follows:

```
public interface BookstoreDto {

    public Author getAuthor();
    public String getTitle();
}
```

Fetching data is accomplished in the following repository via JPQL (the fetched data lands in a List<BookstoreDto>):

```
@Repository
@Transactional(readOnly = true)
public interface AuthorRepository extends JpaRepository<Author, Long> {

    @Query("SELECT a AS author, b.title AS title
        FROM Author a JOIN a.books b")
    List<BookstoreDto> fetchAll();
}
```

Calling this method will trigger the following SQL:

```
SELECT
  author0_.id AS col_0_0_,
  books1_.title AS col_1_0_,
```

181

```
author0_.id AS id1_0_,
author0_.age AS age2_0_,
author0_.genre AS genre3_0_,
author0_.name AS name4_0_
FROM author author0_
INNER JOIN book books1_
  ON author0_.id = books1_.author_id
```

The following service-method calls `fetchAll()` in a read-write transaction. Notice that the fetched Author instances are managed by Hibernate and the potential changes will be propagated to the database via the Dirty Checking mechanism (Hibernate will trigger UPDATE statements on your behalf):

```
@Transactional
public List<BookstoreDto> fetchAuthors() {
    List<BookstoreDto> dto = authorRepository.fetchAll();

    // the fetched Author are managed by Hibernate
    // the following line of code will trigger an UPDATE
    dto.get(0).getAuthor().setGenre("Poetry");

    return dto;
}
```

Displaying the fetched data to the console is quite simple:

```
List<BookstoreDto> authors = ...;
authors.forEach(a -> System.out.println(a.getAuthor()
                                + ", Title: " + a.getTitle()));
```

The source code is available on GitHub[24].

# Not Materialized Association

This time, consider that there is no materialized association between the Author and Book entities. However, as Figure 3-3 reveals, both entities share a genre attribute.

---

[24]HibernateSpringBootDtoEntityViaProjection

**Figure 3-3.** *No materialized association*

This attribute can be used to join Author with Book and fetch the data in the same Spring projection, BookstoreDto. This time, the JPQL uses the genre attribute in order to join these two tables as follows:

```
@Repository
@Transactional(readOnly = true)
public interface AuthorRepository extends JpaRepository<Author, Long> {

    @Query("SELECT a AS author, b.title AS title FROM Author a
            JOIN Book b ON a.genre=b.genre ORDER BY a.id")
    List<BookstoreDto> fetchAll();
}
```

Calling fetchAll() will trigger the following SQL:

```
SELECT
  author0_.id AS col_0_0_,
  book1_.title AS col_1_0_,
  author0_.id AS id1_0_,
  author0_.age AS age2_0_,
  author0_.genre AS genre3_0_,
  author0_.name AS name4_0_
FROM author author0_
INNER JOIN book book1_
  ON (author0_.genre = book1_.genre)
ORDER BY author0_.id
```

The following service-method calls fetchAll() in a read-write transaction. Notice that the fetched Authors are managed and Hibernate will propagate to the database the modifications of these Authors:

```
@Transactional
public List<BookstoreDto> fetchAuthors() {

    List<BookstoreDto> dto = authorRepository.fetchAll();

    // the fetched Author are managed by Hibernate
    // the following line of code will trigger an UPDATE
    dto.get(0).getAuthor().setAge(47);

    return dto;
}
```

Displaying the fetched data to the console is quite simple:

```
List<BookstoreDto> authors = ...;
authors.forEach(a -> System.out.println(a.getAuthor()
                              + ", Title: " + a.getTitle()));
```

The source code is available on GitHub[25].

# Item 27: How to Enrich Spring Projections with Virtual Properties That Are/Aren't Part of Entities

Consider reading **Item 25** before continuing.

Spring projections can be enriched with *virtual* properties that are or are not part of the Domain Model. Commonly, when they are not part of the Domain Model, they are computed at runtime via SpEL expressions.

An interface-based Spring projection that contains methods with unmatched names in the Domain Model and with returns computed at runtime is referenced as an *interface-based open projection*.

---

[25]HibernateSpringBootDtoEntityViaProjectionNoAssociation

For example, the following Spring projection contains three *virtual* properties (years, rank, and books):

```java
public interface AuthorNameAge {

    String getName();

    @Value("#{target.age}")
    String years();

    @Value("#{ T(java.lang.Math).random() * 10000 }")
    int rank();

    @Value("5")
    String books();
}
```

In the Spring projection, AuthorNameAge relies on @Value and Spring SpEL to point to a backing property from the Domain Model (in this case, the Domain Model property age is exposed via the *virtual* property years). Moreover, use the @Value and Spring SpEL to enrich the result with two *virtual* properties that don't have a match in the Domain Model (in this case, rank and books).

The Spring repository is pretty simple and it contains a query that fetches the author name and age older than the given age:

```java
@Repository
@Transactional(readOnly = true)
public interface AuthorRepository extends JpaRepository<Author, Long> {

    @Query("SELECT a.name AS name, a.age AS age
            FROM Author a WHERE a.age >= ?1")
    List<AuthorNameAge> fetchByAge(int age);
}
```

Calling fetchByAge() for the given age will trigger the following SQL:

```sql
SELECT
  author0_.name AS col_0_0_,
  author0_.age AS col_1_0_
```

```
FROM author author0_
WHERE author0_.age >= ?
```

Printing the fetched data uses years() for age, rank(), and books():

```
List<AuthorNameAge> authors = ...;

for (AuthorNameAge author : authors) {
    System.out.println("Author name: " + author.getName()
        + " | Age: " + author.years()
        + " | Rank: " + author.rank()
        + " | Books: " + author.books());
}
```

An output to the console is (author's name and age have been fetched from the database):

```
Author name: Olivia Goy | Age: 43 | Rank: 3435 | Books: 5
Author name: Quartis Young | Age: 51 | Rank: 2371 | Books: 5
Author name: Katy Loin | Age: 56 | Rank: 2826 | Books: 5
```

The source code is available on GitHub[26].

# Item 28: How to Efficiently Fetch Spring Projection Including *-to-One Associations

Assume that Author and Book are again involved in a bidirectional lazy @OneToMany association. You want to fetch a read-only result set containing the title of each book and the name and genre of the author. Such a read-only result set is the perfect candidate for a DTO, and, being in Spring, the main way to fetch this DTO involves Spring projections.

Let's use the data snapshot shown in Figure 3-4.

---

[26]HibernateSpringBootDtoViaProjectionsAndVirtualProperties

**author**

| id | age | genre | name |
|----|-----|-------|------|
| 1 | 23 | Anthology | Mark Janel |
| 2 | 43 | Horror | Olivia Goy |
| 3 | 51 | Anthology | Quartis Young |
| 4 | 34 | History | Joana Nimar |

+⊢─⊩⊢⊂

**book**

| id | isbn | title | author_id |
|----|------|-------|-----------|
| 1 | 001-JN | A History of Ancient Prague | 4 |
| 2 | 002-JN | A People's History | 4 |
| 3 | 003-JN | History Now | 4 |
| 4 | 001-MJ | The Beatles Anthology | 1 |
| 5 | 001-OG | Carrie | 2 |
| 6 | 002-OG | Nightmare Of A Day | 2 |

***Figure 3-4.*** *Data snapshot*

## Using Nested Closed Projections

The book title is fetched from the book table, while the author name and genre are fetched from the author table. This means that you can write an interface-based, nested Spring closed projection, as follows:

```
public interface BookDto {

    public String getTitle();
    public AuthorDto getAuthor();

    interface AuthorDto {

        public String getName();
        public String getGenre();
    }
}
```

Now all you need is the proper query to populate this Spring projection. The quickest approach relies on the Spring Data Query Builder mechanism, as follows:

```
@Repository
@Transactional(readOnly=true)
public interface BookRepository extends JpaRepository<Book, Long> {

    List<BookDto> findBy();
}
```

187

From an implementation point of view, this was really fast! But, is this approach working? Let's see the result set as a JSON representation (imagine that this is returned by a REST controller endpoint):

```
[
  {
     "title":"A History of Ancient Prague",
     "author":{
        "genre":"History",
        "name":"Joana Nimar"
     }
  },
  {
     "title":"A People's History",
     "author":{
        "genre":"History",
        "name":"Joana Nimar"
     }
  },
  ...
]
```

Yes, it's working! But is it efficient? Without inspecting the triggered SQL and the Persistence Context contents, you may think that this approach is great. But the generated SELECT fetches more data than required (e.g., you didn't require the id and the age of the author):

```
SELECT
   book0_.title AS col_0_0_,
   author1_.id AS col_1_0_,
   author1_.id AS id1_0_,
   author1_.age AS age2_0_,
   author1_.genre AS genre3_0_,
   author1_.name AS name4_0_
FROM book book0_
```

```
LEFT OUTER JOIN author author1_
  ON book0_.author_id = author1_.id
```

It is obvious that this query fetches all the attributes of the author (the more attributes the entity has, the more unneeded data is fetched). Moreover, if you inspect the Persistence Context contents, you'll notice that it contains three entries in READ_ONLY status and none of them has the hydrated state (the hydrated state was discarded since this transaction was marked as readOnly):

Here are the Persistence Context contents:

```
Total number of managed entities: 3
Total number of collection entries: 3

EntityKey[com.bookstore.entity.Author#1]:
    Author{id=1, name=Mark Janel, genre=Anthology, age=23}
EntityKey[com.bookstore.entity.Author#2]:
    Author{id=2, name=Olivia Goy, genre=Horror, age=43}
EntityKey[com.bookstore.entity.Author#4]:
    Author{id=4, name=Joana Nimar, genre=History, age=34}
```

The road of the result set from the database to the projection passes partially through the Persistence Context. The authors are fetched as read-only entities as well. Generally speaking, the amount of data may impact performance (e.g., a relatively large number of unneeded fetched columns and/or a relatively large number of fetched rows). But since we are in the read-only mode, there is no hydrated state in the Persistence Context and no Dirty Checking is executed for the authors. Nevertheless, the Garbage Collector needs to collect these instances after the Persistence Context is closed.

Writing an explicit JPQL produces the same output as the query generated via the Query Builder mechanism):

```
@Repository
@Transactional(readOnly=true)
public interface BookRepository extends JpaRepository<Book, Long> {
```

```
@Query("SELECT b.title AS title, a AS author "
    + "FROM Book b LEFT JOIN b.author a")
// or as a INNER JOIN
// @Query("SELECT b.title AS title, b.author AS author FROM Book b")
List<BookDto> findByViaQuery();
}
```

## Using a Simple Closed Projection

Relying on nested Spring projection can lead to performance penalties. How about using a simple Spring closed projection that fetches raw data as follows:

```
public interface SimpleBookDto {

    public String getTitle(); // of book
    public String getName();   // of author
    public String getGenre(); // of author
}
```

This time the Query Builder mechanism cannot help you. You can write a LEFT JOIN as follows:

```
@Repository
@Transactional(readOnly=true)
public interface BookRepository extends JpaRepository<Book, Long> {

    @Query("SELECT b.title AS title, a.name AS name, a.genre AS genre "
        + "FROM Book b LEFT JOIN b.author a")
    List<SimpleBookDto> findByViaQuerySimpleDto();
}
```

This time, the JSON representation of the result set looks as follows:

```
[
   {
      "title":"A History of Ancient Prague",
      "genre":"History",
      "name":"Joana Nimar"
   },
```

```
{
    "title":"A People's History",
    "genre":"History",
    "name":"Joana Nimar"
},
...
]
```

The books and authors data is mixed. Depending on the case, this kind of output can be accepted (as in this case) or not. But how efficient is it? Let's look at the triggered SQL:

```
SELECT
    book0_.title AS col_0_0_,
    author1_.name AS col_1_0_,
    author1_.genre AS col_2_0_
FROM book book0_
LEFT OUTER JOIN author author1_
    ON book0_.author_id = author1_.id
```

The query looks exactly as expected. Notice that this query fetches only the requested columns. Further, the Persistence Context is empty. Here is the Persistence Context content:

```
Total number of managed entities: 0
Total number of collection entries: 0
```

From a performance perspective, this approach is better than relying on nested Spring projections. The SQL fetches only the requested columns and the Persistence Context is bypassed. The drawback is in data representation (*raw data*), which doesn't maintain the tree structure of parent-child entities. In some cases, this is not an issue; in other cases, it is. You have to process this data to be shaped as needed (on the server-side or client-side). When no further processing is needed, you can even drop the projection and return List<Object[]>:

```
@Query("SELECT b.title AS title, a.name AS name, a.genre AS genre "
    + "FROM Book b LEFT JOIN b.author a")
List<Object[]> findByViaQueryArrayOfObjects();
```

# Using a Simple Open Projection

Relying on a simple Spring closed projection is okay as long as you don't care to maintain the data structure (tree structure of parent-child entities). If this is an issue, you can rely on a simple Spring open projection. Remember from **Item 27** that an open projection allows you to define methods with unmatched names in the Domain Model and with returns that are computed at runtime. Essentially, an open projection supports *virtual* properties.

This time, we write a Spring open projection as follows:

```
public interface VirtualBookDto {

    public String getTitle(); // of book

    @Value("#{@authorMapper.buildAuthorDto(target.name, target.genre)}")
    AuthorClassDto getAuthor();
}
```

The highlighted SpEL expression refers to the bean `AuthorMapper` that invokes the `buildAuthorDto()` method and forwards the projection name and genre as the method parameters. So, at runtime, the name and genre of the author should be used to create an instance of `AuthorClassDto` listed here:

```
public class AuthorClassDto {

    private String genre;
    private String name;

    // getters, setters, equals() and hashCode() omitted for brevity
}
```

The job is accomplished by a helper class named `AuthorMapper`, as shown here:

```
@Component
public class AuthorMapper {

    public AuthorClassDto buildAuthorDto(String genre, String name) {
        AuthorClassDto authorClassDto = new AuthorClassDto();
        authorClassDto.setName(name);
        authorClassDto.setGenre(genre);

        return authorClassDto;
    }
}
```

How efficient is this implementation? Is it worth the effort? The triggered SQL is obtained from the following JPQL:

```
@Repository
@Transactional(readOnly=true)
public interface BookRepository extends JpaRepository<Book, Long> {

    @Query("SELECT b.title AS title, a.name AS name, a.genre AS genre "
        + "FROM Book b LEFT JOIN b.author a")
    List<VirtualBookDto> findByViaQueryVirtualDto();
}
```

The SQL looks exactly as expected:

```
SELECT
  book0_.title AS col_0_0_,
  author1_.name AS col_1_0_,
  author1_.genre AS col_2_0_
FROM book book0_
LEFT OUTER JOIN author author1_
  ON book0_.author_id = author1_.id
```

The Persistence Context was untouched, as shown.:

```
Total number of managed entities: 0
Total number of collection entries: 0
```

The JSON representation maintains the data structure:

```
[
  {
    "title":"A History of Ancient Prague",
    "author":{
      "genre":"Joana Nimar",
      "name":"History"
    }
  },
```

```
{
    "title":"A People's History",
    "author":{
        "genre":"Joana Nimar",
        "name":"History"
    }
},
...
]
```

Even if it requires a little more work than the preceding approaches, relying on a simple Spring open projection maintains the data structure. Unfortunately, as you can see from Figure 3-5, this approach has the worse time-performance trend.

The time-performance trend graphic shown in Figure 3-5 puts these four approaches head-to-head for 100, 500, and 1,000 authors with five books each. It looks like fetching raw data is the fastest approach, while using an open projection is the slowest.

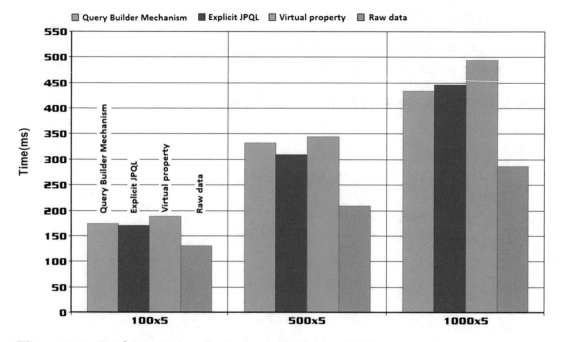

***Figure 3-5.***  *Fetching @ManyToOne association as DTO*

The time-performance trend graphic in Figure 3-5 was obtained against MySQL, on a Windows 7 machine with the following characteristics: Intel i7, 2.10GHz, and 6GB RAM. The application and MySQL ran on the same machine.

The complete code is available on GitHub[27].

# Item 29: Why to Pay Attention to Spring Projections that Include Associated Collections

Assume that `Author` and `Book` are involved in a bidirectional lazy `@OneToMany` association. You want to fetch the `name` and the `genre` of each author, as well as the `title` of all associated books. Since you need a read-only result set containing a subset of columns from the author and book tables, let's try to use a Spring projection (DTO).

Let's use the data snapshot shown in Figure 3-6.

**author**

| id | age | genre | name |
|----|-----|-----------|--------------|
| 1  | 23  | Anthology | Mark Janel |
| 2  | 43  | Horror | Olivia Goy |
| 3  | 51  | Anthology | Quartis Young |
| 4  | 34  | History | Joana Nimar |

**book**

| id | isbn | title | author_id |
|----|--------|----------------------------|-----------|
| 1  | 001-JN | A History of Ancient Prague | 4 |
| 2  | 002-JN | A People's History | 4 |
| 3  | 003-JN | History Now | 4 |
| 4  | 001-MJ | The Beatles Anthology | 1 |
| 5  | 001-OG | Carrie | 2 |
| 6  | 002-OG | Nightmare Of A Day | 2 |

*Figure 3-6.* *Data snapshot*

## Using Nested Spring Closed Projection

The books `title` is fetched from the `book` table, while the author `name` and `genre` are fetched from the `author` table. This means that you can write an interface-based, nested Spring closed projection, as shown here (this approach is very tempting, thanks to its simplicity):

```
public interface AuthorDto {

    public String getName();
```

---

[27]HibernateSpringBootNestedVsVirtualProjection

```
    public String getGenre();
    public List<BookDto> getBooks();

    interface BookDto {
        public String getTitle();
    }
}
```

Notice that the book titles are mapped as a List<BookDto>. So, calling
AuthorDto#getBooks() should return a List<BookDto> that contains only the book titles.

## Use the Query Builder Mechanism

From an implementation point of view, the quickest approach to populating the
projection relies on the Query Builder mechanism, as shown here:

```
@Repository
@Transactional(readOnly=true)
public interface AuthorRepository extends JpaRepository<Author, Long> {

    List<AuthorDto> findBy();
}
```

Is this approach working? Let's see the result set as a JSON representation (imagine that
this is returned by a REST controller endpoint):

```
[
  {
    "genre":"Anthology",
    "books":[
      {
        "title":"The Beatles Anthology"
      }
    ],
    "name":"Mark Janel"
  },
  {
    "genre":"Horror",
    "books":[
```

```
        {
            "title":"Carrie"
        },
        {
            "title":"Nightmare Of A Day"
        }
    ],
    "name":"Olivia Goy"
},
{
    "genre":"Anthology",
    "books":[

    ],
    "name":"Quartis Young"
},
{
    "genre":"History",
    "books":[
        {
            "title":"A History of Ancient Prague"
        },
        {
            "title":"A People's History"
        },
        {
            "title":"History Now"
        }
    ],
    "name":"Joana Nimar"
}
]
```

The result looks perfect! So, you've used a Spring projection and a query generated via the Query Builder mechanism to fetch a read-only result set. Is this efficient? Are you triggering a single SELECT query? Have you managed to bypass the Persistence Context? Well, no, no, and no!

Checking the triggered SQL queries reveals the following:

```
SELECT
  author0_.id AS id1_0_,
  author0_.age AS age2_0_,
  author0_.genre AS genre3_0_,
  author0_.name AS name4_0_
FROM author author0_

-- for each author there is an additional SELECT
SELECT
  books0_.author_id AS author_i4_1_0_,
  books0_.id AS id1_1_0_,
  books0_.id AS id1_1_1_,
  books0_.author_id AS author_i4_1_1_,
  books0_.isbn AS isbn2_1_1_,
  books0_.title AS title3_1_1_
FROM book books0_
WHERE books0_.author_id = ?
```

> This solution triggers five SELECT statements! It's quite obvious that this is
> an N+1 issue. The association between Author and Book is lazy, and Spring
> needs to fetch the authors and the associated books as entities in order to
> populate the projections with the requested data. This is confirmed by the
> Persistence Context content as well.

The Persistence Context contains 10 entities (four of them being collection entries) with READ_ONLY status and no hydrated state.

Persistence Context content:

```
Total number of managed entities: 10
Total number of collection entries: 4

EntityKey[com.bookstore.entity.Book#1]:
    Book{id=1, title=A History of Ancient Prague, isbn=001-JN}
EntityKey[com.bookstore.entity.Book#3]:
```

```
    Book{id=3, title=History Now, isbn=003-JN}
EntityKey[com.bookstore.entity.Book#2]:
    Book{id=2, title=A People's History, isbn=002-JN}
EntityKey[com.bookstore.entity.Book#5]:
    Book{id=5, title=Carrie, isbn=001-OG}
EntityKey[com.bookstore.entity.Book#4]:
    Book{id=4, title=The Beatles Anthology, isbn=001-MJ}
EntityKey[com.bookstore.entity.Book#6]:
    Book{id=6, title=Nightmare Of A Day, isbn=002-OG}

EntityKey[com.bookstore.entity.Author#1]:
    Author{id=1, name=Mark Janel, genre=Anthology, age=23}
EntityKey[com.bookstore.entity.Author#2]:
    Author{id=2, name=Olivia Goy, genre=Horror, age=43}
EntityKey[com.bookstore.entity.Author#3]:
    Author{id=3, name=Quartis Young, genre=Anthology, age=51}
EntityKey[com.bookstore.entity.Author#4]:
    Author{id=4, name=Joana Nimar, genre=History, age=34}
```

> In addition to the N+1 issue, the Persistence Context is not bypassed either.
> So, this approach is really bad and should be avoided.

## Use an Explicit JPQL

You can sweeten the situation a little by dropping the Query Builder mechanism and
employing an explicit JPQL, as follows:

```
@Repository
@Transactional(readOnly=true)
public interface AuthorRepository extends JpaRepository<Author, Long> {

    @Query("SELECT a.name AS name, a.genre AS genre, b AS books "
        + "FROM Author a INNER JOIN a.books b")
    List<AuthorDto> findByViaQuery();
}
```

This time, there is a single SELECT triggered. Conforming to the JPQL, the books are fully loaded, not only the titles:

```
SELECT
    author0_.name AS col_0_0_,
    author0_.genre AS col_1_0_,
    books1_.id AS col_2_0_,
    books1_.id AS id1_1_,
    books1_.author_id AS author_i4_1_,
    books1_.isbn AS isbn2_1_,
    books1_.title AS title3_1_
FROM author author0_
INNER JOIN book books1_
    ON author0_.id = books1_.author_id
```

Moreover, the Persistence Context was populated with six entities (and no collection entries) of type Book in READ_ONLY status and no hydrated state (this time, less data was loaded in the Persistence Context).

Persistence Context content:

```
Total number of managed entities: 6
Total number of collection entries: 0

EntityKey[com.bookstore.entity.Book#3]:
    Book{id=3, title=History Now, isbn=003-JN}
EntityKey[com.bookstore.entity.Book#2]:
    Book{id=2, title=A People's History, isbn=002-JN}
EntityKey[com.bookstore.entity.Book#5]:
    Book{id=5, title=Carrie, isbn=001-OG}
EntityKey[com.bookstore.entity.Book#4]:
    Book{id=4, title=The Beatles Anthology, isbn=001-MJ}
EntityKey[com.bookstore.entity.Book#6]:
    Book{id=6, title=Nightmare Of A Day, isbn=002-OG}
EntityKey[com.bookstore.entity.Book#1]:
    Book{id=1, title=A History of Ancient Prague, isbn=001-JN}
```

Moreover, we lost the data structure (the tree structure of the parent-child entities), and each title is wrapped in its own List:

```
[
    {
        "genre":"History",
        "books":[
            {
                "title":"A History of Ancient Prague"
            }
        ],
        "name":"Joana Nimar"
    },
    {
        "genre":"History",
        "books":[
            {
                "title":"A People's History"
            }
        ],
        "name":"Joana Nimar"
    },
    {
        "genre":"History",
        "books":[
            {
                "title":"History Now"
            }
        ],
        "name":"Joana Nimar"
    },
    {
        "genre":"Anthology",
        "books":[
            {
                "title":"The Beatles Anthology"
```

```
        }
    ],
    "name":"Mark Janel"
},
...
]
```

As a little tweak here, you can remove the List from the nested projection, as follows:

```
public interface AuthorDto {

    public String getName();
    public String getGenre();
    public BookDto getBooks();

    interface BookDto {
        public String getTitle();
    }
}
```

This will not create the Lists, but it's pretty confusing.

## Use JPA JOIN FETCH

As **Item 39** highlights, JOIN FETCH is capable of initializing the associated collections along with their parent objects using a single SQL SELECT. So, you can write a query as follows:

```
@Repository
@Transactional(readOnly=true)
public interface AuthorRepository extends JpaRepository<Author, Long> {

    @Query("SELECT a FROM Author a JOIN FETCH a.books")
    Set<AuthorDto> findByJoinFetch();
}
```

> Notice that this example uses Set instead of List to avoid duplicates. In this case, adding the SQL DISTINCT clause doesn't work. If you add an ORDER BY clause (e.g., ORDER BY a.name ASC), behind the scenes, Hibernate uses a LinkedHashSet. Therefore, the order of items is preserved as well.

Calling findByJoinFetch() triggers the following SELECT (notice the INNER JOIN between author and book):

**SELECT**
```
    author0_.id AS id1_0_0_,
    books1_.id AS id1_1_1_,
    author0_.age AS age2_0_0_,
    author0_.genre AS genre3_0_0_,
    author0_.name AS name4_0_0_,
    books1_.author_id AS author_i4_1_1_,
    books1_.isbn AS isbn2_1_1_,
    books1_.title AS title3_1_1_,
    books1_.author_id AS author_i4_1_0__,
    books1_.id AS id1_1_0__
```
**FROM** author author0_
**INNER JOIN** book books1_
    **ON** author0_.id = books1_.author_id

This time, there is a single SELECT triggered. Conforming to this SQL, the authors and books are fully loaded, not only the names, genres, and titles. Let's check out the Persistence Context (we have nine entities in READ_ONLY status and no hydrated state, and three of them are collection entries). This is not a surprise, since by its meaning JOIN FETCH fetches entities, and combined with @Transactional(readOnly=true), this results in read-only entities. So, the Set<AuthorDto> is obtained from these entities via the Persistence Context. Persistence Context content:

```
Total number of managed entities: 9
Total number of collection entries: 3

EntityKey[com.bookstore.entity.Book#3]:
    Book{id=3, title=History Now, isbn=003-JN}
```

```
EntityKey[com.bookstore.entity.Book#2]:
    Book{id=2, title=A People's History, isbn=002-JN}
EntityKey[com.bookstore.entity.Book#5]:
    Book{id=5, title=Carrie, isbn=001-OG}
EntityKey[com.bookstore.entity.Book#4]:
    Book{id=4, title=The Beatles Anthology, isbn=001-MJ}
EntityKey[com.bookstore.entity.Book#6]:
    Book{id=6, title=Nightmare Of A Day, isbn=002-OG}
EntityKey[com.bookstore.entity.Book#1]:
    Book{id=1, title=A History of Ancient Prague, isbn=001-JN}

EntityKey[com.bookstore.entity.Author#1]:
    Author{id=1, name=Mark Janel, genre=Anthology, age=23}
EntityKey[com.bookstore.entity.Author#2]:
    Author{id=2, name=Olivia Goy, genre=Horror, age=43}
EntityKey[com.bookstore.entity.Author#4]:
    Author{id=4, name=Joana Nimar, genre=History, age=34}
```

This time, we preserve the data as the tree structure of parent-child entities. Fetching data as a JSON outputs the expected result without duplicates:

```
[
  {
    "genre":"Anthology",
    "books":[
      {
          "title":"The Beatles Anthology"
      }
    ],
    "name":"Mark Janel"
  },
  {
    "genre":"Horror",
    "books":[
      {
          "title":"Carrie"
      },
```

```
        {
            "title":"Nightmare Of A Day"
        }
    ],
    "name":"Olivia Goy"
},
{
    "genre":"History",
    "books":[
        {
            "title":"A History of Ancient Prague"
        },
        {
            "title":"A People's History"
        },
        {
            "title":"History Now"
        }
    ],
    "name":"Joana Nimar"
}
]
```

As you can see, JOIN FETCH maintains the tree structure of parent-child entities, but it brings more unneeded data into the Persistence Context than explicit JPQL. How this will affect overall performance depends on how much unneeded data is fetched and how you stress the Garbage Collector, which will have to clean up these objects after the Persistence Context is disposed.

# Using a Simple Closed Projection

Nested Spring projection is prone to performance penalties. How about using a simple Spring closed projection, as follows:

```
public interface SimpleAuthorDto {

    public String getName();  // of author
    public String getGenre(); // of author
    public String getTitle(); // of book
}
```

And a JPQL, as shown here:

```
@Repository
@Transactional(readOnly=true)
public interface AuthorRepository extends JpaRepository<Author, Long> {

    @Query("SELECT a.name AS name, a.genre AS genre, b.title AS title "
        + "FROM Author a INNER JOIN a.books b")
    List<SimpleAuthorDto> findByViaQuerySimpleDto();
}
```

This time, there is a single SELECT that fetches only the requested data:

```
SELECT
  author0_.name AS col_0_0_,
  author0_.genre AS col_1_0_,
  books1_.title AS col_2_0_
FROM author author0_
INNER JOIN book books1_
  ON author0_.id = books1_.author_id
```

The Persistence Context is bypassed. Persistence Context content:

```
Total number of managed entities: 0
Total number of collection entries: 0
```

But, as the following JSON reveals, the data structure is totally lost (this is raw data):

```
[
    {
        "genre":"History",
        "title":"A History of Ancient Prague",
        "name":"Joana Nimar"
    },
    {

        "genre":"History",
        "title":"A People's History",
        "name":"Joana Nimar"
    },
    {

        "genre":"History",
        "title":"History Now",
        "name":"Joana Nimar"
    },
    ...
]
```

While this approach fetches only the needed data and doesn't involve the Persistence Context, it seriously suffers at the data representation level. In some cases, this is not an issue, in other cases it is. You have to process this data to shape it as needed (on the server-side or client-side). When no further processing is needed, you can even drop the projection and return List<Object[]>:

```
@Query("SELECT a.name AS name, a.genre AS genre, b.title AS title "
        + "FROM Author a INNER JOIN a.books b")
List<Object[]> findByViaArrayOfObjects();
```

# Transform List<Object[]> in DTO

You can fetch List<Object[]> and transform it into DTO via the following custom transformer:

```
@Component
public class AuthorTransformer {

    public List<AuthorDto> transform(List<Object[]> rs) {

        final Map<Long, AuthorDto> authorsDtoMap = new HashMap<>();

        for (Object[] o : rs) {

            Long authorId = ((Number) o[0]).longValue();

            AuthorDto authorDto = authorsDtoMap.get(authorId);
            if (authorDto == null) {
                authorDto = new AuthorDto();
                authorDto.setId(((Number) o[0]).longValue());
                authorDto.setName((String) o[1]);
                authorDto.setGenre((String) o[2]);
            }

            BookDto bookDto = new BookDto();
            bookDto.setId(((Number) o[3]).longValue());
            bookDto.setTitle((String) o[4]);

            authorDto.addBook(bookDto);
            authorsDtoMap.putIfAbsent(authorDto.getId(), authorDto);
        }

        return new ArrayList<>(authorsDtoMap.values());
    }
}
```

The AuthorDto and BookDto are simple POJOs defined as follows:

```
public class AuthorDto implements Serializable {

    private static final long serialVersionUID = 1L;

    private Long authorId;
    private String name;
    private String genre;

    private List<BookDto> books = new ArrayList<>();

    // constructors, getters, setters omitted for brevity

}

public class BookDto implements Serializable {

    private static final long serialVersionUID = 1L;

    private Long bookId;
    private String title;

    // constructors, getters, setters omitted for brevity
}
```

In order to write a simple transformer, the executed query fetches the IDs of authors and books as well. The executed query is shown here:

```
@Repository
@Transactional(readOnly=true)
public interface AuthorRepository extends JpaRepository<Author, Long> {
@Query("SELECT a.id AS authorId, a.name AS name, a.genre AS genre, "
            + "b.id AS bookId, b.title AS title FROM Author a "
            + "INNER JOIN a.books b")
    List<Object[]> findByViaArrayOfObjectsWithIds();
}
```

The service-method executes the query and applies the transformer as follows:

```
...
List<Object[]> authors = authorRepository.findByViaArrayOfObjectsWithIds();
List< AuthorDto> authorsDto = authorTransformer.transform(authors);
...
```

This time, there is a single SELECT that fetches only the requested data:

```
SELECT
    author0_.id AS col_0_0_,
    author0_.name AS col_1_0_,
    author0_.genre AS col_2_0_,
    books1_.id AS col_3_0_,
    books1_.title AS col_4_0_
FROM author author0_
INNER JOIN book books1_
    ON author0_.id = books1_.author_id
```

The Persistence Context is bypassed. Persistence Context content:

```
Total number of managed entities: 0
Total number of collection entries: 0
```

The JSON representation of the DTO looks okay:

```
[
  {
    "name":"Mark Janel",
    "genre":"Anthology",
    "books":[
      {
        "title":"The Beatles Anthology",
        "id":4
      }
    ],
    "id":1
  },
  {
```

```
    "name":"Olivia Goy",
    "genre":"Horror",
    "books":[
        {
            "title":"Carrie",
            "id":5
        },
        {
            "title":"Nightmare Of A Day",
            "id":6
        }
    ],
    "id":2
},
{

    "name":"Joana Nimar",
    "genre":"History",
    "books":[
        {
            "title":"A History of Ancient Prague",
            "id":1
        },
        {
            "title":"A People's History",
            "id":2
        },
        {
            "title":"History Now",
            "id":3
        }
    ],
    "id":4
}
]
```

Figure 3-7 shows a head-to-head comparison between these six approaches for 100, 500, and 1,000 authors with five books each. As expected, the Query Builder mechanism and the nested projections have the worse time-performance trend. The execution times for explicit JPQL and JOIN FETCH are approximately the same, but remember that JOIN FETCH fetches more unneeded data than an explicit JPQL. Finally, a raw projection—List<Object[]> and List<Object[]>—transformed in DTO has almost the same execution times. So, to fetch only the needed data and maintain the data structure (the tree structure of parent-child entities), the fastest approach is to rely on a custom transformer of List<Object[]>.

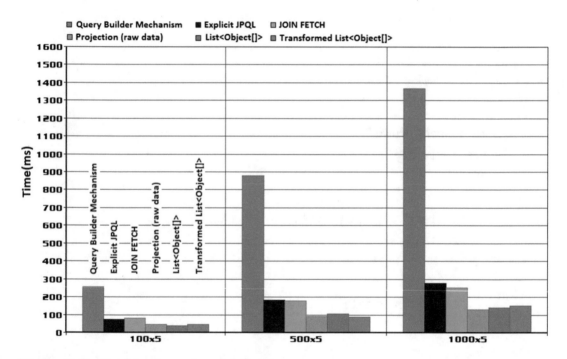

***Figure 3-7.***  *Fetching associated collections*

The time-performance trend graphic shown in Figure 3-7 was obtained against MySQL, on a Windows 7 machine with the following characteristics: Intel i7, 2.10GHz, and 6GB RAM. The application and MySQL ran on the same machine.

The complete application is available on GitHub[28].

---

[28]HibernateSpringBootProjectionAndCollections

# Item 30: How to Fetch All Entity Attributes via Spring Projection

Consider an Author entity with the following four attributes: id, age, genre, and name. The data snapshot is shown in Figure 3-8.

**author**

| id | age | genre | name |
|----|-----|-----------|---------------|
| 1 | 23 | Anthology | Mark Janel |
| 2 | 43 | Horror | Olivia Goy |
| 3 | 51 | Anthology | Quartis Young |
| 4 | 34 | History | Joana Nimar |
| 5 | 33 | History | Marin Kyrab |

***Figure 3-8.*** *Data snapshot*

We already know that it's very simple to fetch a read-only result set containing a subset of these attributes via an interface/class-based Spring closed projection (e.g., fetch only the name and the age).

But sometimes you'll need a read-only result set containing all the entity attributes (a DTO that mirrors the entity). This section depicts several approaches based on read-only entities and Spring projections and highlights their pros and cons from a performance perspective.

Since you need all attributes of Author, you can easily trigger a read-only query that fetches the result set as entities via the built-in findAll() method:

```
List<Author> authors = authorRepository.findAll();
```

The built-in findAll() is annotated with @Transactional(readOnly=true). Therefore, the Persistence Context will be populated with Author entities in read-only mode.

Persistence Context content:

```
Total number of managed entities: 5

EntityKey[com.bookstore.entity.Author#1]:
    Author{id=1, name=Mark Janel, genre=Anthology, age=23}
EntityKey[com.bookstore.entity.Author#2]:
    Author{id=2, name=Olivia Goy, genre=Horror, age=43}
```

```
EntityKey[com.bookstore.entity.Author#3]:
    Author{id=3, name=Quartis Young, genre=Anthology, age=51}
EntityKey[com.bookstore.entity.Author#4]:
    Author{id=4, name=Joana Nimar, genre=History, age=34}
EntityKey[com.bookstore.entity.Author#5]:
    Author{id=5, name=Marin Kyrab, genre=History, age=33}
```

```
Entity name: com.bookstore.entity.Author | Status: READ_ONLY | State: null
Entity name: com.bookstore.entity.Author | Status: READ_ONLY | State: null
Entity name: com.bookstore.entity.Author | Status: READ_ONLY | State: null
Entity name: com.bookstore.entity.Author | Status: READ_ONLY | State: null
Entity name: com.bookstore.entity.Author | Status: READ_ONLY | State: null
```

The read-only mode instructs Hibernate to discard the hydrated state. Moreover, there is no automatic flush time and no Dirty Checking. At the end of this section, we will add this approach in a head-to-head comparison with the other approaches discussed earlier.

> Keep in mind that this is a read-only entity, not a DTO that mirrors the entity and bypasses the Persistence Context. The meaning of a read-only entity is that it will be modified at some point in the current or subsequent requests (see **Item 22**). Otherwise, it should be a projection (DTO).

Now, let's involve a Spring projection and different query types. Let's start with the interface-based Spring closed projection that contains the corresponding getters:

```
public interface AuthorDto {

    public Long getId();
    public int getAge();
    public String getName();
    public String getGenre();
}
```

Now, let's focus on different query types.

# Using the Query Builder Mechanism

A straightforward query can be written as follows:

```
@Repository
@Transactional(readOnly=true)
public interface AuthorRepository extends JpaRepository<Author, Long> {

    List<AuthorDto> findBy();
}
```

Calling findBy() will trigger the following SELECT statement:

```
SELECT
    author0_.id AS col_0_0_,
    author0_.age AS col_1_0_,
    author0_.name AS col_2_0_,
    author0_.genre AS col_3_0_
FROM author author0_
```

The Persistence Context remains untouched. Persistence Context content:

```
Total number of managed entities: 0
```

> This approach is easy to implement and is quite efficient.
>
> As a tip, note that returning List<Object[]> instead of List<AuthorDto> is not efficient because it will load the data in the Persistence Context as well.

# Using JPQL and @Query

An improper approach will rely on @Query and JPQL as follows:

```
@Repository
@Transactional(readOnly=true)
public interface AuthorRepository extends JpaRepository<Author, Long> {

    @Query("SELECT a FROM Author a")
    List<AuthorDto> fetchAsDto();
}
```

Calling `fetchAsDto()` will trigger the following `SELECT` statement:

**SELECT**
  author0_.id **AS** id1_0_,
  author0_.age **AS** age2_0_,
  author0_.genre **AS** genre3_0_,
  author0_.name **AS** name4_0_
**FROM** author author0_

This `SELECT` is exactly the same as the one triggered in the previous approach, but the Persistence Context is not empty. It contains five entries in `READ_ONLY` status and with a `null` loaded state.

Persistence Context content:

```
Total number of managed entities: 5

EntityKey[com.bookstore.entity.Author#1]:
    Author{id=1, name=Mark Janel, genre=Anthology, age=23}
EntityKey[com.bookstore.entity.Author#2]:
    Author{id=2, name=Olivia Goy, genre=Horror, age=43}
EntityKey[com.bookstore.entity.Author#3]:
    Author{id=3, name=Quartis Young, genre=Anthology, age=51}
EntityKey[com.bookstore.entity.Author#4]:
    Author{id=4, name=Joana Nimar, genre=History, age=34}
EntityKey[com.bookstore.entity.Author#5]:
    Author{id=5, name=Marin Kyrab, genre=History, age=33}
```

> This time, the data is loaded in the Persistence Context as in the read-only entities case. However, this time, Spring must also create the `AuthorDto` list.
>
> As a tip, fetching the result set as a `List<Object[]>` instead of as a `List<AuthorDto>` produces the same behavior.

# Using JPQL with an Explicit List of Columns and @Query

You can use JPQL and @Query by explicitly listing the columns to be fetches,
as shown here:

```
@Repository
@Transactional(readOnly=true)
public interface AuthorRepository extends JpaRepository<Author, Long> {

    @Query("SELECT a.id AS id, a.age AS age, a.name AS name,
                    a.genre AS genre FROM Author a")
    List<AuthorDto> fetchAsDtoColumns();
}
```

The triggered SQL is efficient and quite obvious:

```
SELECT
    author0_.id AS col_0_0_ ,
    author0_.age AS col_1_0_ ,
    author0_.name AS col_2_0_ ,
    author0_.genre AS col_3_0_
FROM author author0_
```

Moreover, the Persistence Context remains untouched. Persistence Context content:

```
Total number of managed entities: 0
```

> This approach is quite efficient. If you use @Query and JPQL, then pay attention to how the JPQL is written. Explicitly listing the columns to be fetched eliminates the performance penalty caused by loading data in the Persistence Context.
>
> As a tip, fetching the result set as a List<Object[]> instead of as a List<AuthorDto> produces the same behavior.

217

# Using a Native Query and @Query

You can use @Query and native queries, as follows:

```
@Repository
@Transactional(readOnly=true)
public interface AuthorRepository extends JpaRepository<Author, Long> {

    @Query(value = "SELECT id, age, name, genre FROM author",
            nativeQuery = true)
    List<AuthorDto> fetchAsDtoNative();
}
```

Being a native query, the triggered SQL is obvious:

```
SELECT
  id,
  age,
  name,
  genre
FROM author
```

The Persistence Context remains untouched. Persistence Context content:

```
Total number of managed entities: 0
```

As you can see in Figure 3-9, this approach is less efficient than the others.

Figure 3-9 shows a time-performance trend graphic of a head-to-head comparison between these approaches for 100, 500, and 1,000 authors. It looks like JPQL with an explicit list of columns and the Query Builder mechanism are the fastest approaches.

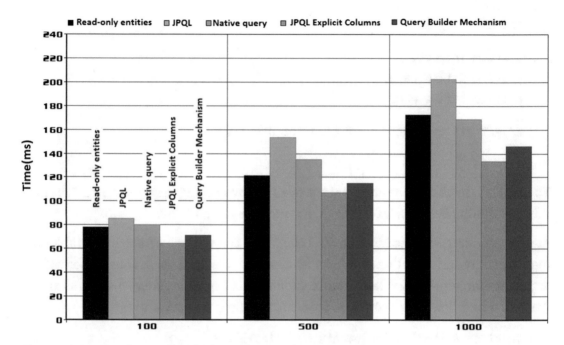

***Figure 3-9.*** *Fetching all basic attributes of an entity*

The time-performance trend shown in Figure 3-9 was obtained against MySQL, on a Windows 7 machine with the following characteristics: Intel i7, 2.10GHz, and 6GB RAM. The application and MySQL ran on the same machine.

The complete application is available on GitHub[29].

# Item 31: How to Fetch DTO via Constructor Expression

Assume that the application contains the following Author entity. This entity maps an author profile:

```
@Entity
public class Author implements Serializable {

    private static final long serialVersionUID = 1L;

    @Id
    @GeneratedValue(strategy = GenerationType.IDENTITY)
```

---

[29]HibernateSpringBootJoinDtoAllFields

```
    private Long id;

    private int age;
    private String name;
    private String genre;

    // getters and setters omitted for brevity
}
```

The goal is to fetch only the name and age of all authors having the same genre. This time, the application relies on a DTO with a constructor and arguments.

The first step consists of writing the DTO class. This class contains instance variables that map the entity attributes that should be fetched from the database, a constructor with arguments for initializing these instance variables, and specific getters (no setters are needed). The following AuthorDto is proper for fetching the name and age:

```
public class AuthorDto implements Serializable {

    private static final long serialVersionUID = 1L;

    private final String name;
    private final int age;

    public AuthorDto(String name, int age) {
        this.name = name;
        this.age = age;
    }

    public String getName() {
        return name;
    }

    public int getAge() {
        return age;
    }
}
```

The second step consists of writing a typical Spring repository. The needed SQL is generated via the Spring Data Query Builder mechanism and the result set is mapped to List<AuthorDto>:

```
@Repository
@Transactional(readOnly = true)
public interface AuthorRepository extends JpaRepository<Author, Long> {

    List<AuthorDto> findByGenre(String genre);
}
```

Calling findByGenre() will trigger the following SQL:

```
SELECT
    author0_.name AS col_0_0_,
    author0_.age AS col_1_0_
FROM
    author author0_
WHERE
    author0_.genre = ?
```

Displaying the results is pretty straightforward:

```
List<AuthorDto> authors =...;
for (AuthorDto author : authors) {
    System.out.println("Author name: " + author.getName()
                            + " | Age: " + author.getAge());
}
```

Here's a possible output:

```
Author name: Mark Janel | Age: 23
Author name: Quartis Young | Age: 51
Author name: Alicia Tom | Age: 38
...
```

The source code is available on GitHub[30].

---

[30]HibernateSpringBootDtoConstructor

The Spring Data Query Builder mechanism is great, but it has some limitations. If this mechanism is not preferred or is simply not applicable, then JPQL can be used as well. In JPQL, a constructor can be used in the SELECT clause to return an instance of a non-entity Java object —this is known as the *Constructor Expression*:

```
@Repository
@Transactional(readOnly = true)
public interface AuthorRepository extends JpaRepository<Author, Long> {

    @Query(value="SELECT new com.bookstore.dto.AuthorDto(a.name, a.age)
                FROM Author a")
    List<AuthorDto> fetchAuthors();
}
```

> Hibernate 6 will have support for Constructor Expressions mixed with other select expressions (HHH-9877[31]). For more details about the Hibernate 6 goodies, see **Appendix K.**

Calling fetchAuthors() will trigger the following SQL:

```
SELECT
    author0_.name AS col_0_0_,
    author0_.age AS col_1_0_
FROM author author0_
```

Displaying the results is pretty straightforward:

```
List<AuthorDto> authors =...;

for (AuthorDto author : authors) {
    System.out.println("Author name: " + author.getName()
                            + " | Age: " + author.getAge());
}
```

---

[31]https://hibernate.atlassian.net/browse/HHH-9877

Possible output will be:

```
Author name: Mark Janel | Age: 23
Author name: Olivia Goy | Age: 43
Author name: Quartis Young | Age: 51
...
```

The source code is available on GitHub[32].

> If (for any reason) the goal needs to be accomplished directly via
> EntityManager then follow this example:
>
> ```
> Query query = entityManager.createQuery(
>     "SELECT new com.bookstore.dto.AuthorDto(a.name, a.age)
>      FROM Author a", AuthorDto.class);
>
> List<AuthorDto> authors = query.getResultList();
> ```

# Item 32: Why You Should Avoid Fetching Entities in DTO via the Constructor Expression

Consider two entities, Author and Book. There is no materialized association between them, but both entities share an attribute named genre. See Figure 3-10.

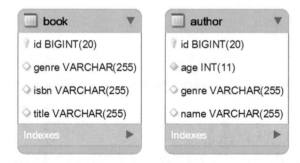

***Figure 3-10.***  *No materialized association*

---

[32]HibernateSpringBootDtoConstructorExpression

The goal consists of using this attribute to join the tables corresponding to Author and Book, and fetching the result in a DTO. The result should contain the Author entity and only the title attribute from Book.

We've already solved this scenario in **Item 26**, "How to Add an Entity in a Spring Projection". However, this scenario can be solved via DTO and a Constructor Expression as well. Nevertheless, the involved performance penalty is a clear signal that this approach should be avoided.

Consider the classical DTO implementation used with a Constructor Expression:

```java
public class BookstoreDto implements Serializable {

    private static final long serialVersionUID = 1L;

    private final Author author;
    private final String title;

    public BookstoreDto(Author author, String title) {
        this.author = author;
        this.title = title;
    }

    public Author getAuthor() {
        return author;
    }

    public String getTitle() {
        return title;
    }
}
```

The JPQL used to populate this DTO is written in the following repository:

```java
@Repository
@Transactional(readOnly = true)
public interface AuthorRepository extends JpaRepository<Author, Long> {

    @Query("SELECT new com.bookstore.dto.BookstoreDto(a, b.title)"
            + "FROM Author a JOIN Book b ON a.genre=b.genre ORDER BY a.id")
    List<BookstoreDto> fetchAll();
}
```

Calling the fetchAll() method reveals that the data cannot be fetched in a single SELECT. Each author needs a secondary SELECT. Therefore, it's prone to the N+1 problem:

```
SELECT
  author0_.id AS col_0_0_,
  book1_.title AS col_1_0_
FROM author author0_
INNER JOIN book book1_
  ON (author0_.genre = book1_.genre)
ORDER BY author0_.id
```

```
SELECT
  author0_.id AS id1_0_0_,
  author0_.age AS age2_0_0_,
  author0_.genre AS genre3_0_0_,
  author0_.name AS name4_0_0_
FROM author author0_
WHERE author0_.id = ?
```

The source code is available on GitHub[33].

This approach cannot fetch the data in a single SELECT, and it's prone to N+1. Using Spring projections, a JPA Tuple, or even a Hibernate-specific ResultTransformer are all better approaches. These approaches will fetch the data in a single SELECT.

Although Hibernate 5.3.9.Final still behaves this way, future Hibernate releases (most probably, Hibernate 6.0) will address this limitation.

---

[33]HibernateSpringBootAvoidEntityInDtoViaConstructor

# Item 33: How to Fetch DTO via a JPA Tuple

Assume that the application contains the following Author entity. This entity maps an author profile:

```
@Entity
public class Author implements Serializable {

    private static final long serialVersionUID = 1L;

    @Id
    @GeneratedValue(strategy = GenerationType.IDENTITY)
    private Long id;

    private int age;
    private String name;
    private String genre;

    // getters and setters omitted for brevity
}
```

The goal is to fetch only the name and age of all authors. This time, the application relies on DTO and JPA, javax.persistence.Tuple. Essentially, Tuple doesn't require a DTO class and is a more convenient approach than fetching data as Object[], because:

- Tuple retains the alias of property that gets filled out by the query (e.g., from AS name, Tuple retains name). With Object[], the alias information is lost.

- Tuple automatically casts the value.

- TupleElement supports Java Generics, so it provides more type safety than Objects.

> Based on these three bullets, we can say that Tuple is one of the best ways to deal with scalar projections. It works with JPQL, Criteria API, and for native SQL.

The first step consists of writing a typical Spring repository and mapping the fetched data into a List<Tuple>. The triggered SQL can be expressed via JPQL or native SQL (starting from Hibernate ORM 5.2.11). Check out the JPQL-based repository:

```
@Repository
@Transactional(readOnly = true)
public interface AuthorRepository extends JpaRepository<Author, Long> {

    @Query(value = "SELECT a.name AS name, a.age AS age FROM Author a")
    List<Tuple> fetchAuthors();
}
```

Calling the fetchAuthors() method will trigger the following SQL:

```
SELECT
  author0_.name AS col_0_0_,
  author0_.age AS col_1_0_
FROM author author0_
```

Here's the native SQL-based repository:

```
@Repository
@Transactional(readOnly = true)
public interface AuthorRepository extends JpaRepository<Author, Long> {

    @Query(value = "SELECT name, age FROM author",
            nativeQuery = true)
    List<Tuple> fetchAuthors();
}
```

Calling the fetchAuthors() method will trigger the following SQL:

```
SELECT
  name, age
FROM author
```

Combining Tuple with the Spring Data Query Builder mechanism will result in SQL statements that fetch all attributes of the entity.

You can access the data mapped in a Tuple via a suite of dedicated methods. One of them is Object get(String alias), where alias is the alias of a certain attribute. For example, you can display the fetched names and ages as follows (aliases and attribute names are the same here, but this is not mandatory):

```
List<Tuple> authors = ...;
for (Tuple author : authors) {
    System.out.println("Author name: " + author.get("name")
                                + " | Age: " + author.get("age"));
}
```

A possible output will be:

```
Author name: Mark Janel | Age: 23
Author name: Olivia Goy | Age: 43
Author name: Quartis Young | Age: 51
...
```

Moreover, you can check the type of values:

```
// true
System.out.println(author.get("name") instanceof String);

// true
System.out.println(author.get("age") instanceof Integer);
```

The source code that uses JPQL is available on GitHub[34].

The source code that uses native SQL is available on GitHub[35].

---

[34]HibernateSpringBootDtoTupleAndJpql
[35]HibernateSpringBootDtoTupleAndSql

> If (for any reason) the goal must be accomplished directly via
> EntityManager then follow these examples:
>
> ```
> // using native SQL
> Query query = entityManager.createNativeQuery(
>     "SELECT name, age FROM author", Tuple.class);
> List<Tuple> authors = query.getResultList();
>
> // using JPQL
> TypedQuery<Tuple> query = entityManager.createQuery(
>     "SELECT a.name AS name, a.age AS age FROM Author a", Tuple.class);
> List<Tuple> authors = query.getResultList();
> ```
>
> The Criteria API provides CriteriaQuery<Tuple> createTupleQuery().

# Item 34: How to Fetch DTO via @SqlResultSetMapping and @NamedNativeQuery

If you are not familiar with using named (native) queries in Spring Boot applications, then I suggest you postpone this section until you read **Item 127**.

Assume that the application contains the following Author entity. This entity maps an author profile:

```
@Entity
public class Author implements Serializable {

    private static final long serialVersionUID = 1L;

    @Id
    @GeneratedValue(strategy = GenerationType.IDENTITY)
    private Long id;

    private int age;
    private String name;
    private String genre;

    // getters and setters omitted for brevity
}
```

JPA @SqlResultSetMapping and @NamedNativeQuery is a combination that works for scalar (ColumnResult), constructor (ConstructorResult), and entity (EntityResult) mappings.

## Scalar Mappings

Via ColumnResult, you can map any column to a scalar result type. For example, let's map the name column as follows:

```
@SqlResultSetMapping(
    name = "AuthorsNameMapping",
    columns = {
        @ColumnResult(name = "name")
    }
)
@NamedNativeQuery(
    name = "Author.fetchName",
    query = "SELECT name FROM author",
    resultSetMapping = "AuthorsNameMapping"
)
@Entity
public class Author implements Serializable {
...
}
```

The Spring repository uses the @Query annotation to note that this is a native query:

```
@Repository
@Transactional(readOnly = true)
public interface AuthorRepository extends JpaRepository<Author, Long> {

    @Query(nativeQuery = true)
    List<String> fetchName();
}
```

# Constructor Mapping

This time, the goal is to fetch only the name and age of all authors. So, you need to fetch a DTO via @SqlResultSetMapping and @NamedNativeQuery and we will rely on ConstructorResult. This is especially useful for native queries where Constructor Expression cannot be used.

The first step consists of decorating the Author entity with the corresponding @SqlResultSetMapping and @NamedNativeQuery to fetch name and age in a DTO class named AuthorDto:

```
@NamedNativeQuery(
    name = "Author.fetchNameAndAge",
    query = "SELECT name, age FROM author",
    resultSetMapping = "AuthorDtoMapping"
)
@SqlResultSetMapping(
    name = "AuthorDtoMapping",
    classes = @ConstructorResult(
        targetClass = AuthorDto.class,
        columns = {
            @ColumnResult(name = "name"),
            @ColumnResult(name = "age")
        }
    )
)
@Entity
public class Author implements Serializable {
    ...
}
```

The AuthorDto is a simple class that maps name and age, as follows:

```
public class AuthorDto implements Serializable {

    private static final long serialVersionUID = 1L;

    private final String name;
    private final int age;
```

231

```
    public AuthorDto(String name, int age) {
        this.name = name;
        this.age = age;
    }

    public String getName() {
        return name;
    }

    public int getAge() {
        return age;
    }
}
```

The Spring repository uses the @Query annotation to note that this is a native query:

```
@Repository
@Transactional(readOnly = true)
public interface AuthorRepository extends JpaRepository<Author, Long> {

    @Query(nativeQuery = true)
    List<AuthorDto> fetchNameAndAge();
}
```

Calling fetchNameAndAge() will trigger the following SQL (this is the native SQL provided in @NamedNativeQuery):

```
SELECT
    name,
    age
FROM author
```

The source code is available on GitHub[36]. If you don't want to use the {*EntityName*}.{*RepositoryMethodName*} convention and you prefer @Query(name="...") then check out this application[37]. Moreover, you you prefer the XML approach based on orm.xml, this application[38] is for you.

---

[36]HibernateSpringBootDtoSqlResultSetMappingAndNamedNativeQuery2
[37]HibernateSpringBootDtoSqlResultSetMappingAndNamedNativeQuery
[38]HibernateSpringBootDtoSqlResultSetMappingNamedNativeQueryOrmXml

If (for any reason) the goal must be accomplished  directly via
EntityManager without @NamedNativeQuery then consider this[39].

## Entity Mapping

You can fetch a single entity or multiple entities via EntityResult. A complete kickoff application is available on GitHub[40]. Or, If you don't want to rely on the {EntityName}. {RepositoryMethodName} convention and you prefer @Query(name="..."), then check out this application[41].

# Item 35: How to Fetch DTO via ResultTransformer

Hibernate's result transformers are one of the most powerful mechanisms for customizing result set mappings. Result transformers allows you to transform the result set in any way you like.

Assume that the application contains the following Author entity. This entity maps an author profile:

```
@Entity
public class Author implements Serializable {

    private static final long serialVersionUID = 1L;

    @Id
    @GeneratedValue(strategy = GenerationType.IDENTITY)
    private Long id;

    private int age;
```

---

[39]HibernateSpringBootDtoViaSqlResultSetMappingEm
[40]HibernateSpringBootDtoSqlResultSetMappingAndNamedNativeQueryEntity2
[41]HibernateSpringBootDtoSqlResultSetMappingAndNamedNativeQueryEntity

```
    private String name;
    private String genre;

    // getters and setters omitted for brevity
}
```

The goal is to fetch only the name and age of all authors. This time, the application relies on DTO and on the Hibernate-specific ResultTransformer. This interface is the Hibernate-specific way to transform query results into the actual application-visible query result list. It works for JPQL and native queries and is a really powerful feature.

The first step consists of defining the DTO class. ResultTransformer can fetch data in a DTO with a constructor and no setters or in a DTO with no constructor but with setters. Fetching the name and age in a DTO with a constructor and no setters requires a DTO, as shown here:

```
public class AuthorDtoNoSetters implements Serializable {

    private static final long serialVersionUID = 1L;

    private final String name;
    private final int age;

    public AuthorDtoNoSetters(String name, int age) {
        this.name = name;
        this.age = age;
    }

    public String getName() {
        return name;
    }

    public int getAge() {
        return age;
    }

}
```

Further, the application uses AliasToBeanConstructorResultTransformer. This is useful for this kind of DTO. You can write a JPQL query to fetch the name and age attributes via the EntityManager#createQuery() and unwrap(org.hibernate.query. Query.class) methods as follows:

```
@Repository
public class Dao implements AuthorDao {

    @PersistenceContext
    private EntityManager entityManager;

    @Override
    @Transactional(readOnly = true)
    public List<AuthorDtoNoSetters> fetchAuthorsNoSetters() {

        Query query = entityManager
            .createQuery("SELECT a.name as name, a.age as age FROM Author a")
            .unwrap(org.hibernate.query.Query.class)
            .setResultTransformer(
                new AliasToBeanConstructorResultTransformer(
                        AuthorDtoNoSetters.class.getConstructors()[0]
                )
            );

        List<AuthorDtoNoSetters> authors = query.getResultList();

        return authors;
    }
}
```

ResultTransformer can fetch the data in a DTO with setters and no constructor as well. Such a DTO can be as follows:

```
public class AuthorDtoWithSetters implements Serializable {

    private static final long serialVersionUID = 1L;

    private String name;
    private int age;
```

```
    public String getName() {
        return name;
    }

    public int getAge() {
        return age;
    }

    public void setName(String name) {
        this.name = name;
    }

    public void setAge(int age) {
        this.age = age;
    }
}
```

This time, the application relies on Transformers.aliasToBean(). The JPQL query that fetches the name and age attributes uses the EntityManager#createQuery() and unwrap(org.hibernate.query.Query.class) methods, as follows:

```
@Repository
public class Dao implements AuthorDao {

    PersistenceContext
    private EntityManager entityManager;

    @Override
    @Transactional(readOnly = true)
    public List<AuthorDtoWithSetters> fetchAuthorsWithSetters() {
        Query query = entityManager
            .createQuery("SELECT a.name as name, a.age as age FROM Author a")
            .unwrap(org.hibernate.query.Query.class)
            .setResultTransformer(
                Transformers.aliasToBean(AuthorDtoWithSetters.class)
        );

    List<AuthorDtoWithSetters> authors = query.getResultList();
```

```
    return authors;
    }
}
```

Calling fetchAuthorsNoSetters() or fetchAuthorsWithSetters() will trigger the next SQL:

```
SELECT
  author0_.name AS col_0_0_,
  author0_.age AS col_1_0_
FROM author author0_
```

Since both kinds of DTO have getters, the access to the fetched data is very simple.

The source code is available on GitHub[42].

Besides JPQL, native SQL queries can be used as well. In this case, use EntityManager.createNativeQuery() instead of EntityManager.createQuery() and unwrap(org.hibernate.query.NativeQuery.class). A complete example is available on GitHub[43].

Starting with Hibernate 5.2, ResultTransformer is deprecated, but until a replacement is available (in Hibernate 6.0), it can be used (read further[44]). The ResultTransformer is being split into TupleTransformer and ResultListTransformer (HHH-11104[45]). For more details about Hibernate 6 goodies, check out **Appendix K**. But don't worry, the migration will be quite smooth.

---

[42]HibernateSpringBootDtoResultTransformerJpql

[43]HibernateSpringBootDtoResultTransformer

[44]https://discourse.hibernate.org/t/hibernate-resulttransformer-is-deprecated-what-to-use-instead/232

[45]https://hibernate.atlassian.net/browse/HHH-11104

# Item 36: How to Fetch DTO via a custom ResultTransformer

If you are not familiar with Hibernate-specific ResultTransformer then consider **Item 35** before continuing.

Sometimes you need a custom ResultTransformer in order to obtain the desired DTO. Consider the Author (with id, name, genre, age, and books) and Book (with id, title, and isbn) entities involved in a bidirectional lazy @OneToMany association. You want to fetch the id, name, and age of each author, including the id and title of their associated books.

The most intuitive DTO will be a class written as follows:

```
public class AuthorDto implements Serializable {

    private static final long serialVersionUID = 1L;

    private Long authorId;
    private String name;
    private int age;

    private List<BookDto> books = new ArrayList<>();

    // constructor, getter, setters, etc omitted for brevity
}
```

As you can see, besides ID, name, and age, this DTO also declares a List<BookDto>. The BookDto maps the ID and the title of a book as follows:

```
public class BookDto implements Serializable {

    private static final long serialVersionUID = 1L;

    private Long bookId;
    private String title;

    // constructor, getter, setters, etc omitted for brevity
}
```

Further, an SQL JOIN can help you fetch the desired result set:

```
@Repository
public class Dao implements AuthorDao {

    @PersistenceContext
    private EntityManager entityManager;

    @Override
    @Transactional(readOnly = true)
    public List<AuthorDto> fetchAuthorWithBook() {

        Query query = entityManager
            .createNativeQuery(
                "SELECT a.id AS author_id, a.name AS name, a.age AS age, "
                + "b.id AS book_id, b.title AS title "
                + "FROM author a JOIN book b ON a.id=b.author_id")
            .unwrap(org.hibernate.query.NativeQuery.class)
            .setResultTransformer(new AuthorBookTransformer());

        List<AuthorDto> authors = query.getResultList();

        return authors;
    }
}
```

Trying to map the result set to AuthorDto is not achievable via a built-in ResultTransformer. You need to transform the result set from Object[] to List<AuthorDto> and, for this, you need the AuthorBookTransformer, which represents an implementation of the ResultTransformer interface. This interface defines two methods—transformTuple() and transformList(). The transformTuple() allows you to transform tuples, which are the elements making up each row of the query result. The transformList() method allows you to perform transformation on the query result as a whole.

Starting with Hibernate 5.2, `ResultTransformer` is deprecated. Until a replacement is available (in Hibernate 6.0), it can be used (read further[46]). For more details about Hibernate 6 goodies, check out **Appendix K**.

You need to override `transformTuple()` to obtain the needed transformation of each row of the query result:

```java
public class AuthorBookTransformer implements ResultTransformer {

    private Map<Long, AuthorDto> authorsDtoMap = new HashMap<>();

    @Override
    public Object transformTuple(Object[] os, String[] strings) {

        Long authorId = ((Number) os[0]).longValue();
        AuthorDto authorDto = authorsDtoMap.get(authorId);

        if (authorDto == null) {
            authorDto = new AuthorDto();
            authorDto.setId(((Number) os[0]).longValue());
            authorDto.setName((String) os[1]);
            authorDto.setAge((int) os[2]);
        }

        BookDto bookDto = new BookDto();
        bookDto.setId(((Number) os[3]).longValue());
        bookDto.setTitle((String) os[4]);

        authorDto.addBook(bookDto);

        authorsDtoMap.putIfAbsent(authorDto.getId(), authorDto);

        return authorDto;
    }
```

---

[46]https://discourse.hibernate.org/t/hibernate-resulttransformer-is-deprecated-what-to-use-instead/232

```
    @Override
    public List<AuthorDto> transformList(List list) {
        return new ArrayList<>(authorsDtoMap.values());
    }
}
```

Feel free to optimize this implementation further. For now, let's write a REST controller endpoint as follows:

```
@GetMapping("/authorWithBook")
public List<AuthorDto> fetchAuthorWithBook() {
    return bookstoreService.fetchAuthorWithBook();
}
```

Accessing localhost:8080/authorWithBook returns the following JSON:

```
[
  {
    "name":"Mark Janel",
    "age":23,
    "books":[
      {
        "title":"The Beatles Anthology",
        "id":3
      },
      {
        "title":"Anthology Of An Year",
        "id":7
      },
      {
        "title":"Anthology From A to Z",
        "id":8
      },
      {
        "title":"Past Anthology",
        "id":9
      }
    ],
```

```
      "id":1
   },
   {
      "name":"Olivia Goy",
      "age":43,
      "books":[
         {
            "title":"Carrie",
            "id":4
         },
         {
            "title":"Horror Train",
            "id":6
         }
      ],
      "id":2
   },
   {
      "name":"Joana Nimar",
      "age":34,
      "books":[
         {
            "title":"A History of Ancient Prague",
            "id":1
         },
         {
            "title":"A People's History",
            "id":2
         },
         {
            "title":"History Today",
            "id":5
         }
      ],
```

```
      "id":4
    }
]
```

The complete application is available on GitHub[47].

# Item 37: How to Map an Entity to a Query via @Subselect

> Consider using @Subselect only after you've evaluated potential solutions based on DTO, DTO + extra queries, or mapping a database view to an entity.

This item talks about mapping an entity to a query via the Hibernate-specific @Subselect. Consider these two entities in a bidirectional lazy @OneToMany association, as follows:

```
@Entity
public class Author implements Serializable {

    private static final long serialVersionUID = 1L;

    @Id
    @GeneratedValue(strategy = GenerationType.IDENTITY)
    private Long id;

    private String name;
    private String genre;
    private int age;

    @OneToMany(cascade = CascadeType.ALL,
                mappedBy = "author", orphanRemoval = true)
    private List<Book> books = new ArrayList<>();
    ...
}
```

---

[47]HibernateSpringBootDtoCustomResultTransformer

```
@Entity
public class Book implements Serializable {

    private static final long serialVersionUID = 1L;

    @Id
    @GeneratedValue(strategy = GenerationType.IDENTITY)
    private Long id;

    private String title;
    private String isbn;

    @ManyToOne(fetch = FetchType.LAZY)
    @JoinColumn(name = "author_id")
    private Author author;
    ...
}
```

An Author wrote several Books. The idea is to write a read-only query to fetch from the Author some fields (e.g., id, name, and genre), but to have the possibility to call getBooks() and fetch the List<Book> in a lazy manner as well. As you know, a classic DTO cannot be used, since such a DTO is not managed and we cannot navigate the associations (this doesn't support any managed associations to other entities).

The Hibernate-specific @Subselect provides a solution to this problem. Via @Subselect, the application can map an immutable and read-only entity to a given SQL SELECT. Via this entity, the application can fetch the associations on demand (you can lazy navigate the associations). The steps to follow are:

- Define a new entity that contains only the needed fields from the Author (it's very important to include the association to Book as well).

- For all these fields, define only getters.

- Mark this entity as @Immutable since no write operations are allowed.

- Flush pending state transitions for the used entities using @Synchronize. Hibernate will perform the synchronization before fetching AuthorDto entities.

- Use @Subselect to write the needed query (map an entity to an SQL query that fetches id, name, and genre, but not books).

Gluing these steps into code produces the following entity:

```
@Entity
@Subselect(
    "SELECT a.id AS id, a.name AS name, a.genre AS genre FROM Author a")
@Synchronize({"author", "book"})
@Immutable
public class AuthorSummary implements Serializable {

    private static final long serialVersionUID = 1L;

    @Id
    private Long id;

    private String name;
    private String genre;

    @OneToMany(mappedBy = "author")
    private Set<Book> books = new HashSet<>();

    public Long getId() {
        return id;
    }

    public String getName() {
        return name;
    }

    public String getGenre() {
        return genre;
    }

    public Set<Book> getBooks() {
        return books;
    }
}
```

Further, write a classical Spring repository for AuthorSummary:

```
@Repository
public interface AuthorDtoRepository
        extends JpaRepository<AuthorSummary, Long> {
}
```

245

A service-method can fetch an author by ID, and, if the genre of the fetched author is equal to the given genre, it fetches the books as well by explicitly calling getBooks():

```
@Transactional(readOnly = true)
public void fetchAuthorWithBooksById(long id, String genre) {

    AuthorSummary author = authorSummaryRepository
        .findById(id).orElseThrow();

    System.out.println("Author: " + author.getName());

    if (author.getGenre().equals(genre)) {
        // lazy loading the books of this author
        Set<Book> books = author.getBooks();
        books.forEach((b) -> System.out.println("Book: "
            + b.getTitle() + "(" + b.getIsbn() + ")"));
    }
}
```

Consider fetching the author with an ID of *4* and a genre of *History*. Figure 3-11 shows the fetched rows (the first SELECT will fetch the author id, name, and genre; the secondary SELECT will fetch the books of this author).

**Author**

| id | age | genre | name |
|----|-----|-------|------|
| 1 | 23 | Anthology | Mark Janel |
| 2 | 43 | Horror | Olivia Goy |
| 3 | 51 | Anthology | Quartis Young |
| 4 | 34 | History | Joana Nimar |
| 5 | 38 | Anthology | Alicia Tom |
| 6 | 56 | Anthology | Katy Loin |

**Book**

| id | isbn | title | author_id |
|----|------|-------|-----------|
| 1 | 001-JN | A History of Ancient Prague | 4 |
| 2 | 002-JN | A People's History | 4 |
| 3 | 001-MJ | The Beatles Anthology | 1 |
| 4 | 001-OG | Carrie | 2 |

***Figure 3-11.*** *Fetching the author with an ID of 4 and a genre of History*

The SQL statements triggered to fetch this data are (this time, instead of a database table name, Hibernate uses the provided SQL statement as a sub-SELECT in the FROM clause):

**SELECT**
```
  authordto0_.id AS id1_0_,
  authordto0_.genre AS genre2_0_,
  authordto0_.name AS name3_0_
```

```
FROM (SELECT
    a.id AS id,
    a.name AS name,
    a.genre AS genre
FROM Author a) authordto0_
SELECT
    books0_.author_id AS author_i4_1_0_,
    books0_.id AS id1_1_0_,
    books0_.id AS id1_1_1_,
    books0_.author_id AS author_i4_1_1_,
    books0_.isbn AS isbn2_1_1_,
    books0_.title AS title3_1_1_
FROM book books0_
WHERE books0_.author_id = ?
```

The source code is available on GitHub[48].

# Item 38: How to Fetch DTO via Blaze-Persistence Entity Views

Assume that the application contains the following Author entity. This entity maps an author profile:

```
@Entity
public class Author implements Serializable {

    private static final long serialVersionUID = 1L;

    @Id
    @GeneratedValue(strategy = GenerationType.IDENTITY)
    private Long id;
```

---

[48]HibernateSpringBootSubselect

```
    private int age;
    private String name;
    private String genre;

    // getters and setters omitted for brevity
}
```

The goal is to fetch only the name and age of all authors. This time, the application relies on Blaze Persistence[49] entity views. Blaze Persistence is an open source project meant to represent a Rich Criteria API for JPA providers. Being external to Spring Boot, it must be added in the application as a dependency. For example, via Maven, you can add the following dependencies to pom.xml:

```
<dependency>
    <groupId>com.blazebit</groupId>
    <artifactId>blaze-persistence-integration-entity-view-spring</artifactId>
    <version>${blaze-persistence.version}</version>
    <scope>compile</scope>
</dependency>
<dependency>
    <groupId>com.blazebit</groupId>
    <artifactId>blaze-persistence-integration-spring-data-2.0</artifactId>
    <version>${blaze-persistence.version}</version>
    <scope>compile</scope>
</dependency>
<dependency>
    <groupId>com.blazebit</groupId>
    <artifactId>blaze-persistence-jpa-criteria-api</artifactId>
    <version>${blaze-persistence.version}</version>
    <scope>compile</scope>
</dependency>
```

---

[49]https://persistence.blazebit.com/

```xml
<dependency>
    <groupId>com.blazebit</groupId>
    <artifactId>blaze-persistence-integration-hibernate-5.2</artifactId>
    <version>${blaze-persistence.version}</version>
    <scope>runtime</scope>
</dependency>

<dependency>
    <groupId>com.blazebit</groupId>
    <artifactId>blaze-persistence-jpa-criteria-impl</artifactId>
    <version>${blaze-persistence.version}</version>
    <scope>runtime</scope>
</dependency>
```

Further, configure Blaze-Persistence, `CriteriaBuilderFactory`, and `EntityViewManager`. This can be accomplished via a classical Spring configuration class and @Bean as follows:

```java
@Configuration
@EnableEntityViews("com.bookstore")
@EnableJpaRepositories(
    basePackages = "com.bookstore",
    repositoryFactoryBeanClass = BlazePersistenceRepositoryFactoryBean.class)
public class BlazeConfiguration {

    private final LocalContainerEntityManagerFactoryBean
        localContainerEntityManagerFactoryBean;

    public BlazeConfiguration(LocalContainerEntityManagerFactoryBean
                                localContainerEntityManagerFactoryBean) {
        this.localContainerEntityManagerFactoryBean =
            localContainerEntityManagerFactoryBean;
    }

    @Bean
    @Scope(ConfigurableBeanFactory.SCOPE_SINGLETON)
    @Lazy(false)
```

```
    public CriteriaBuilderFactory createCriteriaBuilderFactory() {
        CriteriaBuilderConfiguration config = Criteria.getDefault();

        return config.createCriteriaBuilderFactory(
            localContainerEntityManagerFactoryBean.getObject());
    }

    @Bean
    @Scope(ConfigurableBeanFactory.SCOPE_SINGLETON)
    @Lazy(false)
    public EntityViewManager createEntityViewManager(
        CriteriaBuilderFactory cbf, EntityViewConfiguration
                                    entityViewConfiguration) {

        return entityViewConfiguration.createEntityViewManager(cbf);
    }
}
```

All the settings are in place. It's time to exploit Blaze Persistence goodies. The
application should fetch from the database only the name and age of the authors.
Therefore, it's time to write a DTO, or more precisely, an *entity view* via an interface in
Blaze-Persistence fashion. The key here consists of annotating the view with
@EntityView(Author.class):

```
@EntityView(Author.class)
public interface AuthorView {

    public String getName();
    public int getAge();
}
```

Further, write a Spring-centric repository by extending EntityViewRepository (this is a
Blaze Persistence interface):

```
@Repository
@Transactional(readOnly = true)
public interface AuthorViewRepository
    extends EntityViewRepository<AuthorView, Long> {
}
```

The EntityViewRepository interface is a base interface that inherits the most commonly used repository methods. Basically, it can be used as any other Spring Data repository. For example, you can call findAll() to fetch all authors in AuthorView as follows:

```
@Service
public class BookstoreService {

    private final AuthorViewRepository authorViewRepository;

    public BookstoreService(AuthorViewRepository authorViewRepository) {
        this.authorViewRepository = authorViewRepository;
    }

    public Iterable<AuthorView> fetchAuthors() {
        return authorViewRepository.findAll();
    }
}
```

Calling the fetchAuthors() method will trigger the following SQL:

```
SELECT
  author0_.age AS col_0_0_,
  author0_.name AS col_1_0_
FROM author author0_
```

The source code is available on GitHub[50].

# Item 39: How to Effectively Fetch Parent and Association in One SELECT

Assume that the following two entities, Author and Book, are in a bidirectional lazy @OneToMany association (it can be another type of association as well, or it can be unidirectional):

```
@Entity
public class Author implements Serializable {
```

---

[50]HibernateSpringBootDtoBlazeEntityView

```java
    private static final long serialVersionUID = 1L;

    @Id
    private Long id;

    private String name;
    private String genre;
    private int age;

    @OneToMany(cascade = CascadeType.ALL,
                mappedBy = "author", orphanRemoval = true)
    private List<Book> books = new ArrayList<>();
    ...
}

@Entity
public class Book implements Serializable {

    private static final long serialVersionUID = 1L;

    @Id
    private Long id;

    private String title;
    private String isbn;

    @ManyToOne(fetch = FetchType.LAZY)
    @JoinColumn(name = "author_id")
    private Author author;
    ...
}
```

This is a lazy association from both directions. Loading an Author will not load its Books, and vice versa (loading a Book doesn't load its Author). This behavior may be okay in some cases and not okay in others, depending on the requirements of the current feature.

This time, the goal is to perform the following two queries:

- Fetch an author by name, including their books

- Fetch a book by ISBN, including the author

Having a lazy association between authors and books, the goal can be accomplished in two SQL SELECTs. Fetching the author in a SELECT and calling getBooks() will trigger a second SELECT to fetch the books. Or, fetching a book in a SELECT and calling getAuthor() will trigger a second SELECT to fetch the author. This approach highlights at least two drawbacks:

- The application triggers two SELECTs instead of one.

- The lazy fetching (the second SELECT) must take place in an active Hibernate session to avoid LazyInitializationException (this exception occurs if the application calls author.getBooks() or book.getAuthor() outside of a Hibernate session).

Obviously, in this case, it will be preferable to fetch the author and book data in a single SELECT instead of two. However, the application cannot use an SQL JOIN + DTO because it plans to modify these entities. Therefore, they should be managed by Hibernate. Using an SQL JOIN to fetch these entities is not a practical option as well (for this, consider **Item 40**). A naive approach consists of switching the association from LAZY to EAGER at the entities-level. This will work, but **DON'T DO THIS**! As a rule of thumb, use LAZY associations and fetch these associations at the query-level via JOIN FETCH (if the application plans to modify the fetched entities) or via JOIN + DTO (if the fetched data is read-only). In this case, JOIN FETCH is the right choice.

JOIN FETCH is specific to JPA and it allows associations (especially useful for collections) of values to be initialized along with their parent objects using a single SELECT. In Spring style, the goal can be accomplished via two classical repositories and JPQL:

```
@Repository
@Transactional(readOnly = true)
public interface AuthorRepository extends JpaRepository<Author, Long> {

    @Query(value = "SELECT a FROM Author a JOIN FETCH a.books
                    WHERE a.name = ?1")
    Author fetchAuthorWithBooksByName(String name);
}

@Repository
@Transactional(readOnly = true)
public interface BookRepository extends JpaRepository<Book, Long> {
```

```
    @Query(value = "SELECT b FROM Book b JOIN FETCH b.author
                    WHERE b.isbn = ?1")
    Book fetchBookWithAuthorByIsbn(String isbn);
}
```

Calling fetchAuthorWithBooksByName() will trigger the following SQL (the Author and their Books are loaded in a single SELECT):

```
SELECT
  author0_.id AS id1_0_0_,
  books1_.id AS id1_1_1_,
  author0_.age AS age2_0_0_,
  author0_.genre AS genre3_0_0_,
  author0_.name AS name4_0_0_,
  books1_.author_id AS author_i4_1_1_,
  books1_.isbn AS isbn2_1_1_,
  books1_.title AS title3_1_1_,
  books1_.author_id AS author_i4_1_0__,
  books1_.id AS id1_1_0__
FROM author author0_
INNER JOIN book books1_
  ON author0_.id = books1_.author_id
WHERE author0_.name = ?
```

And calling fetchBookWithAuthorByIsbn() will trigger the following SQL (the Book and its Author are loaded in a single SELECT):

```
SELECT
  book0_.id AS id1_1_0_,
  author1_.id AS id1_0_1_,
  book0_.author_id AS author_i4_1_0_,
  book0_.isbn AS isbn2_1_0_,
  book0_.title AS title3_1_0_,
  author1_.age AS age2_0_1_,
  author1_.genre AS genre3_0_1_,
  author1_.name AS name4_0_1_
```

```
FROM book book0_
INNER JOIN author author1_
  ON book0_.author_id = author1_.id
WHERE book0_.isbn = ?
```

Especially with @OneToMany and @ManyToMany associations, it's better to set up associations as LAZY at the entity-level and fetch this association eagerly at the query-level via JOIN FETCH (if the application plans to modify the fetched entities) or via JOIN + DTO (if the fetched data is read-only). The eager fetching strategy cannot be overridden on a query-basis. Only the lazy fetching strategy can be overridden on a query-basis.

Joining tables may result in Cartesian products (e.g., CROSS JOIN, where each row in the first table is matched with every row in the second table) or large result sets. On the other hand, FetchType.LAZY causes secondary queries (N+1). If there are 100 authors and each of them has written five books then the Cartesian product query fetches 100 x 5 = 500 rows. On the other hand, relying on FetchType.LAZY will cause 100 secondary queries (one secondary query for each author). Fetching multiple one-to-many or many-to-many associations may lead to complex Cartesian products or a large number of secondary queries. It is better to have a large Cartesian product than a large number of database round trips. Nevertheless, if you can avoid a large Cartesian product with just a few queries then use these queries.

The source code is available on GitHub[51].

---

[51]HibernateSpringBootJoinFetch

# Item 40: How to Decide Between JOIN and JOIN FETCH

Typically, JOIN and JOIN FETCH come into play when the application has lazy associations but some data must be fetched eagerly. Relying on FetchType.EAGER at the entities-level is a *code smell*. Assume the well-known Author and Book entities that are involved in a bidirectional lazy @OneToMany association:

```
 @Entity
public class Author implements Serializable {

    private static final long serialVersionUID = 1L;

    @Id
    private Long id;

    private String name;
    private String genre;
    private int age;

    @OneToMany(cascade = CascadeType.ALL,
                mappedBy = "author", orphanRemoval = true)
    private List<Book> books = new ArrayList<>();
    ...
}

@Entity
public class Book implements Serializable {

    private static final long serialVersionUID = 1L;

    @Id
    private Long id;

    private String title;
    private String isbn;

    @ManyToOne(fetch = FetchType.LAZY)
    @JoinColumn(name = "author_id")
    private Author author;
    ...
}
```

Consider the sample data shown in Figure 3-12.

| id | age | genre | name | | id | isbn | price | title | author_id |
|----|-----|-------|------|---|----|------|-------|-------|-----------|
| 1 | 23 | Anthology | Mark Janel | | 1 | 001-JN | 36 | A History of Ancient Prague | 4 |
| 2 | 43 | Horror | Olivia Goy | | 2 | 002-JN | 41 | A People's History | 4 |
| 3 | 51 | Anthology | Quartis Young | | 3 | 001-MJ | 11 | The Beatles Anthology | 1 |
| 4 | 34 | History | Joana Nimar | | 4 | 001-OG | 23 | Carrie | 2 |
| 5 | 38 | Anthology | Alicia Tom | | | | | | |
| 6 | 56 | Anthology | Katy Loin | | | | | | |

***Figure 3-12.***  *Data snapshot*

The goal is to fetch the following data as entities:

- All Authors and their Books that are more expensive than the given price

- All the Books and their Authors

# Fetch All Authors and Their Books that Are More Expensive than the Given Price

To satisfy the first query (fetch all the Authors and their Books that are more expensive than the given price), you can write a Spring repository, AuthorRepository, and add a JOIN and a JOIN FETCH query meant to fetch the same data:

```
@Repository
@Transactional(readOnly = true)
public interface AuthorRepository extends JpaRepository<Author, Long> {

    // INNER JOIN
    @Query(value = "SELECT a FROM Author a INNER JOIN a.books b
                    WHERE b.price > ?1")
    List<Author> fetchAuthorsBooksByPriceInnerJoin(int price);

    // JOIN FETCH
    @Query(value = "SELECT a FROM Author a JOIN FETCH a.books b
                    WHERE b.price > ?1")
    List<Author> fetchAuthorsBooksByPriceJoinFetch(int price);
}
```

You can call these repository-methods and display the fetched data to the console, as follows:

```
public void fetchAuthorsBooksByPriceJoinFetch() {

    List<Author> authors =
            authorRepository.fetchAuthorsBooksByPriceJoinFetch(40);

    authors.forEach((e) -> System.out.println("Author name: "
        + e.getName() + ", books: " + e.getBooks()));
}

@Transactional(readOnly = true)
public void fetchAuthorsBooksByPriceInnerJoin() {

    List<Author> authors =
            authorRepository.fetchAuthorsBooksByPriceInnerJoin(40);

    authors.forEach((e) -> System.out.println("Author name: "
        + e.getName() + ", books: " + e.getBooks()));
}
```

## How JOIN FETCH Will Act

JOIN FETCH is specific to JPA and it allows associations to be initialized along with their parent objects using a single SELECT. As you will see soon, this is particularly useful when fetching associated collections. This means that calling fetchAuthorsBooksByPriceJoinFetch() will trigger a single SELECT, as follows:

```
SELECT
  author0_.id AS id1_0_0_,
  books1_.id AS id1_1_1_,
  author0_.age AS age2_0_0_,
  author0_.genre AS genre3_0_0_,
  author0_.name AS name4_0_0_,
  books1_.author_id AS author_i5_1_1_,
  books1_.isbn AS isbn2_1_1_,
  books1_.price AS price3_1_1_,
  books1_.title AS title4_1_1_,
```

```
    books1_.author_id AS author_i5_1_0__,
    books1_.id AS id1_1_0__
FROM author author0_
INNER JOIN book books1_
    ON author0_.id = books1_.author_id
WHERE books1_.price > ?
```

Running this SQL against the data sample for a given price of *40* dollars will fetch the following data (displays the authors' names and books):

```
Author name: Joana Nimar,
      books: [Book{id=2, title=A People's History, isbn=002-JN, price=41}]
```

This looks correct! There is a single book in the database more expensive than *40* dollars and its author is *Joana Nimar*.

## How JOIN Will Act

On the other hand, JOIN doesn't allow associated collections to be initialized along with their parent objects using a single SELECT. This means that calling fetchAuthorsBooksByPriceInnerJoin() will result in the following SELECT (the SQL reveals that no book was loaded):

```
SELECT
    author0_.id AS id1_0_,
    author0_.age AS age2_0_,
    author0_.genre AS genre3_0_,
    author0_.name AS name4_0_
FROM author author0_
INNER JOIN book books1_
    ON author0_.id = books1_.author_id
WHERE books1_.price > ?
```

Running this SQL against the data sample will fetch a single author (*Joana Nimar*), which is correct. Attempting to display the books written by *Joana Nimar* via getBooks() will trigger an additional SELECT, as follows:

**SELECT**
```
  books0_.author_id AS author_i5_1_0_,
  books0_.id AS id1_1_0_,
  books0_.id AS id1_1_1_,
  books0_.author_id AS author_i5_1_1_,
  books0_.isbn AS isbn2_1_1_,
  books0_.price AS price3_1_1_,
  books0_.title AS title4_1_1_
FROM book books0_
WHERE books0_.author_id = ?
```

> Writing this query doesn't help either:
>
> ```
> @Query(value = "SELECT a, b FROM Author a
>                        INNER JOIN a.books b WHERE b.price > ?1")
> ```

Display the author name and the fetched books:

```
Author name: Joana Nimar,
    books: [
      Book{id=1, title=A History of Ancient Prague, isbn=001-JN, price=36},
      Book{id=2, title=A People's History, isbn=002-JN, price=41}
    ]
```

Two things must be highlighted here: an important drawback and a potential confusion.

First, the drawback. Notice that JOIN has fetched the books in an additional SELECT. This can be considered a performance penalty in comparison to JOIN FETCH, which needs a single SELECT, and therefore a single database round trip.

Second, a potential confusion. Pay extra attention to the interpretation of the WHERE books1_.price > ? clause in the first SELECT. While the application fetches only the authors who have written books that are more expensive than *40* dollars, when calling getBooks(), the application fetches all the books of these authors, not only the books more expensive than *40* dollars. This is normal since, when getBooks() is called, the WHERE clause is not there anymore. Therefore, in this case, JOIN produced a different result than JOIN FETCH.

# Fetch All Books and their Authors

To satisfy the second query (all the Books and their Authors), write a Spring repository and a BookRepository and then add two JOINs and a JOIN FETCH query:

```
@Repository
@Transactional(readOnly = true)
public interface BookRepository extends JpaRepository<Book, Long> {

    // INNER JOIN BAD
    @Query(value = "SELECT b FROM Book b INNER JOIN b.author a")
    List<Book> fetchBooksAuthorsInnerJoinBad();

    // INNER JOIN GOOD
    @Query(value = "SELECT b, a FROM Book b INNER JOIN b.author a")
    List<Book> fetchBooksAuthorsInnerJoinGood();

    // JOIN FETCH
    @Query(value = "SELECT b FROM Book b JOIN FETCH b.author a")
    List<Book> fetchBooksAuthorsJoinFetch();
}
```

You can call these methods and display the fetched data to the console, as follows:

```
public void fetchBooksAuthorsJoinFetch() {

    List<Book> books = bookRepository.fetchBooksAuthorsJoinFetch();

    books.forEach((e) -> System.out.println("Book title: " + e.getTitle()
        + ", Isbn:" + e.getIsbn() + ", author: " + e.getAuthor()));
}

@Transactional(readOnly = true)
public void fetchBooksAuthorsInnerJoinBad/Good() {

    List<Book> books = bookRepository.fetchBooksAuthorsInnerJoinBad/Good();

    books.forEach((e) -> System.out.println("Book title: " + e.getTitle()
        + ", Isbn: " + e.getIsbn() + ", author: " + e.getAuthor()));
}
```

# How JOIN FETCH Will Act

Calling fetchBooksAuthorsJoinFetch() will trigger a single SQL triggered as follows (all authors and books are fetched in a single SELECT):

```
SELECT
  book0_.id AS id1_1_0_,
  author1_.id AS id1_0_1_,
  book0_.author_id AS author_i5_1_0_,
  book0_.isbn AS isbn2_1_0_,
  book0_.price AS price3_1_0_,
  book0_.title AS title4_1_0_,
  author1_.age AS age2_0_1_,
  author1_.genre AS genre3_0_1_,
  author1_.name AS name4_0_1_
FROM book book0_
INNER JOIN author author1_
  ON book0_.author_id = author1_.id
```

Running this SQL against the data sample will output the following (displays only the book title, ISBN, and author):

```
Book title: A History of Ancient Prague, Isbn:001-JN,
    author: Author{id=4, name=Joana Nimar, genre=History, age=34}

Book title: A People's History, Isbn:002-JN,
    author: Author{id=4, name=Joana Nimar, genre=History, age=34}

Book title: The Beatles Anthology, Isbn:001-MJ,
    author: Author{id=1, name=Mark Janel, genre=Anthology, age=23}

Book title: Carrie, Isbn:001-OG,
    author: Author{id=2, name=Olivia Goy, genre=Horror, age=43}
```

Everything looks as expected! There are four books and each of them has an author.

# How JOIN Will Act

On the other hand, calling fetchBooksAuthorsInnerJoinBad() will trigger a single SQL as follows (the SQL reveals that no author was loaded):

```
SELECT
    book0_.id AS id1_1_,
    book0_.author_id AS author_i5_1_,
    book0_.isbn AS isbn2_1_,
    book0_.price AS price3_1_,
    book0_.title AS title4_1_
FROM book book0_
INNER JOIN author author1_
    ON book0_.author_id = author1_.id
```

The returned List<Book> contains four Books. Looping this list and fetching the author of each book via getAuthor() will trigger three additional SELECT statements. There are three SELECT statements instead of four because two of the books have the same author. Therefore, for the second of these two books, the author will be fetched from the Persistence Context. So, this SELECT is triggered three times with different id values:

```
SELECT
    author0_.id AS id1_0_0_,
    author0_.age AS age2_0_0_,
    author0_.genre AS genre3_0_0_,
    author0_.name AS name4_0_0_
FROM author author0_
WHERE author0_.id = ?
```

Displaying the title, ISBN, and author of each book will output the following:

```
Book title: A History of Ancient Prague, Isbn: 001-JN,
    author: Author{id=4, name=Joana Nimar, genre=History, age=34}

Book title: A People's History, Isbn: 002-JN,
    author: Author{id=4, name=Joana Nimar, genre=History, age=34}

Book title: The Beatles Anthology, Isbn: 001-MJ,
    author: Author{id=1, name=Mark Janel, genre=Anthology, age=23}
```

```
Book title: Carrie, Isbn: 001-OG,
    author: Author{id=2, name=Olivia Goy, genre=Horror, age=43}
```

In this case, the performance penalty is obvious. While JOIN FETCH needs a single SELECT, JOIN needs four SELECT statements.

How about calling fetchBooksAuthorsInnerJoinGood()? Well, this will produce the exact same query and result as JOIN FETCH. This is working because the fetched association is not a collection. So, in this case, you can use JOIN or JOIN FETCH.

> As a rule of thumb, use JOIN FETCH (not JOIN) whenever the data should be fetched as entities (because the application plans to modify them) and Hibernate should include the associations in the SELECT clause. This is particularly useful when fetching associated collections. In such scenarios, using JOIN is prone to N+1 performance penalties. On the other hand, whenever you're fetching read-only data (you don't plan to modify it), it's better rely on JOIN + DTO instead of JOIN FETCH.

> Note that while a query such as SELECT a FROM Author a JOIN FETCH a.books is correct, the following attempts will not work:
>
> SELECT a.age as age FROM Author a JOIN FETCH a.books
>
> Causes: *org.hibernate.QueryException: query specified join fetching, but the owner of the fetched association was not present in the select list*
>
> SELECT a FROM Author a JOIN FETCH a.books.title
>
> Causes: *org.hibernate.QueryException: illegal attempt to dereference collection [author0_.id.books] with element property reference [title]*

The source code is available on GitHub[52].

---

# Item 41: How to Fetch All Left Entities

Consider the well-known `Author` and `Book` entities that are involved in a bidirectional lazy one-to-many association, shown in Figure 3-13.

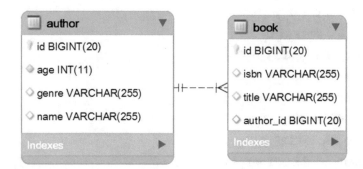

***Figure 3-13.*** *The @OneToMany table relationship*

From **Item 39**, it's clear that fetching an entity and its lazy associations (specifically, the associated collections) in a single `SELECT` is the perfect job for `JOIN FETCH`.

`JOIN FETCH` is transformed in an `INNER JOIN`. Therefore, the result set includes the rows of the entity or table referenced on the left side of the statement that match the entity or table referenced on the right side of the statement. You can fetch all rows of the entity or table referenced on the left side of the statement in plain SQL via `LEFT JOIN`. `LEFT JOIN` will not fetch the associated collections in the same `SELECT`.

So, the solution should combine the advantages brought by `JOIN FETCH` and `LEFT JOIN` and should eliminate their disadvantages. This is perfectly achievable via `LEFT JOIN FETCH` as in the following repository:

```
@Repository
@Transactional(readOnly = true)
public interface AuthorRepository extends JpaRepository<Author, Long> {

    @Query(value = "SELECT a FROM Author a LEFT JOIN FETCH a.books")
    List<Author> fetchAuthorWithBooks();
}
```

Calling fetchAuthorWithBooks() will trigger the following SQL (notice the presence of LEFT OUTER JOIN):

```
SELECT
  author0_.id AS id1_0_0_,
  books1_.id AS id1_1_1_,
  author0_.age AS age2_0_0_,
  author0_.genre AS genre3_0_0_,
  author0_.name AS name4_0_0_,
  books1_.author_id AS author_i4_1_1_,
  books1_.isbn AS isbn2_1_1_,
  books1_.title AS title3_1_1_,
  books1_.author_id AS author_i4_1_0__,
  books1_.id AS id1_1_0__
FROM author author0_
LEFT OUTER JOIN book books1_
  ON author0_.id = books1_.author_id
```

Or the BookRepository:

```
@Repository
@Transactional(readOnly = true)
public interface BookRepository extends JpaRepository<Book, Long> {

    @Query(value = "SELECT b FROM Book b LEFT JOIN FETCH b.author")

    // or, via JOIN
    // @Query(value = "SELECT b, a FROM Book b LEFT JOIN b.author a")
    List<Book> fetchBookWithAuthor();
}
```

Calling fetchBookWithAuthor() will trigger the following SQL (notice the presence of LEFT OUTER JOIN):

```
SELECT
  book0_.id AS id1_1_0_,
  author1_.id AS id1_0_1_,
  book0_.author_id AS author_i4_1_0_,
  book0_.isbn AS isbn2_1_0_,
```

```
    book0_.title AS title3_1_0_,
    author1_.age AS age2_0_1_,
    author1_.genre AS genre3_0_1_,
    author1_.name AS name4_0_1_
FROM book book0_
LEFT OUTER JOIN author author1_
    ON book0_.author_id = author1_.id
```

The source code is available on GitHub[53].

# Item 42: How to Fetch DTO from Unrelated Entities

Unrelated entities are entities that don't have an explicit association between them.
For example, Figure 3-14 represents the tables corresponding to two unrelated entities,
Author and Book.

***Figure 3-14.*** *Tables without relationships*

However, notice that both tables have the name column. This is the name of the author.
The goal is to fetch a DTO (Spring projection) that contains the author's names and book
titles where the price is equal to the given value.

Hibernate 5.1 introduced explicit joins on unrelated entities and the syntax and behavior
are similar to SQL JOIN statements. For example, the following query is useful in this
case:

---

[53]HibernateSpringBootLeftJoinFetch

```
@Repository
@Transactional(readOnly = true)
public interface AuthorRepository extends JpaRepository<Author, Long> {

    @Query(value = "SELECT a.name AS name, b.title AS title "
                + "FROM Author a INNER JOIN Book b ON a.name = b.name "
                + "WHERE b.price = ?1")
    List<BookstoreDto> fetchAuthorNameBookTitleWithPrice(int price);
}
```

The SQL statement is:

```
SELECT
  author0_.name AS col_0_0_,
  book1_.title AS col_1_0_
FROM author author0_
INNER JOIN book book1_
  ON (author0_.name = book1_.name)
WHERE book1_.price = ?
```

The source code is available on GitHub[54].

# Item 43: How to Write JOIN Statements

A brief overview of JOIN statements should bring into discussion the three main types of joins:

- INNER

- OUTER

- CROSS

---

[54]HibernateSpringBootDtoUnrelatedEntities

INNER JOIN is useful for fetching data if it's present in both tables.

OUTER JOIN can be:

- LEFT OUTER JOIN: Fetches data present in the left table

- RIGHT OUTER JOIN: Fetches data present in the right table

- FULL OUTER JOIN: fetches data present in either of the two tables (can be inclusive or exclusive)

- CROSS JOIN: Joins everything with everything; a CROSS JOIN that does not have an ON or WHERE clause gives the Cartesian product

In a query (JPQL/SQL), specifying JOIN means INNER JOIN. Specifying LEFT/RIGHT/FULL JOIN means LEFT/RIGHT/FULL OUTER JOIN.

SQL JOIN statements are the best approach for mitigating the famous LazyInitializationException. Moreover, in the case of read-only data, combining SQL JOIN statements and DTO (e.g., Spring projections) represents the best approach for fetching data from multiple tables. Commonly, SQL JOIN statements are represented via Venn diagrams (even if this may not be the best representation, it's very easy to understand). Venn diagrams for SQL JOINs are shown in Figure 3-15.

SELECT select_list
FROM TableA A
LEFT JOIN TableB B
ON A.Key = B.Key

SELECT select_list
FROM TableA A
LEFT JOIN TableB B
ON A.Key = B.Key
WHERE B.Key IS NULL

SELECT select_list
FROM TableA A
INNER JOIN TableB
ON A.Key = B.Key

SELECT select_list
FROM TableA A
RIGHT JOIN TableB B
ON A.Key = B.Key

SELECT select_list
FROM TableA A
RIGHT JOIN TableB B
ON A.Key = B.Key
WHERE A.Key IS NULL

SELECT select_list
FROM TableA A
FULL OUTER JOIN TableB B
ON A.Key = B.Key
WHERE A.Key IS NULL
OR B.Key IS NULL

SELECT select_list
FROM TableA A
FULL OUTER JOIN TableB B
ON A.Key = B.Key

***Figure 3-15.** JOINs*

Using the Author and Book entities involved in a bidirectional lazy @OneToMany association, consider a Spring projection (DTO) that fetches the names of authors and titles of books:

```
public interface AuthorNameBookTitle {

    String getName();
    String getTitle();
}
```

# INNER JOIN

Considering that the author table is table A and the book table is table B, an INNER JOIN expressed via JPQL can be written as follows:

```
@Query(value = "SELECT b.title AS title, a.name AS name "
        + "FROM Author a INNER JOIN a.books b")
List<AuthorNameBookTitle> findAuthorsAndBooksJpql();
```

Or assume that book is table A and author is table B:

```
@Query(value = "SELECT b.title AS title, a.name AS name "
        + "FROM Book b INNER JOIN b.author a")
List<AuthorNameBookTitle> findBooksAndAuthorsJpql();
```

As native SQL:

```
@Query(value = "SELECT b.title AS title, a.name AS name "
        + "FROM author a INNER JOIN book b ON a.id = b.author_id",
      nativeQuery = true)
List<AuthorNameBookTitle> findAuthorsAndBooksSql();
```

```
@Query(value = "SELECT b.title AS title, a.name AS name "
      + "FROM book b INNER JOIN author a ON a.id = b.author_id",
    nativeQuery = true)
List<AuthorNameBookTitle> findBooksAndAuthorsSql();
```

Adding a WHERE clause can help you filter the result set. For example, let's filter the result set by the author's genre and the book's price:

```
@Query(value = "SELECT b.title AS title, a.name AS name "
        + "FROM Author a INNER JOIN a.books b "
        + "WHERE a.genre = ?1 AND b.price < ?2")
List<AuthorNameBookTitle> findAuthorsAndBooksByGenreAndPriceJpql(
    String genre, int price);
```

In native SQL:

```
@Query(value = "SELECT b.title AS title, a.name AS name "
        + "FROM author a INNER JOIN book b ON a.id = b.author_id "
        + "WHERE a.genre = ?1 AND b.price < ?2",
      nativeQuery = true)
List<AuthorNameBookTitle> findBooksAndAuthorsByGenreAndPriceSql(
    String genre, int price);
```

The complete code is available on GitHub[55].

# LEFT JOIN

Considering that the author table is table A and the book table is table B, a LEFT JOIN expressed via JPQL can be written as follows:

```
@Query(value = "SELECT b.title AS title, a.name AS name "
        + "FROM Author a LEFT JOIN a.books b")
List<AuthorNameBookTitle> findAuthorsAndBooksJpql();
```

Or assume that book is table A and author is table B:

```
@Query(value = "SELECT b.title AS title, a.name AS name "
        + "FROM Book b LEFT JOIN b.author a")
List<AuthorNameBookTitle> findBooksAndAuthorsJpql();
```

As native SQL:

```
@Query(value = "SELECT b.title AS title, a.name AS name "
        + "FROM author a LEFT JOIN book b ON a.id = b.author_id",
```

---

[55]HibernateSpringBootDtoViaInnerJoins

```
            nativeQuery = true)
List<AuthorNameBookTitle> findAuthorsAndBooksSql();

@Query(value = "SELECT b.title AS title, a.name AS name "
        + "FROM book b LEFT JOIN author a ON a.id = b.author_id",
        nativeQuery = true)
List<AuthorNameBookTitle> findBooksAndAuthorsSql();
```

The complete code is available on GitHub[56]. In addition, this[57] application is a sample of writing exclusive LEFT JOINs.

# RIGHT JOIN

Assume that the author table is table A and the book table is table B. A RIGHT JOIN expressed via JPQL can be written as follows:

```
@Query(value = "SELECT b.title AS title, a.name AS name "
        + "FROM Author a RIGHT JOIN a.books b")
List<AuthorNameBookTitle> findAuthorsAndBooksJpql();
```

Or assume that book is table A and author is table B:

```
@Query(value = "SELECT b.title AS title, a.name AS name "
        + "FROM Book b RIGHT JOIN b.author a")
List<AuthorNameBookTitle> findBooksAndAuthorsJpql();
```

As native SQL:

```
@Query(value = "SELECT b.title AS title, a.name AS name "
        + "FROM author a RIGHT JOIN book b ON a.id = b.author_id",
    nativeQuery = true)
List<AuthorNameBookTitle> findAuthorsAndBooksSql();

@Query(value = "SELECT b.title AS title, a.name AS name "
        + "FROM book b RIGHT JOIN author a ON a.id = b.author_id",
        nativeQuery = true)
List<AuthorNameBookTitle> findBooksAndAuthorsSql();
```

---

[56]HibernateSpringBootDtoViaLeftJoins

[57]HibernateSpringBootDtoViaLeftExcludingJoins

The complete code is available on GitHub[58]. In addition, this[59] application is a sample of writing exclusive RIGHT JOINs.

# CROSS JOIN

A CROSS JOIN does not have an ON or WHERE clause and returns the Cartesian product. Let's assume that you have the Book and the Format entities (the Format entity has a formatType field that represents a specific book format—e.g., *paperback, PDF, kindle,* etc.). There is no relationship between these entities.

Considering that the book table is table A and the format table is table B, a CROSS JOIN expressed via JPQL can be written as follows:

```
@Query(value = "SELECT b.title AS title, f.formatType AS formatType "
        + "FROM Book b, Format f")
List<BookTitleAndFormatType> findBooksAndFormatsJpql();
```

Or assume that format is table A and book is table B:

```
@Query(value = "SELECT b.title AS title, f.formatType AS formatType "
        + "FROM Format f, Book b")
List<BookTitleAndFormatType> findFormatsAndBooksJpql();
```

As native SQL:

```
@Query(value = "SELECT b.title AS title, f.format_type AS formatType "
        + "FROM format f CROSS JOIN book b",
      nativeQuery = true)
List<BookTitleAndFormatType> findFormatsAndBooksSql();
```

```
@Query(value = "SELECT b.title AS title, f.format_type AS formatType "
        + "FROM book b CROSS JOIN format f",
      nativeQuery = true)
List<BookTitleAndFormatType> findBooksAndFormatsSql();
```

---

[58]HibernateSpringBootDtoViaRightJoins

[59]HibernateSpringBootDtoViaRightExcludingJoins

The BookTitleAndFormatType is a simple Spring projection:

```
public interface BookTitleAndFormatType {

    String getTitle();
    String getFormatType();
}
```

Pay attention to *implicit* JOIN statements in *-to-one associations. These kinds of JOIN statements will execute a CROSS JOIN not an INNER JOIN as you may expect. For example, consider the following JPQL:

```
@Query(value = "SELECT b.title AS title, b.author.name
            AS name FROM Book b")
List<AuthorNameBookTitle> findBooksAndAuthorsJpql();
```

This implicit JOIN results in a CROSS JOIN with an WHERE clause, not in a INNER JOIN:

```
SELECT
    book0_.title AS col_0_0_,
    author1_.name AS col_1_0_
FROM book book0_
CROSS JOIN author author1_
WHERE book0_.author_id = author1_.id
```

As a rule of thumb, to avoid such cases, it's better to rely on explicit JOIN statements. If you fetch entities, rely on JOIN FETCH (**Item 39**). Also, always check the SQL statements generated via Criteria API, since they are prone to contain unwanted CROSS JOINs as well.

The complete code is available on GitHub[60].

---

[60]HibernateSpringBootDtoViaCrossJoins

# FULL JOIN

> MySQL doesn't support FULL JOINs. The examples in this section were tested on PostgreSQL.

Assume the author table is table A and the book table is table B. An inclusive FULL JOIN expressed via JPQL can be written as follows:

```
@Query(value = "SELECT b.title AS title, a.name AS name "
        + "FROM Author a FULL JOIN a.books b")
List<AuthorNameBookTitle> findAuthorsAndBooksJpql();
```

Or assume that book is table A and author is table B:

```
@Query(value = "SELECT b.title AS title, a.name AS name "
        + "FROM Book b FULL JOIN b.author a")
List<AuthorNameBookTitle> findBooksAndAuthorsJpql();
```

As native SQL:

```
@Query(value = "SELECT b.title AS title, a.name AS name "
        + "FROM author a FULL JOIN book b ON a.id = b.author_id",
      nativeQuery = true)
List<AuthorNameBookTitle> findAuthorsAndBooksSql();
```

```
@Query(value = "SELECT b.title AS title, a.name AS name "
        + "FROM book b FULL JOIN author a ON a.id = b.author_id",
      nativeQuery = true)
List<AuthorNameBookTitle> findBooksAndAuthorsSql();
```

The complete code is available on GitHub[61]. In addition, this[62] application is a sample of writing exclusive FULL JOINs.

---

[61]HibernateSpringBootDtoViaFullJoins
[62]HibernateSpringBootDtoViaFullOuterExcludingJoins

# Simulate a FULL JOIN in MySQL

MySQL doesn't provide support for FULL JOINs, but there are a few ways you can simulate FULL JOINs. The best approach relies on UNION or UNION ALL. The difference between them consists of the fact that UNION removes duplicates while UNION ALL returns duplicates as well.

JPA doesn't support the UNION clause; therefore, you need to use native SQL. The idea is to simulate an inclusive FULL JOIN via a UNION of two outer joins, as follows:

```
@Repository
@Transactional(readOnly = true)
public interface AuthorRepository extends JpaRepository<Author, Long> {

    @Query(value = "(SELECT b.title AS title, a.name AS name FROM author a "
            + "LEFT JOIN book b ON a.id = b.author_id) "
            + "UNION "
            + "(SELECT b.title AS title, a.name AS name FROM author a "
            + "RIGHT JOIN book b ON a.id = b.author_id "
            + "WHERE a.id IS NULL)",
        nativeQuery = true)
    List<AuthorNameBookTitle> findAuthorsAndBooksSql();
}
```

> This query uses UNION; therefore, it removes duplicates. Nevertheless, there are legitimate cases where duplicate results are expected. For such cases, use UNION ALL instead of UNION.

The complete code is available on GitHub[63].

---

[63]HibernateSpringBootDtoViaFullJoinsMySQL

# Item 44: How to Paginate JOINs

Consider the well known `Author` and `Book` entities in a bidirectional lazy `@OneToMany` association. Now, let's assume that the fetched result set should be read-only and it should contain only the names and ages of authors of the given genre and the ISBNs and titles of the associated books. Moreover, you want to fetch the result set in pages. This is a perfect job for `JOIN` + projections (DTO); therefore, start by writing a Spring projection as follows:

```
public interface AuthorBookDto {

    public String getName();  // of author
    public int getAge();      // of author
    public String getTitle(); // of book
    public String getIsbn();  // of book
}
```

Further, write a JPQL relying on a `LEFT JOIN`, as follows:

```
@Transactional(readOnly = true)
@Query(value = "SELECT a.name AS name, a.age AS age,
                b.title AS title, b.isbn AS isbn
                FROM Author a LEFT JOIN a.books b WHERE a.genre = ?1")
Page<AuthorBookDto> fetchPageOfDto(String genre, Pageable pageable);
```

The service-method that calls `fetchPageOfDto()` can be written as follows:

```
public Page<AuthorBookDto> fetchPageOfAuthorsWithBooksDtoByGenre(
                                        int page, int size) {

    Pageable pageable = PageRequest.of(page, size,
        Sort.by(Sort.Direction.ASC, "name"));
    Page<AuthorBookDto> pageOfAuthors
        = authorRepository.fetchPageOfDto("Anthology", pageable);

    return pageOfAuthors;
}
```

The trigger SQL statements are as follows:

```
SELECT
    author0_.name AS col_0_0_,
    author0_.age AS col_1_0_,
    books1_.title AS col_2_0_,
    books1_.isbn AS col_3_0_
FROM author author0_
LEFT OUTER JOIN book books1_
    ON author0_.id = books1_.author_id
WHERE author0_.genre = ?
ORDER BY author0_.name ASC LIMIT ? ?

SELECT
    COUNT(author0_.id) AS col_0_0_
FROM author author0_
LEFT OUTER JOIN book books1_
    ON author0_.id = books1_.author_id
WHERE author0_.genre = ?
```

A JSON representation of a possible result set is as follows:

```
{
    "content":[
        {
            "title":"The Beatles Anthology",
            "isbn":"001-MJ",
            "age":23,
            "name":"Mark Janel"
        },
        {
            "title":"Anthology From Zero To Expert",
            "isbn":"002-MJ",
            "age":23,
            "name":"Mark Janel"
        }
    ],
```

```
    "pageable":{
        "sort":{
            "sorted":true,
            "unsorted":false,
            "empty":false
        },
        "pageSize":2,
        "pageNumber":0,
        "offset":0,
        "paged":true,
        "unpaged":false
    },
    "totalElements":7,
    "totalPages":4,
    "last":false,
    "numberOfElements":2,
    "first":true,
    "sort":{
        "sorted":true,
        "unsorted":false,
        "empty":false
    },
    "number":0,
    "size":2,
    "empty":false
}
```

Notice that this is the raw result. Sometimes this is all you need. Otherwise, it can be further processed in memory to give it different shapes (e.g., group all books of an author under a list). You can do this on the server side or on the client side.

As **Item 95** and **Item 96** highlight, this SELECT COUNT can be assimilated in a single query via a SELECT subquery or using the COUNT(*) OVER() window function. In order to rely on COUNT(*) OVER(), add an additional field in AuthorBookDto to store the total number of rows:

```
public interface AuthorBookDto {

    public String getName();  // of author
    public int getAge();      // of author
    public String getTitle(); // of book
    public String getIsbn();  // of book

    @JsonIgnore
    public long getTotal();
}
```

Further, trigger a native query as follows:

```
@Transactional(readOnly = true)
@Query(value = "SELECT a.name AS name, a.age AS age, b.title AS title,
                b.isbn AS isbn, COUNT(*) OVER() AS total FROM author a
                LEFT JOIN book b ON a.id = b.author_id WHERE a.genre = ?1",
        nativeQuery = true)
List<AuthorBookDto> fetchListOfDtoNative(
                String genre, Pageable pageable);
```

The service-method for calling fetchListOfDtoNative() is shown here:

```
public Page<AuthorBookDto> fetchPageOfAuthorsWithBooksDtoByGenreNative(
        int page, int size) {

    Pageable pageable = PageRequest.of(page, size,
        Sort.by(Sort.Direction.ASC, "name"));

    List<AuthorBookDto> listOfAuthors = authorRepository
        .fetchListOfDtoNative("Anthology", pageable);
    Page<AuthorBookDto> pageOfAuthors = new PageImpl(listOfAuthors,
        pageable, listOfAuthors.isEmpty() ? 0 :
```

```
            listOfAuthors.get(0).getTotal());

    return pageOfAuthors;
}
```

This time, fetching a page requires only a single SQL statement:

```
SELECT
  a.name AS name,
  a.age AS age,
  b.title AS title,
  b.isbn AS isbn,
  COUNT(*) OVER() AS total
FROM author a
LEFT JOIN book b
  ON a.id = b.author_id
WHERE a.genre = ?
ORDER BY a.name ASC LIMIT ? ?
```

Sometimes there is no need to trigger a SELECT COUNT for each page because new inserts or removes are very rare. Therefore the number of rows remains fixed for a long time. In such cases, trigger a single SELECT COUNT when the first page is fetched and use Slice or List for pagination, as in the following two approaches.

As long as the total number of rows is not relevant for each page, using Slice instead of Page is also an option:

```
@Transactional(readOnly = true)
@Query(value = "SELECT a.name AS name, a.age AS age, b.title AS title,
                b.isbn AS isbn FROM Author a LEFT JOIN a.books b
                WHERE a.genre = ?1")
Slice<AuthorBookDto> fetchSliceOfDto(
    String genre, Pageable pageable);

public Slice<AuthorBookDto> fetchSliceOfAuthorsWithBooksDtoByGenre(
        int page, int size) {
```

```
    Pageable pageable = PageRequest.of(page, size,
        Sort.by(Sort.Direction.ASC, "name"));
    Slice<AuthorBookDto> sliceOfAuthors = authorRepository
        . fetchSliceOfDto("Anthology", pageable);

    return sliceOfAuthors;
}
```

Again a single SELECT is needed:

```
SELECT
  author0_.name AS col_0_0_,
  author0_.age AS col_1_0_,
  books1_.title AS col_2_0_,
  books1_.isbn AS col_3_0_
FROM author author0_
LEFT OUTER JOIN book books1_
  ON author0_.id = books1_.author_id
WHERE author0_.genre = ?
ORDER BY author0_.name ASC LIMIT ? ?
```

Of course, relying on List instead of Page/Slice will trigger a single SQL statement as well, but then there will no page metadata available:

```
@Transactional(readOnly = true)
@Query(value = "SELECT a.name AS name, a.age AS age, b.title AS title,
               b.isbn AS isbn FROM Author a LEFT JOIN a.books b
               WHERE a.genre = ?1")
List<AuthorBookDto> fetchListOfDto(String genre, Pageable pageable);

public List<AuthorBookDto> fetchListOfAuthorsWithBooksDtoByGenre(
                                              int page, int size) {

    Pageable pageable = PageRequest.of(page, size,
        Sort.by(Sort.Direction.ASC, "name"));
    List<AuthorBookDto> listOfAuthors
        = authorRepository.fetchListOfDto("Anthology", pageable);

    return listOfAuthors;
}
```

Calling `fetchListOfAuthorsWithBooksDtoByGenre()` triggers the same `SELECT` as in the case of `Slice`. This time the produced JSON doesn't contain any page metadata.

This time, we use `Pageable` just to add the SQL clauses for ordering and paging via Spring help. Especially when paging, Spring will choose the proper SQL clause depending on the dialect (e.g., for MySQL, it will add `LIMIT`).

So far, you have seen several approaches for fetching a read-only result set that contains a subset of columns for authors and the associated books. Because of the pagination, the main issue with these approaches is that they are prone to truncate the result set. Therefore, an author can be fetched with only a subset of their books. Figure 3-16 shows how *Mark Janel* has three books, but two of them are listed on the first page, while the third book is listed on second page.

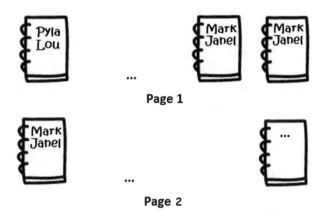

*Figure 3-16.* *Pagination of a truncated result set*

Sometimes this is not an issue at all. For example, the output from Figure 3-16 is okay. How can you avoid truncation of the result set? What can be done if this is a requirement of your application design?

## The DENSE_RANK() Window Function to the Rescue

DENSE_RANK is a window function that assigns a sequential number to different values of a within each group b. For this, DENSE_RANK adds a new column, as shown in Figure 3-17 (na_rank).

SELECT * FROM bookstoredb.author;

| id | age | genre | name |
|----|-----|-------|------|
| 1 | 23 | Anthology | Mark Janel |
| 2 | 43 | Horror | Olivia Goy |
| 3 | 51 | Anthology | Quartis Young |
| 4 | 34 | History | Joana Nimar |
| 5 | 41 | Anthology | Pyla Lou |
| 6 | 31 | Anthology | Merci Umaal |

SELECT * FROM bookstoredb.book;

| id | isbn | title | author_id |
|----|------|-------|-----------|
| 1 | 001-JN | A History of Ancient Prague | 4 |
| 2 | 002-JN | A People's History | 4 |
| 3 | 001-MJ | The Beatles Anthology | 1 |
| 4 | 001-OG | Carrie | 2 |
| 5 | 001-QY | Anthology Of An Year | 3 |
| 6 | 001-KL | Personal Anthology | 5 |
| 7 | 001-MU | Ultimate Anthology | 6 |
| 8 | 002-MJ | Anthology From Zero To Expert | 1 |
| 9 | 003-MJ | Quick Anthology | 1 |
| 10 | 002-MU | 1959 Anthology | 6 |

SELECT * FROM (SELECT *, DENSE_RANK() OVER (ORDER BY name, age) na_rank
FROM (SELECT a.name AS name, a.age AS age, b.title AS title, b.isbn AS isbn
FROM author a LEFT JOIN book b ON a.id = b.author_id WHERE a.genre = "Anthology"
ORDER BY a.name) ab ) ab_r;

| name | age | title | isbn | na_rank |
|------|-----|-------|------|---------|
| Mark Janel | 23 | The Beatles Anthology | 001-MJ | 1 |
| Mark Janel | 23 | Anthology From Zero To Expert | 002-MJ | 1 |
| Mark Janel | 23 | Quick Anthology | 003-MJ | 1 |
| Merci Umaal | 31 | Ultimate Anthology | 001-MU | 2 |
| Merci Umaal | 31 | 1959 Anthology | 002-MU | 2 |
| Pyla Lou | 41 | Personal Anthology | 001-KL | 3 |
| Quartis Young | 51 | Anthology Of An Year | 001-QY | 4 |

***Figure 3-17.*** *Applying DENSE_RANK()*

Once DENSE_RANK() has done its job, the query can simply fetch the authors in pages by adding a WHERE clause, as in the following native query:

```
@Transactional(readOnly = true)
@Query(value = "SELECT * FROM (SELECT *,
             DENSE_RANK() OVER (ORDER BY name, age) na_rank
             FROM (SELECT a.name AS name, a.age AS age, b.title AS title,
             b.isbn AS isbn FROM author a LEFT JOIN book b ON a.id =
             b.author_id WHERE a.genre = ?1 ORDER BY a.name) ab ) ab_r
             WHERE ab_r.na_rank > ?2 AND ab_r.na_rank <= ?3",
     nativeQuery = true)
List<AuthorBookDto> fetchListOfDtoNativeDenseRank(
    String genre, int start, int end);
```

As a rule of thumb, use native queries to write complex queries. This way, you can take advantage of window functions, Common Table Expressions (CTE), PIVOT[64], and so on. Using native queries in the proper cases can seriously boost the performance of your application. And don't forget to analyze your SQL queries and execution plans to optimize their results.

The service-method that calls `fetchListOfDtoNativeDenseRank()` can be:

```
public List<AuthorBookDto> fetchListOfAuthorsWithBooksDtoNativeDenseRank(
        int start, int end) {

    List<AuthorBookDto> listOfAuthors = authorRepository
        .fetchListOfDtoNativeDenseRank("Anthology", start, end);

    return listOfAuthors;
}
```

For example, you can fetch the first two authors with books without truncating the books as follows:

```
fetchListOfAuthorsWithBooksDtoNativeDenseRank(0, 2);
```

Representing the result set as a JSON reveals that two authors have been fetched (*Mark Janel* with three books and *Merci Umaal* with two books):

```
[
  {
     "title":"The Beatles Anthology",
     "isbn":"001-MJ",
     "age":23,
     "name":"Mark Janel"
  },
```

---

[64]https://vladmihalcea.com/how-to-map-table-rows-to-columns-using-sql-pivot-or-case-expressions/

```
    {
        "title":"Anthology From Zero To Expert",
        "isbn":"002-MJ",
        "age":23,
        "name":"Mark Janel"
    },
    {
        "title":"Quick Anthology",
        "isbn":"003-MJ",
        "age":23,
        "name":"Mark Janel"
    },
    {
        "title":"Ultimate Anthology",
        "isbn":"001-MU",
        "age":31,
        "name":"Merci Umaal"
    },
    {
        "title":"1959 Anthology",
        "isbn":"002-MU",
        "age":31,
        "name":"Merci Umaal"
    }
]
```

Notice that this is the raw result. It can be further processed in memory to give it different shapes (e.g., group all books of an author under a list). This time, Pageable is not used and there is no page metadata available, but you can easily add some information (e.g., by adjusting the query to fetch the maximum value assigned by DENSE_RANK(), you can obtain the total number of authors). The complete application is available on GitHub[65] (each query is exposed by a REST endpoint in BookstoreController).

---

[65]HibernateSpringBootJoinPagination

# Item 45: How to Stream the Result Set (in MySQL) and How to Use the Streamable Utility

In this item, we discuss streaming the result set (in MySQL) and using the `Streamable` utility class.

## Stream the Result Set (in MySQL)

Spring Data JPA 1.8 provides support for streaming the result set via the Java 8 Stream API (this feature is available in JPA 2.2 as well). For databases that fetch the entire result set in a single round trip (e.g., MySQL, SQL Server, PostgreSQL), streaming can cause performance penalties. This happens especially when dealing with large result sets. In some cases (require benchmarks to identify such cases), the developer can avoid these performance issues by:

- *Forward-only* result set (default in Spring Data)

- *Read-only* statement (add `@Transactional(readOnly=true)`)

- Set the *fetch-size* value (e.g. 30, or row-by-row)

- For MySQL, set *fetch-size* to `Integer.MIN_VALUE`, or use cursor-based streaming by adding `useCursorFetch=true` to the JDBC URL and then set the `HINT_FETCH_SIZE` hint or call `setFetchSize(size)` with `size` being the desired number of rows to be fetched each time

Nevertheless, in the case of streaming, the response time grows exponentially with the result set size. In such cases, pagination and batching (poll in batches) can perform better than streaming a large result set (which requires benchmarks). Data processing can be done by stored procedures.

> As a rule of thumb, strive to keep the JDBC result set as small as possible. In web applications, pagination should be preferable! JPA 2.2 supports Java 1.8 Stream methods, but the execution plan might not be as efficient as when using SQL-level pagination.

Okay, let's look at an example based on a simple Author entity. The repository, AuthorRepository, exposes a method named streamAll() that returns a Stream<Author>:

```
@Repository
public interface AuthorRepository extends JpaRepository<Author, Long> {

    @Query("SELECT a FROM Author a")
    @QueryHints(value = @QueryHint(name = HINT_FETCH_SIZE,
                value = "" + Integer.MIN_VALUE))
    Stream<Author> streamAll();
}
```

A service method can call streamAll() as follows:

```
@Transactional(readOnly = true)
public void streamDatabase() {

    try ( Stream<Author> authorStream = authorRepository.streamAll()) {

        authorStream.forEach(System.out::println);
    }
}
```

The complete code is available on GitHub[66]. This application contains the useCursorFetch=true case as well.

## Do Not Confuse Stream with the Streamable Utility

Spring Data allows you to return Streamable (org.springframework.data.util. Streamable). This is an alternative to Iterable or any collection type (e.g., List, Set, etc.). Streamable comes with several methods that allow you to directly filter (filter()), map (map()), flat-map (flatMap()), and so on, over the elements of a Streamable. In addition, it allows you to concatenate one or more Streamables via the and() method.

---

[66]HibernateSpringBootStreamAndMySQL

Consider the Author entity and the following query-methods that return Streamable (even if these methods rely on the Query Builder mechanism, using @Query is also allowed):

```
Streamable<Author> findByGenre(String genre);
```

```
Streamable<Author> findByAgeGreaterThan(int age);
```

Or you can combine Streamable with Spring projections, as follows:

```
public interface AuthorName {

    public String getName();
}
```

```
Streamable<AuthorName> findBy();
```

Calling these methods from service-methods is quite straightforward:

```
public void fetchAuthorsAsStreamable() {

    Streamable<Author> authors
        = authorRepository.findByGenre("Anthology");
    authors.forEach(System.out::println);
}
```

```
public void fetchAuthorsDtoAsStreamable() {

    Streamable<AuthorName> authors
        = authorRepository.findBy();
    authors.forEach(a -> System.out.println(a.getName()));
}
```

Further, you can call the Streamable API methods. From a performance perspective, pay attention to the fact that using Streamable in a defective manner is very easy. It is very tempting and comfortable to fetch a Streamable result set and chop it via filter(), map(),flatMap(), and so on until you obtain only the needed data instead of writing a query (e.g., JPQL) that fetches exactly the needed result set from the database. You're just throwing away some of the fetched data to keep only the needed data. Fetching more data than needed can cause significant performance penalties.

## Don't Fetch More Columns than Needed Just to Drop a Part of them via map()

Fetching more columns than needed may cause serious performance penalties. Therefore don't use Streamable, as in the following example. You need a read-only result set containing only the names of the authors of genre *Anthology*, but this example fetches entities (all columns) and applies the map() method:

```
// don't do this
public void fetchAuthorsNames() {

    Streamable<String> authors
        = authorRepository.findByGenre("Anthology")
            .map(Author::getName);

    authors.forEach(System.out::println);
}
```

In such a case, use Streamable and a Spring projection to fetch only the name column:

```
Streamable<AuthorName> queryByGenre(String genre);

public void fetchAuthorsNames() {

    Streamable<AuthorName> authors
        = authorRepository.queryByGenre("Anthology");

    authors.forEach(a -> System.out.println(a.getName()));
}
```

## Don't Fetch More Rows than Needed Just to Drop a Part of Them via filter()

Fetching more rows than needed may cause serious performance penalties as well. Therefore don't use Streamable, as in the following example. You need a result set containing only the authors of genre *Anthology* who are older than *40*, but you fetched all authors of genre *Anthology* and then applied the filter() method to keep those older than *40*:

```
// don't do this
public void fetchAuthorsOlderThanAge() {

    Streamable<Author> authors
        = authorRepository.findByGenre("Anthology")
            .filter(a -> a.getAge() > 40);

    authors.forEach(System.out::println);
}
```

In such a case, simply write the proper JPQL (via the Query Builder mechanism or @Query) that filters the data at the database-level and returns only the needed result set:

```
Streamable<Author> findByGenreAndAgeGreaterThan(String genre, int age);
```

```
public void fetchAuthorsOlderThanAge() {

    Streamable<Author> authors
        = authorRepository.findByGenreAndAgeGreaterThan("Anthology", 40);

    authors.forEach(System.out::println);
}
```

## Pay Attention to Concatenating Streamable via and()

Streamable can be used to concatenate/combine query-method results via the and() method. For example, let's concatenate the findByGenre() and findByAgeGreaterThan() query-methods:

```
@Transactional(readOnly = true)
public void fetchAuthorsByGenreConcatAge() {

    Streamable<Author> authors
        = authorRepository.findByGenre("Anthology")
            .and(authorRepository.findByAgeGreaterThan(40));

    authors.forEach(System.out::println);
}
```

Don't assume that concatenating these two Streamables trigger a single SQL SELECT statement! Each Streamable produces a separate SQL SELECT, as follows:

```
SELECT
  author0_.id AS id1_0_,
  author0_.age AS age2_0_,
  author0_.genre AS genre3_0_,
  author0_.name AS name4_0_
FROM author author0_
WHERE author0_.genre = ?

SELECT
  author0_.id AS id1_0_,
  author0_.age AS age2_0_,
  author0_.genre AS genre3_0_,
  author0_.name AS name4_0_
FROM author author0_
WHERE author0_.age > ?
```

The resulting Streamable concatenates the two result sets into a single one. It's like saying that the first result set contains all authors of the given genre (*Anthology*), while the second result set contains all authors older than the given age (*40*). The final result set contains the concatenation of these results sets.

**In other words, if an author has the genre *Anthology* and is older than *40*, then they will appear twice in the final result set. This is NOT the same thing (doesn't produce the same result set) as writing something like the following:**

```
@Query("SELECT a FROM Author a WHERE a.genre = ?1 AND a.age > ?2")
Streamable<Author> fetchByGenreAndAgeGreaterThan(String genre, int age);

@Query("SELECT a FROM Author a WHERE a.genre = ?1 OR a.age > ?2")
Streamable<Author> fetchByGenreAndAgeGreaterThan(String genre, int age);
```

Or via the Query Builder mechanism:

```
Streamable<Author> findByGenreAndAgeGreaterThan(String genre, int age);

Streamable<Author> findByGenreOrAgeGreaterThan(String genre, int age);
```

So, pay attention to what you are expecting and how you are interpreting the result of concatenating two or more `Streamables`.

Moreover, as a rule of thumb, don't concatenate `Streamables` if you can obtain the needed result set via single `SELECT`. Additional `SELECT` statements add pointless overhead.

The complete application is available on GitHub[67].

# How to Return Custom Streamable Wrapper Types

A common practice consists of exposing dedicated wrapper types for collections that result from mapping a query result set. This way, upon a single query execution, the API can return multiple results. After you call a query-method that returns a collection, you can pass it to a wrapper class by manual instantiation of that wrapper-class. You can avoid the manual instantiation if the code respects the following key points.

- The type implements `Streamable`

- The type exposes a constructor (used next) or a static factory method named `of(...)` or `valueOf(...)` and takes `Streamable` as an argument

Consider the Book entity with the following persistent fields: `id`, `price`, and `title`. The `BookRepository` contains a single query-method:

```
Books findBy();
```

Notice the return type of the `findBy()` method. We don't return a `Streamable`! We return a class representing a custom `Streamable` wrapper type. The `Books` class follows the two bullets and is shown here:

```
public class Books implements Streamable<Book> {

    private final Streamable<Book> streamable;

    public Books(Streamable<Book> streamable) {
```

---

[67]HibernateSpringBootStreamable

```java
        this.streamable = streamable;
    }

    public Map<Boolean, List<Book>> partitionByPrice(int price) {

        return streamable.stream()
            .collect(Collectors.partitioningBy((Book a)
                -> a.getPrice() >= price));
    }

    public int sumPrices() {
        return streamable.stream()
            .map(Book::getPrice)
            .reduce(0, (b1, b2) -> b1 + b2);
    }

    public List<BookDto> toBookDto() {
        return streamable
            .map(b -> new BookDto(b.getPrice(), b.getTitle()))
            .toList();
    }

    @Override
    public Iterator<Book> iterator() {
        return streamable.iterator();
    }
}
```

As you can see, this class exposes three methods that manipulate the passed Streamable to return different results: partitionByPrice(), sumPrices(), and toBookDto(). Further, a service-method can exploit the Books class:

```java
@Transactional
public List<BookDto> updateBookPrice() {

    Books books = bookRepository.findBy();

    int sumPricesBefore = books.sumPrices();
    System.out.println("Total prices before update: " + sumPricesBefore);

    Map<Boolean, List<Book>> booksMap = books.partitionByPrice(25);
```

```
booksMap.get(Boolean.TRUE).forEach(
    a -> a.setPrice(a.getPrice() + 3));

booksMap.get(Boolean.FALSE).forEach(
    a -> a.setPrice(a.getPrice() + 5));

int sumPricesAfter = books.sumPrices();
System.out.println("Total prices after update: " + sumPricesAfter);

return books.toBookDto();
}
```

That's all! The complete application is available on GitHub[68].

---

# CHAPTER 4

# Batching

## Item 46: How to Batch Inserts in Spring Boot Style

Batching is a mechanism capable of grouping INSERT, UPDATE, and DELETE statements and, as a consequence, it significantly reduces the number of database/network round trips. Fewer round trips usually results in better performance.

> Batching can be the perfect solution for avoiding performance penalties caused by a significant number of separate database/network round trips representing inserts, deletes, or updates in a database. For example, without batching, having 1,000 inserts requires 1,000 separate round trips, while employing batching with a batch size of 30 will result in 34 separate round trips. The more inserts we have, the more helpful batching is.

## Enabling Batching and Preparing the JDBC URL

Enabling batch inserts support in a Spring Boot + Hibernate + (MySQL in this example) application starts with several settings in `application.properties`, discussed next.

## Setting the Batch Size

The batch size can be set via the `spring.jpa.properties.hibernate.jdbc.batch_size` property. The recommended value ranges between 5 and 30. The default value can be fetched via `Dialect.DEFAULT_BATCH_SIZE`. Setting the batch size to 30 can be done as follows:

```
spring.jpa.properties.hibernate.jdbc.batch_size=30
```

297

© Anghel Leonard 2020
A. Leonard, *Spring Boot Persistence Best Practices*, https://doi.org/10.1007/978-1-4842-5626-8_4

Do not confuse `hibernate.jdbc.batch_size` with `hibernate.jdbc.fetch_size`. The latter is used to set the JDBC `Statement.setFetchSize()`, as described in **Item 45**. As a rule of thumb, `hibernate.jdbc.fetch_size` is not recommended for Hibernate (which navigates the entire result set) and databases that fetch the whole result set in a single database round trip. Therefore, you should avoid it when using MySQL or PostgreSQL. But it can be useful for databases that support fetching the result set in multiple database round trips (such as Oracle).

## Batching Optimizations for MySQL

For MySQL, there are several properties that can be used to optimize batching performance. First, there is the JDBC URL optimization flag-property, `rewriteBatchedStatements` (this can be used in PostgreSQL as well as in **Item 55**). Once this property is enabled, the SQL statements are rewritten into a single string buffer and sent into a single request to the database. Otherwise, the batched statements (e.g., INSERTs) look like this:

```
insert into author (age, genre, name, id) values (828, 'Genre_810',
'Name_810', 810)
insert into author (age, genre, name, id) values (829, 'Genre_811',
'Name_811', 811)
...
```

With this setting, these SQL statements are rewritten as follows:

```
insert into author (age, genre, name, id) values (828, 'Genre_810',
'Name_810', 810),(829, 'Genre_811', 'Name_811', 811),...
```

Another JDBC URL optimization flag-property is `cachePrepStmts`. This property enables caching and works well with `prepStmtCacheSize`, `prepStmtCacheSqlLimit`, etc. Without this setting, the cache is disabled.

Finally, the JDBC URL optimization flag-property `useServerPrepStmts` is used to enable the server-side prepared statements (this may lead to a significant performance boost).

MySQL supports client (enabled by default) and server (disabled by default) prepared statements.

With client prepared statements, the SQL statement is prepared on the client side before it's sent to the server for execution. The SQL statement is prepared by replacing the placeholders with literal values. At each execution, the client sends a complete SQL statement ready to be executed via a COM_QUERY command.

Server prepared statements is enabled when you set useServerPrepStmts=true. This time the SQL query text is sent only once from client to server via a COM_STMT_PREPARE command. The server prepares the query and sends the result (e.g., placeholders) to the client. Further, at each execution, the client will send to the server only the literal values to be used in place of placeholders via a COM_STMT_EXECUTE command. At this point, the SQL is executed.

Most connection pools (e.g., Apache DBCP, Vibur, and C3P0) will cache prepared statements across connections. In other words, successive calls of the same statement string will use the same instance of PreparedStatement. So, the same PreparedStatement is used across connections (connections that are used and returned to the pool) to avoid preparing the same string on the server side. Other connection pools don't support a prepared statement cache at the connection pool level and prefer to take advantage of JDBC driver caching capabilities (e.g., HikariCP[1]).

The MySQL driver offers a client-side statement cache, which is disabled by default. It can be enabled via the JDBC option, cachePrepStmts=true. Once it is enabled, MySQL will provide caches for both client and server prepared statements. You can get a snapshot of the current caching status via the following query:

SHOW GLOBAL STATUS LIKE '%stmt%';

---

[1]https://github.com/brettwooldridge/HikariCP#statement-cache

This will return the table shown here:

| Variable_name | Value |
|---|---|
| com_stmt_execute | ... |
| com_stmt_prepare | ... |
| prepared_stmt_count | ... |
| ... | ... |

Note that older MySQL versions will not tolerate having rewriting and server-side prepared statements activated at the same time. To be sure that these statements are still valid, check the notes of the Connector/J that you are using.

Having these settings in place results in the following JDBC URL:

```
jdbc:mysql://localhost:3306/bookstoredb?
cachePrepStmts=true
&useServerPrepStmts=true
&rewriteBatchedStatements=true
```

For other RDBMS, just remove/replace the settings specific to MySQL.

As a rule of thumb, if the Second Level Cache is not needed, then make sure it's disabled via `spring.jpa.properties.hibernate.cache.use_second_level_cache=false`.

## Preparing the Entities for Batching Inserts

Next, prepare the entities involved in batching inserts. Set the *assigned generator* since the Hibernate IDENTITY generator will cause batching inserts to be disabled. The Author entity is as follows:

```
@Entity
public class Author implements Serializable {

    private static final long serialVersionUID = 1L;
```

```
@Id
private Long id;

private String name;
private String genre;
private int age;

// getters and setters omitted for brevity
}
```

**Don't** add this:

```
@GeneratedValue(strategy = GenerationType.IDENTITY)
```

For the Hibernate IDENTITY generator (e.g., MySQL AUTO_INCREMENT and PostgreSQL (BIG)SERIAL), Hibernate disables JDBC batching for INSERTs only (as an alternative, the developer can rely on JOOQ, which supports batching in this case as well).

On the other hand, `GenerationType.AUTO` and UUID can be used for insert batching:

```
@Entity
public class Author implements Serializable {

    @Id
    @GeneratedValue(strategy = GenerationType.AUTO)
    private UUID id;
    ...
}
```

Nevertheless, in a nutshell, UUID identifiers should be avoided. Further details are available in **Item 74**, in the section titled, "How About the Universally Unique Identifier (UUID)?".

# Identify and Avoid the Built-In saveAll(Iterable<S> entities) Drawbacks

Spring comes with the built-in saveAll(Iterable<S> entities) method. While this method can be quite convenient for saving relatively small Iterables, when you are dealing with batching, and especially with a high volume of entities, you need to be aware of several aspects:

- **The developer cannot control the flush and clear of Persistence Context in the current transaction:** The saveAll(Iterable<S> entities) method will cause a single flush before the transaction commits; therefore, during the preparation of JDBC batches, the entities are accumulated in the current Persistence Context. For a significant number of entities (large Iterable), this can "overwhelm" the Persistence Context causing performance penalties (e.g., the flush become slow) or even memory-specific errors. The solution is to chunk your data and call saveAll() with an Iterable whose size is equal to the batch size. This way, each Iterable runs in a separate transaction and Persistence Context. You don't risk overwhelming the Persistence Context and, in the case of a failure, the rollback will not affect the previous commits. Moreover, you avoid long-running transactions that are not in favor of MVCC (Multi-Version Concurrency Control[2]) and affect scalability. However, it will be better to simply reuse the Persistence Context in flush-clear cycles and the same transaction in begin-commit cycles (you'll do this in the next section).

- **The developer cannot rely on persist() instead of merge():** Behind the scenes, the saveAll(Iterable<S> entities) method calls the built-in save(S s) method, which calls EntityManager#merge(). This means that, before triggering the INSERTs, the JPA persistence provider will trigger SELECTs. The more SELECTs that are triggered, the more significant the performance penalty will be. Each triggered SELECT is needed to ensure that the database doesn't already

---

[2]https://vladmihalcea.com/how-does-mvcc-multi-version-concurrency-control-work/

contain a record having the same primary key as the one to insert (in such cases, Hibernate will trigger an UPDATE instead of an INSERT). Calling persist() instead of merge() will trigger only the INSERTs. Nevertheless, adding a @Version property to entities will prevent these extra-SELECTs from being fired before batching.

- **The saveAll() method returns a List<S> containing the persisted entities:** For each Iterable, saveAll() creates a list where it adds the persisted entities. If you don't need this list then it is created for nothing. For example, if you batch 1,000 entities with a batch size of 30 then 34 lists will be created. If you don't need these List objects, you just add more work to the Garbage Collector for nothing.

An example of batching inserts via saveAll(Iterable<S> entities) can be found on GitHub[3]. Next, let's talk about an approach meant to give you more control.

## Custom Implementation Is the Way to Go

By writing a custom implementation of batching, you can control and tune the process. You expose to the client a saveInBatch(Iterable<S> entities) method that takes advantage of several optimizations. This custom implementation can rely on EntityManager and has several main objectives:

- Commit the database transaction after each batch

- Use persist() instead of merge()

- Don't require the presence of @Version in entities to avoid extra-SELECTs

- Don't return a List of the persisted entities

- Expose batching in Spring style via a method named saveInBatch(Iterable<S>)

Before we continue, let's highlight the best practices for batching inserts.

---

[3]HibernateSpringBootBatchInsertsJpaRepository

The recommended batch size is between 5 and 30.

Commit the database transaction for each batch (this will flush the current batch to the database). This way, you avoid long-running transactions (which are not in favor of MVCC and affect scalability) and, in the case of a failure, the rollback will not affect the previous commits. Before starting a new batch, begin the transaction again and clear the entity manager. This will prevent the accumulation of managed entities and possible memory errors, which are performance penalties caused by slow flushes. Reuse the transaction in begin-commit cycles and the entity manager in flush-clear cycles.

Nevertheless, if you decide to commit the transaction only at the end, then, inside the transaction, explicitly flush and clear the records after each batch. This way, the Persistence Context releases some memory and prevents memory exhaustion and slow flushes. Watch your code for long-running transactions.

## Writing the BatchRepository Contract

The implementation starts with a non-repository interface that holds the needed methods. This interface is annotated with @NoRepositoryBean:

```
@NoRepositoryBean
public interface BatchRepository<T, ID extends Serializable>
                                 extends JpaRepository<T, ID> {
    <S extends T> void saveInBatch(Iterable<S> entitles);
}
```

## Writing the BatchRepository Implementation

Next, you can extend the SimpleJpaRepository repository base class and implement the BatchRepository. By extending SimpleJpaRepository, you can customize the base repository by adding the needed methods. Mainly, you extend the persistence *technology-specific* repository base class and use this extension as the custom base class for the repository proxies. Notice that you set transaction propagation to NEVER because you don't want to allow Spring to start a potentially long-running transaction (for a hypersonic guide about Spring transaction propagation, check out **Appendix G**):

```
@Transactional(propagation = Propagation.NEVER)
public class BatchRepositoryImpl<T, ID extends Serializable>
    extends SimpleJpaRepository<T, ID> implements BatchRepository<T, ID> {
    ...
    @Override
    public <S extends T> void saveInBatch(Iterable<S> entities) {

        BatchExecutor batchExecutor
            = SpringContext.getBean(BatchExecutor.class);
        batchExecutor.saveInBatch(entities);
    }
    ...
}
```

This extension helps expose the batching inserts implementation in Spring style. The batching takes place in a Spring component named `BatchExecutor`. While the complete code is available on GitHub[4], the following method (`BatchExecutor.saveInBatch()`) shows the implementation (notice that it obtains the `EntityManager` from the `EntityManagerFactory` and controls the transaction begin-commit cycles):

```
@Component
public class BatchExecutor<T> {

    private static final Logger logger =
        Logger.getLogger(BatchExecutor.class.getName());

    @Value("${spring.jpa.properties.hibernate.jdbc.batch_size}")
    private int batchSize;

    private final EntityManagerFactory entityManagerFactory;

    public BatchExecutor(EntityManagerFactory entityManagerFactory) {
        this.entityManagerFactory = entityManagerFactory;
    }

    public <S extends T> void saveInBatch(Iterable<S> entities) {
        EntityManager entityManager
            = entityManagerFactory.createEntityManager();
```

---

[4]HibernateSpringBootBatchInsertsSpringStyleBatchPerTransaction

```
    EntityTransaction entityTransaction = entityManager.
    getTransaction();

    try {
        entityTransaction.begin();

        int i = 0;
        for (S entity : entities) {
            if (i % batchSize == 0 && i > 0) {
                logger.log(Level.INFO,
                    "Flushing the EntityManager
                        containing {0} entities ...", batchSize);

                entityTransaction.commit();
                entityTransaction.begin();

                entityManager.clear();
            }

            entityManager.persist(entity);
            i++;
        }

        logger.log(Level.INFO,
            "Flushing the remaining entities ...");

        entityTransaction.commit();
    } catch (RuntimeException e) {
        if (entityTransaction.isActive()) {
            entityTransaction.rollback();
        }

        throw e;
    } finally {
        entityManager.close();
    }
}
}
```

## Setting BatchRepositoryImpl as the Base Class

Next, you need to instruct Spring to rely on this customized repository base class. In a Java configuration, this can be done via the repositoryBaseClass attribute:

```
@SpringBootApplication
@EnableJpaRepositories(
    repositoryBaseClass = BatchRepositoryImpl.class)
public class MainApplication {

    ...

}
```

# Testing Time

Consider using this implementation in Spring Boot style. First, define a classic repository for the Author entity (this time, extend BatchRepository):

```
@Repository
public interface AuthorRepository extends BatchRepository<Author, Long> {
}
```

Further, inject this repository in a service and call saveInBatch() as follows:

```
public void batchAuthors() {

    List<Author> authors = new ArrayList<>();

    for (int i = 0; i < 1000; i++) {

        Author author = new Author();

        author.setId((long) i + 1);
        author.setName("Name_" + i);
        author.setGenre("Genre_" + i);
        author.setAge(18 + i);

        authors.add(author);
    }

    authorRepository.saveInBatch(authors);
}
```

Possible output will reveal that 1,000 authors are processed in 34 batches and 34 flushes (if you need a refresher about how flush works, see **Appendix H**). See Figure 4-1.

```
519998 nanoseconds spent acquiring 1 JDBC connections;
0 nanoseconds spent releasing 0 JDBC connections;
19727668 nanoseconds spent preparing 34 JDBC statements;
0 nanoseconds spent executing 0 JDBC statements;
8624954427 nanoseconds spent executing 34 JDBC batches;
0 nanoseconds spent performing 0 L2C puts;
0 nanoseconds spent performing 0 L2C hits;
0 nanoseconds spent performing 0 L2C misses;
9428708483 nanoseconds spent executing 34 flushes (flushing a total of 1000 entities and 0 collections);
0 nanoseconds spent executing 0 partial-flushes (flushing a total of 0 entities and 0 collections)
```

***Figure 4-1.*** *Batch inserts*

> As a rule of thumb, always ensure that the application (the data access layer) is really using batching and it is used as expected. Since batching can be silently disabled or not optimized correctly, don't assume that it just works. It's better to rely on tools (e.g., `DataSource-Proxy`; see **Item 83**) that are capable of logging the batch size and count the executed statements.

The source code is available on GitHub[5]. If you just want to commit at the end of the batching process but still take advantage of flush and clear after each batch, consider this code[6].

You may also like to check:

- Batch inserts via `EntityManager` and a DAO layer[7]

- Batch inserts via `JpaContext` and `EntityManager`[8]

---

[5]HibernateSpringBootBatchInsertsEntityManagerViaJpaContext

[6]HibernateSpringBootBatchInsertsSpringStyleBatchPerTransaction

[7]HibernateSpringBootBatchInsertsSpringStyle

[8]HibernateSpringBootBatchInsertsEntityManager

# Item 47: How to Optimize Batch Inserts of Parent-Child Relationships

To get familiar with batching inserts, consider reading **Item 46** before continuing. Consider a @OneToMany association between the Author and Book entities. Saving an author saves their books as well, thanks to cascading persist (or all). If the number of authors and books is significantly high, you can use the batch inserts technique to improve performance.

By default, this will result in batching each author and the books per author. For example, consider 40 authors, each of whom has written five books. Inserting this data into the database requires 240 inserts (40 authors and 200 books). Batching these inserts with a batch size of 15 should result in 17 JDBC batches. Why 17? The answer is coming soon.

Without *ordering the inserts*, the following SQL statements will be grouped in batches in this order (the highlighted inserts are meant to visually demarcate each author):

**insert into author (age, genre, name, id) values (?, ?, ?, ?)**
insert into book (author_id, isbn, title, id) values (?, ?, ?, ?)
-- 4 more

**insert into author (age, genre, name, id) values (?, ?, ?, ?)**
insert into book (author_id, isbn, title, id) values (?, ?, ?, ?)
-- 4 more

...

So, there is an insert targeting the author table followed by five inserts targeting the book table. Since there are 40 authors, this is repeated 40 times. In the end, the statistics reveal a number of 80 JDBC batches, as shown in Figure 4-2.

```
471614 nanoseconds spent acquiring 1 JDBC connections;
0 nanoseconds spent releasing 0 JDBC connections;
25202794 nanoseconds spent preparing 80 JDBC statements;
0 nanoseconds spent executing 0 JDBC statements;
3065506548 nanoseconds spent executing 80 JDBC batches;
0 nanoseconds spent performing 0 L2C puts;
0 nanoseconds spent performing 0 L2C hits;
0 nanoseconds spent performing 0 L2C misses;
3238487470 nanoseconds spent executing 3 flushes (flushing a total of 240 entities and 40 collections);
0 nanoseconds spent executing 0 partial-flushes (flushing a total of 0 entities and 0 collections)
```

***Figure 4-2.*** *Batch inserts (including associations) without ordering the inserts*

309

Why 80 JDBC batches? The answer lies in how batching works. More precisely, a JDBC batch can target one table only. When another table is targeted, the current batch ends and a new one is created. In this case, targeting the author table creates a batch, while targeting the book table creates another batch. The first batch groups only one insert, while the second batch groups five inserts. So, there are 40 x 2 batches.

## Ordering Inserts

The solution to this problem relies in *ordering the inserts*. This can be accomplished by adding application.properties to the following setting:

spring.jpa.properties.hibernate.order_inserts=true

This time, the inserts are ordered as follows:

```
insert into author (age, genre, name, id) values (?, ?, ?, ?)
-- 14 more

insert into book (author_id, isbn, title, id) values (?, ?, ?, ?)
-- 74 more (15 x 5)
...
```

The first batch groups 15 inserts targeting the author table. Each of the following five batches groups 15 inserts targeting the book table. So, there are six batches so far. Another six will cover the next group of 15 authors. So, 12 batches. The last 10 authors are grouped in a new batch; therefore, there are 13 so far. The last 10 authors have written 50 books, which results in four more batches. In total, that's 17 JDBC batches, as shown in Figure 4-3.

```
460863 nanoseconds spent acquiring 1 JDBC connections;
0 nanoseconds spent releasing 0 JDBC connections;
18206769 nanoseconds spent preparing 6 JDBC statements;
0 nanoseconds spent executing 0 JDBC statements;
761763240 nanoseconds spent executing 17 JDBC batches;
0 nanoseconds spent performing 0 L2C puts;
0 nanoseconds spent performing 0 L2C hits;
0 nanoseconds spent performing 0 L2C misses;
870081646 nanoseconds spent executing 3 flushes (flushing a total of 240 entities and 40 collections);
0 nanoseconds spent executing 0 partial-flushes (flushing a total of 0 entities and 0 collections)
```

*Figure 4-3.* *Batch inserts (including associations) with ordered inserts*

The time-performance trend graph shown in Figure 4-4 reveals that ordering inserts can result in substantial benefits. Here, we increase the number of authors from 5 to 500 while keeping the number of books per author equal to 5.

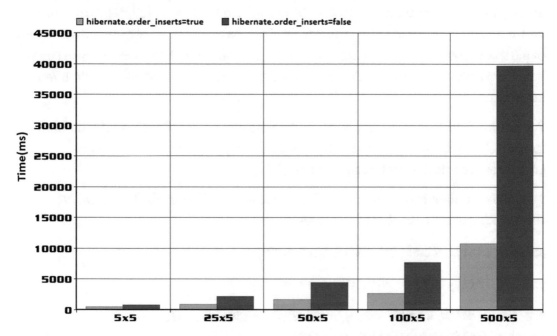

***Figure 4-4.*** *Batch inserts including associations with and without ordering*

This time-performance trend graphic was obtained against MySQL, on a Windows 7 machine with the following characteristics: Intel i7, 2.10GHz, and 6GB RAM. The application and MySQL ran on the same machine.

The source code is available on GitHub[9]. Or, if you want to run batching in a single transaction, check out this GitHub[10] application.

[9]HibernateSpringBootBatchInsertOrderBatchPerTransaction
[10]HibernateSpringBootBatchInsertOrder

# Item 48: How to Control Batch Size at the Session Level

Setting the batch size at the application-level can be done in `application.properties` via the `spring.jpa.properties.hibernate.jdbc.batch_size`. In other words, the same batch size is used for all Hibernate sessions. But, starting with Hibernate 5.2, you can set batch size at the session-level. This allows you to have Hibernate sessions with different batch sizes.

You set the batch size at session-level via the `Session.setJdbcBatchSize()` method. In Spring Boot, accessing the `Session` implies unwrapping it from the current `EntityManager` via `EntityManager#unwrap()`.

The following snippet of code shows all the pieces needed to set the batch size at session-level in the case of batching inserts:

```
private static final int BATCH_SIZE = 30;

private EntityManager entityManager = ...;

Session session = entityManager.unwrap(Session.class);
session.setJdbcBatchSize(BATCH_SIZE);

...
int i = 0;
for (S entity: entities) {
    if (i % session.getJdbcBatchSize() == 0 && i > 0) {

        ...
    }
}
...
```

The source code is available on GitHub[11]. Or, if you want to run batching in a single transaction, then check out this GitHub[12] application.

---

[11]HibernateSpringBootBatchInsertsViaSessionPerTransaction
[12]HibernateSpringBootBatchInsertsViaSession

# Item 49: How to Fork-Join JDBC Batching

Most databases provide support for *bulk* inserting many millions of records. Before deciding to go with batching/bulking at the application-level, it is advisable to check out what options your database vendor provides. For example, MySQL provides LOAD DATA INFILE, which is a highly optimized feature that directly inserts data into a table from a CSV/TSV file at great speeds.

The previous items have covered several aspects of persisting entities via batching. But there are cases where entities are not needed and you have to employ JDBC plain batching. For example, assume that you have a file (`citylots.json`) that contains information about city lots in JSON. You need to transfer this file to a database table (`lots`) via an INSERT statement of type (the placeholder is a line from the file):

```
INSERT INTO lots (lot) VALUES (?)
```

In Spring Boot, JDBC batching can be easily done via JdbcTemplate; more precisely via the JdbcTemplate.batchUpdate() methods. A flavor of this method takes as its second argument an instance of BatchPreparedStatementSetter, which is useful for setting the literal values of the PreparedStatement passed as the first argument via a String. Essentially, batchUpdate() issues multiple update statements on a single PreparedStatement, using batch updates and a BatchPreparedStatementSetter to set the values.

The following component represents a JDBC batching implementation using batchUpdate():

```
@Component
public class JoiningComponent {

    private static final String SQL_INSERT
        = "INSERT INTO lots (lot) VALUES (?)";

    private final JdbcTemplate jdbcTemplate;

    public JoiningComponent(JdbcTemplate jdbcTemplate) {
        this.jdbcTemplate = jdbcTemplate;
    }
```

```
@Transactional(propagation = Propagation.REQUIRES_NEW)
public void executeBatch(List<String> jsonList) {

    jdbcTemplate.batchUpdate(SQL_INSERT,
                new BatchPreparedStatementSetter() {

        @Override
        public void setValues(PreparedStatement pStmt, int i)
        throws SQLException {
            String jsonLine = jsonList.get(i);
            pStmt.setString(1, jsonLine);
        }

        @Override
        public int getBatchSize() {
            return jsonList.size();
        }
    });
}
}
```

The action takes place in the executeBatch() method. The received jsonList is iterated, and for each item, the PreparedStatement is prepared accordingly (in setValues()) and the update is issued.

This implementation works just fine as long as the jsonList is not significantly large. The citylots.json file has 200,000+ lines, so the implementation needs a long transaction in order to iterate a list of 200,000+ items and issue 200,000+ updates. With a batch size of 30, there are 6,600+ batches to execute. Even with batch support, it will take a significant amount of time to sequentially execute 6,600+ batches.

# Fork-Join Batching

In such scenarios, instead of performing batching sequentially, it will be better to perform it concurrently. Java comes with several approaches that can be employed, here such as Executors, a fork/join framework, CompletableFuture, and so on. In this case, let's use the fork/join framework.

Although it's beyond the scope of this book to dissect the fork/join framework, this section quickly highlights several aspects:

- The fork/join framework is meant to take a big task (typically, "big" means a large amount of data) and recursively split (fork) it into smaller tasks (subtasks) that can be performed in parallel. In the end, after all the subtasks have been completed, their results are combined (joined) into a single result.

- In API terms, a fork/join can be created via `java.util.concurrent.ForkJoinPool`.

- A `ForkJoinPool` object manipulates tasks. The base type of task executed in `ForkJoinPool` is `ForkJoinTask<V>`. There are three types of tasks, but we are interested in `RecursiveAction`, which is for the tasks that return `void`.

- The logic of a task is happening in an `abstract` method named `compute()`.

- Submitting tasks to `ForkJoinPool` can be done via a bunch of methods, but we are interested in `invokeAll()`. This method is used to fork a bunch of tasks (e.g., a collection).

- Typically, the number of available processors (cores) gives the fork/join parallelism level.

Based on these points, you can employ the fork/join framework to fork a list of 200,000+ items in subtasks of a maximum of 30 items (30 is the size of a batch, represented as a configuration property in `application.properties`). Further, the `JoiningComponent.executeBatch()` method will execute each subtask (batch):

```
@Component
@Scope("prototype")
public class ForkingComponent extends RecursiveAction {

    @Value("${jdbc.batch.size}")
    private int batchSize;
```

```
    @Autowired
    private JoiningComponent joiningComponent;

    @Autowired
    private ApplicationContext applicationContext;

    private final List<String> jsonList;

    public ForkingComponent(List<String> jsonList) {
        this.jsonList = jsonList;
    }

    @Override
    public void compute() {
        if (jsonList.size() > batchSize) {
            ForkJoinTask.invokeAll(createSubtasks());
        } else {
            joiningComponent.executeBatch(jsonList);
        }
    }

    private List<ForkingComponent> createSubtasks() {
        List<ForkingComponent> subtasks = new ArrayList<>();

        int size = jsonList.size();

        List<String> jsonListOne = jsonList.subList(0, (size + 1) / 2);
        List<String> jsonListTwo = jsonList.subList((size + 1) / 2, size);

        subtasks.add(applicationContext.getBean(
            ForkingComponent.class, new ArrayList<>(jsonListOne)));
        subtasks.add(applicationContext.getBean(
            ForkingComponent.class, new ArrayList<>(jsonListTwo)));

        return subtasks;
    }
}
```

Finally, you need to fire up everything via ForkJoinPool:

```
public static final int NUMBER_OF_CORES =
    Runtime.getRuntime().availableProcessors();
public static final ForkJoinPool forkJoinPool = new
    ForkJoinPool(NUMBER_OF_CORES);

// fetch 200000+ lines from file
List<String> allLines = Files.readAllLines(Path.of(fileName));

private void forkjoin(List<String> lines) {
    ForkingComponent forkingComponent
        = applicationContext.getBean(ForkingComponent.class, lines);

    forkJoinPool.invoke(forkingComponent);
}
```

Each batch will run in its own transaction/connection, so you need to ensure that the connection pool (e.g., HikariCP) can serve the necessary number of connections to avoid contentions between the fork/join threads. Typically, the number of available processors (cores) gives the fork/join parallelism level (this is not a rule; you need to benchmark it). Therefore, the number of connections should be the same as or more than the number of fork/join threads that will execute batches. For example, if you have eight cores, then the connection pool must provide at least eight connections if you want to avoid idle fork/join threads. For HikariCP, you can set 10 connections:

```
spring.datasource.hikari.maximumPoolSize=10
spring.datasource.hikari.minimumIdle=10
```

Figure 4-5 shows the time-performance trend when batching 1,000, 10,000, and 25,000 items using one thread, four threads, eight threads, respectively, and a batch size of 30. It's quite obvious that using concurrent batching can seriously speed up the process. Of course, for a particular job, tuning and finding the best values for the number of threads, the number of connections, batch size, subtask size, etc., can optimize this implementation further.

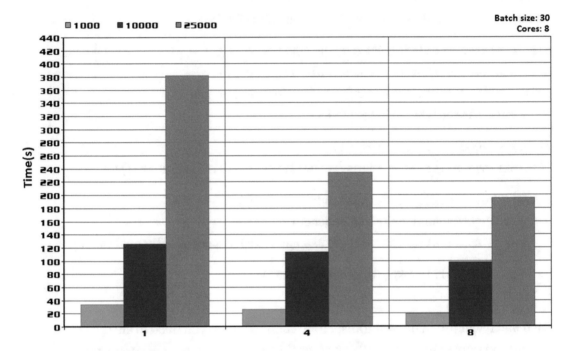

***Figure 4-5.*** *Fork/join and JDBC batch inserts*

The time-performance trend graphic shown in Figure 4-5 was obtained against MySQL on a Windows 7 machine with the following characteristics: Intel i7, 2.10GHz, and 6GB RAM. The application and MySQL ran on the same machine.

The complete application is available on GitHub[13].

> For complex batching scenarios, it is advisable to rely on a dedicated tool. For example, the Spring Batch[14] project can be a proper choice.

# Item 50: Batching Entities via CompletableFuture

This item uses the code base from **Item 46**, in the section entitled "Custom Implementation Is the Way to Go," so consider getting familiar with it before reading this item.

---

[13]HibernateSpringBootBatchJsonFileForkJoin

[14]https://spring.io/projects/spring-batch

When you need to speed up the entity-batching process, think of performing the batching concurrently instead of performing it sequentially, as in **Item 46**. Java comes with several approaches, such as Executors, the fork/join framework, CompletableFuture, and so on. You can easily employ the fork/join framework as you did in **Item 49**, but for the sake of variation, this time let's use the CompletableFuture API.

While it's beyond the scope of this book to dissect the CompletableFuture API, the following list quickly highlights several aspects:

- CompletableFuture was added in JDK 8 as an enhancement of Future API.

- CompletableFuture comes with a solid asynchronous API materialized in a significant number of methods.

- From these methods, we are interested in CompletableFuture.allOf(). This method allows you to asynchronously execute a bunch of tasks and wait for them to complete. In this case, the tasks are the insert batches.

- Another method that you need is CompletableFuture.runAsync(). This method can run a task asynchronously and doesn't return a result. In this case, the task is a transaction that executes a single batch. If you need to return a result, then you can simply employ the supplyAsync() method.

Remember that in **Item 49**, you created the BatchExecutor, which reuses the same transaction in begin-commit cycles. This time, you need concurrent batching, so a single transaction is not enough. In other words, you need one transaction/connection per batch. This can be shaped via TransactionTemplate. The retrofitted BatchExecutor is listed here:

```
@Component
public class BatchExecutor<T> {

    private static final Logger logger =
        Logger.getLogger(BatchExecutor.class.getName());

    @Value("${spring.jpa.properties.hibernate.jdbc.batch_size}")
    private int batchSize;
```

```
    private final TransactionTemplate txTemplate;
    private final EntityManager entityManager;

    private static final ExecutorService executor
        = Executors.newFixedThreadPool(
            Runtime.getRuntime().availableProcessors() - 1);

    public BatchExecutor(TransactionTemplate txTemplate,
                         EntityManager entityManager) {
        this.txTemplate = txTemplate;
        this.entityManager = entityManager;
    }

    public <S extends T> void saveInBatch(List<S> entities)
              throws InterruptedException, ExecutionException {

        txTemplate.setPropagationBehavior(
            TransactionDefinition.PROPAGATION_REQUIRES_NEW);

        final AtomicInteger count = new AtomicInteger();
        CompletableFuture[] futures = entities.stream()
            .collect(Collectors.groupingBy(
                c -> count.getAndIncrement() / batchSize))
            .values()
            .stream()
            .map(this::executeBatch)
            .toArray(CompletableFuture[]::new);

        CompletableFuture<Void> run = CompletableFuture.allOf(futures);

        run.get();
    }

    public <S extends T> CompletableFuture<Void>
        executeBatch(List<S> list) {

        return CompletableFuture.runAsync(() -> {
            txTemplate.execute(new TransactionCallbackWithoutResult() {
```

```
            @Override
            protected void doInTransactionWithoutResult(
                                    TransactionStatus status) {

                for (S entity : list) {
                    entityManager.persist(entity);
                }
            }
        });
    }, executor);
    }
}
```

Notice that we chunk the initial list into an array of CompletableFuture using the batch size. While the chunking technique used here is quite slow, it's very easy to write. Nevertheless, many other solutions are available, as you can see in the application[15].

Also, notice that we use a custom ExecutorService. This can be useful for controlling the parallelism level, but you can skip it as well. If you skip it, then the asynchronous tasks are executed in threads obtained from the global ForkJoinPool.commonPool(). Finally, for the HikariCP connection pool, you can set 10 connections, as shown here (this will easily accommodate the eight threads used for batching):

```
spring.datasource.hikari.maximumPoolSize=10
spring.datasource.hikari.minimumIdle=10
```

Figure 4-6 shows the performance trend for batching 1,000, 5,000, and 10,000 entities using one thread, four threads, and eight threads, respectively, and a batch size of 30. It's quite obvious that using concurrent batching can seriously speed up the process. Of course, for a particular job, tuning and finding the best values for the number of threads, the number of connections, batch size, subtasks size, etc., can optimize this implementation further.

---

[15]ChunkList

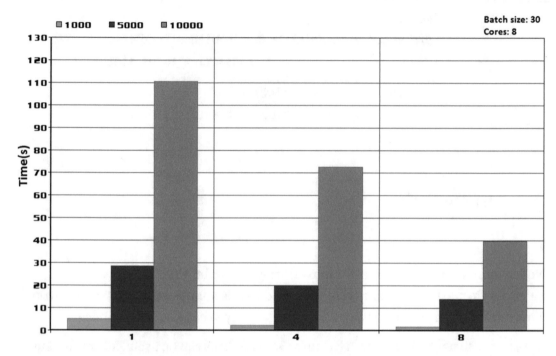

*Figure 4-6.* *CompletableFuture and JPA batch inserts*

The time-performance trend graphic in Figure 4-6 was obtained against MySQL on a Windows 7 machine with the following characteristics: Intel i7, 2.10GHz, and 6GB RAM. The application and MySQL ran on the same machine.

The complete application is available on GitHub[16].

> For a complex batching scenario, it is advisable to rely on a dedicated tool. For example, the Spring Batch[17] project can be a good choice.

# Item 51: How to Efficiently Batch Updates

Batching updates is a matter of settings. First, the JDBC URL for MySQL can be prepared as in **Item 46**:

---

[16]HibernateSpringBootBatchInsertsCompletableFuture
[17]https://spring.io/projects/spring-batch

322

```
jdbc:mysql://localhost:3306/bookstoredb?
cachePrepStmts=true
&useServerPrepStmts=true
&rewriteBatchedStatements=true
```

For other RDBMS, you just remove the settings specific to MySQL.

You can also set the batch size via `spring.jpa.properties.hibernate.jdbc.batch_size`.

Next, there are two main aspects that need to be considered.

## Versioned Entities

If the entities that should be updated are versioned (contain a property annotated with `@Version` for preventing *lost updates*), then make sure that the following property is set:

`spring.jpa.properties.hibernate.jdbc.batch_versioned_data=true`

> `spring.jpa.properties.hibernate.jdbc.batch_versioned_data` should be explicitly set before Hibernate 5. Starting with Hibernate 5, this setting is enabled by default.

## Batch Updates of Parent-Child Relationships

When updates affect a parent-child relationship with cascade all/persist, it is advisable to *order the updates* via the following setting:

`spring.jpa.properties.hibernate.order_updates=true`

If you don't order the updates, the application will be prone to the issue described in **Item 47**. As a quick reminder, a JDBC batch can target one table only. When another table is targeted, the current batch ends and a new one is created.

The source code bundled with this book contains two applications. One is useful for batching updates that don't involve associations (GitHub[18]) and the other one involves associations (GitHub[19]). Both applications use the well known entities, Author and Book.

---

[18]HibernateSpringBootBatchUpdateOrderSingleEntity
[19]HibernateSpringBootBatchUpdateOrder

# Bulk Updates

*Bulk* operations (delete and updates) are also useful for modifying a set of records. *Bulk* operations are fast, but they have three main drawbacks:

- *Bulk* updates (and deletes) may leave the Persistence Context in an outdated state (it's up to you to prevent this issue by flushing the Persistence Context before the update/delete and then close/clear it after the update/delete to avoid issues created by potentially un-flushed or outdated entities).

- *Bulk* updates (and deletes) don't benefit from automatic Optimistic Locking (e.g., @Version is ignored). Therefore, the *lost updates* are not prevented. Nevertheless, other queries may benefit from the Optimistic Locking mechanism. Therefore, it is advisable to signal these updates by explicitly incrementing versions (if any are present).

- *Bulk* deletes cannot take advantage of cascading removals (CascadeType.REMOVE) or of orphanRemoval.

That being said, let's assume that Author and Book are involved in a bidirectional lazy @OneToMany association. The Author persistent fields are id, name, genre, age, version, and books. The Book persistent fields are id, title, isbn, version, and author. Now, let's update!

Let's update all the authors by incrementing their age by *1* and update the books by setting their isbns to *None*. There is no need to load the authors and books in the Persistence Context to perform these updates. You can just trigger two *bulk* operations as follows (notice how the query explicitly increments the version as well):

```
// add this query in AuthorRepository
@Transactional
@Modifying(flushAutomatically = true, clearAutomatically = true)
@Query(value = "UPDATE Author a SET a.age = a.age + 1,
               a.version = a.version + 1")
public int updateInBulk();

// add this query in BookRepository
@Transactional
@Modifying(flushAutomatically = true, clearAutomatically = true)
```

```
@Query(value = "UPDATE Book b SET b.isbn='None',
               b.version=b.version + 1")
public int updateInBulk();
```

And a service-method triggers the updates:

```
@Transactional
public void updateAuthorsAndBooks() {

    authorRepository.updateInBulk();
    bookRepository.updateInBulk();
}
```

The triggered SQL statements are:

```
UPDATE author
SET age = age + 1,
    version = version + 1

UPDATE book
SET isbn = 'None',
    version = version + 1
```

Bulk operations can be used for entities as well. Let's assume that the Persistence Context contains the Author and the associated Book for all authors older than *40*. This time, the *bulk* operations can be written as follows:

```
// add this query in AuthorRepository
@Transactional
@Modifying(flushAutomatically = true, clearAutomatically = true)
@Query(value = "UPDATE Author a SET a.age = a.age + 1,
               a.version = a.version + 1 WHERE a IN ?1")
public int updateInBulk(List<Author> authors);

// add this query in BookRepository
@Transactional
@Modifying(flushAutomatically = true, clearAutomatically = true)
@Query(value = "UPDATE Book b SET b.isbn='None',
               b.version = b.version + 1 WHERE b.author IN ?1")
public int updateInBulk(List<Author> authors);
```

And a service-method triggers the updates:

```
@Transactional
public void updateAuthorsGtAgeAndBooks() {

    List<Author> authors = authorRepository.findGtGivenAge(40);

    authorRepository.updateInBulk(authors);
    bookRepository.updateInBulk(authors);
}
```

The triggered SQL statements are as follows:

```
UPDATE author
SET age = age + 1,
    version = version + 1
WHERE id IN (?, ?, ?, ..., ?)
```

```
UPDATE book
SET isbn = 'None',
    version = version + 1
WHERE author_id IN (?, ?, ..., ?)
```

The complete application is available on GitHub[20].

# Item 52: How to Efficiently Batch Deletes (No Associations)

To batch deletes against MySQL, you can prepare the JDBC URL, as explained in **Item 46**:

```
jdbc:mysql://localhost:3306/bookstoredb?
cachePrepStmts=true
&useServerPrepStmts=true
&rewriteBatchedStatements=true
```

For other RDBMS, just remove the settings specific to MySQL.

---

[20]HibernateSpringBootBulkUpdates

Set the batch size via `spring.jpa.properties.hibernate.jdbc.batch_size` (e.g., to 30). For versioned entities, set the `spring.jpa.properties.hibernate.jdbc.batch_versioned_data` to `true`.

Batching deletes can be efficiently accomplished in several ways. To decide which approach fits the best, it's important to know that batching affects associations and how much data will be deleted. This item tackles batching deletes that don't affect associations.

Consider the `Author` entity from Figure 4-7.

***Figure 4-7.*** *The Author entity table*

Spring Boot exposes a bunch of methods that can be used to delete records. Further, each of these methods is used to delete 100 authors. Let's start with two methods that trigger *bulk* operations—`deleteAllInBatch()` and `deleteInBatch(Iterable<T> entities)`.

> Generally speaking, notice that the *bulk* operations are faster than batching and can use indexes, but they don't benefit from cascading mechanisms (e.g., `CascadeType.ALL` is ignored) or automatic application-level Optimistic Locking mechanisms (e.g., `@Version` is ignored). Their modifications over entities are not automatically reflected in the Persistence Context.

# Delete via the Built-In deleteAllInBatch() Method

You can easily call the built-in `deleteAllInBatch()` method from a service-method via a classical Spring repository (`AuthorRepository`), as follows:

```
public void deleteAuthorsViaDeleteAllInBatch() {
    authorRepository.deleteAllInBatch();
}
```

The SQL statement generated by `deleteAllInBatch()` is as follows:

**DELETE FROM** author

Adding this SQL in the context of `DataSource-Proxy` (this library was introduced in **Item 83**) reveals the following output:

```
Name:DATA_SOURCE_PROXY, Connection:6, Time:21, Success:True
Type:Prepared, Batch:False, QuerySize:1, BatchSize:0
Query:["delete from author"]
Params:[()]
```

Batching is not used, but all the records from the `author` table have been deleted.

> Even if batching is not used, this is a very efficient way to delete all records from the database. It requires a single database round trip. Nevertheless, `deleteAllInBatch()` doesn't benefit from the automatic application-level Optimistic Locking mechanism (if this mechanism was enabled for preventing *lost updates* (e.g., via `@Version`)) and relies on `Query`'s `executeUpdate()` to trigger a *bulk* operation. These operations are faster than batching, but Hibernate doesn't know which entities are removed. Therefore, the Persistence Context is not automatically updated/synchronized accordingly. It's up to you to decide if, in order to avoid an outdated Persistence Context, you need to trigger the flush operation before deletions and, after deletions, to discard (clear or close) the Persistence Context. For example, `deleteAuthorsViaDeleteAllInBatch()` doesn't require any explicit flush or clear. Before deletions, there is nothing to flush, and after deletions, the Persistence Context is automatically closed.

# Delete via the Built-In deleteInBatch(Iterable<T> entities)

The deleteInBatch(Iterable<T> entities) method can also trigger *bulk* deletes. You can easily call the built-in deleteInBatch(Iterable<T> entities) method from a service-method via a classical Spring repository (AuthorRepository), as follows (delete all authors younger than *60*):

```
@Transactional
public void deleteAuthorsViaDeleteInBatch() {

    List<Author> authors = authorRepository.findByAgeLessThan(60);

    authorRepository.deleteInBatch(authors);
}
```

This time, the SQL statement generated by deleteInBatch(Iterable<T> entities) is as follows:

```
DELETE FROM author
WHERE id = ?
   OR id = ?
   OR id = ?
   OR id = ?
   OR id = ?
   OR id = ?
   ...
```

Adding this SQL to the context of DataSource-Proxy reveals the following output:

```
Name:DATA_SOURCE_PROXY, Connection:6, Time:27, Success:True
Type:Prepared, Batch:False, QuerySize:1, BatchSize:0
Query:["delete from author where id=? or id=? or id=? ...]
Params:[(1,12,23, ...)]
```

Batching is not used. Spring Boot simply chains the corresponding ids under the WHERE clause using the OR operator.

Exactly as with deleteAllInBatch(), this method triggers a *bulk* operation via Query's executeUpdate().

> Don't use deleteInBatch(Iterable<T> entities) to delete all records. For such cases, use deleteAllInBatch(). If you use this method to delete a set of records that satisfy a given filtering criteria, you don't have the benefit of the automatic application-level Optimistic Locking mechanism (to prevent *lost updates*). While this approach is very fast, keep in mind that it's also prone to cause issues if the generated DELETE statement exceeds the maximum accepted size/length (e.g., get an StackOverflowError). Typically, the maximum accepted size is generous, but since you are employing batching, the amount of data to delete is likely generous as well.
>
> Exactly as in the case of deleteAllInBatch(), it's up to you to decide if, before deletions, you have to flush any unflushed entities, and after deletions, you have to discard (close or clear) the Persistence Context. For example, deleteAuthorsViaDeleteInBatch() doesn't require any explicit flush or clear. Before deletions, there is nothing to flush, and after deletions, the Persistence Context is automatically closed.

If you have issues regarding the size of the generated query, you can consider several alternatives. For example, you can rely on the IN operator to write your own *bulk* operation as shown here (this will result in a query of type, IN (?, ..., ?):

```
@Transactional
@Modifying(flushAutomatically = true, clearAutomatically = true)
@Query("DELETE FROM Author a WHERE a IN ?1")
public int deleteInBulk(List<Author> authors);
```

Some RDBMS (e.g., SQL Sever) convert internally from IN to OR, while others don't (e.g., MySQL). In terms of performance, IN and OR are pretty similar, but it is better to benchmark against a specific RDBMS (e.g., in MySQL, IN should perform better than OR). Moreover, in MySQL 8, I rely on IN to manage 500,000 deletes with no issues, while OR has caused a StackOverflowError when used with 10,000 deletes.

Another alternative consists of chunking the fetched result set to accommodate deleteInBatch(Iterable<T> entities). For example, this can be quickly accomplished via functional-programming style, as shown here (if you need to optimize the chunking process, consider this application[21]):

```
@Transactional
public void deleteAuthorsViaDeleteInBatch() {

    List<Author> authors = authorRepository.findByAgeLessThan(60);

    final AtomicInteger count = new AtomicInteger();
    Collection<List<Author>> chunks = authors.parallelStream()
        .collect(Collectors.groupingBy(c -> count.getAndIncrement() / size))
        .values();

    chunks.forEach(authorRepository::deleteInBatch);
}
```

Obviously, the drawback of this approach is the duplication of data in memory. It also doesn't benefit from the automatic Optimistic Locking mechanism (it doesn't prevent *lost updates*). But chunking data can take advantage of parallelization of deletions via fork-join, CompletableFuture, or any other specific API. You can pass a data chuck per transaction and run several transactions in a concurrent fashion. For example, in **Item 49** you saw how to do this to parallelize batching inserts.

Alternatively, you can fetch the result set in chunks and call deleteInBatch(Iterable<T> entities) for each fetched chunk. In this case, the drawback is represented by the extra SELECT per chunk and no *lost updates* prevention.

## Delete via the Built-In deleteAll() Methods

You can easily call the built-in deleteAll(Iterable<? extends T> entities) method from a service-method via a classical Spring repository (AuthorRepository), as follows (delete all authors younger than *60*):

---

[21]ChunkList

```
@Transactional
public void deleteAuthorsViaDeleteAll() {

    List<Author> authors = authorRepository.findByAgeLessThan(60);

    authorRepository.deleteAll(authors);
}
```

This time, the SQL statement generated by deleteAll(Iterable<? extends T> entities) is as follows:

```
DELETE FROM author
WHERE id = ?
  AND version = ?
```

Adding this SQL in the context of DataSource-Proxy (this library is introduced in **Item 83**) reveals the following output (check out the highlighted parts):

```
Name:DATA_SOURCE_PROXY, Connection:6, Time:1116, Success:True
Type:Prepared, Batch:True, QuerySize:1, BatchSize:30
Query:["delete from author where id=? and version=?"]
Params:[(2,0),(3,0),(6,0),(11,0),(13,0),(15,0),(17,0) ...]
```

Finally, batching is used as expected! It benefits from the automatic Optimistic Locking mechanism, so it also prevents lost updates.

> Behind the scenes, deleteAll(Iterable<? extends T> entities) and delete(T entity) rely on EntityManager.remove(). Therefore, the Persistence Context is updated accordingly. In other words, Hibernate transitions the lifecycle state of each entity from *managed* to *removed*.

> You can delete all records via batching by calling deleteAll() without arguments. Behind the scenes, this method calls findAll().

# Delete via the Built-In delete(T entity) Method

Behind the scenes, the deleteAll(Iterable<? extends T> entities) methods rely on the built-in delete(T entity) method. The deleteAll() method, without arguments, calls findAll() and, while looping the result set, it calls delete(T entity) for each element. On the other hand, deleteAll(Iterable<? extends T> entities) loops the entities and calls delete(T entity) for each element.

You can easily call the built-in delete(T entity) method from a service-method via a Spring repository (AuthorRepository), as follows (delete all authors younger than *60*):

```
@Transactional
public void deleteAuthorsViaDelete() {

    List<Author> authors = authorRepository.findByAgeLessThan(60);

    authors.forEach(authorRepository::delete);
}
```

This time, the SQL statement generated by delete(T entity) is as follows:

```
DELETE FROM author
WHERE id = ? AND version = ?
```

Adding this SQL in the context of DataSource-Proxy reveals the following output:

```
Name:DATA_SOURCE_PROXY, Connection:6, Time:1116, Success:True
Type:Prepared, Batch:True, QuerySize:1, BatchSize:30
Query:["delete from author where id=? and version=?"]
Params:[(2,0),(3,0),(6,0),(11,0),(13,0),(15,0),(17,0) ...]
```

As expected, the output is similar to using deleteAll(Iterable<? extends T> entities).

---

In conclusion, deleteAllInBatch() and deleteInBatch(Iterable<T> entities) don't use delete batching. Therefore, there is no need to perform the settings specific for enabling batching. They trigger *bulk* operations that don't benefit from the automatic Optimistic Locking mechanism (if it was enabled, such as via @Version, to prevent *lost updates*) and the Persistence

Context is not synchronized with the database. It is advisable to flush the
Persistence Context before deleting and clear/close it after deleting to avoid
issues created by any unflushed or outdated entities. Batching is employed if
the developer uses the `deleteAll()` or `deleteAll(Iterable<? extends
T> entities)` methods or `delete(T entity)`. As long as all the records
should be deleted, the best approach is to use `deleteAllInBatch()`. Choosing
between `deleteInBatch(Iterable<T> entities)` and `deleteAll()`,
`deleteAll(Iterable<? extends T> entities)`/`delete(T entity)` is a
decision to make based on all these considerations.

The source code is available on GitHub[22].

# Item 53: How to Efficiently Batch Deletes (with Associations)

To batch deletes against MySQL, the JDBC URL can be prepared, as shown in **Item 46**:

```
jdbc:mysql://localhost:3306/bookstoredb?
cachePrepStmts=true
&useServerPrepStmts=true
&rewriteBatchedStatements=true
```

For other RDBMS, you just remove the settings specific to MySQL.

Set the batch size via `spring.jpa.properties.hibernate.jdbc.batch_size` (e.g., to 30).
For versioned entities, set `spring.jpa.properties.hibernate.jdbc.batch_versioned_data` to `true`.

Consider the Author and Book entities involved in a lazy bidirectional @OneToMany
association, as shown in Figure 4-8.

---

[22]HibernateSpringBootBatchDeleteSingleEntity

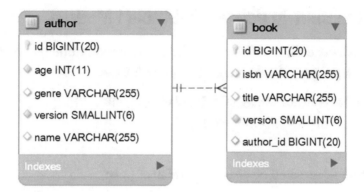

***Figure 4-8.*** *The @OneToMany table relationship*

Deleting authors should delete the associated books as well. For example, deleting all authors should automatically delete all books.

## Relying on orphanRemoval = true

By default, orphanRemoval is set to false. You can enable it to instruct the JPA persistence provider to remove the child-entities that are no longer referenced from the parent-entity.

> Do not confuse orphanRemoval with CascadeType.REMOVE. They are not the same! While orphanRemoval is responsible for automatically removing a disassociated entity instance, the CascadeType.REMOVE doesn't take action, because disassociating the relationship is not a remove operation.

The Author code that matters is listed here:

```
@OneToMany(cascade = CascadeType.ALL,
          mappedBy = "author", orphanRemoval = true)
private List<Book> books = new ArrayList<>();
```

Next, let's consider the Spring Boot delete capabilities.

## Delete via the Built-In deleteAllInBatch() Method

You can easily call the built-in deleteAllInBatch() method from a service-method via a classical Spring repository (AuthorRepository), as follows:

```
public void deleteAuthorsAndBooksViaDeleteAllInBatch() {
    authorRepository.deleteAllInBatch();
}
```

The SQL statement generated by deleteAllInBatch() is:

**DELETE FROM** author

Adding this SQL in the context of DataSource-Proxy (this library is introduced in **Item 83**) reveals the following output:

```
Name:DATA_SOURCE_PROXY, Connection:6, Time:21, Success:True
Type:Prepared, Batch:False, QuerySize:1, BatchSize:0
Query:["delete from author"]
Params:[()]
```

Batching is not used and doesn't benefit from the automatic Optimistic Locking mechanism (prevent *lost updates*), but all records from the author table have been deleted. However, the records from the book table have not been deleted. Therefore, as expected, the deleteAllInBatch() doesn't use orphanRemoval or cascading. It just triggers a *bulk* delete via Query's executeUpdate() and the Persistence Context is not synchronized with the database. The only way to use it to delete all the books is to call it explicitly, as follows:

```
@Transactional
public void deleteAuthorsAndBooksViaDeleteAllInBatch() {
    authorRepository.deleteAllInBatch();
    bookRepository.deleteAllInBatch();
}
```

Even if batching and the *lost updates* prevention mechanism are not used, and the Persistence Context is not synchronized with the database, this is a very efficient way to delete all records from the database. It is up to you to flush (before the delete) and close/clear (after the delete) the Persistence Context to avoid issues created by any unflushed or outdated entities.

# Delete via the Built-In deleteInBatch(Iterable<T> entities)

The deleteInBatch(Iterable<T> entities) is another method that can trigger *bulk* deletes. You can easily call the built-in deleteInBatch(Iterable<T> entities) method from a service-method via a classical Spring repository (AuthorRepository), as follows (delete all authors younger than *60* and their books):

```
@Transactional
public void deleteAuthorsAndBooksViaDeleteInBatch() {
    List<Author> authors = authorRepository.fetchAuthorsAndBooks(60);

    authorRepository.deleteInBatch(authors);
}
```

This time, the SQL statement generated by deleteInBatch(Iterable<T> entities) is as follows:

```
DELETE FROM author
WHERE id = ?
  OR id = ?
  OR id = ?
  OR id = ?
  OR id = ?
  OR id = ?
  ...
```

Adding this SQL in the context of DataSource-Proxy reveals the following output:

```
Name:DATA_SOURCE_PROXY, Connection:6, Time:27, Success:True
Type:Prepared, Batch:False, QuerySize:1, BatchSize:0
Query:["delete from author where id=? or id=? or id=? ...]
Params:[(1,12,23, ...)]
```

Again, batching and the *lost updates* prevention mechanism are not used, but all authors younger than *60* have been deleted. However, the associated records from the book table have not been deleted. Therefore, deleteInBatch(Iterable<T> entities) doesn't take advantage of orphanRemoval or of cascading. It just triggers a *bulk* delete via Query's executeUpdate() and the Persistence Context is not synchronized with the database. The only way to use it to delete all the books is to call it explicitly, as follows:

```
@Transactional
public void deleteAuthorsAndBooksViaDeleteInBatch() {
    List<Author> authors = authorRepository.fetchAuthorsAndBooks(60);

    authorRepository.deleteInBatch(authors);
    authors.forEach(a -> bookRepository.deleteInBatch(a.getBooks()));
}
```

This time, for each deleted author, there will be an extra DELETE to delete the associated books. This is an N+1 issue. The more Ns that are added, the less efficient it will be. Eventually, you can solve this N+1 issue by joining the books of all authors into a single list and passing this list to deleteInBatch(Iterable<T> entities)):

```
DELETE FROM book
WHERE id = ?
   OR id = ?
   OR id = ?
   OR id = ?
   OR id = ?
```

Moreover, keep in mind that this approach is prone to cause issues if the generated DELETE statement exceeds the maximum accepted size. More details about this are in **Item 52.**

## Delete via the Built-In deleteAll(Iterable<? extends T> entities) and delete(T entity) Methods

You can easily call the built-in deleteAll(Iterable<? extends T> entities) method from a service-method via a classical Spring repository (AuthorRepository), as follows (delete all authors younger than *60* and the associated books):

```
@Transactional
public void deleteAuthorsAndBooksViaDeleteAll() {
    List<Author> authors = authorRepository.fetchAuthorsAndBooks(60);

    authorRepository.deleteAll(authors);
}
```

The same thing can be done via delete(T entity), as follows:

```
@Transactional
public void deleteAuthorsAndBooksViaDeleteAll() {
    List<Author> authors = authorRepository.fetchAuthorsAndBooks(60);

    authors.forEach(authorRepository::delete);
}
```

Both of these methods lead to the same SQL statements (notice the Optimistic Locking Mechanism at work via the presence of version in the query):

```
DELETE FROM book
WHERE id = ?
  AND version = ?
-- since each author has written 5 books, there will be 4 more DELETEs here

DELETE FROM author
WHERE id = ?
  AND version = ?
```

These SQL statements are repeated for each author that should be deleted. Adding these SQL statements in the context of DataSource-Proxy reveals the following output (check out the highlighted parts and keep in mind that, for each deleted author, there are two batches):

```
Name:DATA_SOURCE_PROXY, Connection:6, Time:270, Success:True
Type:Prepared, Batch:True, QuerySize:1, BatchSize:5
Query:["delete from book where id=? and version=?"]
Params:[(1,0),(2,0),(3,0),(4,0),(5,0)]

Name:DATA_SOURCE_PROXY, Connection:6, Time:41, Success:True
Type:Prepared, Batch:True, QuerySize:1, BatchSize:1
Query:["delete from author where id=? and version=?"]
Params:[(1,0)]
```

Finally, batching is used, but is not quite optimized. Batching is used because of CascadeType.ALL, which includes CascadeType.REMOVE. To ensure state transitions of each Book from *managed* to *removed*, there is a DELETE statement per Book. But batching has grouped these DELETE statements into a batch.

Nevertheless, the problem is represented by the number of batches. The DELETE statements are not sorted and this causes more batches than needed for this job. Remember that a batch can target one table only. Targeting the book and author tables alternatively results in the following statement: deleting 10 authors with five books each requires 10 x 2 batches. You need 20 batches because each author is deleted in his own batch and his five books are deleted in another batch. The following approach will optimize the number of batches.

First, the code:

```
@Transactional
public void deleteAuthorsAndBooksViaDelete() {
    List<Author> authors = authorRepository.fetchAuthorsAndBooks(60);

    authors.forEach(Author::removeBooks);
    authorRepository.flush();

    // or, authorRepository.deleteAll(authors);
    authors.forEach(authorRepository::delete);
}
```

Check out the bold lines. The code dissociates all Books from their corresponding Authors via the helper method removeBooks(), as shown here (this method is in Author):

```
public void removeBooks() {
    Iterator<Book> iterator = this.books.iterator();
    while (iterator.hasNext()) {
        Book book = iterator.next();

        book.setAuthor(null);
        iterator.remove();
    }
}
```

Further, the code explicitly (manually) flushes the Persistence Context. It's time for orphanRemoval=true to enter the scene. Thanks to this setting, all disassociated books will be deleted. The generated DELETE statements are batched (if orphanRemoval is set to false, a bunch of updates will be executed instead of deletes). Finally, the code deletes all Authors via the deleteAll(Iterable<? extends T> entities) or delete(T entity) method. Since all Books are dissociated, the Author deletion will take advantage of batching as well.

This time, the number of batches is considerably fewer in comparison to the previous approach. Remember that, when deleting 10 authors and the associated books, there were 20 batches needed. Relying on this approach will result in only three batches.

Batches that delete all the associated books are executed first (since each author has five books, there are 10 authors x 5 book records to delete):

```
Name:DATA_SOURCE_PROXY, Connection:6, Time:1071, Success:True
Type:Prepared, Batch:True, QuerySize:1, BatchSize:30
Query:["delete from book where id=? and version=?"]
Params:[(1,0),(2,0),(3,0),(4,0),(5,0),(6,0),(7,0),(8,0), ... ,(30,0)]
```

```
Name:DATA_SOURCE_PROXY, Connection:6, Time:602, Success:True
Type:Prepared, Batch:True, QuerySize:1, BatchSize:20
Query:["delete from book where id=? and version=?"]
Params:[(31,0),(32,0),(33,0),(34,0),(35,0),(36,0), ... ,(50,0)]
```

Further, a batch that deletes 10 authors is executed:

```
Name:DATA_SOURCE_PROXY, Connection:6, Time:432, Success:True
Type:Prepared, Batch:True, QuerySize:1, BatchSize:10
Query:["delete from author where id=? and version=?"]
Params:[(1,0),(2,0),(3,0),(4,0),(5,0),(6,0),(7,0),(8,0),(9,0),(10,0)]
```

The source code is available on GitHub[23].

---

[23]HibernateSpringBootBatchDeleteOrphanRemoval

# Relying on SQL, ON DELETE CASCADE

ON DELETE CASCADE is an SQL directive that uses SQL cascade deletion.

ON DELETE CASCADE is a database-specific action that deletes the child-row in the database when the parent-row is deleted. You can add this directive via the Hibernate-specific @OnDelete annotation, as follows:

```
@OneToMany(cascade = {CascadeType.PERSIST, CascadeType.MERGE},
          mappedBy = "author", orphanRemoval = false)
@OnDelete(action = OnDeleteAction.CASCADE)
private List<Book> books = new ArrayList<>();
```

Notice that the cascading (CascadeType) effect is reduced to PERSIST and MERGE. In addition, orphanRemoval was set to false (or, simply remove it, since false is default). This means that this approach doesn't involve JPA entity state propagations or entity removal events. This approach relies on a database automatic action, therefore, the Persistence Context is not synchronized accordingly. Let's see what happens via each built-in deletion mechanism.

The presence of @OnDelete will alter the author table as follows:

```
ALTER TABLE book
  ADD CONSTRAINT fkklnrv3weler2ftkweewlky958
  FOREIGN KEY (author_id) REFERENCES author (id)
  ON DELETE CASCADE
```

In the case of MySQL, the ON DELETE CASCADE is considered if spring.jpa.properties. hibernate.dialect is set to use the InnoDB engine as follows:

```
spring.jpa.properties.hibernate.dialect=
    org.hibernate.dialect.MySQL5InnoDBDialect
```

Or, for MySQL 8:

```
org.hibernate.dialect.MySQL8Dialect
```

# Delete via the Built-In deleteAllInBatch() Method

You can easily call the built-in deleteAllInBatch() method from a service-method via a classical Spring repository (AuthorRepository), as follows:

```
public void deleteAuthorsAndBooksViaDeleteAllInBatch() {
    authorRepository.deleteAllInBatch();
}
```

The SQL statement generated by deleteAllInBatch() is as follows:

**DELETE FROM** author

Adding this SQL in the context of DataSource-Proxy reveals the following output:

```
Name:DATA_SOURCE_PROXY, Connection:6, Time:21, Success:True
Type:Prepared, Batch:False, QuerySize:1, BatchSize:0
Query:["delete from author"]
Params:[()]
```

Batching is not used and *lost updates* are not prevented, but the triggered *bulk* operation will trigger the database cascade deletion. Therefore, the rows from the book table are also deleted. This is a very efficient approach when deleting all rows from author and book tables.

# Delete via the Built-In deleteInBatch(Iterable<T> entities)

You can easily call the built-in deleteInBatch(Iterable<T> entities) method from a service-method via a classical Spring repository (AuthorRepository), as follows (delete all authors younger than *60* and their books):

```
@Transactional
public void deleteAuthorsAndBooksViaDeleteInBatch() {
    List<Author> authors = authorRepository.fetchAuthorsAndBooks(60);

    authorRepository.deleteInBatch(authors);
}
```

This time, the SQL statement generated by `deleteInBatch(Iterable<T> entities)` is as follows:

```
DELETE FROM author
WHERE id = ?
  OR id = ?
  OR id = ?
  OR id = ?
  OR id = ?
  OR id = ?
  ...
```

Adding this SQL in the context of `DataSource-Proxy` reveals the following output:

```
Name:DATA_SOURCE_PROXY, Connection:6, Time:27, Success:True
Type:Prepared, Batch:False, QuerySize:1, BatchSize:0
Query:["delete from author where id=? or id=? or id=? ...]
Params:[(1,12,23, ...)]
```

Batching is not used and *lost updates* are not prevented, but the triggered *bulk* operation will trigger the database cascade deletion. The associated rows from the book table are also deleted. This is a very efficient approach. The only thing to pay attention to consists of avoiding `DELETE` string statements that exceed the maximum accepted size of a query.

## Delete via the Built-In deleteAll(Iterable<? extends T> entities) and delete(T entity) Methods

You can easily call the built-in `deleteAll(Iterable<? extends T> entities)` method from a service-method via a classical Spring repository (`AuthorRepository`), as follows (delete all authors younger than *60* and the associated books):

```
@Transactional
public void deleteAuthorsAndBooksViaDeleteAll() {
    List<Author> authors = authorRepository.fetchAuthorsAndBooks(60);

    authorRepository.deleteAll(authors);
}
```

The same thing can be done via delete(T entity), as follows:

```
@Transactional
public void deleteAuthorsAndBooksViaDelete() {
    List<Author> authors = authorRepository.fetchAuthorsAndBooks(60);

    authors.forEach(authorRepository::delete);
}
```

Both methods lead to the same SQL statements:

```
DELETE FROM author
WHERE id = ?
  AND version = ?
-- this DELETE is generated for each author that should be deleted
```

These SQL statements are repeated for each author that should be deleted. Adding these SQL statements in the context of DataSource-Proxy reveals the following output (check out the highlighted parts):

```
Name:DATA_SOURCE_PROXY, Connection:6, Time:35, Success:True
Type:Prepared, Batch:True, QuerySize:1, BatchSize:6
Query:["delete from author where id=? and version=?"]
Params:[(5,0),(6,0),(7,0),(8,0),(9,0),(10,0)]
```

Batching is used and *lost updates* prevention for Author is provided via the Optimistic Locking mechanism! Moreover, removing the authors will trigger the database cascade deletion. The associated rows from the book table are also deleted. This time, there is a mix between entity state transitions and database automatic actions. Therefore, the Persistence Context is partially synchronized. Again, this is quite efficient.

The source code is available on GitHub[24].

---

[24]HibernateSpringBootBatchDeleteCascadeDelete

# Item 54: How to Fetch Association in Batches

**Item 39** describes how to fetch the associations (especially collections) in the same query with its parent via JOIN FETCH. Moreover, **Item 7** describes the mighty feature of JPA 2.1 @NamedEntityGraph useful for avoiding N+1 issues and solving lazy loading problems, while **Item 43** tackles fetching associations via SQL JOIN.

Hibernate allows you to fetch associations in batches as well via the Hibernate-specific @BatchSize annotation. However, it is advisable to evaluate the approaches mentioned previously before considering @BatchSize. Having all these approaches under your tool belt will help you decide wisely.

Now, let's continue with @BatchSize, and let's approach a learning by example technique. Consider the Author and Book entities involved in a bidirectional-lazy @OneToMany association. Figure 4-9 represents a data snapshot useful for tracking and better understanding the result sets of the queries.

author

| id | age | genre | name |
|----|-----|-------|------|
| 1 | 23 | Anthology | Mark Janel |
| 2 | 43 | Horror | Olivia Goy |
| 3 | 51 | Anthology | Quartis Young |
| 4 | 34 | History | Joana Nimar |
| 5 | 38 | Anthology | Alicia Tom |
| 6 | 56 | Anthology | Katy Loin |
| 7 | 23 | Anthology | Wuth Troll |

book

| id | isbn | title | author_id |
|----|------|-------|-----------|
| 1 | 001-JN | A History of Ancient Prague | 4 |
| 2 | 002-JN | A People's History | 4 |
| 3 | 003-JN | History Day | 4 |
| 4 | 001-MJ | The Beatles Anthology | 1 |
| 5 | 001-OG | Carrie | 2 |
| 6 | 002-OG | House Of Pain | 2 |
| 7 | 001-WT | Anthology 2000 | 5 |

***Figure 4-9.*** *Data snapshot*

## @BatchSize at the Collection-Level

Check out the Author entity source code:

```
@Entity
public class Author implements Serializable {
    ...
    @OneToMany(cascade = CascadeType.ALL,
            mappedBy = "author", orphanRemoval = true)
```

```
@BatchSize(size = 3)
private List<Book> books = new ArrayList<>();
...
}
```

The books associated collection was annotated with @BatchSize(size = 3). This means that Hibernate should initialize the books collection for up to three Author entities in one batch. Before inspecting the SQL statements, let's consider the following service-method that takes advantage of @BatchSize at the collection-level:

```
@Transactional(readOnly = true)
public void displayAuthorsAndBooks() {

    List<Author> authors = authorRepository.findAll();

    for (Author author : authors) {
        System.out.println("Author: " + author.getName());
        System.out.println("No of books: "
            + author.getBooks().size() + ", " + author.getBooks());
    }
}
```

This method fetches all Author entities via a SELECT query. Further, calling the getBooks() method of the first Author entity will trigger another SELECT query that initializes the collections of the first three Author entities returned by the previous SELECT query. This is the effect of @BatchSize at the collection-level.

So, first SELECT fetches all Authors:

```
SELECT
  author0_.id AS id1_0_,
  author0_.age AS age2_0_,
  author0_.genre AS genre3_0_,
  author0_.name AS name4_0_
FROM author author0_
```

Calling getBooks() for the first Author will trigger the following SELECT:

```
SELECT
  books0_.author_id AS author_i4_1_1_,
  books0_.id AS id1_1_1_,
  books0_.id AS id1_1_0_,
  books0_.author_id AS author_i4_1_0_,
  books0_.isbn AS isbn2_1_0_,
  books0_.title AS title3_1_0_
FROM book books0_
WHERE books0_.author_id IN (?, ?, ?)
```

Hibernate uses an IN clause to efficiently reference the identifiers of the three entity authors (this is the size of the batch). The output is as follows:

```
Author: Mark Janel
No of books: 1, [Book{id=4, title=The Beatles Anthology, isbn=001-MJ}]

Author: Olivia Goy
No of books: 2, [Book{id=5, title=Carrie, isbn=001-OG}, Book{id=6,
title=House Of Pain, isbn=002-OG}]

Author: Quartis Young
No of books: 0, []
```

Reaching the fourth author, *Joana Nimar,* will require a new SELECT for the next batch of Books. The result set of this SELECT is as follows:

```
Author: Joana Nimar
No of books: 3, [Book{id=1, title=A History of Ancient Prague, isbn=001-JN},
Book{id=2, title=A People's History, isbn=002-JN}, Book{id=3, title=History
Day, isbn=003-JN}]

Author: Alicia Tom
No of books: 1, [Book{id=7, title=Anthology 2000, isbn=001-WT}]

Author: Katy Loin
No of books: 0, []
```

Reaching the last author, *Wuth Troll*, will require a new SELECT. There is not enough data to populate another batch of Books; therefore, the IN clause is not needed:

```
SELECT
  books0_.author_id AS author_i4_1_1_,
  books0_.id AS id1_1_1_,
  books0_.id AS id1_1_0_,
  books0_.author_id AS author_i4_1_0_,
  books0_.isbn AS isbn2_1_0_,
  books0_.title AS title3_1_0_
FROM book books0_
WHERE books0_.author_id = ?
```

The output is as follows:

```
No of books: 0, []
```

> Be sure not to misinterpret how @BatchSize works at the collection-level.
> Do not conclude that @BatchSize of size *n* at the collection-level will load *n* items
> (e.g., books) in the collection. It loads *n* collections. Hibernate cannot truncate a
> collection (this is tackled in **Item 97** when we discuss pagination of JOIN FETCH).

## @BatchSize at Class/Entity-Level

Check out the Author entity source code:

```
@Entity
@BatchSize(size = 3)
public class Author implements Serializable {
    ...
    @OneToMany(cascade = CascadeType.ALL,
               mappedBy = "author", orphanRemoval = true)
    private List<Book> books = new ArrayList<>();
    ...
}
```

349

The Author entity was annotated with @BatchSize(size = 3). This means that Hibernate should initialize up to three referenced authors when a book is fetched. In other words, if we iterate through all books and call getAuthor() on each without @BatchSize presence then Hibernate will execute four SELECT statements to retrieve the proxied owners (there are seven books but some of them have the same author, therefore certain SELECT statements will hit the Persistence Context instead of the database). Performing the same action in presence of @BatchSize at Author entity-level, will result in two SELECT statements.

Before inspecting some SQL statements, let's consider the following service-method that takes advantage of @BatchSize at the entity-level:

```
@Transactional(readOnly = true)
public void displayBooksAndAuthors() {

    List<Book> books = bookRepository.findAll();

    for (Book book : books) {
        System.out.println("Book: " + book.getTitle());
        System.out.println("Author: " + book.getAuthor());
    }
}
```

This method fetches all Book entities via a SELECT query. Further, calling the getAuthor() method of the first Book entity will trigger another SELECT query that initializes the associations of the first three Book entities returned by the previous SELECT query. This is the effect of @BatchSize at the entity-level.

So, the first SELECT fetches all Books:

```
SELECT
  book0_.id AS id1_1_,
  book0_.author_id AS author_i4_1_,
  book0_.isbn AS isbn2_1_,
  book0_.title AS title3_1_
FROM book book0_
```

Further, calling getAuthor() for the first Book will trigger the following SELECT:

**SELECT**
    author0_.id **AS** id1_0_0_,
    author0_.age **AS** age2_0_0_,
    author0_.genre **AS** genre3_0_0_,
    author0_.name **AS** name4_0_0_
**FROM** author author0_
**WHERE** author0_.id **IN** (?, ?, ?)

Hibernate uses an IN clause to efficiently reference the identifiers of the three entity authors (this is the size of the batch). The output will be as follows:

```
Book: A History of Ancient Prague
Author: Author{id=4, name=Joana Nimar, genre=History, age=34}
Book: A People's History
Author: Author{id=4, name=Joana Nimar, genre=History, age=34}
Book: History Day
Author: Author{id=4, name=Joana Nimar, genre=History, age=34}

Book: The Beatles Anthology
Author: Author{id=1, name=Mark Janel, genre=Anthology, age=23}

Book: Carrie
Author: Author{id=2, name=Olivia Goy, genre=Horror, age=43}
Book: House Of Pain
Author: Author{id=2, name=Olivia Goy, genre=Horror, age=43}
```

Reaching the next book, *Anthology 2000*, will require a new SELECT for the next batch of Authors. There is not enough data to populate another batch of Authors, therefore, the IN clause is not needed:

**SELECT**
    author0_.id **AS** id1_0_0_,
    author0_.age **AS** age2_0_0_,
    author0_.genre **AS** genre3_0_0_,
    author0_.name **AS** name4_0_0_
**FROM** author author0_
**WHERE** author0_.id = ?

The output is as follows:

```
Book: Anthology 2000
Author: Author{id=5, name=Alicia Tom, genre=Anthology, age=38}
```

> Generally speaking, note that using @BatchSize at the collection-level with a size of *n* will initialize up to *n* lazy collections at a time. On the other hand, using @BatchSize at the entity-level with a size of *n* will initialize up to *n* lazy entity proxies at a time.

> Obviously, loading the associated entities in batches is better than loading them one by one (this way, you avoid the potential N+1 issues). Nevertheless, before going with @BatchSize, be ready to provide arguments against using SQL JOIN, JPA JOIN FETCH, or entity graphs in your particular case.

The complete application is available on GitHub[25].

# Item 55: Why to Avoid PostgreSQL (BIG)SERIAL in Batching Inserts via Hibernate

In PostgreSQL, using GenerationType.IDENTITY will disable Hibernate insert batching. The (BIG)SERIAL acts "almost" like MySQL's AUTO_INCREMENT. In other words, when insert batching is used, avoid the following:

```
@Entity
public class Author implements Serializable {

    @Id
    @GeneratedValue(strategy = GenerationType.IDENTITY)
    private Long id;

    ...
}
```

---

[25]HibernateSpringBootLoadBatchAssociation

PostgreSQL's (BIG)SERIAL is a syntactic sugar expression for emulating an identity column. Behind this emulation, PostgreSQL uses a database sequence.

One solution to this problem consists of relying on GenerationType.AUTO. In PostgreSQL, the GenerationType.AUTO setting will pick up the SEQUENCE generator; therefore, batching inserts will work as expected. The following code works fine:

```
@Entity
public class Author implements Serializable {

    @Id
    @GeneratedValue(strategy = GenerationType.AUTO)
    private Long id;
    ...
}
```

## Optimize the Identifier-Fetching Process

This time, the batching inserts mechanism works fine but, for each insert, Hibernate must fetch its identifier in a separate database round trip. If there are 30 inserts in a single batch, then there will be 30 database round trips needed to fetch 30 identifiers, as in the following example:

```
select nextval ('hibernate_sequence')
select nextval ('hibernate_sequence')
-- 28 more
...
insert into author (age, genre, name, id) values (?, ?, ?, ?)
insert into author (age, genre, name, id) values (?, ?, ?, ?)
...
```

Commonly, batching inserts is employed when the number of inserts is considerably high (e.g., 10,000 inserts). For 10,000 inserts, there are 10,000 extra database round trips, which represents a performance penalty. You can eliminate this performance penalty via the hi/lo algorithm, which can generate in-memory identifiers (**Item 66**). Even better is the great pooled or pooled-lo algorithms (**Item 67**). You can employ the hi/lo algorithm as follows:

```
@Entity
public class Author implements Serializable {

    @Id
    @GeneratedValue(
        strategy = GenerationType.SEQUENCE,
        generator = "hilo"
    )

    @GenericGenerator(
        name = "hilo",
        strategy = "org.hibernate.id.enhanced.SequenceStyleGenerator",
        parameters = {
            @Parameter(name = "sequence_name", value = "hilo_sequence"),
            @Parameter(name = "initial_value", value = "1"),
            @Parameter(name = "increment_size", value = "1000"),
            @Parameter(name = "optimizer", value = "hilo")
        }
    )
    private Long id;
    ...
}
```

This time, an increment of 1,000 means that hi/lo can generate 1,000 in-memory identifiers. So, for 10,000 inserts, there will be only 10 database round trips needed to fetch the identifiers. Obviously, you can further optimize this by adjusting `increment_size`.

## Optimize Batching via reWriteBatchedInserts

**Item 46** introduced the `reWriteBatchedInserts` optimization for MySQL, and it said that this optimization can be used for PostgreSQL as well. Once this property is enabled, the SQL statements are rewritten into a single string buffer and sent in a single request to the database.

In a Spring Boot application that relies on HikariCP, you can set `reWriteBatchedInserts` via `application.properties`:

`spring.datasource.hikari.data-source-properties.reWriteBatchedInserts=true`

This setting can also be achieved programmatically:

```
PGSimpleDataSource ds = ...;
ds.setReWriteBatchedInserts(true);
```

The complete application in available on GitHub[26].

---

[26]HibernateSpringBootBatchingAndSerial

# CHAPTER 5

# Collections

## Item 56: How to JOIN FETCH an @ElementCollection Collection

Especially when defining a unidirectional one-to-many association to a Basic type (e.g., String) or Embeddable type, JPA has a simple solution in the form of @ElementCollection. These types are mapped in a separate table that can be customized via @CollectionTable. Let's assume that an online bookstore shopping cart is mapped via the ShoppingCart entity and the embeddable Book is mapped via @ElementCollection, as shown in Figure 5-1.

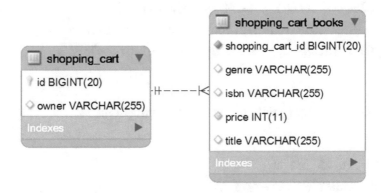

***Figure 5-1.*** *The @ElementCollection table relationship*

The relevant part is the @ElementCollection mapping:

```
@Entity
public class ShoppingCart implements Serializable {

    ...

    @ElementCollection(fetch = FetchType.LAZY) // lazy is default
```

© Anghel Leonard 2020

A. Leonard, *Spring Boot Persistence Best Practices*, https://doi.org/10.1007/978-1-4842-5626-8_5

```
@CollectionTable(name = "shopping_cart_books",
    joinColumns = @JoinColumn(name = "shopping_cart_id"))
private List<Book> books = new ArrayList<>();
...
}
```

By default, books is lazy loaded. Sometimes, modeling certain functional requirements may require that the program fetch the books attribute eagerly. Obviously, switching to FechType.EAGER at entity-level is a *code smell* that must be avoided.

The solution comes from JOIN FETCH, which can be used for @ElementCollection in the same way as for associations. In other words, the following two JPQL queries use JOIN FETCH to fetch books in the same SELECT that fetches the ShoppingCart:

```
@Repository
public interface ShoppingCartRepository
                extends JpaRepository<ShoppingCart, Long> {

    @Query(value = "SELECT p FROM ShoppingCart p JOIN FETCH p.books")
    ShoppingCart fetchShoppingCart();

    @Query(value = "SELECT p FROM ShoppingCart p
                    JOIN FETCH p.books b WHERE b.price > ?1")
    ShoppingCart fetchShoppingCartByPrice(int price);
}
```

Calling fetchShoppingCart() will trigger the following SQL:

```
SELECT
  shoppingca0_.id AS id1_1_,
  shoppingca0_.owner AS owner2_1_,
  books1_.shopping_cart_id AS shopping1_0_0__,
  books1_.genre AS genre2_0_0__,
  books1_.isbn AS isbn3_0_0__,
  books1_.price AS price4_0_0__,
  books1_.title AS title5_0_0__
FROM shopping_cart shoppingca0_
INNER JOIN shopping_cart_books books1_
  ON shoppingca0_.id = books1_.shopping_cart_id
```

Calling fetchShoppingCartByPrice() will trigger the following SQL:

```
SELECT
  shoppingca0_.id AS id1_1_,
  shoppingca0_.owner AS owner2_1_,
  books1_.shopping_cart_id AS shopping1_0_0__,
  books1_.genre AS genre2_0_0__,
  books1_.isbn AS isbn3_0_0__,
  books1_.price AS price4_0_0__,
  books1_.title AS title5_0_0__
FROM shopping_cart shoppingca0_
INNER JOIN shopping_cart_books books1_
  ON shoppingca0_.id = books1_.shopping_cart_id
WHERE books1_.price > ?
```

The source code is available on GitHub[1].

## Item 57: How to DTO an @ElementCollection

This item assumes that an online bookstore shopping cart is mapped via the
ShoppingCart entity and the embeddable Book is mapped via @ElementCollection, as
shown in Figure 5-2.

***Figure 5-2.***  *The @ElementCollection table relationship*

---

The relevant part is the @ElementCollection mapping:

```
@Entity
public class ShoppingCart implements Serializable {

    ...

    @ElementCollection(fetch = FetchType.LAZY) // lazy is default
    @CollectionTable(name = "shopping_cart_books",
        joinColumns = @JoinColumn(name = "shopping_cart_id"))
    private List<Book> books = new ArrayList<>();

    ...
}
```

Further, the goal is to fetch a result set of read-only data containing the owner from shopping_cart, and the title and price from shopping_cart_books (the collection table). Since it's read-only data, a JOIN and DTO will do the job. Since JOIN and Spring projections work fine for @ElementCollection, the solution relies on the following projection:

```
public interface ShoppingCartDto {

    public String getOwner();
    public String getTitle();
    public int getPrice();
}
```

The projection can be used further in a repository, as follows:

```
@Repository
public interface ShoppingCartRepository
        extends JpaRepository<ShoppingCart, Long> {

    @Query(value = "SELECT a.owner AS owner, b.title AS title,
                    b.price AS price FROM ShoppingCart a JOIN a.books b")
    List<ShoppingCartDto> fetchShoppingCart();

    @Query(value = "SELECT a.owner AS owner, b.title AS title,
                    b.price AS price FROM ShoppingCart a JOIN a.books b
                    WHERE b.price > ?1")
    List<ShoppingCartDto> fetchShoppingCartByPrice(int price);
}
```

Calling fetchShoppingCart() will trigger the following SQL (notice that only owner, title, and price have been selected):

```
SELECT
    shoppingca0_.owner AS col_0_0_,
    books1_.title AS col_1_0_,
    books1_.price AS col_2_0_
FROM shopping_cart shoppingca0_
INNER JOIN shopping_cart_books books1_
    ON shoppingca0_.id = books1_.shopping_cart_id
```

Calling fetchShoppingCartByPrice() will trigger the following SQL:

```
SELECT
    shoppingca0_.owner AS col_0_0_,
    books1_.title AS col_1_0_,
    books1_.price AS col_2_0_
FROM shopping_cart shoppingca0_
INNER JOIN shopping_cart_books books1_
    ON shoppingca0_.id = books1_.shopping_cart_id
WHERE books1_.price > ?
```

> Note that @ElementCollection is not an entity association type, even if you may think so. Mainly, as you will see in the next item, @Element Collection acts as a unidirectional @OneToMany (**Item 2**). Therefore, it suffers the same performance penalties. Best practices advise you to use @ElementCollection to represent basic types (e.g., integers or strings) or embeddable types, but not entity classes.

The source code is available on GitHub[2].

---

[2]HibernateSpringBootDtoElementCollection

# Item 58: Why and When to Use @OrderColumn with @ElementCollection

This item assumes that an online bookstore shopping cart is mapped via the ShoppingCart entity and the embeddable Book via @ElementCollection, as in the following code:

```
@Entity
public class ShoppingCart implements Serializable {

    ...

    @Id
    @GeneratedValue(strategy = GenerationType.IDENTITY)
    private Long id;

    private String owner;

    @ElementCollection
    @CollectionTable(name = "shopping_cart_books",
                    joinColumns = @JoinColumn(name = "shopping_cart_id"))
    @Column(name="title")
    private List<String> books = new ArrayList<>();

    // getters and setters omitted for brevity
}
```

This entity is mapped via two tables (shopping_cart and shopping_cart_books). Figure 5-3 represents a snapshot of the data (basically, there is one shopping cart with three books).

shopping_cart

| id | owner |
|----|-------|
| 1  | Mark Juno |

shopping_cart_books

| shopping_cart_id | title |
|------------------|-------|
| 1 | A History of Ancient Prague |
| 1 | Carrie |
| 1 | The Beatles Anthology |

*Figure 5-3.*  *Data snapshot (@ElementCollection)*

The repository for this entity contains a query that fetches ShoppingCart by the owner name:

```
@Repository
@Transactional(readOnly = true)
public interface ShoppingCartRepository
            extends JpaRepository<ShoppingCart, Long> {

    ShoppingCart findByOwner(String owner);
}
```

Further, the application runs several queries (three INSERTs and three DELETEs) to:

- Add one book to the beginning of the current cart

- Add one book to the end of the current cart

- Add one book to the middle of the current cart

- Remove the first book from the cart

- Remove the last book from the cart

- Remove the middle book from the cart

Each of the following scenarios starts with the data snapshot from Figure 5-3.

In order to add a new book to the current cart (INSERT a book), Hibernate will need to delete everything from shopping_cart_books and then re-insert the values, including the new book. For example, the following method will add a new book to the beginning of books:

```
@Transactional
public void addToTheBeginning() {
    ShoppingCart cart = shoppingCartRepository.findByOwner("Mark Juno");

    cart.getBooks().add(0, "Modern history");
}
```

Calling this method will result in the following suite of SQL statements. First, all the books are deleted; second, they are re-inserted, including the new book:

```
DELETE FROM shopping_cart_books
WHERE shopping_cart_id = ?
Binding: [1]
```

```
INSERT INTO shopping_cart_books (shopping_cart_id, title)
  VALUES (?, ?)
Binding: [1, Modern history]
```

```
INSERT INTO shopping_cart_books (shopping_cart_id, title)
  VALUES (?, ?)
Binding: [1, A History of Ancient Prague]
```

```
INSERT INTO shopping_cart_books (shopping_cart_id, title)
  VALUES (?, ?)
Binding: [1, Carrie]
```

```
INSERT INTO shopping_cart_books (shopping_cart_id, title)
  VALUES (?, ?)
Binding: [1, The Beatles Anthology]
```

> Each INSERT must delete all records from the @CollectionTable for the *Entity*, and then re-insert them.

Similarly, the following attempts at inserting a book at the end and in the middle will result in a bunch of SQL statements, as previously:

```
@Transactional
public void addToTheEnd() {
    ShoppingCart cart = shoppingCartRepository.findByOwner("Mark Juno");

    cart.getBooks().add("The last day");
}
```

```
@Transactional
public void addInTheMiddle() {
    ShoppingCart cart = shoppingCartRepository.findByOwner("Mark Juno");

    cart.getBooks().add(cart.getBooks().size() / 2, "Middle man");
}
```

Removing a book from books is not efficient either. As with the case of INSERT, each remove needs to delete everything from shopping_cart_books and then re-insert all the values. For example, the following method will delete the first book:

```
@Transactional
public void removeFirst() {
    ShoppingCart cart = shoppingCartRepository.findByOwner("Mark Juno");

    cart.getBooks().remove(0);
}
```

Calling this method will result in the following suite of SQL statements. First, all the books are deleted; second, they are all re-inserted, excluding the deleted book:

```
DELETE FROM shopping_cart_books
WHERE shopping_cart_id = ?
Binding: [1]

INSERT INTO shopping_cart_books (shopping_cart_id, title)
  VALUES (?, ?)
Binding: [1, Carrie]

INSERT INTO shopping_cart_books (shopping_cart_id, title)
  VALUES (?, ?)
Binding: [1, The Beatles Anthology]
```

> Each DELETE must delete all records from the @CollectionTable for the *Entity*, and then re-insert them.

Similarly, the following attempts at removing a book from the end and from the middle will result in a bunch of SQL statements, as you saw previously:

```
@Transactional
public void removeLast() {
    ShoppingCart cart = shoppingCartRepository.findByOwner("Mark Juno");

    cart.getBooks().remove(cart.getBooks().size() - 1);
}
```

```
@Transactional
public void removeMiddle() {
    ShoppingCart cart = shoppingCartRepository.findByOwner("Mark Juno");

    cart.getBooks().remove(cart.getBooks().size() / 2);
}
```

> A collection that needs to be updated frequently leads to obvious performance
> penalties. It's better to rely on an explicit one-to-many association. On the
> other hand, a collection that needs few (or no) updates is a good candidate for
> `@ElementCollection`, since it doesn't represent a foreign key side.

The source code is available on GitHub[3].

## Optimizing @ElementCollection via @OrderColumn

An `@OrderColumn` can be used to define an order `List` on any collection mapping.
Adding `@OrderColumn` to an `@ElementCollection` is an optimization reflected in certain
INSERTs and DELETEs. The code that matters is modified as follows:

```
@Entity
public class ShoppingCart implements Serializable {

    ...

    @ElementCollection
    @OrderColumn(name = "index_no")
    @CollectionTable(name = "shopping_cart_books",
                    joinColumns = @JoinColumn(name = "shopping_cart_id"))
    @Column(name="title")
    private List<String> books = new ArrayList<>();
    ...

}
```

The presence of @OrderColumn is reflected in a new column (index_no) in the shopping_
cart_books table, as shown in Figure 5-4.

---

[3]HibernateSpringBootElementCollectionNoOrderColumn

| shopping_cart | | shopping_cart_books | | |
|---|---|---|---|---|
| id | owner | shopping_cart_id | title | index_no |
| 1 | Mark Juno | 1 | A History of Ancient Prague | 0 |
| | | 1 | Carrie | 1 |
| | | 1 | The Beatles Anthology | 2 |

***Figure 5-4.*** *Data snapshot (@ElementCollection and @OrderColumn)*

So, in order to uniquely identify each row, the @OrderColumn is mapped in the target table as a new column. Now, let's see how @OrderColumn can optimize @ElementCollection. Each of the following scenarios starts from the data snapshot shown in Figure 5-4.

## Adding One Book to the Beginning of the Current Cart

Adding one book (*Modern History*) to the beginning of the current cart will trigger the following SQL statements (under each SQL statement is a list of binding parameters):

```
UPDATE shopping_cart_books
SET title = ?
WHERE shopping_cart_id = ?
AND index_no = ?
Binding: [Modern History, 1, 0]
```

```
UPDATE shopping_cart_books
SET title = ?
WHERE shopping_cart_id = ?
AND index_no = ?
Binding: [A History of Ancient Prague, 1, 1]
```

```
UPDATE shopping_cart_books
SET title = ?
WHERE shopping_cart_id = ?
AND index_no = ?
Binding: [Carrie, 1, 2]
```

```
INSERT INTO shopping_cart_books (shopping_cart_id, index_no, title)
  VALUES (?, ?, ?)
Binding: [1, 3, The Beatles Anthology]
```

Adding a new book to the beginning of books (at index 0) pushes down the existing books by one position. This is happening in memory and is flushed into the database via a suite of UPDATE statements. Each existing row has a corresponding UPDATE statement. In the end, after these updates complete, the last book is re-inserted via an INSERT statement. Figure 5-5 shows the shopping_cart_books table before (left side) and after (right side) inserting the *Modern History* book.

| shopping_cart_id | title | index_no |
|---|---|---|
| 1 | A History of Ancient Prague | 0 |
| 1 | Carrie | 1 |
| 1 | The Beatles Anthology | 2 |

before insert

| shopping_cart_id | title | index_no |
|---|---|---|
| 1 | Modern History | 0 |
| 1 | A History of Ancient Prague | 1 |
| 1 | Carrie | 2 |
| 1 | The Beatles Anthology | 3 |

after insert

***Figure 5-5.*** *Insert at the beginning (@ElementCollection and @OrderColumn)*

> Without @OrderColumn, the application triggered five SQL statements (one DELETE and four INSERTs). With @OrderColumn, the application triggered four SQL statements (three UPDATEs and one INSERT).

## Adding One Book to the End of the Current Cart

Adding one book (*The Last Day*) to the end of the current cart will trigger the following SQL statement:

```
INSERT INTO shopping_cart_books (shopping_cart_id, index_no, title)
  VALUES (?, ?, ?)
Binding: [1, 3, The Last Day]
```

Adding to the end of the collection doesn't affect the order of it; therefore, a single INSERT will do the job. This is way better than the case without @OrderColumn.

> Without @OrderColumn, the application triggered five SQL statements (one DELETE and four INSERTs). With @OrderColumn, the application triggered one INSERT statement.

# Adding One Book to the Middle of the Current Cart

Adding one book (*Middle Man*) to the middle of the current cart will trigger the following SQL statements:

```
UPDATE shopping_cart_books
SET title = ?
WHERE shopping_cart_id = ?
AND index_no = ?
Binding: [Middle Man, 1, 1]
```

```
UPDATE shopping_cart_books
SET title = ?
WHERE shopping_cart_id = ?
AND index_no = ?
Binding: [Carrie, 1, 2]
```

```
INSERT INTO shopping_cart_books (shopping_cart_id, index_no, title)
  VALUES (?, ?, ?)
Binding: [1, 3, The Beatles Anthology]
```

Adding a new book to the middle of books pushes all the existing books situated between the middle and the end of the collection down one position. This is happening in memory and is flushed into the database via a suite of UPDATE statements. Each such row has a corresponding UPDATE statement. In the end, the last book is re-inserted via an INSERT statement. Figure 5-6 shows the shopping_cart_books table before (left side) and after (right side) inserting the *Middle Man* book.

| shopping_cart_id | title | index_no |
|---|---|---|
| 1 | A History of Ancient Prague | 0 |
| 1 | Carrie | 1 |
| 1 | The Beatles Anthology | 2 |

before insert

| shopping_cart_id | title | index_no |
|---|---|---|
| 1 | A History of Ancient Prague | 0 |
| 1 | Middle Man | 1 |
| 1 | Carrie | 2 |
| 1 | The Beatles Anthology | 3 |

after insert

***Figure 5-6.*** *Insert in the middle (@ElementCollection and @OrderColumn)*

> Without @OrderColumn, the application triggered five SQL statements (one DELETE and four INSERTs). With @OrderColumn, the application triggered three SQL statements (two UPDATEs and one INSERT).

## Removing the First Book from the Current Cart

Removing the first book from the current cart (*A History of Ancient Prague*) will trigger the following SQL statements:

```
DELETE FROM shopping_cart_books
WHERE shopping_cart_id = ?
  AND index_no = ?
Binding: [1, 2]
```

```
UPDATE shopping_cart_books
SET title = ?
WHERE shopping_cart_id = ?
AND index_no = ?
Binding: [The Beatles Anthology, 1, 1]
```

```
UPDATE shopping_cart_books
SET title = ?
WHERE shopping_cart_id = ?
AND index_no = ?
Binding: [Carrie, 1, 0]
```

Removing the first book from books (at index 0) pushes all the existing books up one position. This is happening in memory and is flushed into the database via a suite of UPDATE statements triggered after deleting the last row via a DELETE statement. Figure 5-7 shows the shopping_cart_books table before (left side) and after (right side) deleting the *A History of Ancient Prague* book.

| shopping_cart_id | title | index_no |
|---|---|---|
| 1 | A History of Ancient Prague | 0 |
| 1 | Carrie | 1 |
| 1 | The Beatles Anthology | 2 |

before remove

| shopping_cart_id | title | index_no |
|---|---|---|
| 1 | Carrie | 0 |
| 1 | The Beatles Anthology | 1 |

after remove

***Figure 5-7.*** *Remove the first book (@ElementCollection and @OrderColumn)*

> Without @OrderColumn, the application triggered three SQL statements (one DELETE and two INSERTs). With @OrderColumn, the application triggered three SQL statements as well (one DELETE and two UPDATEs).

## Removing the Last Book from the Current Cart

Removing the last book (*The Beatles Anthology*) from the current cart will trigger the following SQL statement:

```
DELETE FROM shopping_cart_books
WHERE shopping_cart_id = ?
  AND index_no = ?
Binding: [1, 2]
```

Removing a book from the end of the collection doesn't affect the order of it; therefore, a single DELETE will do the job. This is way better than the case without @OrderColumn.

> Without @OrderColumn, the application triggered three SQL statements (one DELETE and two INSERTs). With @OrderColumn, the application triggered one DELETE statement.

## Removing One Book from the Middle of the Current Cart

Removing one book (*Carrie*) from the middle of the current cart will trigger the following SQL statements:

```
DELETE FROM shopping_cart_books
WHERE shopping_cart_id = ?
  AND index_no = ?
Binding: [1, 2]

UPDATE shopping_cart_books
SET title = ?
WHERE shopping_cart_id = ?
AND index_no = ?
Binding: [The Beatles Anthology, 1, 1]
```

Removing a book from the middle of books pushes the existing books situated between the middle and the end of the collection up one position. This is happening in memory and is flushed into the database via a DELETE and a suite of UPDATE statements. First, the last row is deleted. Second, each row situated between the end and the middle of the table is updated. Figure 5-8 shows the shopping_cart_books table before (left side) and after (right side) removing the *Carrie* book.

| shopping_cart_id | title | index_no |
|---|---|---|
| 1 | A History of Ancient Prague | 0 |
| 1 | Carrie | 1 |
| 1 | The Beatles Anthology | 2 |
| | before remove | |

| shopping_cart_id | title | index_no |
|---|---|---|
| 1 | A History of Ancient Prague | 0 |
| 1 | The Beatles Anthology | 1 |
| | after remove | |

***Figure 5-8.*** *Remove from the middle (@ElementCollection and @OrderColumn)*

> Without @OrderColumn, the application triggered three SQL statements (one DELETE and two INSERTs). With @OrderColumn, the application triggered two SQL statements as well (one DELETE and one UPDATE).

The final conclusion is that @OrderColumn can mitigate some performance penalties when operations take place near the collection tail (e.g., add/remove at/from the end of the collection). All elements situated before the adding/removing entry are essentially left untouched, so the performance penalty can be ignored if the application affects rows close to the collection tail.

> As a rule of thumb, element collections are a proper choice when there are very few changes to the data and adding a new entity has the purpose only of mapping the foreign key side. Otherwise, a one-to-many association is a better option.
>
> Note that the unidirectional @OneToMany and @ManyToMany and the bidirectional @ManyToMany fall in the same umbrella as @ElementCollection.

The source code is available on GitHub[4].

---

[4]HibernateSpringBootElementCollectionWithOrderColumn

# Item 59: How to Merge Entity Collections

This item illustrates one good way to merge entity collections.

For starters, assume that Author and Book are involved in a bidirectional lazy @OneToMany association. The Domain Model is shown in Figure 5-9.

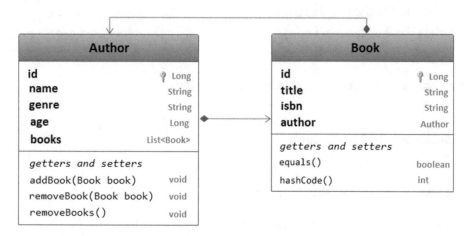

***Figure 5-9.***  *Bidirectional @OneToMany relationship*

In code, the Author class looks as follows:

```
@Entity
public class Author implements Serializable {

    private static final long serialVersionUID = 1L;

    @Id
    @GeneratedValue(strategy = GenerationType.IDENTITY)
    private Long id;

    private String name;
    private String genre;
    private int age;

    @OneToMany(cascade = CascadeType.ALL,
            mappedBy = "author", orphanRemoval = true)
    private List<Book> books = new ArrayList<>();
```

```java
    public void addBook(Book book) {
        this.books.add(book);
        book.setAuthor(this);
    }

    public void removeBook(Book book) {
        book.setAuthor(null);
        this.books.remove(book);
    }

    // getters and setters omitted for brevity
}
```

And the Book entity looks as follows:

```java
@Entity
public class Book implements Serializable {

    private static final long serialVersionUID = 1L;

    @Id
    @GeneratedValue(strategy = GenerationType.IDENTITY)
    private Long id;

    private String title;
    private String isbn;

    @ManyToOne(fetch = FetchType.LAZY)
    @JoinColumn(name = "author_id")
    private Author author;

    // getters and setters omitted for brevity

    @Override
    public boolean equals(Object obj) {

        if(obj == null) {
            return false;
        }
```

```java
        if (this == obj) {
            return true;
        }

        if (getClass() != obj.getClass()) {
            return false;
        }

        return id != null && id.equals(((Book) obj).id);
    }

    @Override
    public int hashCode() {
        return 2021;
    }
}
```

The database is already populated with the entities from Figure 5-10.

**author**

| id | age | genre | name |
|----|-----|-------|------|
| 1 | 23 | Anthology | Mark Janel |
| 2 | 34 | History | Joana Nimar |

**book**

| id | isbn | title | author_id |
|----|------|-------|-----------|
| 1 | 001-JN | A History of Ancient Prague | 2 |
| 2 | 002-JN | A People's History | 2 |
| 3 | 001-MJ | The Beatles Anthology | 1 |
| 4 | 007-JN | Carrie | 2 |

***Figure 5-10.*** *Data snapshot (before merge)*

Now, let's fetch a List of Book entities associated with a given Author record (e.g., *Joana Nimar*). Fetching the Author and an associated Book can be easily accomplished via a JOIN, as shown here:

```java
@Repository
public interface BookRepository extends JpaRepository<Book, Long> {

    @Query(value = "SELECT b FROM Book b JOIN b.author a WHERE a.name = ?1")
    List<Book> booksOfAuthor(String name);
}
```

Calling booksOfAuthor("Joana Nimar") will trigger the following SELECT:

```
SELECT
  book0_.id AS id1_1_,
  book0_.author_id AS author_i4_1_,
  book0_.isbn AS isbn2_1_,
  book0_.title AS title3_1_
FROM book book0_
INNER JOIN author author1_
  ON book0_.author_id = author1_.id
WHERE author1_.name = ?
```

The List<Book> returned by this SELECT contains three books.

At this point, the List<Book> is in a *detached* state; therefore, let's store it in a variable named detachedBooks:

```
Book{id=1, title=A History of Ancient Prague, isbn=001-JN}
Book{id=2, title=A People's History, isbn=002-JN}
Book{id=4, title=Carrie, isbn=007-JN}
```

Next, let's perform the following modifications on this collection (since the collection is in a *detached* state, the modifications will not be automatically propagated to the database):

- Update the first book title from *A History of Ancient Prague to A History of Ancient Rome:*

  ```
  detachedBooks.get(0).setTitle("A History of Ancient Rome");
  ```

- Remove the second book:

  ```
  detachedBooks.remove(1);
  ```

- Add a new book (*History In 100 Minutes*):

  ```
  Book book = new Book();
  book.setTitle("History In 100 Minutes");
  book.setIsbn("005-JN");
  detachedBooks.add(book);
  ```

Displaying the detachedBooks collection after modifications reveals the following content (check out the last new book, which has a null id):

```
Book{id=1, title=A History of Ancient Rome, isbn=001-JN}
Book{id=4, title=Carrie, isbn=007-JN}
Book{id=null, title=History In 100 Minutes, isbn=005-JN}
```

## Merging the Detached Collection

The final step in this item is to merge the *detached* collection using the minimum number of database round trips as possible. First of all, the developer must fetch the Author and the associated Book. This can be easily done via JOIN FETCH:

```
@Repository
public interface AuthorRepository extends JpaRepository<Author, Long> {

    @Query(value="SELECT a FROM Author a JOIN FETCH a.books
                WHERE a.name = ?1")
    Author authorAndBooks(String name);
}
```

Calling authorAndBooks() triggers the following SELECT (the author and the associated books are fetched from the database):

```
SELECT
  author0_.id AS id1_0_0_,
  books1_.id AS id1_1_1_,
  author0_.age AS age2_0_0_,
  author0_.genre AS genre3_0_0_,
  author0_.name AS name4_0_0_,
  books1_.author_id AS author_i4_1_1_,
  books1_.isbn AS isbn2_1_1_,
  books1_.title AS title3_1_1_,
  books1_.author_id AS author_i4_1_0__,
  books1_.id AS id1_1_0__
FROM author author0_
INNER JOIN book books1_
  ON author0_.id = books1_.author_id
WHERE author0_.name = ?
```

Consider that the returned `Author` is stored in a variable named `author`.

Next, let's set the `detachedBooks` to `author`! First, let's quickly eliminate the bad approaches.

> Mixing *managed* and *detached* entities is a bad combination that leads to errors. Therefore, trying to do something as `author.setBooks` `(detachedBooks)` will simply not work. On the other hand, detaching the author, setting the `detachedBooks`, and then merging the author will work fine, but will result in an extra `SELECT` query generated by the merging process. This extra `SELECT` can be avoided by using manual merging.

Manual merging requires three steps:

- Remove the existing database rows that are no longer found in the incoming collection (`detachedBooks`). First, filter the books of `author` that are not in `detachedBooks`. Second, every `author` book that cannot be found in `detachedBooks` should be removed as follows:

```
List<Book> booksToRemove = author.getBooks().stream()
    .filter(b -> !detachedBooks.contains(b))
    .collect(Collectors.toList());
```

```
booksToRemove.forEach(b -> author.removeBook(b));
```

- Update the existing database rows found in the incoming collection (`detachedBooks`). First, filter the new books (`newBooks`). These are books present in `detachedBooks` but not present in the `author` books. Second, filter the `detachedBooks` to obtain the books that are in `detachedBooks` but are not in `newBooks`. These are the books that should be updated as follows:

```
List<Book> newBooks = detachedBooks.stream()
    .filter(b -> !author.getBooks().contains(b))
    .collect(Collectors.toList());
```

```
detachedBooks.stream()
    .filter(b -> !newBooks.contains(b))
    .forEach((b) -> {
        b.setAuthor(author);
        Book mergedBook = bookRepository.save(b);
        author.getBooks().set(
            author.getBooks().indexOf(mergedBook), mergedBook);
    });
```

- Finally, add the rows found in the incoming collection that cannot be found in the current result set (newBooks):

```
newBooks.forEach(b -> author.addBook(b));
```

Gluing these three steps together in a service-method will result in the following:

```
@Transactional
public void updateBooksOfAuthor(String name, List<Book> detachedBooks) {

    Author author = authorRepository.authorAndBooks(name);

    // Remove the existing database rows that are no
    // longer found in the incoming collection (detachedBooks)
    List<Book> booksToRemove  = author.getBooks().stream()
        .filter(b -> !detachedBooks.contains(b))
        .collect(Collectors.toList());
    booksToRemove .forEach(b -> author.removeBook(b));

    // Update the existing database rows which can be found
    // in the incoming collection (detachedBooks)
    List<Book> newBooks = detachedBooks.stream()
        .filter(b -> !author.getBooks().contains(b))
        .collect(Collectors.toList());

    detachedBooks.stream()
        .filter(b -> !newBooks.contains(b))
        .forEach((b) -> {
            b.setAuthor(author);
```

```
            Book mergedBook = bookRepository.save(b);
            author.getBooks().set(
                author.getBooks().indexOf(mergedBook), mergedBook);
        });

    // Add the rows found in the incoming collection,
    // which cannot be found in the current database snapshot
    newBooks.forEach(b -> author.addBook(b));
}
```

## Testing Time

Calling updateBooksOfAuthor() can be done as follows:

updateBooksOfAuthor("Joana Nimar", detachedBooks);

The triggered SQL statements, except for the SELECT that fetches the author and associated books, are:

```
INSERT INTO book (author_id, isbn, title)
  VALUES (?, ?, ?)
Binding: [2, 005-JN, History In 100 Minutes]
```

```
UPDATE book
SET author_id = ?,
    isbn = ?,
    title = ?
WHERE id = ?
Binding: [2, 001-JN, A History of Ancient Rome, 1]
```

```
DELETE FROM book
WHERE id = ?
Binding: [2]
```

Figure 5-11 shows the current snapshot of the data.

| author | | | | | book | | | |
|---|---|---|---|---|---|---|---|---|
| id | age | genre | name | | id | isbn | title | author_id |
| 1 | 23 | Anthology | Mark Janel | | 1 | 001-JN | A History of Ancient Rome | 2 |
| 2 | 34 | History | Joana Nimar | | 3 | 001-MJ | The Beatles Anthology | 1 |
| | | | | | 4 | 007-JN | Carrie | 2 |
| | | | | | 5 | 005-JN | History In 100 Minutes | 2 |

***Figure 5-11.*** *Data snapshot (after merge)*

Done! The complete code is available on GitHub[5].

You may think of this case as a *corner-case*. It's not a daily task to fetch a collection of child entities and work with them independent of the associated parent. It is more common to fetch the parent entity and the associated collection of child entities, modify the collection in a *detached* state, and merge the parent entity. In such cases, CascadeType.ALL will be used and the resulting SQL statements are exactly as you would expect.

---

[5]HibernateSpringBootMergeCollections

# CHAPTER 6

# Connections and Transactions

## Item 60: How to Delay Connection Acquisition Until It's Really Needed

Starting with Hibernate 5.2.10, the database connection acquisition can be delayed until it's really needed.

For a hypersonic guide about Spring transaction propagation, check out **Appendix G**. In the case of *resource-local* (a single datasource), Hibernate will acquire the database connection of a JDBC transaction right after the transaction starts (e.g., in Spring, a method annotated with @Transactional acquires the database connection immediately after it is called).

> In *resource-local*, a database connection is acquired immediately because Hibernate needs to check the JDBC Connection auto-commit status. If this is true then Hibernate will disable it.

Practically, the database connection is useless to the application until the first JDBC statement of the current transaction is triggered; holding the database connection unused for this time induces a performance penalty that can have a big impact if there are many or/and time-consuming tasks before the first JDBC statement.

© Anghel Leonard 2020
A. Leonard, *Spring Boot Persistence Best Practices*, https://doi.org/10.1007/978-1-4842-5626-8_6

In order to prevent this performance penalty, you can inform Hibernate that you disabled auto-commit, so no check is needed. To do this, follow these two steps:

- Turn off auto-commit. For example, check your pool connection for a method of type `setAutoCommit(boolean commit)` and set it to false, e.g., `HikariConfiguartion#setAutoCommit(false)`.

- Set to true the Hibernate-specific property: `hibernate.connection. provider_disables_autocommit`

By default, Spring Boot relies on HikariCP, and you can turn off auto-commit in `application.properties` via the `spring.datasource.hikari.auto-commit` property. So, the following two settings need to be added to `application.properties`:

```
spring.datasource.hikari.auto-commit=false
spring.jpa.properties.hibernate.connection.provider_disables_
autocommit=true
```

> As a rule of thumb, for *resource-local* JPA transactions, it is always good practice to configure the connection pool (e.g., HikariCP) to disable the auto-commit and set `hibernate.connection.provider_disables_ autocommit` to `true`. So, go for it in all your applications using *resource-local*!
>
> Be careful not to set `hibernate.connection.provider_disables_ autocommit` to `true` and then forget to disable the auto-commit mode! Hibernate will not disable it either! This means that every SQL statement will be executed in auto-commit mode, and no unit-of-work transaction will be available.

To see how a connection acquisition is delayed, consider the following method meant to isolate the main timeslots when a connection is obtained from the HikariCP connection pool. Consider reading the comments of this method, as they explain what is going on:

```
@Transactional
public void doTimeConsumingTask() throws InterruptedException {

    System.out.println("Waiting for a time-consuming
                        task that doesn't need a database connection ...");
```

```
// we use a sleep of 40 seconds just to capture HikariCP logging status
// which take place at every 30 seconds - this will reveal if
// the connection was opened (acquired from the connection pool) or not
Thread.sleep(40000);

System.out.println("Done, now query the database ...");
System.out.println("The database connection should be acquired now ...");

Author author = authorRepository.findById(1L).get();

// at this point, the connection should be open
Thread.sleep(40000);

author.setAge(44);
}
```

Calling this method without delaying the connection acquisition will reveal the output
shown in Figure 6-1 (the connection is obtained immediately and is kept open until the
first SQL is triggered).

**@Transactional**                                    **Acquire connection immediately**

```
Waiting for a time-consuming task that doesn't need a database connection
HikariPool-1 - Pool stats (total=10, active=1, idle= 9 , waiting=0)
Done, now query the database ...                          the connection was acquired even
                                                          if we don't need it at this point
The database connection should be acquired now ...
SELECT
    author0_.id AS id1_0_0_,
    author0_.age AS age2_0_0_,
    author0_.genre AS genre3_0_0_,                   at this point the database connection is used
    author0_.name AS name4_0_0_                      (until now, the connection was open for nothing)
FROM author author0_
WHERE author0_.id = ?
UPDATE author
SET age = ?,
    genre = ?,
    name = ?        the connection was released back in the connection pool
WHERE id = ?
HikariPool-1 - Pool stats (total=10, active=0, idle=10, waiting=0)
```

***Figure 6-1.*** *Acquire connection immediately*

Calling the same method with connection acquisition enabled will reveal that the connection is obtained right before the first SQL is triggered. Meanwhile, this connection can be used by another thread, as shown in Figure 6-2.

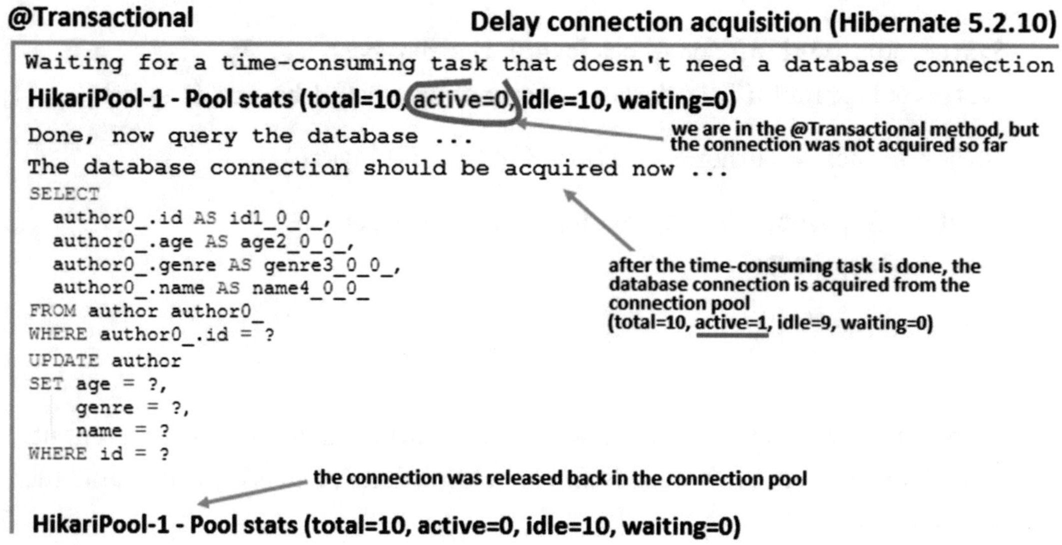

**Figure 6-2.**  *Delay connection acquisition*

The source code is available on GitHub[1].

# Item 61: How @Transactional(readOnly=true) Really Works

Consider the Author entity with the id  age, name, and genre fields.

Next, with the classical AuthorRepository and BookstoreService entities, you can quickly load the first Author by genre, as follows:

```
@Repository
public interface AuthorRepository extends JpaRepository<Author, Long> {

    Author findFirstByGenre(String genre);
}

@Service
public class BookstoreService {
```

---

[1]HibernateSpringBootDelayConnection

```
    public void fetchAuthor() {
        Author author = authorRepository.findFirstByGenre("Anthology");
    }
}
```

But, is something missing here?! Yes, there is no transactional-context. The findFirstByGenre() method must be wrapped in a transactional-context; therefore, you should consider @Transactional.

Via @Transactional, you explicitly demarcate the database transaction boundaries and ensure that one database connection will be used for the whole database transaction duration. All SQL statements will use this single isolation connection and all of them will run in the scope of the same Persistence Context.

Generally speaking, JPA doesn't impose transactions for read operations (it does it only for write operations by throwing a meaningful exception), but this means that:

- You allow the auto-commit mode to control the behavior of data access (this behavior may differ depending on the JDBC driver, the database, and the connection pool implementations and settings).

- Generally speaking, if auto-commit is set to true, then each SQL statement will have to be executed in a separate physical database transaction, which may imply a different connection per statement (e.g., in an environment that doesn't support *connection-per-thread*, a method with two SELECT statements requires two physical database transactions and two separate database connections). Each SQL statement is automatically committed right after it is executed.

- Explicitly setting the transaction isolation level may lead to unexpected behaviors.

- Setting auto-commit to true makes sense only if you execute a single read-only SQL statement (as we do above), but it doesn't lead to any significant benefit. Therefore, even in such cases, it's better to rely on explicit (declarative) transactions.

As a rule of thumb, use explicit (declarative) transactions even for read-only statements (e.g., `SELECT`) to define the proper transactional-contexts. A non-transactional-context refers to a context with no explicit transaction boundaries, **not** to a context with no physical database transaction. All database statements are executed in the context of a physical database transaction. By omitting the explicit transaction boundaries (transactional-context, begin/commit/rollback), you expose the application to at least the following drawbacks with implications in performance:

- By default, Hibernate will turn off `autocommit` mode anyway (`autocommit=false`) and a JDBC transaction is opened. The SQL statement runs inside this JDBC transaction and, afterwards, Hibernate closes the connection. But it doesn't close the transaction, which remains uncommitted (remains in the pending state), and this allows the database vendor implementation or the connection pool to take action. (The JDBC specification doesn't impose a certain behavior for pending transactions. For example, MySQL rolls back the transaction while Oracle commits it.) You shouldn't take this risk because, as a rule of thumb, you always must ensure that the transaction ends by committing it or rolling it back.

- In the case of many small transactions (very common in applications with many concurrent requests), starting and ending a physical database transaction for every SQL statement implies a performance overhead.

- A method running in a non-transactional-context is prone to be altered by developers in order to write data. (Having a transactional-context via `@Transactional(readOnly=true)` at the class/method-level acts as a flag for the team members signaling that no writes should be added to this method and prevents writes if this flag is ignored.)

- You cannot benefit from Spring optimizations for the underlying data access layer (e.g., flush mode is set to MANUAL, so Dirty Checking is skipped).

- You cannot benefit from database-specific optimizations for read-only transactions.

- You don't follow the read-only Spring built-in query-methods that are by default annotated with `@Transactional (readOnly=true)`.

- Starting with Hibernate 5.2.10, you can delay connection acquisition (**Item 60**) and this requires disabling `autocommit`.

- There is no ACID support for a group of read-only SQL statements.

Being aware of these drawbacks (this list is not exhaustive) should help you to decide wisely between non-transactional contexts and classical database ACID transactions for read-only statements.

Okay, so `@Transactional` should be added, but should `readOnly` be set to `false` (default) or to `true`? Depending on this setting, the entities are loaded in *read-write* mode or *read-only* mode. Besides the obvious difference between read-write and read-only modes, another major difference takes place at the Hibernate underlying level. Loading an entity in the Persistence Context is accomplished by Hibernate via what is called the *hydrated state* or *loaded state*. The *hydration* is the process of materializing the fetched database result set into an `Object[]`. The entity is materialized in the Persistence Context. What's happening next depends on the read mode:

- *Read-write* mode: In this mode, both the entity and its hydrated state are available in the Persistence Context. They are available during the Persistence Context lifespan (until the Persistence Context is closed) or until the entity is detached. The *hydrated state* is needed by the Dirty Checking mechanism, the Versionless Optimistic Locking mechanism, and the Second Level Cache. The Dirty Checking mechanism takes advantage of the hydrated state at flush time

(if you need a refresher about how flush works, consider **Appendix H**).
It simply compares the current entity's state with the corresponding
hydrated state and, if they are not the same, then Hibernate triggers
the proper UPDATE statements. The Versionless Optimistic Locking
mechanism takes advantage of the hydrated state to build the WHERE
clause filtering predicates. The Second Level Cache represents the
cache entries via the disassembled hydrated state. In read-write
mode, the entities have the MANAGED status.

- *Read-only* mode: In this mode, the hydrated state is discarded
  from memory and only the entities are kept in the Persistence
  Context (these are *read-only* entities). Obviously, this means that
  the automatic Dirty Checking and Versionless Optimistic Locking
  mechanisms are disabled. In read-only mode, the entities have the
  READ_ONLY status. Moreover, there is no automatic flush because
  Spring Boot sets flush mode to MANUAL.

The read-only mode acts as this way only if the Spring version is 5.1 or higher
and you use @Transactional(readOnly=true). Or, if the read-only
mode is set via @QueryHint, Session.setDefaultReadOnly(true), or
org.hibernate.readOnly, the JPA query hint is as below:

```
// @QueryHint in repository at query-level
@QueryHints(value = {
    @QueryHint(
        name = org.hibernate.jpa.QueryHints.HINT_READONLY,
        value = "true")
})

// setDefaultReadOnly
Session session = entityManager.unwrap(Session.class);
session.setDefaultReadOnly(true);

// JPA hint
List<Foo> foo = entityManager.createQuery("", Foo.class)
    .setHint(QueryHints.HINT_READONLY, true).getResultList();
```

In versions prior to 5.1, Spring doesn't propagate the read-only mode to Hibernate. Therefore, the hydrated state remains in memory in the Persistence Context. Spring only sets `FlushType.MANUAL`, so the automatic Dirty Checking mechanism will not take action since there is no automatic flush time. The performance penalty of keeping the hydrated state in memory is present (the Garbage Collector must collect this data). This is a solid reason to upgrade to at least Spring 5.1.

Further, let's try both read modes and see what the Persistence Context reveals. The following code was run against Spring Boot 2.1.4, which requires Spring Framework 5.1.x. To inspect the Persistence Context, the following helper method will be used (this method returns the current Persistence Context as an instance of org.hibernate. engine.spi.PersistenceContext):

```
private org.hibernate.engine.spi.PersistenceContext
        getPersistenceContext() {

    SharedSessionContractImplementor sharedSession = entityManager.unwrap(
        SharedSessionContractImplementor.class
    );

    return sharedSession.getPersistenceContext();
}
```

Using `PersistenceContext` allows you to explore its API and inspect the Persistence Context content. For example, let's display the following information:

- The current phase (this is just a string that marks the timeslot when the Persistence Context is inspected)

- The fetched entity via `toString()`

- If the Persistence Context contains only non-read-only entities

- The entity status (`org.hibernate.engine.spi.Status`)

- The hydrated/loaded state of the entity

Let's group this information into a helper method:

```
private void displayInformation(String phase, Author author) {

    System.out.println("Phase:" + phase);
    System.out.println("Entity: " + author);

    org.hibernate.engine.spi.PersistenceContext
        persistenceContext = getPersistenceContext();
    System.out.println("Has only non read entities : "
        + persistenceContext.hasNonReadOnlyEntities());

    EntityEntry entityEntry = persistenceContext.getEntry(author);
    Object[] loadedState = entityEntry.getLoadedState();
    Status status = entityEntry.getStatus();

    System.out.println("Entity entry : " + entityEntry);
    System.out.println("Status: " + status);
    System.out.println("Loaded state: " + Arrays.toString(loadedState));
}
```

Further, set the readOnly to false and run the following service-method (in the following examples, we force flush for the sake of testing, but manual flushing is a *code smell* and it should be avoided):

```
@Transactional
public void fetchAuthorReadWriteMode() {
    Author author = authorRepository.findFirstByGenre("Anthology");

    displayInformation("After Fetch", author);

    author.setAge(40);

    displayInformation("After Update Entity", author);

    // force flush - triggering manual flush is
    // a code smell and should be avoided
    // in this case, by default, flush will take
```

```
    // place before transaction commit
    authorRepository.flush();

    displayInformation("After Flush", author);
}
```

Calling fetchAuthorReadWriteMode() triggers a SELECT and an UPDATE statement. The output is as follows:

```
-------------------------------------
```
**Phase:After Fetch**
```
Entity: Author{id=1, age=23, name=Mark Janel, genre=Anthology}
-------------------------------------
Has only non read entities : true
Entity entry : EntityEntry[com.bookstore.entity.Author#1](MANAGED)
Status:MANAGED
Loaded state: [23, Anthology, Mark Janel]

-------------------------------------
```
**Phase:After Update Entity**
```
Entity: Author{id=1, age=40, name=Mark Janel, genre=Anthology}
-------------------------------------
Has only non read entities : true
Entity entry : EntityEntry[com.bookstore.entity.Author#1](MANAGED)
Status:MANAGED
Loaded state: [23, Anthology, Mark Janel]
```
**Hibernate: update author set age=?, genre=?, name=? where id=?**

```
-------------------------------------
```
**Phase:After Flush**
**// this flush was manually forced for the sake of testing**
**// by default, the flush will take place before transaction commits**
```
Entity: Author{id=1, age=40, name=Mark Janel, genre=Anthology}
-------------------------------------
Has only non read entities : true
Entity entry : EntityEntry[com.bookstore.entity.Author#1](MANAGED)
Status:MANAGED
Loaded state: [40, Anthology, Mark Janel]
```

The interpretation of this output is straightforward. The hydrated/loaded state is kept in the Persistence Context and the Dirty Checking mechanism uses it at flush time to update the author (triggers an UPDATE on your behalf). The fetched entity status is MANAGED. Further, set the readOnly to true and run the following service-method:

```
@Transactional(readOnly = true)
public void fetchAuthorReadOnlyMode() {
    ...
}
```

Calling fetchAuthorReadOnlyMode() triggers a single SELECT statement. The output is as follows:

```
----------------------------------------
Phase:After Fetch
Entity: Author{id=1, age=23, name=Mark Janel, genre=Anthology}
----------------------------------------
Has only non read entities : false
Entity entry : EntityEntry[com.bookstore.entity.Author#1](READ_ONLY)
Status:READ_ONLY
Loaded state: null


----------------------------------------
Phase:After Update Entity
Entity: Author{id=1, age=40, name=Mark Janel, genre=Anthology}
----------------------------------------
Has only non read entities : false
Entity entry : EntityEntry[com.bookstore.entity.Author#1](READ_ONLY)
Status:READ_ONLY
Loaded state: null


----------------------------------------
Phase:After Flush
// be default, for readOnly=true, there is no flush
// this flush was manually forced for the sake of testing
Entity: Author{id=1, age=40, name=Mark Janel, genre=Anthology}
----------------------------------------
```

```
Has only non read entities : false
Entity entry : EntityEntry[com.bookstore.entity.Author#1](READ_ONLY)
Status:READ_ONLY
Loaded state: null
```

This time, after fetching the Author entity, the hydrated/loaded state is immediately discarded (it's null). The fetched entity is in READ_ONLY status and the automatic flush is disabled. Even if you force flush by explicitly calling flush(), the Dirty Checking mechanism is not used because it is disabled (no UPDATE will be triggered).

> Setting readOnly=true for read-only data is a good optimization of performance since the hydrated/loaded state is discarded. This allows Spring to optimize the underlying data access layer operations. Nevertheless, fetching read-only data via DTO (Spring projection) is still a better way to do it if you never plan to modify this data.

Consider the following Spring projection:

```
public interface AuthorDto {

    public String getName();
    public int getAge();
}
```

And the following query:

```
@Repository
public interface AuthorRepository extends JpaRepository<Author, Long> {

    AuthorDto findTopByGenre(String genre);
}
```

Calling findTopByGenre() and inspecting the Persistence Context reveals that the Persistence Context is empty:

```
@Transactional
public void fetchAuthorDtoReadWriteMode() {
    AuthorDto authorDto = authorRepository.findTopByGenre("Anthology");
```

```
    org.hibernate.engine.spi.PersistenceContext
        persistenceContext = getPersistenceContext();

    System.out.println("No of managed entities : "
        + persistenceContext.getNumberOfManagedEntities());
}

@Transactional(readOnly = true)
public void fetchAuthorDtoReadOnlyMode() {
    AuthorDto authorDto = authorRepository.findTopByGenre("Anthology");

    org.hibernate.engine.spi.PersistenceContext
        persistenceContext = getPersistenceContext();

    System.out.println("No of managed entities : "
        + persistenceContext.getNumberOfManagedEntities());
}
```

Both service-methods return the same result:

```
No of managed entities : 0
```

The complete application is available on GitHub[2]. As a bonus, you can get a transaction ID (in MySQL only read-write transactions get an ID) in this application.[3]

# Item 62: Why Spring Ignores @Transactional

Consider the following simple service:

```
@Service
public class BookstoreService {

    private static final Logger log =
        Logger.getLogger(BookstoreService.class.getName());

    private final AuthorRepository authorRepository;
```

---

[2]HibernateSpringBootTransactionalReadOnlyMeaning
[3]HibernateSpringBootTransactionId

```
public BookstoreService(AuthorRepository authorRepository) {
    this.authorRepository = authorRepository;
}

public void mainAuthor() {
    Author author = new Author();
    persistAuthor(author);
    notifyAuthor(author);
}

@Transactional(propagation = Propagation.REQUIRES_NEW)
private long persistAuthor(Author author) {
    authorRepository.save(author);
    return authorRepository.count();
}

private void notifyAuthor(Author author) {
    log.info(() -> "Saving author: " + author);
}
}
```

Calling the mainAuthor() method will create a new author, persist the author (via persistAuthor()), and notify them that the account was created (via notifyAuthor()). As you can see, the persistAuthor() method was annotated with @Transactional and a new transaction is required (REQUIRES_NEW). Therefore, when persistAuthor() is called, Spring Boot should start a new transaction and run into it the save() and count() query-methods. In order to check this assumption, let's log these transaction details (add application.properties):

```
logging.level.ROOT=INFO
logging.level.org.springframework.orm.jpa=DEBUG
logging.level.org.springframework.transaction=DEBUG

# for Hibernate only
logging.level.org.hibernate.engine.transaction.internal.
TransactionImpl=DEBUG
```

Running the code outputs the following relevant lines:

**Creating new transaction with name [org.springframework.data.
jpa.repository.support.SimpleJpaRepository.save]: PROPAGATION_
REQUIRED,ISOLATION_DEFAULT**
Opened new EntityManager [SessionImpl(343534938<open>)] for JPA transaction

insert into author (age, genre, name) values (?, ?, ?)

Initiating transaction commit
Committing JPA transaction on EntityManager [SessionImpl(343534938<open>)]
Closing JPA EntityManager [SessionImpl(343534938<open>)] after transaction

**Creating new transaction with name [org.springframework.data.
jpa.repository.support.SimpleJpaRepository.count]: PROPAGATION_
REQUIRED,ISOLATION_DEFAULT,readOnly**
Opened new EntityManager [SessionImpl(940130302<open>)] for JPA transaction

select count(*) as col_0_0_ from author author0_

Initiating transaction commit
Committing JPA transaction on EntityManager [SessionImpl(940130302<open>)]
Closing JPA EntityManager [SessionImpl(940130302<open>)] after transaction

There is no transaction that runs the persistAuthor() method as a
unit-of-work. The save() and count() methods run in separate transactions. Why was
@Transactional ignored?

---

Why was @Transactional ignored? There are two main reasons:

- @Transactional was added to a private, protected, or
  package-protected method.

- @Transactional was added to a method defined in the
  same class as where it is invoked.

Therefore, as a rule of thumb, @Transactional works only on public
methods, and the method should be added in a class different from where it is
invoked.

---

Following this tip, the persistAuthor() method can be moved to a helper-service and marked as public:

```
@Service
public class HelperService {

    private final AuthorRepository authorRepository;

    public HelperService(AuthorRepository authorRepository) {
        this.authorRepository = authorRepository;
    }

    @Transactional(propagation = Propagation.REQUIRES_NEW)
    public long persistAuthor(Author author) {
        authorRepository.save(author);
        return authorRepository.count();
    }
}
```

Call it from BookstoreService as follows:

```
@Service
public class BookstoreService {

    private static final Logger log =
        Logger.getLogger(BookstoreService.class.getName());

    private final HelperService helperService;

    public BookstoreService(HelperService helperService) {
        this.helperService = helperService;
    }

    public void mainAuthor() {
        Author author = new Author();
        helperService.persistAuthor(author);
        notifyAuthor(author);
    }
```

```
    private void notifyAuthor(Author author) {
        log.info(() -> "Saving author: " + author);
    }
}
```

This time, running the code outputs the following relevant lines:

**Creating new transaction with name [com.bookstore.service.HelperService.
persistAuthor]: PROPAGATION_REQUIRES_NEW,ISOLATION_DEFAULT**
```
Opened new EntityManager [SessionImpl(1973372401<open>)] for JPA
transaction
```

**Participating in existing transaction**
```
insert into author (age, genre, name) values (?, ?, ?)
```

**Participating in existing transaction**
```
select count(*) as col_0_0_ from author author0_
```

```
Initiating transaction commit
Committing JPA transaction on EntityManager [SessionImpl(1973372401<open>)]
Closing JPA EntityManager [SessionImpl(1973372401<open>)] after transaction
```

Finally, things are working as expected. The @Transactional was not ignored.
The complete application is available on GitHub[4].

# Item 63: How to Set and Check that Transaction Timeout and Rollback at Expiration Work as Expected

Spring supports several approaches for explicitly setting a transaction timeout. The most popular approach relies on the timeout element of the @Transactional annotation, as in the following trivial service-method:

**@Transactional(timeout = 10)**
```
public void newAuthor() {
```

---

[4]HibernateSpringBootWhyTransactionalIsIgnored

```
    Author author = new Author();
    author.setAge(23);
    author.setGenre("Anthology");
    author.setName("Mark Janel");
    authorRepository.saveAndFlush(author);

    System.out.println("The end!");
}
```

In this method, the transaction timeout is set to 10 seconds. Obviously, this simple insert cannot take so long to cause the transaction expiration. So, how do you know that it works? A naive attempt will sneak in a Thread.sleep() with a value larger than the transaction timeout:

```
@Transactional(timeout = 10)
public void newAuthor() {

    Author author = new Author();
    author.setAge(23);
    author.setGenre("Anthology");
    author.setName("Mark Janel");
    authorRepository.saveAndFlush(author);

    Thread.sleep(15000); // 15 seconds

    System.out.println("The end!");
}
```

Since the current thread delays the transaction commit for 15 seconds and the transaction times out in 10 seconds, you may expect to see a timeout-specific exception and a transaction rollback. But, this will not act as expected; instead, the transaction will commit after 15 seconds.

Another attempt may rely on two concurrent transactions. Transaction A can hold an exclusive lock long enough to cause Transaction B to time out. This will work, but there is a simpler way to do it!

Simply sneak an SQL query into the transactional service-method that uses the SQL SLEEP function that's specific to your RDBMS. Most RDBMS come with a SLEEP function flavor. For example, MySQL uses SLEEP(n), while PostgreSQL uses PG_SLEEP(n).

A SLEEP function pauses the current statements for the specified duration of time (the SLEEP() and PG_SLEEP() duration is in seconds), which pauses the transaction. If it pauses the transaction for a time longer than the transaction timeout, the transaction should expire and roll back.

The following repository defines a SLEEP() based query that delays the current transaction for 15 seconds, while the timeout is set to 10 seconds:

```
@Repository
public interface AuthorRepository extends JpaRepository<Author, Long> {

    @Query(value = "SELECT SLEEP(15)", nativeQuery = true)
    public void sleepQuery();
}
```

So, by sneaking this query in your transaction, the transaction should be delayed for the specified time:

```
@Transactional(timeout = 10)
public void newAuthor() {

    Author author = new Author();
    author.setAge(23);
    author.setGenre("Anthology");
    author.setName("Mark Janel");
    authorRepository.saveAndFlush(author);

    authorRepository.sleepQuery();

    System.out.println("The end!");
}
```

Calling newAuthor() will run for 10 seconds and throw the following timeout-specific exception:

```
org.springframework.dao.QueryTimeoutException
Caused by: org.hibernate.QueryTimeoutException
```

# Setting Transaction and Query Timeouts

Relying on the `timeout` element of `@Transactional` is a very handy way to set a transaction timeout at the method-level or class-level. You can explicitly set a global timeout as well, via the `spring.transaction.default-timeout` property in `application-properties`, as shown here (you can override the global setting via the `timeout` element of the `@Transactional` annotation):

`spring.transaction.default-timeout=10`

You can set a timeout at the query-level via two hints:

- Via a `org.hibernate.timeout` Hibernate-specific hint, which is equivalent to `setTimeout()` from `org.hibernate.query.Query` (the timeout is specified in seconds):

```
@QueryHints({
    @QueryHint(name = "org.hibernate.timeout", value = "10")
})
@Query(value = "SELECT SLEEP(15)", nativeQuery = true)
public void sleepQuery();
```

- Via the `javax.persistence.query.timeout` JPA hint, which is equivalent to `setTimeout()` from `org.hibernate.query.Query` (the timeout is specified in milliseconds):

```
@QueryHints({
    @QueryHint(name = "javax.persistence.query.timeout",
               value = "10000")
})
@Query(value = "SELECT SLEEP(15)", nativeQuery = true)
public void sleepQuery();
```

Finally, if you are using `TransactionTemplate`, then the timeout can be set via `TransactionTemplate.setTimeout(int n)`, which is in seconds.

## Check That a Transaction Was Rolled Back

After a transaction times out, it should be rolled back. You can check this at the database-level, via specific tools, or in the application log. First, enable transaction logging in application.properties as follows:

```
logging.level.ROOT=INFO
logging.level.org.springframework.orm.jpa=DEBUG
logging.level.org.springframework.transaction=DEBUG
```

Now, an expired transaction will log something as shown here:

```
Creating new transaction with name ...
Opened new EntityManager [SessionImpl(1559444773<open>)] for JPA
transaction
...
```

***At this point the transaction times out !!!***

```
...
Statement cancelled due to timeout or client request
Initiating transaction rollback
Rolling back JPA transaction on EntityManager [SessionImpl(1559444773<open>)]
Closing JPA EntityManager [SessionImpl(1559444773<open>)] after transaction
```

The complete application is available on GitHub[5].

# Item 64: Why and How to Use @Transactional in a Repository Interface

The way that you handle transactions in the data access layer is one of the key aspects that can make the difference between a supersonic application and one that barely works.

Generally speaking, the speed of a database is given by the *transaction throughput*, expressed as a number of transactions per second. This means that databases were built to accommodate a lot of short transactions rather than long-running transactions. Follow

---

[5]HibernateSpringBootTransactionTimeout

the techniques exposed in this item to boost your data access layer by striving to obtain short transactions.

As a first step of defining the query-methods (read-only and read-write query-methods), you define a domain class-specific repository interface. The interface must extend `Repository` and be typed to the domain class and an ID type. Commonly, you would extend `CrudRepository`, `JpaRepository`, or `PagingAndSortingRepository`. Further, in this custom interface, you list the query-methods.

For example, consider the `Author` entity and its simple repository interface:

```
@Repository
public interface AuthorRepository extends JpaRepository<Author, Long> {
}
```

There are voices that advice developers to use `@Transactional` only on services (`@Service`) and avoid adding it to repository interfaces. But, from a performance perspective, is this good advice to follow in production? Or, should you be more flexible and consider using `@Transactional` in interface repositories as well? Some of these voices will even encourage you to add `@Transactional` only at the services-class-level or, even worse, at the controllers-class-level. It's clear that such advice doesn't consider the mitigation of long-running transactions and/or are targeting small applications. Of course, following this advice may speed up the development curve and quickly create a comfortable development environment for most developer levels.

Let's see how these transactions work and look at the involved performance penalties depending on where you place the `@Transactional` annotation. Let's start with a myth formulated as a question.

# Does Query-methods listed in an interface repository run by default in a transactional-context?

As a quick remainder, *non-transactional-context* refers to context with no explicit transaction boundaries, **not** to context with no physical database transaction. All database statements are triggered in the context of a physical database transaction. By omitting the explicit transaction boundaries, you expose the application to a bunch of performance penalties detailed in **Item 61**. In a nutshell, it is recommended to use explicit transactions for your read-only queries as well.

Now, let's try to answer the question from the title of this section by writing a JPQL SELECT into the AuthorRepository:

```
@Query("SELECT a FROM Author a WHERE a.name = ?1")
public Author fetchByName(String name);
```

Now, a service-method can call this query-method. Notice that the service-method doesn't declare an explicit transactional-context. This was done on purpose to see if Spring will supply a transactional-context for you (in reality, developers forget to add @Transactional(readOnly = true)):

```
public void callFetchByNameMethod() {

    Author author = authorRepository.fetchByName("Joana Nimar");
    System.out.println(author);
}
```

By simply inspecting the transaction flow in the application log (**Item 85**), we notice that there is no transactional-context available, therefore Spring did not provide a default transactional-context. Moreover, it flags this behavior via a message as follows:

```
Don't need to create transaction for [...fetchByName]: This method isn't
transactional.
```

But, how about a query generated via the Spring Data Query Builder mechanism? Well, consider the next query-method in AuthorRepository:

```
public Author findByName(String name);
```

Let's call it from a proper service-method:

```
public void callFindByNameMethod() {

    Author author = authorRepository.findByName("Joana Nimar");
    System.out.println(author);
}
```

Again, inspecting the application log reveals that there is no default transactional-context.

Finally, let's add a query-method that modifies data to `AuthorRepository`:

```
@Modifying
@Query("DELETE FROM Author a WHERE a.genre <> ?1")
public int deleteByNeGenre(String genre);
```

And a service-method:

```
public void callDeleteByNeGenreMethod() {

    int result = authorRepository.deleteByNeGenre("Anthology");
    System.out.println(result);
}
```

This time, you don't need to inspect the application log. The service-method will throw a meaningful exception, as follows:

```
Caused by: org.springframework.dao.InvalidDataAccessApiUsageException:
Executing an update/delete query;
nested exception is javax.persistence.TransactionRequiredException:
Executing an update/delete query

Caused by: javax.persistence.TransactionRequiredException: Executing an
update/delete query
```

> In conclusion, Spring doesn't supply a default transactional-context for user-defined query-methods. On the other hand, the built-in query-methods (e.g., `save()`, `findById()`, `delete()`, etc.) don't have this issue. They are inherited from the extended built-in repository interfaces (e.g., `JpaRepository`) and come with default transactional-contexts.

Let's quickly call the built-in `findById()` to see this aspect:

```
public void callFindByIdMethod() {

    Author author = authorRepository.findById(1L).orElseThrow();
    System.out.println(author);
}
```

The application log reveals that Spring automatically supplies a transactional-context in this case:

Creating new transaction with name [...**SimpleJpaRepository.findById**]: PROPAGATION_REQUIRED,ISOLATION_DEFAULT,readOnly

Opened new EntityManager [SessionImpl(854671988<open>)] for JPA transaction

**begin**

Exposing JPA transaction as JDBC [...HibernateJpaDialect$HibernateConnection Handle@280099a0]

**select author0_.id as id1_0_0_, author0_.age as age2_0_0_, author0_.genre as genre3_0_0_, author0_.name as name4_0_0_ from author author0_ where author0_.id=?**

Initiating transaction commit
Committing JPA transaction on EntityManager [SessionImpl(854671988<open>)]

**committing**

Closing JPA EntityManager [SessionImpl(854671988<open>)] after transaction

This example triggered a SELECT statement. Now, let's update the selected author via setGenre():

```
public void callFindByIdMethodAndUpdate() {

    Author author = authorRepository.findById(1L).orElseThrow();
    author.setGenre("History");

    authorRepository.save(author);
}
```

This time, the application log reveals that this code requires two separate physical transactions (two database round trips) to accommodate the SELECT triggered via findById(), and the SELECT and UPDATE triggered via save(). The Persistence Context used by findById() is closed after this method execution. Therefore, the save() method needs another Persistence Context. In order to update the author, Hibernate needs to merge the detached author. Basically, it loads the author in this Persistence Context via a prior SELECT. Obviously, these two SELECT statements may return different result sets if a concurrent transaction performs modifications on the concerned data, but this can be eliminated via Versioned Optimistic Locking to prevent *lost updates*. Let's examine the application log:

Creating new transaction with name [...**SimpleJpaRepository.findById**]: PROPAGATION_REQUIRED,ISOLATION_DEFAULT,readOnly

Opened new EntityManager [SessionImpl(1403088342<open>)] for JPA transaction

**begin**

Exposing JPA transaction as JDBC [...HibernateJpaDialect$HibernateConnection Handle@51fa09c7]

**select author0_.id as id1_0_0_, author0_.age as age2_0_0_, author0_.genre as genre3_0_0_, author0_.name as name4_0_0_ from author author0_ where author0_.id=?**

Initiating transaction commit
Committing JPA transaction on EntityManager [SessionImpl(1403088342<open>)]

**committing**

Closing JPA EntityManager [SessionImpl(1403088342<open>)] after transaction

Creating new transaction with name [...**SimpleJpaRepository.save**]: PROPAGATION_REQUIRED,ISOLATION_DEFAULT

Opened new EntityManager [SessionImpl(94617220<open>)] for JPA transaction

**begin**

Exposing JPA transaction as JDBC [...HibernateJpaDialect$HibernateConnection Handle@4850d66b]

**select author0_.id as id1_0_0_, author0_.age as age2_0_0_, author0_.genre as genre3_0_0_, author0_.name as name4_0_0_ from author author0_ where author0_.id=?**

Committing JPA transaction on EntityManager [SessionImpl(94617220<open>)]

**committing**

**update author set age=?, genre=?, name=? where id=?**

Closing JPA EntityManager [SessionImpl(94617220<open>)] after transaction

In other words, Spring has automatically supplied transactional-contexts for the `findById()` and `save()` methods, but it doesn't supply a transactional-context for the `callFindByIdMethodAndUpdate()` service-method. Among the drawbacks, this service-method doesn't take advantage of ACID properties as a unit-of-work, needs two physical transactions and database round trips, and triggers three SQL statements instead of two.

Most of the time, you would implement a service-method containing query-method invocations with the assumption that the triggered SQL statements will run as a unit-of-work in a transaction having ACID properties. Obviously, this assumption doesn't validate the previous case.

How about calling `fetchByName()` and `deleteByNeGenre()` in the same service-method, as follows:

```
public void callFetchByNameAndDeleteByNeGenreMethods() {

    Author author = authorRepository.fetchByName("Joana Nimar");
    authorRepository.deleteByNeGenre(author.getGenre());
}
```

Since `AuthorRepository` doesn't provide a transactional-context for the query-methods, `deleteByNeGenre()` will cause a `javax.persistence.TransactionRequiredException` exception. So, this time, the code doesn't run silently in a non-transactional-context.

## Okay, So All I Have to Do Is Add @Transactional at the Service-Method Level, Right?

To provide an explicit transactional-context, you can add `@Transactional` at the service-method level. This way the SQL statements that run in the boundaries of this transactional-context will take advantage of ACID properties as a unit-of-work. For example, let's add `@Transactional` to `callFetchByNameMethod()`:

```
@Transactional(readOnly = true)
public void callFetchByNameMethod() {

    Author author = authorRepository.fetchByName("Joana Nimar");
    System.out.println(author);
}
```

This time, the application log confirms the presence of the transactional-context:

Creating new transaction with name [...**BookstoreService.
callFetchByNameMethod**]: PROPAGATION_REQUIRED,ISOLATION_DEFAULT,readOnly

Opened new EntityManager [SessionImpl(2012237082<open>)] for JPA
transaction

**begin**

Exposing JPA transaction as JDBC [...HibernateJpaDialect$HibernateConnection
Handle@7d3815f7]

**select author0_.id as id1_0_, author0_.age as age2_0_, author0_.genre as
genre3_0_, author0_.name as name4_0_ from author author0_ where author0_.name=?
Author{id=4, age=34, name=Joana Nimar, genre=History}**

Initiating transaction commit

Committing JPA transaction on EntityManager [SessionImpl(2012237082<open>)]

**committing**

Closing JPA EntityManager [SessionImpl(2012237082<open>)] after transaction

Cool! Now you can define a unit-of-work by joining multiple logical related SQL
statements under the umbrella of a transactional-context and take advantage of
ACID properties. For example, you can rewrite callFindByIdMethodAndUpdate(), as
shown here:

**@Transactional**
```
public void callFindByIdMethodAndUpdate() {

    Author author = authorRepository.findById(1L).orElseThrow();
    author.setGenre("History");
}
```

This time, there is a single transaction (a single database round trip), two SQL
statements (a SELECT and an UPDATE), and there is no need to explicitly call save()
(see **Item 107**).

The callFindByIdMethodAndUpdate() takes advantage of ACID properties as well. Here's the log:

Creating new transaction with name [...**BookstoreService. callFindByIdMethodAndUpdate**]: PROPAGATION_REQUIRED,ISOLATION_DEFAULT

Opened new EntityManager [SessionImpl(1115708094<open>)] for JPA transaction

**begin**

Exposing JPA transaction as JDBC [...HibernateJpaDialect$HibernateConnection Handle@78ea700f]

Found thread-bound EntityManager [SessionImpl(1115708094<open>)] for JPA transaction

**Participating in existing transaction**

**select author0_.id as id1_0_0_, author0_.age as age2_0_0_, author0_.genre as genre3_0_0_, author0_.name as name4_0_0_ from author author0_ where author0_.id=?**

Initiating transaction commit

Committing JPA transaction on EntityManager [SessionImpl(1115708094<open>)]

**committing**

**update author set age=?, genre=?, name=? where id=?**

Closing JPA EntityManager [SessionImpl(1115708094<open>)] after transaction

Finally, let's call the callFetchByNameAndDeleteByNeGenreMethods() method in an explicit transactional-context:

```
@Transactional
public void callFetchByNameAndDeleteByNeGenreMethods() {

    Author author = authorRepository.fetchByName("Joana Nimar");
    authorRepository.deleteByNeGenre(author.getGenre());
```

```
if (new Random().nextBoolean()) {
    throw new RuntimeException("Some DAO exception occurred!");
}
}
```

Now, notice that after the triggered SELECT (via fetchByName()) and DELETE (via deleteByNeGenre()), we have emulated a random exception that should cause transaction rollback. This reveals the atomicity of the transaction. So, if an exception occurs, the application log will reveal the following:

Creating new transaction with name [**...BookstoreService.callFetchBy NameAndDeleteByNeGenreMethods**]: PROPAGATION_REQUIRED,ISOLATION_DEFAULT

Opened new EntityManager [SessionImpl(654609843<open>)] for JPA transaction

**begin**

Exposing JPA transaction as JDBC [...HibernateJpaDialect$Hibernate ConnectionHandle@7f94541b]

**select author0_.id as id1_0_, author0_.age as age2_0_, author0_.genre as genre3_0_, author0_.name as name4_0_ from author author0_ where author0_. name=?**

**delete from author where genre<>?**

**Initiating transaction rollback**

**Rolling back JPA transaction on EntityManager [SessionImpl(654609843<open>)]**

**rolling back**

Closing JPA EntityManager [SessionImpl(654609843<open>)] after transaction

**Caused by: java.lang.RuntimeException: Some DAO exception occurred!**

Okay, it looks like adding @Transactional at the service-method level fixes all the issues. This solution has transactional-context available for the service-method and it takes advantage of ACID properties.

# But, Generally Speaking, Is this Approach Always Enough?

In order to answer to this question, let's tackle the following service-method:

```
@Transactional(readOnly = true)
public void longRunningServiceMethod() {

    System.out.println("Service-method start ...");
    System.out.println("Sleeping before triggering SQL
                    to simulate a long running code ...");
    Thread.sleep(40000);

    Author author = authorRepository.fetchByName("Joana Nimar");
    System.out.println(author);

    System.out.println("Service-method done ...");
}
```

Notice that, just for testing purposes, we use a very long sleep of 40 seconds. When we talk about long-running versus short transactions, we should discuss them in terms of milliseconds. For example, Figure 6-3 shows five long-running transactions.

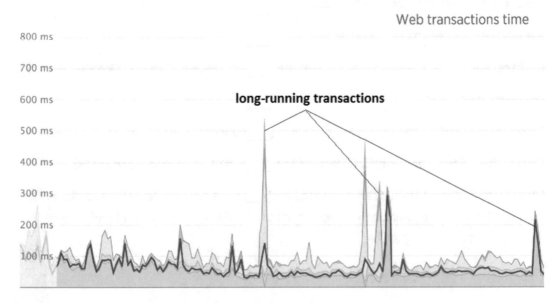

***Figure 6-3.*** *Time sample of web transactions*

At the end of the service-method, you call the fetchByName() query-method. Therefore, the service-method is annotated with @Transactional(readOnly = true) to explicitly define the transactional-context boundaries. Check out the application log:

Creating new transaction with name [**...BookstoreService.
longRunningServiceMethod**]: PROPAGATION_REQUIRED,ISOLATION_DEFAULT,readOnly

Opened new EntityManager [SessionImpl(1884806106<open>)] for JPA transaction

**begin**

Exposing JPA transaction as JDBC [...HibernateJpaDialect$Hibernate
ConnectionHandle@63ad5fe7]

**Service-method start ...**
**Sleeping before triggering SQL to simulate a long running code ...**

HikariPool-1 - Pool stats (total=10, **active=1**, idle=9, waiting=0)

**select author0_.id as id1_0_, author0_.age as age2_0_, author0_.genre as
genre3_0_, author0_.name as name4_0_ from author author0_ where author0_.
name=?**
**Author{id=4, age=34, name=Joana Nimar, genre=History}**

**Service-method done ...**

Initiating transaction commit

Committing JPA transaction on EntityManager [SessionImpl(1884806106<open>)]

**committing**

Closing JPA EntityManager [SessionImpl(1884806106<open>)] after transaction

HikariPool-1 - Pool stats (total=10, **active=0**, idle=10, waiting=0)

So, what is happening here? Spring starts the transaction and acquires the database connection immediately, before starting to run the longRunningServiceMethod() method code. The database connection is opened right away and is ready to be used. But we don't use it right away, we just keep it open! We run some other tasks (simulated via Thread.sleep()) before calling fetchByName(), which is before the first interaction with the database connection. Meanwhile, the database connection remains open and linked to the transaction (check out the HikariCP log, `active=1`). Finally, the transaction is committed and the database connection is released back to the connection pool. This scenario represents a long-running transaction that may affect scalability and is not in favor of MVCC (Multi-Version Concurrency Control). The main reason for this problem is because we've annotated the service-method with `@Transactional`. But, if we remove this `@Transactional` then `fetchByName()` will run outside a transactional-context! Hmm!

# I Know! Let's Move @Transactional in the Repository Interface!

The solution will consist of moving `@Transactional` into the repository interface as follows:

```
@Repository
@Transactional(readOnly = true)
public interface AuthorRepository extends JpaRepository<Author, Long> {

    @Query("SELECT a FROM Author a WHERE a.name = ?1")
    public Author fetchByName(String name);
}
```

Or, like this (of course, the drawback shown here is represented by the fact that if we have more read-only query-methods then we need to repeat the `@Transactional(readOnly = true)` annotation):

```
@Repository
public interface AuthorRepository extends JpaRepository<Author, Long> {

    @Transactional(readOnly = true)
    @Query("SELECT a FROM Author a WHERE a.name = ?1")
    public Author fetchByName(String name);
}
```

The service-method doesn't contain `@Transactional`:

```
public void longRunningServiceMethod() {

    // remains unchanged
}
```

This time, the application log reveals the expected result:

**Service-method start ...**
**Sleeping before triggering SQL to simulate a long running code ...**

HikariPool-1 - Pool stats (total=10, **active=0,** idle=10, waiting=0)

Creating new transaction with name [...SimpleJpaRepository.fetchByName]:
PROPAGATION_REQUIRED,ISOLATION_DEFAULT,readOnly

Opened new EntityManager [SessionImpl(508317658<open>)] for JPA transaction

**begin**

Exposing JPA transaction as JDBC [...HibernateJpaDialect$HibernateConnection
Handle@3ba1f56e]

**select author0_.id as id1_0_, author0_.age as age2_0_, author0_.genre as**
**genre3_0_, author0_.name as name4_0_ from author author0_ where author0_.**
**name=?**

Initiating transaction commit

Committing JPA transaction on EntityManager [SessionImpl(508317658<open>)]

**committing**

Closing JPA EntityManager [SessionImpl(508317658<open>)] after transaction

**Author{id=4, age=34, name=Joana Nimar, genre=History}**

**Service-method done ...**

So, this time, the transaction is wrapping only the SQL SELECT statement triggered via the query-method. Since this leads to a short transaction, it's pretty clear that this is the way to go.

# But What If I Want to Call More Query-Methods in the Service-Method? Do I Lose ACID?

The previous scenario runs as expected because we called a single query-method in the longRunningServiceMethod() service-method. However, you will most likely need to call several query-methods that produce a bunch of SQL statements that define a logical transaction. For example, after fetching an author by name (fetchByName()), you might want to delete all the authors who have a different genre than this author (deleteByNeGenre()). Calling these two query-methods in the service-method that is not annotated with @Transactional will lose ACID properties for this unit-of-work. Therefore, you need to add @Transactional at the service-method as well.

First, let's look at the best way to shape the repository interface, AuthorRepository. You should follow **Oliver Drotbohm's** advice:

> *Thus we recommend using @Transactional(readOnly = true)*
> *for query-methods as well, which you can easily achieve adding*
> *that annotation to your repository interface. Make sure you add*
> *a plain @Transactional to the manipulating methods you might*
> *have declared or re-decorated in that interface.*

Further, Oliver is asked: "So in short, I should use @Transactional on add/edit/delete queries and @Transaction(readOnly = true) on SELECT queries on all my DAO-methods?" **Oliver** answers as follows:

> *Exactly. The easiest way to do so is by using @Transactional*
> *(readOnly = true) on the interface (as it usually contains mostly*
> *finder methods) and override this setting for each modifying query-*
> *method with a plain @Transactional. That's actually the way it's*
> *done in SimpleJpaRepository.*

So, we should have:

```
@Repository
@Transactional(readOnly = true)
public interface AuthorRepository extends JpaRepository<Author, Long> {

    @Query("SELECT a FROM Author a WHERE a.name = ?1")
    public Author fetchByName(String name);

    @Transactional
    @Modifying
    @Query("DELETE FROM Author a WHERE a.genre <> ?1")
    public int deleteByNeGenre(String genre);
}
```

So, we ensure that all query-methods are running in a read-only transactional-context by annotating the repository interface with @Transactional(readOnly = true). Further, for query-methods that can modify data, we switch to a transactional-context that allows data modifications by adding @Transactional without a readOnly flag. Mainly, what we've done here is exactly what Spring Data does internal for its built-in query-methods.

Further, the service-method is annotated with @Transactional because we will trigger a SELECT and an UPDATE:

```
@Transactional
public void longRunningServiceMethod() {

    System.out.println("Service-method start ...");
    System.out.println("Sleeping before triggering SQL
                        to simulate a long running code ...");
    Thread.sleep(40000);

    Author author = authorRepository.fetchByName("Joana Nimar");
    authorRepository.deleteByNeGenre(author.getGenre());

    System.out.println("Service-method done ...");
}
```

Let's check out the application log now:

Creating new transaction with name [...**BookstoreService.
longRunningServiceMethod**]: PROPAGATION_REQUIRED,ISOLATION_DEFAULT

Opened new EntityManager [SessionImpl(138303640<open>)] for JPA transaction

**begin**

Exposing JPA transaction as JDBC [...HibernateJpaDialect$Hibernate
ConnectionHandle@7c4a03a]

Service-method start ...
Sleeping before triggering SQL to simulate a long running code ...

HikariPool-1 - Pool stats (total=10, **active=1**, idle=9, waiting=0)

**Found thread-bound EntityManager [SessionImpl(138303640<open>)] for JPA
transaction
Participating in existing transaction**

**select author0_.id as id1_0_, author0_.age as age2_0_, author0_.genre as
genre3_0_, author0_.name as name4_0_ from author author0_ where author0_.name=?**

**Found thread-bound EntityManager [SessionImpl(138303640<open>)] for JPA
transaction
Participating in existing transaction**

**delete from author where genre<>?**

Service-method done ...

Initiating transaction commit

Committing JPA transaction on EntityManager [SessionImpl(138303640<open>)]

**committing**

Closing JPA EntityManager [SessionImpl(138303640<open>)] after transaction
HikariPool-1 - Pool stats (total=10, active=0, idle=10, waiting=0)

Check the following highlighted output:

**Found thread-bound EntityManager [SessionImpl(138303640<open>)] for JPA
transaction
Participating in existing transaction**

This time, each called query-method (fetchByName() and deleteByNeGenre())
participates in the existing transaction opened when you call the longRunningService
Method() service-method. So, don't get confused and think that the @Transactional
annotations from the repository interface will start new transactions or will consume
new database connections. Spring will automatically *invite* the called query-methods to
participate in the existing transaction. Everything works like a charm! Spring relies on
its transaction propagation mechanisms detailed in **Appendix G**. More precisely, in the
default mode, Spring applies the transaction propagation rules that are specific to the
default transaction propagation mechanism, Propagation.REQUIRED. Of course, if you
explicitly set another transaction propagation mechanism (see **Appendix G**), then you
have to evaluate your transaction flow in the corresponding context.

Okay, but now we are back to a long-running transaction! Well, in such cases we should refactor the code and redesign the implementation to obtain shorter transactions. Or, if we are using Hibernate 5.2.10+, we can delay the database connection acquisition. Based on **Item 60**, we can delay the connection acquisition via the following two settings (it's recommended to always use these settings in *resource-local* (specific to single data source)):

```
spring.datasource.hikari.auto-commit=false
spring.jpa.properties.hibernate.connection.provider_disables_
autocommit=true
```

Now the database connection acquisition is delayed until the first SQL statement is executed:

Creating new transaction with name [...**BookstoreService.
longRunningServiceMethod**]: PROPAGATION_REQUIRED,ISOLATION_DEFAULT

Opened new EntityManager [SessionImpl(138303640<open>)] for JPA transaction

**begin**

Exposing JPA transaction as JDBC [...HibernateJpaDialect$HibernateConnection
Handle@7c4a03a]

Service-method start ...
Sleeping before triggering SQL to simulate a long running code ...

HikariPool-1 - Pool stats (total=10, **active=0**, idle=10, waiting=0)

**Found thread-bound EntityManager [SessionImpl(138303640<open>)] for JPA
transaction
Participating in existing transaction**

**select author0_.id as id1_0_, author0_.age as age2_0_, author0_.genre as
genre3_0_, author0_.name as name4_0_ from author author0_ where author0_.
name=?**

**Found thread-bound EntityManager [SessionImpl(138303640<open>)] for JPA
transaction
Participating in existing transaction**

**delete from author where genre<>?**

Service-method done ...

Initiating transaction commit

Committing JPA transaction on EntityManager [SessionImpl(138303640<open>)]

**committing**

Closing JPA EntityManager [SessionImpl(138303640<open>)] after transaction

HikariPool-1 - Pool stats (total=10, active=0, idle=10, waiting=0)

Notice that until the first query-method is called, HikariCP reports 0 active connections. So, our time-consuming tasks (simulated via Thread.sleep()) are executed without keeping a database connection open. Nevertheless, after the connection is acquired, it remains open until the end of the service-method execution (until the transaction completes). This is a strong reason to pay extra attention to your service-method design to avoid any long-running tasks.

> As a rule of thumb, strive to avoid transactions that interleave heavy business logic that doesn't interact with the database with query-method invocations. This can result in long-running transactions and complex service-methods that become time-consuming and are hard to understand, debug, refactor, and review. There are almost always better solutions, just take your time to find them.

The complete code covering the long-running method case is available on GitHub[6].

# So, If I Delay the Connection Acquisition then I Can Avoid @Transactional in Repository Interfaces?

If you can, upgrade to Hibernate 5.2.10+ and perform the settings from **Item 60** to delay the connection acquisition. Then, in most of these cases, you can use @Transactional only at the service-level and not in repository interfaces. But this means that you are

---

[6]HibernateSpringBootTransactionalInRepository

still prone to forget adding @Transactional(readOnly=true) to service-methods that contain read-only database operations (**Item 61**). Now, let's look at two cases that generate shorter transactions if you add @Transactional to the repository interfaces as well.

## Case 1

Consider the following repository and two service-methods in BookstoreService:

```
@Repository
public interface AuthorRepository extends JpaRepository<Author, Long> {

    @Query("SELECT a FROM Author a WHERE a.name = ?1")
    public Author fetchByName(String name);
}

@Service
public class BookstoreService {

    public void displayAuthor() {
        Author author = fetchAuthor();
        System.out.println(author);
    }

    @Transactional(readOnly = true)
    public Author fetchAuthor() {
        return authorRepository.fetchByName("Joana Nimar");
    }
}
```

This code falls under the **Item 62** umbrella. In other words, @Transactional was added to a method defined in the same class where it is invoked and Spring will ignore it. But, if we followed the best practices and declare @Transactional(readOnly=true) in the repository interface then everything works perfectly:

```
@Repository
@Transactional(readOnly = true)
public interface AuthorRepository extends JpaRepository<Author, Long> {
```

```
    @Query("SELECT a FROM Author a WHERE a.name = ?1")
    public Author fetchByName(String name);
}

@Service
public class BookstoreService {

    public void displayAuthor() {
        Author author = fetchAuthor();
        System.out.println(author);
    }

    public Author fetchAuthor() {
        return authorRepository.fetchByName("Joana Nimar");
    }
}
```

Alternatively, you can use two services, as in **Item 62**.

# Case 2

Consider the following repository and service-method in BookstoreService:

```
@Repository
public interface AuthorRepository extends JpaRepository<Author, Long> {

    @Query("SELECT a FROM Author a WHERE a.name = ?1")
    public Author fetchByName(String name);
}

@Service
public class BookstoreService {

    @Transactional(readOnly = true)
    public Royalty computeRoyalties() {

        Author author = authorRepository.fetchByName("Joana Nimar");

        // computing royalties is a slow task
        // that requires interaction with other services
        // (e.g., revenue and financial services)
```

```
        return royalties;
    }
}
```

In this case, delaying the connection acquisition doesn't come with a significant benefit. We call fetchByName() immediately; therefore, the database connection is acquired right away. After executing the fetchByName() query-method, the database connection remains open until the royalties are computed.

But, if we had prepared the AuthorRepository as follows:

```
@Repository
@Transactional(readOnly = true)
public interface AuthorRepository extends JpaRepository<Author, Long> {

    @Query("SELECT a FROM Author a WHERE a.name = ?1")
    public Author fetchByName(String name);
}
```

Then there is no need to annotate the service-method with @Transactional (readOnly = true) and the transaction will encapsulate only the execution of fetchByName(), while royalties are computed outside of the transactions:

```
@Service
public class BookstoreService {

    public Royalty computeRoyalties() {

        Author author = authorRepository.fetchByName("Joana Nimar");

        // computing royalties is a slow task
        // that requires interaction with other services
        // (e.g., revenue and financial services)

        return royalties;
    }
}
```

Alternatively, you can split computeRoyalties() into two methods, as shown here:

```
@Repository
public interface AuthorRepository extends JpaRepository<Author, Long> {

    @Query("SELECT a FROM Author a WHERE a.name = ?1")
    public Author fetchByName(String name);
}

@Service
public class BookstoreService {

    public Royalty computeRoyalties() {

        Author author = fetchAuthorByName("Joana Nimar");

        // computing royalties is a slow task
        // that requires interaction with other services
        // (e.g., revenue and financial services)

        return royalties;
    }

    @Transactional(readOnly = true)
    public Author fetchAuthorByName(String name) {

        return authorRepository.fetchByName(name);
    }
}
```

But now we are back to Case 1.

# Three Simple and Common Scenarios

Let's tackle three simple and common scenarios that are easy to mess it up.

## Roll Back a Service-Method at Exception Thrown by the Code that Doesn't Interact with the Database

Consider the following service-method:

```
public void foo() {

    // call a query-method that triggers DML statements (e.g., save())
```

```
    // follows tasks that don't interact with the database but
    // are prone to throw RuntimeException
}
```

Should this service-method be annotated with @Transactional or not? If the highlighted code that doesn't interact with the database fails via a RuntimeException, then the current transaction should be rolled back. The first impulse would be to annotate this service-method as @Transactional. This scenario is common for *checked* exception as well, by using @Transactional(rollbackFor = Exception.class).

But, before deciding to add @Transactional to the service-method, it's advisable to think twice. Maybe there is another solution. For example, maybe you can change the order of tasks without affecting the behavior:

```
public void foo() {

    // follows tasks that don't interact with the database but
    // are prone to throw RuntimeException

    // call a query-method that triggers DML statements (e.g., save())
}
```

Now there is no need to annotate this service-method with @Transactional. If the tasks that don't interact with the database throw a RuntimeException, then save() will not be called at all, so you save a database round trip.

Moreover, if these tasks are time-consuming then they don't affect the duration of the transaction opened for the save() method. In the worst case scenario, we cannot change the order of the tasks and these tasks are time-consuming. Even worse, this can be a heavily called method in your application. Under these circumstances, the service-method will cause long-running transactions. In such cases, you have to redesign your solution to avoid annotating the service-method with @Transactional (e.g., explicitly catch the exception and provide manual rollback via explicit DML statements or refactor the service-method into several service-methods to mitigate the long-running transaction).

## Cascading and @Transactional

Consider Foo and Buzz involved in a bidirectional lazy association. Persisting a Foo will cascade the persist operations to the associated Buzz. And to the following service-method:

```
public void fooAndBuzz() {

    Foo foo = new Foo();

    Buzz buzz1 = new Buzz();
    Buzz buzz2 = new Buzz();

    foo.addBuzz(buzz1);
    foo.addBuzz(buzz2);

    fooRepository.save(foo);
}
```

We call save() only once but it will trigger three INSERT statements. So, should we annotate this method with @Transactional to provide ACID properties? The answer is no! We shouldn't annotate this service-method with @Transactional because the INSERT statement triggered to persist the Buzz instances associated with Foo are the effect of cascading via CascadeType.ALL/PERSIST. All three INSERT statements are executed in the context of the same transaction. If any of these INSERT statements fails, the transaction is automatically rolled back.

## Select ➤ Modify ➤ Save and an Interleaved Long-Running Task

Remember the callFindByIdMethodAndUpdate() from earlier?

```
public void callFindByIdMethodAndUpdate() {

    Author author = authorRepository.findById(1L).orElseThrow();
    author.setGenre("History");

    authorRepository.save(author);
}
```

Let's abstract this method as follows:

```
public void callSelectModifyAndSave () {

    Foo foo = fooRepository.findBy...(...);
    foo.setFooProperty(...);

    fooRepository.save(foo);
}
```

Earlier, we annotated this kind of method with @Transactional to demarcate the transaction boundaries. Among the benefits, we said that there will be two SQL statements (SELECT and UPDATE) instead of three (SELECT, SELECT, and UPDATE), we save a database round trip, and there is no need to explicitly call save():

```
@Transactional
public void callSelectModifyAndSave () {

    Foo foo = fooRepository.findBy...(...);
    foo.setFooProperty(...);
}
```

However, is this approach useful in the following case?

```
@Transactional
public void callSelectModifyAndSave() {

    Foo foo = fooRepository.findBy...(...);

    // long-running task using foo data

    foo.setFooProperty(...);
}
```

If we sneak a long-running task between the SELECT and UPDATE, then we cause a long-running transaction. For example, we may need to select a book, use the selected data to generate a PDF version of the book (this is the long-running task), and update the book's available formats. If we choose to do it as above (which is a pretty common case), then we have a long-running transaction since the transaction will contain the long-running task as well.

In such cases, it's better to drop @Transactional and allow two short transactions separated by a long running-task and an additional SELECT:

```
public void callSelectModifyAndSave() {

    Foo foo = fooRepository.findBy...(...);

    // long-running task using foo data

    foo.setFooProperty(...);
    fooRepository.save(foo);
}
```

Commonly, when a long-running task is involved as here, we have to consider that the selected data may get modified by another transaction (*lost update*) between the SELECT and UPDATE. This may happen in both cases—a long-running transaction or two short transactions separated by a long-running task. In both cases, we can rely on Versioned Optimistic Locking and retry mechanisms (**Item 131**). Since this method is not annotated with @Transactional, we can apply @Retry (notice that @Retry shouldn't be applied to a method annotated with @Transactional—details are explained in **Item 131**):

```
@Retry(times = 10, on = OptimisticLockingFailureException.class)
public void callSelectModifyAndSave() {

    Foo foo = fooRepository.findBy...(...);

    // long-running task using foo data

    foo.setFooProperty(...);
    fooRepository.save(foo);
}
```

Done! This is much better than a single long-running transaction.

> In order to obtain optimal and ACID-based transactional-contexts that mitigate major performance penalties, especially long-running transactions, it is advisable to follow these guidelines:

**Prepare your repository interfaces:**

- Annotate the repository interfaces with `@Transactional` `(readOnly=true)`.

- Override `@Transactional(readOnly=true)` with `@Transactional` for query-methods that modify data/generate DML (such as `INSERT`, `UPDATE`, and `DELETE`).

**Delay database connection acquisition:**

- For Hibernate 5.2.10+, delay the database connection acquisition until it's really needed (see **Item 60**).

**Evaluate each service-method:**

- Evaluate each service-method to decide if it should be annotated with `@Transactional` or not.

- If you decide to annotate a service-method with `@Transactional` then add the proper `@Transactional`. You should add `@Transactional(readOnly=true)` if you call just read-only query-methods and add `@Transactional` if you call at least one query-method that can modify data.

**Measure and monitor transaction duration:**

- Be sure to evaluate the transaction duration and behavior in the context of the current transaction propagation mechanism (**Appendix G**) and strive for short and short/fast transactions.

- Once the database connection is acquired it remains open until the transaction completes. Therefore, design your solutions to avoid long-running transactions.

- Avoid adding `@Transactional` at the controller-class-level or the service-class-level since this may lead to long-running or even unneeded transactions (such a class is prone to open transactional-contexts and acquires database connections for methods that don't need to interact with the database). For example, a developer may add `public` methods that contain business logic that doesn't interact with the database; in such cases, if you delay the database connection acquisition, then Spring Boot will still prepare the transactional-context but will never acquire a database connection for it. On the other hand, if you don't rely on delaying the database connection acquisition, then Spring Boot will prepare the transactional-context and will acquire the database connection for it as well.

That's all!

# CHAPTER 7

# Identifiers

## Item 65: Why to Avoid the Hibernate 5 AUTO Generator Type in MySQL

Consider the following Author entity, which relies on the Hibernate 5 AUTO generator type to generate identifiers:

```
@Entity
public class AuthorBad implements Serializable {

    private static final long serialVersionUID = 1L;

    @Id
    @GeneratedValue(strategy = GenerationType.AUTO)
    // or
    @GeneratedValue
    private Long id;
    ...
}
```

In MySQL and Hibernate 5, the GenerationType.AUTO generator type will result in using the TABLE generator. This adds a significant performance penalty. The TABLE generator type doesn't scale well and is much slower than the IDENTITY and SEQUENCE (not supported in MySQL) generators types, even with a single database connection.

For example, persisting a new AuthorBad will result in three SQL statements, as follows:

```
SELECT
  next_val AS id_val
FROM hibernate_sequence
FOR UPDATE
```

© Anghel Leonard 2020
A. Leonard, *Spring Boot Persistence Best Practices*, https://doi.org/10.1007/978-1-4842-5626-8_7

```
UPDATE hibernate_sequence
SET next_val = ?
WHERE next_val = ?

INSERT INTO author_bad (age, genre, name, id)
  VALUES (?, ?, ?, ?)
```

> As a rule of thumb, **always** avoid the TABLE generator.

Obviously, it's better to persist new authors via a single INSERT statement. To accomplish this goal, rely on IDENTITY or on the *native* generator type. The IDENTITY generator type can be employed as follows:

```
@Entity
public class AuthorGood implements Serializable {

    private static final long serialVersionUID = 1L;

    @Id
    @GeneratedValue(strategy=GenerationType.IDENTITY)
    private Long id;
    ...
}
```

The *native* generator type can be employed as follows:

```
@Entity
public class AuthorGood implements Serializable {

    private static final long serialVersionUID = 1L;

    @Id
    @GeneratedValue(strategy=GenerationType.AUTO, generator="native")
    @GenericGenerator(name="native", strategy="native")
    private Long id;
    ...
}
```

This time, persisting an AuthorGood will produce the following INSERT:

```
INSERT INTO author_good (age, genre, name)
  VALUES (?, ?, ?)
```

The source code is available on GitHub[1].

# Item 66: How to Optimize the Generation of Sequence Identifiers via the hi/lo Algorithm

This item relies on PostgreSQL, which supports the SEQUENCE generator. MySQL provides the TABLE alternative, but don't use it! See **Item 65**.

> Whenever supported, *database sequences* represent the proper way (in JPA and Hibernate ORM) to generate identifiers. The SEQUENCE generator sustains batching, is table free, can take advantage of database sequence pre-allocation, and supports an incremental step.
>
> Do not forget to avoid the TABLE identifier generator, which is counterproductive (for details, see **Item 65**).

By default, the SEQUENCE generator must hit the database for each new sequence value via a SELECT statement. Assuming the following Author entity:

```
@Entity
public class Author implements Serializable {
    ...
    @Id
    @GeneratedValue(strategy = GenerationType.SEQUENCE)
    private Long id;
    ...
}
```

---

[1]HibernateSpringBootAutoGeneratorType

Each persisted Author requires an identifier (the current sequence value) fetched via a database round trip materialized in the following SELECT:

**SELECT**

```
nextval('hibernate_sequence')
```

> Relying on cached sequences or database sequence pre-allocation doesn't help. For cached sequences, the application still requires a database round trip for every new sequence value. On the other hand, the database sequence pre-allocation still has a significant database round trip score.

This can be optimized via the Hibernate-specific *hi/lo* algorithm (especially with a high number of inserts). This algorithm is part of the Hibernate built-in optimizers capable of computing identifiers values in-memory. Therefore, using hi/lo reduces the number of database round trips and, as a consequence, increases application performance.

This algorithm splits the sequence domains into synchronously *hi* groups. The *hi* value can be provided by the database sequence (or the table generator), and its initial value is configurable (`initial_value`). Basically, at a single database round trip, the hi/lo algorithm fetches from the database a new *hi* value and uses it to generate a number of identifiers given by a configurable increment (`increment_size`) representing the number of *lo* entries. While *lo* is in this range, no database round trip that fetches a new *hi* is needed and the in-memory generated identifiers can be safely used. When all the *lo* values are used, a new *hi* value is fetched via a new database round trip.

In code, the hi/lo algorithm can be employed for the Author entity, as shown here:

```
@Entity
public class Author implements Serializable {

    private static final long serialVersionUID = 1L;

    @Id
    @GeneratedValue(strategy = GenerationType.SEQUENCE, generator = "hilo")
    @GenericGenerator(name = "hilo", strategy =
                    "org.hibernate.id.enhanced.SequenceStyleGenerator",
        parameters = {
            @Parameter(name = "sequence_name", value = "hilo_sequence"),
```

```
            @Parameter(name = "initial_value", value = "1"),
            @Parameter(name = "increment_size", value = "100"),
            @Parameter(name = "optimizer", value = "hilo")
        }
    )
    private Long id;
    ...
}
```

The hi/lo algorithm requires several parameters:

- sequence_name: This is the name of the database sequence (e.g., hilo_sequence); the database sequence is created via the following statement:

  **CREATE**
      sequence hilo_sequence start 1 increment 1

- initial_value: This is the first sequence value or the first *hi* (e.g., 1)

- increment_size: This is the number of identifiers (number of *lo* entries) that will be computed in memory before fetching the next *hi* (e.g., 100)

- optimizer: This is the name of the Hibernate built-in optimizers (in this case, hilo)

To generate identifiers in memory, the hi/lo algorithm uses the following formula to compute the valid range of values:

[increment_size x (hi - 1) + 1, increment_size x hi]

For example, conforming to these settings, the ranges of in-memory generated identifiers will be:

- For hi=1, the range is [1, 100]

- For hi=2, the range is [101, 200]

- For hi=3, the range is [201, 300]

- ...

The *lo* value ranges from [0, increment_size) starting at (hi - 1) * increment_size) + 1.

Figure 7-1 shows a graphical step-by-step representation of how hi/lo works for Ned and Jo (`initial_value` of *hi* is 1 and `increment_size` is 2).

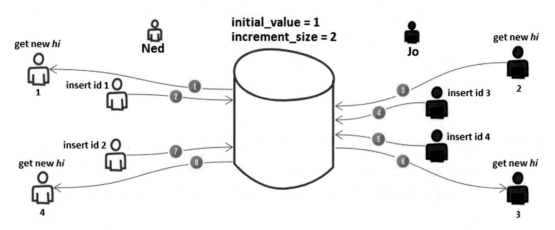

***Figure 7-1.***  *The hi/lo algorithm*

1. Ned starts a transaction and fetches from the database a new *hi* and obtains the value 1.

2. Ned has two in-memory generated identifiers (1 and 2). He uses the identifier with a value of 1 to insert a row.

3. Jo starts her transaction and fetches from the database a new *hi*. She obtains the value 2.

4. Jo has two in-memory generated identifiers (3 and 4). She uses the identifier with value 3 to insert a row.

5. Jo triggers one more insert having the in-memory identifier with a value of 4.

6. Jo doesn't have more in-memory generated identifiers; therefore, the program must fetch a new *hi*. This time, she gets from the database the value 3. Based on this *hi*, Jo can generate in-memory the identifiers with values 5 and 6.

7. Ned uses the in-memory generated identifier with value 2 to insert a new row.

8.  Ned has no more in-memory generated identifiers; therefore, the program must fetch a new *hi*. This time, he gets from the database the value 4. Based on this *hi*, Ned can generate in-memory the identifiers with values 7 and 8.

This being said, a simple way to test the hi/lo algorithm consists of employing a quick batching process. Let's insert in batches 1,000 `Author` instances (in the `author` table). The following service-method batches 1,000 inserts with a batch size of 30 via the `saveAll()` built-in method (while `saveAll()` is okay for examples, it's not the proper choice for production; more details are in **Item 46**):

```
public void batch1000Authors() {

    List<Author> authors = new ArrayList<>();

    for (int i = 1; i <= 1000; i++) {
        Author author = new Author();
        author.setName("Author_" + i);

        authors.add(author);
    }

    authorRepository.saveAll(authors);
}
```

Thanks to the hi/lo algorithm, all 1,000 identifiers are generated using only 10 database round trips. The code fetches only 10 *hi* and, for each *hi*, it generates 100 identifiers in memory. This is way better than 1,000 database round trips. Each round trip for fetching a new *hi* looks as follows:

**SELECT**
  nextval('hilo_sequence')

The complete application is available on GitHub[2].

---

[2]HibernateSpringBootHiLo

# Dealing with External Systems

The *hi* values are provided by the database. Concurrent transactions will receive unique *hi* values; therefore, you don't have to worry about *hi* uniqueness. Two consecutive transactions will receive two consecutive *hi* values.

Now, let's assume a scenario that involves a system external to our application that needs to inserts rows in the author table. This system doesn't use the hi/lo algorithm.

First, the application fetches a new *hi* (e.g., 1) and uses it to generate 100 in-memory identifiers. Let's insert three Authors with the generated in-memory identifiers 1, 2, and 3:

```
@Transactional
public void save3Authors() {

    for (int i = 1; i <= 3; i++) {
        Author author = new Author();
        author.setName("Author_" + i);

        authorRepository.save(author); // uses ids: 1, 2 and 3
    }
}
```

Further, the external system tries to insert a row in the author table. Simulating this behavior can be easily accomplished via a native INSERT as follows:

```
@Repository
public interface AuthorRepository extends JpaRepository<Author, Long> {

    @Modifying
    @Query(value = "INSERT INTO author (id, name)
                    VALUES (NEXTVAL('hilo_sequence'), ?1)",
    nativeQuery = true)
    public void saveNative(String name);
}
```

Executing the NEXTVAL('hilo_sequence') to fetch the next sequence value will return 2. But this application has already used this identifier to insert an Author; therefore, the attempt of the external system will fail with the following error:

```
ERROR: duplicate key value violates unique constraint "author_pkey"
Detail: Key (id)=(2) already exists.
```

> The hi/lo algorithm is not the proper choice in the presence of external systems that act as in the scenario presented previously. Because the database sequence is not aware of the highest in-memory generated identifier, it returns sequence values that might be already used as identifiers. This leads to duplicate identifier errors. There are two options to avoid this kind of issue:
>
> - The external systems should be aware of the hi/lo presence and act accordingly
>
> - Use another Hibernate-specific built-in optimizer (see **Item 67**)

The complete application is available on GitHub[3].

# Item 67: How to Optimize the Generation of Sequence Identifiers via Pooled (-lo) Algorithms

If you are not familiar with the hi/lo algorithm, then consider reading **Item 66** before this one.

The *pooled* and *pooled-lo* algorithms are hi/lo algorithms with different strategies meant to prevent the issues presented in **Item 66**. As a quick remainder, the classical hi/lo algorithm can cause duplicate identifiers errors when external systems, which are not aware of hi/lo presence and/or behavior, try to insert rows in the involved tables.

---

[3]HibernateSpringBootHiLoIssue

# The Pooled Algorithm

Considering the Author entity, the pooled algorithm can be set up as follows:

```
@Entity
public class Author implements Serializable {

    private static final long serialVersionUID = 1L;

    @Id
    @GeneratedValue(strategy = GenerationType.SEQUENCE,
                generator = "hilopooled")
    @GenericGenerator(name = "hilopooled",
                strategy = "org.hibernate.id.enhanced.SequenceStyleGenerator",
        parameters = {
            @Parameter(name = "sequence_name", value = "hilo_sequence"),
            @Parameter(name = "initial_value", value = "1"),
            @Parameter(name = "increment_size", value = "100"),
            @Parameter(name = "optimizer", value = "pooled")
        }
    )
    private Long id;
    ...
}
```

Notice the value of the optimizer parameter, which instructs Hibernate to use the pooled built-in optimizer. Employing this algorithm results in the following CREATE statement for the hilo_sequence:

**CREATE**
```
  sequence hilo_sequence start 1 increment 100
```

Notice the increment 100 part (or, generally speaking, the increment increment_size part).

The pooled algorithm fetched from the database the current sequence value as the top boundary identifier. The current sequence value is computed as the previous sequence value, plus the increment_size. This way, the application will use in-memory identifiers generated between the previous top boundary exclusive (aka, the lowest boundary) and the current top boundary, inclusive.

Let's put these words in a graphical representation. Figure 7-2 shows, step-by-step, how pooled works for Ned and Jo (`initial_value` of *hi* is 1, and `increment_size` is 2).

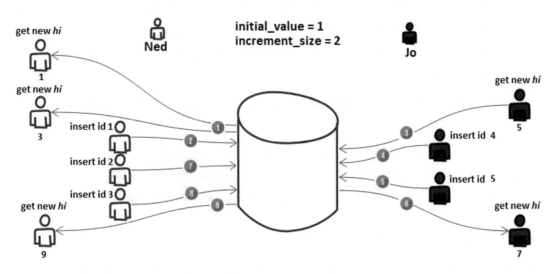

**Figure 7-2.** *The pooled algorithm*

1. Ned starts a transaction and fetches from the database a new *hi* and obtains the value 1 (this is the `initial_value`). In order to determine the top boundary identifier, a new *hi* is fetched automatically, and the value is 3 (this is the `initial_value` + `increment_size`). Only this time, the number of in-memory generated identifiers will equal `increment_size` + 1.

2. Since pooled uses the fetched *hi* as the top boundary identifier, Ned has three in-memory generated identifiers (1, 2, and 3). He uses the identifier with value 1 to insert a row.

3. Jo starts her transaction and fetches from the database a new *hi*. She obtains the value 5.

4. Jo has two in-memory generated identifiers (4 and 5). She uses the identifier with value 4 to insert a row.

5. Jo triggers one more insert with the in-memory identifier of value 5.

6.  Jo doesn't have more in-memory generated identifiers; therefore, she must fetch a new *hi*. This time, she gets from the database the value 7. Based on this *hi*, Jo can generate in-memory the identifiers with values 6 and 7.

7.  Ned uses the in-memory generated identifier with value 2 to insert a new row.

8.  Ned uses the in-memory generated identifier with value 3 to insert a new row.

9.  Ned has no more in-memory generated identifier; therefore, he must fetch a new *hi*. This time, he gets from the database the value 9. Based on this *hi*, Ned can generate in-memory the identifiers with values 8 and 9.

## Dealing with External Systems

Now, let's revisit the section titled "Dealing with External Systems" from **Item 66**. Remember that the initial_value is 1 and the increment_size is 100.

First, the application fetches a new *hi* (e.g., 101). Next, the application inserts three Authors with the generated in-memory identifiers 1, 2, and 3.

Further, the external system tries to insert a row in the author table. This action was simulated by a native INSERT that relies on NEXTVAL('hilo_sequence') to fetch the next sequence value. Executing the NEXTVAL('hilo_sequence') to fetch the next sequence value will return 201. This time, the external system will successfully insert a row with identifier 201. If our application continues to insert more rows (while the external system doesn't) then, at some moment, the new *hi* 301 will be fetched. This *hi* will be the new top boundary identifier while the exclusive lower boundary identifier will be 301 - 100 = 201; therefore, the next row identifier will be 202.

Looks like the external system can live happily and work next to this application, thanks to the pooled algorithm.

> In contrast to the classical hi/lo algorithm, the Hibernate-specific pooled algorithm doesn't cause issues to external systems that want to interact with our tables. In other words, external systems can concurrently insert rows in

the tables relying on pooled algorithm. Nevertheless, old versions of Hibernate can raise exceptions caused by INSERT statements that are triggered by external systems that use the lowest boundary as an identifier. This is a good reason to update to Hibernate's latest versions (e.g., Hibernate 5.x), which have fixed this issue. This way, you can take advantage of the pooled algorithm with no worries.

The complete application is available on GitHub[4].

## The Pooled-Lo Algorithm

Considering the Author entity, the pooled-lo algorithm can be set up as follows:

```
@Entity
public class Author implements Serializable {

    private static final long serialVersionUID = 1L;

    @Id
    @GeneratedValue(strategy = GenerationType.SEQUENCE,
                generator = "hilopooled")
    @GenericGenerator(name = "hilopooled",
                strategy = "org.hibernate.id.enhanced.SequenceStyleGenerator",
        parameters = {
            @Parameter(name = "sequence_name", value = "hilo_sequence"),
            @Parameter(name = "initial_value", value = "1"),
            @Parameter(name = "increment_size", value = "100"),
            @Parameter(name = "optimizer", value = "pooled-lo")
        }
    )
    private Long id;
    ...
}
```

---

[4]HibernateSpringBootPooled

Notice the value of the `optimizer` parameter, which instructs Hibernate to use the pooled-lo built-in optimizer. Employing this algorithm results in the following CREATE statement for the `hilo_sequence` (the same statement as in the case of the pooled algorithm):

**CREATE**

```
sequence hilo_sequence start 1 increment 100
```

Notice the `increment 100` part (or, generally speaking, the `increment increment_size` part).

The pooled-lo is an optimization of hi/lo similar with pooled. This time, the strategy of this algorithm fetches from the database the current sequence value and uses it as the in-memory inclusive lowest boundary identifier. The number of in-memory generated identifiers is equal to `increment_size`.

Let's put these words in a graphical representation. Figure 7-3 shows the step-by-step process for how pooled-lo works for Ned and Jo (`initial_value` of *hi* is 1, and `increment_size` is 2).

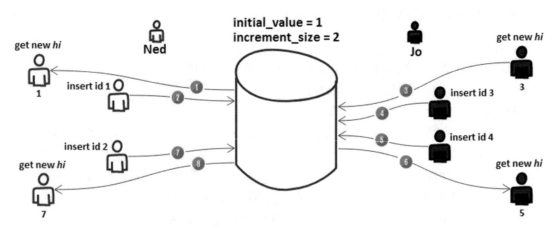

***Figure 7-3.*** *The pooled-lo algorithm*

1. Ned starts a transaction, fetches from the database a new *hi*, and obtains the value 1.

2. Ned has two in-memory generated identifiers (1 and 2). He uses the identifier with value 1 to insert a row.

3. Jo starts her transaction and fetches from the database a new *hi*. She obtains the value 3.

4. Jo has two in-memory generated identifiers (3 and 4). She uses the identifier with value 3 to insert a row.

5. Jo triggers one more insert having the in-memory identifier with value 4.

6. Jo doesn't have more in-memory generated identifiers; therefore, it must fetch a new *hi*. This time, she gets from the database the value 5. Based on this *hi*, Jo can generate in-memory the identifiers with values 5 and 6.

7. Ned uses the in-memory generated identifier with value 2 to insert a new row.

8. Ned has no more in-memory generated identifiers; therefore, he must fetch a new *hi*. This time, he gets from the database the value 7. Based on this *hi*, Ned can generate in-memory the identifiers with values 7 and 8.

## Dealing with External Systems

Now, let's revisit the section titled "Dealing with External Systems" from **Item 66**. Remember that the `initial_value` is 1 and the `increment_size` is 100.

First, the application fetches a new *hi* (e.g., 1). Next, the application inserts three `Authors` with the generated in-memory identifiers 1, 2, and 3.

Further, the external system tries to insert a row into the `author` table. This action was simulated by a native `INSERT` that relies on `NEXTVAL('hilo_sequence')` to fetch the next sequence value. Executing `NEXTVAL('hilo_sequence')` to fetch the next sequence value will return 101. This time, the external system will successfully insert a row with identifier 101. If the application continues to insert more rows (while the external system doesn't), then, at some moment, the new *hi* 201 will be fetched. This *hi* will be the new inclusive lower boundary identifier.

Again, it looks like the external system can live happily and work next to this application, thanks to the pooled-lo algorithm.

The complete application is available on GitHub[5].

---

[5]HibernateSpringBootPooledLo

# Item 68: How to Correctly Override equals() and hashCode()

Overriding equals() and hashCode() in entities can be a delicate task because it's not the same as in the case of Plain Old Java Objects (POJO) and Java Beans. The main statement to consider is that **Hibernate requires that an entity must be equal to itself across all its state transitions (*transient(new), managed(persistent), detached and removed*)**. If you need a quick remainder about Hibernate entity state transitions, consider reading **Appendix A** (at the end of it).

To detect the entity changes, Hibernate uses its internal mechanism known as Dirty Checking. This mechanism doesn't use equals() and hashCode(), but, conforming to Hibernate documentation, if entities are stored in a Set or are reattached to a new Persistence Context, then the developer should override equals() and hashCode(). Moreover, synchronizing both sides of a bidirectional association via the helper methods requires you to override equals() and hashCode() as well. So, there are three scenarios that involve overriding equals() and hashCode().

In order to learn how to override equals() and hashCode() to respect the consistency of entity equality across all its state transitions, the developer must test several scenarios.

## Building the Unit Test

Start by creating a new entity instance (in *transient* state) and adding it into a Set. The purpose of the unit test is to check the consistency of equality of this *transient* entity from the Set against different state transitions. Consider a *transient* instance of the Book entity stored in a Set, as in the following unit test (the content of the Set don't change during the test):

```
Book book = new Book();
Set<Book> books = new HashSet<>();

@BeforeClass
public static void setUp() {
```

```
    book.setTitle("Modern History");
    book.setIsbn("001-100-000-111");

    books.add(book);
}
```

Let's start by checking the consistency of equality between the book that has never been persisted and the Set content:

```
@Test
public void A_givenBookInSetWhenContainsThenTrue() throws Exception {

    assertTrue(books.contains(book));
}
```

Further, the book passes from the *transient* to *managed* state transition. At first assertion point, the state of book is *transient*. For a database-generated identifier, the id of book should be null. For an assigned identifier, the id of book should be non-null. Therefore, depending on the case, the test relies on assertNull() or assertNotNull(). After persisting the book entity (state *managed*), the test checks that the identifier of book is non-null and the Set contains book:

```
@Test
public void B_givenBookWhenPersistThenSuccess() throws Exception {

    assertNull(book.getId());
    // for assigned identifier, assertNotNull(book.getId());

    entityManager.persistAndFlush(book);
    assertNotNull(book.getId());

    assertTrue(books.contains(book));
}
```

The next test sets a new title for the detached book. Further, the book entity is merged (in other words, Hibernate loads in the Persistence Context an entity containing the latest data from the database and updates it to mirror the book entity). At the

449

assertion point, the test checks the consistency of equality between the returned (*managed*) mergedBook entity and the Set contents:

```
@Test
public void C_givenBookWhenMergeThenSuccess() throws Exception {

    book.setTitle("New Modern History");
    assertTrue(books.contains(book));

    Book mergedBook = entityManager.merge(book);
    entityManager.flush();

    assertTrue(books.contains(mergedBook));
}
```

Further, the foundBook entity is loaded via EntityManager#find(Book.class, book. getId()). At the assertion point, the test checks the consistency of equality between foundBook (*managed* entity) and the Set content:

```
@Test
public void D_givenBookWhenFindThenSuccess() throws Exception {

    Book foundBook = entityManager.find(Book.class, book.getId());
    entityManager.flush();

    assertTrue(books.contains(foundBook));
}
```

Further, the foundBook entity is fetched via EntityManager#find(Book.class, book. getId()). Afterward, it's explicitly detached via the detach() method. Finally, the test checks the consistency of equality between this detached entity and the Set contents:

```
@Test
public void E_givenBookWhenFindAndDetachThenSuccess() throws Exception {

    Book foundBook = entityManager.find(Book.class, book.getId());
    entityManager.detach(foundBook);

    assertTrue(books.contains(foundBook));
}
```

In the last test, the foundBook entity is fetched via EntityManager#find(Book.class, book.getId()). Afterward, this entity is removed via the EntityManager#remove() method and the test checks the consistency of equality between the removed entity and the Set contents. Finally, the entity is removed from Set and asserted again:

```
@Test
public void F_givenBookWhenFindAndRemoveThenSuccess() throws Exception {

    Book foundBook = entityManager.find(Book.class, book.getId());
    entityManager.remove(foundBook);
    entityManager.flush();

    assertTrue(books.contains(foundBook));

    books.remove(foundBook);

    assertFalse(books.contains(foundBook));
}
```

Okay, so far so good! Now, let's override equals() and hashCode() in different ways and see which approaches pass the test.

# Best Approaches for Overriding equals( ) and hashCode( )

An entity that passes the test is an entity equal to itself across all its state transitions (*transient, attached, detached,* and *removed*).

## Using a Business Key

A *business key* is an entity field that is unique. It's not nullable or updatable, meaning that it is assigned when the entity is created and remains unchanged (e.g., SSN, ISBN, CNP, etc.). For example, the following entity has an isbn field as its business key:

```
@Entity
public class BusinessKeyBook implements Serializable {

    private static final long serialVersionUID = 1L;
```

```
    @Id
    @GeneratedValue(strategy = GenerationType.IDENTITY)
    private Long id;

    private String title;

    @Column(nullable = false, unique = true, updatable = false, length = 50)
    private String isbn;

    // getter and setters omitted for brevity
}
```

Since isbn is known from the moment of creating the entity, it can be used in equals()
and hashCode() as follows:

```
@Override
public boolean equals(Object obj) {

    if (this == obj) {
        return true;
    }

    if (obj == null) {
        return false;
    }

    if (getClass() != obj.getClass()) {
        return false;
    }

    BusinessKeyBook other = (BusinessKeyBook) obj;
    return Objects.equals(isbn, other.getIsbn());
}

@Override
public int hashCode() {
    return Objects.hash(isbn);
}
```

> Business key equality passes the test. This is the best choice for overriding equals() and hashCode(). However, there are entities that don't have a business key. In such cases, other approaches should be considered.

## Using @NaturalId

Annotating a business key with @NaturalId transforms this field in a natural identifier of the entity (by default, the natural identifier is immutable). The isbn number of a book is a typical natural identifier. The natural identifier is not a replacement for the entity identifier. The entity identifier can be a surrogate key that is the perfect fit for not pressuring memory for both table and index pages. The entity identifier can be used to fetch entities as usual. In addition, Hibernate-specific APIs allow you to fetch the entity by the associated natural key via dedicated methods. **Item 69** dissects this topic in detail.

```
@Entity
public class NaturalIdBook implements Serializable {

    private static final long serialVersionUID = 1L;

    @Id
    @GeneratedValue(strategy = GenerationType.IDENTITY)
    private Long id;

    private String title;

    @NaturalId
    @Column(nullable = false, updatable = false, unique = true, length = 50)
    private String isbn;

    // getters and setters omitted for brevity
}
```

Since isbn is known from the moment of creating the entity, it can be used in equals() and hashCode() as follows:

```
@Override
public boolean equals(Object obj) {
```

```
    if (this == obj) {
        return true;
    }

    if (obj == null) {
        return false;
    }

    if (getClass() != obj.getClass()) {
        return false;
    }

    BusinessKeyBook other = (BusinessKeyBook) obj;
    return Objects.equals(isbn, other.getIsbn());
}

@Override
public int hashCode() {
    return Objects.hash(isbn);
}
```

@NaturalId equality passes the test. This is the best choice for overriding equals() and hashCode() when the business key should be used for fetching entities via the Hibernate ORM API as well.

## Manually Assigned Identifier

When the entity identifier is manually assigned, the entity looks as follows:

```
@Entity
public class IdManBook implements Serializable {

    private static final long serialVersionUID = 1L;

    @Id
    private Long id;
```

```
    private String title;
    private String isbn;

    // getters and setters omitted for brevity
}
```

During the creation of this entity, the code must call setId() to explicitly set an identifier. So, the entity identifier is known from the first moment. This means that the entity identifier can be used to override equals() and hashCode() as follows:

```
@Override
public boolean equals(Object obj) {

    if (this == obj) {
        return true;
    }

    if (obj == null) {
        return false;
    }

    if (getClass() != obj.getClass()) {
        return false;
    }

    IdManBook other = (IdManBook) obj;
    return Objects.equals(id, other.getId());
}

@Override
public int hashCode() {
    return Objects.hash(id);
}
```

The manually assigned identifiers equality pass the test. This is a good choice for overriding equals() and hashCode() when there is no need to use an auto-incremented entity identifier.

# Database-Generated Identifiers

The auto-incremented entity identifier is usually the most commonly used entity. The entity identifier of a *transient* entity is known only after a database round trip. A typical entity relies on the IDENTITY generator as follows:

```
@Entity
public class IdGenBook implements Serializable {

    private static final long serialVersionUID = 1L;

    @Id
    @GeneratedValue(strategy = GenerationType.IDENTITY)
    private Long id;

    private String title;
    private String isbn;

    // getters and setters omitted for brevity
}
```

Relying on the generated entity identifier for overriding equals() and hashCode() is a little bit tricky. The correct implementation is listed here:

```
@Override
public boolean equals(Object obj) {

    if(obj == null) {
        return false;
    }

    if (this == obj) {
        return true;
    }

    if (getClass() != obj.getClass()) {
        return false;
    }

    IdGenBook other = (IdGenBook) obj;
    return id != null && id.equals(other.getId());
}
```

```
@Override
public int hashCode() {
    return 2021;
}
```

There are two important lines in this implementation. Both of them are constructed with respect to the fact that a *transient* object has a null ID, and after it is persisted and become *managed*, it has a valid (non-null) ID. This means that the same object can have different IDs in different state transitions; therefore a hashCode() based on an ID (e.g., Objects.hash(getId())) will return two different values (in other words, this object is not equal to itself across the state transitions; it will not be found in the Set). Returning a constant from hashCode() will solve the problem.

```
return 2021;
```

Further, the equality test should be done as follows:

```
return id != null && id.equals(other.getId());
```

If the current object ID is null then equals() returns false. If equals() was executed, it means that the involved objects are not references of the same object; therefore they are two *transient* objects or a *transient* and a non-*transient* object and such objects cannot be equal. Two objects are considered equal only if the current object ID is not null and is equal with the other object ID. This means that two objects with null IDs are considered equal only if they are references of the same object. This is achievable because hashCode() returns a constant; therefore, for null IDs, we rely on Object reference equality.

> Returning a constant value from hashCode() will help you meet the Hibernate requirement mentioned here, but may affect the performance in the case of huge Sets (or Maps), since all objects will land in the same hash bucket. Nevertheless, combining huge Sets and Hibernate will lead to performance penalties that surpass this concern. Therefore, there is no problem in returning a constant value from hashCode(). As a rule of thumb, it's better to use small result sets to avoid a plethora of performance penalties.

This implementation passes the test. This is the recommended way to override `equals()` and `hashCode()` based on the database-generated identifier.

# Approaches for Overriding equals( ) and hashCode( ) that Must Be Avoided

An entity that doesn't pass the test is an entity considered not equal to itself across all its state transitions (*transient, attached, detached,* and *removed*).

## Default Implementation (JVM)

Relying on the default `equals()` and `hashCode()` means not overriding any of them explicitly:

```
@Entity
public class DefaultBook implements Serializable {

    private static final long serialVersionUID = 1L;

    @Id
    @GeneratedValue(strategy = GenerationType.IDENTITY)
    private Long id;

    private String title;
    private String isbn;

    // getters and setters omitted for brevity
    // no explicit equals() and hashCode()
}
```

When these methods are not overridden, Java will use their default implementations. Unfortunately, the default implementation is not really serving the goal of determining if two objects have the same value. By default, `equals()` considers that two objects are equal if and only if they are represented by the same memory address (same object references), while hashCode() returns an integer representation of the object memory address. This is a native function known as the *identity hash code*.

In these coordinates, the default implementation of equals() and hashCode() will fail the following tests with java.lang.AssertionError: C_givenBookWhenMergeThenSuccess(), D_givenBookWhenFindThenSuccess(), E_givenBookWhenFindAndDetachThenSuccess() and F_givenBookWhenFindAndRemoveThenSuccess(). This happens because tests C, D, E, and F assert equality between objects as mergedBook and foundBook, which have different memory addresses than book.

> Relying on default equals() and hashCode() is a bad decision.

## Database-Generated Identifiers

A database-generated identifier is commonly employed via the IDENTITY generator as follows:

```
@Entity
public class IdBook implements Serializable {

    private static final long serialVersionUID = 1L;

    @Id
    @GeneratedValue(strategy = GenerationType.IDENTITY)
    private Long id;

    private String title;
    private String isbn;

    // getters and setters omitted for brevity
}
```

You can override equals() and hashCode() based on the database-generated identifiers as follows:

```
@Override
public boolean equals(Object obj) {
```

```
    if (this == obj) {
        return true;
    }

    if (obj == null) {
        return false;
    }

    if (getClass() != obj.getClass()) {
        return false;
    }

    final IdBook other = (IdBook) obj;
    if (!Objects.equals(this.id, other.id)) {
        return false;
    }

    return true;
}

@Override
public int hashCode() {
    int hash = 3;
    hash = 89 * hash + Objects.hashCode(this.id);

    return hash;
}
```

The A_givenBookInSetWhenContainsThenTrue() is the only test that passes. The rest of them will fail with java.lang.AssertionError. This happens because tests B, C, D, E, and F asserts equality between objects that have non-null IDs and the book stored in the Set whose ID is null.

> Avoid relying on database-generated identifiers to override equals() and hashCode().

# Lombok @EqualsAndHashCode

Since Lombok is so popular these days, it is commonly used in entities as well. One of the most often used Lombok annotation in entities is @EqualsAndHashCode. This annotation generates equals() and hashCode() conforming to the Lombok documentation. However, are the generated equals() and hashCode() correct/proper for these entities? Typically, the following code is encountered in production:

```
@Entity
@EqualsAndHashCode
public class LombokDefaultBook implements Serializable {

    private static final long serialVersionUID = 1L;

    @Id
    @GeneratedValue(strategy = GenerationType.IDENTITY)
    private Long id;

    private String title;
    private String isbn;

    // getters and setters omitted for brevity
}
```

Lombok will generate something as follows:

```
public boolean equals(Object o) {
    if (o == this) {
        return true;
    }

    if (!(o instanceof LombokDefaultBook)) {
        return false;
    }

    LombokDefaultBook other = (LombokDefaultBook) o;
    if (!other.canEqual(this)) {
        return false;
    }
```

```
    Object this$id = getId();
    Object other$id = other.getId();
    if (this$id == null ? other$id != null : !this$id.equals(other$id)) {
        return false;
    }

    Object this$title = getTitle();
    Object other$title = other.getTitle();
    if (this$title == null ? other$title != null :
                        !this$title.equals(other$title)) {
        return false;
    }

    Object this$isbn = getIsbn();
    Object other$isbn = other.getIsbn();
    return this$isbn == null ? other$isbn == null :
                        this$isbn.equals(other$isbn);
}

protected boolean canEqual(Object other) {
    return other instanceof LombokDefaultBook;
}

public int hashCode() {
    int PRIME = 59; int result = 1;
    Object $id = getId();
    result = result * 59 + ($id == null ? 43 : $id.hashCode());
    Object $title = getTitle();
    result = result * 59 + ($title == null ? 43 : $title.hashCode());
    Object $isbn = getIsbn();
    result = result * 59 + ($isbn == null ? 43 : $isbn.hashCode());

    return result;
}
```

By default, Lombok uses all these fields to generate equals() and hashCode().
Obviously, this is not okay for consistency of equality. Running these tests reveals that
this implementation passes only the A_givenBookInSetWhenContainsThenTrue() test.

---

Relying on the default Lombok @EqualsAndHashCode to override equals()
and hashCode() is a bad decision. Another common scenario consists
of excluding fields such as title and isbn and relying only on id,
@EqualsAndHashCode(exclude = {"title", "isbn"}). This can be
useful in the case of manually assigned identifiers, but is useless in the case
of database-generated identifiers.

---

Some of the Lombok annotations are shortcuts for other Lombok annotations.
In the case of entities, avoid using @Data, which is a shortcut for
@ToString, @EqualsAndHashCode, @Getter on all fields, @Setter on all
non-final fields, and @RequiredArgsConstructor. Rather only use the
@Getter and @Setter methods and implement equals(), hashCode(),
and toString() methods as you saw in this item.

---

Done! The source code is available on GitHub[6].

# Item 69: How to Use Hibernate-Specific @NaturalId in Spring Style

Hibernate ORM provides support for declaring a business key as a natural ID via the
@NaturalId annotation. This feature is specific to Hibernate, but it can be adapted to be
used in Spring style.

The business keys must be unique (e.g., book ISBN, people SSN, CNP, etc.). An entity
can have at the same time an identifier (e.g., auto-generated identifier) and one or more
natural IDs.

---

[6]HibernateSpringBootLombokEqualsAndHashCode

If the entity has a single @NaturalId, then the developer can find it via the Session.bySimpleNaturalId() method (and its flavors). If the entity has more than one @NaturalId (an entity can have a compound natural ID), then the developer can find it via the Session.byNaturalId() method (and its flavors).

Natural IDs can be mutable or immutable (default). You can switch between mutable and immutable by writing: @NaturalId(mutable = true). It is advisable that a field marked as @NaturalId be marked with @Column as well, most commonly like this:

- Immutable natural ID:

  ```
  @Column(nullable = false, updatable = false, unique = true)
  ```

- Mutable natural ID:

  ```
  @Column(nullable = false, updatable = true, unique = true)
  ```

In addition, equals() and hashCode() should be implemented to be natural ID-centric.

Natural IDs can be cached in the Second Level Cache, as explained in **Item 70**. This can be very useful in web applications. Natural IDs are a perfect fit as part of bookmarkable URLs (e.g., isbn is a natural ID and query parameter in the http://bookstore.com/books?isbn=001 request); therefore, the data can be fetched based on the information sent by the client.

Based on these statements, the following Book entity contains a natural ID named isbn:

```
@Entity
public class Book implements Serializable {

    private static final long serialVersionUID = 1L;

    @Id
    @GeneratedValue(strategy = GenerationType.IDENTITY)
    private Long id;

    private String title;
    private int price;
```

```
@NaturalId(mutable = false)
@Column(nullable = false, updatable = false, unique = true, length = 50)
private String isbn;

// getters and setters omitted for brevity

@Override
public boolean equals(Object o) {

    if (this == o) {
        return true;
    }

    if (getClass() != o.getClass()) {
        return false;
    }

    Book other = (Book) o;
    return Objects.equals(isbn, other.getIsbn());
}

@Override
public int hashCode() {
    return Objects.hash(isbn);
}

@Override
public String toString() {
    return "Book{" + "id=" + id + ", title=" + title
            + ", isbn=" + isbn + ", price=" + price + '}';
}
}
```

Finding Books by natural ID in Spring style starts by defining an interface suggestively named NaturalRepository. This is needed to fine tune the built-in JpaRepository repository by adding two more methods: findBySimpleNaturalId() and findByNaturalId():

```
@NoRepositoryBean
public interface NaturalRepository<T, ID extends Serializable>
                                    extends JpaRepository<T, ID> {

    // use this method when your entity has a single field annotated with
    @NaturalId
    Optional<T> findBySimpleNaturalId(ID naturalId);

    // use this method when your entity has more than one field annotated with
    @NaturalId
    Optional<T> findByNaturalId(Map<String, Object> naturalIds);
}
```

Next, you extend the SimpleJpaRepository class and implement the
NaturalRepository. This allows you to customize the base repository by adding the
methods. In other words, you can extend the persistence *technology-specific* repository
base class and use this extension as the custom base class for the repository proxies:

```
@Transactional(readOnly = true)
public class NaturalRepositoryImpl<T, ID extends Serializable>
    extends SimpleJpaRepository<T, ID> implements NaturalRepository<T, ID> {

    private final EntityManager entityManager;

    public NaturalRepositoryImpl(JpaEntityInformation entityInformation,
                                    EntityManager entityManager) {
        super(entityInformation, entityManager);

        this.entityManager = entityManager;
    }

    @Override
    public Optional<T> findBySimpleNaturalId(ID naturalId) {

        Optional<T> entity = entityManager.unwrap(Session.class)
            .bySimpleNaturalId(this.getDomainClass())
            .loadOptional(naturalId);

        return entity;
    }
```

```
    @Override
    public Optional<T> findByNaturalId(Map<String, Object> naturalIds) {

        NaturalIdLoadAccess<T> loadAccess
            = entityManager.unwrap(Session.class)
                .byNaturalId(this.getDomainClass());
        naturalIds.forEach(loadAccess::using);

        return loadAccess.loadOptional();
    }
}
```

Further, you have to tell Spring to use this customized repository base class in place of the default one. This can be accomplished pretty easily via the repositoryBaseClass attribute of the @EnableJpaRepositories annotation:

```
@SpringBootApplication
@EnableJpaRepositories(repositoryBaseClass = NaturalRepositoryImpl.class)
public class MainApplication {

    ...
}
```

# Testing Time

Now, let's try to use @NaturalId in Spring style based on the previous implementation. First, define a classical Spring repository for the Book entity. This time, extend NaturalRepository as follows:

```
@Repository
public interface BookRepository<T, ID>
        extends NaturalRepository<Book, Long> {
}
```

Further, let's persist two books (two Book instances). One with isbn equal to *001-AR* and other with isbn equal to *002-RH*. Since isbn is the natural ID, let's fetch the first Book as follows:

```
Optional<Book> foundArBook
    = bookRepository.findBySimpleNaturalId("001-AR");
```

The SQL statements triggered behind the scenes are as follows:

```
SELECT
  book_.id AS id1_0_
FROM book book_
WHERE book_.isbn = ?
```

```
SELECT
  book0_.id AS id1_0_0_,
  book0_.isbn AS isbn2_0_0_,
  book0_.price AS price3_0_0_,
  book0_.title AS title4_0_0_
FROM book book0_
WHERE book0_.id = ?
```

There are two queries?! Yes, you saw right! The first SELECT is triggered to fetch the entity identifier that corresponds to the specified natural ID. The second SELECT is triggered to fetch the entity by the identifier fetched via the first SELECT. Mainly, this behavior is dictated by how the entities are stored by their identifier in the Persistence Context.

> Obviously, triggering two SELECT statements can be interpreted as a potential performance penalty. Nevertheless, if the entity is present (already loaded) in the current Persistence Context, then neither of these two statements is triggered. In addition, the Second Level Cache can be used to optimize the entity identifier retrieval, as described in **Item 70**.

## Compound Natural ID

A compound natural ID is obtained when multiple fields are annotated with @NaturalId. For a compound natural ID, the developer must perform the find operations by specifying all of them; otherwise, the result is an exception of type: Entity [...] defines its natural-id with n properties but only k were specified.

For example, let's say the Book entity has the sku field as another natural ID. So, isbn and sku represent a compound natural ID:

```java
@Entity
public class Book implements Serializable {

    private static final long serialVersionUID = 1L;

    @Id
    @GeneratedValue(strategy = GenerationType.IDENTITY)
    private Long id;

    private String title;
    private int price;

    @NaturalId(mutable = false)
    @Column(nullable = false, updatable = false, unique = true, length = 50)
    private String isbn;

    @NaturalId(mutable = false)
    @Column(nullable = false, updatable = false, unique = true)
    private Long sku;

    //getters and setters omitted for brevity

    @Override
    public boolean equals(Object o) {

        if (this == o) {
            return true;
        }

        if (getClass() != o.getClass()) {
            return false;
        }

        Book other = (Book) o;
        return Objects.equals(isbn, other.getIsbn())
            && Objects.equals(sku, other.getSku());
    }

    @Override
    public int hashCode() {
        return Objects.hash(isbn, sku);
    }
```

```
    @Override
    public String toString() {
        return "Book{" + "id=" + id + ", title=" + title
                + ", isbn=" + isbn + ", price=" + price + ", sku=" + sku + '}';
    }
}
```

Let's assume the existence of a Book identified by the isbn *001-AR* and sku *1*. You can find this Book via findByNaturalId() as follows:

```
Map<String, Object> ids = new HashMap<>();
ids.put("sku", 1L);
ids.put("isbn", "001-AR");

Optional<Book> foundArBook = bookRepository.findByNaturalId(ids);
```

The SQL statements triggered behind the scenes are:

```
SELECT
    book_.id AS id1_0_
FROM book book_
WHERE book_.isbn = ? AND book_.sku = ?

SELECT
    book0_.id AS id1_0_0_,
    book0_.isbn AS isbn2_0_0_,
    book0_.price AS price3_0_0_,
    book0_.sku AS sku4_0_0_,
    book0_.title AS title5_0_0_
FROM book book0_
WHERE book0_.id = ?
```

The complete code is available on GitHub[7].

---

[7]HibernateSpringBootNaturalIdImpl

# Item 70: How to Use Hibernate-Specific @NaturalId and Skip the Entity Identifier Retrieval

Consider **Item 69** before continuing with this one. Further, the Book entity from **Item 69** is considered well known.

Fetching an entity by natural ID requires two SELECT statements. One SELECT fetches the identifier of the entity associated with the given natural ID, and one SELECT fetches the entity by this identifier. The second SELECT statement has nothing special. This SELECT is triggered when the developer calls findById() as well. If the entity associated with the given identifier is not in the Persistence Context or Second Level Cache then this SELECT will fetch it from the database. But, the first SELECT is specific only to entities that are fetched by natural ID. Triggering this SELECT every time the entity identifier is unknown represents a performance penalty.

However, Hibernate provides a workaround to this. This workaround is @NaturalIdCache. This annotation is used at the entity level to specify that the natural ID values associated with the annotated entity should be cached in the Second Level Cache (if no region is specified then {*entity-name*}##NaturalId is used). Besides @NaturalIdCache, the entity can be annotated with @Cache as well (it's not mandatory to have both annotations at the same time). This way, the entity itself is cached as well. Nevertheless, when @Cache is used, it is important to be aware of the following notice referring to choosing the cache strategy.

> The READ_ONLY caching strategy is an option only for immutable entities. The TRANSACTIONAL caching strategy is specific to JTA environments and has bad performance caused by its synchronous caching mechanism. The NONSTRICT_READ_WRITE caching strategy will rely on the *read-through* data fetching strategy; therefore, the first SELECT is still needed to bring data into the Second Level Cache. Finally, the READ_WRITE caching strategy is an asynchronous *write-through* cache concurrency strategy that serves the purpose here. Details are available in **Appendix G**.

At persist time, if the entity identifier is known (e.g., there are manually assigned IDs, SEQUENCE and TABLE generators, etc.) then, next to the natural ID, the entity itself is cached via *write-through*. Therefore, fetching this entity by its natural ID will not hit the database (no SQL statements are needed). On the other hand, if the entity identifier is unknown at persist time, then the entity itself is not cached via *write-through*. With the IDENTITY generator (or the *native* generator type), only the specified natural ID and the database returned natively generated identity value are cached. At fetching time, the identifier of the entity associated with this natural ID is fetched from the Second Level Cache. Further, the corresponding entity is fetched from the database via a SELECT statement and is stored in the Second Level Cache via the *read-through* data fetching strategy. Subsequent fetches will not hit the database. However, putting entities with database-generated IDs in the Second Level Cache on insert is an open issue with major priority at HHH-7964[8].

## Using @NaturalIdCache Solely

Adding only @NaturalIdCache to the Book entity will result in the following code:

```
@Entity
@NaturalIdCache
public class Book implements Serializable {

    private static final long serialVersionUID = 1L;

    @Id
    @GeneratedValue(strategy = GenerationType.IDENTITY)
    private Long id;

    private String title;
    private int price;
```

---

[8]https://hibernate.atlassian.net/browse/HHH-7964

```
@NaturalId(mutable = false)
@Column(nullable = false, updatable = false, unique = true, length = 50)
private String isbn;

// code omitted for brevity
}
```

Consider that a Book was persisted in the database with the database-generated id *1* and the isbn *001-AR*. The log output reveals the following sequence of relevant actions in the current transaction:

```
begin
    Executing identity-insert immediately
    insert into book (isbn, price, title) values (?, ?, ?)
    Natively generated identity: 1
committing
```

You can fetch (for the first time) this entity by natural ID as follows:

```
Optional<Book> foundArBook
    = bookRepository.findBySimpleNaturalId("001-AR");
```

The natural ID is fetched from the Second Level Cache. The relevant log is shown here:

```
begin
    Getting cached data from region [`Book##NaturalId` (AccessType[read-
        write])] by key [com.bookstore.entity.Book##NaturalId[001-AR]]
    Cache hit : region = `Book##NaturalId`, key =
        `com.bookstore.entity.Book##NaturalId[001-AR]`
    ...
```

The Book was not cached in the Second Level Cache; therefore, it is fetched from the database:

```
    ...
    select book0_.id as id1_0_0_, book0_.isbn as isbn2_0_0_, book0_.price as
        price3_0_0_, book0_.title as title4_0_0_ from book book0_ where
        book0_.id=?
    Done materializing entity [com.bookstore.entity.Book#1]
committing
```

> Using only @NaturalIdCache will cache the natural IDs in the Second Level
> Cache. Therefore, it eliminates the SELECT needed to fetch the unknown
> identifier of the entity associated with the given natural ID. The entities are
> not cached in the Second Level Cache. Of course, they are still cached in the
> Persistence Context.

## Using @NaturalIdCache and @Cache

Adding @NaturalIdCache and @Cache to the Book entity will result in the following
code:

```
@Entity
@NaturalIdCache
@Cache(usage = CacheConcurrencyStrategy.READ_WRITE, region = "Book")
public class Book implements Serializable {

    private static final long serialVersionUID = 1L;

    @Id
    @GeneratedValue(strategy = GenerationType.IDENTITY)
    private Long id;

    private String title;
    private int price;

    @NaturalId(mutable = false)
    @Column(nullable = false, updatable = false, unique = true, length = 50)
    private String isbn;

    // code omitted for brevity
}
```

Consider that a Book was persisted in the database with the database-generated id *1* and
the isbn *001-AR*. The log output reveals the following sequence of relevant actions in the
current transaction:

```
begin
    Executing identity-insert immediately
    insert into book (isbn, price, title) values (?, ?, ?)
    Natively generated identity: 1
committing
```

You can fetch (for the first time) this entity by natural ID as follows:

```
Optional<Book> foundArBook
    = bookRepository.findBySimpleNaturalId("001-AR");
```

The natural ID is fetched from the Second Level Cache. The relevant log is shown here:

```
begin
    Getting cached data from region [`Book##NaturalId` (AccessType[read-
        write])] by key [com.bookstore.entity.Book##NaturalId[001-AR]]
    Cache hit : region = `Book##NaturalId`, key =
        `com.bookstore.entity.Book##NaturalId[001-AR]`
    ...
```

Further, the JPA persistence provider tries to fetch the Book entity, but this was not cached in the Second Level Cache yet (remember HHH-7964[9]). The log output is pretty clear:

```
    ...
    Getting cached data from region [`Book` (AccessType[read-write])]
        by key [com.bookstore.entity.Book#1]
    Cache miss : region = `Book`, key = `com.bookstore.entity.Book#1`
    ...
```

Since the Book is not in the Second Level Cache, the Book must be loaded from the database:

```
    ...
    select book0_.id as id1_0_0_, book0_.isbn as isbn2_0_0_, book0_.price as
        price3_0_0_, book0_.title as title4_0_0_ from book book0_
        where book0_.id=?
    ...
```

---

[9]https://hibernate.atlassian.net/browse/HHH-7964

This time the Book is cached via *read-through*. The log is relevant again:

```
...
Adding entity to second-level cache: [com.bookstore.entity.Book#1]
Caching data from load [region=`Book` (AccessType[read-write])] :
    key[com.bookstore.entity.Book#1] ->
    value[CacheEntry(com.bookstore.entity.Book)]
Done entity load : com.bookstore.entity.Book#1
committing
```

Subsequent fetches will not hit the database. Both the natural ID and the entity are in the Second Level Cache.

> Using @NaturalIdCache will cache the natural IDs in the Second Level Cache; therefore, it eliminates the SELECT needed to fetch the unknown identifier of the entity associated with the given natural ID. Adding @Cache to the equation with a READ_WRITE strategy leads to the following two behaviors:
>
> - For IDENTITY (or the *native* generator type), entities will be cached via *read-through* (remember HHH-7964[9]).
>
> - For manually assigned IDs, SEQUENCE and TABLE generators, etc., the entities will be cached via *write-through*, which is obviously the preferable way.
>
> *Database sequences* are the best identifier generator choice when using JPA and Hibernate ORM, but not all databases support them (e.g., while databases such as PostgreSQL, Oracle, SQL Server 2012, DB2, HSQLDB support database sequences, MySQL doesn't). Alternatively, MySQL can rely on the TABLE generator, but this is not a good choice (see **Item 65**). Therefore, in the case of MySQL, it's better to rely on the IDENTITY generator and *read-through* than on the TABLE generator and *write-through*.

The complete code is available on GitHub[10]. This code uses MySQL.

---

[10]HibernateSpringBootNaturalIdCache

# Item 71: How to Define an Association that References a @NaturalId Column

If you are not familiar with Hibernate-specific @NaturalId and how to use it in Spring Boot, consider **Item 69** and **Item 70**.

Consider the following Author entity that defines a natural ID via the email field:

```
@Entity
public class Author implements Serializable {

    private static final long serialVersionUID = 1L;

    @Id
    @GeneratedValue(strategy = GenerationType.IDENTITY)
    private Long id;

    private int age;
    private String name;
    private String genre;

    @NaturalId(mutable = false)
    @Column(nullable = false, updatable = false, unique = true, length = 50)
    private String email;

    ...
}
```

Now, let's assume that the Book entity should define an association that doesn't reference the primary key of the Author. More precisely, this association references the email natural ID. For this, you can rely on @JoinColumn and the referencedColumnName element. The value of this element is the name of the database column that should be used as the foreign key:

```
@Entity
public class Book implements Serializable {

    private static final long serialVersionUID = 1L;

    @Id
    @GeneratedValue(strategy = GenerationType.IDENTITY)
    private Long id;
```

```
    private String title;
    private String isbn;

    @ManyToOne(fetch = FetchType.LAZY)
    @JoinColumn(referencedColumnName = "email")
    private Author author;

    ...
}
```

> Generally speaking, an association can reference any column (not just natural
> ID columns) as long as that column contains unique values.

## Testing Time

Consider the data snapshot shown in Figure 7-4.

**author**

| id | age | email | genre | name |
|----|-----|-------|-------|------|
| 1 | 38 | alicia.tom@gmail.com | Anthology | Alicia Tom |
| 2 | 34 | joana.nimar@gmail.com | History | Joana Nimar |

**book**

| id | isbn | title | author_email |
|----|------|-------|--------------|
| 1 | AT-001 | Anthology of a day | alicia.tom@gmail.com |
| 2 | AT-002 | Anthology gaps | alicia.tom@gmail.com |
| 3 | JN-001 | History of Prague | joana.nimar@gmail.com |

*Figure 7-4.  Data snapshot*

Notice the book.author_email column, which represents the foreign key and references
the author.email column. The following service-method fetches a book by title and calls
getAuthor() to lazy fetch the author as well:

```
@Transactional(readOnly = true)
public void fetchBookWithAuthor() {

    Book book = bookRepository.findByTitle("Anthology gaps");
    Author author = book.getAuthor();
```

```
    System.out.println(book);
    System.out.println(author);
}
```

The SELECT triggered to fetch the author is as follows:

```
SELECT
  author0_.id AS id1_0_0_,
  author0_.age AS age2_0_0_,
  author0_.email AS email3_0_0_,
  author0_.genre AS genre4_0_0_,
  author0_.name AS name5_0_0_
FROM author author0_
WHERE author0_.email = ?
```

The complete application is available on GitHub[11].

# Item 72: How to Obtain Auto-Generated Keys

Consider the following Author entity, which delegates the key generation to the database system:

```
@Entity
public class Author implements Serializable {

    @Id
    @GeneratedValue(strategy = GenerationType.IDENTITY)
    private Long id;

    private int age;
    private String name;
    private String genre;
    ...
}
```

---

[11]HibernateSpringBootReferenceNaturalId

Now, let's see how to retrieve the database auto-generated primary keys via getId(),
JdbcTemplate, and SimpleJdbcInsert.

## Retrieve Auto-Generated Keys via getId()

In JPA style, you can retrieve the auto-generated keys via getId(), as in the following
example:

```
public void insertAuthorGetAutoGeneratedKeyViaGetId() {

    Author author = new Author();

    author.setAge(38);
    author.setName("Alicia Tom");
    author.setGenre("Anthology");

    authorRepository.save(author);

    long pk = author.getId();
    System.out.println("Auto generated key: " + pk);
}
```

## Retrieve Auto-Generated Keys via JdbcTemplate

You can use JdbcTemplate to retrieve the auto-generated keys via the update() method.
This method comes in different flavors, but the signature needed here is:

```
public int update(PreparedStatementCreator psc, KeyHolder
generatedKeyHolder) throws DataAccessException
```

The PreparedStatementCreator is a functional interface that takes an instance
of java.sql.Connection and returns a java.sql.PreparedStatement object.
The KeyHolder object contains the auto-generated key returned by the update()
method. In code, it's as follows:

```
@Repository
public class JdbcTemplateDao implements AuthorDao {

    private static final String SQL_INSERT
        = "INSERT INTO author (age, name, genre) VALUES (?, ?, ?);";
```

```java
private final JdbcTemplate jdbcTemplate;

public JdbcTemplateDao(JdbcTemplate jdbcTemplate) {
    this.jdbcTemplate = jdbcTemplate;
}

@Override
@Transactional
public long insertAuthor(int age, String name, String genre) {

    KeyHolder keyHolder = new GeneratedKeyHolder();

    jdbcTemplate.update(connection -> {
        PreparedStatement ps = connection
            .prepareStatement(SQL_INSERT, Statement.RETURN_GENERATED_KEYS);
        ps.setInt(1, age);
        ps.setString(2, name);
        ps.setString(3, genre);

        return ps;
    }, keyHolder);

    return keyHolder.getKey().longValue();
}
}
```

In this example, the PreparedStatement is instructed to return the auto-generated keys via Statement.RETURN_GENERATED_KEYS. Alternatively, the same thing can be accomplished as follows:

```java
// alternative 1
PreparedStatement ps = connection
    .prepareStatement(SQL_INSERT, new String[]{"id"});

// alternative 2
PreparedStatement ps = connection
    .prepareStatement(SQL_INSERT, new int[] {1});
```

## Retrieve Auto-Generated Keys via SimpleJdbcInsert

Consequently, you can call the `SimpleJdbcInsert.executeAndReturnKey()` method to insert a new record to the author table and get back the auto-generated key:

```
@Repository
public class SimpleJdbcInsertDao implements AuthorDao {

    private final SimpleJdbcInsert simpleJdbcInsert;

    public SimpleJdbcInsertDao(DataSource dataSource) {
        this.simpleJdbcInsert = new SimpleJdbcInsert(dataSource)
            .withTableName("author").usingGeneratedKeyColumns("id");
    }

    @Override
    @Transactional
    public long insertAuthor(int age, String name, String genre) {
        return simpleJdbcInsert.executeAndReturnKey(
            Map.of("age", age, "name", name, "genre", genre)).longValue();
    }
}
```

The complete application is available on GitHub[12].

# Item 73: How to Generate Custom Sequence IDs

**Item 66** and **Item 67** discussed in depth the hi/lo algorithm and its optimizations. Now, let's assume that the application needs custom sequence-based IDs. For example, IDs of type A-0000000001, A-0000000002, A-0000000003... You can generate these kinds of IDs (and any other custom pattern) by extending the Hibernate-specific SequenceStyleGenerator and overriding the generate() and configure() methods, as follows:

```
public class CustomSequenceIdGenerator extends SequenceStyleGenerator {
```

---

[12]HibernateSpringBootReturnGeneratedKeys

```java
public static final String PREFIX_PARAM = "prefix";
public static final String PREFIX_DEFAULT_PARAM = "";
private String prefix;

public static final String NUMBER_FORMAT_PARAM = "numberFormat";
public static final String NUMBER_FORMAT_DEFAULT_PARAM = "%d";
private String numberFormat;

@Override
public Serializable generate(SharedSessionContractImplementor session,
            Object object) throws HibernateException {
    return prefix + String.format(numberFormat,
        super.generate(session, object));
}

@Override
public void configure(Type type, Properties params,
            ServiceRegistry serviceRegistry) throws MappingException {
    super.configure(LongType.INSTANCE, params, serviceRegistry);

    prefix = ConfigurationHelper.getString(
        PREFIX_PARAM, params, PREFIX_DEFAULT_PARAM);
    numberFormat = ConfigurationHelper.getString(
        NUMBER_FORMAT_PARAM, params, NUMBER_FORMAT_DEFAULT_PARAM);
    }
}
```

As the name suggests, the generate() method is called to generate an ID. Its implementation has two steps: it extracts the next value from the sequence via super. generate() and then uses the extracted value to generate a custom ID.

The configure() method is called at instantiation of CustomSequenceIdGenerator. Its implementation has two steps: it sets the Type to LongType since the sequence produces Long values and then it handles the generator parameters set as follows:

```java
@Id
@GeneratedValue(strategy = GenerationType.SEQUENCE,
    generator = "hilopooledlo")
```

```
@GenericGenerator(name = "hilopooledlo",
    strategy = "com.bookstore.generator.id.StringPrefixedSequenceIdGenerator",
    parameters = {
        @Parameter(name = CustomSequenceIdGenerator.SEQUENCE_PARAM,
                    value = "hilo_sequence"),
        @Parameter(name = CustomSequenceIdGenerator.INITIAL_PARAM,
                    value = "1"),
        @Parameter(name = CustomSequenceIdGenerator.OPT_PARAM,
                    value = "pooled-lo"),
        @Parameter(name = CustomSequenceIdGenerator.INCREMENT_PARAM,
                    value = "100"),
        @Parameter(name = CustomSequenceIdGenerator.PREFIX_PARAM,
                    value = "A-"),
        @Parameter(name = CustomSequenceIdGenerator.NUMBER_FORMAT_PARAM,
                    value = "%010d")
    }
)
private String id;
```

Starting from this example, you can implement any kind of custom sequence-based IDs. The complete application is available on GitHub[13].

# Item 74: How to Efficiently Implement a Composite Primary Key

A composite primary key consists of two (or more) columns that together act as the primary key of a given table.

Let's quickly consider several issues about simple and composite primary keys:

- Typically, primary keys (and foreign keys) have a default index, but you can create other indexes as well.

---

[13]HibernateSpringBootCustomSequenceGenerator

- Small primary keys (e.g., numerical keys) result in small indexes. Big primary keys (e.g., composite and UUID keys) result in big indexes. Keeping primary keys small is better. **From a performance perspective (required space and index usage), numerical primary keys are the best choice.**

- Composite primary keys result in big indexes. Since they are slow (think to JOIN statements), they should be avoided. Or, at least minimize the number of involved columns as much as possible since multi-column indexes have a bigger memory footprint too.

- Primary keys can be used in JOIN statements, which is another reason to keep them small.

- Primary keys should be small but still unique. This can be a problem in a clustered environment, where numerical primary keys are prone to conflicts. **To avoid conflicts in clustered environments, most relational databases rely on numerical sequences. In other words, each node from the cluster has its own offset used to generate identifiers.** Alternatively, but not better, is the use of UUID primary keys. UUIDs come with performance penalties in clustered indexes because their lack of sequentiality and the fact that they have a bigger memory footprint too (for details, check the last section of this item).

- Sharing primary keys between tables reduces memory footprint by using fewer indexes and no foreign key columns (see @MapsId, **Item 11**). **Therefore, go for shared primary keys!**

As the third bullet highlights, composite keys are not quite efficient and they should be avoided. If you can simply cannot avoid them, at least implement them correctly. A composite key should respect four rules as follows:

- The composite key class must be `public`
- The composite key class must implement `Serializable`
- The composite key must define `equals()` and `hashCode()`
- The composite key must define a no-arguments constructor

Now, let's assume that `Author` and `Book` are two entities involved a lazy bidirectional @OneToMany association. The `Author` identifier is a composite identifier consisting of name and age columns. The `Book` entity uses this composite key to reference its own `Author`. The `Book` identifier is a typical database-generated numeric identifier.

To define the composite primary key of `Author`, you can rely on the `@Embeddable` - `@EmbeddedId` pair or `@IdClass` JPA annotations.

## Composite key via @Embeddable and @EmbeddedId

The first step consists of extracting the composite key columns in a separate class and annotating it with @Embeddable. So, extract the name and age columns in a class named AuthorId as follows:

```
@Embeddable
public class AuthorId implements Serializable {

    private static final long serialVersionUID = 1L;

    @Column(name = "name")
    private String name;

    @Column(name = "age")
    private int age;

    public AuthorId() {
    }

    public AuthorId(String name, int age) {
        this.name = name;
        this.age = age;
    }
```

```java
public String getName() {
    return name;
}

public int getAge() {
    return age;
}

@Override
public int hashCode() {
    int hash = 3;
    hash = 23 * hash + Objects.hashCode(this.name);
    hash = 23 * hash + this.age;
    return hash;
}

@Override
public boolean equals(Object obj) {

    if (this == obj) {
        return true;
    }

    if (obj == null) {
        return false;
    }

    if (getClass() != obj.getClass()) {
        return false;
    }

    final AuthorId other = (AuthorId) obj;
        if (this.age != other.age) {
        return false;
    }

    if (!Objects.equals(this.name, other.name)) {
        return false;
    }
```

```
        return true;
    }

    @Override
    public String toString() {
        return "AuthorId{" + "name=" + name + ", age=" + age + '}';
    }
}
```

So, AuthorId is the composite primary key of the Author entity. In code, this is equivalent to adding a field of type AuthorId annotated with @EmbeddedId, as follows:

```
@Entity
public class Author implements Serializable {

    private static final long serialVersionUID = 1L;

    @EmbeddedId
    private AuthorId id;

    private String genre;

    @OneToMany(cascade = CascadeType.ALL,
                mappedBy = "author", orphanRemoval = true)
    private List<Book> books = new ArrayList<>();

    public void addBook(Book book) {
        this.books.add(book);
        book.setAuthor(this);
    }

    public void removeBook(Book book) {
        book.setAuthor(null);
        this.books.remove(book);
    }

    public void removeBooks() {
        Iterator<Book> iterator = this.books.iterator();
```

```
        while (iterator.hasNext()) {
            Book book = iterator.next();

            book.setAuthor(null);
            iterator.remove();
        }
    }

    public AuthorId getId() {
        return id;
    }

    public void setId(AuthorId id) {
        this.id = id;
    }

    public String getGenre() {
        return genre;
    }

    public void setGenre(String genre) {
        this.genre = genre;
    }

    public List<Book> getBooks() {
        return books;
    }

    public void setBooks(List<Book> books) {
        this.books = books;
    }

    @Override
    public String toString() {
        return "Author{" + "id=" + id + ", genre=" + genre + '}';
    }
}
```

The Book entity uses the `AuthorId` composite key to reference its own `Author`. For this, the @ManyToOne mapping uses the two columns that are part of the composite key:

```
@Entity
public class Book implements Serializable {

    private static final long serialVersionUID = 1L;

    @Id
    @GeneratedValue(strategy = GenerationType.IDENTITY)
    private Long id;

    private String title;
    private String isbn;

    @ManyToOne(fetch = FetchType.LAZY)
    @JoinColumns({
        @JoinColumn(
            name = "name",
            referencedColumnName = "name"),
        @JoinColumn(
            name = "age",
            referencedColumnName = "age")
    })
    private Author author;

    public Long getId() {
        return id;
    }

    public void setId(Long id) {
        this.id = id;
    }

    public String getTitle() {
        return title;
    }

    public void setTitle(String title) {
        this.title = title;
    }
```

```java
    public String getIsbn() {
        return isbn;
    }
    public void setIsbn(String isbn) {
        this.isbn = isbn;
    }

    public Author getAuthor() {
        return author;
    }

    public void setAuthor(Author author) {
        this.author = author;
    }

    @Override
    public boolean equals(Object obj) {

        if (this == obj) {
            return true;
        }

        if (getClass() != obj.getClass()) {
            return false;
        }

        return id != null && id.equals(((Book) obj).id);
    }

    @Override
    public int hashCode() {
        return 2021;
    }

    @Override
    public String toString() {
        return "Book{" + "id=" + id + ", title="
            + title + ", isbn=" + isbn +      '}';
    }
}
```

## Testing Time

Let's consider several common operations that involve the manipulation of the Author entity. Let's look at the triggered SQL statements.

## Persist an Author and Three Books

First, let's persist an author with three books. Notice how we instantiate AuthorId to create the primary key of the author:

```
@Transactional
public void addAuthorWithBooks() {

    Author author = new Author();
    author.setId(new AuthorId("Alicia Tom", 38));
    author.setGenre("Anthology");

    Book book1 = new Book();
    book1.setIsbn("001-AT");
    book1.setTitle("The book of swords");

    Book book2 = new Book();
    book2.setIsbn("002-AT");
    book2.setTitle("Anthology of a day");

    Book book3 = new Book();
    book3.setIsbn("003-AT");
    book3.setTitle("Anthology today");

    author.addBook(book1);
    author.addBook(book2);
    author.addBook(book3);

    authorRepository.save(author);
}
```

Calling addAuthorWithBooks() will trigger the following SQL statements:

```
SELECT
  author0_.age AS age1_0_1_,
  author0_.name AS name2_0_1_,
```

```
  author0_.genre AS genre3_0_1_,
  books1_.age AS age4_1_3_,
  books1_.name AS name5_1_3_,
  books1_.id AS id1_1_3_,
  books1_.id AS id1_1_0_,
  books1_.age AS age4_1_0_,
  books1_.name AS name5_1_0_,
  books1_.isbn AS isbn2_1_0_,
  books1_.title AS title3_1_0_
FROM author author0_
LEFT OUTER JOIN book books1_
  ON author0_.age = books1_.age
  AND author0_.name = books1_.name
WHERE author0_.age = ?
AND author0_.name = ?

INSERT INTO author (genre, age, name)
  VALUES (?, ?, ?)

INSERT INTO book (age, name, isbn, title)
  VALUES (?, ?, ?, ?)

INSERT INTO book (age, name, isbn, title)
  VALUES (?, ?, ?, ?)

INSERT INTO book (age, name, isbn, title)
  VALUES (?, ?, ?, ?)
```

The things happen exactly as in the case of a simple primary key. Since this is an explicitly assigned primary key, Hibernate triggers a SELECT to ensure that there are no other records in the database with this ID. Once it is sure about this aspect, Hibernate triggers the proper INSERT statements, one against the author table and three against the book table.

## Find an Author by Name

The name column is part of the composite primary key, but it can be used in queries as well. The following query finds an author by name. Notice how we reference the name column via id:

```
@Query("SELECT a FROM Author a WHERE a.id.name = ?1")
public Author fetchByName(String name);
```

A service-method calling fetchByName() can be written as follows:

```
@Transactional(readOnly = true)
public void fetchAuthorByName() {
    Author author = authorRepository.fetchByName("Alicia Tom");

    System.out.println(author);
}
```

Calling fetchAuthorByName() will trigger the following SELECT statement:

```
SELECT
    author0_.age AS age1_0_,
    author0_.name AS name2_0_,
    author0_.genre AS genre3_0_
FROM author author0_
WHERE author0_.name = ?
```

The things happen exactly as in the case of a simple primary key. A single SELECT is needed to fetch an author by name. Similarly, we can fetch an author by age, which is the other column that is part of the composite key.

## Remove a Book of an Author

Consider that we've loaded an author and their associated books via the following JOIN FETCH query:

```
@Query("SELECT a FROM Author a "
    + "JOIN FETCH a.books WHERE a.id = ?1")
public Author fetchWithBooks(AuthorId id);
```

494

Let's remove the first book via a service-method:

```
@Transactional
public void removeBookOfAuthor() {

    Author author = authorRepository.fetchWithBooks(
        new AuthorId("Alicia Tom", 38));
    author.removeBook(author.getBooks().get(0));
}
```

Calling removeBookOfAuthor() triggers the following SQL statements:

```
SELECT
  author0_.age AS age1_0_0_,
  author0_.name AS name2_0_0_,
  books1_.id AS id1_1_1_,
  author0_.genre AS genre3_0_0_,
  books1_.age AS age4_1_1_,
  books1_.name AS name5_1_1_,
  books1_.isbn AS isbn2_1_1_,
  books1_.title AS title3_1_1_,
  books1_.age AS age4_1_0__,
  books1_.name AS name5_1_0__,
  books1_.id AS id1_1_0__
FROM author author0_
INNER JOIN book books1_
  ON author0_.age = books1_.age
  AND author0_.name = books1_.name
WHERE (author0_.age, author0_.name)=(?, ?)

DELETE FROM book WHERE id = ?
```

The things happen exactly as in the case of a simple primary key. Only notice the WHERE clause of the SELECT statement. The WHERE a.id = ?1 was interpreted as WHERE (author0_.age, author0_.name)=(?, ?).

# Remove an Author

Removing an author will cascade to the associated books as well:

```
@Transactional
public void removeAuthor() {
    authorRepository.deleteById(new AuthorId("Alicia Tom", 38));
}
```

The triggered SQL statements are as follows:

```
SELECT
  author0_.age AS age1_0_0_,
  author0_.name AS name2_0_0_,
  author0_.genre AS genre3_0_0_
FROM author author0_
WHERE author0_.age = ? AND author0_.name = ?

SELECT
  books0_.age AS age4_1_0_,
  books0_.name AS name5_1_0_,
  books0_.id AS id1_1_0_,
  books0_.id AS id1_1_1_,
  books0_.age AS age4_1_1_,
  books0_.name AS name5_1_1_,
  books0_.isbn AS isbn2_1_1_,
  books0_.title AS title3_1_1_
FROM book books0_ WHERE books0_.age = ? AND books0_.name = ?

-- the below DELETE is triggered for each associated book
DELETE FROM book WHERE id = ?

DELETE FROM author
WHERE age = ? AND name = ?
```

The things happen exactly as in the case of a simple primary key. Since the data to delete is not available in the Persistence Context, Hibernate loads this data via two SELECT statements (one SELECT for the author and one for the associated books). Further,

Hibernate performs the deletes. Obviously, relying on deleteById() in this context is not efficient, so to optimize deletion, consider **Item 6**. The complete application is available on GitHub[14].

## Composite key via @IdClass

Relying on @Embeddable is quite simple but is not always possible. Imagine a case in which you cannot modify the class that should become a composite key, so you cannot add @Embeddable. Fortunately, such cases can take advantage of another annotation named @IdClass. This annotation is applied at class-level to the entity that uses the composite key as @IdClass(*name_of_the_composite_key_class*). So, if the AuthorId is the composite key of Author entity, then @IdClass is used as follows:

```
@Entity
@IdClass(AuthorId.class)
public class Author implements Serializable {

    private static final long serialVersionUID = 1L;

    @Id
    private String name;

    @Id
    private int age;

    private String genre;

    @OneToMany(cascade = CascadeType.ALL,
            mappedBy = "author", orphanRemoval = true)
    private List<Book> books = new ArrayList<>();
    ...
}
```

Besides @IdClass, notice that the composite key columns are annotated with @Id. This is needed in place of @EmbeddedId.

---

[14]HibernateSpringBootCompositeKeyEmbeddable

That's all! The rest of code remains the same as in the @Embeddable case, including the testing results. The complete application is available on GitHub[15].

## How About the Universally Unique Identifier (UUID)?

> The most commonly used *synthetic* identifiers (or *surrogate* identifiers) are numerical or UUIDs. In comparison with *natural* keys, the *surrogate* identifiers doesn't have a meaning or a correspondent in our world. A *surrogate* identifier can be generated by a Numerical Sequence Generator (e.g., an identity or sequence) or by a Pseudorandom Number Generator (e.g., a GUID and UUID).

Most commonly, UUID[16] *surrogate* identifiers come into discussion in clustered environments where *surrogate* numerical primary keys are prone to conflicts. UUID primary keys are less prone to conflicts in such environments and simplify replication. For example, in the case of MySQL, UUIDs are used as an alternative to the AUTO_INCREMENT primary key, while in PostgreSQL, as an alternative to (BIG)SERIAL.

> Recall that in clustered environments, most relational databases rely on *numerical sequences* and different offsets per node to avoid the risk of conflicts. Use *numerical sequences* over UUIDs because they require less memory than UUIDs (an UUID requires 16 bytes, while BIGINT requires 8 bytes and INTEGER 4 bytes) and the index usage is more performant. Moreover, since UUID are not sequential, they introduce performance penalties at clustered indexes level. More precisely, we discuss an issue known as *index fragmentation,* which is caused by the fact that UUIDs are random. Some databases (e.g., MySQL 8.0) come with significant improvement of

---

[15]HibernateSpringBootCompositeKeyIdClass
[16]https://www.ietf.org/rfc/rfc4122.txt

mitigating UUID performance penalties (there are three new functions: UUID_ TO_BIN, BIN_TO_UUID, and IS_UUID) while other databases are still prone to these issues. As Rick James highlights, "If you cannot avoid UUIDs (which would be my first recommendation)..." then it is recommended to read his article[17] for a deep understanding of the main issues and potential solutions.

Assuming that you have to use UUID, let's look at the best ways to do it.

## Generate UUID via GenerationType.AUTO

When using JPA, you can assign UUID automatically via GenerationType.AUTO, as in the following example:

```java
import java.util.UUID;
...
@Entity
public class Author implements Serializable {

    private static final long serialVersionUID = 1L;

    @Id
    @GeneratedValue(strategy = GenerationType.AUTO)
    private UUID id;
    ...

    public UUID getId() {
        return id;
    }

    public void setId(UUID id) {
        this.id = id;
    }
    ...
}
```

---

[17]http://mysql.rjweb.org/doc.php/uuid

You can insert an author easily via a service-method, as follows (authorRepository is just a classic Spring repository for the Author entity):

```
public void insertAuthor() {

    Author author = new Author();
    author.setName("Joana Nimar");
    author.setGenre("History");
    author.setAge(34);

    authorRepository.save(author);
}
```

Calling insertAuthor() will lead to the following INSERT statement (notice the highlighted UUID):

```
INSERT INTO author (age, genre, name, id)
  VALUES (?, ?, ?, ?)
Binding:[34, History, Joana Nimar, 3636f5d5-2528-4a17-9a90-758aa416da18]
```

> By default, MySQL 8 maps a java.util.UUID identifier to a BINARY(255) column type, which is way too much. A BINARY(16) should be preferable. So, be sure to adjust your schema accordingly. Via JPA annotations (not recommended in production) you can use columnDefinition as follows:
>
> ```
> @Id
> @GeneratedValue(strategy = GenerationType.AUTO)
> @Column(columnDefinition = "BINARY(16)")
> private UUID id;
> ```
>
> Generally speaking, when the database doesn't have a dedicated type for UUID, use BINARY(16). For Oracle, use RAW(16). PostgreSQL and SQL Server have dedicated data types for UUID.

The GenerationType.AUTO and UUIDs work just fine with insert batching as well.

The complete application is available on GitHub[18].

---

[18]HibernateSpringBootAutoUUID

# Manually Assigned UUID

A UUID can be manually assigned by simply omitting the @GeneratedValue:

```
import java.util.UUID;
...
@Entity
public class Author implements Serializable {

    private static final long serialVersionUID = 1L;

    @Id
    @Column(columnDefinition = "BINARY(16)")
    private UUID id;

    ...

    public UUID getId() {
        return id;
    }

    public void setId(UUID id) {
        this.id = id;
    }
    ...
}
```

Further, you can manually assign a UUID. For example, via the UUID#randomUUID()
method:

```
public void insertAuthor() {

    Author author = new Author();
    author.setId(UUID.randomUUID());
    author.setName("Joana Nimar");
    author.setGenre("History");
    author.setAge(34);

    authorRepository.save(author);
}
```

Calling insertAuthor() will lead to the following INSERT statement (notice the highlighted UUID):

```
INSERT INTO author (age, genre, name, id)
  VALUES (?, ?, ?, ?)
Binding:[34, History, Joana Nimar, 24de5cbe-a542-432e-9e08-b77964dbf0d0]
```

The complete application is available on GitHub[19].

## Hibernate-Specific uuid2

Hibernate can also generate a UUID identifier on your behalf, as follows:

```
import java.util.UUID;
...
@Entity
public class Author implements Serializable {

    private static final long serialVersionUID = 1L;

    @Id
    @Column(columnDefinition = "BINARY(16)")
    @GeneratedValue(generator = "uuid2")
    @GenericGenerator(name = "uuid2", strategy = "uuid2")
    private UUID id;
    ...

    public UUID getId() {
        return id;
    }

    public void setId(UUID id) {
        this.id = id;
    }
    ...
}
```

---

[19]HibernateSpringBootAssignedUUID

> The Hibernate-specific uuid2 generator is compliant with the RFC 4122[20] standard. It works with java.util.UUID, byte[] and String Java types. Hibernate ORM also has a non-compliant RFC 4122 UUID generator named uuid. This legacy UUID generator should be avoided.

The complete application is available on GitHub[21].

# Item 75: How to Define a Relationship in a Composite Key

If you are not familiar with composite primary keys, it is advisable to read **Item 74** before this one. That being said, consider the Author and Book entities in a bidirectional lazy @OneToMany association. The Author has a composite key that consists of the publisher and the name of the author. While the name of the author is a String, the publisher is actually an entity and more authors can have the same publisher. The Publisher entity maps the publisher name and an Unique Registration Code (URC):

```
@Entity
public class Publisher implements Serializable {

    private static final long serialVersionUID = 1L;

    @Id
    @GeneratedValue(strategy = GenerationType.IDENTITY)
    private Long id;

    private int urc;
    private String name;

    public Long getId() {
        return id;
    }
}
```

---

[20]https://www.ietf.org/rfc/rfc4122.txt
[21]HibernateSpringBootUUID2

```java
public void setId(Long id) {
    this.id = id;
}

public int getUrc() {
    return urc;
}

public void setUrc(int urc) {
    this.urc = urc;
}

public String getName() {
    return name;
}

public void setName(String name) {
    this.name = name;
}

@Override
public int hashCode() {
    int hash = 3;
    hash = 79 * hash + this.urc;
    hash = 79 * hash + Objects.hashCode(this.name);
    return hash;
}

@Override
public boolean equals(Object obj) {

    if (this == obj) {
        return true;
    }

    if (obj == null) {
        return false;
    }
```

```
        if (getClass() != obj.getClass()) {
            return false;
        }

        final Publisher other = (Publisher) obj;
        if (this.urc != other.urc) {
            return false;
        }

        if (!Objects.equals(this.name, other.name)) {
            return false;
        }

        return true;
    }

    @Override
    public String toString() {
        return "Publisher{" + "id=" + id + ", urc=" + urc
            + ", name=" + name + '}';
    }
}
```

An author primary key contains the Publisher, so the composite primary key class should define a @ManyToOne relationship, as shown here:

```
@Embeddable
public class AuthorId implements Serializable {

    private static final long serialVersionUID = 1L;

    @ManyToOne
    @JoinColumn(name = "publisher")
    private Publisher publisher;

    @Column(name = "name")
    private String name;

    public AuthorId() {
    }
```

```java
    public AuthorId(Publisher publisher, String name) {
        this.publisher = publisher;
        this.name = name;
    }

    public Publisher getPublisher() {
        return publisher;
    }

    public String getName() {
        return name;
    }

    @Override
    public int hashCode() {
        int hash = 7;
        hash = 97 * hash + Objects.hashCode(this.publisher);
        hash = 97 * hash + Objects.hashCode(this.name);
        return hash;
    }

    @Override
    public boolean equals(Object obj) {

        if (this == obj) {
            return true;
        }

        if (obj == null) {
            return false;
        }

        if (getClass() != obj.getClass()) {
            return false;
        }

        final AuthorId other = (AuthorId) obj;
        if (!Objects.equals(this.name, other.name)) {
            return false;
        }
```

```
        if (!Objects.equals(this.publisher, other.publisher)) {
            return false;
        }

        return true;
    }

    @Override
    public String toString() {
        return "AuthorId{ " + "publisher=" + publisher
                + ", name=" + name + '}';
    }
}
```

Further, the Author entity uses the AuthorId class as its identifier in the same way as you saw in the "Composite key via @Embeddable and @EmbeddedId" section:

```
@Entity
public class Author implements Serializable {

    private static final long serialVersionUID = 1L;

    @EmbeddedId
    private AuthorId id;

    private String genre;

    @OneToMany(cascade = CascadeType.ALL,
                mappedBy = "author", orphanRemoval = true)
    private List<Book> books = new ArrayList<>();
    ...
}
```

Finally, the Book entity references the Author identifier:

```
@Entity
public class Book implements Serializable {

    private static final long serialVersionUID = 1L;
```

```
@Id
@GeneratedValue(strategy = GenerationType.IDENTITY)
private Long id;

private String title;
private String isbn;

@ManyToOne(fetch = FetchType.LAZY)
@JoinColumns({
    @JoinColumn(
        name = "publisher",
        referencedColumnName = "publisher"),
    @JoinColumn(
        name = "name",
        referencedColumnName = "name")
})
private Author author;
...
}
```

## Testing Time

This section considers several common operations that involve the manipulation of the Author entity. Let's see the triggered SQL statements.

## Persist a Publisher

To define a composite key for the Author, you need at least one Publisher to exist, so let's persist one:

```
@Transactional
public void addPublisher() {
    Publisher publisher = new Publisher();
    publisher.setName("GreatBooks Ltd");
    publisher.setUrc(92284434);

    publisherRepository.save(publisher);
}
```

This method triggers a simple INSERT:

```
INSERT INTO publisher (name, urc)
  VALUES (?, ?)
```

## Persist Two Authors

Now, let's use the publisher persisted earlier to define the composite primary keys of two authors:

```
@Transactional
public void addAuthorsWithBooks() {

    Publisher publisher = publisherRepository.findByUrc(92284434);

    Author author1 = new Author();
    author1.setId(new AuthorId(publisher, "Alicia Tom"));
    author1.setGenre("Anthology");

    Author author2 = new Author();
    author2.setId(new AuthorId(publisher, "Joana Nimar"));
    author2.setGenre("History");

    Book book1 = new Book();
    book1.setIsbn("001-AT");
    book1.setTitle("The book of swords");

    Book book2 = new Book();
    book2.setIsbn("002-AT");
    book2.setTitle("Anthology of a day");

    Book book3 = new Book();
    book3.setIsbn("003-AT");
    book3.setTitle("Anthology today");

    author1.addBook(book1);
    author1.addBook(book2);
    author2.addBook(book3);
```

```
    authorRepository.save(author1);
    authorRepository.save(author2);
}
```

Calling addAuthorsWithBooks() triggers the following SQL statements:

```
-- fetch the publisher used to shape the composite key
SELECT
  publisher0_.id AS id1_2_,
  publisher0_.name AS name2_2_,
  publisher0_.urc AS urc3_2_
FROM publisher publisher0_
WHERE publisher0_.urc = ?
```

```
-- ensure that the first author is not in the database
SELECT
  author0_.name AS name1_0_1_,
  author0_.publisher AS publishe3_0_1_,
  author0_.genre AS genre2_0_1_,
  books1_.name AS name4_1_3_,
  books1_.publisher AS publishe5_1_3_,
  books1_.id AS id1_1_3_,
  books1_.id AS id1_1_0_,
  books1_.name AS name4_1_0_,
  books1_.publisher AS publishe5_1_0_,
  books1_.isbn AS isbn2_1_0_,
  books1_.title AS title3_1_0_
FROM author author0_
LEFT OUTER JOIN book books1_
  ON author0_.name = books1_.name
  AND author0_.publisher = books1_.publisher
WHERE author0_.name = ?
AND author0_.publisher = ?
```

```
-- persist the first author
INSERT INTO author (genre, name, publisher)
  VALUES (?, ?, ?)
```

```
-- this author has two books
INSERT INTO book (name, publisher, isbn, title)
  VALUES (?, ?, ?, ?)

INSERT INTO book (name, publisher, isbn, title)
  VALUES (?, ?, ?, ?)

-- ensure that the second author is not in the database
SELECT
  author0_.name AS name1_0_1_,
  author0_.publisher AS publishe3_0_1_,
  author0_.genre AS genre2_0_1_,
  books1_.name AS name4_1_3_,
  books1_.publisher AS publishe5_1_3_,
  books1_.id AS id1_1_3_,
  books1_.id AS id1_1_0_,
  books1_.name AS name4_1_0_,
  books1_.publisher AS publishe5_1_0_,
  books1_.isbn AS isbn2_1_0_,
  books1_.title AS title3_1_0_
FROM author author0_
LEFT OUTER JOIN book books1_
  ON author0_.name = books1_.name
  AND author0_.publisher = books1_.publisher
WHERE author0_.name = ?
AND author0_.publisher = ?

-- persist the second author
INSERT INTO author (genre, name, publisher)
  VALUES (?, ?, ?)

-- this author has a single book
INSERT INTO book (name, publisher, isbn, title)
  VALUES (?, ?, ?, ?)
```

# Find an Author by Name

The name column is part of the composite primary key but it can be used in queries as well. The following query finds an author by name. Notice how we reference the name column via id:

```
@Query("SELECT a FROM Author a WHERE a.id.name = ?1")
public Author fetchByName(String name);
```

A service-method calling fetchByName() can be written as follows:

```
@Transactional(readOnly = true)
public void fetchAuthorByName() {
    Author author = authorRepository.fetchByName("Alicia Tom");

    System.out.println(author);
}
```

Calling fetchAuthorByName() will trigger the following SELECT statements:

```
SELECT
   author0_.name AS name1_0_,
   author0_.publisher AS publishe3_0_,
   author0_.genre AS genre2_0_
FROM author author0_
WHERE author0_.name = ?

SELECT
   publisher0_.id AS id1_2_0_,
   publisher0_.name AS name2_2_0_,
   publisher0_.urc AS urc3_2_0_
FROM publisher publisher0_
WHERE publisher0_.id = ?
```

The second SELECT is needed to fetch the publisher of the just fetched author. Obviously, this is not very efficient, but it is the price to pay for fetching the Author identifier.

# Remove a Book of an Author

Consider that we've loaded an author and the associated books via the following JOIN FETCH query:

```
@Query("SELECT a FROM Author a "
    + "JOIN FETCH a.books WHERE a.id = ?1")
public Author fetchWithBooks(AuthorId id);
```

Further, let's remove the first book via a service-method:

```
@Transactional
public void removeBookOfAuthor() {

    Publisher publisher = publisherRepository.findByUrc(92284434);
    Author author = authorRepository.fetchWithBooks(
        new AuthorId(publisher, "Alicia Tom"));

    author.removeBook(author.getBooks().get(0));
}
```

Calling removeBookOfAuthor() triggers the following SQL statements:

```
SELECT
  publisher0_.id AS id1_2_,
  publisher0_.name AS name2_2_,
  publisher0_.urc AS urc3_2_
FROM publisher publisher0_
WHERE publisher0_.urc = ?

SELECT
  author0_.name AS name1_0_0_,
  author0_.publisher AS publishe3_0_0_,
  books1_.id AS id1_1_1_,
  author0_.genre AS genre2_0_0_,
  books1_.name AS name4_1_1_,
  books1_.publisher AS publishe5_1_1_,
  books1_.isbn AS isbn2_1_1_,
  books1_.title AS title3_1_1_,
```

```
   books1_.name AS name4_1_0__,
   books1_.publisher AS publishe5_1_0__,
   books1_.id AS id1_1_0__
FROM author author0_
INNER JOIN book books1_
  ON author0_.name = books1_.name
  AND author0_.publisher = books1_.publisher
WHERE (author0_.name, author0_.publisher)=(?, ?)

DELETE FROM book
WHERE id = ?
```

## Remove an Author

Removing an author will cascade to the associated books as well:

```
@Transactional
public void removeAuthor() {
    Publisher publisher = publisherRepository.findByUrc(92284434);
    authorRepository.deleteById(new AuthorId(publisher, "Alicia Tom"));
}
```

The triggered SQL statements are pretty straightforward. After three SELECT statements that fetch the publisher, the author, and their associated books, are two DELETE statements. Since this author has a single book, there is a single DELETE triggered against the book table. Finally, the second DELETE deletes the corresponding row from the author table:

```
SELECT
  publisher0_.id AS id1_2_,
  publisher0_.name AS name2_2_,
  publisher0_.urc AS urc3_2_
FROM publisher publisher0_
WHERE publisher0_.urc = ?

SELECT
  author0_.name AS name1_0_0_,
  author0_.publisher AS publishe3_0_0_,
  author0_.genre AS genre2_0_0_
FROM author author0_
```

```
WHERE author0_.name = ?
AND author0_.publisher = ?

SELECT
    books0_.name AS name4_1_0_,
    books0_.publisher AS publishe5_1_0_,
    books0_.id AS id1_1_0_,
    books0_.id AS id1_1_1_,
    books0_.name AS name4_1_1_,
    books0_.publisher AS publishe5_1_1_,
    books0_.isbn AS isbn2_1_1_,
    books0_.title AS title3_1_1_
FROM book books0_
WHERE books0_.name = ?
AND books0_.publisher = ?

DELETE FROM book
WHERE id = ?

DELETE FROM author
WHERE name = ?
    AND publisher = ?
```

> Looks like mapping relationships in composite keys is technically working,
> but, at the query-level, it's not efficient. Every time Hibernate needs to
> construct the entity identifier, it must trigger an additional SELECT. But, if this
> part of the entity identifier can be stored in the Second Level Cache, then this
> additional SELECT can be mitigated.

The complete application is available on GitHub[22].

---

[22]HibernateSpringBootCompositeKeyEmbeddableMapRel

# Item 76: How to Use an Entity for the Junction Table

Consider the junction table of a many-to-many association shown in Figure 7-5.

***Figure 7-5.*** *The many-to-many table relationship*

As expected, the author_book table maps the primary keys of the author and book tables. But how do you add more columns to this table? For example, how do you add a column as publishedOn to store the date when each book was published? So far, this is not possible!

Adding more columns in the author_book junction table is possible if you define an entity for this table.

## Define a Composite Primary Key for the Junction Table

If you are not familiar with composite keys, consider **Item 74**.

The first step consists of joining the author_id and book_id keys in a composite key via @Embeddable, as follows (this is the primary key of the entity corresponding to the junction table):

```
@Embeddable
public class AuthorBookId implements Serializable {

    private static final long serialVersionUID = 1L;

    @Column(name = "author_id")
    private Long authorId;
```

```java
@Column(name = "book_id")
private Long bookId;

public AuthorBookId() {
}

public AuthorBookId(Long authorId, Long bookId) {
    this.authorId = authorId;
    this.bookId = bookId;
}

// getters omitted for brevity

@Override
public int hashCode() {
    int hash = 7;
    hash = 31 * hash + Objects.hashCode(this.authorId);
    hash = 31 * hash + Objects.hashCode(this.bookId);
    return hash;
}

@Override
public boolean equals(Object obj) {
    if (this == obj) {
        return true;
    }

    if (obj == null) {
        return false;
    }

    if (getClass() != obj.getClass()) {
        return false;
    }

    final AuthorBookId other = (AuthorBookId) obj;
    if (!Objects.equals(this.authorId, other.authorId)) {
        return false;
    }
```

```
        if (!Objects.equals(this.bookId, other.bookId)) {
            return false;
        }

        return true;
    }
}
```

## Define an Entity for the Junction Table

Further, map the junction table using a dedicated entity:

```
@Entity
public class AuthorBook implements Serializable {

    private static final long serialVersionUID = 1L;

    @EmbeddedId
    private AuthorBookId id;

    @MapsId("authorId")
    @ManyToOne(fetch = FetchType.LAZY)
    private Author author;

    @MapsId("bookId")
    @ManyToOne(fetch = FetchType.LAZY)
    private Book book;

    private Date publishedOn = new Date();

    public AuthorBook() {
    }

    public AuthorBook(Author author, Book book) {
        this.author = author;
        this.book = book;
        this.id = new AuthorBookId(author.getId(), book.getId());
    }
```

```java
    // getters and setters omitted for brevity

    @Override
    public int hashCode() {
        int hash = 7;
        hash = 29 * hash + Objects.hashCode(this.author);
        hash = 29 * hash + Objects.hashCode(this.book);
        return hash;
    }

    @Override
    public boolean equals(Object obj) {
        if (this == obj) {
            return true;
        }

        if (obj == null) {
            return false;
        }

        if (getClass() != obj.getClass()) {
            return false;
        }

        final AuthorBook other = (AuthorBook) obj;
        if (!Objects.equals(this.author, other.author)) {
            return false;
        }

        if (!Objects.equals(this.book, other.book)) {
            return false;
        }

        return true;
    }
}
```

# Plug In the Author and Book

Finally, we need to plug the Author and Book into AuthorBook. In other words, Author and Book should define a @OneToMany for the author and book attributes:

```
@Entity
public class Author implements Serializable {

    private static final long serialVersionUID = 1L;

    @Id
    @GeneratedValue(strategy = GenerationType.IDENTITY)
    private Long id;

    private String name;
    private String genre;
    private int age;

    @OneToMany(mappedBy = "author",
            cascade = CascadeType.ALL, orphanRemoval = true)
    private List<AuthorBook> books = new ArrayList<>();

    // getters and setters omitted for brevity

    @Override
    public boolean equals(Object obj) {

        if (this == obj) {
            return true;
        }

        if (getClass() != obj.getClass()) {
            return false;
        }

        return id != null && id.equals(((Author) obj).id);
    }
```

```
    @Override
    public int hashCode() {
        return 2021;
    }
}
```

And, here's the Book:

```
@Entity
public class Book implements Serializable {

    private static final long serialVersionUID = 1L;

    @Id
    @GeneratedValue(strategy = GenerationType.IDENTITY)
    private Long id;

    private String title;
    private String isbn;

    @OneToMany(mappedBy = "book",
            cascade = CascadeType.ALL, orphanRemoval = true)
    private List<AuthorBook> authors = new ArrayList<>();

    // getters and setters omitted for brevity

    @Override
    public boolean equals(Object obj) {

        if (this == obj) {
            return true;
        }

        if (getClass() != obj.getClass()) {
            return false;
        }

        return id != null && id.equals(((Book) obj).id);
    }
```

```
    @Override
    public int hashCode() {
        return 2021;
    }
}
```

At this point, the junction table has an entity and the many-to-many association has been transformed in two bidirectional one-to-many associations.

# CHAPTER 8

# Calculating Properties

## Item 77: How to Map Calculated Non-Persistent Properties

This item is about mapping calculated non-persistent properties of an entity based on the persistent entity attributes. It uses the Book entity mapping shown in Figure 8-1.

*Figure 8-1.* *Book class diagram*

Each book has a price mapped via the persistent field, called price. And, based on the price, the developer must calculate the value of the non-persistent field, discounted. This is the price with a discount applied. Let's assume that each book has a 25% discount. In other words, after a Book is loaded, the getDiscounted() property should return the price with the discount applied, price - price * 0.25.

## JPA Quick Approach

A JPA quick approach consists of annotating the getDiscounted() property with JPA @Transient as follows:

© Anghel Leonard 2020
A. Leonard, *Spring Boot Persistence Best Practices*, https://doi.org/10.1007/978-1-4842-5626-8_8

```
@Transient
public double getDiscounted() {
    return this.price - this.price * 0.25;
}
```

This means that the computation is performed every time the getDiscounted() method is called. If the computation is fairly complex (e.g., depends on other computations) or the property must be called multiple times, this implementation is less efficient than the following one.

# JPA @PostLoad

A better approach consists of two steps:

- Annotate the discounted field with @Transient

- Declare a private method annotated with @PostLoad and calculate the discounted value

In code lines, these two bullets appear as follows:

```
@Entity
public class Book implements Serializable {
    ...
    @Transient
    private double discounted;
    ...

    public double getDiscounted() {
        return discounted;
    }

    @PostLoad
    private void postLoad() {
        this.discounted = this.price - this.price * 0.25;
    }
}
```

> For more details about JPA callbacks, consider **Item 104.**

This time, the computation is performed after the entity is loaded. Calling getDiscounted()
will return the value of discounted without repeating the computation at every call.

The complete code is available on GitHub[1].

## Hibernate-specific @Formula

The computation of discounted can be written as an SQL query expression as well. For
this, rely on the @Formula annotation specific to Hibernate. The following snippet of code
shows how @Formula can be used in this case:

```
@Entity
public class Book implements Serializable {

    ...

    @Formula("price - price * 0.25")
    private double discounted;

    ...

    @Transient
    public double getDiscounted() {
        return discounted;
    }
}
```

Fetching a Book entity will be accomplished via the following SQL statement (notice that
the given formula is part of the query):

```
SELECT
  book0_.id AS id1_0_,
  book0_.isbn AS isbn2_0_,
  book0_.price AS price3_0_,
```

---

[1]HibernateSpringBootCalculatePropertyPostLoad

```
book0_.title AS title4_0_,
book0_.price - book0_.price * 0.25 AS formula0_
FROM book book0_
```

Calling getDiscounted() will return the computed discounted value at query time.

The complete code is available on GitHub[2].

These two approaches of computing discounted can be placed in the same category. Both of them assume that a Book entity is loaded and its persistent attributes are used to compute the value of the non-persistent field, discounted. The main difference is in how the formula was written. @PostLoad was written in Java, and @Formula was written as an SQL query expression.

# Item 78: How to Map Calculated Persistent Properties via @Generated

This item is about mapping calculated persistent properties of an entity based on other persistent entity attributes. It uses the Book entity mapping shown in Figure 8-2.

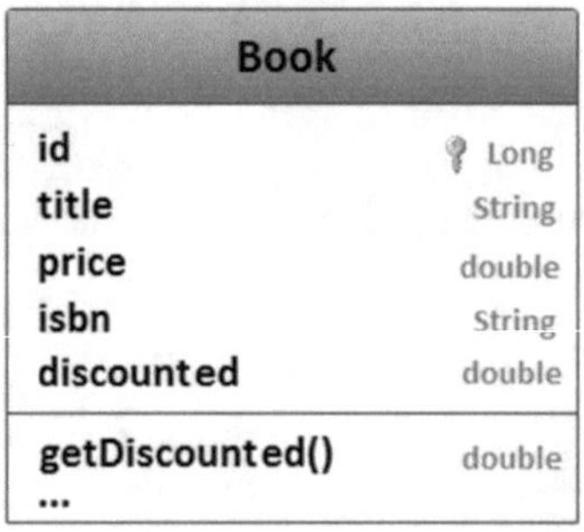

| Book | | |
|---|---|---|
| id | 🔑 Long | |
| title | String | |
| price | double | |
| isbn | String | |
| discounted | double | |
| getDiscounted() | double | |
| ... | | |

*Figure 8-2.  Book class diagram*

Each book has a price mapped via the persistent field, called price. And, based on the price, the developer must calculate the value of the persistent field, discounted. This is the price with a discount applied. Each book has a 25% discount. In other words, persisting a Book with a given price should persist discounted as price - price * 0.25. Updating the price should update the discounted field as well.

Further, let's see how to compute discounted at INSERT and/or UPDATE time.

---

[2]HibernateSpringBootCalculatePropertyFormula

# Hibernate-Specific @Generated

Consider that discounted is a persistent field of the Book entity that must be computed based on the price persistent field. So, the discounted field is materialized in a column of the book table, and its value will be computed at INSERT or/and UPDATE time. This is a generated column; it's for columns what a view is for tables.

Hibernate provides the @Generated annotation. Via this annotation, the developer instructs Hibernate (NOT the database) when the associated column value is calculated. The value of this annotation can be GenerationTime.INSERT (only INSERT time) or GenerationTime.ALWAYS (INSERT and UPDATE times). If the value should not be generated, GenerationTime.NEVER is the proper choice.

Further, you can provide a custom @Column definition for the discounted field. As a rule of thumb, a generated column cannot be written directly via the INSERT or UPDATE statements. In code, this looks as follows:

```
@Entity
public class Book implements Serializable {

    @Generated(value = GenerationTime.ALWAYS)
    @Column(insertable = false, updatable = false)
    private double discounted;
    ...
    public double getDiscounted() {
        return discounted;
    }
}
```

> For GenerationTime.INSERT, the column should be annotated with @Column(insertable = false).

Where is the formula for calculating the discounted value? Well, there are two ways to specify the formula.

## Formula via columnDefinition Element

The formula can be specified as an SQL query expression via the columnDefinition element of the @Column annotation, as follows:

```
@Generated(value = GenerationTime.ALWAYS)
@Column(insertable = false, updatable = false,
    columnDefinition = "double AS (price - price * 0.25)")
private double discounted;
```

If the database schema is generated from JPA annotations (e.g., spring.jpa.hibernate. ddl-auto=create) then the columnDefinition presence is reflected in the CREATE TABLE query, as shown here (the same query is generated for GenerationTime.INSERT):

```
CREATE TABLE book (
    id BIGINT NOT NULL AUTO_INCREMENT,
    discounted DOUBLE AS (price - price * 0.25),
    isbn VARCHAR(255),
    price DOUBLE PRECISION NOT NULL,
    title VARCHAR(255),
    PRIMARY KEY (id)
)
```

> Relying on columnDefinition requires to generate the database schema from JPA annotations; therefore, this cannot represent a production solution. In production, spring.jpa.hibernate.ddl-auto should be disabled (not specified) or set to validate, and the database migration should be managed via dedicated tools such as Flyway or Liquibase.
>
> Obviously, this applies to eclipselink.ddl-generation (specific to EclipseLink persistence provider) and any other similar mechanism used for generating DDL for the database schema. Such mechanisms should be used only for prototyping your database schema.

Databases (e.g., MySQL, PostgreSQL) typically recognize two kinds of generated columns: *stored* and *virtual*. Via `columnDefinition`, the column will take the default value set for the used database (in MySQL and PostgreSQL, the default is *virtual*). These two notions are explained in the next section.

## Formula via CREATE TABLE

In production, the formula should be specified as part of database schema via `CREATE TABLE`, not in `columnDefinition`. The syntax for defining a generated column in MySQL is as follows (for other database considerations, read the documentation):

```
column_name data_type [GENERATED ALWAYS] AS (expression)
   [VIRTUAL | STORED] [UNIQUE [KEY]]
```

First, specify the column name and its data type.

Next, add the optional `GENERATED ALWAYS` clause to indicate that the column is a generated column. Actually, `AS (expression)` indicates that the column is generated, while the optional `GENERATED ALWAYS` just highlights this in a more explicit way. There is no `GENERATED INSERT`!

The type of the column can be `VIRTUAL` or `STORED`. By default, MySQL uses `VIRTUAL` if you don't explicitly specify the type:

- `VIRTUAL`: Column values are not stored, but are evaluated when rows are read, immediately after any `BEFORE` triggers. A *virtual* column takes no storage (InnoDB supports secondary indexes on *virtual* columns).

- `STORED`: Column values are evaluated and stored when rows are inserted or updated. A *stored* column does require storage space and can be indexed.

After that, specify the expression. The expression can contain operators, literals, built-in functions with no parameters, or references to any column within the same table. Functions must be scalar and deterministic.

Finally, if the generated column is *stored*, you can define a unique constraint for it.

> Specifying a formula in a CREATE TABLE is more flexible than using columnDefinition and sustains the maintainability of the database schema via dedicated tools such as Flyway or Liquibase.

A MySQL CREATE TABLE sample for having a *stored* generated column can be written as follows:

```
CREATE TABLE book (
  id BIGINT NOT NULL AUTO_INCREMENT,
  discounted DOUBLE GENERATED ALWAYS AS ((`price` - `price` * 0.25))
  STORED,
  isbn VARCHAR(255),
  price DOUBLE PRECISION NOT NULL,
  title VARCHAR(255),
  PRIMARY KEY (id)
)
```

In the application bundled to this book, this DDL was added in schema-sql.sql. But remember that, in production, you should rely on Flyway or Liquibase, which provide automatic schema migration.

## Testing Time

Persisting a book that's *$13.99* will generate the following SQL statements:

```
INSERT INTO book (isbn, price, title)
  VALUES (?, ?, ?)
Binding:[OO1-AH, 13.99, Ancient History]
```

```
SELECT
  book_.discounted AS discount2_0_
FROM book book_
WHERE book_.id = ?
Binding:[1], Extracted:[10.4925]
```

After triggering the INSERT and flushing it, Hibernate automatically triggers a SELECT to fetch the computed discounted value. This is needed to synchronize the managed entity with the underlying table row. Calling getDiscounted() will return *10.4925*. This is the effect of @Generated.

Further, let's trigger an UPDATE to set the new price to $*9.99*. The resulted SQL statements are:

```
UPDATE book
SET isbn = ?,
    price = ?,
    title = ?
WHERE id = ?
Binding:[001-AH, 9.99, Ancient History, 1]

SELECT
  book_.discounted AS discount2_0_
FROM book book_
WHERE book_.id = ?
Binding:[1], Extracted:[7.4925]
```

After triggering the UPDATE and flushing it, Hibernate automatically triggers a SELECT to fetch the computed discounted value. This is needed to synchronize the managed entity with the underlying table row. Calling getDiscounted() will return *7.4925*. This is the effect of @Generated.

The complete code is available on GitHub[3].

# Item 79: How to Use SQL Functions with Multiple Parameters in JPQL Queries

The presence of SQL functions (MySQL, PostgreSQL, etc.) in JPQL queries may lead to exceptions if Hibernate cannot recognize them.

---

[3]HibernateSpringBootCalculatePropertyGenerated

# Function in the SELECT Part

For example, the MySQL concat_ws() function (used for concatenating multiple strings by a delimiter/separator) is not recognized by Hibernate. Starting with Hibernate 5.3 (or, to be precise, 5.2.18), such functions can be registered via MetadataBuilderContributor and can inform Hibernate about it via the metadata_builder_contributor property.

Figure 8-3 depicts a usage case of concat_ws().

***Figure 8-3.*** *MySQL concat_ws() function*

The concat_ws() function is used for concatenating the title and price of a Book (from the database), with the $ symbol and current date (from the application) separated by space.

In Spring style, you can write the query via @Query as follows:

```
@Repository
@Transactional(readOnly = true)
public interface BookRepository extends JpaRepository<Book, Long> {

    @Query(value = "SELECT concat_ws(b.title, ?1, b.price, ?2) "
            + "FROM Book b WHERE b.id = 1")
    String fetchTitleAndPrice(String symbol, Instant instant);
}
```

In pure JPA style, you can write the query via EntityManager as follows:

```
@Repository
public class Dao<T, ID extends Serializable> implements GenericDao<T, ID> {
```

```
@PersistenceContext
private EntityManager entityManager;

@Override
@Transactional(readOnly = true)
public String fetchTitleAndPrice(String symbol, Instant instant) {

    return (String) entityManager.createQuery(
        "SELECT concat_ws(b.title, :symbol, b.price, :instant) "
        + "FROM Book b WHERE b.id = 1"
    )
        .setParameter("symbol", symbol)
        .setParameter("instant", instant)
        .getSingleResult();
}
}
```

But, none of these attempts will work until the concat_ws() function is registered via MetadataBuilderContributor, as follows:

```
public class SqlFunctionsMetadataBuilderContributor
                implements MetadataBuilderContributor {

    @Override
    public void contribute(MetadataBuilder metadataBuilder) {
        metadataBuilder.applySqlFunction(
            "concat_ws",
            new SQLFunctionTemplate(
                StandardBasicTypes.STRING,
                "concat_ws(' ', ?1, ?2, ?3, ?4)"
            )
        );
    }
}
```

Similar to the previous example, you can register any other SQL function. For example, you can register the famous `date_trunc()` as follows:

```
@Override
public void contribute(MetadataBuilder metadataBuilder) {
    metadataBuilder.applySqlFunction(
        "date_trunc", new SQLFunctionTemplate(
            StandardBasicTypes.TIMESTAMP, "date_trunc('minute', ?1)"
        )
    );
}
```

Finally, set `spring.jpa.properties.hibernate.metadata_builder_contributor` in `application.properties`, as shown here:

```
spring.jpa.properties.hibernate.metadata_builder_contributor
    =com.bookstore.config.SqlFunctionsMetadataBuilderContributor
```

Running the code will reveal output similar to this:

```
A People's History  $  32  2019-07-16 11:17:49.949732
```

The complete code is available on GitHub[4].

# Function in the WHERE Part

In JPA 2.1, functions can be used in the WHERE part of a JPQL query without registering the function. JPA 2.1 introduced `function()`, which takes as arguments:

- The name of the function to call as the first argument
- All parameters of the function

---

[4]HibernateSpringBootJpqlFunctionsParams

Let's call the same `concat_ws()` function, but this time in the `WHERE` clause:

```
@Transactional(readOnly = true)
@Query(value = "SELECT b FROM Book b WHERE b.isbn "
            + "= function('concat_ws', '-', ?1, ?2)")
Book fetchByIsbn(String code, String author);
```

Calling `fetchByIsbn()` from a service-method can be done as follows:

```
public Book fetchBookByIsbn() {
    return bookRepository.fetchByIsbn("001", "JN");
}
```

The SQL triggered is as follows:

```
SELECT
  book0_.id AS id1_0_,
  book0_.isbn AS isbn2_0_,
  book0_.price AS price3_0_,
  book0_.title AS title4_0_
FROM book book0_
WHERE book0_.isbn = concat_ws('-', ?, ?)
Binding:[001, JN]
```

You can call SQL functions (standard or custom ones) as follows:

- In JPQL queries, as long as you refer to the standard functions from here[5]

- In a WHERE part and in JPA 2.1, the SQL functions can be called out of the box via `function()`

- In a SELECT part, the unrecognized SQL functions must be registered

Done! The complete application is available on GitHub[6].

---

[5]https://en.wikibooks.org/wiki/Java_Persistence/JPQL#JPQL_supported_functions
[6]HibernateSpringBootJpqlFunction

# Item 80: How to Map @ManyToOne Relationship to an SQL Query Via @JoinFormula

Let's consider the Author and Book entities involved in an unidirectional @ManyToOne relationship reflected by the tables in Figure 8-4 and the data in Figure 8-5.

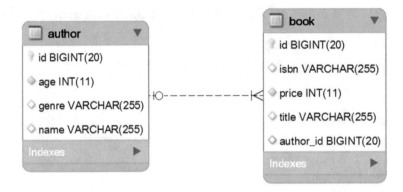

***Figure 8-4.*** *The one-to-many table relationship*

**author**

| id | age | genre | name |
|----|-----|-------|------|
| 1 | 23 | Anthology | Mark Janel |
| 2 | 43 | Horror | Olivia Goy |
| 3 | 51 | Anthology | Quartis Young |
| 4 | 34 | History | Joana Nimar |

**book**

| id | isbn | price | title | author_id |
|----|------|-------|-------|-----------|
| 1 | 001-JN | 23 | A History of Ancient Prague | 4 |
| 2 | 002-JN | 34 | A People's History | 4 |
| 3 | 001-MJ | 55 | The Beatles Anthology | 1 |
| 4 | 002-MJ | 44 | Anthology Of '99 | 1 |
| 5 | 001-OG | 33 | Carrie | 2 |
| 6 | 002-OG | 25 | Last Day | 2 |
| 7 | 003-JN | 41 | History Today | 4 |
| 8 | 003-MJ | 21 | Anthology Of A Game | 1 |

***Figure 8-5.*** *Data snapshot*

This scenario requires you to figure out which book is cheaper than the given book. In other words, while fetching a book by its ID (let's call it book *A*), you want to fetch another book, called book *B,* by the same author whose price is the next cheapest in comparison to book *A's* price. Accomplishing this can be done as follows:

```
@Transactional(readOnly = true)
public void fetchBooks() {

    Book book = bookRepository.findById(7L).orElseThrow();
```

```
    Book nextBook = bookRepository.fetchNextSmallerPrice(
        book.getPrice(), book.getAuthor().getId());

    System.out.println("Fetched book with id 7: " + book);
    System.out.println("Fetched book with next smallest price: " + nextBook);
}
```

Where fetchNextSmallerPrice() is the following native query:

```
@Transactional(readOnly = true)
@Query(value="SELECT * FROM book WHERE price < ?1 AND author_id = ?2 "
            + "ORDER BY price DESC LIMIT 1",
        nativeQuery = true)
Book fetchNextSmallerPrice(int price, long authorId);
```

Two SELECT statements are needed to fetch book and nextBook. Alternatively, it will be simpler to map @ManyToOne to the previous query via Hibernate-specific @JoinFormula:

```
@Entity
public class Book implements Serializable {

    private static final long serialVersionUID = 1L;

    @Id
    @GeneratedValue(strategy = GenerationType.IDENTITY)
    private Long id;

    private String title;
    private String isbn;
    private int price;

    @ManyToOne(fetch = FetchType.LAZY)
    @JoinColumn(name = "author_id")
    private Author author;

    @ManyToOne(fetch = FetchType.LAZY)
    @JoinFormula("(SELECT b.id FROM book b "
        + "WHERE b.price < price AND b.author_id = author_id "
        + "ORDER BY b.price DESC LIMIT 1)")
    private Book nextBook;
```

```
    public Book getNextBook() {
        return nextBook;
    }

    public void setNextBook(Book nextBook) {
        this.nextBook = nextBook;
    }
    ...
}
```

Based on this mapping, the service-method fetchBooks() becomes:

```
@Transactional(readOnly = true)
public void fetchBooks() {

    Book book = bookRepository.findById(7L).orElseThrow();
    Book nextBook = book.getNextBook();

    System.out.println("Fetched book with id 7: " + book);
    System.out.println("Fetched book with next smallest price: " +
                        nextBook);
}
```

The following SELECT statement is executed twice for fetching book and nextBook:

```
SELECT
  book0_.id AS id1_1_0_,
  book0_.author_id AS author_i5_1_0_,
  book0_.isbn AS isbn2_1_0_,
  book0_.price AS price3_1_0_,
  book0_.title AS title4_1_0_,
  (SELECT
    b.id
  FROM book b
  WHERE b.price < book0_.price AND b.author_id = book0_.author_id
  ORDER BY b.price DESC LIMIT 1)
  AS formula1_0_
FROM book book0_
WHERE book0_.id = ?
Binding:[7] Extracted:[4, 003-JN, 2, 41, History Today]
```

538

The third extracted value, which is *2*, corresponds to the formula result. This is the ID of nextBook. So, this query is executed again to fetch nextBook with the following parameters:

Binding:[2] Extracted:[4, 002-JN, **1**, 34, A People's History]

Again, notice that the third extracted value (*1*) corresponds to the formula result. This allows you to continue calling getNextBook(). When there is no other cheaper book, the formula result will be *null*.

Generally speaking, the Hibernate-specific @JoinFormula annotation can be used to define any SELECT query to provide the relationship between two entities. For example, you can use it to fetch the cheapest book of an author. For this, you add an @ManyToOne to Author as well:

```
@Entity
public class Author implements Serializable {
    ...
    @ManyToOne(fetch = FetchType.LAZY)
    @JoinFormula("(SELECT b.id FROM book b "
        + "WHERE b.author_id = id "
        + "ORDER BY b.price ASC LIMIT 1)")
    private Book cheapestBook;
    ...
}
```

Usage:

```
Author author = authorRepository.findById(1L).orElseThrow();
Book cheapestBook = author.getCheapestBook();
```

The complete application is available on GitHub[7].

---

[7]HibernateSpringBootJoinFormula

# CHAPTER 9

# Monitoring

## Item 81: Why and How to Count and Assert SQL Statements

Assuming that you have the Author entity mapped to the table, as shown in Figure 9-1, the goal is to atomically perform the following simple scenario:

- Load an Author from the database

- Update the genre of this Author

***Figure 9-1.*** *The Author entity table*

A simple service-method can implement this scenario, as follows:

```
@Service
public class BookstoreService {

    private final AuthorRepository authorRepository;
    ...

    public void updateAuthor() {

        Author author = authorRepository.findById(1L).orElseThrow();
```

© Anghel Leonard 2020
A. Leonard, *Spring Boot Persistence Best Practices*, https://doi.org/10.1007/978-1-4842-5626-8_9

```
        author.setGenre("History");

        authorRepository.save(author);
    }
}
```

But, are these operations, atomically? They are not, because the developer accidentally forgot to add @Transactional at the method level and there is no inherited transactional-context. Each operation will run in a separate transaction, which will result in a performance penalty. The code will also be prone to unexpected behaviors and data inconsistencies. However, does this accident has a negative impact on the number and/ or type of triggered SQLs? Counting and asserting the number of SQL statements against the expectations will answer this question.

Empowering the mechanism for counting and asserting the triggered SQL statements requires two libraries. Counting is the responsibility of the DataSource-Proxy library. Among this library's goodies (check **Item 83**), it will proxy the data source and extract important information such as the bind parameters' values and number of executed SQL statements.

The key is to call the countQuery() method before building the proxy. This instructs DataSource-Proxy to create a DataSourceQueryCountListener. Besides the data source name, this listener provides metrics such as the number of database calls, total query execution time, and number of queries by type:

```
public ProxyDataSourceInterceptor(final DataSource dataSource) {

    super();

    this.dataSource = ProxyDataSourceBuilder.create(dataSource)
        .name("DATA_SOURCE_PROXY")
        .logQueryBySlf4j(SLF4JLogLevel.INFO)
        .multiline()
        .countQuery()
        .build();
}
```

Having this listener in place, the triggered SQL statements can be counted directly via the QueryCount API. Or, even better, you can use the db-util library. The advantage of using this library is the out-of-the-box automated validator named SQLStatementCountValidator. This validator exposes the following static assertions: assertSelectCount(), assertInsertCount(), assertUpdateCount(), and assertDeleteCount().

Using this validator requires three main steps:

- Reset the QueryCount via SQLStatementCountValidator.reset()

- Execute the SQL statements

- Apply the proper assertions

Getting back to updateAuthor() method, the developer is not aware about forgetting to add @Transactional, therefore, judging the code in the context of a transaction, the expected number of SQL statements is equal with two, a SELECT and an UPDATE. No INSERTs or DELETEs are expected. You can assert the expected queries as follows:

```
private final BookstoreService bookstoreService;
...

SQLStatementCountValidator.reset();

bookstoreService.updateAuthor();

assertSelectCount(1);
assertUpdateCount(1);
assertInsertCount(0);
assertDeleteCount(0);
```

> As a rule of thumb, these assertions can be added in unit tests. It is advisable to assert all types of operations, not just those that you expect to occur. For example, if an unexpected DELETE is triggered and you skipped the assertDeleteCount(0) then you will not catch it.

Running the application will cause the following exception:

```
com.vladmihalcea.sql.exception.SQLSelectCountMismatchException: Expected 1
statements but recorded 2 instead!
```

> If the number of expected SQL statements differs from the number of executed SQL statements, then the SQLStatementCountValidator will throw an exception of type SQL*Foo*CountMismatchException, where *Foo* is one of Select, Insert, Update, or Delete, depending on the SQL type.

So, the application asserts one SELECT, but two were triggered. Why isn't the number of expected SQL statements correct? Because each statement runs in a separate transaction, the following SQL statements are actually triggered (checking the right-side comments reveals that the reality is far away from the expectation):

```
Author author = authorRepository.findById(1L).orElseThrow(); // 1 select
author.setGenre("History");
authorRepository.save(author);    // 1 select, 1 update
```

Listing these SQL statements will reveal the following:

```
-- fetch the author
SELECT
   author0_.id AS id1_0_0_,
   author0_.age AS age2_0_0_,
   author0_.genre AS genre3_0_0_,
   author0_.name AS name4_0_0_
FROM author author0_
WHERE author0_.id = ?

-- the fetched author is not managed,
-- therefore it must be fetched again before updating it
SELECT
   author0_.id AS id1_0_0_,
   author0_.age AS age2_0_0_,
   author0_.genre AS genre3_0_0_,
   author0_.name AS name4_0_0_
FROM author author0_
WHERE author0_.id = ?
```

```
-- update the author
UPDATE author
SET age = ?,
    genre = ?,
    name = ?
WHERE id = ?
```

So, the developer expects two SQL statements, but in reality, there are three SQL statements. Therefore, there are three database round trips instead of two. This is not okay, but, thanks to counting and asserting the SQL statements, this mistake doesn't remain undiscovered. Realizing the mistake, the developer fixes the updateAuthor() method, as follows:

```
@Service
public class BookstoreService {

    private final AuthorRepository authorRepository;

    ...

    @Transactional
    public void updateAuthor() {

        Author author = authorRepository.findById(1L).orElseThrow();
        author.setGenre("History");

        authorRepository.save(author);
    }
}
```

Counting and asserting again reveals that the expected number and type of SQL statements meets the reality. This time, only one SELECT and one UPDATE are triggered. No INSERTs and no DELETEs. This is way better.

But, wait! Now, since you provided a transactional-context, is it necessary to explicitly call the save() method? The answer is no! As you can see in **Item 107**, calling save() is redundant in this case. By removing this explicit call, you don't affect the number of triggered SQL because the Hibernate Dirty Checking mechanism will trigger the UPDATE on your behalf. Therefore, the best way to write the updateAuthor() method is as follows (of course, in reality, you will pass the author ID as a parameter to this method and you won't rely on orElseThrow(); they are used here just for brevity):

```
@Transactional
public void updateAuthor() {

    Author author = authorRepository.findById(1L).orElseThrow();
    author.setGenre("History");
}
```

The source code is available on GitHub[1].

# Item 82: How to Log the Binding and Extracted Parameters of a Prepared Statement

Consider the Author entity and two prepared statements built from an INSERT and a SELECT. Displaying the corresponding SQL statements will look as follows:

```
INSERT INTO author (age, genre, name)
  VALUES (?, ?, ?)
```

```
SELECT
  author0_.id AS id1_0_0_,
  author0_.age AS age2_0_0_,
  author0_.genre AS genre3_0_0_,
  author0_.name AS name4_0_0_
FROM author author0_
WHERE author0_.id = ?
```

Notice all those question marks (?). They are placeholders for the *binding* and *extracted* parameters. Most of the time, it's useful to see the real values of these parameters in place of these placeholders. There are several approaches for accomplishing this. Let's look at three of them.

## TRACE

Probably the quickest approach to this problem consists of enabling the TRACE logging level in application.properties as follows:

```
logging.level.org.hibernate.type.descriptor.sql=TRACE
```

---

[1]HibernateSpringBootCountSQLStatements

This time, the output will be as follows:

```
insert into author (age, genre, name) values (?, ?, ?)
binding parameter [1] as [INTEGER] - [34]
binding parameter [2] as [VARCHAR] - [History]
binding parameter [3] as [VARCHAR] - [Joana Nimar]
```

```
select author0_.id as id1_0_0_, author0_.age as age2_0_0_, author0_.genre
as genre3_0_0_, author0_.name as name4_0_0_ from author author0_ where
author0_.id=?
binding parameter [1] as [BIGINT] - [1]
extracted value ([age2_0_0_] : [INTEGER]) - [34]
extracted value ([genre3_0_0_] : [VARCHAR]) - [History]
extracted value ([name4_0_0_] : [VARCHAR]) - [Joana Nimar]
```

For each parameter, the output contains its type (*binding parameter* or *extracted value*), position or name, data type, and value.

The source code is available on GitHub[2].

> When you use starters, Spring Boot relies on Logback by default. If you don't want to set the TRACE logging level in `application.properties`, then simply add your Logback configuration file or create one. The `logback-spring.xml`, `logback.xml`, `logback-spring.groovy`, or `logback.groovy` files in classpath will be automatically recognized and processed accordingly by Spring Boot. Here is a sample from `logback-spring.xml` (the complete file is available on GitHub[3]):
>
> ```
> ...
> <logger name="org.hibernate.type.descriptor.sql"
>         level="trace" additivity="false">
>     <appender-ref ref="Console" />
> </logger>
> ...
> ```

---

[2]HibernateSpringBootLogTraceViewBindingParameters
[3]HibernateSpringBootLogTraceViewBindingParameters

# Log4j 2

The same result can be obtained via Log4j 2. To enable it, first exclude Spring Boot's default logging and add the Log4j 2 dependency as follows:

```
<!-- Exclude Spring Boot's Default Logging -->
<dependency>
    <groupId>org.springframework.boot</groupId>
    <artifactId>spring-boot-starter</artifactId>
    <exclusions>
        <exclusion>
            <groupId>org.springframework.boot</groupId>
            <artifactId>spring-boot-starter-logging</artifactId>
        </exclusion>
    </exclusions>
</dependency>

<!-- Add Log4j2 Dependency -->
<dependency>
    <groupId>org.springframework.boot</groupId>
    <artifactId>spring-boot-starter-log4j2</artifactId>
</dependency>
```

Further, configure the TRACE level in log4j.xml as follows (this file should be placed in the /resources folder next to application.properties):

```
<Loggers>
    <Logger name="org.hibernate.type.descriptor.sql" level="trace"/>
    ...
</Loggers>
```

Of course, the logging can be further tuned, as conforming to the Log4j 2 documentation.

The source code is available on GitHub[4].

---

[4]HibernateSpringBootLog4j2ViewBindingParameters

Beside the *binding* and *extracted* parameters, other approaches can provide more details about the queries. Details such as the execution time, batching information, query type, and so on can be obtained with the approaches presented in **Item 83**.

## MySQL and profileSQL=true

For MySQL only, the binding parameters (not the extracted ones) are visible via two steps:

- Turn off `spring.jpa.show-sql` (omit it or set it to `false`)

- Shape the JDBC URL by appending
  `logger=Slf4JLogger&profileSQL=true` to it

The source code is available on GitHub[5].

# Item 83: How to Log Query Details

To log only the *binding parameters* and *extracted values* of a prepared statement, see **Item 82.**

You can obtain details about SQL queries in several ways. Let's look at three of them.

## Via DataSource-Proxy

The `DataSource-Proxy` is an open source project that "provides a listener framework for JDBC interactions and query executions via proxy". It doesn't have dependencies to other libraries; everything is optional. It's highly configurable, flexible, extensible, and is the way to go.

Enabling this library in a Spring Boot application requires several steps. First, add the `datasource-proxy` dependency to `pom.xml`:

```
<dependency>
    <groupId>net.ttddyy</groupId>
    <artifactId>datasource-proxy</artifactId>
    <version>${datasource-proxy.version}</version>
</dependency>
```

---

[5]HibernateSpringBootLogBindingParametersMySQL

Next, create a bean post processor to intercept the DataSource bean and wrap the
DataSource bean via ProxyFactory and an implementation of MethodInterceptor. The
end result is shown in the following snippet of code:

```
private static class ProxyDataSourceInterceptor
                        implements MethodInterceptor {

    private final DataSource dataSource;

    public ProxyDataSourceInterceptor(final DataSource dataSource) {
        super();
        this.dataSource = ProxyDataSourceBuilder.create(dataSource)
            .name("DATA_SOURCE_PROXY")
            .logQueryBylf4j(SLF4JLogLevel.INFO)
            .multiline()
            .build();
    }
    ...
}
```

This is where the level of details can be customized. A rich and fluent API can be used
to tune the details (check documentation). After all the settings are in place, just call
build(). A typical output will look as follows:

```
Name:DATA_SOURCE_PROXY, Connection:5, Time:131, Success:True
Type:Prepared, Batch:False, QuerySize:1, BatchSize:0
Query:["insert into author (age, genre, name) values (?, ?, ?)"]
Params:[(34,History,Joana Nimar)]
```

The source code is available on GitHub[6].

# Via log4jdbc

The officials behind log4jdbc state that "log4jdbc is a Java JDBC driver that can log SQL
and/or JDBC calls (and optionally SQL timing information) for other JDBC drivers using
the Simple Logging Facade For Java (SLF4J) logging system".

---

[6]HibernateSpringBootDataSourceProxy

A Spring Boot application can take advantage of log4jdbc immediately after adding its dependency to pom.xml:

```
<dependency>
    <groupId>com.integralblue</groupId>
    <artifactId>log4jdbc-spring-boot-starter</artifactId>
    <version>1.0.2</version>
</dependency>
```

The official documentation provides details about customizing the output. A typical output contains the SQL (including execution time), an audit of the involved methods, and the result set as a table, as shown in Figure 9-2.

```
|---------|----|--------|------------|
|id       |age |genre   |name        |
|---------|----|--------|------------|
|[unread] |34  |History |Joana Nimar |
|---------|----|--------|------------|
```

***Figure 9-2.*** *log4jdbc output sample*

The source code is available on GitHub[7].

# Via P6spy

The documentation says that P6Spy "...is a framework that enables database data to be seamlessly intercepted and logged with no code changes to the application". Enabling P6spy requires you to add pom.xml to the corresponding dependency:

```
<dependency>
    <groupId>p6spy</groupId>
    <artifactId>p6spy</artifactId>
    <version>${p6spy.version}</version>
</dependency>
```

---

[7]HibernateSpringBootLog4JdbcViewBindingParameters

Further, in `application.properties`, you set up the JDBC URL and driver class name, as follows:

```
spring.datasource.url=jdbc:p6spy:mysql://localhost:3306/bookstoredb
spring.datasource.driverClassName=com.p6spy.engine.spy.P6SpyDriver
```

Finally, to the application root folder, you add the `spy.properties` file. This file contains P6Spy configurations. In this application, the logs will be outputted to the console, but there is a pretty easy way to switch to a file. More details about P6Spy configurations can be found in the documentation.

The output can look as follows:

```
insert into author (age, genre, name) values (?, ?, ?)
insert into author (age, genre, name) values (34, 'History', 'Joana Nimar');
#1562161760396 | took 0ms | commit | connection 0| url jdbc:p6spy:mysql://
localhost:3306/bookstoredb?createDatabaseIfNotExist=true
```

The source code is available on GitHub[8].

# Item 84: How to Log Slow Queries with Threshold

You can log slow queries using threshold via `DataSource-Proxy`. To get familiar with `DataSource-Proxy`, consider **Item 83**.

Having `DataSource-Proxy` ready to go, consider the following steps to log slow queries:

- In the bean post processor, define a constant representing the threshold of a slow query in milliseconds:

  ```
  private static final long THRESHOLD_MILLIS = 30;
  ```

- Further, define a `SLF4JQueryLoggingListener` listener and override the `afterQuery()` method as follows:

  ```
  SLF4JQueryLoggingListener listener
      = new SLF4JQueryLoggingListener() {
  ```

---

[8]HibernateSpringBootP6spy

```
    @Override
    public void afterQuery(ExecutionInfo execInfo,
                           List<QueryInfo> queryInfoList) {
        // call query logging logic only
        // when it took more than threshold
        if (THRESHOLD_MILLIS <= execInfo.getElapsedTime()) {
            logger.info("Slow SQL detected ...");
            super.afterQuery(execInfo, queryInfoList);
        }
    }
};

listener.setLogLevel(SLF4JLogLevel.WARN);
```

- Finally, use this `listener` to configure the datasource proxy:

```
this.dataSource = ProxyDataSourceBuilder.create(dataSource)
    .name("DATA_SOURCE_PROXY")
    .multiline()
    .listener(listener)
    .build();
```

Done! Now, the logged SQL will be just those that exceed the threshold. The source code is available on GitHub[9].

Starting with Hibernate 5.4.5, you can log slow queries with threshold in milliseconds via a new property named, `hibernate.session.events.log.LOG_QUERIES_SLOWER_THAN_MS`. All you have to do is to add in `application.properties` this property and to specify the threshold in milliseconds as in the following example:

```
spring.jpa.properties.hibernate.session
    .events.log.LOG_QUERIES_SLOWER_THAN_MS=25
```

A complete example is available on GitHub[10]. If you are not using Hibernate 5.4.5+ then logging slow queries can be done using a third-part library.

---

[9]HibernateSpringBootLogSlowQueries
[10]HibernateSpringBootLogSlowQueries545

# Item 85: Log Transactions and Query-Methods Details

Sometimes, in order to understand what's happening in the data access layer, you need to log more details about the running transactions (e.g., you may need to understand a certain transaction propagation scenario) and query-methods (e.g., you may need to log the execution time of a `query-method`).

## Log Transactions Details

By default, the logger `INFO` level doesn't reveal details about the running transactions. But you can easily expose transaction details by adding `application.properties` to the following lines:

```
logging.level.ROOT=INFO
logging.level.org.springframework.orm.jpa=DEBUG
logging.level.org.springframework.transaction=DEBUG
logging.level.org.hibernate.engine.transaction.internal.
TransactionImpl=DEBUG
```

Sometimes it's useful to log connection pool status as well. For HikariCP (the recommended and default connection pool in Spring Boot applications), you can do this by adding `application.properties` to the following settings:

```
logging.level.com.zaxxer.hikari.HikariConfig=DEBUG
logging.level.com.zaxxer.hikari=DEBUG
```

If you need more detail, replace `DEBUG` with `TRACE`.

## Take Control via Transaction Callbacks

Spring Boot allows you to enable a set of callbacks useful for taking control before transaction commits/completes and after transaction commits/completes. Globally (at the application-level), you can do it via a AOP component, as shown here:

```
@Aspect
@Component
public class TransactionProfiler extends TransactionSynchronizationAdapter {
```

```
Logger logger = LoggerFactory.getLogger(this.getClass());

@Before("@annotation(
    org.springframework.transaction.annotation.Transactional)")
public void registerTransactionSyncrhonization() {
    TransactionSynchronizationManager.registerSynchronization(this);
}

@Override
public void afterCompletion(int status) {
    logger.info("After completion (global) ...");
}

@Override
public void afterCommit() {
    logger.info("After commit (global) ...");
}

@Override
public void beforeCompletion() {
    logger.info("Before completion (global) ...");
}

@Override
public void beforeCommit(boolean readOnly) {
    logger.info("Before commit (global) ...");
}
}
```

For example, you could call this service-method:

```
@Transactional
public void updateAuthor() {

    Author author = authorRepository.findById(1L).orElseThrow();

    author.setAge(49);
}
```

The log will then contain something similar to this:

```
Hibernate: select author0_.id as id1_0_0_, author0_.age as age2_0_0_,
author0_.genre as genre3_0_0_, author0_.name as name4_0_0_ from author
author0_ where author0_.id=?
```

```
c.b.profiler.TransactionProfiler: Before commit (global) ...
c.b.profiler.TransactionProfiler: Before completion (global) ...
```

```
Hibernate: update author set age=?, genre=?, name=? where id=?
```

```
c.b.profiler.TransactionProfiler: After commit (global) ...
c.b.profiler.TransactionProfiler: After completion (global) ...
```

You can also take advantage of these callbacks at the method-level via
TransactionSynchronizationManager#registerSynchronization(), as shown here:

```
@Transactional
public void updateAuthor() {

    TransactionSynchronizationManager.registerSynchronization(
        new TransactionSynchronizationAdapter() {

        @Override
        public void afterCompletion(int status) {
            logger.info("After completion (method) ...");
        }

        @Override
        public void afterCommit() {
            logger.info("After commit (method) ...");
        }

        @Override
        public void beforeCompletion() {
            logger.info("Before completion (method) ...");
        }

        @Override
        public void beforeCommit(boolean readOnly) {
```

```
            logger.info("Before commit (method) ...");
        }
    });

    Author author = authorRepository.findById(1L).orElseThrow();

    author.setAge(51);
}
```

This time, the output is as follows:

```
Hibernate: select author0_.id as id1_0_0_, author0_.age as age2_0_0_,
author0_.genre as genre3_0_0_, author0_.name as name4_0_0_ from author
author0_ where author0_.id=?
```

```
c.b.profiler.TransactionProfiler: Before commit (method) ...
c.b.profiler.TransactionProfiler: Before completion (method) ...
```

```
Hibernate: update author set age=?, genre=?, name=? where id=?
```

```
c.b.profiler.TransactionProfiler: After commit (method) ...
c.b.profiler.TransactionProfiler: After completion (method) ...
```

The TransactionSynchronizationManager class provides other useful methods, such as isActualTransactionActive(), getCurrentTransactionName(), isCurrentTransactionReadOnly(), and getCurrentTransactionIsolationLevel(). Each of these methods has a corresponding setter as well.

The complete application is available on GitHub[11].

## Log Query-Methods Execution Time

You can easily log query-method execution times via AOP. The following component is pretty straightforward:

```
@Aspect
@Component
public class RepositoryProfiler {

    Logger logger = LoggerFactory.getLogger(this.getClass());
```

---

[11]HibernateSpringBootTransactionCallback

```
@Pointcut("execution(public *
    org.springframework.data.repository.Repository+.*(..))")
public void intercept() {
}

@Around("intercept()")
public Object profile(ProceedingJoinPoint joinPoint) {

long startMs = System.currentTimeMillis();

Object result = null;
try {
    result = joinPoint.proceed();
} catch (Throwable e) {
    logger.error(e.getMessage(), e);
    // do whatever you want with the exception
}

long elapsedMs = System.currentTimeMillis() - startMs;

// you may like to use logger.debug
logger.info(joinPoint.getTarget()+"."+joinPoint.getSignature()
    + ": Execution time: " + elapsedMs + " ms");

// pay attention that this line may return null
return result;
    }
}
```

For example, you could call this service-method:

```
@Transactional
public void updateAuthor() {

    Author author = authorRepository.findById(1L).orElseThrow();

    author.setAge(49);
}
```

Then the log will contain something similar to this:

```
c.bookstore.profiler.RepositoryProfiler  : org.springframework.data.
jpa.repository.support.SimpleJpaRepository@780dbed7.Optional org.
springframework.data.repository.CrudRepository.findById(Object):
Execution time: 47 ms
```

The complete application is available on GitHub[12].

---

[12]HibernateSpringBootRepoIntercept

# CHAPTER 10

# Configuring DataSource and Connection Pool

## Item 86: How to Customize HikariCP Settings

Spring Boot relies on HikariCP as the default connection pool.

Adding in your project `spring-boot-starter-jdbc` or `spring-boot-starter-data-jpa` "starters" will automatically add a dependency to HikariCP with the default settings.

> It's important to know how to alter the configuration of your connection pool. Most of the time, the default settings don't satisfy the production requirements. The best way to tune the connection pool parameters for production is using FlexyPool[1] by Vlad Mihalcea. FlexyPool can determine the optimal settings needed to sustain the high performance of the connection pool. FlexyPool is just one of several amazing tools. For more details, check out **Appendix J**.
>
> Assuming that you have set the optimal values for your connection pool, this chapter shows you several approaches for setting them in production for HikariCP.

---

[1]https://github.com/vladmihalcea/flexy-pool

© Anghel Leonard 2020
A. Leonard, *Spring Boot Persistence Best Practices*, https://doi.org/10.1007/978-1-4842-5626-8_10

# Tuning HikariCP Parameters via application.properties

You can tune HikariCP's parameters in the `application.properties` file. Each parameter value can be altered by appending its name as a suffix to a Spring property starting with `spring.datasource.hikari.*`. The * is a placeholder for the parameter name. The list of parameters and their meanings can be found in the HikariCP documentation. The following snippet of code shows example settings for the most common parameters:

```
spring.datasource.hikari.connectionTimeout=50000
spring.datasource.hikari.idleTimeout=300000
spring.datasource.hikari.maxLifetime=900000
spring.datasource.hikari.maximumPoolSize=8
spring.datasource.hikari.minimumIdle=8
spring.datasource.hikari.poolName=MyPool
spring.datasource.hikari.connectionTestQuery=select 1 from dual
# disable auto-commit
spring.datasource.hikari.autoCommit=false
# more settings can be added as spring.datasource.hikari.*
```

Or, like this:

```
spring.datasource.hikari.connection-timeout=50000
spring.datasource.hikari.idle-timeout=300000
spring.datasource.hikari.max-lifetime=900000
spring.datasource.hikari.maximum-pool-size=8
spring.datasource.hikari.minimum-idle=8
spring.datasource.hikari.pool-name=MyPool
spring.datasource.hikari.connection-test-query=select 1 from dual
```

Spring Boot processes `application.properties` and configures the HikariCP connection pool according to those values. The complete code is available on GitHub[2].

---

[2]HibernateSpringBootHikariCPPropertiesKickoff

# Tuning HikariCP Parameters via application.properties and DataSourceBuilder

You can tune HikariCP's parameters by using the application.properties file and DataSourceBuilder. This class provides support for building a DataSource with common implementations and properties. This time, in application.properties, the parameter names are specified as suffixes of a custom property (e.g., app.datasource.*):

```
app.datasource.connection-timeout=50000
app.datasource.idle-timeout=300000
app.datasource.max-lifetime=900000
app.datasource.maximum-pool-size=8
app.datasource.minimum-idle=8
app.datasource.pool-name=MyPool
app.datasource.connection-test-query=select 1 from dual
# disable auto-commit
app.datasource.auto-commit=false
# more settings can be added as app.datasource.*
```

Further, configuring the DataSource requires two steps:

- Use @ConfigurationProperties to load the properties of type app.datasource

- Use DataSourceBuilder to build an instance of HikariDataSource

The following code speaks for itself:

```
@Configuration
public class ConfigureDataSource {

    @Bean
    @Primary
    @ConfigurationProperties("app.datasource")
    public DataSourceProperties dataSourceProperties() {
        return new DataSourceProperties();
    }
```

```
@Bean
@ConfigurationProperties("app.datasource")
public HikariDataSource dataSource(DataSourceProperties properties) {
    return properties.initializeDataSourceBuilder()
        .type(HikariDataSource.class)
        .build();
    }
}
```

The complete code is available on GitHub[3].

# Tuning HikariCP Parameters via DataSourceBuilder

You can tune HikariCP parameters programmatically via DataSourceBuilder. In other words, the connection pool's parameters are set directly via the DataSourceBuilder API. This can be done in two steps:

- Create an instance of HikariDataSource

- Call dedicated methods for shaping this data source

In addition to the setJdbcUrl(), setUsername(), and setPassword() methods, the DataSourceBuilder API exposes dedicated methods for the HikariCP parameters, as shown in the following snippet of code:

```
@Configuration
public class ConfigureDataSource {

    @Bean
    public HikariDataSource dataSource() {

        HikariDataSource hds = new HikariDataSource();
            hds.setJdbcUrl("jdbc:mysql://localhost:3306/numberdb"
                                + "?createDatabaseIfNotExist=true");
        hds.setUsername("root");
        hds.setPassword("root");
```

---

[3]HibernateSpringBootDataSourceBuilderHikariCPKickoff

```
        hds.setConnectionTimeout(50000);
        hds.setIdleTimeout(300000);
        hds.setMaxLifetime(900000);
        hds.setMaximumPoolSize(8);
        hds.setMinimumIdle(8);
        hds.setPoolName("MyPool");
        hds.setConnectionTestQuery("select 1 from dual");
        hds.setAutoCommit(false);

        return hds;
    }
}
```

The complete code is available on GitHub[4].

# Tuning Other Connection Pools

This item dissertation can be applied to other connection pools as well. While the big picture remains the same, the developer needs to make small adjustments, as in the following list of examples (the following examples use `application.properties` and DataSourceBuilder): BoneCP[5], C3P0[6], DBCP2[7], Tomcat,[8] and ViburDBCP[9].

Mainly, these examples follow three steps:

- In `pom.xml` (for Maven), add the dependency corresponding to the connection pool

- In `application.properties`, configure the connection pool via a custom prefix, e.g., `app.datasource.*`

- Write a @Bean that returns the `DataSource` via `DataSourceBuilder`

---

[4]HibernateSpringBootDataSourceBuilderProgHikariCPKickoff
[5]HibernateSpringBootDataSourceBuilderBoneCPKickoff
[6]HibernateSpringBootDataSourceBuilderC3P0Kickoff
[7]HibernateSpringBootDataSourceBuilderDBCP2Kickoff
[8]HibernateSpringBootDataSourceBuilderTomcatKickoff
[9]HibernateSpringBootDataSourceBuilderViburDBCPKickoff

# Item 87: How to Configure Two Data Sources with Two Connection Pools

This item tackles the configuration of two databases with two connections pools. More precisely, an entity named Author is mapped to a table named author in a database named authorsdb, while another entity named Book is mapped to a table named book in a database named booksdb. The entities are not related and are very straightforward:

```
@Entity
public class Author implements Serializable {

    private static final long serialVersionUID = 1L;

    @Id
    @GeneratedValue(strategy = GenerationType.IDENTITY)
    private Long id;

    private String name;
    private String genre;
    private int age;
    private String books;

    // getters and setters omitted for brevity
}

@Entity
public class Book implements Serializable {

    private static final long serialVersionUID = 1L;

    @Id
    @GeneratedValue(strategy = GenerationType.IDENTITY)
    private Long id;

    private String title;
    private String isbn;
    private String authors;

    // getters and setters omitted for brevity
}
```

Calling query-methods from AuthorRepository will result in SQL statements triggered against the authorsdb database, while calling query-methods from BookRepository will result in SQL statements triggered against the booksdb database.

First, focus on application.properties. Here, let's add the configurations for the data sources. More precisely, let's add the configurations for the two JDBC URLs and connection pools. Notice that the first data source uses the app.datasource.ds1 prefix, while the second data source uses the app.datasource.ds2 prefix:

```
app.datasource.ds1.url=jdbc:mysql://localhost:3306/authorsdb
                                    ?createDatabaseIfNotExist=true
app.datasource.ds1.username=root
app.datasource.ds1.password=root
app.datasource.ds1.connection-timeout=50000
app.datasource.ds1.idle-timeout=300000
app.datasource.ds1.max-lifetime=900000
app.datasource.ds1.maximum-pool-size=8
app.datasource.ds1.minimum-idle=8
app.datasource.ds1.pool-name=MyPoolDS1
app.datasource.ds1.connection-test-query=select 1 from dual

app.datasource.ds2.url=jdbc:mysql://localhost:3306/booksdb
                                    ?createDatabaseIfNotExist=true
app.datasource.ds2.username=root
app.datasource.ds2.password=root
app.datasource.ds2.connection-timeout=50000
app.datasource.ds2.idle-timeout=300000
app.datasource.ds2.max-lifetime=900000
app.datasource.ds2.maximum-pool-size=4
app.datasource.ds2.minimum-idle=4
app.datasource.ds2.pool-name=MyPoolDS2
app.datasource.ds2.connection-test-query=select 1 from dual
```

These configurations can be set programmatically in a @Configuration class as well. Here is an example:

```
@Bean
public HikariDataSource dataSource() {

    HikariDataSource hds = new HikariDataSource();
    hds.setJdbcUrl("jdbc:mysql://localhost:3306/numberdb
                    ?createDatabaseIfNotExist=true");
    ...
    return hds;
}
```

Further, these settings are loaded and used to create instances of HikariDataSource in a class annotated with @Configuration. Each database has an associated HikariDataSource:

```
@Configuration
public class ConfigureDataSources {

    // first database, authorsdb
    @Primary
    @Bean(name = "configAuthorsDb")
    @ConfigurationProperties("app.datasource.ds1")
    public DataSourceProperties firstDataSourceProperties() {
        return new DataSourceProperties();
    }

    @Primary
    @Bean(name = "dataSourceAuthorsDb")
    @ConfigurationProperties("app.datasource.ds1")
    public HikariDataSource firstDataSource(
            @Qualifier("configAuthorsDb") DataSourceProperties properties) {
        return properties.initializeDataSourceBuilder()
            .type(HikariDataSource.class)
            .build();
    }
```

```
// second database, booksdb
@Bean(name = "configBooksDb")
@ConfigurationProperties("app.datasource.ds2")
public DataSourceProperties secondDataSourceProperties() {
    return new DataSourceProperties();
}

@Bean(name = "dataSourceBooksDb")
@ConfigurationProperties("app.datasource.ds2")
public HikariDataSource secondDataSource(
        @Qualifier("configBooksDb") DataSourceProperties properties) {
    return properties.initializeDataSourceBuilder()
        .type(HikariDataSource.class)
        .build();
}
}
```

Next, for each HikariDataSource, configure a LocalContainerEntityManager
FactoryBean and a PlatformTransactionManager. Tell Spring Boot that the entities
mapped to authorsdb are in the com.bookstore.ds1 package:

```
@Configuration
@EnableJpaRepositories(
    entityManagerFactoryRef = "ds1EntityManagerFactory",
    transactionManagerRef = "ds1TransactionManager",
    basePackages = "com.bookstore.ds1"
)
@EnableTransactionManagement
public class FirstEntityManagerFactory {

    @Bean
    @Primary
    public LocalContainerEntityManagerFactoryBean ds1EntityManagerFactory(
                EntityManagerFactoryBuilder builder,
                @Qualifier("dataSourceAuthorsDb") DataSource
                dataSource) {
```

```java
        return builder
            .dataSource(dataSource)
            .packages(packagesToScan())
            .persistenceUnit("ds1-pu")
            .properties(hibernateProperties())
            .build();
    }

    @Bean
    @Primary
    public PlatformTransactionManager ds1TransactionManager(
                    @Qualifier("ds1EntityManagerFactory")
                    EntityManagerFactory ds1EntityManagerFactory) {
        return new JpaTransactionManager(ds1EntityManagerFactory);
    }

    protected String[] packagesToScan() {
        return new String[]{
            "com.bookstore.ds1"
        };
    }

    protected Map<String, String> hibernateProperties() {
        return new HashMap<String, String>() {
            {
                put("hibernate.dialect",
                    "org.hibernate.dialect.MySQL5Dialect");
                put("hibernate.hbm2ddl.auto", "create");
            }
        };

    }
}
```

Next, configure a LocalContainerEntityManagerFactoryBean and a PlatformTransactionManager for the second data source. This time, tell Spring Boot that the entities mapped to booksdb are in the com.bookstore.ds2 package:

```java
@Configuration
@EnableJpaRepositories(
    entityManagerFactoryRef = "ds2EntityManagerFactory",
    transactionManagerRef = "ds2TransactionManager",
    basePackages = "com.bookstore.ds2"
)
@EnableTransactionManagement
public class SecondEntityManagerFactory {

    @Bean
    public LocalContainerEntityManagerFactoryBean ds2EntityManagerFactory(
                EntityManagerFactoryBuilder builder,
                @Qualifier("dataSourceBooksDb") DataSource dataSource) {

        return builder
            .dataSource(dataSource)
            .packages(packagesToScan())
            .persistenceUnit("ds2-pu")
            .properties(hibernateProperties())
            .build();
    }

    @Bean
    public PlatformTransactionManager ds2TransactionManager(
                @Qualifier("ds2EntityManagerFactory") EntityManager
                Factory secondEntityManagerFactory) {
        return new JpaTransactionManager(secondEntityManagerFactory);
    }

    protected String[] packagesToScan() {
        return new String[]{
            "com.bookstore.ds2"
        };
    }

    protected Map<String, String> hibernateProperties() {
        return new HashMap<String, String>() {
            {
```

```
                    put("hibernate.dialect",
                        "org.hibernate.dialect.MySQL5Dialect");
                    put("hibernate.hbm2ddl.auto", "create");
                }
        };
    }
}
```

# Testing Time

The AuthorRepository is added to the com.bookstore.ds1 package, while BookRepository is added to the com.bookstore.ds2 package:

```
package com.bookstore.ds1;

@Repository
public interface AuthorRepository extends JpaRepository<Author, Long> {
}

package com.bookstore.ds2;

@Repository
public interface BookRepository extends JpaRepository<Book, Long> {
}
```

Persisting an author can be done in a service-method as follows:

```
public Author persistAuthor() {

    Author author = new Author();

    author.setName("Joana Nimar");
    author.setGenre("History");
    author.setAge(34);
    author.setBooks("A History of Ancient Prague, A People's History");

    return authorRepository.save(author);
}
```

Calling persistAuthor() will save the author in the authorsdb database.

Persisting a book can be done in a service-method as follows:

```
public Book persistBook() {

    Book book = new Book();

    book.setIsbn("001-JN");
    book.setTitle("A History of Ancient Prague");
    book.setAuthors("Joana Nimar");

    return bookRepository.save(book);
}
```

Calling persistBook() will save the book in the booksdb database.

The complete application in available on GitHub[10].

---

[10]HibernateSpringBootTwoDataSourceBuilderKickoff

# CHAPTER 11

# Audit

## Item 88: How to Track the Creation and Modification Times and Entity Users

This item explains how to add auto-generated persistent fields to track the creation and modification times and the users. Auditing is useful for maintaining history of records. This can help you track user activities.

Let's consider the following names for these persistent fields (feel free to alter these names as you like):

- `created`: The timestamp when the row was inserted in the database
- `createdBy`: The current logged-in user(s) who triggered the insertion of this row
- `lastModified`: The timestamp of the last update of this row
- `lastModifiedBy`: The current logged-in user(s) who triggered the last update

---

By default, the timestamps will be saved in the local time zone, but let's save them in UTC (or GMT) instead. In MySQL, storing timestamps in UTC (or GMT) can be accomplished in two steps (see **Item 111**):

- Add `useLegacyDatetimeCode=false` to JDBC URL
- Add `spring.jpa.properties.hibernate.jdbc.time_zone=UTC` to `application.properties`

---

© Anghel Leonard 2020

A. Leonard, *Spring Boot Persistence Best Practices*, https://doi.org/10.1007/978-1-4842-5626-8_11

Adding these auto-generated persistent fields to entities can be done via Spring Data JPA auditing or Hibernate support. In both cases, these fields are added to an abstract non-entity class annotated with @MappedSuperclass (which designates a class whose mapping information is applied to the entities that inherit from it).

Let's name this class BaseEntity, as shown in Figure 11-1.

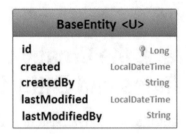

**Figure 11-1.**  *The base entity class diagram*

Entities can inherit these fields by extending BaseEntity. For example, let's track the user activity for the Author and Book entities.

Figure 11-2 speaks for itself.

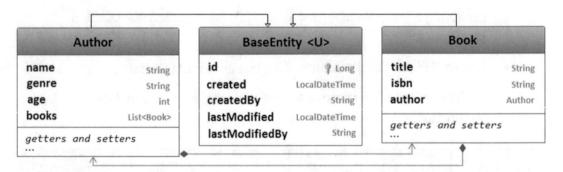

**Figure 11-2.**  *Domain Model*

Now, let's put this in code via Spring Data JPA auditing.

# Rely on Spring Data JPA Auditing

Spring Data provides four annotations that serve this goal. These annotations are @CreatedBy (for the createdBy field), @CreatedDate (for the created field), @LastModifiedBy (for the lastModifiedBy field), and @LastModifiedDate (for the lastModified field). Having the fields annotated accordingly is just half of the solution.

In addition, next to the @MappedSuperclass annotation, the BaseEntity should be annotated with @EntityListeners({AuditingEntityListener.class}). The class specified as the listener (AuditingEntityListener) is a Spring Data JPA entity listener class. It uses callback methods (annotated with the @PrePersist and @PreUpdate annotations) to persist and update the created, createdBy, lastModified, and lastModifiedBy fields. This happens whenever the entity is persisted or updated. That being said, here's the code:

```
@MappedSuperclass
@EntityListeners({AuditingEntityListener.class})
public abstract class BaseEntity<U> {

    @Id
    @GeneratedValue(strategy = GenerationType.IDENTITY)
    protected Long id;

    @CreatedDate
    protected LocalDateTime created;

    @CreatedBy
    protected U createdBy;

    @LastModifiedDate
    protected LocalDateTime lastModified;

    @LastModifiedBy
    protected U lastModifiedBy;
}
```

The Author and Book extend BaseEntity as follows:

```
@Entity
public class Author extends BaseEntity<String> implements Serializable {

    ...
}

@Entity
public class Book extends BaseEntity<String> implements Serializable {

    ...
}
```

But this is not all! at this point, JPA can populate the created and lastModified fields using the current system time, but it cannot populate createdBy and lastModifiedBy. For this task, JPA needs to know the currently logged-in user(s). In other words, the developer needs to provide an implementation of AuditorAware and override the getCurrentAuditor() method.

The currently logged-in user is fetched inside getCurrentAuditor() via Spring Security. In this example, there is a dummy implementation with hard-coded users, but it should be very easy to hook your real users as long as you already have Spring Security in place:

```java
public class AuditorAwareImpl implements AuditorAware<String> {

    @Override
    public Optional<String> getCurrentAuditor() {

        // use Spring Security to retrieve the currently logged-in user(s)
        return Optional.of(Arrays.asList("mark1990", "adrianm", "dan555")
            .get(new Random().nextInt(3)));
    }
}
```

The final step consists of enabling JPA auditing by specifying @EnableJpaAuditing on a configuration class. @EnableJpaAuditing accepts one element, auditorAwareRef. The value of this element is the name of the AuditorAware bean:

```java
@SpringBootApplication
@EnableJpaAuditing(auditorAwareRef = "auditorAware")
public class MainApplication {
    ...
}
```

Done! Check out the "Testing Time" section for a quick run and output of the application. The complete code is available on GitHub[1].

---

[1]HibernateSpringBootAudit

# Relying on Hibernate Support

If, from some reason, this approach is not suitable, you can rely on Hibernate support.

## The created and lastModified Fields

For the created and lastModified fields, Hibernate provides two built-in annotations (@CreationTimestamp and @UpdateTimestamp) that can be used out of the box.

> Both @CreationTimestamp and @UpdateTimestamp perform in-memory generation of the timestamp (using the VM time).

The createdBy and lastModifiedBy fields need annotations that must be implemented, as you will see soon. For now, let's consider that the annotation for createdBy is @CreatedBy and for lastModifiedBy it's @ModifiedBy. Putting it all together in BaseEntity results in the following code:

```
import org.hibernate.annotations.CreationTimestamp;
import org.hibernate.annotations.UpdateTimestamp;
...
@MappedSuperclass
public abstract class BaseEntity<U> {

    @Id
    @GeneratedValue(strategy = GenerationType.IDENTITY)
    protected Long id;

    @CreationTimestamp
    protected LocalDateTime created;

    @UpdateTimestamp
    protected LocalDateTime lastModified;

    @CreatedBy
    protected U createdBy;

    @ModifiedBy
    protected U lastModifiedBy;
}
```

# The createdBy and lastModifiedBy Fields

For the createdBy and lastModifiedBy fields, there is no Hibernate-specific built-in annotation. But you can build the @CreatedBy and @ModifiedBy annotations via the Hibernate-specific AnnotationValueGeneration interface. This interface represents a ValueGeneration based on a custom Java generator annotation type, where ValueGeneration describes the generation of property values. First, let's define the @CreatedBy annotation using @ValueGenerationType as follows:

```
@ValueGenerationType(generatedBy = CreatedByValueGeneration.class)
@Retention(RetentionPolicy.RUNTIME)
public @interface CreatedBy {
}
```

Then the @ModifiedBy annotation:

```
@ValueGenerationType(generatedBy = ModifiedByValueGeneration.class)
@Retention(RetentionPolicy.RUNTIME)
public @interface ModifiedBy {
}
```

> Starting with Hibernate 4.3, a new approach for declaring generated attributes and custom generators is available via the @ValueGenerationType meta-annotation. The @Generated annotation has been retrofitted to use @ValueGenerationType.

The CreatedByValueGeneration class implements AnnotationValueGeneration and provides the generator for the user's name (the user who created the entity). The relevant code is listed here (this timestamp should be generated only when the entity is persisted for the first time; therefore, set generation timing to GenerationTiming.INSERT):

```
public class CreatedByValueGeneration
              implements AnnotationValueGeneration<CreatedBy> {

    private final ByValueGenerator generator
        = new ByValueGenerator(new UserService());

    ...
```

```
@Override
public GenerationTiming getGenerationTiming() {
    return GenerationTiming.INSERT;
}

@Override
public ValueGenerator<?> getValueGenerator() {
    return generator;
}
...
}
```

The ModifiedByValueGeneration class implements AnnotationValueGeneration and provides the generator for the user's name (the user who modified the entity). The relevant code is listed here (this timestamp should be generated at every update of the entity; therefore, set generation timing to GenerationTiming.ALWAYS):

```
public class ModifiedByValueGeneration
                    implements AnnotationValueGeneration<ModifiedBy> {

    private final ModifiedByValueGenerator generator
        = new ModifiedByValueGenerator(new UserService());
    ...
    @Override
    public GenerationTiming getGenerationTiming() {
        return GenerationTiming.ALWAYS;
    }

    @Override
    public ValueGenerator<?> getValueGenerator() {
        return generator;
    }
    ...
}
```

The generator returned by CreatedByValueGeneration and ModifiedByValue Generation is ByValueGenerator. This represents a straightforward implementation of the ValueGenerator interface. The result of this class is the generateValue() method:

```
public class ByValueGenerator implements ValueGenerator<String> {

    public final UserService userService;

    public ByValueGenerator(UserService userService) {
        this.userService = userService;
    }

    @Override
    public String generateValue(Session session, Object entity) {
        // Hook into a service to get the current user, etc.
        return userService.getCurrentUserName();
    }
}
```

The UserService should use Spring Security to return the currently logged user via getCurrentUserName(). For now, let's simply use a dummy implementation:

```
@Service
public class UserService {

    public String getCurrentUserName() {
        // use Spring Security to retrieve the currently logged-in user(s)
        return Arrays.asList("mark1990", "adrianm", "dan555")
            .get(new Random().nextInt(3));
    }
}
```

Obviously, you can quickly hook your own service that deals with logged-in users.

The complete code is available on GitHub[2].

---

[2]HibernateSpringBootTimestampGeneration

# Testing Time

Both of these approaches produce the same SQL statements and results; therefore, the following discussion covers both.

Persisting an author triggers the following SQL statement:

```
INSERT INTO author (created, created_by, last_modified,
                    last_modified_by, age, genre, name)
  VALUES (?, ?, ?, ?, ?, ?, ?)
```

Persisting a book triggers the following SQL statement:

```
INSERT INTO book (created, created_by, last_modified,
                  last_modified_by, author_id, isbn, title)
  VALUES (?, ?, ?, ?, ?, ?, ?)
```

Updating an author triggers the following SQL statement:

```
UPDATE author
SET created = ?,
    created_by = ?,
    last_modified = ?,
    last_modified_by = ?,
    age = ?,
    genre = ?,
    name = ?
WHERE id = ?
```

Updating a book triggers the following SQL statement:

```
UPDATE book
SET created = ?,
    created_by = ?,
    last_modified = ?,
    last_modified_by = ?,
    author_id = ?,
    isbn = ?,
    title = ?
WHERE id = ?
```

Figure 11-3 shows a snapshot of the author and book tables. Notice the created, created_by, last_modified, and last_modified_by columns.

**author**

| id | created | created_by | last_modified | last_modified_by | age | genre | name |
|----|---------|-----------|---------------|------------------|-----|-------|------|
| 1 | 2019-07-24 06:30:58 | dan555 | 2019-07-24 06:30:58 | dan555 | 34 | Anthology | Quartis Young |
| 2 | 2019-07-24 06:30:58 | dan555 | 2019-07-24 06:31:04 | adrianm | 45 | Anthology | Mark Janel |

**book**

| id | created | created_by | last_modified | last_modified_by | isbn | title | author_id |
|----|---------|-----------|---------------|------------------|------|-------|-----------|
| 1 | 2019-07-24 06:30:58 | adrianm | 2019-07-24 06:31:09 | adrianm | not available | The Beatles Anthology | 1 |
| 2 | 2019-07-24 06:30:58 | adrianm | 2019-07-24 06:31:09 | adrianm | not available | A People's Anthology | 1 |
| 3 | 2019-07-24 06:30:58 | adrianm | 2019-07-24 06:30:58 | adrianm | 003 | Anthology Myths | 2 |

*Figure 11-3.* *Data snapshot from the author and book tables*

# Item 89: How to Enable Hibernate-Specific Envers Auditing

**Item 88** talks about how to track the creation and modification times and the users for entities via the Spring Data JPA auditing and Hibernate value generators. Hibernate ORM has a module named Hibernate Envers that's dedicated to auditing/versioning entity classes. Among its features, Hibernate Envers provides auditing, logging data for each *revision*, and querying historical snapshots of an entity and its associations.

This item iterates the best practices for enabling Hibernate Envers. But not before adding Hibernate Envers dependency to pom.xml (for Maven):

```
<dependency>
    <groupId>org.hibernate</groupId>
    <artifactId>hibernate-envers</artifactId>
</dependency>
```

Hibernate Envers uses Java Architecture for the XML Binding (JAXB) API; therefore, if you get an exception of this type:

```
Caused by: javax.xml.bind.JAXBException: Implementation of JAXB-API has
not been found on module path or classpath
```

That means the following dependencies are needed as well:

```
<dependency>
    <groupId>javax.xml.bind</groupId>
    <artifactId>jaxb-api</artifactId>
</dependency>
<dependency>
    <groupId>org.glassfish.jaxb</groupId>
    <artifactId>jaxb-runtime</artifactId>
</dependency>
```

## Auditing Entities

Preparing the entities that should be audited via Hibernate Envers is a simple task that requires you to add the @Audited annotation at the entity class-level. Each entity is audited in a separate database table. To explicitly specify the name of the audit-table per entity, rely on the @AuditTable annotation (by default, the name is of type *entity*_AUD). This can be done as shown here for the Author and Book entities:

```
@Entity
@Audited
@AuditTable("author_audit")
public class Author implements Serializable {

    ...

}

@Entity
@Audited
@AuditTable("book_audit")
public class Book implements Serializable {

    ...

}
```

The database schema reveals the tables from Figure 11-4, including the author_audit table.

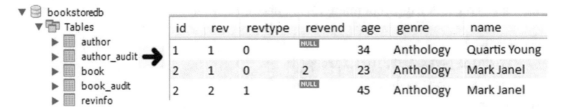

| | id | rev | revtype | revend | age | genre | name |
|---|---|---|---|---|---|---|---|
| bookstoredb | | | | | | | |
| ▼ 🗄 Tables | | | | | | | |
| ▶ 📋 author | 1 | 1 | 0 | NULL | 34 | Anthology | Quartis Young |
| ▶ 📋 author_audit → | 2 | 1 | 0 | 2 | 23 | Anthology | Mark Janel |
| ▶ 📋 book | | | | | | | |
| ▶ 📋 book_audit | 2 | 2 | 1 | NULL | 45 | Anthology | Mark Janel |
| ▶ 📋 revinfo | | | | | | | |

***Figure 11-4.*** *The author_audit table*

> *Revision* is a term specific to Hibernate Envers. It refers to a database transaction that has modified the audited entity (INSERT, UPDATE, or DELETE). The revinfo table (last table in Figure 11-4) stores the *revision* number and its epoch timestamp.

The author_audit (and book_audit) table stores the snapshot of the entity for a certain revision. The rev column holds the revision number.

The revtype column value is taken from the RevisionType enum, and it's defined as follows:

- 0 (or ADD): A database table row was inserted.

- 1 (or MOD): A database table row was updated.

- 2 (or DEL): A database table row was deleted.

The revend column holds the end revision number in audit entities. This column appears only if the validity audit strategy is used. ValidityAuditStrategy is discussed a little bit later.

## Schema Generation

Using Hibernate Envers requires a suite of tables besides the actual entity tables. These tables can be generated from JPA annotations (e.g., @Audited and @AuditedTable) as long as spring.jpa.hibernate.ddl-auto is set up to export schema DDL into the database. Such an application can be found on GitHub[3].

---

[3]HibernateSpringBootEnvers

But, in production, relying on this practice is a bad idea. If automatic schema migration is not needed, then schema-*.sql can do the job for you. Otherwise, it's better to rely on tools like Flyway or Liquibase.

In both cases, the developer needs the CREATE TABLE statements for the Envers tables. In this case, these statements are as follows (notice that the names of the tables correspond to the names specified via @AuditedTable):

```sql
CREATE TABLE author_audit (
  id BIGINT(20) NOT NULL,
  rev INT(11) NOT NULL,
  revtype TINYINT(4) DEFAULT NULL,
  revend INT(11) DEFAULT NULL,
  age INT(11) DEFAULT NULL,
  genre VARCHAR(255) DEFAULT NULL,
  name VARCHAR(255) DEFAULT NULL,
  PRIMARY KEY (id,rev),
  KEY FKp4vbplw134mimnk3nlxfvmcho (rev),
  KEY FKdtg6l7ccqhpsdnkltcoisi9l9 (revend));

CREATE TABLE book_audit (
  id BIGINT(20) NOT NULL,
  rev INT(11) NOT NULL,
  revtype TINYINT(4) DEFAULT NULL,
  revend INT(11) DEFAULT NULL,
  isbn VARCHAR(255) DEFAULT NULL,
  title VARCHAR(255) DEFAULT NULL,
  author_id BIGINT(20) DEFAULT NULL,
  PRIMARY KEY (id,rev),
  KEY FKjx5fxkthrd6kxbxb3ukwbo4mf (rev),
  KEY FKr9ed64q1nek7vjfbcxmo4v8ic (revend));

CREATE TABLE revinfo (
  rev INT(11) NOT NULL AUTO_INCREMENT,
  revtstmp BIGINT(20) DEFAULT NULL,
  PRIMARY KEY (rev));
```

If Envers doesn't automatically recognize the used schema then the schema name should be passed as follows:

- For MySQL: `spring.jpa.properties.org.hibernate.envers.default_catalog`

- For others: `spring.jpa.properties.org.hibernate.envers.default_schema`

The complete code is available on GitHub[4].

## Querying the Entity Snapshots

Hibernate Envers provides support for querying the entity snapshots. The starting point is represented by the `AuditReaderFactory`, which is a factory for `AuditReader` objects.

You can build an `AuditReader` via a JPA `EntityManager` or Hibernate `Session` as shown:

```
EntityManager em;
...
// via EntityManager
AuditReader reader = AuditReaderFactory.get(em);

// via Session
AuditReader reader = AuditReaderFactory.get(em.unwrap(Session.class));
```

The `AuditReader` is the entry point to a wide range of features against the audit log. Among its features, `AuditReader` allows you query the audit log via the `createQuery()` method. Here are two examples:

- Get all Book instances modified at revision #3:

    ```
    List<Book> books = reader.createQuery()
        .forEntitiesAtRevision(Book.class, 3).getResultList();
    ```

---

[4]HibernateSpringBootEnversSchemaSql

- Get all Book instances in all the states in which they were audited:

```
List<Book> books = reader.createQuery()
    .forRevisionsOfEntity(Book.class, true, true).getResultList();
```

I strongly recommend that you take some time and overview this API since it has a plethora of features. Especially if you need more advanced queries.

## ValidityAuditStrategy Audit Logging Strategy

By default, Hibernate Envers uses an audit logging strategy implemented under the name DefaultAuditStrategy. Let's use the following query (get all Book instances modified at revision *#3*):

```
List<Book> books = reader.createQuery()
    .forEntitiesAtRevision(Book.class, 3).getResultList();
```

The **SELECT** triggered behind the scenes is as follows:

```
SELECT
  book_aud0_.id AS id1_3_,
  book_aud0_.rev AS rev2_3_,
  book_aud0_.revtype AS revtype3_3_,
  book_aud0_.isbn AS isbn4_3_,
  book_aud0_.title AS title5_3_,
  book_aud0_.author_id AS author_i6_3_
FROM book_audit book_aud0_
WHERE book_aud0_.rev =
  (
    SELECT MAX(book_aud1_.rev)
    FROM book_audit book_aud1_
    WHERE book_aud1_.rev <= ?
    AND book_aud0_.id = book_aud1_.id
  )
AND book_aud0_.revtype <> ?
```

It's pretty obvious that this query is not very performant, especially if the audit log is quite big (check out the SELECT subquery).

But DefaultAuditStrategy is just one of the AuditStrategy implementations. Another one is ValidityAuditStrategy. You can enable this strategy in a Spring Boot application using application.properties, as follows:

```
spring.jpa.properties.org.hibernate.envers.audit_strategy
    =org.hibernate.envers.strategy.ValidityAuditStrategy
```

> Before Hibernate version 5.4, the correct value is org.hibernate.envers. strategy.internal.ValidityAuditStrategy.

Once ValidityAuditStrategy is enabled, you can try the same query again. This time, the SQL statement is more efficient:

```
SELECT
  book_aud0_.id AS id1_3_,
  book_aud0_.rev AS rev2_3_,
  book_aud0_.revtype AS revtype3_3_,
  book_aud0_.revend AS revend4_3_,
  book_aud0_.isbn AS isbn5_3_,
  book_aud0_.title AS title6_3_,
  book_aud0_.author_id AS author_i7_3_
FROM book_audit book_aud0_
WHERE book_aud0_.rev <= ?
AND book_aud0_.revtype <> ?
AND (book_aud0_.revend > ?
OR book_aud0_.revend IS NULL)
```

This time, there is no SELECT subquery! Nice! Further, this can be improved by adding an index for the revend and rev columns. This way, the sequential scan is avoided and the Envers becomes even more performant. However, the revend column appears only when you're using ValidityAuditStrategy and it references the revinfo table. Its purpose is to mark the last revision for which this entity snapshot was still valid.

Keep in mind that `ValidityAuditStrategy` is very good at fast entity snapshot fetching, but it performs worse than `DefaultAuditStrategy` while preserving the entity states in the database. It's usually worth it to spend extra time during writing and have faster reads, but this is not a general rule. It's not wrong to prefer `DefaultAuditStrategy`, if it's what you need.

# Item 90: How to Inspect the Persistence Context

Have you ever wondered what is in the Persistence Context? Or whether a certain entity or collection is in the current Persistence Context or not? You can inspect the Hibernate Persistence Context via `org.hibernate.engine.spi.PersistenceContext`. First, a helper method exploits the `SharedSessionContractImplementor` to get the `PersistenceContext`, as shown here:

```
@PersistenceContext
private final EntityManager entityManager;
...
private org.hibernate.engine.spi.PersistenceContext getPersistenceContext() {

    SharedSessionContractImplementor sharedSession = entityManager.unwrap(
        SharedSessionContractImplementor.class
    );

    return sharedSession.getPersistenceContext();
}
```

Further, `PersistenceContext` provides a generous number of methods for adding, removing, and inspecting its content. For example, the following method displays the number of total managed entities and some information about them, including their status and hydrated state:

```
private void briefOverviewOfPersistentContextContent() {

    org.hibernate.engine.spi.PersistenceContext persistenceContext
        = getPersistenceContext();
```

```
int managedEntities
    = persistenceContext.getNumberOfManagedEntities();
int collectionEntriesSize
    = persistenceContext.getCollectionEntriesSize();

System.out.println("Total number of managed entities: "
    + managedEntities);
System.out.println("Total number of collection entries: "
    + collectionEntriesSize);

// getEntitiesByKey() will be removed and probably replaced
// with #iterateEntities()
Map<EntityKey, Object> entitiesByKey
    = persistenceContext.getEntitiesByKey();

if (!entitiesByKey.isEmpty()) {
    System.out.println("\nEntities by key:");
    entitiesByKey.forEach((key, value) -> System.out.println(key
        + ": " + value));

    System.out.println("\nStatus and hydrated state:");
    for (Object entry : entitiesByKey.values()) {
        EntityEntry ee = persistenceContext.getEntry(entry);
        System.out.println(
            "Entity name: " + ee.getEntityName()
                + " | Status: " + ee.getStatus()
                + " | State: " + Arrays.toString(ee.getLoadedState()));
    }
}

if (collectionEntriesSize > 0) {
    System.out.println("\nCollection entries:");
    persistenceContext.forEachCollectionEntry(
        (k, v) -> System.out.println("Key:" + k
            + ", Value:" + (v.getRole() == null ? "" : v)), false);
}
}
```

Let's look at the Author and Book entities in a bidirectional lazy @OneToMany association. The following service-method:

- Fetches an author

- Fetches the associated books

- Deletes the author and the associated books

- Creates a new author with a single book

After each of these operations, the briefOverviewOfPersistentContextContent() method call is executed:

```
@Transactional
public void sqlOperations() {

    briefOverviewOfPersistentContextContent();

    Author author = authorRepository.findByName("Joana Nimar");
    briefOverviewOfPersistentContextContent();

    author.getBooks().get(0).setIsbn("not available");
    briefOverviewOfPersistentContextContent();

    authorRepository.delete(author);
    authorRepository.flush();
    briefOverviewOfPersistentContextContent();

    Author newAuthor = new Author();
    newAuthor.setName("Alicia Tom");
    newAuthor.setAge(38);
    newAuthor.setGenre("Anthology");

    Book book = new Book();
    book.setIsbn("001-AT");
    book.setTitle("The book of swords");

    newAuthor.addBook(book); // use addBook() helper

    authorRepository.saveAndFlush(newAuthor);
    briefOverviewOfPersistentContextContent();
}
```

Calling sqlOperations() outputs:

Initially the Persistence Context is empty:

```
Total number of managed entities: 0
Total number of collection entities: 0
```

After the SELECT for *Joana Nimar* was triggered:

```
Total number of managed entities: 1
Total number of collection entries: 1
```

**Entities by key:**
```
EntityKey[com.bookstore.entity.Author#4]:
    Author{id=4, name=Joana Nimar, genre=History, age=34}
```

**Status and hydrated state** (because we required the hydrated state, Hibernate will trigger a SELECT to fetch the books of this author):
```
Entity name: com.bookstore.entity.Author
    | Status: MANAGED
    | State: [34, [Book{id=1, title=A History of Ancient Prague,
                isbn=001-JN}, Book{id=2, title=A People's History,
                isbn=002-JN}], History, Joana Nimar]
```

**Collection entries:**
```
Key:[Book{id=1, title=A History of Ancient Prague, isbn=001-JN}, Book{id=2,
title=A People's History, isbn=002-JN}], Value:CollectionEntry[com.
bookstore.entity.Author.books#4]
```

After the SELECT statement for the books of *Joana Nimar* is triggered (there are two books):

```
Total number of managed entities: 3
Total number of collection entries: 1
```

**Entities by key:**
```
EntityKey[com.bookstore.entity.Book#2]:
    Book{id=2, title=A People's History, isbn=002-JN}
EntityKey[com.bookstore.entity.Author#4]:
    Author{id=4, name=Joana Nimar, genre=History, age=34}
```

```
EntityKey[com.bookstore.entity.Book#1]:
    Book{id=1, title=A History of Ancient Prague, isbn=not available}
```

**Status and hydrated state:**
```
Entity name: com.bookstore.entity.Book
    | Status: MANAGED
    | State: [Author{id=4, name=Joana Nimar, genre=History, age=34},
                002-JN, A People's History]

Entity name: com.bookstore.entity.Author
    | Status: MANAGED
    | State: [34, [Book{id=1, title=A History of Ancient Prague,
                isbn=not available}, Book{id=2, title=A People's History,
                isbn=002-JN}], History, Joana Nimar]

Entity name: com.bookstore.entity.Book
    | Status: MANAGED
    | State: [Author{id=4, name=Joana Nimar, genre=History, age=34},
                001-JN, A History of Ancient Prague]
```

**Collection entries:**
```
Key:[Book{id=1, title=A History of Ancient Prague, isbn=not
available}, Book{id=2, title=A People's History, isbn=002-JN}],
Value:CollectionEntry[com.bookstore.entity.Author.books#4]
```

After the DELETE statements of the author and the associated books are triggered:

```
Total number of managed entities: 0
Total number of collection entities: 0
```

After the INSERT statements that persist the new author and their book are triggered:

```
Total number of managed entities: 2
Total number of collection entries: 1
```

**Entities by key:**
```
EntityKey[com.bookstore.entity.Book#5]:
    Book{id=5, title=The book of swords, isbn=001-AT}
EntityKey[com.bookstore.entity.Author#5]:
    Author{id=5, name=Alicia Tom, genre=Anthology, age=38}
```

**Status and hydrated state:**

Entity name: com.bookstore.entity.Book
    | Status: MANAGED
    | State: [Author{id=5, name=Alicia Tom, genre=Anthology, age=38},
                001-AT, The book of swords]

Entity name: com.bookstore.entity.Author
    | Status: MANAGED
    | State: [38, [Book{id=5, title=The book of swords,
                isbn=001-AT}], Anthology, Alicia Tom]

**Collection entries:**

Key:[Book{id=5, title=The book of swords, isbn=001-AT}],
Value:CollectionEntry[com.bookstore.entity.Author.books#5]
    ->[com.bookstore.entity.Author.books#5]

This is just an example to get you familiar with the PersistenceContext API. Peruse the documentation to discover more useful methods.

The complete application is available on GitHub[5].

# Item 91: How to Extract Table Metadata

You can extract table metadata (or, generally speaking, database metadata) via the Hibernate SPI, org.hibernate.integrator.spi.Integrator. Implementing Integrator consists of overriding the integrate() method and returning metadata.getDatabase(), as follows:

```
public class DatabaseTableMetadataExtractor
          implements org.hibernate.integrator.spi.Integrator {

    public static final DatabaseTableMetadataExtractor EXTRACTOR
        = new DatabaseTableMetadataExtractor();

    private Database database;

    // this method will be deprecated starting with Hibernate 6.0
```

---

[5]HibernateSpringBootInspectPersistentContext

```
    @Override
    public void integrate(
        Metadata metadata,
        SessionFactoryImplementor sessionImplementor,
        SessionFactoryServiceRegistry serviceRegistry) {

        database = metadata.getDatabase();
    }

    @Override
    public void disintegrate(
        SessionFactoryImplementor sessionImplementor,
        SessionFactoryServiceRegistry serviceRegistry) {
    }

    public Database getDatabase() {
        return database;
    }
}
```

Next, register this Integrator via LocalContainerEntityManagerFactoryBean, as follows:

```
@Configuration
@EnableJpaRepositories(
    entityManagerFactoryRef = "entityManagerFactory",
    transactionManagerRef = "transactionManager",
    basePackages = "com.bookstore.*"
)
@EnableTransactionManagement
public class EntityManagerFactoryConfig {

    @Bean
    @Primary
    public LocalContainerEntityManagerFactoryBean entityManagerFactory(
            EntityManagerFactoryBuilder builder, DataSource dataSource) {

        return builder
            .dataSource(dataSource)
```

```
            .packages(packagesToScan())
            .persistenceUnit("ds-pu")
            .properties(hibernateProperties())
            .build();
    }

    @Bean
    @Primary
    public PlatformTransactionManager transactionManager(
            @Qualifier("entityManagerFactory") EntityManagerFactory
            entityManagerFactory) {

        return new JpaTransactionManager(entityManagerFactory);
    }

    protected String[] packagesToScan() {
        return new String[]{
            "com.bookstore.*"
        };
    }

    protected Map<String, Object> hibernateProperties() {
        return new HashMap<String, Object>() {
            {
                put("hibernate.dialect",
                    "org.hibernate.dialect.MySQL5Dialect");
                put("hibernate.hbm2ddl.auto", "create");
                put("hibernate.integrator_provider",
                    (IntegratorProvider) () -> Collections.singletonList(
                        DatabaseTableMetadataExtractor.EXTRACTOR
                    ));
            }
        };
    }
}
```

Done! Now, let's use the Domain Model shown in Figure 11-5.

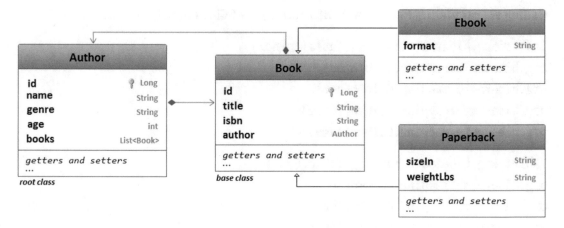

***Figure 11-5.***  *Domain Model*

You can extract and display the metadata of the mapping tables as follows (there is one mapping table per entity class):

```
public void extractTablesMetadata() {
    for (Namespace namespace :
                DatabaseTableMetadataExtractor.EXTRACTOR
                    .getDatabase()
                    .getNamespaces()) {

        namespace.getTables().forEach(this::displayTablesMetdata);
    }
}

private void displayTablesMetdata(Table table) {

    System.out.println("\nTable: " + table);
    Iterator it = table.getColumnIterator();
    while (it.hasNext()) {
        System.out.println(it.next());
    }
}
```

Calling extractTablesMetadata() will produce the following output:

```
Table: org.hibernate.mapping.Table(Author)
org.hibernate.mapping.Column(id)
org.hibernate.mapping.Column(age)
org.hibernate.mapping.Column(genre)
org.hibernate.mapping.Column(name)
```

```
Table: org.hibernate.mapping.Table(Book)
org.hibernate.mapping.Column(id)
org.hibernate.mapping.Column(isbn)
org.hibernate.mapping.Column(title)
org.hibernate.mapping.Column(author_id)
```

```
Table: org.hibernate.mapping.Table(Ebook)
org.hibernate.mapping.Column(format)
org.hibernate.mapping.Column(ebook_book_id)
```

```
Table: org.hibernate.mapping.Table(Paperback)
org.hibernate.mapping.Column(sizeIn)
org.hibernate.mapping.Column(weightLbs)
org.hibernate.mapping.Column(paperback_book_id)
```

The complete application is available on GitHub[6].

---

[6]HibernateSpringBootTablesMetadata

# CHAPTER 12

# Schemas

## Item 92: How to Set Up Flyway in Spring Boot

For production, don't rely on `hibernate.ddl-auto` (or counterparts) to export schema DDL to the database. Simply remove (disable) `hibernate.ddl-auto` or set it to `validate` and rely on Flyway or Liquibase. This item presents several aspects of setting Flyway as the database migration tool in Spring Boot.

> This section contains applications for MySQL and PostgreSQL.
>
> In this context, is important to know that the terms *database*, *schema*, and *catalog* represent the same thing in MySQL, while in PostgreSQL, a *database* is the same as a *catalog* and can have multiple *schemas* (two tables with the same name can live in the same *database* but in different *schemas*).

### Quickest Flyway Setup (MySQL and PostgreSQL)

The quickest setup with default settings is achievable by adding a Flyway dependency to the project. For Maven, add `pom.xml` to the following dependency:

```
<dependency>
    <groupId>org.flywaydb</groupId>
    <artifactId>flyway-core</artifactId>
</dependency>
```

Spring Boot has a flag-setting named `spring.flyway.enabled`. This flag-setting is set by default to `true`; therefore, when Spring Boot gets acknowledgment about the Flyway presence, it will rely on default settings for Flyway to migrate the database.

601

A. Leonard, *Spring Boot Persistence Best Practices*, https://doi.org/10.1007/978-1-4842-5626-8_12

By default, Spring Boot looks up the SQL files in the `classpath:db/migration` path (configurable via `spring.flyway.locations`). Files names should respect the Flyway naming conventions (e.g., `V1.1__Description.sql`). In addition, the developer can add in this location the SQL files corresponding to Flyway callbacks (e.g., `afterMigrate.sql`, `beforeClean.sql`, etc.). These files will be taken into consideration accordingly.

A kickoff application using Flyway and MySQL is available on GitHub[1].

The MySQL database is created via the specific parameter `createDatabaseIf NotExist=true` to the JDBC URL. Flyway will connect to this database present in the JDBC URL and will run the SQL files against it.

Moreover, a kickoff application using Flyway and PostgreSQL is also available on GitHub[2].

This application relies on the default `postgres` database and a `public` schema. The SQL files are executed against this schema.

> If the names of the tables used in `CREATE TABLE` are not the same as the names of the entities (e.g., for the `Author` entity, the table name should be `author`), you must use `@Table(name="`*table name*`")` to instruct JPA about the corresponding tables. For example, for a table named `author_ history` the entity name should be `AuthorHistory` or the `@Table` should be specified at entity level as `@Table(name="author_history")`.

## Instruct Flyway to Create the Database

This time, you'll instruct Flyway to create the MySQL database on your behalf.

> Flyway was not designed to create the database (e.g., execute `CREATE DATABASE` statements). It was designed to connect to an existing (empty or not) database and, once the connection is established, to execute all the given scripts against this database. Nevertheless, Flyway can create schemas via `CREATE SCHEMA`.

---

[1]HibernateSpringBootFlywayMySQLQuick

[2]HibernateSpringBootFlywayPostgreSQLQuick

Mainly, Flyway can be instructed to update schemas via the `spring.flyway.schemas` setting. If there is more than one schema, their names should be separated by commas. If the schemas don't exist, Flyway will automatically create them.

## MySQL

In MySQL, *schema* is equivalent to *database*; therefore, Flyway can create a MySQL database. Three steps are needed to accomplish this task:

- Remove the database name from the JDBC URL:

  ```
  spring.datasource.url=jdbc:mysql://localhost:3306/
  ```

- Instruct Flyway to update (and, since it doesn't exist, to create) the database via `spring.flyway.schemas`:

  ```
  spring.flyway.schemas=bookstoredb
  ```

- Inform entities about the database name, as in the following example:

  ```
  @Entity
  @Table(schema = "bookstoredb") // or @Table(catalog = "bookstoredb")
  public class Author implements Serializable {
      ...
  }
  ```

Done! Now Flyway will create the `bookstoredb` database on your behalf.

The complete application is available on GitHub[3].

## PostgreSQL

In comparison to MySQL, things are different in PostgreSQL because a PostgreSQL database can have multiple schemas. This time, creating a schema doesn't result in creating a database. It results in creating a schema.

In PostgreSQL, a connection is always to a certain database. Switching to another database requires a new connection. Flyway connects to an existing database and `CREATE SCHEMA` (triggered via `spring.flyway.schemas`) will create a schema in this database.

---

[3]HibernateSpringBootFlywayMySQLDatabase

The steps for accomplishing this behavior are listed here:

- Specify the database to connect to in the JDBC URL (e.g., the convenient default `postgres` database or your own database)

  ```
  spring.datasource.url=jdbc:postgresql://localhost:5432/
  postgres
  ```

- Instruct Flyway to update (and, since it doesn't exist, to create) the database via `spring.flyway.schemas`:

  ```
  spring.flyway.schemas=bookstore
  ```

- Inform entities about the database name, as in the following example:

  ```
  @Entity
  @Table(schema = "bookstore")
  public class Author implements Serializable {
      ...
  }
  ```

Done! Now Flyway will create the `bookstore` schema on your behalf. The complete application is available on GitHub[4].

A comparison of results can be seen in Figure 12-1.

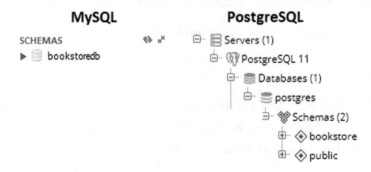

***Figure 12-1.***  *Schemas in MySQL and PostgreSQL*

---

[4]HibernateSpringBootFlywayPostgreSqlSchema

# Set Up Flyway via @FlywayDataSource

Flyway can be configured via Spring Boot properties prefixed with `spring.flyway.*` and placed in the `application.properties` file. Another approach consists of using the `@FlywayDataSource` annotation and the Flyway-fluent API.

In this context, most probably the `DataSource` is configured programmatically as well; therefore, let's consider the following MySQL `DataSource` (more details in **Item 86**):

```
@Bean(name = "dataSource")
public HikariDataSource dataSource() {

    HikariDataSource hds = new HikariDataSource();
        hds.setJdbcUrl("jdbc:mysql://localhost:3306/bookstoredb
                                ?createDatabaseIfNotExist=true");

    hds.setUsername("root");
    hds.setPassword("root");
    hds.setConnectionTimeout(50000);
    hds.setIdleTimeout(300000);
    hds.setMaxLifetime(900000);
    hds.setMaximumPoolSize(8);
    hds.setMinimumIdle(8);
    hds.setPoolName("MyPool");
    hds.setConnectionTestQuery("select 1 from dual");
    hds.setAutoCommit(false);

    return hds;
}
```

Next, this `DataSource` must be passed to Flyway. For this, you define a method that receives the `DataSource` as an argument, annotate it with `@FlywayDataSource`, and implement it as follows:

```
@FlywayDataSource
@Bean(initMethod = "migrate")
public Flyway flyway(@Qualifier("dataSource")
        HikariDataSource dataSource) {

    return Flyway.configure()
        .dataSource(dataSource)
```

```
        .locations("classpath:db/migration") // this path is default
        .load();
}
```

Flyway will connect to the database found in the JDBC URL of dataSource and run the SQL files from classpath:db/migration against it.

Feel free to explore the fluent API to see what settings can be customized.

The complete application is available on GitHub for MySQL[5] and PostgreSQL[6].

## Flyway and Multiple Schemas

Flyway can be set up to migrate multiple schemas of the same vendor or different vendors. For such examples, please consider:

- Automatically creating and migrating two databases in MySQL[7]

- Automatically creating and migrating two databases in PostgreSQL[8]

- Automatically creating and migrating two DataSources (MySQL and PostgreSQL)[9]

# Item 93: How to Generate Two Databases via schema-*.sql and Match Entities to Them

For production, don't rely on hibernate.ddl-auto (or counterparts) to export schema DDL to the database. Simply remove (disable) hibernate.ddl-auto or set it to validate and rely on schema-*.sql or, for production, on Flyway (**Item 92**) or Liquibase.

Relying on schema-*.sql is useful for avoiding generating schema from JPA annotations. However, it's not versioned, so schema migration is not supported. In schema-*.sql the developer can call the SQL statements that will be executed at each run of the application.

---

[5]HibernateSpringBootFlywayMySQLProg
[6]HibernateSpringBootFlywayPostgreSQLProg
[7]HibernateSpringBootFlywayMySQLTwoDatabases
[8]HibernateSpringBootFlywayPostgreSqlTwoSchemas
[9]HibernateSpringBootFlywayTwoVendors

For example, the following schema-mysql.sql contains the DDL statements that are specific to MySQL for creating two databases and two tables (the author table in authorsdb database and the book table in the booksdb database):

```
CREATE DATABASE IF NOT EXISTS authorsdb;

CREATE TABLE IF NOT EXISTS authorsdb.author
  (
    id BIGINT(20) NOT NULL auto_increment,
    age INT(11) NOT NULL,
    genre VARCHAR(255) DEFAULT NULL,
    name VARCHAR(255) DEFAULT NULL,
    PRIMARY KEY (id)
  );

CREATE DATABASE IF NOT EXISTS booksdb;

CREATE TABLE IF NOT EXISTS booksdb.book
  (
    id BIGINT(20) NOT NULL auto_increment,
    isbn VARCHAR(255) DEFAULT NULL,
    title VARCHAR(255) DEFAULT NULL,
    PRIMARY KEY (id)
  );
```

To instruct Spring Boot to execute the DDL statements from schema-mysql.sql just add application.properties to the following settings:

```
spring.datasource.initialization-mode=always
spring.datasource.platform=mysql
```

Possible values of spring.datasource.initialization-mode are always, embedded, and never. While always and never are quite clear, the embedded value (which is the default) instructs Spring Boot to initialize the schema only if you are relying on an embedded database (e.g., H2).

Moreover, in application.properties, set the JDBC URL without an explicit database:

```
spring.datasource.url=jdbc:mysql://localhost:3306
```

Further, the Author entity should be explicitly mapped to the authorsdb.author table and the Book entity should be mapped to booksdb.book table. For this, annotate the Author entity with @Table(schema="authorsdb") and the Book entity with @Table(schema="booksdb"):

```
@Entity
@Table(schema="authorsdb")
public class Author implements Serializable {
    ...
}

@Entity
@Table(schema="booksdb")
public class Book implements Serializable {
    ...
}
```

That's all! Now, you can use the AuthorRepository and BookRepository as usual. The query-methods from AuthorRepository will be triggered against the authorsdb, while the query-methods from BookRepository will be triggered against the booksdb.

The complete application in available on GitHub[10].

If you want to import SQL script files via Hibernate then you have to use the hibernate.hbm2ddl.import_files property. Simple pass the files to be loaded as the value of this property. Or, you can do it via JPA 2.1 schema generation features. For loading a script simply use javax.persistence.sql-load-script-source property. A complete example is available on GitHub[11].

---

[10]HibernateSpringBootMatchEntitiesToTablesTwoSchemas
[11]HibernateSpringBootSchemaGeneration

# CHAPTER 13

# Pagination

## Item 94: When and Why Offset Pagination May Become a Performance Penalty

Offset pagination is very popular and Spring Boot (more precisely, Spring Data Commons) provides support for it via the Page and Slice APIs. However, while your project evolves and data is accumulating, relying on offset pagination may lead to performance penalties even if it was not an issue at the start of the project.

Dealing with offset pagination means you can ignore the performance penalty induced by throwing away $n$ records before reaching the desired offset. A larger $n$ leads to a significant performance penalty. Another penalty is the extra SELECT needed to count the total number of records (especially if you need to count every fetched page). While keyset (seek) pagination can be the way to go (as a different approach), offset pagination can be optimized to avoid this extra SELECT, as explained in **Item 95** and **Item 96**. So, if you are familiar with this topic and all you need is an optimized offset pagination, you can simply jump to **Item 95** and **Item 96**. Okay, now let's continue...

With relatively small datasets, offset and keyset provide almost the same performance. But, can you guarantee that the dataset will not grow over time or can you control the growing process? Most businesses start with a small amount of data, but when success accelerates, the amount of data can increase very quickly as well.

## Index Scan in Offset and Keyset

Index scan in offset will traverse the range of indexes from the beginning to the specified offset. Basically, the offset represents the number of records that must be skipped before including them in the result, which means that a count has to be involved as well.

© Anghel Leonard 2020
A. Leonard, *Spring Boot Persistence Best Practices*, https://doi.org/10.1007/978-1-4842-5626-8_13

In offset, depending on how much data must be fetched and skipped (and keep in mind that tables usually "grow" quickly), this approach may lead to a significant performance degradation. The offset approach will traverse the already shown records. See Figure 13-1.

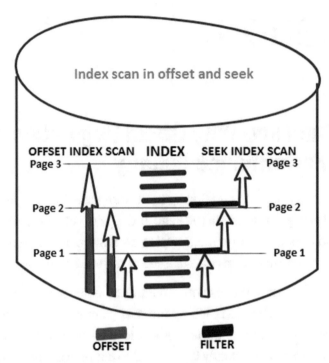

***Figure 13-1.*** *Index scan in offset vs. keyset pagination*

On the other hand, index scan in keyset will traverse only the required values, starting with the last previous value (it skips the values until the last value previously fetched). In keyset, the performance remains approximately constant in relation to the increase of the table records.

## Offset Pagination Pros and Cons

Consider the following pros and cons of offset pagination.

Cons:

- Inserts may cause pages leeway

- Each time, it numbers the rows from the beginning

- It applies a filter to drop out the unnecessary rows

- If the offset is greater than the number of rows in the ordered results, then no rows are returned

Pros:

- It can fetch arbitrary pages

An important reference and compelling argument against using offset pagination is represented by the USE THE INDEX, LUKE![1] website. I strongly suggest you take some time and watch this great presentation[2] of Markus Winand, which covers important topics for tuning pagination-SQL, like using indexes and *row values* (supported in PostgreSQL) in offset and keyset pagination.

Before jumping into a pagination implementation, it is advisable to consider at least the following two aspects:

- Sometimes there is no need to trigger a SELECT COUNT for every page (inserts/deletes are rare). In such cases, it's better to trigger SELECT COUNT periodically or only once.

- It's better to use powerful filtering capabilities instead of returning tons of pages. Think about when you last navigated beyond a few pages of a website and, if you don't remember, it means that your clients acts the same. They prefer to polish their filters instead of navigating tons of pages. Therefore, boost your filters until the returned results fits into a few pages.

---

[1]https://use-the-index-luke.com/no-offset
[2]https://www.slideshare.net/MarkusWinand/p2d2-pagination-done-the-postgresql-way?ref=https://use-the-index-luke.com/no-offset

# Spring Boot Offset Pagination

If the winner is offset pagination, then Spring Boot provides built-in support for offset pagination via the Page API. Consider the author table corresponding to the Author entity in Figure 13-2.

***Figure 13-2.***  *The Author entity table*

The following examples rely on the Author entity and the AuthorRepository repository to shape a simple way of implementing pagination. For starters, there at least five ways to fetch the result set, as follows:

> If you need to suppress pagination in a query-method that takes as an argument Pageable, then simply pass it Pageable.unpaged().

- Invoke a built-in findAll(Pageable) without explicit ordering (**not recommended**):

    authorRepository.findAll(PageRequest.of(page, size));

- Invoke a built-in findAll(Pageable) with ordering:

    authorRepository.findAll(PageRequest.of(page, size,
                        Sort.by(Sort.Direction.ASC, "price")));

- Use the Spring Data Query Builder mechanism to define new methods in your repository:

```
Page<Author> findByName(String name, Pageable pageable);
Page<Author> queryFirst10ByName(String name, Pageable pageable);
```

- Use JPQL and @Query with and without explicit SELECT COUNT:

```
@Query(value = "SELECT a FROM Author a WHERE a.genre = ?1",
        countQuery = "SELECT COUNT(*) FROM Author a WHERE a.genre = ?1")
public Page<Author> fetchByGenreExplicitCount(
                        String genre, Pageable pageable);

@Query("SELECT a FROM Author a WHERE a.genre = ?1")
public Page<Author> fetchByGenre(String genre, Pageable pageable);
```

- Use native query and @Query with and without explicit SELECT COUNT:

```
@Query(value = "SELECT * FROM author WHERE genre = ?1",
        countQuery = "SELECT COUNT(*) FROM author WHERE genre = ?1",
        nativeQuery = true)
public Page<Author> fetchByGenreNativeExplicitCount(
                            String genre, Pageable pageable);
@Query(value = "SELECT * FROM author WHERE genre = ?1",
        nativeQuery = true)
public Page<Author> fetchByGenreNative(String genre, Pageable
pageable);
```

Further, the classical repository needed to support pagination of Author will extend PagingAndSortingRepository, as follows:

```
@Repository
public interface AuthorRepository
            extends PagingAndSortingRepository<Author, Long> {
}
```

Next, a service-method can fetch pages of Author in ascending order by age, as follows:

```
public Page<Author> fetchNextPage(int page, int size) {
```

```
    return authorRepository.findAll(PageRequest.of(page, size,
                               Sort.by(Sort.Direction.ASC, "age")));
}
```

Next, call this from a controller as follows:

```
@GetMapping("/authors/{page}/{size}")
public Page<Author> fetchAuthors(@PathVariable int page,
                                  @PathVariable int size) {

    return bookstoreService.fetchNextPage(page, size);
}
```

Here is one possible request and its output (fetch the first page containing five authors and a pageable element with details):

```
http://localhost:8080/authors/1/5

{
    "content":[
        {
            "id":22,
            "age":24,
            "name":"Kemal Ilias",
            "genre":"History"
        },
        {
            "id":28,
            "age":24,
            "name":"Sandra Ostapenco",
            "genre":"History"
        },
        {
            "id":16,
            "age":24,
            "name":"Joana Leonte",
            "genre":"History"
        },
```

```
    {
        "id":46,
        "age":24,
        "name":"Alp Ran",
        "genre":"History"
    },
    {
        "id":12,
        "age":26,
        "name":"Katre Mun",
        "genre":"Anthology"
    }
],
"pageable":{
    "sort":{
        "sorted":true,
        "unsorted":false,
        "empty":false
    },
    "pageNumber":1,
    "pageSize":5,
    "offset":5,
    "paged":true,
    "unpaged":false
},
"totalPages":11,
"totalElements":51,
"last":false,
"numberOfElements":5,
"first":false,
"sort":{
    "sorted":true,
    "unsorted":false,
    "empty":false
},
```

```
    "number":1,
    "size":5,
    "empty":false
}
```

Two SQL statements are needed to fetch this result (the second SELECT counts the records and is triggered for every fetched page):

```
SELECT
    author0_.id AS id1_0_,
    author0_.age AS age2_0_,
    author0_.genre AS genre3_0_,
    author0_.name AS name4_0_
FROM author author0_
ORDER BY author0_.age ASC
LIMIT 5, 5

SELECT
    Count(author0_.id) AS col_0_0_
FROM author author0_
```

> Sometimes there is no need to trigger a SELECT COUNT for each page because new inserts or removes are very rare; therefore, the number of rows remains fix for a long time. In such cases, trigger a SELECT COUNT only once, when the first page is fetched, and rely on Slice or List for pagination instead of Page. Or you can trigger SELECT COUNT periodically (e.g., every 15 minutes, at every 10 pages, etc.).

> In the case of pagination, a deterministic sort order is mandatory. Therefore, do not forget the ORDER BY clause.

Notice that Spring can derive the Pageable object if you add it to the controller. The request's parameters follow these conventions:

- The page request parameter indicates the page to retrieve (the default is 0)

- The size request parameter indicates the size of the page to retrieve (the default is 20)

- The sort request parameter indicates sorting properties as property, property (,ASC|DESC) (the ascending direction is the default)

Here is a controller endpoint sample:

```
@GetMapping("/authors")
public Page<Author> fetchAuthors(Pageable pageable) {

    return bookstoreService.fetchNextPagePageable(pageable);
}
```

Here is a request of page 1 with size of 3 and sorted descending by name:

```
http://localhost:8080/authors?page=1&size=3&sort=name,desc
```

Or sorting by name descending and genre ascending:

```
http://localhost:8080/authors?page=1&size=3&sort=name,desc&sort=genre,asc
```

The source code is available on GitHub[3].

Before deciding which pagination type fits best, please consider reading this entire chapter. Most probably, the approach presented in this item will be most prone to performance penalties, so use it only as a landmark for what is coming next. The next two items—**Item 95** and **Item 96**—discuss optimizations of offset pagination.

More precisely, try to avoid the additional SELECT COUNTs via the COUNT(*) OVER() window function and the SELECT COUNT subquery.

The time-performance trend graphic shown in Figure 13-3 highlights that COUNT(*) OVER() tends to perform better than using two SELECT statements or a SELECT COUNT subquery. On the other hand, a SELECT COUNT subquery doesn't seem to come with an important benefit over triggering two SELECT statements. This is happening because the application and the database run on the same machine. If you access the database over a network, then triggering two SELECT statements will add the network overhead twice,

---

[3]HibernateSpringBootOffsetPagination

while a SELECT  COUNT subquery will add this overhead only once. In Figure 13-3, we assume the author table with 1 million records, and we try to fetch a page of 100 entities. More precisely, we fetch the first page (0), the 5,000th page, and the 9,999th page.

The time-performance trend graphic shown in Figure 13-3 was obtained against MySQL on a Windows 7 machine with the following characteristics: Intel i7, 2.10GHz, and 6GB RAM. The application and MySQL ran on the same machine.

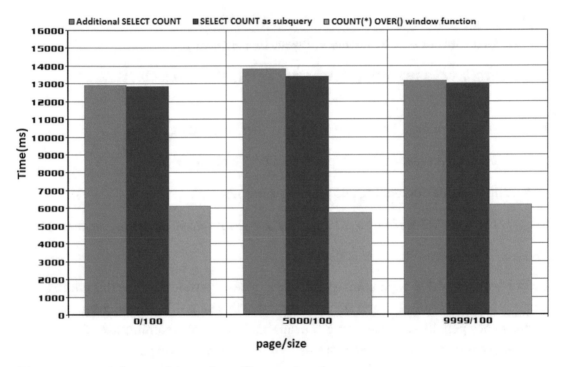

*Figure 13-3.* *Select entities using offset pagination*

In MySQL, to count records, you also have the SQL_CALC_FOUND_ROWS query modifier and the accompanying FOUND_ROWS() function. This approach was skipped in this book since it was marked to be deprecated in MySQL 8.0.17 and will be removed in a future MySQL version. Nevertheless, an interesting dissertation about SQL_CALC_FOUND_ROWS performance can be found here[4].

---

[4]https://www.percona.com/blog/2007/08/28/to-sql_calc_found_rows-or-not-to-sql_calc_found_rows/

# Item 95: How to Optimize Offset Pagination with COUNT(*) OVER and Page<entity/dto>

**Item 94** highlights the two potential performance penalties of offset pagination: traversing the already shown records and two separate SELECT statements per page (two database round trips). One SELECT fetches the data and another one counts the total records. Further, let's try to fetch the information obtained via these two SELECTs in only one query (one database round trip). This way, the performance penalty added by the second round trip is eliminated. As a trade-off, the SELECT that fetches the data will require some time for counting as well.

## COUNT(*) OVER( ) Windowed Aggregate

The COUNT(*) OVER() is a combination between the COUNT() aggregate function and the OVER() clause, which differentiates window functions from other functions. OVER specifies the window clauses for the aggregation functions.

Using COUNT(*) OVER() windowed aggregate to eliminate the second database round trip needed to fetch the total number of records can be used when the RDBMS supports window functions (e.g., MySQL 8). If your RDBMS doesn't support window functions, consider **Item 96**, which uses the SELECT COUNT subquery.

You can write a COUNT(*) OVER() query via a native query. COUNT(*) OVER() is part of the query that fetches the data. Its purpose is to count the total number of records. Further, each fetched page of data can be a page of entities (but only if there are plans to modify them) or a page of DTO (for read-only data). Let's see how to fetch a Page<*dto*>.

## Pages as Page<*dto*>

An uninspired approach for fetching Page<*dto*> is something as follows:

```
public Page<AuthorDto> findAll(Pageable pageable) {
    Page<Author> page = authorRepository.findAll(pageable);
```

```
    return new PageImpl<AuthorDto>(AuthorConverter/Mapper.convert/map(
        page.getContent()), pageable, page.getTotalElements());
}
```

> Some developers claim that the previous example is the way to go, based on a variety of reasons that are more or less true. However, before you decide, consider reading Vlad Mihalcea's tweet[5], which argues against this anti-pattern. Vlad says: "Don't fetch entities, only to use a mapper to create DTOs. That's very inefficient, yet I keep on seeing this anti-pattern being promoted."

While this method returns a Page<AuthorDto>, it still fetches the data into the Persistence Context when authorRepository.findAll() is called. Since the built-in findAll() is annotated with @Transactional(readOnly = true) the Persistence Context will not save the hydrated state. Therefore, the entities will be loaded in read-only mode.

It's better to avoid fetching the data as read-only entities with the single purpose of converting them to DTOs. In such cases, the DTO contains all properties of the entity (it mirrors the entity). Most of the time, we extract a subset of properties (common scenario in web applications), which means we extract only the needed properties from entities to DTOs and throw away the rest. Fetching more data than needed is a bad practice. So, in both scenarios, fetching entities with the single purpose of using a mapper to DTOs will cause performance penalties.

A Page<*dto*> requires a DTO; therefore, you define a Spring projection (DTO) containing the getters corresponding to the data that should be fetched. In this case, it's the age and name of the Author entity:

```
public interface AuthorDto {
    public String getName();

    public int getAge();
```

---

[5]https://twitter.com/vlad_mihalcea/status/1207887006883340288

```
@JsonIgnore
public long getTotal();
}
```

Check the highlighted two lines of code. The getTotal() is needed to map the result of COUNT(*) OVER(). This is not a property of the Author entity. Moreover, it is annotated with @JsonIgnore because it will not be serialized in the JSON response sent to the client. It will be used in the constructor of PageImpl to create a Page<AuthorDto>. But, before that, the JPQL query that fetches the data and the total number of records in a single database round trip are both listed here (the WHERE clause can be used as well):

```
@Repository
public interface AuthorRepository
            extends PagingAndSortingRepository<Author, Long> {

    @Query(value = "SELECT name, age, COUNT(*) OVER() AS total FROM
                  author", nativeQuery = true)
    List<AuthorDto> fetchAll(Pageable pageable);
}
```

Notice that the query doesn't explicitly set the ORDER BY and LIMIT clauses needed to order and limit the result set. However, using the passed Pageable, which contains the page, size, and sorting information, will do the job pretty nicely. This Pageable will add to the generated SQL statement the missing ORDER BY and LIMIT clauses based on the given size, page, and sort information. It will be no problem to replace the Pageable object with two integers and add ORDER BY age LIMIT ?1, ?2 to the query.

> The LIMIT clause is recognized by MySQL and PostgreSQL. SQL Server supports the SELECT TOP clause, while Oracle uses ROWNUM or ROWS FETCH NEXT *n* ROWS ONLY.

Calling fetchAll() will trigger the following SQL statement:

```
SELECT
  name,
  age,
  COUNT(*) OVER() AS total
```

```
FROM author
ORDER BY age ASC
LIMIT ? ?
```

The COUNT(*) OVER() result is stored via getTotal(). Since fetchAll() returns a List<AuthorDto>, it has to be converted to a Page<AuthorDto>. A service-method creates a Pageable and calls fetchAll(). The result of fetchAll() is used to create a Page<AuthorDto> via the following PageImpl constructor:

```
public PageImpl(List<T> content, Pageable pageable, long total)
```

The service-method is quite straightforward:

```
public Page<AuthorDto> fetchNextPage(int page, int size) {

    Pageable pageable = PageRequest.of(page, size,
                Sort.by(Sort.Direction.ASC, "age"));

    List<AuthorDto> authors = authorRepository.fetchAll(pageable);
    Page<AuthorDto> pageOfAuthors = new PageImpl(authors, pageable,
                authors.isEmpty() ? 0 : authors.get(0).getTotal());

    return pageOfAuthors;
}
```

A REST controller endpoint can call the fetchNextPage() method as follows:

```
@GetMapping("/authors/{page}/{size}")
public Page<AuthorDto> fetchAuthors(
            @PathVariable int page, @PathVariable int size) {

    return bookstoreService.fetchNextPage(page, size);
}
```

Here is some possible JSON output (notice that the total number of records is 51):

```
http://localhost:8080/authors/1/3
```

```
{
    "content":[
```

```
    {
        "age":23,
        "name":"Wuth Troll"
    },
    {
        "age":23,
        "name":"Nagir Turok"
    },
    {
        "age":24,
        "name":"Alp Ran"
    }
],
"pageable":{
    "sort":{
        "sorted":true,
        "unsorted":false,
        "empty":false
    },
    "pageSize":3,
    "pageNumber":1,
    "offset":3,
    "paged":true,
    "unpaged":false
},
"totalPages":17,
"totalElements":51,
"last":false,
"numberOfElements":3,
"first":false,
"sort":{
    "sorted":true,
    "unsorted":false,
    "empty":false
},
```

```
        "number":1,
        "size":3,
        "empty":false
}
```

The source code is available on GitHub[6].

You can easily fetch only the data (without the `pageable` element) as a `List<AuthorDto>`, as in this application[7].

# Pages as Page<*entity*>

While Page<*dto*> is a perfect fit for pagination of read-only data, Page<*entity*> is preferable for entities that will be modified.

Fetching an entity will not map the `COUNT(*) OVER()` result. The entity defines its set of properties (`id`, `age`, `name`, and `genre`), but it doesn't have a special property for representing the total number of records in the database. To fix this problem, there is at least one approach discussed further.

## Use a Dedicated Property

One way to map the total number of records returned by the `COUNT(*) OVER()` is to add a dedicated property in the corresponding entity. This property can be mapped to a column that is not *insertable* or *updatable,* as in the following example (there is no setter for the `total` property):

```
@Entity
public class Author implements Serializable {

    private static final long serialVersionUID = 1L;

    @Id
    @GeneratedValue(strategy = GenerationType.IDENTITY)
    private Long id;
```

---

```
    private int age;
    private String name;
    private String genre;

    @Column(insertable = false, updatable = false)
    long total;

    ...

    public long getTotal() {
        return total;
    }
}
```

Further, in the AuthorRepository, you can rely on a native SQL that contains COUNT(*) OVER(), as follows:

```
@Repository
public interface AuthorRepository
                    extends PagingAndSortingRepository<Author, Long> {

    @Query(value = "SELECT id, name, age, genre, COUNT(*) OVER() AS total
             FROM author", nativeQuery = true)
    List<Author> fetchAll(Pageable pageable);
}
```

Calling fetchAll() will trigger the following SELECT statement (notice that there is a single query for fetching a page of data as a List<Author>):

```
SELECT
  id,
  name,
  age,
  genre,
  COUNT(*) OVER() AS total
FROM author
ORDER BY age ASC
LIMIT ?, ?
```

The service-method that calls `fetchAll()` is responsible for preparing the Page<Author> as follows:

```
public Page<Author> fetchNextPage(int page, int size) {

    Pageable pageable = PageRequest.of(page, size,
                    Sort.by(Sort.Direction.ASC, "age"));

    List<Author> authors = authorRepository.fetchAll(pageable);
    Page<Author> pageOfAuthors = new PageImpl(authors, pageable,
                    authors.isEmpty() ? 0 : authors.get(0).getTotal());

    return pageOfAuthors;
}
```

The source code is available on GitHub[8]. The application exposes a REST endpoint of type `http://localhost:8080/authors/{page}/{size}`. The returned result is a JSON, as shown in the following example (there are 51 records in the author table and this is exposed by the total field):

```
http://localhost:8080/authors/1/3

{
    "content":[
        {
            "id":7,
            "age":23,
            "name":"Wuth Troll",
            "genre":"Anthology"
        },
        {
            "id":48,
            "age":23,
            "name":"Nagir Turok",
            "genre":"Anthology"
        },
```

---

[8]HibernateSpringBootPageEntityOffsetPaginationExtraColumnWF

```
        {
            "id":46,
            "age":24,
            "name":"Alp Ran",
            "genre":"History"
        }
    ],
    "pageable":{
        "sort":{
            "sorted":true,
            "unsorted":false,
            "empty":false
        },
        "pageSize":3,
        "pageNumber":1,
        "offset":3,
        "paged":true,
        "unpaged":false
    },
    "totalPages":17,
    "totalElements":51,
    "last":false,
    "numberOfElements":3,
    "first":false,
    "sort":{
        "sorted":true,
        "unsorted":false,
        "empty":false
    },
    "number":1,
    "size":3,
    "empty":false
}
```

You can easily fetch only the data (without the pageable element) as a List<Author>, as in this application[9].

---

[9]HibernateSpringBootListEntityOffsetPaginationExtraColumnWF

# Item 96: How to Optimize Offset Pagination with SELECT COUNT subquery and Page<entity/dto>

**Item 94** highlights two potential performance penalties of offset pagination: traversing the already shown records and two separate SELECT statements per page (two database round trips). One SELECT fetches the data and the other one counts the records. Let's try to trigger these two SELECTs in only one query (one database round trip). This way, the performance penalty of the second round trip is eliminated. As a trade-off, the SELECT that fetches the data will consume some time for counting as well.

## SELECT COUNT Subquery

Use the SELECT  COUNT subquery to eliminate the second database round trip needed to fetch the total number of records if your RDBMS doesn't support window functions (e.g., MySQL prior to version 8). If your RDBMS supports window functions, consider the method in **Item 95**.

You can write a SELECT  COUNT subquery via a native query or JPQL. Being a subquery, this SELECT  COUNT is nested in the SELECT that fetches the data, and its purpose is to count the total number of records. Further, each fetched page of data can be a page of entities (but only if there are plans to modify them) or a page of DTOs (for read-only data). Let's see how to fetch a Page<*dto*>.

## Pages as Page<*dto*>

An uninspired approach to fetching Page<*dto*> is something as follows:

```
public Page<AuthorDto> findAll(Pageable pageable) {
    Page<Author> page = authorRepository.findAll(pageable);
    return new PageImpl<AuthorDto>(AuthorConverter/Mapper.convert/map(
        page.getContent()), pageable, page.getTotalElements());
}
```

While this method returns a Page<AuthorDto>, it still fetches the data into the Persistence Context when authorRepository.findAll() is called. It will be a better way to avoid fetch the data as read-only entities, and afterward, to convert it to a DTO. Moreover, in this case, the DTO contains all the properties of the entity (it mirrors the entity). Extracting a subset of properties imposes the thrown away data that was fetched with no purpose.

A Page<*dto*> requires a DTO; therefore, you need to define a Spring projection (DTO) containing the getters that correspond to the data that should be fetched. In this case, it's the age and name of the Author entity:

```
public interface AuthorDto {

    public String getName();

    public int getAge();

    @JsonIgnore
    public long getTotal();
}
```

Check the highlighted two lines of code. getTotal() is needed to map the result of the SELECT COUNT subquery. This is not a property of the Author entity. Moreover, it is annotated with @JsonIgnore because it will not be serialized in the JSON response sent to the client. It will be used in the constructor of PageImpl to create a Page<AuthorDto>. But, before that, the JPQL query that fetches the data and the total number of records in a single database round trip is listed here:

```
@Repository
public interface AuthorRepository
            extends PagingAndSortingRepository<Author, Long> {

    @Query(value = "SELECT a.name as name, a.age as age, "
        + "(SELECT count(a) FROM Author a) AS total FROM Author a")
    List<AuthorDto> fetchAllJpql(Pageable pageable);
}
```

Notice that fetchAllJpql() takes an argument of type Pageable (an object that wraps metadata about a page of data such as page size, total elements, page number, sorting, etc.). JPQL does not provide a mechanism to limit queries; therefore, explicitly adding

LIMIT (or its counterparts) is not possible. This is most often achieved by using the setMaxResults() method on the Query. However, using Pageable will do the job pretty nicely. The passed Pageable will add to the generated SQL statement the ORDER BY and LIMIT clauses.

Calling fetchAllJpql() will trigger the following SQL statement:

**SELECT**
  author0_.name **AS** col_0_0_,
  author0_.age **AS** col_1_0_,
  (**SELECT COUNT**(author1_.id)
  **FROM** author author1_)
  **AS** col_2_0_
**FROM** author author0_
**ORDER BY** author0_.age **ASC**
**LIMIT** ? ?

---

The same effect can be obtained via the following native query:

```
@Repository
public interface AuthorRepository
            extends PagingAndSortingRepository<Author, Long> {
    @Query(value = "SELECT t.total, name, age FROM author, "
            + "(SELECT count(*) AS total FROM author) AS t",
            nativeQuery = true)
    List<AuthorDto> fetchAllNative(Pageable pageable);
}
```

---

The SELECT COUNT subquery result is stored via getTotal(). Since fetchAllJqpl() returns a List<AuthorDto>, it has to be converted to a Page<AuthorDto>. A service-method creates Pageable and calls fetchAllJpql(). The result of fetchAllJpql() is used to create a Page<AuthorDto> via the following PageImpl constructor:

```
public PageImpl(List<T> content, Pageable pageable, long total)
```

The service-method is quite straightforward:

```
public Page<AuthorDto> fetchNextPageJpql(int page, int size) {

    Pageable pageable = PageRequest.of(page, size,
                        Sort.by(Sort.Direction.ASC, "age"));

    List<AuthorDto> authors = authorRepository.fetchAllJpql(pageable);
    Page<AuthorDto> pageOfAuthors = new PageImpl(authors, pageable,
        authors.isEmpty() ? 0 : authors.get(0).getTotal());

    return pageOfAuthors;
}
```

A REST controller endpoint can call the fetchNextPageJpql() method, as follows:

```
@GetMapping("/authors/{page}/{size}")
public Page<AuthorDto> fetchAuthorsJpql(
            @PathVariable int page, @PathVariable int size) {

    return bookstoreService.fetchNextPageJpql(page, size);
}
```

Possible output is the following JSON (notice that the total number of records is 51):

```
http://localhost:8080/authors/1/3

{
    "content":[
        {
            "age":23,
            "name":"Tylor Ruth"
        },
        {
            "age":23,
            "name":"Wuth Troll"
        },
        {
            "age":24,
            "name":"Kemal Ilias"
        }
    ],
```

```
    "pageable":{
        "sort":{
            "unsorted":false,
            "sorted":true,
            "empty":false
        },
        "pageSize":3,
        "pageNumber":1,
        "offset":3,
        "paged":true,
        "unpaged":false
    },
    "totalPages":17,
    "totalElements":51,
    "last":false,
    "numberOfElements":3,
    "first":false,
    "sort":{
        "unsorted":false,
        "sorted":true,
        "empty":false
    },
    "number":1,
    "size":3,
    "empty":false
}
```

The source code is available on GitHub[10].

You can easily fetch only the data (without the pageable element) as a List<AuthorDto>, as in this application[11].

---

[10]HibernateSpringBootPageDtoOffsetPagination
[11]HibernateSpringBootListDtoOffsetPagination

# Pages as Page<*entity*>

While Page<*dto*> is the perfect fit for paginating read-only data, the Page<*entity*> is preferable for entities that will be modified.

Fetching an entity will not map the SELECT COUNT subquery result. An entity defines a set of properties, but it doesn't have a special property for representing the total number of records in the database. To fix this problem, there is at least one approach, discussed next.

## Use an Extra Property

One way to map the total number of records returned by the SELECT COUNT subquery is to add an extra property to the corresponding entity. This property can be mapped to a column that is not *insertable* or *updatable*, as in the following example (there is no setter for the total property):

```
@Entity
public class Author implements Serializable {

    private static final long serialVersionUID = 1L;

    @Id
    @GeneratedValue(strategy = GenerationType.IDENTITY)
    private Long id;
    private int age;
    private String name;
    private String genre;

    @Column(insertable = false, updatable = false)
    long total;

    ...

    public long getTotal() {
        return total;
    }
}
```

Further, in AuthorRepository, you can rely on a native SQL that contains the SELECT COUNT subquery, as follows:

```
@Repository
public interface AuthorRepository
            extends PagingAndSortingRepository<Author, Long> {

    @Query(value = "SELECT t.total, id, name, age, genre FROM author, "
        + "(SELECT count(*) AS total FROM author) AS t",
        nativeQuery = true)
    List<Author> fetchAll(Pageable pageable);
}
```

Calling fetchAll() will trigger the following SELECT statement (notice that there is a single query for fetching a page of data as a List<Author>):

```
SELECT
  t.total,
  id,
  name,
  age,
  genre
FROM author,
     (SELECT COUNT(*) AS total
     FROM author) AS t
ORDER BY age ASC
LIMIT ?, ?
```

The service-method that calls fetchAll() is responsible for preparing the Page<Author>, as follows:

```
public Page<Author> fetchNextPage(int page, int size) {

    Pageable pageable = PageRequest.of(page, size,
                    Sort.by(Sort.Direction.ASC, "age"));

    List<Author> authors = authorRepository.fetchAll(pageable);
    Page<Author> pageOfAuthors = new PageImpl(authors, pageable,
                    authors.isEmpty() ? 0 : authors.get(0).getTotal());

    return pageOfAuthors;
}
```

The source code is available on GitHub[12]. The application exposes a REST endpoint of type `http://localhost:8080/authors/{page}/{size}`. The returned result is a JSON, as in the following example (there are 51 records in the `author` table and this is exposed by the `total` field):

`http://localhost:8080/authors/1/3`

```
{
    "content":[
        {
            "id":25,
            "age":23,
            "name":"Tylor Ruth",
            "genre":"Anthology"
        },
        {
            "id":7,
            "age":23,
            "name":"Wuth Troll",
            "genre":"Anthology"
        },
        {
            "id":22,
            "age":24,
            "name":"Kemal Ilias",
            "genre":"History"
        }
    ],
    "pageable":{
        "sort":{
            "sorted":true,
            "unsorted":false,
            "empty":false
        },
```

---

[12]HibernateSpringBootPageEntityOffsetPaginationExtraColumn

```
        "pageSize":3,
        "pageNumber":1,
        "offset":3,
        "paged":true,
        "unpaged":false
    },
    "totalPages":17,
    "totalElements":51,
    "last":false,
    "numberOfElements":3,
    "first":false,
    "sort":{
        "sorted":true,
        "unsorted":false,
        "empty":false
    },
    "number":1,
    "size":3,
    "empty":false
}
```

You can easily fetch only the data (without the pageable element) as a List<Author>, as in this application[13].

# Item 97: How to Use JOIN FETCH and Pageable

Consider two entities (Author and Book) involved in a bidirectional lazy @OneToMany association. You can efficiently fetch the authors with the associated books in the same query via (LEFT) JOIN FETCH (**Item 39** and **Item 41**). You can apply pagination to the result set by combining (LEFT) JOIN FETCH and Pageable. But attempting to implement this combination results in an exception. For example, consider the following query:

---

[13]HibernateSpringBootListEntityOffsetPaginationExtraColumn

```
@Transactional(readOnly = true)
@Query(value = "SELECT a FROM Author a
                JOIN FETCH a.books WHERE a.genre = ?1")
Page<Author> fetchWithBooksByGenre (String genre, Pageable pageable);
```

Calling fetchWithBooksByGenre() results in the following exception:

```
org.hibernate.QueryException: query specified join fetching,but the owner
of the fetched association was not present in the select list [FromElement
{explicit, not a collection join, fetch join, fetch non-lazy properties,
classAlias = null, role = com.bookstore.entity.Author.books, tableName = book,
tableAlias = books1_, origin = author author0_, columns = {author0_.id,
className = com.bookstore.entity.Book}}]
```

The main cause of this exception is represented by the missing count query from Spring Data.

> If you don't actually need a Page (e.g., you  don't care about the total number of records and so on), then just replace Page with Slice or List. This will eliminate this exception.

You can add the missing SELECT COUNT via the countQuery element, as follows:

```
@Transactional
@Query(value = "SELECT a FROM Author a
                LEFT JOIN FETCH a.books WHERE a.genre = ?1",
       countQuery = "SELECT COUNT(a) FROM Author a WHERE a.genre = ?1")
Page<Author> fetchWithBooksByGenre(String genre, Pageable pageable);
```

Or you can add it via an ad hoc entity graph, as follows (more details about entity graphs are available in **Item 7**, **Item 8**, and **Item 9**):

```
@Transactional
@EntityGraph(attributePaths = {"books"},
             type = EntityGraph.EntityGraphType.FETCH)
@Query(value = "SELECT a FROM Author a WHERE a.genre = ?1")
Page<Author> fetchWithBooksByGenre(String genre, Pageable pageable);
```

This time, calling one of these `fetchWithBooksByGenre()` methods results in the following SQL statements:

```
SELECT
    author0_.id AS id1_0_0_,
    books1_.id AS id1_1_1_,
    author0_.age AS age2_0_0_,
    author0_.genre AS genre3_0_0_,
    author0_.name AS name4_0_0_,
    books1_.author_id AS author_i4_1_1_,
    books1_.isbn AS isbn2_1_1_,
    books1_.title AS title3_1_1_,
    books1_.author_id AS author_i4_1_0__,
    books1_.id AS id1_1_0__
FROM author author0_
LEFT OUTER JOIN book books1_
    ON author0_.id = books1_.author_id
WHERE author0_.genre = ?
ORDER BY author0_.name ASC

SELECT
    COUNT(author0_.id) AS col_0_0_
FROM author author0_
WHERE author0_.genre = ?
```

Notice that the pagination takes place in memory (there is no database pagination in these SQL statements). Moreover, this will be signaled as a message of type HHH000104:

`firstResult/maxResults specified with collection fetch; applying in memory!.`

Relying on pagination in memory can cause performance penalties, especially if the fetched collection is big. Therefore, use this code with extra care. For understanding and fixing HHH000104, please consider **Item 98**.

On the other hand, let's fetch all the books with the associated authors. For example:

```
@Transactional(readOnly = true)
@Query(value = "SELECT b FROM Book b
                LEFT JOIN FETCH b.author WHERE b.isbn LIKE ?1%",
       countQuery = "SELECT COUNT(b) FROM Book b WHERE b.isbn LIKE ?1%")
Page<Book> fetchWithAuthorsByIsbn(String isbn, Pageable pageable);

@Transactional(readOnly = true)
@EntityGraph(attributePaths = {"author"},
             type = EntityGraph.EntityGraphType.FETCH)
@Query(value = "SELECT b FROM Book b WHERE b.isbn LIKE ?1%")
Page<Book> fetchWithAuthorsByIsbn(String isbn, Pageable pageable);
```

Both queries trigger the following queries:

```
SELECT
  book0_.id AS id1_1_0_,
  author1_.id AS id1_0_1_,
  book0_.author_id AS author_i4_1_0_,
  book0_.isbn AS isbn2_1_0_,
  book0_.title AS title3_1_0_,
  author1_.age AS age2_0_1_,
  author1_.genre AS genre3_0_1_,
  author1_.name AS name4_0_1_
FROM book book0_
LEFT OUTER JOIN author author1_
  ON book0_.author_id = author1_.id
WHERE book0_.isbn LIKE ?
ORDER BY book0_.title ASC LIMIT ?

SELECT
  COUNT(book0_.id) AS col_0_0_
FROM book book0_
WHERE book0_.isbn LIKE ?
```

This time pagination is done by the database, which is way better than in memory.

The complete application is available on GitHub[14].

---

[14]HibernateSpringBootJoinFetchPageable

# Item 98: How to Fix HHH000104

In **Item 97**, you saw that HHH000104 is a warning that tell you that pagination of a result set is taking place in memory. For example, consider the Author and Book entities in a bidirectional lazy @OneToMany association and the following query:

```
@Transactional
@Query(value = "SELECT a FROM Author a
                  LEFT JOIN FETCH a.books WHERE a.genre = ?1",
        countQuery = "SELECT COUNT(a) FROM Author a WHERE a.genre = ?1")
Page<Author> fetchWithBooksByGenre(String genre, Pageable pageable);
```

Calling fetchWithBooksByGenre() works fine except that the following warning is signaled: HHH000104: firstResult/maxResults specified with collection fetch; applying in memory! Obviously, having pagination in memory cannot be good from a performance perspective.

Generally speaking, it is not possible to limit the size of a fetched collection with Hibernate ORM/JPA annotations. For example, it is not possible to limit the size of a @OneToMany collection. Hibernate cannot operate on subsets of a collection since it must manage the whole collection entity state transitions.

In this case, Hibernate cannot simply truncate the result set using SQL-level pagination because it's prone to truncate some Book rows. This may result in an Author having only a subset of Book. This is why pagination is done in memory, where Hibernate can control the entire result set. Unfortunately, especially with large result sets, this can result in significant performance penalties.

Since HHH000104 is reported as a warning, it is very possible to miss it in the log. Starting with Hibernate 5.2.13, HHH000104 is reported as an exception if hibernate.query.fail_on_pagination_over_collection_fetch property is enabled. In Spring Boot, this property can be enabled in application. properties as follows:

spring.jpa.properties.hibernate.query.fail_on_pagination_
over_collection_fetch=true

This time, missing HHH000104 is not possible, therefore ensure that you **always** enable this property in your projects.

Further, let's see how to fix HHH000104 and perform pagination on the database.

# Fetching Managed Entities

You can fetch the result set as a Page, a Slice, or a List.

## Fetching Page<Author>

First, let's focus on Page and fetch the IDs of authors of a given genre:

```
@Transactional(readOnly = true)
@Query(value = "SELECT a.id FROM Author a WHERE a.genre = ?1")
Page<Long> fetchPageOfIdsByGenre(String genre, Pageable pageable);
```

Further, let's fetch the books of these authors (the fetched IDs):

```
@Transactional(readOnly = true)
@QueryHints(value = @QueryHint(name = HINT_PASS_DISTINCT_THROUGH,
                              value = "false"))
@Query(value = "SELECT DISTINCT a FROM Author a
               LEFT JOIN FETCH a.books WHERE a.id IN ?1")
List<Author> fetchWithBooks(List<Long> authorIds);
```

Or, you can rely on entity graphs:

```
@Transactional(readOnly = true)
@EntityGraph(attributePaths = {"books"},
            type = EntityGraph.EntityGraphType.FETCH)
@QueryHints(value = @QueryHint(name = HINT_PASS_DISTINCT_THROUGH,
                              value = "false"))
@Query(value = "SELECT DISTINCT a FROM Author a WHERE a.id IN ?1")
List<Author> fetchWithBooksEntityGraph(List<Long> authorIds);
```

A service-method can call these two queries as follows (before calling `fetchWithBooks()`, it is recommended that you ensure that `pageOfIds.getContent()` is not empty):

```
@Transactional
public Page<Author> fetchAuthorsWithBooksByGenre(int page, int size) {

    Pageable pageable = PageRequest.of(
        page, size, Sort.by(Sort.Direction.ASC, "name"));

    Page<Long> pageOfIds = authorRepository
        .fetchPageOfIdsByGenre("Anthology", pageable);
    List<Author> listOfAuthors = authorRepository
        .fetchWithBooks(pageOfIds.getContent());
    Page<Author> pageOfAuthors = new PageImpl(
        listOfAuthors, pageable, pageOfIds.getTotalElements());

    return pageOfAuthors;
}
```

Similarly, you can call `fetchWithBooksEntityGraph()`.

> Notice that the service-method was annotated with @Transactional, which means that the entities will be fetched in read-write mode. If you need read-only entities, then add @Transactional(readOnly=true).

The triggered SQL statements are as follows (this is the same for entity graph usage):

```
SELECT
  author0_.id AS col_0_0_
FROM author author0_
WHERE author0_.genre = ?
ORDER BY author0_.name ASC LIMIT ? ?

SELECT
  COUNT(author0_.id) AS col_0_0_
FROM author author0_
WHERE author0_.genre = ?
```

```
SELECT
    author0_.id AS id1_0_0_,
    books1_.id AS id1_1_1_,
    author0_.age AS age2_0_0_,
    author0_.genre AS genre3_0_0_,
    author0_.name AS name4_0_0_,
    books1_.author_id AS author_i4_1_1_,
    books1_.isbn AS isbn2_1_1_,
    books1_.title AS title3_1_1_,
    books1_.author_id AS author_i4_1_0__,
    books1_.id AS id1_1_0__
FROM author author0_
LEFT OUTER JOIN book books1_
    ON author0_.id = books1_.author_id
WHERE author0_.id IN (?, ?, ?, ?)
```

Here's sample JSON output:

```
{
    "content":[
        {
            "id":1,
            "name":"Mark Janel",
            "genre":"Anthology",
            "age":23,
            "books":[
                {
                    "id":3,
                    "title":"The Beatles Anthology",
                    "isbn":"001-MJ"
                },
                {
                    "id":8,
                    "title":"Anthology From Zero To Expert",
                    "isbn":"002-MJ"
                },
```

```
            {
                "id":9,
                "title":"Quick Anthology",
                "isbn":"003-MJ"
            }
        ]
    },
    {
        "id":6,
        "name":"Merci Umaal",
        "genre":"Anthology",
        "age":31,
        "books":[
            {
                "id":7,
                "title":"Ultimate Anthology",
                "isbn":"001-MU"
            },
            {
                "id":10,
                "title":"1959 Anthology",
                "isbn":"002-MU"
            }
        ]
    }
],
"pageable":{
    "sort":{
        "sorted":true,
        "unsorted":false,
        "empty":false
    },
    "pageSize":2,
    "pageNumber":0,
    "offset":0,
```

```
      "paged":true,
      "unpaged":false
   },
   "totalElements":4,
   "totalPages":2,
   "last":false,
   "numberOfElements":2,
   "first":true,
   "sort":{
      "sorted":true,
      "unsorted":false,
      "empty":false
   },
   "number":0,
   "size":2,
   "empty":false
}
```

Further, you can optimize the implementation to avoid a separate SELECT COUNT for offset pagination. A quick approach is a native query using COUNT(*) OVER() as shown here:

```
@Transactional(readOnly = true)
@Query(value = "SELECT a.id AS id, COUNT(*) OVER() AS total
                FROM Author a WHERE a.genre = ?1",
       nativeQuery = true)
List<Tuple> fetchTupleOfIdsByGenre(String genre, Pageable pageable);
```

The service-method should deal with the List<Tuple> in order to extract the IDs of authors and the total number of elements:

```
@Transactional
public Page<Author> fetchPageOfAuthorsWithBooksByGenreTuple(
           int page, int size) {

   Pageable pageable = PageRequest.of(page, size,
       Sort.by(Sort.Direction.ASC, "name"));
```

```
List<Tuple> tuples = authorRepository.fetchTupleOfIdsByGenre(
    "Anthology", pageable);

List<Long> listOfIds = new ArrayList<>(tuples.size());
for(Tuple tuple: tuples) {
    listOfIds.add(((BigInteger) tuple.get("id")).longValue());
}

List<Author> listOfAuthors
    = authorRepository.fetchWithBooksJoinFetch(listOfIds);
Page<Author> pageOfAuthors = new PageImpl(listOfAuthors, pageable,
    ((BigInteger) tuples.get(0).get("total")).longValue());

return pageOfAuthors;
}
```

This time, the additional SELECT COUNT is eliminated; therefore, you can reduce this from three to two SELECT statements.

## Fetching Slice<Author>

Relying on Slice is also an option. Using Slice instead of Page removes the need of this extra SELECT COUNT query and returns the page (records) and some metadata without the total number of records. This is useful when you need the metadata provided by Slice but you don't need the total number of records, or when you fetched the total number of records via a separate SELECT COUNT executed only once. This is commonly done when inserts/deletes are never or rarely triggered. In that case, the number of records doesn't change between pages navigation, so there is no need to trigger a SELECT COUNT for every page.

This goes from three to two SQL statements. Here is the implementation based on Slice:

```
@Transactional(readOnly = true)
@Query(value = "SELECT a.id FROM Author a WHERE a.genre = ?1")
Slice<Long> fetchSliceOfIdsByGenre(String genre, Pageable pageable);

@Transactional
public Slice<Author> fetchAuthorsWithBooksByGenre(int page, int size) {

    Pageable pageable = PageRequest.of(page, size,
        Sort.by(Sort.Direction.ASC, "name"));
```

```
    Slice<Long> pageOfIds = authorRepository
        .fetchSliceOfIdsByGenre("Anthology", pageable);
    List<Author> listOfAuthors = authorRepository
        .fetchWithBooks(pageOfIds.getContent());
    Slice<Author> sliceOfAuthors = new SliceImpl(
        listOfAuthors, pageable, pageOfIds.hasNext());

    return sliceOfAuthors;
}
```

This will trigger only two SQL SELECT statements. You don't have information about the total number of rows, but you know if there are more pages or not. Sample JSON is shown here (check the last element):

```
{
    "content":[
        {
            "id":1,
            "name":"Mark Janel",
            "genre":"Anthology",
            "age":23,
            "books":[
                {
                    "id":3,
                    "title":"The Beatles Anthology",
                    "isbn":"001-MJ"
                },
                {
                    "id":8,
                    "title":"Anthology From Zero To Expert",
                    "isbn":"002-MJ"
                },
                {
                    "id":9,
                    "title":"Quick Anthology",
                    "isbn":"003-MJ"
                }
```

```
          ]
      },
      {
          "id":6,
          "name":"Merci Umaal",
          "genre":"Anthology",
          "age":31,
          "books":[
            {
                "id":7,
                "title":"Ultimate Anthology",
                "isbn":"001-MU"
            },
            {
                "id":10,
                "title":"1959 Anthology",
                "isbn":"002-MU"
            }
          ]
      }
   ],
   "pageable":{
      "sort":{
          "sorted":true,
          "unsorted":false,
          "empty":false
      },
      "pageSize":2,
      "pageNumber":0,
      "offset":0,
      "paged":true,
      "unpaged":false
   },
   "numberOfElements":2,
   "first":true,
   "last":false,
```

```
  "sort":{
     "sorted":true,
     "unsorted":false,
     "empty":false
  },
  "number":0,
  "size":2,
  "empty":false
}
```

## Fetching List<Author>

We can also fetch data as a List<Author>. This is useful when you don't need any metadata provided by Page or Slice:

```
@Transactional(readOnly = true)
@Query(value = "SELECT a.id FROM Author a WHERE a.genre = ?1")
List<Long> fetchListOfIdsByGenre(String genre, Pageable pageable);
```

This time, you use Pageable just for adding the SQL clauses for ordering and paging via Spring help. Especially when paging, Spring will choose the proper SQL clause depending on the dialect (e.g., for MySQL it will add LIMIT). Removing Pageable and using a native query is also an option.

The service-method that calls fetchListOfIdsByGenre() is now as follows:

```
@Transactional
public List<Author> fetchListOfAuthorsWithBooksByGenre(int page, int size) {
    Pageable pageable = PageRequest.of(page, size,
        Sort.by(Sort.Direction.ASC, "name"));

    List<Long> listOfIds = authorRepository.fetchListOfIdsByGenre(
        "Anthology", pageable);
    List<Author> listOfAuthors
        = authorRepository.fetchWithBooksJoinFetch(listOfIds);

    return listOfAuthors;
}
```

This will trigger the following two SELECT statements:

```
SELECT
    author0_.id AS col_0_0_
FROM author author0_
WHERE author0_.genre = ?
ORDER BY author0_.name
ASC LIMIT ? ?
```

```
SELECT
    author0_.id AS id1_0_0_,
    books1_.id AS id1_1_1_,
    author0_.age AS age2_0_0_,
    author0_.genre AS genre3_0_0_,
    author0_.name AS name4_0_0_,
    books1_.author_id AS author_i4_1_1_,
    books1_.isbn AS isbn2_1_1_,
    books1_.title AS title3_1_1_,
    books1_.author_id AS author_i4_1_0__,
    books1_.id AS id1_1_0__
FROM author author0_
LEFT OUTER JOIN book books1_
    ON author0_.id = books1_.author_id
WHERE author0_.id IN (?, ?)
```

And a JSON representation of a sample result set:

```
[
    {
        "id":3,
        "name":"Quartis Young",
        "genre":"Anthology",
        "age":51,
        "books":[
            {
                "id":5,
                "title":"Anthology Of An Year",
```

```
            "isbn":"001-QY"
          }
        ]
      },
      {
        "id":5,
        "name":"Pyla Lou",
        "genre":"Anthology",
        "age":41,
        "books":[
          {
            "id":6,
            "title":"Personal Anthology",
            "isbn":"001-KL"
          }
        ]
      }
    ]
```

The complete application in available on GitHub[15].

# Item 99: How to Implement Slice<T> findAll( )

Spring Boot provides an offset-based built-in paging mechanism that returns a Page or Slice. Each of these APIs represents a page of data and some page metadata. The main difference is that Page contains the total number of records, while Slice can only tell if there is another page available. For Page, Spring Boot provides a findAll() method capable of taking as arguments a Pageable and/or a Specification or Example. In order to create a Page that contains the total number of records, this method triggers an SELECT COUNT extra query next to the query used to fetch the data of the current page. This can lead to a performance penalty since the SELECT COUNT query is triggered every time a page is requested. In order to avoid this extra query, Spring Boot provides a more relaxed

---

[15]HibernateSpringBootHHH000104

API, the Slice API. Using Slice instead of Page removes the need of this extra SELECT COUNT query and returns the page (records) and some page metadata without the total number of records. So, while Slice doesn't know the total number of records, it still can tell if there is another page available after the current one or this is the last page. The problem is that Slice works fine for queries containing the SQL WHERE clause (including those that use the Query Builder mechanism built into Spring Data), but it doesn't work for findAll(). This method will still return a Page instead of a Slice, so the SELECT COUNT query is triggered for Slice<T> findAll(...).

# Quick Implementation

A quick solution for fetching a Slice of all data consists of defining a method that relies on an explicit query (JPQL) and a Pageable object.

## Fetching Slice<*entity*>

Consider naming this method fetchAll(). You can add this to a repository, as follows (AuthorRepository is the repository corresponding to the Author entity):

```
@Repository
@Transactional(readOnly = true)
public interface AuthorRepository
               extends PagingAndSortingRepository<Author, Long> {

    @Query(value = "SELECT a FROM Author a")
    Slice<Author> fetchAll(Pageable pageable);
}
```

Calling fetchAll() will trigger a single SELECT query as follows:

```
SELECT
  author0_.id AS id1_0_,
  author0_.age AS age2_0_,
  author0_.genre AS genre3_0_,
  author0_.name AS name4_0_
FROM author author0_
ORDER BY author0_.age ASC
LIMIT ? ?
```

652

A service-method calling `fetchAll()` can be written as follows:

```
public Slice<Author> fetchNextSlice(int page, int size) {

    return authorRepository.fetchAll(PageRequest.of(page, size,
                Sort.by(Sort.Direction.ASC, "age")));
}
```

Consider a REST endpoint of type `localhost:8080/authors/{page}/{size}` and a total of 51 records in the author table. A request for the second page of size 3 can be triggered as `localhost:8080/authors/1/3` and the result (as JSON) is as follows:

```
{
    "content":[
        {
            "id":7,
            "age":23,
            "name":"Wuth Troll",
            "genre":"Anthology"
        },
        {
            "id":25,
            "age":23,
            "name":"Tylor Ruth",
            "genre":"Anthology"
        },
        {
            "id":16,
            "age":24,
            "name":"Joana Leonte",
            "genre":"History"
        }
    ],
    "pageable":{
        "sort":{
            "sorted":true,
            "unsorted":false,
            "empty":false
        },
```

```
      "pageSize":3,
      "pageNumber":1,
      "offset":3,
      "paged":true,
      "unpaged":false
   },
   "numberOfElements":3,
   "first":false,
   "last":false,
   "sort":{
      "sorted":true,
      "unsorted":false,
      "empty":false
   },
   "number":1,
   "size":3,
   "empty":false
}
```

There is no information about the total number of records. But, `"last": false` is an indicator that this is not the last page.

## Fetching Slice<*dto*>

Consider the following Spring Boot projection (DTO):

```
public interface AuthorDto {

    public String getName();

    public int getAge();
}
```

Consider naming this method `fetchAllDto()`. You can add this to a repository as follows (AuthorRepository is the repository corresponding to the Author entity):

```
@Repository
@Transactional(readOnly = true)
public interface AuthorRepository
                extends PagingAndSortingRepository<Author, Long> {
```

```
@Query(value = "SELECT a.name as name, a.age as age FROM Author a")
Slice<AuthorDto> fetchAllDto(Pageable pageable);
}
```

Calling `fetchAllDto()` will trigger a single SELECT query as follows:

```
SELECT
  author0_.name AS col_0_0_,
  author0_.age AS col_1_0_
FROM author author0_
ORDER BY author0_.age ASC
LIMIT ? ?
```

A service-method calling `fetchAllDto()` can be written as follows:

```
public Slice<AuthorDto> fetchNextSlice(int page, int size) {

    return authorRepository.fetchAllDto(PageRequest.of(page, size,
                Sort.by(Sort.Direction.ASC, "age")));
}
```

Consider a REST endpoint of type `localhost:8080/authors/{page}/{size}` and a total of 51 records in the author table. A request for the second page of size 3 can be triggered as `localhost:8080/authors/1/3` and the result (as JSON) is as follows:

```
{
   "content":[
      {
         "age":23,
         "name":"Wuth Troll"
      },
      {
         "age":23,
         "name":"Tylor Ruth"
      },
      {
         "age":24,
         "name":"Joana Leonte"
      }
   ],
```

```
  "pageable":{
    "sort":{
        "sorted":true,
        "unsorted":false,
        "empty":false
    },
    "pageSize":3,
    "pageNumber":1,
    "offset":3,
    "paged":true,
    "unpaged":false
  },
  "numberOfElements":3,
  "first":false,
  "last":false,
  "sort":{
    "sorted":true,
    "unsorted":false,
    "empty":false
  },
  "number":1,
  "size":3,
  "empty":false
}
```

The source code is available on GitHub[16].

# Implementation of Slice<T> findAll(Pageable pageable)

Preserving the method name as findAll means you have to create a custom implementation of it. For starters, write an abstract class and define findAll() as follows:

```
@Repository
@Transactional(readOnly = true)
public abstract class SlicePagingRepositoryImplementation<T> {
```

---

[16]HibernateSpringBootSliceAllViaFetchAll

```
@Autowired
private EntityManager entityManager;

private final Class<T> entityClass;

public SlicePagingRepositoryImplementation(Class<T> entityClass) {
    this.entityClass = entityClass;
}

public Slice<T> findAll(Pageable pageable) {

    return findAll(pageable, entityClass);
}
...
```

The findAll(Pageable, Class<T>) is a private method responsible for building the query. A simple approach will be as follows:

```
private Slice<T> findAll(Pageable pageable, Class<T> entityClass) {

    final String sql = "SELECT e FROM " + entityClass.getSimpleName() + " e";
    TypedQuery<T> query = entityManager.createQuery(sql, entityClass);

    return this.readSlice(query, pageable);
}
```

Finally, readSlice() is a private method responsible for creating a Slice<T> via SliceImpl and the given query:

```
private Slice<T> readSlice(final TypedQuery<T> query,
                                        final Pageable pageable) {

    query.setFirstResult((int) pageable.getOffset());
    query.setMaxResults(pageable.getPageSize() + 1);

    final List<T> content = query.getResultList();

    boolean hasNext = content.size() == (pageable.getPageSize() + 1);
    if (hasNext) {
        content.remove(content.size() - 1);
    }
```

```
    return new SliceImpl<>(content, pageable, hasNext);
}
```

The complete implementation is available on GitHub[17]. Next to this one, there are several other implementations, as follows:

- Implementation[18] based on `CriteriaBuilder` instead of hard-coded SQL

- Implementation[19] that allows you to provide a `Sort`

- Implementation[20] that allows you to provide a `Sort` and `Specification`

- Implementation[21] that allows you to provide a `Sort`, `LockModeType`, `QueryHints`, and `Specification`

- Implementation[22] that overrides the `Page<T> readPage(...)` method from `SimpleJpaRepository`

# Item 100: How to Implement Keyset Pagination

It is advisable to read **Item 94** before continuing.

For large datasets, the offset pagination comes with significant performance penalties, especially caused by traversing the already shown records to reach the needed offset. In such cases, it's better to rely on keyset pagination, which maintains a "constant" time over the growing data. The pros and cons of keyset pagination are listed next.

Cons:

- Cannot fetch arbitrary pages

- Writing the `WHERE` clause is not (always) easy

---

[17]HibernateSpringBootSliceAllSimpleSql

[18]HibernateSpringBootSliceAllCriteriaBuilder

[19]HibernateSpringBootSliceAllCriteriaBuilderAndSort

[20]HibernateSpringBootSliceAllCriteriaBuilderSortAndSpecification

[21]HibernateSpringBootSliceAllCriteriaBuilderSortAndSpecificationAndQueryHints

[22]HibernateSpringBootSliceAllCriteriaBuilderSimpleJpaRepository

Pros:

- Searches the last entry of the previous page

- Fetches only the following rows

- Infinite scrolling mechanism

- Inserts will not cause pages leeway

Another con to consider is that Spring Boot doesn't provide built-in support for keyset pagination. Actually, the main reason to rely on offset over keyset pagination is the lack of tool support.

Consider the author table corresponding to the Author entity, shown in Figure 13-4.

***Figure 13-4.*** *The Author entity table*

The goal is to implement keyset pagination to fetch authors as entities and as DTO.

Choose a column to act as the latest visited record/row (e.g., the id column) and use this column in the WHERE and ORDER BY clauses. The idioms relying on id column are as follows (sorting by multiple columns follows this same idea):

```
SELECT ...
  FROM ...
 WHERE id < {last_seen_id}
 ORDER BY id DESC
 LIMIT {how_many_rows_to_fetch}
```

Or, like this:

```
SELECT ...
  FROM ...
 WHERE ...
   AND id < {last_seen_id}
 ORDER BY id DESC
 LIMIT {how_many_rows_to_fetch}
```

For example, applying the first idiom in this case may result in the following native queries (the first queries fetches entities; the second one fetches DTO):

```
@Repository
@Transactional(readOnly = true)
public interface AuthorRepository extends JpaRepository<Author, Long> {

    @Query(value = "SELECT * FROM author AS a WHERE a.id < ?1
            ORDER BY a.id DESC LIMIT ?2", nativeQuery = true)
    List<Author> fetchAll(long id, int limit);

    @Query(value = "SELECT name, age FROM author AS a WHERE a.id < ?1
            ORDER BY a.id DESC LIMIT ?2", nativeQuery = true)
    List<AuthorDto> fetchAllDto(long id, int limit);
}
```

> In the case of pagination, a deterministic sort order is mandatory, so do not forget the ORDER  BY clause.

> The LIMIT clause is recognized by MySQL and PostgreSQL. SQL Server supports the SELECT  TOP clause, while Oracle uses ROWNUM or ROWS  FETCH  NEXT *n* ROWS  ONLY.

The AuthorDto is a simple Spring Boot projection:

```
public interface AuthorDto {

    public String getName();
```

```
    public int getAge();
}
```

Further, service-methods can call `fetchAll()` and `fetchAllDto()`, as follows:

```
public List<Author> fetchNextPage(long id, int limit) {
    return authorRepository.fetchAll(id, limit);
}

public List<AuthorDto> fetchNextPageDto(long id, int limit) {
    return authorRepository.fetchAllDto(id, limit);
}
```

A REST controller endpoint such as `localhost:8080/authors/{id}/{limit}` can help you test these service-methods. For example, calling `fetchNextPage()` via `localhost:8080/authors/5/3` will output the following:

```
[
    {
        "id":4,
        "age":34,
        "name":"Joana Nimar",
        "genre":"History"
    },
    {
        "id":3,
        "age":51,
        "name":"Quartis Young",
        "genre":"Anthology"
    },
    {
        "id":2,
        "age":43,
        "name":"Olivia Goy",
        "genre":"Horror"
    }
]
```

The time-performance trend graphic shown in Figure 13-5 reveals that keyset pagination is much faster than offset pagination. Consider the author table with 1 million records. We fetch first page (0), the 5,000th page, and the 9,999th page with 100 records.

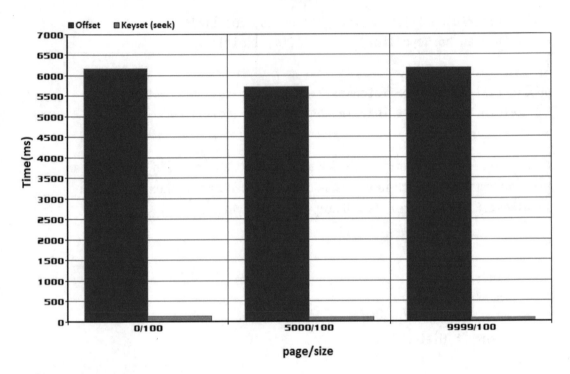

***Figure 13-5.***  *Offset vs. keyset*

The source code is available on GitHub[23].

# Item 101: How to Add a Next Page Button to Keyset Pagination

It is advisable to read **Item 100** before continuing.

Keyset pagination doesn't rely on the total number of elements. But, with a little trick, the response to the client can contain a piece of information that indicates if there are more records to fetch. The client side can use this information to display a Next Page

---

[23]HibernateSpringBootKeysetPagination

button. For example, a REST controller endpoint such as localhost:8080/authors/5/3 will return three records (IDs *4*, *3*, and *2*), but there is one more record in the author table (with ID *1*). The last element of the response indicates that this is not the last page:

```
{
    "authors":[
        {
            "id":4,
            "age":34,
            "name":"Joana Nimar",
            "genre":"History"
        },
        {
            "id":3,
            "age":51,
            "name":"Quartis Young",
            "genre":"Anthology"
        },
        {
            "id":2,
            "age":43,
            "name":"Olivia Goy",
            "genre":"Horror"
        }
    ],
    "last":false
}
```

Therefore, you can fetch the next page via localhost:8080/authors/2/3. This time, the response will contain one record (ID *1*) and the last element is true. This means that this is the last page, so the Next Page button should be disabled:

```
{
    "authors":[
        {
            "id":1,
            "age":23,
```

```
        "name":"Mark Janel",
        "genre":"Anthology"
    }
  ],
  "last":true
}
```

But, how do you add the last element? First, you define a class that groups the fetched data and the extra elements (in this case, last, but more can be added):

```
public class AuthorView {

    private final List<Author> authors;
    private final boolean last;

    public AuthorView(List<Author> authors, boolean last) {
        this.authors = authors;
        this.last = last;
    }

    public List<Author> getAuthors() {
        return authors;
    }

    public boolean isLast() {
        return last;
    }
}
```

Further, the service-method fetches limit + 1 records and determines the value of last as follows:

```
public AuthorView fetchNextPage(long id, int limit) {
    List<Author> authors = authorRepository.fetchAll(id, limit + 1);

    if (authors.size() == (limit + 1)) {
        authors.remove(authors.size() - 1);
        return new AuthorView(authors, false);
    }
```

```
        return new AuthorView(authors, true);
}
```

Finally, you modify the REST controller endpoint to return List<AuthorView> instead of List<Author>:

```
@GetMapping("/authors/{id}/{limit}")
public AuthorView fetchAuthors(
            @PathVariable long id, @PathVariable int limit) {

    return bookstoreService.fetchNextPage(id, limit);
}
```

Done! The source code is available on GitHub[24]. It also contains the DTO case.

# Item 102: How to Implement Pagination via ROW_NUMBER( )

So far, the pagination topic was covered in several items. Another approach for fetching data in pages consists of using the ROW_NUMBER() window function, which is introduced in **Item 119**. If you are not familiar with ROW_NUMBER(), it's better to postpone this item until you read **Item 119**.

Consider the well-known Author entity and the following DTO:

```
public interface AuthorDto {

    public String getName();
    public int getAge();
}
```

The following native query is an example of fetching authors in pages via ROW_NUMBER():

```
@Repository
@Transactional(readOnly = true)
```

---

```
public interface AuthorRepository
        extends PagingAndSortingRepository<Author, Long> {

    @Query(value = "SELECT * FROM (SELECT name, age, "
                + "ROW_NUMBER() OVER (ORDER BY age) AS row_num "
                + "FROM author) AS a WHERE row_num BETWEEN ?1 AND ?2",
            nativeQuery = true)
    List<AuthorDto> fetchPage(int start, int end);
}
```

Or, if you need to fetch the total number of rows as well, then enrich the DTO with the total field and the query with COUNT(*) OVER() window function, as follows:

```
public interface AuthorDto {

    public String getName();
    public int getAge();
    public long getTotal();
}
```

```
@Repository
@Transactional(readOnly = true)
public interface AuthorRepository extends JpaRepository<Author, Long> {

    @Query(value = "SELECT * FROM (SELECT name, age, "
            + "COUNT(*) OVER() AS total, "
            + "ROW_NUMBER() OVER (ORDER BY age) AS row_num FROM author) AS a "
            + "WHERE row_num BETWEEN ?1 AND ?2",
            nativeQuery = true)
    List<AuthorDto> fetchPage(int start, int end);
}
```

The complete application is available on GitHub[25].

---

# CHAPTER 14

# Queries

## Item 103: How to Optimize SELECT DISTINCT via Hibernate-Specific HINT_PASS_DISTINCT_THROUGH

Consider the Author and Book entities involved in a bidirectional lazy one-to-many association. The data snapshot is shown in Figure 14-1 (there is one author who has written two books).

**author**

| id | age | genre | name |
|----|-----|---------|-------------|
| 1  | 34  | History | Joana Nimar |

**book**

| id | isbn | title | author_id |
|----|--------|--------------------------|-----------|
| 1  | 001-JN | A History of Ancient Prague | 1 |
| 2  | 002-JN | A People's History | 1 |

***Figure 14-1.*** *Data snapshot (HINT_PASS_DISTINCT_THROUGH)*

Further, let's fetch the list of Author entities along with all their Book child entities. The fact is that the SQL-level result set size is given by the number of fetched rows from the book table. This can lead to Author duplicates (object reference duplicates). Consider the following query:

```
@Repository
@Transactional(readOnly = true)
public interface AuthorRepository extends JpaRepository<Author, Long> {

    @Query("SELECT a FROM Author a LEFT JOIN FETCH a.books")
    List<Author> fetchWithDuplicates();
}
```

© Anghel Leonard 2020
A. Leonard, *Spring Boot Persistence Best Practices,* https://doi.org/10.1007/978-1-4842-5626-8_14

Calling fetchWithDuplicates() will trigger the following SQL:

```
SELECT
  author0_.id AS id1_0_0_,
  books1_.id AS id1_1_1_,
  author0_.age AS age2_0_0_,
  author0_.genre AS genre3_0_0_,
  author0_.name AS name4_0_0_,
  books1_.author_id AS author_i4_1_1_,
  books1_.isbn AS isbn2_1_1_,
  books1_.title AS title3_1_1_,
  books1_.author_id AS author_i4_1_0__,
  books1_.id AS id1_1_0__
FROM author author0_
LEFT OUTER JOIN book books1_
  ON author0_.id = books1_.author_id
```

The fetched List<Author> contains two identical entries:

```
List<Author> authors = authorRepository.fetchWithDuplicates();

authors.forEach(a -> {
    System.out.println("Id: " + a.getId()
        + ": Name: " + a.getName() + " Books: " + a.getBooks());
});
```

Here's the output:

```
Id: 1: Name: Joana Nimar Books: [Book{id=1, title=A History of Ancient
Prague, isbn=001-JN}, Book{id=2, title=A People's History, isbn=002-JN}]

Id: 1: Name: Joana Nimar Books: [Book{id=1, title=A History of Ancient
Prague, isbn=001-JN}, Book{id=2, title=A People's History, isbn=002-JN}]
```

Just for the record, let's look at the execution plans for PostgreSQL (left side) and for MySQL (right side), shown in Figure 14-2.

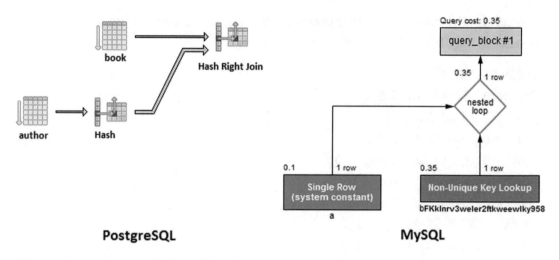

***Figure 14-2.*** *PostgreSQL and MySQL execution plans without DISTINCT*

So, the fetched List<Author> contains two references of the same Author entity object. Imagine a prolific author who has written 20 books. Having 20 references of the same Author entity is a performance penalty that you may not (want to) afford.

Why are there duplicates anyway? Because Hibernate simply returns the result set fetched via the left outer join. If you have five authors and each author has three books, the result set will have 5 x 3 = 15 rows. Therefore, the List<Author> will have 15 elements, all of type Author. Nevertheless, Hibernate will create only five instances, but duplicates are preserved as duplicate references to these five instances. So, there are five instances on the Java heap and 10 references to them.

One workaround consists of using the DISTINCT keyword as follows:

```
@Repository
@Transactional(readOnly = true)
public interface AuthorRepository extends JpaRepository<Author, Long> {

    @Query("SELECT DISTINCT a FROM Author a LEFT JOIN FETCH a.books")
    List<Author> fetchWithoutHint();
}
```

Calling fetchWithoutHint() will trigger the following SQL statement (notice the presence of the DISTINCT keyword in the SQL query):

```
SELECT DISTINCT
  author0_.id AS id1_0_0_,
  books1_.id AS id1_1_1_,
  author0_.age AS age2_0_0_,
  author0_.genre AS genre3_0_0_,
  author0_.name AS name4_0_0_,
  books1_.author_id AS author_i4_1_1_,
  books1_.isbn AS isbn2_1_1_,
  books1_.title AS title3_1_1_,
  books1_.author_id AS author_i4_1_0__,
  books1_.id AS id1_1_0__
FROM author author0_
LEFT OUTER JOIN book books1_
  ON author0_.id = books1_.author_id
```

> In JPQL, the purpose of the DISTINCT keyword is to avoid returning the same parent entities when JOIN FETCH-ing parents with child associations. The duplicate values must be eliminated from the query result.

Checking the output confirms that the duplicates were removed from the List<Author>:

```
Id: 1: Name: Joana Nimar Books: [Book{id=1, title=A History of Ancient
Prague, isbn=001-JN}, Book{id=2, title=A People's History, isbn=002-JN}]
```

But the issue consists of the fact that the DISTINCT keyword was passed to the database as well (check the triggered SQL statement). Now, let's see the PostgreSQL (left side) and MySQL (right side) execution plans again, shown in Figure 14-3.

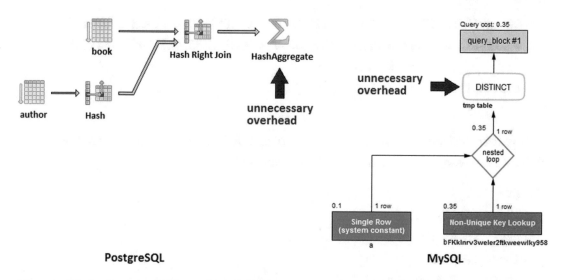

**Figure 14-3.** *PostgreSQL and MySQL execution plans with DISTINCT*

Even if the result set contains unique parent-child records (you don't have duplicated entries in the JDBC result set), the chosen execution plans were affected by the presence of DISTINCT. The PostgreSQL execution plan uses a *HashAggregate* stage for removing duplicates, while the MySQL added a temporary table used for removing duplicates. This is unnecessary overhead. Moreover, most of the databases will actually filter duplicate records automatically.

> In other words, DISTINCT should be passed to the database only if you really need to filter out duplicated records from the result set.

This issue was addressed in HHH-10965[1] and was materialized in Hibernate 5.2.2 in QueryHints.HINT_PASS_DISTINCT_THROUGH. You can add this hint as follows:

```
@Repository
@Transactional(readOnly = true)
public interface AuthorRepository extends JpaRepository<Author, Long> {
```

---

[1]https://hibernate.atlassian.net/browse/HHH-10965

```
    @Query("SELECT DISTINCT a FROM Author a LEFT JOIN FETCH a.books")
    @QueryHints(value = @QueryHint(name = HINT_PASS_DISTINCT_THROUGH,
                 value = "false"))
    List<Author> fetchWithHint();
}
```

Calling fetchWithHint() will trigger the following SQL statement (notice that the DISTINCT keyword in not present in the SQL query):

**SELECT**
```
    author0_.id AS id1_0_0_,
    books1_.id AS id1_1_1_,
    author0_.age AS age2_0_0_,
    author0_.genre AS genre3_0_0_,
    author0_.name AS name4_0_0_,
    books1_.author_id AS author_i4_1_1_,
    books1_.isbn AS isbn2_1_1_,
    books1_.title AS title3_1_1_,
    books1_.author_id AS author_i4_1_0__,
    books1_.id AS id1_1_0__
```
**FROM** author author0_
**LEFT OUTER JOIN** book books1_
   **ON** author0_.id = books1_.author_id

Checking the output confirms that the duplicates were removed from the List<Author>:

Id: 1: Name: Joana Nimar Books: [Book{id=1, title=A History of Ancient Prague, isbn=001-JN}, Book{id=2, title=A People's History, isbn=002-JN}]

Moreover, the execution plan will not contain the unnecessary overhead.

> Keep in mind that this hint is useful only for JPQL query entities. It's not useful for scalar queries (e.g. List<Integer>) or DTO. In such cases, the DISTINCT JPQL keyword needs to be passed to the underlying SQL query. This will instruct the database to remove duplicates from the result set.

Notice that HINT_PASS_DISTINCT_THROUGH does not work if you have the hibernate.use_sql_comments property enabled. More details in HHH-13280[2].

Moreover, keep an eye on HHH-13782[3].

The complete application is available on GitHub[4].

# Item 104: How to Set Up JPA Callbacks

JPA callbacks are user-defined methods that can be used to instruct the application to react to certain events that occur inside the persistence mechanism. In **Item 77**, you saw how to use the JPA @PostLoad callback to calculate a non-persistent property. The complete list of callbacks extracted from the official documentation are shown in Figure 14-4.

| Type | Description |
| --- | --- |
| @PrePersist | Executed before the entity manager persist operation is actually executed or cascaded. This call is synchronous with the persist operation. |
| @PreRemove | Executed before the entity manager remove operation is actually executed or cascaded. This call is synchronous with the remove operation. |
| @PostPersist | Executed after the entity manager persist operation is actually executed or cascaded. This call is invoked after the database INSERT is executed. |
| @PostRemove | Executed after the entity manager remove operation is actually executed or cascaded. This call is synchronous with the remove operation. |
| @PreUpdate | Executed before the database UPDATE operation. |
| @PostUpdate | Executed after the database UPDATE operation. |
| @PostLoad | Executed after an entity has been loaded into the current persistence context or an entity has been refreshed. |

***Figure 14-4.** JPA callbacks*

---

[2]https://hibernate.atlassian.net/browse/HHH-13280
[3]https://hibernate.atlassian.net/browse/HHH-13782
[4]HibernateSpringBootHintPassDistinctThrough

Let's add all these callbacks to the Author entity, as follows:

```java
@Entity
public class Author implements Serializable {

    private static final Logger logger =
        Logger.getLogger(Author.class.getName());
    private static final long serialVersionUID = 1L;

    @Id
    @GeneratedValue(strategy = GenerationType.IDENTITY)
    private Long id;

    private int age;
    private String name;
    private String genre;
    ...
    @PrePersist
    private void prePersist() {
        logger.info("@PrePersist callback ...");
    }

    @PreUpdate
    private void preUpdate() {
        logger.info("@PreUpdate callback ...");
    }

    @PreRemove
    private void preRemove() {
        logger.info("@PreRemove callback ...");
    }

    @PostLoad
    private void postLoad() {
        logger.info("@PostLoad callback ...");
    }

    @PostPersist
    private void postPersist() {
        logger.info("@PostPersist callback ...");
    }
```

```
@PostUpdate
private void postUpdate() {
    logger.info("@PostUpdate callback ...");
}

@PostRemove
private void postRemove() {
    logger.info("@PostRemove callback ...");
}
...
}
```

Persisting a new Author will trigger @PrePersist and @PostPersist. Fetching an Author will trigger the @PostLoad callback. Updating an Author will trigger the @PreUpdate and @PostUpdate callbacks. And, finally, deleting an Author will trigger the @PreRemove and @PostRemove callbacks. The complete code is available on GitHub[5].

## Separate Listener Class via @EntityListeners

Sometimes, you'll need to trigger JPA callbacks for multiple entities. For example, let's assume that you have two entities, Paperback and Ebook, and you want to receive notifications whenever instances of these entities are loaded, persisted, etc. To accomplish this task, you start by defining a non-entity class (Book) via @MappedSuperclass:

```
@MappedSuperclass
public abstract class Book implements Serializable {
    ...
}
```

Next, Paperback and Ebook extend this class:

```
@Entity
public class Ebook extends Book implements Serializable {
    ...
}
```

---

[5]HibernateSpringBootJpaCallbacks

```
@Entity
public class Paperback extends Book implements Serializable {

    ...

}
```

Next, you define a class containing the JPA callbacks. Notice that you use Book as the argument of each callback. This way, the callbacks are notified whenever a Paperback or Ebook (or other entities that extend Book) are persisted, loaded, etc.:

```
public class BookListener {

    @PrePersist
    void onPrePersist(Book book) {
        System.out.println("BookListener.onPrePersist(): " + book);
    }

    @PostPersist
    void onPostPersist(Book book) {
        System.out.println("BookListener.onPostPersist(): " + book);
    }
    ...
}
```

Finally, you use the JPA annotation, @EntityListeners, to link the BookListener and Book entities:

```
@MappedSuperclass
@EntityListeners(BookListener.class)
public abstract class Book implements Serializable {

    ...

}
```

Of course, you can also define multiple listener-classes and annotate only the entities that you want. Do not assume that using @MappedSuperclass is mandatory.

The complete application is available on GitHub[6].

---

[6]HibernateSpringBootEntityListener

# Item 105: How to Use Spring Data Query Builder to limit the Result Set Size and to Count and Delete Derived Queries

Spring Data comes with the Query Builder mechanism for JPA and it's capable of interpreting a query method name (or a derived query—the query derived from the method name) and converting it into an SQL statement. This is possible as long as you follow the naming conventions of this mechanism.

## Limiting the Result Set Size

As a rule of thumb, the developer must control the size of the result set and always be aware of the evolution of its size in time. Never fetch more data than needed. Strive to limit the result set size to the data that will be manipulated. Moreover, strive to work with relatively small result sets (pagination is quite useful for slicing the result set).

Basically, the name of the query method instructs Spring Data on how to add the LIMIT clause (or similar clauses depending on the RDBMS) to the generated SQL queries.

The fetched result set can be limited via the keywords first or top, which can be used interchangeably (use the one that you prefer). Optionally, a numeric value can be appended to top/first to specify the maximum result size to be returned. If the number is left out, a result size of 1 is assumed.

Assume the Author entity shown in Figure 14-5.

*Figure 14-5.* *The Author entity table*

The goal is to fetch the first five authors who are *56* years old. Employing the the Query Builder mechanism is as simple as writing the following query in `AuthorRepository`:

```
List<Author> findTop5ByAge(int age);
```

Or via the first keyword:

```
List<Author> findFirst5ByAge(int age);
```

Behind the scenes, the name of this method is translated to the following SQL query:

```
SELECT
    author0_.id AS id1_0_,
    author0_.age AS age2_0_,
    author0_.genre AS genre3_0_,
    author0_.name AS name4_0_
FROM
    author author0_
WHERE
    author0_.age =? LIMIT ?
```

If the result set should be ordered, then simply use `OrderBy`*Property*`Desc/Asc`. For example, you can fetch the first five authors that are *56* years old in descending order by name, as follows:

```
List<Author> findFirst5ByAgeOrderByNameDesc(int age);
```

This time, the triggered SQL will be as follows:

```
SELECT
    author0_.id AS id1_0_,
    author0_.age AS age2_0_,
    author0_.genre AS genre3_0_,
    author0_.name AS name4_0_
FROM
    author author0_
WHERE
    author0_.age =?
ORDER BY
    author0_.name DESC LIMIT ?
```

How about fetching the first five authors by the *Horror* genre who are younger than *50* in descending name order? Adding the LessThan keyword to the method name will answer this question as follows:

```
List<Author> findFirst5ByGenreAndAgeLessThanOrderByNameDesc(
    String genre, int age);
```

The SQL from this method name is as follows:

```
SELECT
    author0_.id AS id1_0_,
    author0_.age AS age2_0_,
    author0_.genre AS genre3_0_,
    author0_.name AS name4_0_
FROM
    author author0_
WHERE
    author0_.genre =?
    AND author0_.age <?
ORDER BY
    author0_.name DESC LIMIT ?
```

The source code is available on GitHub[7].

The complete list of supported keywords is shown here:

| Keyword | Example | SQL |
| --- | --- | --- |
| And | findByNameAndAge | ...where a.name = ?1 and a.age = ?2 |
| Or | findByNameOrAge | ...where a.name = ?1 or a.age = ?2 |
| Is, Equals | findByName, findByNameIs, findByNameEquals | ...where a.name = ?1 |
| Between | findByStartDateBetween | ...where a.startDate between ?1 and ?2 |

*(continued)*

---

[7]HibernateSpringBootLimitResultSizeViaQueryCreator

| Keyword | Example | SQL |
|---|---|---|
| LessThan | findByAgeLessThan | ...where a.age < ?1 |
| LessThanEquals | findByAgeLessThanEquals | ...where a.age <= ?1 |
| GreaterThan | findByAgeGreaterThan | ...where a.age > ?1 |
| GreaterThanEquals | findByAgeGreaterThanEquals | ...where a.age >= ?1 |
| After | findByStartDateAfter | ...where a.startDate > ?1 |
| Before | findByStartDateBefore | ...where a.startDate < ?1 |
| IsNull | findByAgeIsNull | ...where a.age is null |
| IsNotNull, NotNull | findByAge(Is)NotNull | ...where a.age not null |
| Like | findByNameLike | ...where a.name like ?1 |
| NotLike | findByNameNotLike | ...where a.name not like ?1 |
| StartingWith | findByNameStartingWith | ...where a.name like ?1 (parameter bound with appended %) |
| EndingWith | findByNameEndingWith | ...where a.name like ?1 (parameter bound with appended %) |
| Containing | findByNameContaining | ...where a.name like ?1 (parameter bound with appended %) |
| OrderBy | findByAgeOrderByNameAsc | ...where a.age = ?1 order by a.name asc |
| Not | findByNameNot | ...where a.name <> ?1 |
| In | findByAgeIn(Collection<Age>) | ...where a.age in ?1 |
| NotIn | findByAgeNotIn(Collection<Age>) | ...where a.age not in ?1 |
| True | findByActiveTrue | ...where a.active = true |
| False | findByActiveFalse | ...where a.active = false |
| IgnoreCase | findByNameIgnoreCase | ...where UPPER(a.name) = UPPER(?1) |

If you don't want to add a `WHERE` clause then just use the `findBy()` method. Of course, you can limit the result set via `findFirst5By()` or `findTop5By()`.

Notice that `find...By` is not the only prefix that you can use. The Query Builder mechanism strips the prefixes `find...By`, `read...By`, `query...By`, and `get...By` from the method and starts parsing the rest of it. All these prefixes have the same meaning and work in the same way.

The Query Builder mechanism can be very handy, but it is advisable to avoid complex queries that require long names. Those names get out of control very quickly.

Besides these keywords, you can fetch a `Page` and a `Slice`, as follows:

```
Page<Author> queryFirst10ByName(String name, Pageable p)
Slice<Author> findFirst10ByName(String name, Pageable p)
```

In conclusion, the Query Builder mechanism is pretty flexible and useful. But, wait, this is not all! The awesomeness of this mechanism comes from the fact that it can be used in conjunction with Spring projections (DTO). Assuming the following projection:

```
public interface AuthorDto {

    public String getName();
    public String getAge();
}
```

You can fetch the result set via the Query Builder mechanism as follows (fetch the data for the first five authors in ascending order by age):

```
List<AuthorDto> findFirst5ByOrderByAgeAsc();
```

The generated SQL will fetch only the required data. It will not load anything in the Persistence Context. Avoid using the Query Builder mechanism with nested projections. This is a totally different story. Check out **Item 28** and **Item 29**.

# Count and Delete Derived Queries

Besides the queries of type find...By, the Query Builder mechanism supports derived count queries and derived delete queries.

## Derived Count Queries

A derived count query starts with count...By, as in the following example:

```
long countByGenre(String genre);
```

The triggered SELECT will be:

```
SELECT
  COUNT(author0_.id) AS col_0_0_
FROM author author0_
WHERE author0_.genre = ?
```

Here's another example: `long countDistinctAgeByGenre(String genre);`

## Derived Delete Queries

A derived delete query can return the number of deleted records or the list of the deleted records. A derived delete query that returns the number of deleted records starts with delete...By or remove...By and returns long, as in the following example:

```
long deleteByGenre(String genre);
```

A derived delete query that returns the list of deleted records starts with delete... or remove...By and returns List/Set<*entity*>, as in the following example:

```
List<Author> removeByGenre(String genre);
```

In both examples, the executed SQL statements will consists of a SELECT to fetch the entities in the Persistence Context, and, afterwards, a DELETE for each entity that must be deleted:

```
SELECT
  author0_.id AS id1_0_,
  author0_.age AS age2_0_,
  author0_.genre AS genre3_0_,
  author0_.name AS name4_0_
```

```
FROM author author0_
WHERE author0_.genre = ?
```

```
-- for each author that should be deleted there a DELETE statement as below
DELETE FROM author
WHERE id = ?
```

Here's another example: `List<Author> removeDistinctByGenre(String genre);`

The complete application is available on GitHub[8].

# Item 106: Why You Should Avoid Time-Consuming Tasks in Post-Commits

Typically, the performance issue described in this item is observed directly in production, since it involves heavy loading (but it can be observed in loading tests as well).

It is specific to Spring post-commit hooks and the symptoms are reflected on the pool connection. Most commonly, the symptoms are observed on the pool connection method *some_pool*.getConnection(). The symptoms claim that a connection acquisition is taking around 50% of the response time. Practically, this is unacceptable for a pool connection, especially if your SQL queries are fast (e.g., under 5ms) and there are very good calibrations of the number of available and idle connections.

The real cause may lie on the fact that there are time-consuming tasks in your post-commit hooks. Basically, in Spring implementation, the connection passes through the following sequence:

```
private void processCommit(DefaultTransactionStatus status)
    throws TransactionException {
    try {
        prepareForCommit(status);
        triggerBeforeCommit(status);
        triggerBeforeCompletion(status);
        doCommit(status);
        triggerAfterCommit(status);
        triggerAfterCompletion(status);
```

---

[8]HibernateSpringBootDerivedCountAndDelete

```
    } finally {
        //release connection
        cleanupAfterCompletion(status);
    }
}
```

So, the connection is released back in the pool only after the execution of the post-commit hooks. If your hooks are time-consuming (e.g., sending JMS messages or I/O operations) then there are serious performance issues that should be handled. Re-architecting the entire solution can be the best choice, but trying to implement the hooks asynchronously or involving a pending action can represent acceptable solutions as well.

Nevertheless, the following code reveals this problem. The code updates the age of an Author and executes a dummy sleep of 60 seconds to simulate a time-consuming post-commit task. This should be enough time to capture HikariCP (the pool connection) log and see if the connection is still active in the post-commit:

```
@Transactional
public void updateAuthor() {

    TransactionSynchronizationManager.registerSynchronization(
                        new TransactionSynchronizationAdapter() {

        @Override
        public void afterCommit() {
            logger.info(() -> "Long running task right after commit ...");

            // Right after commit do other stuff but
            // keep in mind that the connection will not
            // return to pool connection until this code is done
            // So, avoid time-consuming tasks here
            try {
                // This sleep() is just proof that the
                // connection is not released
                // Check HikariCP log
                Thread.sleep(60 * 1000);
            } catch (InterruptedException ex) {
                Thread.currentThread().interrupt();
```

```
                logger.severe(() -> "Exception: " + ex);
            }

            logger.info(() -> "Long running task done ...");
        }
    });

    logger.info(() -> "Update the author age and commit ...");
    Author author = authorRepository.findById(1L).get();

    author.setAge(40);
}
```

The output log reveals that the connection is open while the code is sleeping. Therefore, the connection is held open for nothing:

```
Update the author age and commit ...
update author set age=?, name=?, surname=? where id=?
Long running task right after commit ...
Pool stats (total=10, active=1, idle=9, waiting=0)
Long running task done ...
Pool stats (total=10, active=0, idle=10, waiting=0)
```

The complete code is available on GitHub[9].

# Item 107: How to Avoid Redundant save( ) Calls

Consider an entity named Author. Among its properties, it has an age property. Further, the application plans to update the age of an author via the following method:

```
@Transactional
public void updateAuthorRedundantSave() {
    Author author = authorRepository.findById(1L).orElseThrow();
    author.setAge(44);

    authorRepository.save(author);
}
```

---

[9]HibernateSpringBootPostCommit

Calling this method will trigger the following two SQL statements:

```
SELECT
    author0_.id AS id1_0_0_,
    author0_.age AS age2_0_0_,
    author0_.genre AS genre3_0_0_,
    author0_.name AS name4_0_0_
FROM author author0_
WHERE author0_.id = ?

UPDATE author
SET age = ?, genre = ?, name = ?
WHERE id = ?
```

Check out the bold line (**authorRepository.save(author)**)—is this line needed? The correct answer is no! When the application fetches the author from the database, it becomes a managed instance. Among other things, this means that Hibernate will take care of triggering UPDATE statements if the instance is modified. This is accomplished at flush time by the Hibernate Dirty Checking mechanism. In other words, the same behavior can be accomplished via the following method:

```
@Transactional
public void updateAuthorRecommended() {
    Author author = authorRepository.findById(1L).orElseThrow();
    author.setAge(44);
}
```

Calling this method will trigger exactly the same queries. This means that Hibernate has detected that the fetched entity was modified and triggers the UPDATE on your behalf.

The presence or absence of save() doesn't affect the number or type of queries, but it still has a performance penalty, because the save() method fires a MergeEvent behind the scenes, which will execute a bunch of Hibernate-specific internal operations that are useless in this case. So, in scenarios such as these, avoid the explicit call of the save() method.

The source code is available on GitHub[10].

---

[10]HibernateSpringBootRedundantSave

# Item 108: Why and How to Prevent N+1 Issues

> N+1 issues are associated with lazy fetching, but eager fetching is not exempt either.

A classical N+1 scenario starts with a bidirectional lazy @OneToMany association between Author and Book, as shown in Figure 14-6.

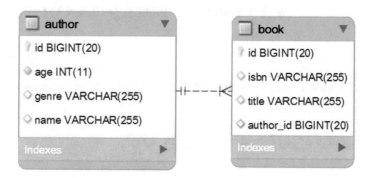

*Figure 14-6.*  *The @OneToMany table relationship*

The developer starts by fetching a collection of entities (e.g., List<Book>, which is query number 1 from N+1), and afterward, for each entity (Book) from this collection, he lazily fetch the Author entity (this results in N queries, where N can reach the size of the Book collection). So, this is a classic N+1.

A snapshot of the data is shown in Figure 14-7.

**author**

| id | age | genre | name |
|----|-----|-------|------|
| 1 | 23 | Anthology | Mark Janel |
| 2 | 43 | Horror | Olivia Goy |
| 3 | 51 | Anthology | Quartis Young |
| 4 | 34 | History | Joana Nimar |

**book**

| id | isbn | title | author_id |
|----|------|-------|-----------|
| 1 | 001-JN | A History of Ancient Prague | 4 |
| 2 | 001-QY | Modern Anthology | 3 |
| 3 | 001-MJ | The Beatles Anthology | 1 |
| 4 | 001-OG | Carrie | 2 |

*Figure 14-7.*  *Data snapshot*

Let's look at the code that causes the N+1 issue. For brevity, let's skip the Author and Book source and jump directly to fetching the authors and books:

```
@Transactional(readOnly = true)
public void fetchBooksAndAuthors() {
    List<Book> books = bookRepository.findAll();

    for (Book book : books) {
        Author author = book.getAuthor();
        System.out.println("Book: " + book.getTitle()
                        + " Author: " + author.getName());
    }
}
```

Calling fetchBooksAndAuthors() against this sample of data will trigger the following SQL statements:

```
-- SELECT that fetches all books (this is 1)
SELECT
  book0_.id AS id1_1_,
  book0_.author_id AS author_i4_1_,
  book0_.isbn AS isbn2_1_,
  book0_.title AS title3_1_
FROM book book0_

-- follows 4 SELECTs, one for each book (this is N)
SELECT
  author0_.id AS id1_0_0_,
  author0_.age AS age2_0_0_,
  author0_.genre AS genre3_0_0_,
  author0_.name AS name4_0_0_
FROM author author0_
WHERE author0_.id = ?
```

Of course, the developer can fetch a List<Author> first, and for each Author to fetch the associated books as a List<Book>. This also results in an N+1 issue.

Obviously, if N is relatively big (keep in mind that collections can "grow" over time), this leads to a significant performance degradation. This is **why** it is important to know about N+1 issues. But how do you avoid them? The solution is to rely on joins (JOIN FETCH or JOIN (for DTO)) or entity graphs that reduce N+1 to 1.

Maybe the hardest part is not fixing N+1 issues but actually discovering them. To catch the N+1 issues during development, monitor the number of generated SQL statements and verify that the reported number is equal to the expected number (see **Item 81**).

The complete code is available on GitHub[11].

# Hibernate-Specific @Fetch(FetchMode.JOIN) and N+1

One of the common scenarios that cause N+1 issues is improper usage of Hibernate-specific @Fetch(FetchMode.JOIN). Hibernate supports three fetch modes via org.hibernate.annotations.FetchMode and org.hibernate.annotations.Fetch annotations:

- FetchMode.SELECT (default): In a parent-child association, for N parents, there will be N+1 SELECT statements to load the parents and their associated children. This fetch mode can be optimized via @BatchSize (**Item 54**).

- FetchMode.SUBSELECT: In a parent-child association, one SELECT loads the parents and one SELECT loads all the associated children. There will be two SELECT statements.

- FetchMode.JOIN: In a parent-child association, the parents and the associated children are loaded in one SELECT statement.

In this section, we focus on FetchMode.JOIN.

---

[11]HibernateSpringBootSimulateNPlus1

> Always evaluate JOIN FETCH (**Item 39**) and entity graphs (**Item 7** and **Item 8**) before deciding to use FetchMode.JOIN. Both of these approaches are used on a query-basis, and both of them support HINT_PASS_DISTINCT_ THROUGH optimization (**Item 103**) to remove duplicates. If you need to use Specification then use entity graphs. Specifications are ignored with JOIN FETCH.
>
> The FetchMode.JOIN fetch mode **always** triggers an EAGER load so the children are loaded when the parents are loaded, even if they are not needed. Besides this drawback, FetchMode.JOIN may return **duplicate results.** You will have to remove the duplicates yourself (e.g., store the result in a Set).
>
> But, if you decide to go with FetchMode.JOIN at least work to avoid N+1 issues discussed next.

Let's consider three entities, Author, Book, and Publisher. Between Author and Book there is a bidirectional lazy @OneToMany association. Between Author and Publisher there is a unidirectional lazy @ManyToOne association (the author has an exclusive contract with a publisher). Between Book and Publisher, there is no association.

You want to fetch all books (via the Spring Data built-in findAll() method), including their authors, and the publishers of these authors. In such cases, you may think that Hibernate-specific FetchMode.JOIN can be used as follows:

```
@Entity
public class Author implements Serializable {

    ...
    @ManyToOne(fetch = FetchType.LAZY)
    @JoinColumn(name = "publisher_id")
    @Fetch(FetchMode.JOIN)
    private Publisher publisher;

    ...
}

@Entity
public class Book implements Serializable {
```

```
    ...
    @ManyToOne(fetch = FetchType.LAZY)
    @JoinColumn(name = "author_id")
    @Fetch(FetchMode.JOIN)
    private Author author;
    ...
}

@Entity
public class Publisher implements Serializable {
    ...
}
```

A service-method can fetch all Books via findAll(), as follows:

```
List<Book> books = bookRepository.findAll();
```

> You may think that, thanks to FetchMode.JOIN, the previous line of code will
> trigger a single SELECT containing the proper JOIN statements for fetching
> authors and the publishers of these authors. But Hibernate @Fetch(FetchMode.
> JOIN) doesn't work for query-methods. It works if you fetch the entity by ID
> (primary key) using EntityManager#find(), Spring Data, findById(), or
> findOne(). Using FetchMode.JOIN in this manner will cause N+1 issues.

Let's see the triggered SQL statements representing the N+1 case:

```
-- Select all books
SELECT
  book0_.id AS id1_1_,
  book0_.author_id AS author_i5_1_,
  book0_.isbn AS isbn2_1_,
  book0_.price AS price3_1_,
  book0_.title AS title4_1_
FROM book book0_
```

```
-- For each book, fetch the author and the author's publisher
SELECT
  author0_.id AS id1_0_0_,
  author0_.age AS age2_0_0_,
  author0_.genre AS genre3_0_0_,
  author0_.name AS name4_0_0_,
  author0_.publisher_id AS publishe5_0_0_,
  publisher1_.id AS id1_2_1_,
  publisher1_.company AS company2_2_1_
FROM author author0_
LEFT OUTER JOIN publisher publisher1_
  ON author0_.publisher_id = publisher1_.id
WHERE author0_.id = ?
```

Obviously, this is not the expected behavior. The performance penalty impact is given by the size of N. The bigger the N, the bigger the performance penalty impact. But you can eliminate this problem by employing JOIN FETCH or entity graphs.

## Using JOIN FETCH Instead of FetchMode.JOIN

You can use JOIN FETCH (**Item 39**) instead of FetchMode.JOIN by overriding findAll():

```
@Override
@Query("SELECT b FROM Book b LEFT JOIN FETCH b.author a
        LEFT JOIN FETCH a.publisher p")
public List<Book> findAll();
```

Or if you want a INNER JOIN as follows:

```
@Override
@Query("SELECT b, b.author, b.author.publisher FROM Book b")
public List<Book> findAll();
```

Now, calling findAll() will trigger a single SELECT:

```
SELECT
  book0_.id AS id1_1_0_,
  author1_.id AS id1_0_1_,
```

```
  publisher2_.id AS id1_2_2_,
  book0_.author_id AS author_i5_1_0_,
  book0_.isbn AS isbn2_1_0_,
  book0_.price AS price3_1_0_,
  book0_.title AS title4_1_0_,
  author1_.age AS age2_0_1_,
  author1_.genre AS genre3_0_1_,
  author1_.name AS name4_0_1_,
  author1_.publisher_id AS publishe5_0_1_,
  publisher2_.company AS company2_2_2_
FROM book book0_
LEFT OUTER JOIN author author1_
  ON book0_.author_id = author1_.id
LEFT OUTER JOIN publisher publisher2_
  ON author1_.publisher_id = publisher2_.id
```

## Using Entity Graphs Instead of FetchMode.JOIN

You can use entity graphs (**Item 7** and **Item 8**) instead of FetchMode.JOIN by overriding findAll() as follows:

```
@Override
@EntityGraph(attributePaths = {"author.publisher"})
public List<Book> findAll();
```

Now, calling findAll() will trigger a single SELECT:

```
SELECT
  book0_.id AS id1_1_0_,
  author1_.id AS id1_0_1_,
  publisher2_.id AS id1_2_2_,
  book0_.author_id AS author_i5_1_0_,
  book0_.isbn AS isbn2_1_0_,
  book0_.price AS price3_1_0_,
  book0_.title AS title4_1_0_,
```

```
    author1_.age AS age2_0_1_,
    author1_.genre AS genre3_0_1_,
    author1_.name AS name4_0_1_,
    author1_.publisher_id AS publishe5_0_1_,
    publisher2_.company AS company2_2_2_
FROM book book0_
LEFT OUTER JOIN author author1_
    ON book0_.author_id = author1_.id
LEFT OUTER JOIN publisher publisher2_
    ON author1_.publisher_id = publisher2_.id
```

The complete application is available on GitHub[12].

# Item 109: How to Use Hibernate-Specific Soft Deletes Support

Soft deletion (or logical delete) refers to marking a record in the database as deleted but not actually (physically) deleting it. While it is marked as deleted, this record is not available (e.g., it's not added in result sets; it acts like it was really deleted). The record can be deleted permanently later (hard delete) or it can be restored (or undeleted).

Commonly, this task is implemented via an extra column that holds a flag-value set to true for a deleted record, or to false for an available (or active) record. But relying on a flag-value is not the only possibility. A soft delete mechanism can be controlled by timestamps or by @Enumerated as well.

Soft deletes are the proper choice in a limited number of cases. Famous usage cases include the idea to temporary deactivate a user, device, service, and so on. For example, you can blacklist a user who adds malicious comments on posts until you discuss with him and eliminate the issue or decide to perform a physical delete of his account. Or you can put a user on hold until he can confirm the registration email address. If the grace period for confirming the email expires, then you perform a physical delete of the registration.

---

[12]HibernateSpringBootFetchJoinAndQueries

From a performance perspective, using soft deletes can be okay as long as the developer takes into account a few things before using this approach:

- While you will not lose any data, if the soft-deleted records represent a considerable amount from the total records and are seldom/never planned to be restored or permanently deleted, then just having "hangout" data will have performance implications. Most of the time, this is data that cannot be deleted such as historical data, financial data, social media data, etc.

- Obviously, having soft deletes in a table means that this table doesn't store only the necessary data; if this become an issue (it is desirable to anticipate this right from the beginning), then moving unnecessary data to an archived table can be the solution. Another solution consists of having a mirror-table that records all deletes/updates via a trigger on the original table; moreover, some RDBMSs provide support that doesn't require you to change the code (e.g., Oracle has Flashback Technology, while SQL Server has Temporal Tables).

- Inevitably, a part of the queries will be "polluted" with a WHERE clause for distinguishing between available and soft-deleted records; having a significant number of such queries can lead to performance penalties.

- Does the employed solution take into account cascading soft deletes? You may need this feature and doing it manually may be prone to errors and data issues.

- A lot of soft deletes can affect indexing.

Until Spring Data provides built-in support for soft deletes (keep an eye on DATAJPA-307[13]), let's see how to tackle this problem via Hibernate support.

---

[13]https://jira.spring.io/browse/DATAJPA-307

# Hibernate Soft Deletes

Soft deletion implementation can be Hibernate-centric. Start by defining an abstract class annotated with @MappedSuperclass and containing a flag-field named deleted. This field is true for a deleted record and false (default) for an available record:

```
@MappedSuperclass
public abstract class BaseEntity {

    @Column(name = "deleted")
    protected boolean deleted;
}
```

Further, the entities that should take advantage of soft deletion will extend BaseEntity. For example, the Author and Book entities—between Author and Book there is a bidirectional lazy @OneToMany association.

Besides extending the BaseEntity, these entities should be:

- Marked with Hibernate-specific @Where annotations, @Where(clause = "deleted = false"); this helps Hibernate filter the soft deleted records by appending this SQL condition to entity queries.

- Marked with Hibernate-specific @SQLDelete annotations to trigger UPDATE SQL statements in place of DELETE SQL statements; removing an entity will result in updating the deleted column to true instead of a physical delete of the record.

In code:

```
@Entity
@SQLDelete(sql
    = "UPDATE author "
    + "SET deleted = true "
    + "WHERE id = ?")
@Where(clause = "deleted = false")
public class Author extends BaseEntity implements Serializable {

    private static final long serialVersionUID = 1L;
```

```java
    @Id
    GeneratedValue(strategy = GenerationType.IDENTITY)
    private Long id;

    private String name;
    private String genre;
    private int age;

    @OneToMany(cascade = CascadeType.ALL,
                mappedBy = "author", orphanRemoval = true)
    private List<Book> books = new ArrayList<>();

    public void removeBook(Book book) {
        book.setAuthor(null);
        this.books.remove(book);
    }

    // getters and setters omitted for brevity
}

@Entity
@SQLDelete(sql
    = "UPDATE book "
    + "SET deleted = true "
    + "WHERE id = ?")
@Where(clause = "deleted = false")
public class Book extends BaseEntity implements Serializable {

    private static final long serialVersionUID = 1L;

    @Id
    @GeneratedValue(strategy = GenerationType.IDENTITY)
    private Long id;

    private String title;
    private String isbn;

    @ManyToOne(fetch = FetchType.LAZY)
    @JoinColumn(name = "author_id")
    private Author author;

    // getters and setters omitted for brevity
}
```

# Testing Time

Consider the snapshot of data shown in Figure 14-8 (all the records are available and active since the deleted value is 0 or false).

author

| id | deleted | age | genre | name |
|---|---|---|---|---|
| 1 | 0 | 23 | Anthology | Mark Janel |
| 2 | 0 | 43 | Horror | Olivia Goy |
| 3 | 0 | 51 | Anthology | Quartis Young |
| 4 | 0 | 34 | History | Joana Nimar |

book

| id | deleted | isbn | title | author_id |
|---|---|---|---|---|
| 1 | 0 | 001-JN | A History of Ancient Prague | 4 |
| 2 | 0 | 002-JN | A People's History | 4 |
| 3 | 0 | 001-MJ | The Beatles Anthology | 1 |
| 4 | 0 | 001-OG | Carrie | 2 |

*Figure 14-8.* *Data snapshot (no record was soft deleted)*

For simplicity, the following examples use hard-coded identifiers and direct fetching.

## Deleting an Author

Deleting an author is quite easy. The following method deletes the author with an ID of *1* via the built-in delete(T entity) method (behind the scenes, this method relies on EntityManager.remove()):

```
@Transactional
public void softDeleteAuthor() {
    Author author = authorRepository.findById(1L).get();

    authorRepository.delete(author);
}
```

Calling softDeleteAuthor() triggers the following SQL statements:

```
SELECT
    author0_.id AS id1_0_0_,
    author0_.deleted AS deleted2_0_0_,
    author0_.age AS age3_0_0_,
    author0_.genre AS genre4_0_0_,
    author0_.name AS name5_0_0_
FROM author author0_
```

```
WHERE author0_.id = ?
AND (author0_.deleted = 0)
SELECT
  books0_.author_id AS author_i5_1_0_,
  books0_.id AS id1_1_0_,
  books0_.id AS id1_1_1_,
  books0_.deleted AS deleted2_1_1_,
  books0_.author_id AS author_i5_1_1_,
  books0_.isbn AS isbn3_1_1_,
  books0_.title AS title4_1_1_
FROM book books0_
WHERE (books0_.deleted = 0)
AND books0_.author_id = ?

UPDATE book
SET deleted = TRUE
WHERE id = ?

UPDATE author
SET deleted = TRUE
WHERE id = ?
```

Both SELECT statements fetch only records that are not soft deleted (check the WHERE clause). Next, the author is deleted (resulting in updating deleted to true). Furthermore, the cascade mechanism is responsible for triggering the child removal, which results in another update. Figure 14-9 highlights the soft deleted records.

**author**

| id | deleted | age | genre | name |
|----|---------|-----|-------|------|
| 1 | 1 | 23 | Anthology | Mark Janel |
| 2 | 0 | 43 | Horror | Olivia Goy |
| 3 | 0 | 51 | Anthology | Quartis Young |
| 4 | 0 | 34 | History | Joana Nimar |

**book**

| id | deleted | isbn | title | author_id |
|----|---------|------|-------|-----------|
| 1 | 0 | 001-JN | A History of Ancient Prague | 4 |
| 2 | 0 | 002-JN | A People's History | 4 |
| 3 | 1 | 001-MJ | The Beatles Anthology | 1 |
| 4 | 0 | 001-OG | Carrie | 2 |

***Figure 14-9.*** *Data snapshot (after soft deleting an author)*

## Deleting a Book

To delete a book let's consider the following service-method:

```
@Transactional
public void softDeleteBook() {
    Author author = authorRepository.findById(4L).get();
    Book book = author.getBooks().get(0);

    author.removeBook(book);
}
```

Calling softDeleteBook() triggers the following SQL statements:

```
SELECT
  author0_.id AS id1_0_0_,
  author0_.deleted AS deleted2_0_0_,
  author0_.age AS age3_0_0_,
  author0_.genre AS genre4_0_0_,
  author0_.name AS name5_0_0_
FROM author author0_
WHERE author0_.id = ?
AND (author0_.deleted = 0)

SELECT
  books0_.author_id AS author_i5_1_0_,
  books0_.id AS id1_1_0_,
  books0_.id AS id1_1_1_,
  books0_.deleted AS deleted2_1_1_,
  books0_.author_id AS author_i5_1_1_,
  books0_.isbn AS isbn3_1_1_,
  books0_.title AS title4_1_1_
FROM book books0_
WHERE (books0_.deleted = 0)
AND books0_.author_id = ?

UPDATE book
SET deleted = TRUE
WHERE id = ?
```

Again, both SELECT statements fetch only records that are not soft deleted (check the WHERE clause). Next, the first book of this author is deleted (resulting in updating deleted to true). Figure 14-10 highlights the soft deleted records.

**author**

| id | deleted | age | genre | name |
|----|---------|-----|-------|------|
| 1 | 1 | 23 | Anthology | Mark Janel |
| 2 | 0 | 43 | Horror | Olivia Goy |
| 3 | 0 | 51 | Anthology | Quartis Young |
| 4 | 0 | 34 | History | Joana Nimar |

**book**

| id | deleted | isbn | title | author_id |
|----|---------|------|-------|-----------|
| 1 | 1 | 001-JN | A History of Ancient Prague | 4 |
| 2 | 0 | 002-JN | A People's History | 4 |
| 3 | 1 | 001-MJ | The Beatles Anthology | 1 |
| 4 | 0 | 001-OG | Carrie | 2 |

***Figure 14-10.*** *Data snapshot (after soft deleting a book)*

## Restoring an Author

Remember that, when the author was removed, the cascade mechanism automatically removed the associated books. Therefore, restoring the author implies restoring its associated books as well.

This can accomplished via JPQL. To restore an author by ID, just trigger an UPDATE statement via JPQL that set deleted to false (or 0). This query can be listed in AuthorRepository:

```
@Transactional
@Query(value = "UPDATE Author a SET a.deleted = false WHERE a.id = ?1")
@Modifying
public void restoreById(Long id);
```

Restoring the books of an author is equivalent to setting the deleted of each associated book to false (or 0). With the author ID, you can do this via JPQL in BookRepository:

```
@Transactional
@Query(value = "UPDATE Book b SET b.deleted = false WHERE b.author.id = ?1")
@Modifying
public void restoreByAuthorId(Long id);
```

The following service-method restores the author deleted earlier:

```
@Transactional
public void restoreAuthor() {
    authorRepository.restoreById(1L);
    bookRepository.restoreByAuthorId(1L);
}
```

The SQL statements are listed here:

```
UPDATE author
SET deleted = 0
WHERE id = ?

UPDATE book
SET     deleted = 0
WHERE   author_id = ?
```

## Restoring a Book

You can restore a certain book by its ID via JPQL, as shown here:

```
@Transactional
@Query(value = "UPDATE Book b SET b.deleted = false WHERE b.id = ?1")
@Modifying
public void restoreById(Long id);
```

The following service-method restore the book deleted earlier:

```
@Transactional
public void restoreBook() {
    bookRepository.restoreById(1L);
}
```

The SQL statement is shown here:

```
UPDATE book
SET deleted = 0
WHERE id = ?
```

## Useful Queries

While working with soft deletes, there are two queries that are very handy. For example, in the context of soft deletion, calling the built-in findAll() method will fetch only the records that have deleted = false. You can fetch all records, including the soft deleted records, via a native query as follows (this query is for authors):

```
@Query(value = "SELECT * FROM author", nativeQuery = true)
List<Author> findAllIncludingDeleted();
```

Another handy native query can fetch only the soft deleted records as follows:

```
@Query(value = "SELECT * FROM author AS a WHERE a.deleted = true",
       nativeQuery = true)
List<Author> findAllOnlyDeleted();
```

> These queries cannot be written via JPQL because the goal is to prevent Hibernate from adding the WHERE clause when filtering soft deletions.

## Update the Deleted Property in the Current Persistence Context

Hibernate will not update the deleted property on your behalf. In other words, the native UPDATE triggered via @SQLDelete will update the deleted column but will not update the deleted property of the soft deleted entity.

Typically, the update of the deleted property is not needed because the referenced entity is released immediately after deletion.

As soon as the database record is updated, all subsequent queries use the new deleted value; therefore, you can ignore the outdated deleted property.

Nevertheless, if the referenced entity is still in use, you should update the deleted property yourself. The best way to do it is via the JPA @PreRemove lifecycle callback (for details about the JPA lifecycle callbacks, see **Item 104**).

The authorRemove() method is added to the Author entity:

```
@PreRemove
private void authorRemove() {

    deleted = true;
}
```

And in the Book entity:

```
@PreRemove
private void bookRemove() {

    deleted = true;
}
```

Now, Hibernate automatically calls these methods before it performs a remove operation on the Author or the Book entities.

> If you notice that the soft deleted entities are fetched as well (e.g., via direct fetching in a @ManyToOne relationship or other relationship), then most probably you need to add at the entities-level a dedicated @Loaded that includes the deleted column as well. For example, in the Author entity, this can be done as follows:
>
> ```
> @Loader(namedQuery = "findAuthorById")
> @NamedQuery(name = "findAuthorById", query =
>     "SELECT a " +
>     "FROM Author a " +
>     "WHERE" +
>     " a.id = ?1 AND " +
>     " a.deleted = false")
> ```

The complete application is available on GitHub[14].

# Item 110: Why and How to Avoid the OSIV Anti-Pattern

Open Session In View (OSIV) is used by default in Spring Boot and this is signaled via a log message as follows:

*spring.jpa.open-in-view is enabled by default. Therefore, database queries may be performed during view rendering. Explicitly configure spring.jpa. open in-view to disable this warning.*

It can be disabled by adding the following configuration to the application.properties file:

- spring.jpa.open-in-view=false

---

[14]HibernateSpringBootSoftDeletes

Open Session In View is an anti-pattern, not a pattern. At the least, OSIV is counterproductive. If this is so, why is OSIV used? Most of the time it is used to avoid the well-known Hibernate-specific `LazyInitializationException`.

A short story of Hibernate-specific `LazyInitializationException`: an entity might have associations, and Hibernate comes with proxies (`Proxy`) that allow the developer to defer fetching until the associations are needed. However, in order to accomplish this successfully, a `Session` needs to be open at fetching time. In other words, trying to initialize proxies when the Persistence Context is closed will lead to `LazyInitializationException`. In a common scenario, the developer fetches an entity without its association, closes the Persistence Context, and, later, tries to fetch the association lazy. This results in the infamous `LazyInitializationException`.

OSIV can prevent `LazyInitializationException` by forcing the Persistence Context to remain open so that the View layer (and the developers) can trigger the proxy initializations. In other words, it binds a JPA `EntityManager` to the thread the entire time the request is processed. Is this good or bad? Well, having a `Session` that lives as long as the request-response lifespan saves you from getting `LazyInitializationException`, but it opens the gate for performance penalties and bad practices. So, it's definitely bad!

Consider two entities, `Author` and `Book`, in a `@OneToMany` bidirectional lazy association (an author has written multiple books). In code:

```
@Entity
public class Author implements Serializable {

    private static final long serialVersionUID = 1L;

    @Id
    @GeneratedValue(strategy = GenerationType.IDENTITY)
    private Long id;

    private String name;
    private String genre;
    private int age;
```

```java
    @OneToMany(cascade = CascadeType.ALL,
             mappedBy = "author", orphanRemoval = true)
    @JsonManagedReference
    private List<Book> books = new ArrayList<>();

    // getters and setters omitted for brevity
}

@Entity
public class Book implements Serializable {

    private static final long serialVersionUID = 1L;

    @Id
    @GeneratedValue(strategy = GenerationType.IDENTITY)
    private Long id;

    private String title;
    private String isbn;

    @ManyToOne(fetch = FetchType.LAZY)
    @JoinColumn(name = "author_id")
    @JsonBackReference
    private Author author;

    // getters and setters omitted for brevity
}
```

@JsonManagedReference and @JsonBackReference are designed to handle this two-way linkage between fields—one for Author, the other for Book. This is a common approach for avoiding the Jackson infinite recursion problem:

- @JsonManagedReference is the forward part of reference (it gets serialized)

- @JsonBackReference is the back part of reference (it's not serialized)

Alternatives to these two annotations are: @JsonIdentityInfo, @JsonIgnore, @JsonView, or a custom serializer.

Further, let's consider a classical `AuthorRepository`, `BookstoreService`, and a `BookstoreController` and let's see how OSIV works internally:

- Step 1: The `OpenSessionInViewFilter` calls the `SessionFactory#openSession()` and obtains a new `Session`.

- Step 2: The `Session` is bound to the `TransactionSynchronizationManager`.

- Step 3: The `OpenSessionInViewFilter` calls the `FilterChain#doFilter()` and the request is further processed.

- Step 4: The `DispatcherServlet` is called.

- Step 5: The `DispatcherServlet` routes the HTTP request to the underlying `BookstoreController`.

- Step 6: The `BookstoreController` calls `BookstoreService` to get a list of `Author` entities.

- Step 7: The `BookstoreService` opens a transaction by using the same `Session` opened by `OpenSessionInViewFilter`.

- Step 8: This transaction uses a new connection from the connection pool.

- Step 9: The `AuthorRepository` fetches a list of `Author` entities without initializing the `Book` association.

- Step 10: The `BookstoreService` commits the underlying transaction, but the `Session` is not closed because it was opened externally by the `OpenSessionInViewFilter`.

- Step 11: The `DispatcherServlet` renders the UI; in order to accomplish this, it needs the lazy `Book` association and thus it triggers the initialization of this lazy association.

- Step 12: The `OpenSessionInViewFilter` can close the `Session`, and the underlying database connection is released to the connection pool.

What are the main drawbacks of OSIV? Well, at least the following:

- Puts a lot of pressure on the connection pool, since concurrent requests sit in the queue waiting for long-running connections to be released. This can lead to a premature depletion of the connection pool.

- Statements issued from the UI rendering phase will run in auto-commit mode since there is no explicit transaction. This forces the database to have a lot of I/O operations (transfers the transaction log to disk). One optimization consists of marking the `Connection` as read-only, which would allow the database server to avoid writing to the transaction log.

- The service and UI layers can trigger statements against the database. This is against SoC (Separation of Concerns) and increases the complexity of testing.

> Of course, the solution to avoid OSIV overhead consists of disabling it and writing the queries by controlling the lazy loading  (e.g., via `JOIN` and/or `JOIN FETCH`) to avoid the potential `LazyInitializationException`. But this will not fix the issues caused by lazy loading triggered from the View layer. When the View layer forces lazy loading, there will be no active Hibernate `Session`, and this will cause lazy loading exceptions. To fix this, use `Hibernate5Module` or explicitly initialize the unfetched lazy associations.

# Hibernate5Module

`Hibernate5Module` is part of the `jackson-datatype-hibernate` project. Conforming to the official statement, the goal of this project is "to build Jackson modules (jar) to support JSON serialization and deserialization of Hibernate specific data types and properties; especially lazy-loading aspects."

The presence of `Hibernate5Module` instructs Jackson to initialize the unfetched lazy associations with default values (e.g., a lazy association will be initialized with `null`). In other words, Jackson will no longer use OSIV to fetch lazy associations. Nevertheless, `Hibernate5Module` works fine with lazy associations but does not work with lazy basic attributes (**Item 23**).

Adding `Hibernate5Module` to a project is a two-step task. First, add the following dependency to `pom.xml`:

```
<dependency>
    <groupId>com.fasterxml.jackson.datatype</groupId>
    <artifactId>jackson-datatype-hibernate5</artifactId>
</dependency>
```

Second, set up the following @Bean:

```
@SpringBootApplication
public class MainApplication {

    public static void main(String[] args) {
        SpringApplication.run(MainApplication.class, args);
    }

    @Bean
    public Hibernate5Module hibernate5Module() {
        return new Hibernate5Module();
    }
}
```

## Testing Time

Let's fetch an Author without the associated Book entities via a trivial service-method of BookstoreService:

```
public Author fetchAuthorWithoutBooks() {
    Author author = authorRepository.findByName("Joana Nimar");

    return author;
}
```

In the BookstoreController, let's call this method:

```
// The View will NOT force lazy initialization of books
@RequestMapping("/fetchwithoutbooks")
public Author fetchAuthorWithoutBooks() {
    Author author = bookstoreService.fetchAuthorWithoutBooks();

    return author;
}
```

Accessing the http://localhost:8080/fetchwithoutbooks URL triggers the following SQL statement:

```
SELECT
    author0_.id AS id1_0_,
    author0_.age AS age2_0_,
    author0_.genre AS genre3_0_,
    author0_.name AS name4_0_
FROM author author0_
WHERE author0_.name = ?
```

The returned JSON is as follows:

```
{
    "id":4,
    "name":"Joana Nimar",
    "genre":"History",
    "age":34,
    "books":null
}
```

The associated books have not been fetched. The books property was initialized to null, and most probably you don't want it to be serialized. For this, just annotate the Author entity with @JsonInclude(Include.NON_EMPTY). Triggering the same request will return the following JSON:

```
{
    "id":4,
    "name":"Joana Nimar",
    "genre":"History",
    "age":34
}
```

The complete code is available on GitHub[15].

# Explicitly (Manually) Initializing the Unfetched Lazy Properties

By explicitly (manually) initializing the unfetched lazy associations, the developer prevents the View from triggering lazy loading of them. The Session kept open by OSIV will no longer be used, so you can disable OSIV with no worries.

## Testing Time

Let's fetch an Author without the associated Book entities via a simple service-method of BookstoreService:

```
public Author fetchAuthorWithoutBooks() {
    Author author = authorRepository.findByName("Joana Nimar");

    // explicitly set Books of the Author to null
    // in order to avoid fetching them from the database
    author.setBooks(null);

    // or, to an empty collection
    // author.setBooks(Collections.emptyList());
    return author;
}
```

---

[15]HibernateSpringBootJacksonHibernate5Module

In the BookstoreController, let's call this method:

```
// The View will NOT force lazy initialization of books
@RequestMapping("/fetchwithoutbooks")
public Author fetchAuthorWithoutBooks() {
    Author author = bookstoreService.fetchAuthorWithoutBooks();

    return author;
}
```

Accessing the http://localhost:8080/fetchwithoutbooks URL triggers the following SQL statement:

```
SELECT
    author0_.id AS id1_0_,
    author0_.age AS age2_0_,
    author0_.genre AS genre3_0_,
    author0_.name AS name4_0_
FROM author author0_
WHERE author0_.name = ?
```

The returned JSON is as follows:

```
{
    "id":4,
    "name":"Joana Nimar",
    "genre":"History",
    "age":34,
    "books":null
}
```

The associated books have not been fetched. Exactly as before, annotate the Author entity with @JsonInclude (Include.NON_EMPTY) to avoid the serialization of books property.

The complete code is available on GitHub[16].

---

[16]HibernateSpringBootSuppressLazyInitInOpenSessionInView

712

If OSIV is enabled, the developer can still initialize the unfetched lazy associations manually as long as they do this outside of a transaction to avoid flushing. Why does this work? Since the Session is open, why doesn't the manual initialization of the associations of a managed entity trigger the flush? The answer can be found in the documentation of OpenSessionInViewFilter, which specifies that: "This filter will by default not flush the Hibernate Session, with the flush mode set to FlushMode.NEVER/MANUAL. It assumes to be used in combination with service layer transactions that care for the flushing: The active transaction manager will temporarily change the flush mode to FlushMode.AUTO during a read-write transaction, with the flush mode reset to FlushMode.NEVER/MANUAL at the end of each transaction. If you intend to use this filter without transactions, consider changing the default flush mode (through the flushMode property)."

## How About the Hibernate-Specific hibernate.enable_lazy_load_no_trans

If you have never heard about the Hibernate-specific hibernate.enable_lazy_load_no_trans setting, then you didn't miss a thing! But, if you heard about it and use it, read this section to learn why you should avoid this setting. In a nutshell, hibernate.enable_lazy_load_no_trans is another hack for avoiding LazyInitializationException.

Consider the following two service-methods:

```
public List<Book> fetchBooks() {

    return bookRepository.findByPriceGreaterThan(30);
}
```

```
public void displayAuthors(List<Book> books) {

    books.forEach(b -> System.out.println(b.getAuthor()));
}
```

Calling fetchBooks() will return a List containing all the books that are more expensive than *$30*. Afterward, you pass this list to the displayAuthors() method. Obviously, calling getAuthor() in this context will cause a LazyInitializationException since the authors are lazy loaded and, at this moment, there is no active Hibernate session.

Now, in application.properties, let's set hibernate.enable_lazy_load_no_trans as follows:

spring.jpa.properties.hibernate.enable_lazy_load_no_trans=true

> This time, the LazyInitializationException doesn't occur and the authors are displayed. What's the catch? Well, Hibernate opens a Session for each fetched author. Moreover, a database transaction and connection is used for each author. Obviously, this comes with a significant performance penalty. Don't even think that annotating the displayAuthors() method with @Transactional(readOnly=true) will sweeten the situation by using a single transaction. Actually, it makes things even worse by consuming one more transaction and database connection in addition to the ones used by Hibernate. Always avoid this setting!

The complete application is available on GitHub[17].

# Item 111: How to Store Date/Time in UTC Time Zone (MySQL)

> Since working with date and time is a sensitive aspect, it is recommended to store date, time, and timestamps in a database only in UTC (or GMT) format and deal with local time zone conversions only in UI.

---

[17]HibernateSpringBootEnableLazyLoadNoTrans

Consider the following entity:

```
@Entity
public class Screenshot implements Serializable {

    private static final long serialVersionUID = 1L;

    @Id
    @GeneratedValue(strategy = GenerationType.IDENTITY)
    private Long id;

    private String name;

    private Timestamp createOn;

    // getters and setters omitted for brevity
}
```

The focus is on the createOn timestamp. Set createOn to *2018-03-30 10:15:55 UTC* from a computer located in the *America/Los_Angeles* time zone (the time zone was arbitrarily chosen) and persist it via the ScreenshotRepository, as follows:

```
public void saveScreenshotInUTC() {

    TimeZone.setDefault(TimeZone.getTimeZone("America/Los_Angeles"));

    Screenshot screenshot = new Screenshot();

    screenshot.setName("Screenshot-1");
    screenshot.setCreateOn(new Timestamp(
        ZonedDateTime.of(2018, 3, 30, 10, 15, 55, 0,
            ZoneId.of("UTC")
        ).toInstant().toEpochMilli()
    ));

    System.out.println("Timestamp epoch milliseconds before insert: "
        + screenshot.getCreateOn().getTime());

    screenshotRepository.save(screenshot);
}
```

Before inserting, the timestamp epoch milliseconds will display the value *1522404955000*.

Later on, in another transaction, the application fetches this data as follows:

```
public void displayScreenshotInUTC() {
    Screenshot fetchScreenshot = screenshotRepository
        .findByName("Screenshot-1");
    System.out.println("Timestamp epoch milliseconds after fetching: "
        + fetchScreenshot.getCreateOn().getTime());
}
```

The timestamp epoch milliseconds after fetching reveals the same value: *1522404955000*.

But, in the database, the timestamp was saved in the *America/Los_Angeles* time zone, not in UTC. In the left side of Figure 14-11 is what we want, while the right side of the figure is what we have.

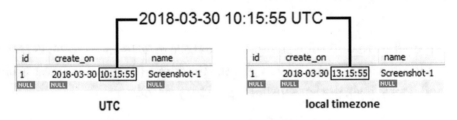

*Figure 14-11.* *Saving date-time in UTC vs. local time zone*

Hibernate 5.2.3 comes with a property that needs to be set up to persist date, time, and timestamps in UTC. This property is `spring.jpa.properties.hibernate.jdbc.time_ zone`. For MySQL only, the JDBC URL needs to be decorated with `useLegacy DatetimeCode=false` as well. Therefore the following settings are needed:

- `spring.jpa.properties.hibernate.jdbc.time_zone=UTC`
- `spring.datasource.url=jdbc:mysql://...?useLegacyDatetime Code=false`

After adding these settings in `application.properties`, the timestamp is saved in the UTC time zone. The timestamp epoch milliseconds reveals the same value (*1522404955000*) before inserting and after fetching.

The source code is available on GitHub[18].

---

[18]HibernateSpringBootUTCTimezone

# Item 112: How to Shuffle Small Result Sets via ORDER BY RAND()

Consider a small result set fetched from the book table (Book entity). The data snapshot is shown in Figure 14-12.

**book**

| id | isbn | title |
|---|---|---|
| 1 | 001-JN | A History of Ancient Prague |
| 2 | 002-JN | A People's History |
| 3 | 001-MJ | The Beatles Anthology |
| 4 | 001-OG | Carrie |
| 5 | 003-JN | World History |

***Figure 14-12.***  *Data snapshot*

The goal is to shuffle this result set. Therefore, executing the same SELECT should produce the same result set but with rows in different order.

A quick approach consists of appending to a SELECT query the ORDER BY clause to sort the SQL result set. Next, pass a database function to ORDER BY that's capable of randomizing the result set. In MySQL, this function is RAND(). Most databases support such a function (e.g., in PostgreSQL, it's random()).

In JPQL, the query for shuffling the result set can be written as follows:

```
@Repository
@Transactional(readOnly = true)
public interface BookRepository extends JpaRepository<Book, Long> {

    @Query("SELECT b FROM Book b ORDER BY RAND()")
    public List<Book> fetchOrderByRnd();
}
```

The generated SQL is:

```
SELECT
  book0_.id AS id1_0_,
  book0_.isbn AS isbn2_0_,
  book0_.title AS title3_0_
FROM book book0_
ORDER BY RAND()
```

Running this query twice will reveal that shuffling is working:

**run 1:**

```
{id=1, title=A History of Ancient Prague, isbn=001-JN},
{id=3, title=The Beatles Anthology, isbn=001-MJ},
{id=2, title=A People's History, isbn=002-JN}
{id=5, title=World History, isbn=003-JN},
{id=4, title=Carrie, isbn=001-OG}]
```

**run 2:**

```
{id=4, title=Carrie, isbn=001-OG},
{id=5, title=World History, isbn=003-JN},
{id=3, title=The Beatles Anthology, isbn=001-MJ},
{id=1, title=A History of Ancient Prague, isbn=001-JN},
{id=2, title=A People's History, isbn=002-JN}]
```

> **DO NOT USE** this technique for large results sets, since it's extremely expensive.
>
> For large results sets, simply rely on other approaches such as TABLESAMPLE or SAMPLE(*n*). The former is supported by PostgreSQL and SQL Server. The latter is supported by Oracle.

The complete application is available on GitHub[19].

# Item 113: How to Use Subqueries in the WHERE/HAVING Clause

JPQL queries can contain subqueries. More precisely, JPQL allows you to use subqueries in WHERE and HAVING clauses. Therefore it's not that versatile as native SQL. But, let's see it at work!

---

[19]HibernateSpringBootOrderByRandom

Consider two unrelated entities, Author and Bestseller. Even if there is no explicit relationships between Author and Bestseller, the Bestseller entity defines a column for storing the author IDs. This column is named authorId. In code:

```
@Entity
public class Author implements Serializable {

    @Id
    @GeneratedValue(strategy = GenerationType.IDENTITY)
    private Long id;

    private int age;
    private String name;
    private String genre;
    ...
}

@Entity
public class Bestseller implements Serializable {

    @Id
    @GeneratedValue(strategy = GenerationType.IDENTITY)
    private Long id;

    private String title;
    private int ranking;
    private Long authorId;
    ...
}
```

Figure 14-13 represents a data snapshot.

**author**

| id | age | genre | name |
|----|-----|-------|------|
| 1 | 23 | Anthology | Mark Janel |
| 2 | 43 | Horror | Olivia Goy |
| 3 | 51 | Anthology | Quartis Young |
| 4 | 34 | History | Joana Nimar |
| 5 | 38 | Anthology | Alicia Tom |
| 6 | 56 | Anthology | Katy Loin |

**bestseller**

| id | author_id | ranking | title |
|----|-----------|---------|-------|
| 1 | 6 | 3022 | Modern Anthology |
| 2 | 4 | 2443 | A History of Ancient Prague |
| 3 | 2 | 1433 | Carrie |

***Figure 14-13.*** *Data snapshot*

So, the best anthology author is *Katy Loin;* the best history author is *Joana Nimar;* and the best horror author is *Olivia Goy.* These authors can be fetched via an INNER JOIN as follows:

```
@Transactional(readOnly = true)
@Query(value = "SELECT a FROM Author a "
            + "INNER JOIN Bestseller b ON a.id = b.authorId")
public List<Author> fetchTheBest();
```

This will trigger the following SQL:

```
SELECT
  author0_.id AS id1_0_,
  author0_.age AS age2_0_,
  author0_.genre AS genre3_0_,
  author0_.name AS name4_0_
FROM author author0_
INNER JOIN bestseller bestseller1_
  ON (author0_.id = bestseller1_.author_id)
```

But, another approach will rely on a SELECT subquery in the WHERE clause, as follows:

```
@Transactional(readOnly = true)
@Query("SELECT a FROM Author a WHERE a.id IN "
     + "(SELECT b.authorId FROM Bestseller b)")
public List<Author> fetchTheBest();
```

This time, the triggered SQL statement is:

```
SELECT
  author0_.id AS id1_0_,
  author0_.age AS age2_0_,
  author0_.genre AS genre3_0_,
  author0_.name AS name4_0_
FROM author author0_
WHERE author0_.id IN (
  SELECT
    bestseller1_.author_id
  FROM bestseller bestseller1_)
```

But, which one is the best? Speaking from the perspective of readability or the logical way to solve problems of type *Fetch from A, conditional from B,* then subqueries (put *B* in a subquery not in a join) are the preferred way. But, if everything comes down to performance, note the MySQL execution plans shown in Figure 14-14.

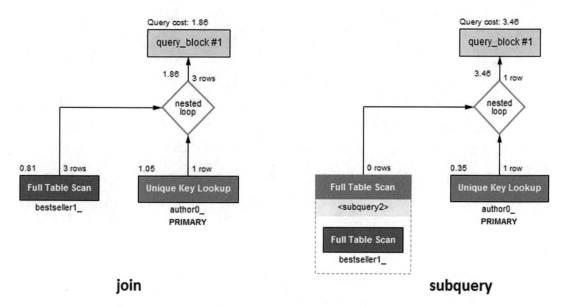

*Figure 14-14.  MySQL JOIN vs. subquery execution plans*

The PostgreSQL execution plan is shown in Figure 14-15.

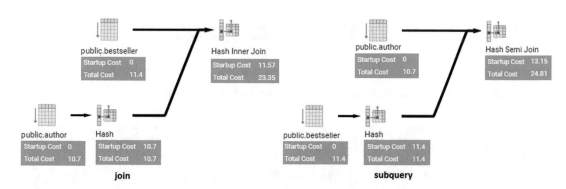

*Figure 14-15.  PostgreSQL JOIN vs. subquery execution plan*

From Figure 14-15, it's quite obvious that using JOIN is faster than using subqueries.

> Keep in mind that subqueries and joins queries may or may not be semantically equivalent (joins may return duplicates that can be removed via `DISTINCT`).

> Even if the execution plan is specific to the database, historically speaking, joins are faster than subqueries among different databases. However, this is not a rule (e.g., the amount of data may significantly influence the results). Of course, do not conclude that subqueries are just a replacement for joins that don't deserve attention. Tuning subqueries can increase their performance as well, but this is an SQL wide topic. So, benchmark! Benchmark! Benchmark!
>
> As a rule of thumb, use subqueries only if you cannot use joins, or if you can prove that they are faster than the alternative joins.

The complete application is available on GitHub[20].

> JPQL supports GROUP BY as well. Commonly, when we use GROUP BY we need to return a Map instead of a `List` or a `Set`. For example, we need to return a Map<*Group, Count*>. If you are in such a case then consider this application[21].

# Item 114: How to Call a Stored Procedure

The best approach for calling a stored procedure depends on its return type. Let's start by calling a stored procedure that returns a value that is not a result set.

> As a rule of thumb, don't implement data-heavy operations in the application. Such operations should be moved to the database-level as stored procedures. While simple operations can be solved by calling specific functions, use stored

---

[20]HibernateSpringBootSubqueryInWhere

[21]HibernateSpringBootResultSetMap

procedures for complex operations. Databases are highly optimized to deal with huge volumes of data, while the application is not. **Typically, stored procedures should save database round trips as well.**

Calling stored procedures that don't return a result is quite simple. The difficult part occurs when you need to call stored procedures that return a result, as a scalar value or as a result set. Further, let's see how you can call several MySQL stored procedures.

## Calling a Stored Procedure that Returns a Value (Scalar Data Types)

Consider the following MySQL stored procedure that counts the authors of the same given genre. This procedure returns an integer:

```
CREATE DEFINER=root@localhost PROCEDURE
  COUNT_AUTHOR_BY_GENRE(IN p_genre CHAR(20), OUT p_count INT)
BEGIN
  SELECT COUNT(*) INTO p_count FROM author WHERE genre = p_genre;
END;
```

You can call this stored procedure in two steps. First, the Author entity defines the stored procedure name and parameters via the JPA, @NamedStoredProcedureQuery, and @StoredProcedureParameter annotations, as follows:

There are four types of parameters that can be defined for a stored procedure: IN, OUT, INOUT, and REF_CURSOR. The first three types are supported by most RDBMS. Ref Cursors are available in some RDBMS (e.g., Oracle, PostgreSQL, etc.) while other RDBMS (e.g., MySQL) don't have Ref Cursors. Setting a REF_CURSOR is commonly accomplished as follows:

```
@StoredProcedureParameter(type = void.class,
                          mode = ParameterMode.REF_CURSOR)
```

```
@Entity
@NamedStoredProcedureQueries({
    @NamedStoredProcedureQuery(
            name = "CountByGenreProcedure",
            procedureName = "COUNT_AUTHOR_BY_GENRE",
            resultClasses = {Author.class},
            parameters = {
                @StoredProcedureParameter(
                        name = "p_genre",
                        type = String.class,
                        mode = ParameterMode.IN),
                @StoredProcedureParameter(
                        name = "p_count",
                        type = Integer.class,
                        mode = ParameterMode.OUT)})
})
public class Author implements Serializable {
  ...
}
```

Second, use Spring @Procedure annotation in AuthorRepository. Simply specify the stored procedure name:

```
@Repository
public interface AuthorRepository extends JpaRepository<Author, Long> {

    @Transactional
    @Procedure(name = "CountByGenreProcedure")
    Integer countByGenre(@Param("p_genre") String genre);
}
```

Calling the countByGenre() method will trigger the following statement:

```
{call COUNT_AUTHOR_BY_GENRE(?,?)}
```

The complete application is available on GitHub[22].

---

[22]HibernateSpringBootCallStoredProcedureReturnValue

# Calling a Stored Procedure that Returns a Result Set

Calling a stored procedure that returns a result set doesn't benefit of @Procedure. You can track the support on JIRA, DATAJPA-1092[23].

The @Procedure will not work as expected (at least, not in Spring Boot 2.3.0, when this book was written).

Consider the following two MySQL stored procedures:

- A stored procedure that returns the nickname and age columns of authors of the same given genre (can be one or multiple authors):

```
CREATE DEFINER=root@localhost
          PROCEDURE FETCH_NICKNAME_AND_AGE_BY_GENRE(
                    IN p_genre CHAR(20))
BEGIN
  SELECT nickname, age FROM author WHERE genre = p_genre;
END;
```

- A stored procedure that returns all authors of the same given genre:

```
CREATE DEFINER=root@localhost
          PROCEDURE FETCH_AUTHOR_BY_GENRE(
                    IN p_genre CHAR(20))
BEGIN
  SELECT * FROM author WHERE genre = p_genre;
END;
```

Now, let's see how you can call these stored procedures via JdbcTemplate, native SQL, and EntityManager.

## Calling a Stored Procedure via JdbcTemplate

First, you prepare a service that benefits JdbcTemplate, as follows:

```
@Service
public class BookstoreService {

    private final JdbcTemplate jdbcTemplate;
```

---

[23]https://jira.spring.io/browse/DATAJPA-1092

```
    public BookstoreService(JdbcTemplate jdbcTemplate) {
        this.jdbcTemplate = jdbcTemplate;
    }

    @PostConstruct
    void init() {
        jdbcTemplate.setResultsMapCaseInsensitive(true);
    }

    // methods that call stored procedures
}
```

Moreover, you prepare the following DTO class:

```
public class AuthorDto implements Serializable {

    private static final long serialVersionUID = 1L;

    private String nickname;
    private int age;

    public AuthorDto() {
    }

    // getters and setters omitted for brevity
}
```

Next, let's see how you can call these two stored procedures.

## Call the Stored Procedure that Returns the Nickname and Age Columns of Authors of the Given Genre (Can Be One or Multiple Authors)

You can fetch the result set in a DTO via BeanPropertyRowMapper. This way, you map the result set to a DTO as follows:

```
public List<AuthorDto> fetchNicknameAndAgeByGenre() {
    SimpleJdbcCall simpleJdbcCall = new SimpleJdbcCall(jdbcTemplate)
        .withProcedureName("FETCH_NICKNAME_AND_AGE_BY_GENRE")
        .returningResultSet("AuthorResultSet",
            BeanPropertyRowMapper.newInstance(AuthorDto.class));
```

```
Map<String, Object> authors = simpleJdbcCall.execute(
    Map.of("p_genre", "Anthology"));

return (List<AuthorDto>) authors.get("AuthorResultSet");
}
```

Obviously, a single AuthorDto can be returned as well. For example, fetch by ID instead of by genre, and the result set will return a single row.

## Call the Stored Procedure that Returns All Authors of the Given Genre

You can call this stored procedure via JdbcTemplate and SimpleJdbcCall to return a List<Author> as follows:

```
public List<Author> fetchAnthologyAuthors() {
    SimpleJdbcCall simpleJdbcCall = new SimpleJdbcCall(jdbcTemplate)
        .withProcedureName("FETCH_AUTHOR_BY_GENRE")
        .returningResultSet("AuthorResultSet",
            BeanPropertyRowMapper.newInstance(Author.class));

    Map<String, Object> authors = simpleJdbcCall.execute(
        Map.of("p_genre", "Anthology"));

    return (List<Author>) authors.get("AuthorResultSet");
}
```

Notice how the result set is mapped to a List<Author> and not to a List<AuthorDto>.

The complete application is available on GitHub[24]. In this application there is also an example of calling a stored procedure that uses the MySQL-specific SELECT-INTO to return a single row. Moreover, there is an example of fetching multiple results sets directly in DTO classes (call a stored procedure that returns multiple results sets). If you don't want to rely on BeanPropertyRowMapper, and you just want to dissect the result set by yourself, then here[25] is an example.

> Until Spring Data @Procedure becomes more flexible, relying on JdbcTemplate is the most versatile way to call stored procedures.

---

[24]HibernateSpringBootCallStoredProcedureJdbcTemplateBeanPropertyRowMapper
[25]HibernateSpringBootCallStoredProcedureJdbcTemplate

# Calling a Stored Procedure via a Native Query

Calling stored procedures via native queries can be a good alternative as well.

## Call the Stored Procedure that Returns the Nickname and Age Columns of Authors of the Given Genre (Can Be One or Multiple Authors)

You can call this stored procedure as shown here:

```
@Repository
@Transactional(readOnly = true)
public interface AuthorRepository extends JpaRepository<Author, Long> {

    @Query(value = "{CALL FETCH_NICKNAME_AND_AGE_BY_GENRE (:p_genre)}",
            nativeQuery = true)
    List<Object[]> fetchNicknameAndAgeByGenreDto(
        @Param("p_genre") String genre);

    @Query(value = "{CALL FETCH_NICKNAME_AND_AGE_BY_GENRE (:p_genre)}",
            nativeQuery = true)
    List<AuthorNicknameAndAge> fetchNicknameAndAgeByGenreProj(
        @Param("p_genre") String genre);
}
```

Calling fetchNicknameAndAgeByGenreDto() fetches the result set as a List<Object[]> and, in the service-method, it's manually mapped to a DTO class as follows:

```
public class AuthorDto implements Serializable {

    private static final long serialVersionUID = 1L;

    private final String nickname;
    private final int age;

    public AuthorDto(String nickname, int age) {
        this.nickname = nickname;
        this.age = age;
    }

    // getters omitted for brevity
}
```

```
public void fetchAnthologyAuthorsNameAndAgeDto() {

    List<Object[]> authorsArray
        = authorRepository.fetchNicknameAndAgeByGenreDto("Anthology");

    List<AuthorDto> authors = authorsArray.stream()
        .map(result -> new AuthorDto(
            (String) result[0],
            (Integer) result[1]
        )).collect(Collectors.toList());

    System.out.println("Result: " + authors);
}
```

Calling fetchNicknameAndAgeByGenreProj() fetches the result set in a
List<AuthorNicknameAndAge>. The result set is automatically mapped to
AuthorNicknameAndAge, which is a simple Spring projection:

```
public interface AuthorNicknameAndAge {

    public String getNickname();
    public int getAge();
}
```

```
public void fetchAnthologyAuthorsNameAndAgeProj() {

    List<AuthorNicknameAndAge> authorsDto
        = authorRepository.fetchNicknameAndAgeByGenreProj("Anthology");

    System.out.println("Result: ");
    authorsDto.forEach(a -> System.out.println(
        a.getNickname() + ", " + a.getAge()));
}
```

## Call the Stored Procedure that Returns All Authors of the Given Genre

You can call this stored procedure as follows:

```
@Repository
@Transactional(readOnly = true)
public interface AuthorRepository extends JpaRepository<Author, Long> {
```

```
@Query(value = "{CALL FETCH_AUTHOR_BY_GENRE (:p_genre)}",
        nativeQuery = true)
List<Author> fetchByGenre(@Param("p_genre") String genre);
}
```

The service-method is quite simple:

```
public void fetchAnthologyAuthors() {

    List<Author> authors = authorRepository.fetchByGenre("Anthology");
    System.out.println("Result: " + authors);
}
```

The complete application is available on GitHub[26].

## Calling a Stored Procedure via EntityManager

EntityManager provides solid support for calling stored procedures. Let's see how to do this for these two stored procedures.

### Call the Stored Procedure that Returns the Nickname and Age Columns of Authors of the Given Genre (Can Be One or Multiple Authors)

This time, the solution relies on a custom repository that injects the EntityManager and works directly with JPA, StoredProcedureQuery. Calling the stored procedure that returns only the nickname and the age of all authors of the same given genre can start by defining a DTO as follows:

```
public class AuthorDto implements Serializable {

    private static final long serialVersionUID = 1L;

    private final String nickname;
    private final int age;

    public AuthorDto(String nickname, int age) {
        this.nickname = nickname;
```

---

[26]HibernateSpringBootCallStoredProcedureNativeCall

```
        this.age = age;
    }

    // getters omitted for brevity
}
```

Further, in the Author entity, use @SqlResultSetMapping to map the result set to AuthorDto:

```
@Entity
@SqlResultSetMapping(name = "AuthorDtoMapping",
    classes = @ConstructorResult(targetClass = AuthorDto.class,
    columns = {
        @ColumnResult(name = "nickname"),
        @ColumnResult(name = "age")}))
public class Author implements Serializable {
    ...
}
```

Finally, use EntityManager and StoredProcedureQuery as follows:

```
@Transactional
public List<AuthorDto> fetchByGenre(String genre) {

    StoredProcedureQuery storedProcedure
        = entityManager.createStoredProcedureQuery(
            "FETCH_NICKNAME_AND_AGE_BY_GENRE", "AuthorDtoMapping");

    storedProcedure.registerStoredProcedureParameter(GENRE_PARAM,
        String.class, ParameterMode.IN);
    storedProcedure.setParameter(GENRE_PARAM, genre);

    List<AuthorDto> storedProcedureResults;
    try {
        storedProcedureResults = storedProcedure.getResultList();
    } finally {
        storedProcedure.unwrap(ProcedureOutputs.class).release();
    }

    return storedProcedureResults;
}
```

Calling this method will result in the following statement:

```
{call FETCH_NICKNAME_AND_AGE_BY_GENRE(?)}
```

Manual mapping of the result set to AuthorDto is also achievable. This time, the Author entity is very simple:

```
@Entity
public class Author implements Serializable {

    ...

}
```

The mapping is accomplished in the fetchByGenre() method:

```
@Transactional
public List<AuthorDto> fetchByGenre(String genre) {

    StoredProcedureQuery storedProcedure
        = entityManager.createStoredProcedureQuery(
            "FETCH_NICKNAME_AND_AGE_BY_GENRE");

    storedProcedure.registerStoredProcedureParameter(GENRE_PARAM,
        String.class, ParameterMode.IN);
    storedProcedure.setParameter(GENRE_PARAM, genre);

    List<AuthorDto> storedProcedureResults;
    try {
        List<Object[]> storedProcedureObjects
            = storedProcedure.getResultList();

        storedProcedureResults = storedProcedureObjects.stream()
            .map(result -> new AuthorDto(
                (String) result[0],
                (Integer) result[1]
        )).collect(Collectors.toList());
    } finally {
        storedProcedure.unwrap(ProcedureOutputs.class).release();
    }

    return storedProcedureResults;
}
```

Calling this method will result in the following statement:

```
{call FETCH_NICKNAME_AND_AGE_BY_GENRE(?)}
```

## Call the Stored Procedure that Returns All Authors of the Given Genre

You can call FETCH_AUTHOR_BY_GENRE in two steps. First, the Author entity defines the stored procedure name and parameters via @NamedStoredProcedureQuery and @StoredProcedureParameter as follows:

```
@Entity
@NamedStoredProcedureQueries({
    @NamedStoredProcedureQuery(
            name = "FetchByGenreProcedure",
            procedureName = "FETCH_AUTHOR_BY_GENRE",
            resultClasses = {Author.class},
            parameters = {
                @StoredProcedureParameter(
                        name = "p_genre",
                        type = String.class,
                        mode = ParameterMode.IN)})
})
public class Author implements Serializable {
    ...
}
```

Second, a custom repository relies on StoredProcedureQuery, as follows:

```
private static final String GENRE_PARAM = "p_genre";

@PersistenceContext
private EntityManager entityManager;

@Transactional
public List<Author> fetchByGenre(String genre) {

    StoredProcedureQuery storedProcedure
        = entityManager.createNamedStoredProcedureQuery(
            "FetchByGenreProcedure");

    storedProcedure.setParameter(GENRE_PARAM, genre);
```

```
    List<Author> storedProcedureResults;
    try {
        storedProcedureResults = storedProcedure.getResultList();
    } finally {
        storedProcedure.unwrap(ProcedureOutputs.class).release();
    }

    return storedProcedureResults;
}
```

Calling this method will result in the following statement:

```
{call FETCH_AUTHOR_BY_GENRE(?)}
```

Another approach consists of defining the stored procedure directly in the custom repository via createStoredProcedureQuery() instead of createNamedStored ProcedureQuery(). This time, the Author entity is very simple:

```
@Entity
public class Author implements Serializable {

    ...

}
```

The fetchByGenre() is written as follows:

```
@Transactional
public List<Author> fetchByGenre(String genre) {

    StoredProcedureQuery storedProcedure
        = entityManager.createStoredProcedureQuery(
            "FETCH_AUTHOR_BY_GENRE", Author.class);

    storedProcedure.registerStoredProcedureParameter(GENRE_PARAM,
        String.class, ParameterMode.IN);
    storedProcedure.setParameter(GENRE_PARAM, genre);

    List<Author> storedProcedureResults;
    try {
        storedProcedureResults = storedProcedure.getResultList();
    } finally {
```

```
        storedProcedure.unwrap(ProcedureOutputs.class).release();
    }

    return storedProcedureResults;
}
```

Calling this method will result in the following statement:

```
{call FETCH_AUTHOR_BY_GENRE(?)}
```

The complete application is available on GitHub[27].

---

Notice that these examples prefer to manually close the `CallableStatement` used behind the scenes for calling a stored procedure in a `finally` clause, as shown here:

```
storedProcedure.unwrap(ProcedureOutputs.class).release();
```

This is needed to avoid the performance penalty of keeping the `CallableStatement` open when it's not needed. The `CallableStatement` is open even after fetching the result set. Calling `release()` will close the `CallableStatement` as soon as possible.

You can easily test if the `CallableStatement` is open, as follows:

```
ProcedureOutputs procedureOutputs = storedProcedure
    .unwrap(ProcedureOutputs.class);
Field csField = procedureOutputs.getClass()
    .getDeclaredField("callableStatement");
csField.setAccessible(true);
CallableStatement cs = (CallableStatement) csField
    .get(procedureOutputs);

System.out.println("Is closed? " + cs.isClosed()); // false
```

This issue will be fixed in Hibernate 6 (HHH-13215[28].)

---

[27]HibernateSpringBootCallStoredProcedureReturnResultSet
[28]https://hibernate.atlassian.net/browse/HHH-13215

# Item 115: How to Unproxy a Proxy

You can get a Hibernate-specific proxy via the `EntityManager#getReference()` method. In Spring Boot, this method is wrapped in the `getOne()` method, as in the following source code:

```
@Override
public T getOne(ID id) {

    Assert.notNull(id, ID_MUST_NOT_BE_NULL);
    return em.getReference(getDomainClass(), id);
}
```

## What Is a Proxy Object?

Sooner or later, every developer that gets in touch with the notion of lazy loading will discover the Hibernate-specific proxies as well. Some developers will ask, "How does lazy loading work?" and another developer will answer, "It uses Hibernate-specific proxies". So, proxy objects facilitate entities lazy loading.

> Do not confuse Hibernate lazy loading with Spring Spring Data JPA deferred bootstrap modes[29]. The latter refers to Spring JPA infrastructure and repository bootstrap.

But, what is a proxy object? First of all, a proxy object is generated by Hibernate at runtime and extends the original entity (the one that you wrote). Moreover, Hibernate replaces the original entity collections (e.g., `List`) with the proper Hibernate-specific persistent wrapper collections (e.g., `PersistentList`). For `Set` it has `PersistentSet` and for `Map` it has `PersistentMap`. They can be found in the `org.hibernate.collection.*` package.

The generated proxy follows the well-known Proxy design pattern. Generally speaking, the intent of this design pattern is to expose a surrogate for another object to provide control to this object. Mainly, a proxy object is an extra level of indirection to support custom access to the original object and wraps the original object complexity.

---

[29]https://github.com/spring-projects/spring-data-examples/tree/master/jpa/deferred

A Hibernate-specific proxy has two main jobs:

- Delegate the calls that access the *basic* properties to the original entity.

- Rely on the persistent wrappers (PersistentList, PersistentSet, PersistentMap) to intercept calls that access the uninitialized collections (List, Set, and Map). When such a call is intercepted, it is handled by an associated listener. This is responsible for issuing the correct initialization query of that collection.

When you get a LazyInitializationException, it means the context in which the Hibernate-specific proxies are living is missing. In other words, there is no Persistence Context or Session available.

## An Entity Object and a Proxy Object Are Not Equal

You can fetch an entity object via the EntityManager#find() method. In Spring Boot, this call is wrapped in the findById() method. While an entity object is populated with data, a proxy object is not. Consider the following Author entity:

```
@Entity
public class Author implements Serializable {

    private static final long serialVersionUID = 1L;

    @Id
    @GeneratedValue(strategy = GenerationType.IDENTITY)
    private Long id;

    private String name;
    private String genre;
    private int age;

    // getters and setters omitted for brevity

    @Override
    public boolean equals(Object obj) {

        if (this == obj) {
            return true;
        }
```

```
        if (obj == null) {
            return false;
        }

        if (getClass() != obj.getClass()) {
            return false;
        }

        return id != null && id.equals(((Author) obj).id);
    }

    @Override
    public int hashCode() {
        return 2021;
    }
}
```

The following code reveals that an entity object is not equal to a proxy object:

```
@Service
public class BookstoreService {

    private final AuthorRepository authorRepository;
    private Author author;
    ...

    public void authorNotEqualsProxy() {

        // behind findById() we have EntityManager#find()
        author = authorRepository.findById(1L).orElseThrow();

        // behind getOne() we have EntityManager#getReference()
        Author proxy = authorRepository.getOne(1L);

        System.out.println("Author class: " + author.getClass().getName());
        System.out.println("Proxy class: " + proxy.getClass().getName());
        System.out.println("'author' equals 'proxy'? "
            + author.equals(proxy));
    }
}
```

Calling authorNotEqualsProxy() produces the following output:

```
Author class: com.bookstore.entity.Author
Proxy class: com.bookstore.entity.Author$HibernateProxy$sfwzCCbF
'author' equals 'proxy'? false
```

## Unproxy a Proxy

Starting with Hibernate 5.2.10 the developer can unproxy a proxy object via the dedicated method, Hibernate.unproxy(). For example, you can unproxy the proxy object as follows:

```
Object unproxy = Hibernate.unproxy(proxy);
```

By unproxying a proxy, that means the proxy becomes an entity object. Therefore the previous code will trigger the following SQL SELECT:

```
SELECT
    author0_.id AS id1_0_0_,
    author0_.age AS age2_0_0_,
    author0_.genre AS genre3_0_0_,
    author0_.name AS name4_0_0_
FROM author author0_
WHERE author0_.id = ?
```

Now, the unproxy can be cast to Author:

```
Author authorViaUnproxy = (Author) unproxy;
```

Obviously, calling getName(), getGenre(), etc. will return the expected data.

---

Before Hibernate 5.2.10, a proxy object can be unproxied via LazyInitializer, as shown here:

```
HibernateProxy hibernateProxy = (HibernateProxy) proxy;
LazyInitializer initializer
    = hibernateProxy.getHibernateLazyInitializer();
Object unproxy = initializer.getImplementation();
```

> To check if a certain property of a proxy object was initialized or not, just call the `Hibernate.isPropertyInitialized()` method. For example, check if the name property of the `proxy` object was initialized before unproxying it:
>
> ```
> // false
> boolean nameIsInitialized
>     = Hibernate.isPropertyInitialized(proxy, "name");
> ```
>
> Calling the same code after unproxying the proxy object will return `true`.

## An Entity Object and an Unproxied Object Are Equal

You can test if an entity object and an unproxied object are equal by adding `BookstoreService` the following method (the author object is the one fetched earlier via `authorNotEqualsProxy()`):

```
@Transactional(readOnly = true)
public void authorEqualsUnproxy() {

    // behind getOne() we have EntityManager#getReference()
    Author proxy = authorRepository.getOne(1L);

    Object unproxy = Hibernate.unproxy(proxy);

    System.out.println("Author class: " + author.getClass().getName());
    System.out.println("Unproxy class: " + unproxy.getClass().getName());
    System.out.println("'author' equals 'unproxy'? "
        + author.equals(unproxy));
}
```

Calling `authorEqualsUnproxy()` outputs the following:

```
Author class: com.bookstore.entity.Author
Unproxy class: com.bookstore.entity.Author
'author' equals 'unproxy'? true
```

The complete application is available on GitHub[30].

---

[30]HibernateSpringBootUnproxyAProxy

740

# Item 116: How to Map a Database View

Let's consider the Author and Book entities involved in a bidirectional lazy @OneToMany relationship. Moreover, let's consider a MySQL database view defined as shown:

```
CREATE OR REPLACE VIEW GENRE_AND_TITLE_VIEW
AS
SELECT
    a.genre,
    b.title
FROM
    author a
INNER JOIN
    book b ON b.author_id = a.id;
```

This view fetched the genres of authors and the titles of books via a INNER JOIN. Now, let's fetch this database view in the application and display its content.

Typically, database views are mapped exactly as database tables. In other words, you need to define an entity that maps the view to the corresponding name and columns. By default, table mapping is not read-only, and this means that content can be modified. Depending on the database, a view can be modified or not (**Item 117**). You can easily prevent Hibernate from modifying the view by annotating the entity-view with @Immutable, as shown here (e.g., MySQL requirements for a database view to be modifiable are available here[31]):

```
@Entity
@Immutable
@Table(name="genre_and_title_view")
public class GenreAndTitleView implements Serializable {

    private static final long serialVersionUID = 1L;

    @Id
    private String title;
```

---

[31]https://dev.mysql.com/doc/refman/8.0/en/view-updatability.html

```
    private String genre;

    public String getTitle() {
        return title;
    }

    public String getGenre() {
        return genre;
    }

    @Override
    public String toString() {
        return "AuthorBookView{" + "title=" + title
            + ", genre=" + genre + '}';
    }
}
```

Further, define a classical Spring repository:

```
@Repository
public interface GenreAndTitleViewRepository
    extends JpaRepository<GenreAndTitleView, Long> {

    List<GenreAndTitleView> findByGenre(String genre);
}
```

Let's trigger a findAll() to fetch and display the view data:

```
private final GenreAndTitleViewRepository genreAndTitleViewRepository;
...
public void displayView() {
    List<GenreAndTitleView> view = genreAndTitleViewRepository.findAll();
    System.out.println("View: " + view);
}
```

Calling displayView() triggers the following SELECT statement:

```
SELECT
  genreandti0_.title AS title1_2_,
  genreandti0_.genre AS genre2_2_
FROM genre_and_title_view genreandti0_
```

Or, you can fetch only records of a certain genre:

```
public void displayViewByGenre() {
    List<GenreAndTitleView> view
        = genreAndTitleViewRepository.findByGenre("History");
    System.out.println("View: " + view);
}
```

This time, calling displayViewByGenre() triggers the following SELECT statement:

**SELECT**
  genreandti0_.title **AS** title1_2_,
  genreandti0_.genre **AS** genre2_2_
**FROM** genre_and_title_view genreandti0_
**WHERE** genreandti0_.genre = ?

The complete application is available on GitHub[32].

# Item 117: How to Update a Database View

Let's consider the author table (corresponding to the Author entity) and the data snapshot shown in Figure 14-16.

| author | | id | age | genre | name | sellrank | royalties | rating |
|--------|--|----|-----|-------|------|----------|-----------|--------|
| id BIGINT(20) | | 1 | 23 | Anthology | Mark Janel | 289 | 1200 | 3 |
| | | 2 | 43 | Horror | Olivia Goy | 490 | 4000 | 5 |
| age INT(11) | | 3 | 51 | Anthology | Quartis Young | 122 | 900 | 4 |
| | | 4 | 34 | History | Joana Nimar | 554 | 5600 | 4 |
| genre VARCHAR(255) | | 5 | 47 | Anthology | Kakki Jou | 231 | 1000 | 5 |
| | | 6 | 56 | Anthology | Fair Pouille | 344 | 3400 | 5 |
| name VARCHAR(255) | | | | | | | | |
| sellrank INT(11) | | | | | | | | |
| royalties INT(11) | | | | | | | | |
| rating INT(11) | | | | | | | | |
| Indexes | ▶ | | | | | | | |

***Figure 14-16.***   *The author table and data snapshot*

---

[32]HibernateSpringBootDatabaseView

Looks like the *Anthology* authors are very popular and successful therefore they have been extracted in a database view as follows:

```
CREATE OR REPLACE VIEW AUTHOR_ANTHOLOGY_VIEW
AS
SELECT
    a.id,
    a.name,
    a.age,
    a.genre
FROM
    author a
WHERE a.genre = "Anthology";
```

This view is mapped to the following entity-view:

```
@Entity
@Table(name = "author_anthology_view")
public class AuthorAnthologyView implements Serializable {

    private static final long serialVersionUID = 1L;

    @Id
    @GeneratedValue(strategy = GenerationType.IDENTITY)
    private Long id;

    private String name;
    private int age;
    private String genre;
    ...
}
```

This is not a read-only database view, so the `AuthorAnthologyView` entity is not annotated with `@Immutable` (details about immutable entities are found in **Item 16**).

# Trigger UPDATE Statements

This database view is seldom modified just for updating the age of authors. When such an update is needed, the application should trigger an UPDATE statement against the database view and the database should automatically update the contents of the underlying table. The following code sample updates the age of an author. First, the repository:

```
@Repository
public interface AuthorAnthologyViewRepository extends
        JpaRepository<AuthorAnthologyView, Long> {

    public AuthorAnthologyView findByName(String name);
}
```

The service-method (*Quartis Young*'s age is updated from *51* to *52*; notice that we are very discrete and we do not request the author's birth information):

```
private final AuthorAnthologyViewRepository authorAnthologyViewRepository;
...
@Transactional
public void updateAuthorAgeViaView() {
    AuthorAnthologyView author
        = authorAnthologyViewRepository.findByName("Quartis Young");

    author.setAge(author.getAge() + 1);
}
```

Calling updateAuthorAgeViaView() triggers the following SQL statements:

```
SELECT
  authorantho0_.id AS id1_1_,
  authorantho0_.age AS age2_1_,
  authorantho0_.genre AS genre3_1_,
  authorantho0_.name AS name4_1_
FROM author_anthology_view authorantho0_
WHERE authorantho0_.name = ?
```

```
UPDATE author_anthology_view
SET age = ?,
    genre = ?,
    name = ?
WHERE id = ?
```

The UPDATE statement will update the database view and the underlying table.

> For a view to be updatable, there must be a one-to-one relationship between the rows in the view and the rows in the underlying table. While this is the main requirement, MySQL has other requirements listed here[33].

## Trigger INSERT Statements

Inserting a new author is also a pretty rare case. But, when it's needed, you can do it, as in the following service-method:

```
public void insertAuthorViaView() {
    AuthorAnthologyView newAuthor = new AuthorAnthologyView();
    newAuthor.setName("Toij Kalu");
    newAuthor.setGenre("Anthology");
    newAuthor.setAge(42);

    authorAnthologyViewRepository.save(newAuthor);
}
```

Again, inserting in the view should be automatically propagated by the database to the underlying author table. Calling insertAuthorViaView() triggers the following INSERT statement:

```
INSERT INTO author_anthology_view (age, genre, name)
  VALUES (?, ?, ?)
```

---

[33]https://dev.mysql.com/doc/refman/8.0/en/view-updatability.html

An updatable view is insertable if it also satisfies the following additional requirements for the view columns: there must be no duplicate view column names, the view must contain all the columns in the base table that do not have a default value, and the view columns must be simple column references (they must not be expressions). Notice that our INSERT works because the schema of the author table specifies default values for the columns that are not present in the database view (see the bold lines shown here):

```
CREATE TABLE author (
  id bigint(20) NOT NULL AUTO_INCREMENT,
  age int(11) NOT NULL,
  genre varchar(255) NOT NULL,
  name varchar(255) NOT NULL,
  sellrank int(11) NOT NULL DEFAULT -1,
  royalties int(11) NOT NULL DEFAULT -1,
  rating int(11) NOT NULL DEFAULT -1,
  PRIMARY KEY (id)
);
```

While this is the main requirement, MySQL has other requirements listed here[33].

At this moment, you can insert an author that has a different genre than *Anthology*. To ensure that INSERTs/UPDATEs conform to the definition of the view, consider **Item 118**, which brings WITH CHECK OPTION into discussion.

## Trigger DELETE Statements

Deleting an author is also a pretty uncommon case. But, when it's needed, you can do it, as in the following example:

```
@Transactional
public void deleteAuthorViaView() {
    AuthorAnthologyView author
        = authorAnthologyViewRepository.findByName("Mark Janel");

    authorAnthologyViewRepository.delete(author);
}
```

Calling `deleteAuthorViaView()` should delete the specified author from the database view and from the underlying table:

```
SELECT
  author anth0_.id AS id1_1_,
  author anth0_.age AS age2_1_,
  author anth0_.genre AS genre3_1_,
  author anth0_.name AS name4_1_
FROM author_anthology_view author anth0_
WHERE author anth0_.name = ?

DELETE FROM author_anthology_view
WHERE id = ?
```

> The tables to be deleted from a `DELETE` statement must be merged views. Join views are not allowed. While this is the main requirement, MySQL has other requirements, listed here[34].

After applying the `UPDATE`, `INSERT`, and `DELETE`s, you should obtain the data snapshot shown in Figure 14-17 (the left side is the database view; the right side is the underlying table).

**author_anthology_view**

| id | name | age | genre |
|----|------|-----|-------|
| 3 | Quartis Young | 52 | Anthology |
| 5 | Kakki Jou | 47 | Anthology |
| 6 | Fair Pouille | 56 | Anthology |
| 7 | Toij Kalu | 42 | Anthology |

**author**

| id | age | genre | name | sellrank | royalties | rating |
|----|-----|-------|------|----------|-----------|--------|
| 2 | 43 | Horror | Olivia Goy | 490 | 4000 | 5 |
| 3 | 52 | Anthology | Quartis Young | 122 | 900 | 4 |
| 4 | 34 | History | Joana Nimar | 554 | 5600 | 4 |
| 5 | 47 | Anthology | Kakki Jou | 231 | 1000 | 5 |
| 6 | 56 | Anthology | Fair Pouille | 344 | 3400 | 5 |
| 7 | 42 | Anthology | Toij Kalu | -1 | -1 | -1 |

***Figure 14-17.*** *Database view and the underlying table*

The complete application is available on GitHub[35].

---

[34]https://dev.mysql.com/doc/refman/8.0/en/view-updatability.html
[35]HibernateSpringBootDatabaseViewUpdateInsertDelete

# Item 118: Why and How to Use WITH CHECK OPTION

In a nutshell, whenever you insert or update a row of the base tables through a database view, MySQL ensures that this operation conforms with the definition of the view as long as the database view definition has explicitly set WITH CHECK OPTION.

Let's reiterate the database view from **Item 117** (mapped to AuthorAnthologyView):

```
CREATE OR REPLACE VIEW AUTHOR_ANTHOLOGY_VIEW
AS
SELECT
    a.id,
    a.name,
    a.age,
    a.genre
FROM
    author a
WHERE a.genre = "Anthology";
```

As you know from **Item 117**, this database view is updatable. Therefore, the application can trigger updates that update data that's not visible through the view. For example, consider the following INSERT via this view:

```
public void insertAnthologyAuthorInView() {
    AuthorAnthologyView author = new AuthorAnthologyView();
    author.setName("Mark Powell");
    author.setGenre("History");
    author.setAge(45);

    authorAnthologyViewRepository.save(author);
}
```

Our view contains only authors of genre *Anthology* and the method inserts an author of genre *History* through the view. What will happen? Well, the newly created author is not visible through the view because their genre is *History*. But, it was inserted in the underlying author table!

But, this may be not what you want! Most probably, the genre of *Mark Powell* is *Anthology* (notice that you call a method named insertAnthologyAuthorInView()), but we mistakenly selected *History*. The result is really confusing because this author is not exposed in the view and was added to the underlying table.

The `WITH CHECK OPTION` to the rescue. The `WITH CHECK OPTION` prevents a view from updating or inserting rows that are not visible through it. Modify the database view definition as follows:

```
CREATE OR REPLACE VIEW AUTHOR_ANTHOLOGY_VIEW
AS
SELECT
    a.id,
    a.name,
    a.age,
    a.genre
FROM
    author a
WHERE a.genre = "Anthology" WITH CHECK OPTION;
```

Calling `insertAnthologyAuthorInView()` again will cause an `SQLException` exception as follows: `CHECK OPTION failed 'bookstoredb.author_anthology_view'`. So, this time the `INSERT` operation is prevented.

But after replacing *History* with *Anthology,* the `INSERT` is successful and the new author is visible in the view and in the underlying table:

```
public void insertAnthologyAuthorInView() {
    AuthorAnthologyView author = new AuthorAnthologyView();
    author.setName("Mark Powell");
    author.setGenre("Anthology");
    author.setAge(45);

    authorAnthologyViewRepository.save(author);
}
```

The complete application is available on GitHub[36].

---

[36]HibernateSpringBootDatabaseViewWithCheckOption

# Item 119: How to Efficiently Assign a Database Temporary Ranking to Rows

Different kinds of tasks (e.g., check **Item 102** and **Item 120**) require you to assign a database temporary sequence of values to rows. An efficient way to accomplish this is using the ROW_NUMBER() window function. This window function is in the same category as the RANK(), DENSE_RANK(), and NTILE() window functions and are known as *ranking functions*.

The ROW_NUMBER() window function produces a sequence of values that starts from value 1 with an increment of 1. This is a temporary sequence of values (non-persistent) that is calculated dynamically at query execution time. The syntax of this window function is as follows:

```
ROW_NUMBER() OVER (<partition_definition> <order_definition>)
```

The OVER clause defines the window of rows that ROW_NUMBER() operates on. The PARTITION BY clause (<partition_definition>) is optional and is used to break the rows into smaller sets (without it, the entire result set is considered a partition). Its syntax is as follows:

```
PARTITION BY <expression>,[{,<expression>}...]
```

The purpose of the ORDER BY clause (<order_definition>) is to set the orders of rows. The sequence of values is applied following this order (in other words, the window function will process the rows in this order). Its syntax is:

```
ORDER BY <expression> [ASC|DESC],[{,<expression>}...]
```

This window function is available in almost all databases, and starting with version 8.x, it's available in MySQL as well.

> The ROW_NUMBER() window function is supported on MySQL 8+, Oracle 9.2+, PostgreSQL 8.4+, SQL Server 2005+, Firebird 3.0+, DB2, Sybase, Teradata, Vertica, and so on.

Figure 14-18 shows the author table (left side) and a data snapshot (right side).

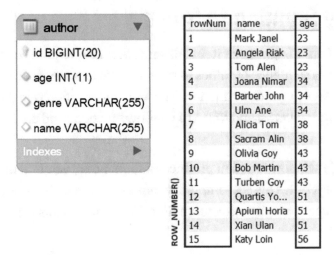

*Figure 14-18.*  *The author table and data snapshot*

To obtain the data snapshot from this figure as a result set, start by defining a Spring projection (DTO), as shown here (the getRowNum() method was added because we want to fetch the rowNum column in the result set):

```
public interface AuthorDto {

    public String getName();
    public int getAge();
    public int getRowNum();
}
```

Further, write a native query as follows:

```
@Repository
@Transactional(readOnly = true)
public interface AuthorRepository extends JpaRepository<Author, Long> {

    @Query(value = "SELECT ROW_NUMBER() OVER(ORDER BY age) "
                 + "rowNum, name, age FROM author",
            nativeQuery = true)
    List<AuthorDto> fetchWithSeqNumber();
}
```

You can call fetchWithSeqNumber() and display the result set via a service-method as follows:

```
public void fetchAuthorsWithSeqNumber() {
    List<AuthorDto> authors = authorRepository.fetchWithSeqNumber();

    authors.forEach(a -> System.out.println(a.getRowNum()
        + ", " + a.getName() + ", " + a.getAge()));
}
```

In the previous query, we used ORDER BY in an OVER clause. We can obtain the same result by using ORDER BY in the query:

```
@Query(value = "SELECT ROW_NUMBER() OVER() "
            + "rowNum, name, age FROM author ORDER BY age",
        nativeQuery = true)
List<AuthorDto> fetchWithSeqNumber();
```

Nevertheless, ORDER BY in the query is not the same as ORDER BY in the OVER clause.

## Using the ORDER BY Clause in the Query and in the OVER Clause

In the previous query, we used the ORDER BY clause in the OVER clause or in the query. Now, let's use it in both places—we want to assign the temporary sequence of values according to ORDER BY in the OVER clause and return the result set ordered according to ORDER BY in the query. The following query and Figure 14-19 highlight that the ORDER BY from the query is not the same as the ORDER BY from OVER. The sequence of values is assigned on the ORDER BY from OVER, but the result set is ordered on the ORDER BY from query:

```
@Query(value = "SELECT ROW_NUMBER() OVER(ORDER BY age) "
            + "rowNum, name, age FROM author ORDER BY name",
        nativeQuery = true)
List<AuthorDto> fetchWithSeqNumber();
```

| rowNum | name | age |
|---|---|---|
| 7 | Alicia Tom | 38 |
| 2 | Angela Riak | 23 |
| 13 | Apium Horia | 51 |
| 5 | Barber John | 34 |
| 10 | Bob Martin | 43 |
| 4 | Joana Nimar | 34 |
| 15 | Katy Loin | 56 |
| 1 | Mark Janel | 23 |
| 9 | Olivia Goy | 43 |
| 12 | Quartis Young | 51 |
| 8 | Sacram Alin | 38 |
| 3 | Tom Alen | 23 |
| 11 | Turben Goy | 43 |
| 6 | Ulm Ane | 34 |
| 14 | Xian Ulan | 51 |

*Figure 14-19.* *The author table and data snapshot*

## Use Multiple Columns with the OVER Clause

The OVER clause supports multiple columns. For example, in the following query, the temporary sequence of values is assigned according to ORDER BY age, name DESC:

```
@Query(value = "SELECT ROW_NUMBER() OVER(ORDER BY age, name DESC) "
          + "rowNum, name, age FROM author",
     nativeQuery = true)
List<AuthorDto> fetchWithSeqNumber();
```

The output is shown in Figure 14-20.

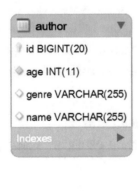

| rowNum | name | age |
|---|---|---|
| 1 | Tom Alen | 23 |
| 2 | Mark Janel | 23 |
| 3 | Angela Riak | 23 |
| 4 | Ulm Ane | 34 |
| 5 | Joana Nimar | 34 |
| 6 | Barber John | 34 |
| 7 | Sacram Alin | 38 |
| 8 | Alicia Tom | 38 |
| 9 | Turben Goy | 43 |
| 10 | Olivia Goy | 43 |
| 11 | Bob Martin | 43 |
| 12 | Xian Ulan | 51 |
| 13 | Quartis Yo... | 51 |
| 14 | Apium Horia | 51 |
| 15 | Katy Loin | 56 |

*Figure 14-20.* *The author table and data snapshot*

Commonly, you don't need to fetch the temporary sequence of values produced by ROW_ NUMBER() in the result set. You will use it internally, in the query. In **Item 120**, you can see an example of using ROW_NUMBER() with PARTITION BY and CTEs (Common Table Expressions) for finding top N rows of every group.

The complete application is available on GitHub[37].

---

This is not an SQL-centric book, so we do not discuss in detail other ranking functions such as RANK(), DENSE_RANK(), and NTILE(). However, it is highly advisable to learn these window functions since they can be extremely useful. MySQL supports all of them starting with version 8.x.

In a nutshell:

- RANK() is useful for specifying the rank for each row in the result set. A sample application is available on GitHub[38].

- In comparison to the RANK() window function, DENSE_RANK() avoids gaps within partition. A sample application is available on GitHub[39].

- NTILE(N) is useful for distributing the number of rows in the specified N number of groups. A sample application is available on GitHub[40].

---

# Item 120: How to Efficiently Find Top N Rows of Every Group

Consider Figure 14-21. On the left side there is a data snapshot of the author table and on the right side is the needed result set. The result set shown in Figure 14-21 contains the first two rows of every author in descending order by sells.

---

[37]HibernateSpringBootAssignSequentialNumber

[38]HibernateSpringBootRankFunction

[39]HibernateSpringBootDenseRankFunction

[40]HibernateSpringBootNTilleFunction

**author table**

| id | name | sold | title |
|----|------|------|-------|
| 1 | Mark Janel | 100 | Anthology of past |
| 2 | Mark Janel | 90 | One summer day |
| 3 | Mark Janel | 110 | Table please |
| 4 | Mark Janel | 290 | Running fast |
| 5 | Olivia Goy | 430 | House of pain |
| 6 | Olivia Goy | 330 | Horror day |
| 7 | Olivia Goy | 130 | Night call |
| 8 | Joana Nimar | 230 | History in a nutshell |
| 9 | Joana Nimar | 70 | Ancient history |
| 10 | Joana Nimar | 170 | Roman history |
| 11 | Joana Nimar | 540 | History of Prague |
| 12 | Joana Nimar | 310 | Modern history |

**result set**

| id | name | sold | title |
|----|------|------|-------|
| 11 | Joana Nimar | 540 | History of Prague |
| 12 | Joana Nimar | 310 | Modern history |
| 4 | Mark Janel | 290 | Running fast |
| 3 | Mark Janel | 110 | Table please |
| 5 | Olivia Goy | 430 | House of pain |
| 6 | Olivia Goy | 330 | Horror day |

***Figure 14-21.*** *Data snapshot*

Generally speaking, fetching the top N rows of every group can be efficiently obtained via CTE (Common Table Expressions) and the ROW_NUMBER() window function (**Item 119**). The native query needed to fetch the result set from Figure 14-21 looks as follows and speaks for itself:

```
@Repository
@Transactional(readOnly = true)
public interface AuthorRepository extends JpaRepository<Author, Long> {

    @Query(value = "WITH sales AS (SELECT *, ROW_NUMBER() "
                + "OVER (PARTITION BY name ORDER BY sold DESC) AS row_num"
                + " FROM author) SELECT * FROM sales WHERE row_num <= 2",
            nativeQuery = true)
    List<Author> fetchTop2BySales();
}
```

Of course, you can easily parameterize the number of rows, as shown here:

```
@Repository
@Transactional(readOnly = true)
public interface AuthorRepository extends JpaRepository<Author, Long> {

    @Query(value = "WITH sales AS (SELECT *, ROW_NUMBER() "
                + "OVER (PARTITION BY name ORDER BY sold DESC) AS row_num"
                + " FROM author) SELECT * FROM sales WHERE row_num <= ?1",
```

```
        nativeQuery = true)
    List<Author> fetchTopNBySales(int n);
}
```

The complete application is available on GitHub[41].

# Item 121: How to Implement Advanced Search via Specification API

It's a common task to fetch data in pages based on multiple filters. For example, an e-commerce website lists the products in pages and provides a suite of filters to help the clients find a specific product or category of products. A typical approach to implementing this kind of dynamic queries relies on JPA Criteria API. On the other hand, a Spring Boot application can rely on the Specification API. This item covers the main steps for accomplishing this task with a generic approach.

Consider that each filter represents a condition (e.g., age > 40, price > 25, name = 'Joana Nimar', etc.). There are simple filters (with a single condition) and compound filters (with multiple conditions joined via logical operators such as AND and OR). Let's consider that a condition (e.g., age > 40) is depicted in three parts: left side (age), right side (40), and an operation (>). Moreover, a condition may contain a logical operator that can be AND or OR. You can map this information in a class named Condition as follows (the END value is not a logical operator; it is used to mark the end of a compound filter):

```
public final class Condition {

    public enum LogicalOperatorType {

        AND, OR, END
    }

    public enum OperationType {

        EQUAL, NOT_EQUAL, GREATER_THAN, LESS_THAN, LIKE
    }

    private final String leftHand;
    private final String rightHand;
```

---

[41]HibernateSpringBootTopNRowsPerGroup

```
    private final OperationType operation;
    private final LogicalOperatorType operator;

    public Condition(String leftHand, String rightHand,
                OperationType operation, LogicalOperatorType operator) {
        this.leftHand = leftHand;
        this.rightHand = rightHand;
        this.operation = operation;
        this.operator = operator;
    }

    public String getLeftHand() {
        return leftHand;
    }

    public String getRightHand() {
        return rightHand;
    }

    public OperationType getOperation() {
        return operation;
    }

    public LogicalOperatorType getOperator() {
        return operator;
    }
}
```

Further, for each supported Condition (of course, more operations can be added in the previous enum), let's define the corresponding Predicate. Each Condition is passed to the Specification implementation and is transformed in a Predicate in the toPredicate() method as follows:

```
public class SpecificationChunk<T> implements Specification<T> {

    private final Condition condition;

    public SpecificationChunk(Condition condition) {
        this.condition = condition;
    }
```

```
@Override
public Predicate toPredicate(Root<T> root,
        CriteriaQuery<?> cquery, CriteriaBuilder cbuilder) {

    switch (condition.getOperation()) {
        case EQUAL:
            return cbuilder.equal(root.get(condition.getLeftHand()),
                condition.getRightHand());
        case NOT_EQUAL:
            return cbuilder.notEqual(root.get(condition.getLeftHand()),
                condition.getRightHand());
        case GREATER_THAN:
            return cbuilder.greaterThan(root.get(condition.getLeftHand()),
                condition.getRightHand());
        case LESS_THAN:
            return cbuilder.lessThan(root.get(condition.getLeftHand()),
                condition.getRightHand());
        case LIKE:
            return cbuilder.like(root.get(condition.getLeftHand()),
                condition.getRightHand());
        default:
            return null;
    }
}
}
```

Finally, the previous SpecificationChunk can be used to implement a Specification builder. The climax of the following implementation consists of chaining the SpecificationChunks conforming to the given logical operators:

```
public class SpecificationBuilder<T> {

    private final List<Condition> conditions;

    public SpecificationBuilder() {
        conditions = new ArrayList<>();
    }
```

```java
    public SpecificationBuilder<T> with(String leftHand, String rightHand,
            OperationType operation, LogicalOperatorType operator) {

        conditions.add(new Condition(leftHand, rightHand,
            operation, operator));
        return this;
    }

    public Specification<T> build() {

        if (conditions.isEmpty()) {
            return null;
        }

        List<Specification<T>> specifications = new ArrayList<>();
        for (Condition condition : conditions) {
            specifications.add(new SpecificationChunk(condition));
        }

        Specification<T> finalSpecification = specifications.get(0);
        for (int i = 1; i < conditions.size(); i++) {
            if (!conditions.get(i - 1).getOperator()
                        .equals(LogicalOperatorType.END)) {
                finalSpecification = conditions.get(i - 1).getOperator()
                        .equals(LogicalOperatorType.OR)
                    ? Specification.where(finalSpecification)
                            .or(specifications.get(i))
                    : Specification.where(finalSpecification)
                            .and(specifications.get(i));
            }
        }

        return finalSpecification;
    }
}
```

# Testing Time

To test this implementation, let's look at the Author and Book entities (there is no association between them) and the following two repositories:

```
@Repository
public interface AuthorRepository extends
    JpaRepository<Author, Long>,
    JpaSpecificationExecutor<Author> {
}

@Repository
public interface BookRepository extends
    JpaRepository<Book, Long>,
    JpaSpecificationExecutor<Book> {
}
```

## Fetch All Authors Older than 40 of Genre Anthology

The following service-method fetches all authors older than *40* and of the genre *Anthology*:

```
public void fetchAuthors() {
    SpecificationBuilder<Author> specBuilder = new SpecificationBuilder();

    Specification<Author> specAuthor = specBuilder
        .with("age", "40", GREATER_THAN, AND)
        .with("genre", "Anthology", EQUAL, END)
        .build();

    List<Author> authors = authorRepository.findAll(specAuthor);

    System.out.println(authors);
}
```

In this case, the triggered SQL SELECT is as follows:

```
SELECT
  author0_.id AS id1_0_,
  author0_.age AS age2_0_,
  author0_.genre AS genre3_0_,
```

```
    author0_.name AS name4_0_,
    author0_.rating AS rating5_0_
FROM author author0_
WHERE author0_.age > 40
AND author0_.genre = ?
```

## Fetch a Page of Books with a Price Less than 60

The following service-method fetches a Page of books with a price less than *60*:

```
public void fetchBooksPage(int page, int size) {
    SpecificationBuilder<Book> specBuilder = new SpecificationBuilder();

    Specification<Book> specBook = specBuilder
        .with("price", "60", LESS_THAN, END)
        .build();

    Pageable pageable = PageRequest.of(page, size,
        Sort.by(Sort.Direction.ASC, "title"));

    Page<Book> books = bookRepository.findAll(specBook, pageable);

    System.out.println(books);
    books.forEach(System.out::println);
}
```

In this case, the triggered SQL SELECT statements are as follows:

```
SELECT
    book0_.id AS id1_1_,
    book0_.isbn AS isbn2_1_,
    book0_.name AS name3_1_,
    book0_.price AS price4_1_,
    book0_.title AS title5_1_
FROM book book0_
WHERE book0_.price < 60
ORDER BY book0_.title ASC LIMIT ?
```

```
SELECT
    COUNT(book0_.id) AS col_0_0_
FROM book book0_
WHERE book0_.price < 60
```

Therefore, it is pretty easy to dynamically create filters.

## What's Next

Taking the implementation further may require the following:

- Adding more operations and operators

- Adding support for complex filters (e.g., using brackets, (x AND y) OR (x AND z))

- Adding joins

- Adding DTO support

- Adding a parser capable of parsing conditions from URL query parameters

The complete application is available on GitHub[42].

# Item 122: How to Enhance SQL Statement Caching via IN Clause Parameter Padding

Consider the Author entity and the following query:

```
@Repository
@Transactional(readOnly = true)
public interface AuthorRepository extends JpaRepository<Author, Long> {

    @Query("SELECT a FROM Author a WHERE a.id IN ?1")
    public List<Author> fetchIn(List<Long> ids);
}
```

---

[42]HibernateSpringBootSearchViaSpecifications

The query selects a list of authors whose IDs match the given list of IDs. The following service-method provides lists of IDs of different sizes (from *2* to *10* IDs):

```java
@Transactional(readOnly=true)
public void fetchAuthorsIn() {

    List twoIds = List.of(1L, 2L);
    List threeIds = List.of(1L, 2L, 3L);
    List fourIds = List.of(1L, 2L, 3L, 4L);
    List fiveIds = List.of(1L, 2L, 3L, 4L, 5L);
    List sixIds = List.of(1L, 2L, 3L, 4L, 5L, 6L);
    List sevenIds = List.of(1L, 2L, 3L, 4L, 5L, 6L, 7L);
    List eightIds = List.of(1L, 2L, 3L, 4L, 5L, 6L, 7L, 8L);
    List nineIds = List.of(1L, 2L, 3L, 4L, 5L, 6L, 7L, 8L, 9L);
    List tenIds = List.of(1L, 2L, 3L, 4L, 5L, 6L, 7L, 8L, 9L, 10L);

    authorRepository.fetchIn(twoIds);
    authorRepository.fetchIn(threeIds);
    authorRepository.fetchIn(fourIds);
    authorRepository.fetchIn(fiveIds);
    authorRepository.fetchIn(sixIds);
    authorRepository.fetchIn(sevenIds);
    authorRepository.fetchIn(eightIds);
    authorRepository.fetchIn(nineIds);
    authorRepository.fetchIn(tenIds);
}
```

Calling fetchAuthorsIn() will produce 10 SELECT statements, which are mainly the same except for the number of bind parameters.

```sql
SELECT
  author0_.id AS id1_0_,
  author0_.age AS age2_0_,
  author0_.genre AS genre3_0_,
  author0_.name AS name4_0_
FROM author author0_
WHERE author0_.id IN (?, ?)
```

...

```
SELECT
  author0_.id AS id1_0_,
  author0_.age AS age2_0_,
  author0_.genre AS genre3_0_,
  author0_.name AS name4_0_
FROM author author0_
WHERE author0_.id IN (?, ?, ?, ?, ?, ?, ?, ?, ?, ?)
```

The 10 SELECT statements may produce 10 execution plans. If the database supports an execution plan cache, the 10 execution plans will be cached (e.g., Oracle, SQL Server). This is happening because each IN clause has a different number of bind parameters.

Reusing an execution plan from cache takes place only if the SQL statement string matches the cached plan. In other words, if you generate the exact same SELECT for a different number of IN clause bind parameters, then you cache fewer execution plans. Again, note that this is useful only for databases that support an execution plan cache, such as Oracle and SQL Server.

Further, let's enable the Hibernate-specific hibernate.query.in_clause_parameter_ padding property:

```
spring.jpa.properties.hibernate.query.in_clause_parameter_padding=true
```

This time, the generated SELECT statements will be these:

```
SELECT
  ...
FROM author author0_
WHERE author0_.id IN (1, 2)

-- for 3 and 4 parameters, it uses 4 bind parameters (2²)
SELECT
  ...
FROM author author0_
WHERE author0_.id IN (1, 2, 3, 3)

SELECT
  ...
FROM author author0_
WHERE author0_.id IN (1, 2, 3, 4)
```

```
-- for 5, 6, 7 and 8 parameters, it uses 8 bind parameters (2³)
SELECT
   ...
FROM author author0_
WHERE author0_.id IN (1, 2, 3, 4, 5, 5, 5, 5)

SELECT
   ...
FROM author author0_
WHERE author0_.id IN (1, 2, 3, 4, 5, 6, 6, 6)

SELECT
   ...
FROM author author0_
WHERE author0_.id IN (1, 2, 3, 4, 5, 6, 7, 7)

SELECT
   ...
FROM author author0_
WHERE author0_.id IN (1, 2, 3, 4, 5, 6, 7, 8)

-- for 9, 10, 11, 12, 13, 14, 15, 16 parameters, it uses 16 parameters (2⁴)
SELECT
   ...
FROM author author0_
WHERE author0_.id IN (1, 2, 3, 4, 5, 6, 7, 8, 9, 9, 9, 9, 9, 9, 9, 9)

SELECT
   ...
FROM author author0_
WHERE author0_.id IN (1, 2, 3, 4, 5, 6, 7, 8, 9, 10, 10, 10, 10, 10, 10, 10)
```

So, in order to generate the same SELECT string, Hibernate uses an algorithm for padding parameters as follows:

- For the 3 and 4 parameters, it uses four bind parameters ($2^2$)

- For the 5, 6, 7, and 8 parameters, it uses eight bind parameters ($2^3$)

- For the 9, 10, 11, 12, 13, 14, 15, and 16 parameters, it uses 16 parameters ($2^4$)

- ...

In this case, a database that supports an execution plan cache will cache and reuse only four plans instead of 10. That's pretty cool! The complete application (for SQL Server) is available on GitHub[43].

# Item 123: How to Create Specification Query Fetch Joins

Consider the Author and Book entities involved in a bidirectional lazy @OneToMany association. The goal of this item is to define a Specification to emulate JPQL join-fetch operations.

## Join Fetch and Pagination in Memory

Joining fetch and pagination in memory is an important topic detailed in **Item 97** and **Item 98**. Consider reading those items if you are not familiar with this topic and the Hibernate-specific HHH000104 warning.

Now you can specify the join fetch in a Specification via JoinType. To accommodate methods as findAll(Specification spec, Pageable pageable) (used in the next examples), you need to check the resultType of CriteriaQuery and apply join only if it is not Long (this is the resultType for the count query specific to offset pagination):

```
public class JoinFetchSpecification<Author>
                    implements Specification<Author> {

    private final String genre;

    public JoinFetchSpecification(String genre) {
        this.genre = genre;
    }
```

---

[43]HibernateSpringBootINListPadding

```
    @Override
    public Predicate toPredicate(Root<Author> root,
            CriteriaQuery<?> cquery, CriteriaBuilder cbuilder) {

        // This is needed to support Pageable queries
        // This causes pagination in memory (HHH000104)
        Class clazz = cquery.getResultType();
        if (clazz.equals(Long.class) || clazz.equals(long.class)) {
            return null;
        }

        root.fetch("books", JoinType.LEFT);
        cquery.distinct(true);

        // in case you need to add order by via Specification
        //cquery.orderBy(cbuilder.asc(root.get("...")));

        return cbuilder.equal(root.get("genre"), genre);
    }
}
```

Having distinct results is enforced by calling the distinct(true) method. To take advantage of the performance optimization discussed in **Item 103**, let's override the findAll() method that is used in this example:

```
@Repository
public interface AuthorRepository
    extends JpaRepository<Author, Long>, JpaSpecificationExecutor<Author> {

    @Override
    @QueryHints(value = @QueryHint(name = HINT_PASS_DISTINCT_THROUGH,
                value = "false"))
    public Page<Author> findAll(Specification<Author> s, Pageable p);
}
```

A service-method that uses JoinFetchSpecification can be written as follows (select a Page of authors of whose genre is *Anthology* and the associated books):

```
public Page<Author> fetchViaJoinFetchSpecification(int page, int size) {

    Pageable pageable = PageRequest.of(page, size,
        Sort.by(Sort.Direction.ASC, "name"));
```

```
    Page<Author> pageOfAuthors = authorRepository
        .findAll(new JoinFetchSpecification("Anthology"), pageable);

    return pageOfAuthors;
}
```

Calling fetchViaJoinFetchSpecification() triggers the following two SELECT statements:

```
SELECT
    author0_.id AS id1_0_0_,
    books1_.id AS id1_1_1_,
    author0_.age AS age2_0_0_,
    author0_.genre AS genre3_0_0_,
    author0_.name AS name4_0_0_,
    books1_.author_id AS author_i4_1_1_,
    books1_.isbn AS isbn2_1_1_,
    books1_.title AS title3_1_1_,
    books1_.author_id AS author_i4_1_0__,
    books1_.id AS id1_1_0__
FROM author author0_
LEFT OUTER JOIN book books1_
    ON author0_.id = books1_.author_id
WHERE author0_.genre = ?
ORDER BY author0_.name ASC

SELECT
    COUNT(author0_.id) AS col_0_0_
FROM author author0_
```

In the end, the result is a Page<Author> but the pagination was performed in memory and it was signaled via the HHH000104 warning.

# Join Fetch and Pagination in Database

Having pagination in memory may cause significant performance penalties, so it is advisable to re-think the implementation for relying on pagination in a database. In **Item 98**, you saw that an approach for solving the HHH000104 warning (that signals that pagination is taking place in memory), which consists of relying on two SELECT queries.

The first SELECT query fetches only a Page of IDs (e.g., a Page of the IDs of authors of the given genre). This query can be added in AuthorRepository:

```
@Repository
@Transactional(readOnly = true)
public interface AuthorRepository
    extends JpaRepository<Author, Long>, JpaSpecificationExecutor<Author> {

    @Query(value = "SELECT a.id FROM Author a WHERE a.genre = ?1")
    Page<Long> fetchPageOfIdsByGenre(String genre, Pageable pageable);
}
```

This time, the database paginates the IDs (check the corresponding SQL to see the LIMIT operation). Having the IDs of the authors solves half of the problem. Further, a Specification is used to define the join:

```
public class JoinFetchInIdsSpecification implements Specification<Author> {

    private final List<Long> ids;

    public JoinFetchInIdsSpecification(List<Long> ids) {
        this.ids = ids;
    }

    @Override
    public Predicate toPredicate(Root<Author> root,
            CriteriaQuery<?> cquery, CriteriaBuilder cbuilder) {

        root.fetch("books", JoinType.LEFT);
        cquery.distinct(true);

        // in case you need to add order by via Specification
        //cquery.orderBy(cbuilder.asc(root.get("...")));

        Expression<String> expression = root.get("id");

        return expression.in(ids);
    }
}
```

Having distinct results is enforced by calling the `distinct(true)` method. To take advantage of the performance optimization discussed in **Item 103**, let's override the `findAll()` method that is used in this example:

```
@Override
@QueryHints(value = @QueryHint(name = HINT_PASS_DISTINCT_THROUGH,
            value = "false"))
public List<Author> findAll(Specification<Author> spec);
```

A service-method that uses `JoinFetchInIdsSpecification` can be written as follows (select a Page of authors of whose genre is *Anthology* and the associated books):

```
@Transactional(readOnly = true)
public Page<Author> fetchViaJoinFetchInIdsSpecification(int page, int size) {

    Pageable pageable = PageRequest.of(page, size,
        Sort.by(Sort.Direction.ASC, "name"));

    Page<Long> pageOfIds = authorRepository.fetchPageOfIdsByGenre(
        "Anthology", pageable);
    List<Author> listOfAuthors = authorRepository.findAll(
        new JoinFetchInIdsSpecification(pageOfIds.getContent()));
    Page<Author> pageOfAuthors = new PageImpl(
        listOfAuthors, pageable, pageOfIds.getTotalElements());

    return pageOfAuthors;
}
```

Calling `fetchViaJoinFetchInIdsSpecification()` triggers the following three SELECT statements:

```
SELECT
  author0_.id AS col_0_0_
FROM author author0_
WHERE author0_.genre = ?
ORDER BY author0_.name ASC LIMIT ?
```

```
SELECT
  COUNT(author0_.id) AS col_0_0_
FROM author author0_
WHERE author0_.genre = ?
```

**SELECT**
  author0_.id **AS** id1_0_0_,
  books1_.id **AS** id1_1_1_,
  author0_.age **AS** age2_0_0_,
  author0_.genre **AS** genre3_0_0_,
  author0_.name **AS** name4_0_0_,
  books1_.author_id **AS** author_i4_1_1_,
  books1_.isbn **AS** isbn2_1_1_,
  books1_.title **AS** title3_1_1_,
  books1_.author_id **AS** author_i4_1_0__,
  books1_.id **AS** id1_1_0__
**FROM** author author0_
**LEFT OUTER JOIN** book books1_
  **ON** author0_.id = books1_.author_id
**WHERE** author0_.id **IN** (?, ?, ?)

Even if this approach triggers three SELECT statements, the database paginates it.

The complete application is available on GitHub[44].

# Item 124: How to Use a Hibernate-Specific Query Plan Cache

Before executing a query, it must be compiled. For example, a query executed 10 times is compiled 10 times. In order to prevent this behavior, Hibernate provides the Query Plan Cache. In this context, a query executed 10 times is compiled once and cached. The subsequent nine executions use the cached plan. By default, Query Plan Cache can cache 2048 plans for entity queries (JPQL and Criteria API) and 128 plans for native queries. The QPC is shared between entity and native queries. For entity queries (JPQL and Criteria API), you can alter the default value via hibernate.query.plan_cache_max_size, while for native queries, we use hibernate.query.plan_parameter_metadata_max_size. Consider the Author entity and the following two JPQL queries:

---

[44]HibernateSpringBootSpecificationQueryFetchJoins

```
@Repository
@Transactional(readOnly = true)
public interface AuthorRepository extends JpaRepository<Author, Long> {

    @Query("SELECT a FROM Author a WHERE a.genre = ?1")
    List<Author> fetchByGenre(String genre);

    @Query("SELECT a FROM Author a WHERE a.age > ?1")
    List<Author> fetchByAge(int age);
}
```

Now let's set the QPC size for entity queries to 2. This means that both of the queries are cached. Next, let's set the QPC size for entity queries to 1. This means that one JPQL plan will be cached and one will be compiled at every execution. Running each scenario 5,000 times reveals a time-performance trend graphic, as shown in Figure 14-22.

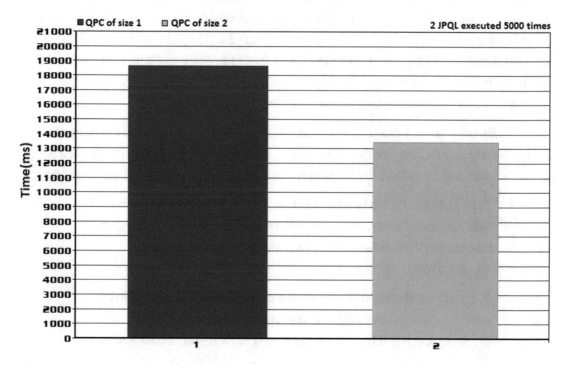

***Figure 14-22.***   *Query Plan Cache*

The time-performance trend graphic shown in Figure 14-22 was obtained against MySQL, on a Windows 7 machine with the following characteristics: Intel i7, 2.10GHz, and 6GB RAM. The application and MySQL ran on the same machine.

Figure 14-22 helps you come to a clear conclusion. Always ensure that the size of your QPC can cache all queries being executed. This is especially necessary for entity queries (JPQL and Criteria API). Once you have queries that are not cached, they will be recompiled at each execution and this will cause serious time performance penalties.

The complete application is available on GitHub[45].

# Item 125: How to Check if a Transient Entity Exists in the Database via Spring Query By Example (QBE)

Consider the Book entity with the following attributes: id, title, genre, price, author, and isbn. A bookstore employee is responsible for checking if a bunch of books where added to the database and then writing a report about it. They simply fill out a form with book details (title, genre, and price) and submits it. The form data is materialized in a transient Book instance via a Spring controller that exposes an endpoint as: public String checkBook(@Validated @ModelAttribute Book book, ...).

To check if a certain book exists in the database, you can use an explicit JPQL or on the Spring Data Query Builder mechanism or, even better, the Query By Example (QBE) API. In this context, this is quite useful if the entity has a significant number of attributes and:

- For all attributes, we need a head-to-head comparison of each attribute value to the corresponding column value (e.g., the given book exists if the title, genre, price, author, and ISBN match a database row).

- For a subset of attributes, we need a head-to-head comparison of each attribute value to the corresponding column value (e.g., the given book exists if the title, author, and ISBN match a database row).

---

[45]HibernateSpringBootQueryPlanCache

- • For a subset of attributes, we return true at first match between an attribute value and the corresponding column value (e.g., the given book exists if the title, author, or ISBN match a database row).

- • Any other scenario.

Spring Data Query by Example (QBE) is a handy approach to query creation that allows you to execute queries based on an example entity instance called *probe*. In Spring Data JPA, you can pass the probe to an org.springframework.data.domain.Example instance. Further, you pass the Example to a query method defined in a repository that extends the QueryByExampleExecutor interface (e.g., BookRepository extends QueryByExampleExecutor):

```
@Repository
public interface BookRepository extends JpaRepository<Book, Long>,
    QueryByExampleExecutor<Book> {
}
```

The QueryByExampleExecutor exposes the following methods (in this case, you are interested in the last one, exists()):

- • <S extends T> Optional<S> findOne(Example<S> ex);

- • <S extends T> Iterable<S> findAll(Example<S> ex);

- • <S extends T> Iterable<S> findAll(Example<S> ex, Sort sort);

- • <S extends T> Page<S> findAll(Example<S> ex, Pageable pg);

- • <S extends T> long count(Example<S> ex);

- • <S extends T> boolean exists(Example<S> ex);

By default, fields having null values are ignored, and strings are matched using the database-specific defaults.

So, let's consider a Book instance (aka, *probe*):

```
Book book = new Book();

book.setTitle("Carrie");
book.setGenre("Horror");
book.setIsbn("001-OG");
book.setAuthor("Olivia Goy");
book.setPrice(23);
```

# Head-to-Head Comparison of All Attributes

You can create an Example by using the of() factory method or by using ExampleMatcher. Here, we use the of() method:

```
public boolean existsBook(Book book) {

    Example<Book> bookExample = Example.of(book);

    return bookRepository.exists(bookExample);
}
```

Calling existsBook() generates the following SQL statement:

```
SELECT
  book0_.id AS id1_0_,
  book0_.author AS author2_0_,
  book0_.genre AS genre3_0_,
  book0_.isbn AS isbn4_0_,
  book0_.price AS price5_0_,
  book0_.title AS title6_0_
FROM book book0_
WHERE book0_.author = ?
AND book0_.title = ?
AND book0_.genre = ?
AND book0_.price = ?
```

**AND** book0_.isbn = ?
Binding: [Olivia Goy, Carrie, Horror, 23, 001-OG]

# Head-to-Head Comparison of Certain Attributes

This time, we want to compare only the book title, author, and ISBN and ignore the price and genre. For this, we use ExampleMatcher, which holds the details on how to match particular attributes. ExampleMatcher is a comprehensive interface with a lots of features that deserve your attention for sure, but for now, we focus on two matchers:

- matchingAll(): Applies the and conjunction to all non-null properties

- withIgnorePaths(): Ignores provided property paths

The existsBook() looks as follows:

```
public boolean existsBook(Book book) {

    Example<Book> bookExample = Example.of(book,
        ExampleMatcher.matchingAll().withIgnorePaths("genre", "price"));

    return bookRepository.exists(bookExample);
}
```

The trigger SQL statement is:

```
SELECT
    book0_.id AS id1_0_,
    book0_.author AS author2_0_,
    book0_.genre AS genre3_0_,
    book0_.isbn AS isbn4_0_,
    book0_.price AS price5_0_,
    book0_.title AS title6_0_
FROM book book0_
WHERE book0_.author = ?
AND book0_.title = ?
```

**AND** book0_.isbn = ?
Binding: [Olivia Goy, Carrie, 001-OG]

## Apply the or Conjunction to a Subset of Attributes

To apply the or conjunction, you need the matchingAny() matcher, as follows:

```
public boolean existsBook(Book book) {

    Example<Book> bookExample = Example.of(book,
        ExampleMatcher.matchingAny().withIgnorePaths("genre", "price"));

    return bookRepository.exists(bookExample);
}
```

The trigger SQL statement is:

**SELECT**
  book0_.id **AS** id1_0_,
  book0_.author **AS** author2_0_,
  book0_.genre **AS** genre3_0_,
  book0_.isbn **AS** isbn4_0_,
  book0_.price **AS** price5_0_,
  book0_.title **AS** title6_0_
**FROM** book book0_
**WHERE** book0_.author = ?
**OR** book0_.title = ?
**OR** book0_.isbn = ?
Binding: [Olivia Goy, Carrie, 001-OG]

Of course, you can easily join these three methods into a single one and exploit QBE to generate a dynamic query.

> Note that the QBE API has some limitations, as follows:
>
> - Query predicates are combined using the AND keyword
>
> - There is no support for nested/grouped property constraints like
>   `author = ?1 or (title = ?2 and isbn = ?3)`
>
> - Only supports starts/contains/ends/regex matching for strings
>   and exact matching for other property types

The complete application is available on GitHub[46].

# Item 126: How to Include in the UPDATE Statement Only the Modified Columns via Hibernate @DynamicUpdate

Let's consider an entity with the following persistent fields: id, name, genre, age, sellrank, royalties, and rating. And the following row:

```
INSERT INTO author (age, name, genre, royalties, sellrank, rating, id)
  VALUES (23, "Mark Janel", "Anthology", 1200, 289, 3, 1);
```

The goal is to update the sellrank to *222*, which you can do via a service-method, as follows:

```
@Transactional
public void updateAuthor() {
    Author author = authorRepository.findById(1L).orElseThrow();

    author.setSellrank(222);
}
```

---

[46]HibernateSpringBootExampleApi

Calling updateAuthor() results in the following UPDATE statement:

```
UPDATE author
SET age = ?,
    genre = ?,
    name = ?,
    rating = ?,
    royalties = ?,
    sellrank = ?
WHERE id = ?
Binding: [23, Anthology, Mark Janel, 3, 1200, 222, 1]
```

Even if you had modified only the sellrank value, the triggered UPDATE contains all columns. To instruct Hibernate to trigger an UPDATE that contains only the modified columns, you can annotate the entity at class-level with the Hibernate-specific @DynamicUpdate as follows:

```
@Entity
@DynamicUpdate
public class Author implements Serializable {
    ...
}
```

This time, the triggered UPDATE is this one:

```
UPDATE author
SET sellrank = ?
WHERE id = ?
Binding: [222, 1]
```

This time, only the sellrank column is present in the triggered UPDATE.

Using this approach has a benefit and a drawback:

- The benefit is quite significant if you avoid updating indexed columns. Triggering an UPDATE that contains all columns will inevitably update the unmodified indexes as well, and this may cause significant performance penalties.

- The drawback is reflected in JDBC statement caching. You cannot reuse the same UPDATE for different subsets of columns via JDBC statement caching (each triggered UPDATE string will be cached and reused accordingly).

The complete application is available on GitHub[47].

# Item 127: How to Use Named (Native) Queries in Spring

A named (native) query is represented by a static predefined unchangeable query string referenced via an associated name. They are commonly used to improve code organization by extracting the JPQL/SQL query strings from the Java code. This is especially useful in Java EE applications, where JPQL/SQL are interleaved with Java code in EJB components. In Spring, you can extract JPQL/SQL in repositories via @Query annotation. Nevertheless, you can use named (native) queries in Spring as well.

Unfortunately, none of the supported approaches provides complete compatibility between Spring features and named (native) queries. At least, not until Spring Boot 2.3.0. So, let's find the most advantageous trade-off. We use the well-known Author entity with the fields: id, name, age, and genre, and Spring Boot 2.3.0.

---

[47]HibernateSpringBootDynamicUpdate

## Referencing a Named (Native) Query

Referencing a named (native) query is accomplished by its name. For example, a named (native) query called AllFooQuery can be referenced from a typical Spring repository via the name element of the @Query annotation, as shown here:

```
AllFooQuery="SELECT f FROM Foo f";

public interface FooRepository extends JpaRepository<Foo, Long> {

    @Query(name="AllFooQuery")
    public List<Foo> fetchAllFoo();
}
```

But Spring Data supports a naming convention that eliminates the need of @Query(name="..."). The name of the named (native) query starts with the name of the entity class, followed by a dot (.), and the name of the repository method. The pattern of this naming convention of named (native) queries is *EntityName. RepositoryMethodName*, and it allows you to define in the repository interface the query-methods with the same name as the named query, *RepositoryMethodName*. For example, if the entity is Foo, then a named (native) query can be used as shown:

```
Foo.fetchAllFoo="SELECT f FROM Foo f";

public interface FooRepository extends JpaRepository<Foo, Long> {

    public List<Foo> fetchAllFoo();
}
```

Let's look at same examples.

## Using @NamedQuery and @NamedNativeQuery

The most popular approach to using named (native) queries relies on @NamedQuery and @NamedNativeQuery annotations added to entities at the class-level.

```
@NamedQueries({
    @NamedQuery(name = "Author.fetchAll",
                query = "SELECT a FROM Author a"),
```

```
    @NamedQuery(name = "Author.fetchByNameAndAge",
                query = "SELECT a FROM Author a
                         WHERE a.name=?1 AND a.age=?2")
})

@NamedNativeQueries({
    @NamedNativeQuery(name = "Author.fetchAllNative",
                      query = "SELECT * FROM author",
                      resultClass = Author.class),

    @NamedNativeQuery(name = "Author.fetchByNameAndAgeNative",
                      query = "SELECT * FROM author
                               WHERE name=?1 AND age=?2",
                      resultClass = Author.class)
})
@Entity
public class Author implements Serializable {
...
}
```

The AuthorRepository references these named (native) queries as follows:

```
@Repository
@Transactional(readOnly = true)
public interface AuthorRepository extends JpaRepository<Author, Long> {

    List<Author> fetchAll();

    Author fetchByNameAndAge(String name, int age);

    @Query(nativeQuery = true)
    List<Author> fetchAllNative();

    @Query(nativeQuery = true)
    Author fetchByNameAndAgeNative(String name, int age);
}
```

> Note that, via this approach, you cannot use named (native) queries with dynamic sorting (Sort). Using Sort in Pageable is ignored, so you need to explicitly add ORDER  BY to the queries. At least this is how it behaves in Spring Boot 2.3.0. The complete application is available on GitHub[48] and it contains use cases for Sort and Pageable that you can test under your Spring Boot release.
>
> A better approach relies on using a properties file to list the named (native) queries. In this case, dynamic Sort works for named queries, but not for named native queries. Using Sort in Pageable works as expected in named (native) queries. You don't need to modify/pollute entities with the previous annotations.

## Using a Properties File ( jpa-named-queries.properties)

Alternatively, you can list the named (native) queries in a properties file called jpa-named-queries.properties. Place this file in the application classpath in a folder named META-INF:

> If you need to alter the location of this file, then use @EnableJpaRepositories (namedQueriesLocation = "...").

```
# Named Queries
# Find all authors
Author.fetchAll
    =SELECT a FROM Author a

# Find the author by name and age
Author.fetchByNameAndAge
    =SELECT a FROM Author a WHERE a.name=?1 AND a.age=?2

...
```

---

[48]HibernateSpringBootNamedQueriesViaAnnotations

```
# Named Native Queries
# Find all authors (native)
Author.fetchAllNative
    =SELECT * FROM author

# Find the author by name and age (native)
Author.fetchByNameAndAgeNative
    =SELECT * FROM author WHERE name=?1 AND age=?2
```

The AuthorRepository is exactly the same as when using @NamedQuery and @NamedNativeQuery.

This time, you can even declare named queries (not named native queries) that use dynamic sorting via Sort, as shown here:

```
# Find the authors older than age ordered via Sort
Author.fetchViaSortWhere
    =SELECT a FROM Author a WHERE a.age > ?1
```

```
// in repository
List<Author> fetchViaSortWhere(int age, Sort sort);
```

```
// service-method calling fetchViaSortWhere()
public List<Author> fetchAuthorsViaSortWhere() {

    return authorRepository.fetchViaSortWhere(
        30, Sort.by(Direction.DESC, "name"));
}
```

The triggered SELECT (notice the presence of ORDER BY author0_.name DESC) is as follows:

```
SELECT
  author0_.id AS id1_0_,
  author0_.age AS age2_0_,
  author0_.genre AS genre3_0_,
  author0_.name AS name4_0_
FROM author author0_
WHERE author0_.age > ?
ORDER BY author0_.name DESC
```

Or, you can use Pageable including Sort (this works for named queries and named native queries):

```
# Find the Pageable of authors older than age ordered via Sort (native)
Author.fetchPageSortWhereNative
    =SELECT * FROM author WHERE age > ?1
```

```
// in repository
@Query(nativeQuery = true)
Page<Author> fetchPageSortWhereNative(int age, Pageable pageable);
```

```
// service-method calling fetchPageSortWhereNative()
public Page<Author> fetchAuthorsPageSortWhereNative() {

    return authorRepository.fetchPageSortWhereNative(
        30, PageRequest.of(1, 3,
        Sort.by(Sort.Direction.DESC, "name")));
}
```

The triggered SELECT statements are as follows (notice the presence of ORDER BY author0_.name DESC LIMIT ?, ? and the generated SELECT COUNT):

```
SELECT
  author0_.id AS id1_0_,
  author0_.age AS age2_0_,
  author0_.genre AS genre3_0_,
  author0_.name AS name4_0_
FROM author author0_
WHERE author0_.age > ?
ORDER BY author0_.name DESC LIMIT ?, ?
```

```
SELECT
  COUNT(author0_.id) AS col_0_0_
FROM author author0_
WHERE author0_.age > ?
```

Note that, via this approach, you cannot use named native queries with dynamic sorting (Sort). This shortcoming is present in the case of using @NamedQuery and @NamedNativeQuery as well. At least this is how it behaves in Spring Boot 2.3.0. The complete application is available on GitHub[49].

Using this approach (using the properties file, jpa-named-queries. properties), you can use dynamic Sort with named queries and Sort in Pageable works as expected. If you need these features, this is the way to go.

---

Another approach consists of using the well-known orm.xml file. This file should be added to the application classpath in a folder called META-INF. This approach provides the same shortcomings as using @NamedQuery and @NamedNativeQuery. At least this is how it behaves in Spring Boot 2.3.0. The complete application is available on GitHub[50].

---

To combine named (native) queries with Spring projections, consider **Item 25**. To work with named (native) queries and result set mappings, consider **Item 34**.

# Item 128: The Best Way to Fetch Parent and Children in Different Queries/Requests

Fetching read-only data should be done via DTO, not via managed entities. But there is no tragedy to fetch read-only entities in a particular context as follows:

- We need all attributes of the entity (so, a DTO will just mirror the entity)

- We manipulate a small number of entities (e.g., an author with several books)

- We use @Transactional(readOnly = true)

---

[49]HibernateSpringBootNamedQueriesInPropertiesFile
[50]HibernateSpringBootNamedQueriesInOrmXml

Under these circumstances, let's tackle a common case that I saw quite a lot.

Let's assume that Author and Book are involved in a bidirectional lazy @OneToMany association. Next, imagine a user that loads a certain Author by ID (without the associated Book). The may or may not be interested in the associated Book; therefore, you don't load them with the Author. If the user is interested in the Book, then they will click the View Books button. Now, you have to return the List<Book> associated with this Author.

So, at first request (query), you fetch an Author as follows:

```
// first query/request
public Author fetchAuthor(long id) {

    return authorRepository.findById(id).orElseThrow();
}
```

This method will trigger a SELECT to load the author with the given ID. At the end of the fetchAuthor() execution, the returned author is detached. If the user clicks on the View Books button, you have to return the associated Book. An uninspired approach that I usually see loads the Author again in order to fetch the associated Book via getBooks(), as shown:

```
// second query/request
@Transactional(readOnly = true)
public List<Book> fetchBooksOfAuthor(Author a) {

    Author author = fetchAuthor(a.getId());
    List<Book> books = author.getBooks();

    Hibernate.initialize(books); // or, books.size();

    return books;
}
```

There are two main two drawbacks to this common approach. First, notice the line:

```
Hibernate.initialize(books); // or, books.size();
```

Here, we *force* the collection initialization because it will not be initialized if we simply return it. In order to trigger the collection initialization, the developer calls books.size() or relies on Hibernate.initialize(books).

Second, this approach triggers two SELECT statements, as follows:

```
SELECT
    author0_.id AS id1_0_0_,
    author0_.age AS age2_0_0_,
    author0_.genre AS genre3_0_0_,
    author0_.name AS name4_0_0_
FROM author author0_
WHERE author0_.id = ?

SELECT
    books0_.author_id AS author_i4_1_0_,
    books0_.id AS id1_1_0_,
    books0_.id AS id1_1_1_,
    books0_.author_id AS author_i4_1_1_,
    books0_.isbn AS isbn2_1_1_,
    books0_.title AS title3_1_1_
FROM book books0_
WHERE books0_.author_id = ?
```

But you don't want to load the Author again (for example, you don't care about *lost updates* of Author), you just want to load the associated Book in a single SELECT.

You can avoid this clumsy solution by relying on an explicit JPQL or on the Query Builder property expressions. This way, there will be a single SELECT and no need to call size() or Hibernate.initialize(). A JPQL can be written as follows in BookRepository:

```
@Repository
@Transactional(readOnly = true)
public interface BookRepository extends JpaRepository<Book, Long> {

    @Query("SELECT b FROM Book b WHERE b.author = ?1")
    List<Book> fetchByAuthor(Author author);
}
```

The service method can be rewritten as follows:

```
// second query/request
public List<Book> fetchBooksOfAuthor(Author a) {

    return bookRepository.fetchByAuthor(a);
}
```

If you don't want to write a JPQL, you can use the Query Builder property expressions, as shown here (the SELECT will be generated on your behalf):

```
@Repository
@Transactional(readOnly = true)
public interface BookRepository extends JpaRepository<Book, Long> {

    List<Book> findByAuthor(Author author);
}
```

The service method is slightly modified to call this query-method:

```
// second query/request
public List<Book> fetchBooksOfAuthor(Author a) {

    return bookRepository.findByAuthor(a);
}
```

If you are not familiar with Query Builder property expressions, then consider this GitHub[51] example. Consider reading the description available there.

This time, both approaches (via JPQL and the Query Builder property expressions) result in a single SELECT:

```
SELECT
  book0_.id AS id1_1_,
  book0_.author_id AS author_i4_1_,
  book0_.isbn AS isbn2_1_,
  book0_.title AS title3_1_
FROM book book0_
WHERE book0_.author_id = ?
```

---

[51]HibernateSpringBootPropertyExpressions

This is much better! The complete application is available on GitHub[52]. The complete application also contains a case when, for the first query, you load a Book, and, for the second query, you load the Author of that Book.

# Item 129: How to Optimize the Merge Operation Using Update

Behind the built-in Spring Data save() method, there is a call of EntityManager#persist() or EntityManager#merge(). The source code of the save() method is listed here:

```
@Transactional
@Override
public <S extends T> S save(S entity) {

    if (entityInformation.isNew(entity)) {
        em.persist(entity);
        return entity;
    } else {
        return em.merge(entity);
    }
}
```

> If you are not familiar with the merge operation, see **Appendix A**.

It is important to know how the save() method works since it's probably the most commonly used Spring Data built-in method. If you know how it works, then you'll know how to use it in your favor and mitigate its performance penalties. In **Item 107**, you saw a case when calling save() was redundant. Now, let's see a case when calling save() can cause serious performance penalties. This is when updating (including update batching) detached entities.

Consider the Author and Book entities involved in a bidirectional lazy @OneToMany association. You load an Author, detach it, and update it in the *detached* state:

---

[52]HibernateSpringBootParentChildSeparateQueries

```
// service-method in BookstoreService class
public Author fetchAuthorById(long id) {

    return authorRepository.findById(id).orElseThrow();
}
```

> If you are not familiar with Hibernate state transitions, see **Appendix A**.

After fetchAuthorById() is executed, the returned Author is in the *detached* state. Therefore, the following code updates the age of this Author in the *detached* state:

```
// fetch an Author and update it in the detached state
Author author = bookstoreService.fetchAuthorById(1L);
author.setAge(author.getAge() + 1);
```

Finally, you propagate the modification to the database via the updateAuthorViaMerge() method:

```
bookstoreService.updateAuthorViaMerge(author);
```

The updateAuthorViaMerge() simply calls the save() method:

```
public void updateAuthorViaMerge(Author author) {

    authorRepository.save(author);
}
```

The SQL triggered by the authorRepository.save(author) line is shown here:

```
SELECT
  author0_.id AS id1_0_1_,
  author0_.age AS age2_0_1_,
  author0_.genre AS genre3_0_1_,
  author0_.name AS name4_0_1_,
  author0_.version AS version5_0_1_,
  books1_.author_id AS author_i5_1_3_,
  books1_.id AS id1_1_3_,
  books1_.id AS id1_1_0_,
  books1_.author_id AS author_i5_1_0_,
```

```
    books1_.isbn AS isbn2_1_0_,
    books1_.title AS title3_1_0_,
    books1_.version AS version4_1_0_
FROM author author0_
LEFT OUTER JOIN book books1_
  ON author0_.id = books1_.author_id
WHERE author0_.id = ?

UPDATE author
SET age = ?,
    genre = ?,
    name = ?,
    version = ?
WHERE id = ?
AND version = ?
```

Therefore, calling save() will come with the following two issues resulting from calling merge() behind the scenes:

- There are two SQL statements, one SELECT (caused by the merge operation) and one UPDATE (the expected update)

- The SELECT will contain a LEFT OUTER JOIN to fetch the associated Books as well (but you don't need the associated books)

There are two performance penalties. First, the SELECT itself, and second, the LEFT OUTER JOIN presence.

How about triggering only the UPDATE and eliminating this potentially expensive SELECT? This is achievable if you inject the EntityManager, unwrap the Session from it, and call the Session#update() method, as shown here:

```
@PersistenceContext
private final EntityManager entityManager;
...
@Transactional
public void updateAuthorViaUpdate(Author author) {

    Session session = entityManager.unwrap(Session.class);
    session.update(author);
}
```

This time, the triggered SQL is only the following UPDATE statement:

```
UPDATE author
SET age = ?,
    genre = ?,
    name = ?,
    version = ?
WHERE id = ?
AND version = ?
```

> The `Session#update()` doesn't work with Versionless Optimistic Locking mechanism. In such a case, the `SELECT` is still triggered.

The complete application is available on GitHub[53].

# Item 130: How to Implement Concurrent Table Based Queues via the SKIP LOCKED Option

Implementing concurrent table based queues (aka, job queues or batch queues) is a difficult task without the SQL SKIP LOCKED option.

Consider the Domain Model shown in Figure 14-23.

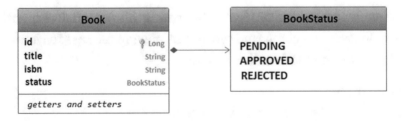

***Figure 14-23.***  *Domain Model*

---

[53]HibernateSpringBootSaveAndMerge

This exclusive bookstore is very careful about the books they sell. To maintain high quality, the bookstore reviewers perform reviews and decide if a certain book is approved or rejected.

Since this is a concurrent process, the challenge consists of coordinating the reviewers so that they don't review the same book at the same time. To pick a book for review, a reviewer should skip the books that have been already reviewed and the books that are currently in review. Figure 14-24 depicts this job queue.

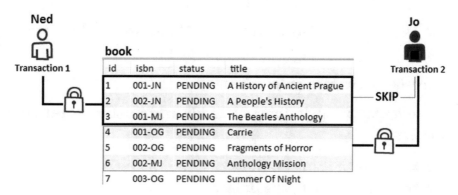

***Figure 14-24.***  *Reviews queue*

This is a job for SKIP  LOCKED. This SQL option instructs the database to skip the locked rows and to lock the rows that have not been locked previously. Let's set up this option for MySQL 8 and PostgreSQL 9.5 (most RDBMSs support this option).

## Set Up SKIP LOCKED

MySQL introduced SKIP  LOCKED starting with version 8, while PostgreSQL started with version 9.5. To set up this SQL option, start from the BookRepository. Here, perform the following settings:

- Set up @Lock(LockModeType.PESSIMISTIC_WRITE)

- Use @QueryHint to set up javax.persistence.lock.timeout to SKIP_LOCKED

The source code of BookRepository is as follows:

```
@Repository
public interface BookRepository extends JpaRepository<Book, Long> {

    @Lock(LockModeType.PESSIMISTIC_WRITE)
    @QueryHints({
        @QueryHint(name = "javax.persistence.lock.timeout",
                   value = "" + LockOptions.SKIP_LOCKED)}
    )
    public List<Book> findTop3ByStatus(BookStatus status, Sort sort);
}
```

Next, focus on the application.properties file.

For MySQL, set up the spring.jpa.properties.hibernate.dialect to point to the MySQL 8 dialect:

```
spring.jpa.properties.hibernate.dialect
    =org.hibernate.dialect.MySQL8Dialect
```

For PostgreSQL, set up the spring.jpa.properties.hibernate.dialect to point to the PostgreSQL 9.5 dialect:

```
spring.jpa.properties.hibernate.dialect
    =org.hibernate.dialect.PostgreSQL95Dialect
```

The setup is done!

## Testing Time

Testing SKIP LOCKED requires at least two concurrent transactions. You can do this in different ways. For example, an easy approach uses TransactionTemplate, as in the following code:

```
private final TransactionTemplate template;
private final BookRepository bookRepository;
...
```

```
public void fetchBooksViaTwoTransactions() {
    template.setPropagationBehavior(
        TransactionDefinition.PROPAGATION_REQUIRES_NEW);

    template.execute(new TransactionCallbackWithoutResult() {
        @Override
        protected void doInTransactionWithoutResult(
                            TransactionStatus status) {
            List<Book> books = bookRepository.findTop3ByStatus(
                BookStatus.PENDING, Sort.by(Sort.Direction.ASC, "id"));

            template.execute(new TransactionCallbackWithoutResult() {
                @Override
                protected void doInTransactionWithoutResult(
                                    TransactionStatus status) {
                    List<Book> books = bookRepository.findTop3ByStatus(
                        BookStatus.PENDING, Sort.by(Sort.Direction.ASC, "id"));
                    System.out.println("Second transaction: " + books);
                }
            });
            System.out.println("First transaction: " + books);
        }
    });
}
```

Running fetchBooksViaTwoTransactions() triggers the following SQL statements:

```sql
SELECT
    book0_.id AS id1_0_,
    book0_.isbn AS isbn2_0_,
    book0_.status AS status3_0_,
    book0_.title AS title4_0_
FROM book book0_
WHERE book0_.status = ?
ORDER BY book0_.id ASC limit ? FOR UPDATE skip locked
```

Notice that Hibernate has appended the SKIP LOCKED option to the FOR UPDATE clause. This query is triggered twice since there are two transactions. The first transaction fetches the books with IDs of *1*, *2*, and *3*:

```
First transaction: [
 Book{id=1, title=A History of Ancient Prague, isbn=001-JN, status=PENDING},
 Book{id=2, title=A People's History, isbn=002-JN, status=PENDING},
 Book{id=3, title=The Beatles Anthology, isbn=001-MJ, status=PENDING}
]
```

While the first transaction is running, the second transactions skips the books with IDs of *1*, *2*, and *3* and fetches the books with IDs of *4*, *5*, and *6*:

```
Second transaction: [
 Book{id=4, title=Carrie, isbn=001-OG, status=PENDING},
 Book{id=5, title=Fragments of Horror, isbn=002-OG, status=PENDING},
 Book{id=6, title=Anthology Mission, isbn=002-MJ, status=PENDING}
]
```

Check out the complete application for MySQL[54] and for PostgreSQL[55].

> From the locking category, it is advisable to read about PostgreSQL *advisory locks*. A great article on this topic can be found here[56].

# Item 131: How to Retry the Transaction After a Versioned (@Version) OptimisticLockException

Optimistic Locking is a concurrency control technique that doesn't use locks. It's extremely useful for preventing *lost updates* (e.g., for long conversations that span across several requests over the stateless HTTP protocol).

---

[54]HibernateSpringBootMySqlSkipLocked

[55]HibernateSpringBootPostgresSqlSkipLocked

[56]https://vladmihalcea.com/how-do-postgresql-advisory-locks-work/

# Versioned Optimistic Locking Exception

Most commonly, Optimistic Locking is implemented by adding a field annotated with @Version to the entity; this is known as *Versioned Optimistic Locking* and it relies on a numerical value that it is automatically managed (incremented by 1 when data is modified) by the JPA persistence provider (Hibernate). In a rude exprimation, based on this value, the JPA persistence provider can check if the data manipulated by the current transaction has been changed by a concurrent transaction. Therefore, it would be prone to a *lost update* (for more details about SQL anomalies, consider **Appendix E**).

> The type of @Version can be any of int, Integer, long, Long, short, Short, java.sql.Timestamp. To maximize efficiency, rely on short/Short. This will result in the database consuming less space (e.g., in MySQL, this type will be stored in a column of type SMALLINT).

> For the *assigned generator* (the generator that doesn't take a @GeneratedValue annotation and the identifiers are manually assigned), use the corresponding wrapper of the chosen primitive type. This will help Hibernate check for nullability. For IDENTITY, SEQUENCE, etc., generator strategies use the primitive type directly.

> Since Hibernate manages the @Version attribute, there is no need to add a setter method.

The following entity uses the *assigned generator* and has a field of type Short annotated with @Version:

```
@Entity
public class Inventory implements Serializable {

    private static final long serialVersionUID = 1L;

    @Id
    private Long id;
```

```
    private String title;
    private int quantity;

    @Version
    private Short version;

    public Short getVersion() {
        return version;
    }

    // getters and setters omitted for brevity
}
```

This entity maps the inventory of a bookstore. For each book, it stores the title and the available quantity. Multiple transactions (representing orders) decrease the quantity with a certain amount. Being concurrent transactions, the developer should mitigate scenarios as follows:

- Initially, the quantity is equal to 3

- Transaction A queries the available quantity, which is 3

- Transaction B queries the available quantity, which is 3

- Before Transaction A commits, Transaction B orders two books and commits (therefore, the quantity is now equal to 1)

- Transaction A orders two books, therefore, it commits and decreases the quantity by 2 (therefore, the quantity is now equal to -1)

Obviously, having a negative quantity means that the client will not receive their order and the application has lost an update. You can mitigate such scenarios via Optimistic Locking (alternatively, a native conditional update of type UPDATE-IF-ELSE may do the trick).

Having @Version in the entity, the last step of this scenario will lead to OptimisticLockException.

More precisely, in Spring Boot, the `OptimisticLockException` will lead to `org.springframework.orm.ObjectOptimisticLockingFailure` `Exception` or its super class, `org.springframework.dao.` `OptimisticLockingFailureException`.

Therefore, the UPDATE triggered by the last step will see that another transaction has modified the involved data. Now, the business logic can decide what to do. Basically, there are two approaches:

- If there are not enough books to satisfy the current transaction then notify the client

- If there are enough books then retry the transaction until it succeeds or until no more books are available

## Simulate an Optimistic Locking Exception

Writing an application that results in an Optimistic Locking exception requires at least two concurrent transactions that try to update the same data. It's like when two concurrent threads (users) try to execute the following service-method:

```
@Transactional
public void run() {

    Inventory inventory = inventoryRepository.findById(1L).orElseThrow();
    inventory.setQuantity(inventory.getQuantity() - 2);
}
```

To reproduce an Optimistic Locking exception, the previous method can be transformed into a Runnable. Furthermore, two threads will concurrently call it:

```
@Service
public class InventoryService implements Runnable {

    private final InventoryRepository inventoryRepository;
```

```
    public InventoryService(InventoryRepository inventoryRepository) {
        this.inventoryRepository = inventoryRepository;
    }

    @Override
    @Transactional
    public void run() {

        Inventory inventory = inventoryRepository
            .findById(1L).orElseThrow();
        inventory.setQuantity(inventory.getQuantity() - 2);
    }
}
```

And two threads (users) call this Runnable via an Executor (this instructs the transaction manager to create two transactions and two entity managers):

```
ExecutorService executor = Executors.newFixedThreadPool(2);
executor.execute(inventoryService);
executor.execute(inventoryService);
```

The complete source code is available on GitHub[57]. Running the code should result in an ObjectOptimisticLockingFailureException. Both threads will trigger a SELECT and will fetch the same value for quantity and version. Further, only one thread will trigger a successful UPDATE and will update the quantity (decreases by 2) and version (increases by 1). The second UPDATE will fail with an Optimistic Locking exception, since the versions don't match (a *lost update* was detected).

## Retrying the Transaction

You can retry the transaction via the db-util library. This library exposes an annotation named @Retry. You can set the type of exception that should trigger the retry, and the number of retries, via the on and times attributes. For example, you can retry the transaction 10 times if OptimisticLockException occurred, as follows:

---

[57]HibernateSpringBootSimulateVersionedOptimisticLocking

```
@Retry(times = 10, on = OptimisticLockException.class)
public void methodProneToOptimisticLockException() { ... }
```

For Spring Boot, the proper exception is OptimisticLockingFailureException:

```
@Retry(times = 10, on = OptimisticLockingFailureException.class)
public void methodProneToOptimisticLockingFailureException() { ... }
```

But, before using @Retry, the developer should add the db-util dependency to the application and perform several settings. For Maven, the dependency that should be added to pom.xml is:

```
<dependency>
    <groupId>com.vladmihalcea</groupId>
    <artifactId>db-util</artifactId>
    <version>1.0.4</version>
</dependency>
```

Further, configure the OptimisticConcurrencyControlAspect bean as follows:

```
@SpringBootApplication
@EnableAspectJAutoProxy
public class MainApplication {

    @Bean
    public OptimisticConcurrencyControlAspect
                    optimisticConcurrencyControlAspect() {

        return new OptimisticConcurrencyControlAspect();
    }
    ...
}
```

An important aspect of @Retry is that it cannot be used on a method annotated with @Transactional (e.g., it cannot be used to annotate the run() method). Trying to do this will result in an exception of type:

```
IllegalTransactionStateException: You shouldn't retry an operation from
within an existing Transaction. This is because we can't retry if the
current Transaction was already rolled back!.
```

The official explanation stands that "it's safer to retry the business logic operation when you are not within a running transaction". Therefore, a simple approach consists of writing an intermediate service as follows:

```
@Service
public class BookstoreService implements Runnable {

    private final InventoryService inventoryService;

    public BookstoreService(InventoryService inventoryService) {
        this.inventoryService = inventoryService;
    }

    @Override
    @Retry(times = 10, on = OptimisticLockingFailureException.class)
    public void run() {
        inventoryService.updateQuantity();
    }
}
```

The InventoryService becomes:

```
@Service
public class InventoryService {

    private final InventoryRepository inventoryRepository;

    public InventoryService(InventoryRepository inventoryRepository) {
        this.inventoryRepository = inventoryRepository;
    }

    @Transactional
    public void updateQuantity() {

        Inventory inventory = inventoryRepository.findById(1L).orElseThrow();
        inventory.setQuantity(inventory.getQuantity() - 2);
    }
}
```

The Executor will become:

```
ExecutorService executor = Executors.newFixedThreadPool(2);
executor.execute(bookstoreService);
executor.execute(bookstoreService);
```

The complete code is available on GitHub[58].

You can avoid the intermediate service by relying on TransactionTemplate instead of @Transactional. For example:

```
@Service
public class InventoryService implements Runnable {

    private final InventoryRepository inventoryRepository;
    private final TransactionTemplate transactionTemplate;

    public InventoryService(InventoryRepository inventoryRepository,

    TransactionTemplate transactionTemplate) {
        this.inventoryRepository = inventoryRepository;
        this.transactionTemplate = transactionTemplate;
    }

    @Override
    @Retry(times = 10, on = OptimisticLockingFailureException.class)
    public void run() {

        transactionTemplate.execute(new TransactionCallbackWithoutResult() {
            @Override
            public void doInTransactionWithoutResult(
                    TransactionStatus status){
```

---

```
                Inventory inventory
                    = inventoryRepository.findById(1L).orElseThrow();
                inventory.setQuantity(inventory.getQuantity() - 2);
            }
        });
    }
}
```

The complete code is available on GitHub[59].

## Testing Scenario

Consider an initial quantity of *10* books of the title, *A People's History*. The `version` field is initially equal to *0*.

Transaction A triggers a `SELECT` to fetch an `Inventory` entity as follows:

**SELECT**
```
  inventory0_.id AS id1_0_0_,
  inventory0_.quantity AS quantity2_0_0_,
  inventory0_.title AS title3_0_0_,
  inventory0_.version AS version4_0_0_
FROM inventory inventory0_
WHERE inventory0_.id = ?
Binding:[1] Extracted:[10, A People's History, 0]
```

Transaction B triggers a similar `SELECT` and fetches the same data. While transaction A is still active, Transaction B triggers an `UPDATE` to order two books (commits):

**UPDATE** inventory
**SET** quantity = ?,
    title = ?,
    version = ?

---

[59]HibernateSpringBootRetryVersionedOptimisticLockingTT

```
WHERE id = ?
AND version = ?
Binding:[8, A People's History, 1, 1, 0]
```

Transaction B has decreased the quantity from *10* to *8* and has increased the version from *0* to *1*. Further, Transaction A attempts to trigger an UPDATE to order two books as well. Transaction A is not aware of Transaction B, so it tries to decrease the quantity from *10* to *8* and to increase the version from *0* to *1*:

```
UPDATE inventory
SET quantity = ?,
    title = ?,
    version = ?
WHERE id = ?
AND version = ?
Binding:[8, A People's History, 1, 1, 0]
```

The version value from UPDATE is not the same as the version value from the database, so an OptimisticLockException is thrown. This will bring the retry mechanism into the scene. This mechanism retries Transaction A (the number of retries is decreased by 1). Conforming to Transaction A, it triggers the SELECT again:

```
SELECT
    inventory0_.id AS id1_0_0_,
    inventory0_.quantity AS quantity2_0_0_,
    inventory0_.title AS title3_0_0_,
    inventory0_.version AS version4_0_0_
FROM inventory inventory0_
WHERE inventory0_.id = ?
Binding:[1] Extracted:[8, A People's History, 1]
```

This time, the fetched quantity is *8* and version is *1*. So, the data updated by Transaction B is visible to Transaction A. Further, Transaction A trigger an UPDATE to decrease the quantity from *8* to *6* and to increase the version from *1* to *2*:

```
UPDATE inventory
SET quantity = ?,
    title = ?,
    version = ?
```

```
WHERE id = ?
AND version = ?
Binding:[6, A People's History, 2, 1, 1]
```

Meanwhile, no other transaction has altered the data. In other words, no other transaction has modified the version. This means that Transaction A commits and the retry mechanism did an awesome job.

# Item 132: How to Retry a Transaction After a Versionless OptimisticLockException

Besides Versioned Optimistic Locking, Hibernate ORM supports *Versionless Optimistic Locking* (no @Version is needed).

## Versionless Optimistic Locking Exception

Basically, Versionless Optimistic Locking relies on the WHERE clause added to the UPDATE statement. This clause checks if the data that should be updated has been changed since it was fetched in the current Persistence Context.

> Versionless Optimistic Locking works as long as the current Persistence Context is open, which avoids detaching entities (Hibernate can no longer track any changes).

The preferable way to go with Versionless Optimistic Locking is as follows:

```
@Entity
@DynamicUpdate
@OptimisticLocking(type = OptimisticLockType.DIRTY)
public class Inventory implements Serializable {

    private static final long serialVersionUID = 1L;

    @Id
    private Long id;
```

```
    private String title;
    private int quantity;

    // getters and setters omitted for brevity
}
```

This entity maps the inventory of a bookstore. For each book, it stores the title and the available quantity. Multiple transactions (representing orders) decrease the quantity by a certain amount. Being concurrent transactions, the developer should mitigate *lost updates* and avoid ending with a negative value.

Setting `OptimisticLockType.DIRTY` instructs Hibernate to automatically add the modified columns (e.g., the column corresponding to the `quantity` property) to the `UPDATE WHERE` clause. The `@DynamicUpdate` annotation is required in this case and in the case of `OptimisticLockType.ALL` (all properties of the entity will be used to verify the entity version).

You can exclude a certain field from versioning (e.g., children collection changes should not trigger a parent version update) at the field level via the `@OptimisticLock(excluded = true)` annotation.

Here is a generic example:

```
@OneToMany(cascade = CascadeType.ALL, orphanRemoval = true)
@OptimisticLock(excluded = true)
private List<Foo> foos = new ArrayList<>();
```

## Simulate an Optimistic Locking Exception

Consider reading the section "Simulate an Optimistic Locking Exception" from **Item 131** since the code (except the entity code) is exactly the same. The complete application is available on GitHub[60].

---

[60]HibernateSpringBootSimulateVersionlessOptimisticLocking

# Retrying the Transaction

Consider reading the section "Retrying the Transaction" from **Item 131** since it presents the install and configuration of the db-util library used further. The considerations presented there are valid for Versionless Optimistic Locking as well. The code (except the entity code) is the same. The complete applications are available on GitHub here[61] and here[62].

# Testing Scenario

Consider an initial quantity of *10* books of the title, *A People's History*.

Transaction A triggers a SELECT to fetch an Inventory entity as follows:

```
SELECT
  inventory0_.id AS id1_0_0_,
  inventory0_.quantity AS quantity2_0_0_,
  inventory0_.title AS title3_0_0_
FROM inventory inventory0_
WHERE inventory0_.id = ?
Binding:[1] Extracted:[10, A People's History]
```

Transaction B triggers a similar SELECT and fetches the same data. While Transaction A is still active, Transaction B triggers an UPDATE to order two books (commits):

```
UPDATE inventory
SET quantity = ?
WHERE id = ?
AND quantity = ?
Binding:[8, 1, 10]
```

Transaction B has decreased the quantity from *10* to *8*. Further, Transaction A attempts to trigger an UPDATE to order two books as well. Transaction A is not aware of Transaction B, so it tries to decrease the quantity from *10* to *8*:

```
UPDATE inventory
SET quantity = ?
```

---

[61]HibernateSpringBootRetryVersionlessOptimisticLocking
[62]HibernateSpringBootRetryVersionlessOptimisticLockingTT

```
WHERE id = ?
AND quantity = ?
Binding:[8, 1, 10]
```

The quantity value from UPDATE WHERE is not the same as the quantity value from the database. Therefore, an OptimisticLockException is thrown. This will bring the retry mechanism into the scene. This mechanism retries Transaction A (the number of retries is decreased by 1). Conforming to Transaction A, it triggers the SELECT again:

```
SELECT
    inventory0_.id AS id1_0_0_,
    inventory0_.quantity AS quantity2_0_0_,
    inventory0_.title AS title3_0_0_
FROM inventory inventory0_
WHERE inventory0_.id = ?
Binding:[1] Extracted:[8, A People's History]
```

This time, the fetched quantity is 8. So, the data updated by Transaction B is visible to Transaction A. Further, Transaction A triggers an UPDATE to decrease the quantity from 8 to 6:

```
UPDATE inventory
SET quantity = ?
WHERE id = ?
AND quantity = ?
Binding:[6, 1, 8]
```

Meanwhile, no other transaction has altered the data. In other words, no other transaction has modified the quantity. This means that Transaction A commits and the retry mechanism did an awesome job.

# Item 133: How to Handle Versioned Optimistic Locking and Detached Entities

Consider this item as a preamble to **Item 134**.

Versioned Optimistic Locking works with detached entities, while Hibernate ORM Versionless Optimistic Locking doesn't work.

This assumes that the Inventory entity was already prepared with @Version. In addition, an empty (no explicit queries) classical InventoryRepository and an InventoryService are available as well. A quick scenario can lead to an Optimistic Locking exception:

- In the InventoryService, the following method fetches an Inventory entity for ID *1* (this is Transaction A):

```
public Inventory firstTransactionFetchesAndReturn() {
    Inventory firstInventory
        = inventoryRepository.findById(1L).orElseThrow();

    return firstInventory;
}
```

- In the InventoryService, the following method fetches an Inventory entity for the same ID (*1*) and updates the data (this is Transaction B):

```
@Transactional
public void secondTransactionFetchesAndReturn() {
    Inventory secondInventory
        = inventoryRepository.findById(1L).orElseThrow();

    secondInventory.setQuantity(secondInventory.getQuantity() - 1);
}
```

- Finally, in InventoryService, the following method updates the entity fetched in Transaction A (this is Transaction C):

```
public void thirdTransactionMergesAndUpdates(Inventory
firstInventory) {

    // calls EntityManager#merge() behind the scene
    inventoryRepository.save(firstInventory);

    // this ends up in Optimistic Locking exception
}
```

Having these three methods, first call `firstTransactionFetchesAndReturn()`. This will trigger the following SELECT:

```
SELECT
  inventory0_.id AS id1_0_0_,
  inventory0_.quantity AS quantity2_0_0_,
  inventory0_.title AS title3_0_0_,
  inventory0_.version AS version4_0_0_
FROM inventory inventory0_
WHERE inventory0_.id = ?
Binding:[1] Extracted:[10, A People's History, 0]
```

At this point, the fetched `version` is *0*. The transaction commits and the Persistence Context is closed. The returned `Inventory` becomes a detached entity.

Further, call `secondTransactionFetchesAndReturn()`. This will trigger the following SQL statements:

```
SELECT
  inventory0_.id AS id1_0_0_,
  inventory0_.quantity AS quantity2_0_0_,
  inventory0_.title AS title3_0_0_,
  inventory0_.version AS version4_0_0_
FROM inventory inventory0_
WHERE inventory0_.id = ?
Binding:[1] Extracted:[10, A People's History, 0]

UPDATE inventory
SET quantity = ?,
    title = ?,
    version = ?
WHERE id = ?
AND version = ?
Binding:[9, A People's History, 1, 1, 0]
```

At this point, the `version` was updated to *1*. This transaction has modified the quantity as well. The Persistence Context is closed.

Next, call `thirdTransactionMergesAndUpdates()` and pass as an argument the detached entity you fetched earlier. Spring inspects the entity and concludes that this should be merged. Therefore, behind the scenes (behind the save() call), it calls EntityManager#merge().

Further, the JPA provider fetches from the database (via SELECT) a persistent object equivalent to the detached entity (since there is no such object) and copies the detached entity to the persisted one:

```
SELECT
  inventory0_.id AS id1_0_0_,
  inventory0_.quantity AS quantity2_0_0_,
  inventory0_.title AS title3_0_0_,
  inventory0_.version AS version4_0_0_
FROM inventory inventory0_
WHERE inventory0_.id = ?
Binding:[1] Extracted:[9, A People's History, 1]
```

> At the merge operation, the detached entity doesn't become managed. The detached entity is copied into a managed entity (available in the Persistence Context).

At this point, Hibernate concludes that the version of the fetched entity and the version of the detached entity don't match. This will lead to an Optimistic Locking exception reported by Spring Boot as ObjectOptimisticLockingFailureException.

The source code is available on GitHub[63].

> Do not attempt to retry the transaction that uses merge(). Each retry will just fetch from the database the entity whose version doesn't match the version of the detached entity, resulting in an Optimistic Locking exception.

---

[63]HibernateSpringBootVersionedOptimisticLockingAndDettachedEntity

# Item 134: How to Use the Optimistic Locking Mechanism and Detached Entities in long HTTP Conversations

The following scenario is a common case in web applications and is known as a *long conversation*. In other words, a bunch of requests (operations) that are logically related shape a stateful long conversation that contains the client thinking periods as well (e.g., suitable for implementing wizards). Mainly, this *read* ➤ *modify* ➤ *write* flow is perceived as a logical or application-level transaction that may span over multiple physical transactions (e.g., in the following example, the application-level transaction spans over two physical transactions).

Application-level transactions should be suitable for ACID properties as well. In other words, you must control concurrency (e.g., via Optimistic Locking mechanism, which is suitable for both application-level and physical transactions) and have application-level repeatable reads. This way, you prevent *lost updates* (details in **Appendix E**). Remember from **Item 21** that Persistence Context guarantees session-level repeatable reads as long as you use entity queries. Fetching projections will NOT take advantage of session-level repeatable reads.

Moreover, pay attention that, in long conversations, only the last physical transaction is writeable to propagate changes to the database (flush and commit). If an application-level transaction has intermediate physical writable transactions, then it cannot sustain atomicity of the application-level transaction. In other words, in the context of the application-level transaction, while a physical transaction may commit, a subsequent one may roll back.

If you don't want to use a logical transaction made of several physical read-only transactions with a last writable transaction, you can disable auto-flushing and enable it in the last physical transaction:

```
// disable auto-flush
entityManager.unwrap(Session.class)
    .setHibernateFlushMode(FlushMode.MANUAL);
```

Then, in the last physical transaction, enable it:

```
// enable auto-flush
entityManager.unwrap(Session.class)
    .setHibernateFlushMode(FlushMode.AUTO);
```

Detached entities are commonly used in long conversations that span across several requests over the stateless HTTP protocol (another approach relies on the Extended Persistence Context, where entities remain attached across multiple HTTP requests).

A typical scenario is as follows:

- An HTTP request A hits a controller endpoint.

- The controller delegates the job further and results in fetching an entity A in a Persistence Context A (entity A is planned to be modified by the client).

- The Persistence Context A is closed and entity A becomes detached.

- The detached entity A is stored in session and the controller returns it to the client.

- The client modifies the received data and submits the modifications in another HTTP request B.

- The detached entity A is fetched from the session and is synchronized with the data submitted by the client.

- The detached entity is merged, which means that Hibernate loads in a Persistence Context B the latest data from the database (entity B) and updates it to mirror the detached entity A.

- After merging, the application can update the database accordingly.

This scenario works fine without Versioned Optimistic Locking as long as the entity data is not modified between the HTTP requests, A and B. If this is happening, and is not wanted (e.g., because of *lost updates*), then it is time to empower Versioned Optimistic Locking, as in the following Inventory entity (inventory of a bookstore):

```java
@Entity
public class Inventory implements Serializable {

    private static final long serialVersionUID = 1L;

    @Id
    @GeneratedValue(strategy = GenerationType.IDENTITY)
    private Long id;

    private String title;

    @Min(value = 0)
    @Max(value = 100)
    private int quantity;

    @Version
    private short version;

    public short getVersion() {
        return version;
    }

    // getters and setters omitted for brevity
}
```

To update (increase/decrease) the inventory, the administrators of the bookstore load the desired title by id (materialized in an Inventory instance) via a simple HTTP GET request pointing to a controller endpoint (this is the controller endpoint that answers the HTTP request A). The returned Inventory is stored in session via @SessionAttributes, as follows:

```java
@Controller
@SessionAttributes({InventoryController.INVENTORY_ATTR})
public class InventoryController {
```

```
protected static final String INVENTORY_ATTR = "inventory";
private static final String BINDING_RESULT =
    "org.springframework.validation.BindingResult." + INVENTORY_ATTR;

private final InventoryService inventoryService;

public InventoryController(InventoryService inventoryService) {
    this.inventoryService = inventoryService;
}

@GetMapping("/load/{id}")
public String fetchInventory(@PathVariable Long id, Model model) {
    if (!model.containsAttribute(BINDING_RESULT)) {
        model.addAttribute(INVENTORY_ATTR,
            inventoryService.fetchInventoryById(id));
    }

    return "index";
}
...
```

After setting the new quantity (the new stock of this title), the data is submitted via an HTTP POST request to the following controller endpoint (this is the HTTP request B). The detached Inventory is loaded from the HTTP session and is synchronized with the submitted data. Therefore, the detached Inventory is updated to mirror the submitted modifications. This is the job of @ModelAttribute and @SessionAttributes. Further, the service-method updateInventory() is responsible for merging the entity and propagating the modifications to the database. If, in the meanwhile, the data was modified by another administrator, then an Optimistic Locking exception will be thrown. Check out the try-catch block that deals with potential Optimistic Locking exceptions:

```
...
@PostMapping("/update")
public String updateInventory(
    @Validated @ModelAttribute(INVENTORY_ATTR) Inventory
    inventory, BindingResult bindingResult, RedirectAttributes
    redirectAttributes, SessionStatus sessionStatus) {
```

```
    if (!bindingResult.hasErrors()) {
        try {
            Inventory updatedInventory =
                inventoryService.updateInventory(inventory);
            redirectAttributes.addFlashAttribute("updatedInventory",
                updatedInventory);
        } catch (OptimisticLockingFailureException e) {
            bindingResult.reject("", "Another user updated the data.
                                    Press the link above to reload it.");
        }
    }

    if (bindingResult.hasErrors()) {
            redirectAttributes.addFlashAttribute(BINDING_RESULT,
                    bindingResult);
            return "redirect:load/" + inventory.getId();
    }

    sessionStatus.setComplete();

    return "redirect:success";
}
...
```

If the inventory was successfully updated, then the data is displayed in a simple HTML page via the following controller endpoint:

```
@GetMapping(value = "/success")
public String success() {
    return "success";
}
```

The Spring service source code is listed here:

```
@Service
public class InventoryService {

    private final InventoryRepository inventoryRepository;

    public InventoryService(InventoryRepository inventoryRepository) {
```

```
        this.inventoryRepository = inventoryRepository;
    }

    public Inventory fetchInventoryById(Long id) {
        Inventory inventory = inventoryRepository
            .findById(id).orElseThrow();
        return inventory;
    }

    public Inventory updateInventory(Inventory inventory) {
        return inventoryRepository.save(inventory);
    }
}
```

## Testing Time

The purpose of testing is to follow a scenario that leads to an Optimistic Locking exception. More precisely, the goal is to obtain Figure 14-25.

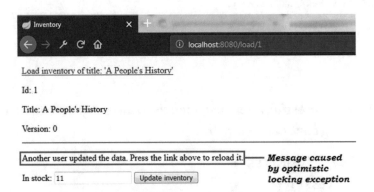

***Figure 14-25.*** *HTTP long conversation and detached entities*

Figure 14-25 can be obtained as follows:

- Start two browsers (to simulate two clients) and access localhost:8080.

- In both browsers, click on the link displayed on screen.

- In the first browser, insert a new stock value and click Update Inventory (the result will be a new page containing the modifications).

- In the second browser, insert another new stock value and click
  `Update Inventory`.

- At this moment, since the first client has modified the data, the
  second client will see the message highlighted in Figure 14-25;
  therefore, there is no *lost update* this time.

The source code is available on GitHub[64].

---

In Spring, it is advisable to avoid using Extended Persistence Context because of
its traps and drawbacks. But if you decide to go with it then pay attention to the
following:

- The `readOnly` flag has no effect. This means that any
  modifications will be propagated to the database even if you
  marked the transaction as `readOnly`. A solution will be to
  disable auto-flushing for all the involved physical transactions
  except the last one where you need to enable it. Nevertheless,
  in Extended Persistence Context, read-only operations (e.g.,
  `find()`, `refresh()`, `detach()`, and read queries) can be
  executed outside a transaction. Even some entity changes
  (e.g., `persist()` and `merge()`) can be executed outside of a
  transaction. They will be queued until the Extended Persistence
  Context joins a transaction. Operations as `flush()`, `lock()`,
  and update/delete queries cannot be executed outside of a
  transaction.

- Memory footprint: Pay attention that each entity that you
  fetch increases the Extended Persistence Context and, as a
  consequence, it slow down the Dirty Checking mechanism. You
  can sweeten the situation by explicitly detaching entities that
  are not needed in the last physical transaction.

---

[64]HibernateSpringBootHTTPLongConversationDetachedEntity

# Item 135: How to Increment the Version of the Locked Entity Even If this Entity Was Not Modified

Consider several editors that prepare a book for printing. They load each chapter and apply specific modifications (formatting, grammar, indentation, etc.). Each of them should be allowed to save their modifications only if, in the meanwhile, the other one didn't save any modifications. In such cases, the chapter should be reloaded before considering modifications. In other words, the modifications should be applied sequentially.

The chapter is mapped by the root entity Chapter, and the modification by the Modification entity. Between Modification (child-side) and Chapter (parent-side), there is a unidirectional lazy @ManyToOne association represented by the tables in Figure 14-26.

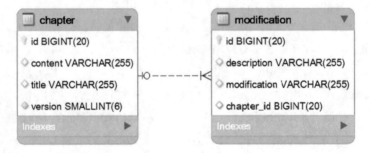

***Figure 14-26.***  *The one-to-many table relationship*

## OPTIMISTIC_FORCE_INCREMENT

To shape this scenario, we can rely on @Version and the OPTIMISTIC_FORCE_INCREMENT locking strategy. Their powers combined can help you increment the version of the locked entity (Chapter) even if this entity was not modified. In other words, each modification (Modification) is forcibly propagated to the parent entity (Chapter) Optimistic Locking version.

So, the Optimistic Locking version should be added to the root entity, Chapter:

```
@Entity
public class Chapter implements Serializable {

    private static final long serialVersionUID = 1L;
```

```
    @Id
    @GeneratedValue(strategy = GenerationType.IDENTITY)
    private Long id;

    private String title;
    private String content;

    @Version
    private short version;
    ...
}
```

The Modification entity is listed here:

```
@Entity
public class Modification implements Serializable {

    private static final long serialVersionUID = 1L;

    @Id
    @GeneratedValue(strategy = GenerationType.IDENTITY)
    private Long id;

    private String description;
    private String modification;

    @ManyToOne(fetch = FetchType.LAZY)
    private Chapter chapter;
    ...
}
```

The editor loads the chapter by ID, using the LockModeType.OPTIMISTIC_FORCE_
INCREMENT lock strategy. For this, we have to override the ChapterRepository.
findById() method to add the locking mode, as shown (by default, findById() doesn't
use locking):

```
@Repository
public interface ChapterRepository extends JpaRepository<Chapter, Long> {
```

```
    @Override
    @Lock(LockModeType.OPTIMISTIC_FORCE_INCREMENT)
    public Optional<Chapter> findById(Long id);
}
```

Further, let's consider the following scenario:

> Step 1: Editor 1 loads chapter 1.

> Step 2: Editor 2 loads chapter 1 as well.

> Step 3: Editor 2 performs a modification and persists it.

> Step 4: Editor 2 forcibly propagates this modification to chapter 1 Optimistic Locking version. The transaction of Editor 2 commits.

> Step 5: Editor 1 performs a modification and attempts to persist it.

> Step 6: Editor 1 causes an Optimistic Locking exception since, in the meanwhile, Editor 2 has added a modification.

You can shape this scenario via two concurrent transactions using TransactionTemplate, as in the following code:

```
@Service
public class BookstoreService {

    private static final Logger log
        = Logger.getLogger(BookstoreService.class.getName());

    private final TransactionTemplate template;
    private final ChapterRepository chapterRepository;
    private final ModificationRepository modificationRepository;

    public BookstoreService(ChapterRepository chapterRepository,
            ModificationRepository modificationRepository,
            TransactionTemplate template) {
        this.chapterRepository = chapterRepository;
        this.modificationRepository = modificationRepository;
        this.template = template;
    }
```

```
public void editChapter() {

    template.setPropagationBehavior(
        TransactionDefinition.PROPAGATION_REQUIRES_NEW);

    template.execute(new TransactionCallbackWithoutResult() {

        @Override
        protected void doInTransactionWithoutResult(
                                    TransactionStatus status) {

            log.info("Starting first transaction ...");

            Chapter chapter = chapterRepository.findById(1L).orElseThrow();

            Modification modification = new Modification();
            modification.setDescription("Rewording first paragraph");
            modification.setModification("Reword: ... Added: ...");
            modification.setChapter(chapter);

            template.execute(new TransactionCallbackWithoutResult() {

                @Override
                protected void doInTransactionWithoutResult(
                                    TransactionStatus status) {

                    log.info("Starting second transaction ...");

                    Chapter chapter
                        = chapterRepository.findById(1L).orElseThrow();

                    Modification modification = new Modification();
                    modification.setDescription(
                        "Formatting second paragraph");
                    modification.setModification("Format ...");
                    modification.setChapter(chapter);

                    modificationRepository.save(modification);

                    log.info("Commit second transaction ...");
                }
            });
```

```
            log.info("Resuming first transaction ...");

            modificationRepository.save(modification);

            log.info("Commit first transaction ...");
        }
    });

    log.info("Done!");
    }
}
```

When running the aforementioned editChapter(), Hibernate generates the following output:

```
Starting first transaction ...

-- Editor 1 load chapter 1
SELECT
  chapter0_.id AS id1_0_0_,
  chapter0_.content AS content2_0_0_,
  chapter0_.title AS title3_0_0_,
  chapter0_.version AS version4_0_0_
FROM chapter chapter0_
WHERE chapter0_.id = 1

Starting second transaction ...

-- Editor 2 loads chapter 1 as well
SELECT
  chapter0_.id AS id1_0_0_,
  chapter0_.content AS content2_0_0_,
  chapter0_.title AS title3_0_0_,
  chapter0_.version AS version4_0_0_
FROM chapter chapter0_
WHERE chapter0_.id = 1

-- Editor 2 perform a modification and persist it
INSERT INTO modification (chapter_id, description, modification)
  VALUES (1, "Formatting second paragraph", "Format")
```

Commit second transaction ...

```
-- Editor 2 forcibly propagate this modification
-- to chapter 1 Optimistic Locking version
UPDATE chapter
SET version = 1
WHERE id = 1
AND version = 0
```

Resuming first transaction ...

```
-- Editor 1 perform a modification and attempts to persist it
INSERT INTO modification (chapter_id, description, modification)
  VALUES (1, "Rewording first paragraph", "Reword: ... Added: ...")
```

```
-- Editor 1 causes an Optimistic Locking exception since,
-- in the meanwhile, Editor 2 has added a modification
UPDATE chapter
SET version = 1
WHERE id = 1
AND version = 0
```

```
-- org.springframework.orm.ObjectOptimisticLockingFailureException
-- Caused by: org.hibernate.StaleObjectStateException
```

Notice the highlighted UPDATE. This is the UPDATE that increment the version. This UPDATE is triggered against the chapter table at the end of the currently running transaction.

> The OPTIMISTIC_FORCE_INCREMENT lock strategy is useful for coordinating child-side state changes in a sequential manner by propagating these changes to the parent-side Optimistic Locking version. You can orchestrate the sequence of state changes of a single child (as shown previously) or of more children.

The complete application is available on GitHub[65].

---

[65]HibernateSpringBootOptimisticForceIncrement

# PESSIMISTIC_FORCE_INCREMENT

While OPTIMISTIC_FORCE_INCREMENT increments the version at the end of the current transaction, PESSIMISTIC_FORCE_INCREMENT increments the version immediately. The entity version update is guaranteed to succeed immediately after acquiring the row-level lock. The increments take place before the entity is returned to the data access layer.

If the entity was previously loaded without being locked and the PESSIMISTIC_FORCE_ INCREMENT version update fails, the currently running transaction can be rolled back right away.

This time, we use @Lock(LockModeType.PESSIMISTIC_FORCE_INCREMENT). We've also added a query that fetches Chapter without locking (findByTitle()):

```
@Repository
public interface ChapterRepository extends JpaRepository<Chapter, Long> {

    @Override
    @Lock(LockModeType.PESSIMISTIC_FORCE_INCREMENT)
    public Optional<Chapter> findById(Long id);

    public Chapter findByTitle(String title);
}
```

Further, let's consider the following scenario:

> Step 1: Editor 1 loads chapter 1 without acquiring a lock (logical or physical).
>
> Step 2: Editor 2 loads chapter 1 as well, but via PESSIMISTIC_ FORCE_INCREMENT.
>
> Step 3: Editor 2 gets a row-lock and increments the version immediately.
>
> Step 4: Editor 2 saves their modifications (the transaction is committed).
>
> Step 5: Editor 1 attempts to acquire a PESSIMISTIC_FORCE_ INCREMENT on the chapter 1 entity loaded during Step 1.
>
> Step 6: Editor 1 causes an Optimistic Locking exception, since, in the meanwhile, Editor 2 has added a modification, which has updated the version.

You can shape this scenario via two concurrent transactions using TransactionTemplate, as shown in the following code:

```
public void editChapterTestVersion() {

    template.setPropagationBehavior(
        TransactionDefinition.PROPAGATION_REQUIRES_NEW);

    template.execute(new TransactionCallbackWithoutResult() {

        @Override
        protected void doInTransactionWithoutResult(
                            TransactionStatus status) {

            log.info("Starting first transaction
                    (no physical or logical lock) ...");

            Chapter chapter = chapterRepository.findByTitle("Locking");

            template.execute(new TransactionCallbackWithoutResult() {

                @Override
                protected void doInTransactionWithoutResult(
                                    TransactionStatus status) {

                    log.info("Starting second transaction ...");

                    Chapter chapter
                        = chapterRepository.findById(1L).orElseThrow();

                    Modification modification = new Modification();
                    modification.setDescription(
                        "Formatting second paragraph");
                    modification.setModification("Format ...");
                    modification.setChapter(chapter);

                    modificationRepository.save(modification);

                    log.info("Commit second transaction ...");
                }
            });
```

```
            log.info("Resuming first transaction ...");

            log.info("First transaction attempts to acquire a "
                + "P_F_I on the existing `chapter` entity");

            entityManager.lock(chapter,
                LockModeType.PESSIMISTIC_FORCE_INCREMENT);

            Modification modification = new Modification();
            modification.setDescription("Rewording first paragraph");
            modification.setModification("Reword: ... Added: ...");
            modification.setChapter(chapter);

            modificationRepository.save(modification);

            log.info("Commit first transaction ...");
        }
    });

    log.info("Done!");
}
```

When running the aforementioned editChapterTestVersion(), Hibernate generates the following output:

```
Starting first transaction (no physical or logical lock) ...

-- Editor 1 loads chapter 1 without acquiring any lock (logical of
physical)
SELECT
  chapter0_.id AS id1_0_,
  chapter0_.content AS content2_0_,
  chapter0_.title AS title3_0_,
  chapter0_.version AS version4_0_
FROM chapter chapter0_
WHERE chapter0_.title = "Locking"
```

Starting second transaction ...

-- *Editor 2 loads chapter 1 as well, but via PESSIMISTIC_FORCE_INCREMENT*
**SELECT**
  chapter0_.id **AS** id1_0_0_,
  chapter0_.content **AS** content2_0_0_,
  chapter0_.title **AS** title3_0_0_,
  chapter0_.version **AS** version4_0_0_
**FROM** chapter chapter0_
**WHERE** chapter0_.id = " Locking" **FOR UPDATE**

-- *Editor 2 gets a row-lock and increment the version immediately*
**UPDATE** chapter
**SET** version = 1
**WHERE** id = 1
**AND** version = 0

-- *Editor 2 save their modifications (transaction is committed)*
**INSERT INTO** modification (chapter_id, description, modification)
  **VALUES** (1, " Formatting second paragraph", "Format ...")

Commit second transaction ...

Resuming first transaction ...

First transaction attempts to acquire a PESSIMISTIC_FORCE_INCREMENT on the
existing `chapter` entity

-- *Editor 1 attempts to acquire a PESSIMISTIC_FORCE_INCREMENT*
-- *on chapter 1 entity loaded at Step 1*
**UPDATE** chapter
**SET** version = 1
**WHERE** id = 1
**AND** version = 0

-- *Editor 1 causes an Optimistic Locking exception since, in the meanwhile,*
-- *Editor 2 has added a modification, therefore updated the version*
-- javax.persistence.OptimisticLockException
-- Caused by: org.hibernate.StaleObjectStateException

Notice that, even if Editor 1 loads Chapter 1 without being locked, the failure of acquiring a `PESSIMISTIC_FORCE_INCREMENT` later rolled back the current transaction immediately.

To acquire an exclusive lock, Hibernate will rely on the underlying `Dialect` lock clause. Pay attention to the MySQL dialect—`MySQL5Dialect` (MyISAM) doesn't support row-level locking, `MySQL5InnoDBDialect` (InnoDB) acquires row-level locks via `FOR UPDATE` (a timeout can be set), and `MySQL8Dialect` (InnoDB) acquires row-level locks via `FOR UPDATE NOWAIT`.

In PostgreSQL, the `PostgreSQL95Dialect` dialect acquires row-level locks via `FOR UPDATE NOWAIT`.

A transaction that increments the entity version will block other transactions to acquire a `PESSIMISTIC_FORCE_INCREMENT` lock until it releases the row-level physical lock (by commit or rollback). In this context, always rely on `NOWAIT` or on explicit short timeouts to avoid deadlocks (notice that the default timeouts are commonly too relaxed and it's good practice to explicitly set short timeouts). The database can detect and fix deadlocks (by killing one of the transactions), but it can do so only after timeout. A long timeout means a busy connection for a long time, and so a performance penalty. Moreover, locking too much data may affect scalability.

Note that MySQL uses `REPEATABLE_READ` as the default isolation level. This means that the acquired locks (explicit locks or not) are held for the duration of the transaction. On the other hand, in the `READ_COMMITTED` isolation level (default in PostgreSQL and other RDBMS), the unneeded locks are released after the `STATEMENT` completes. More details are available here[66].

The complete application is available on GitHub[67].

---

[66]https://www.percona.com/blog/2012/08/28/differences-between-read-committed-and-repeatable-read-transaction-isolation-levels/

[67]HibernateSpringBootPesimisticForceIncrement

# Item 136: How PESSIMISTIC_READ/WRITE Works

When we talk about PESSIMISTIC_READ and PESSIMISTIC_WRITE, we talk about shared and exclusive locks.

Shared locks and read locks allow multiple processes to read at the same time and disallow writes. Exclusive or write locks disallow reads and writes as long as a write operation is in progress. The purpose of a shared/read lock is to prevent other processes from acquiring an exclusive/write lock.

In a nutshell a shared/read lock says:

- *You're welcome to read next to other readers, but if you want to write, you'll have to wait for locks to be released.*

An exclusive/write lock says:

- *Sorry, somebody is writing, so you cannot read or write until the lock is released.*

You can acquire a shared lock in Spring Boot at the query-level via PESSIMISTIC_READ, while you can acquire an exclusive lock via PESSIMISTIC_WRITE as in the following repository associated with the Author entity (in the same way you can acquire shared/exclusive locks for any other query—e.g., queries defined via the Spring Data Query Builder mechanism or via @Query):

```
@Repository
public interface AuthorRepository extends JpaRepository<Author, Long> {

    @Override
    @Lock(LockModeType.PESSIMISTIC_READ/WRITE)
    public Optional<Author> findById(Long id);
}
```

The support and syntax for acquiring shared and exclusive locks is specific to each database. Moreover, these aspects can differ even in the same database, depending on the dialect. Hibernate relies on `Dialect` to choose the proper syntax.

For testing purposes, let's consider the following scenario, which involves two concurrent transactions:

Step 1: Transaction A fetches the author with an ID of *1*.

Step 2: Transaction B fetches the same author.

Step 3: Transaction B updates the author's genre.

Step 4: Transaction B commits.

Step 5: Transaction A commits.

In code, this scenario can be implemented via `TransactionTemplate` as shown here:

```
private final TransactionTemplate template;
...
public void pessimisticReadWrite() {

    template.setPropagationBehavior(
        TransactionDefinition.PROPAGATION_REQUIRES_NEW);
    template.setTimeout(3); // 3 seconds

    template.execute(new TransactionCallbackWithoutResult() {

        @Override
        protected void doInTransactionWithoutResult(
                            TransactionStatus status) {

            log.info("Starting first transaction ...");

            Author author = authorRepository.findById(1L).orElseThrow();
```

```
template.execute(new TransactionCallbackWithoutResult() {

    @Override
    protected void doInTransactionWithoutResult(
                        TransactionStatus status) {

        log.info("Starting second transaction ...");

        Author author
            = authorRepository.findById(1L).orElseThrow();
        author.setGenre("Horror");

        log.info("Commit second transaction ...");
    }
});

log.info("Resuming first transaction ...");
log.info("Commit first transaction ...");
    }
});

log.info("Done!");
}
```

Now, let's see how this scenario works in the context of PESSIMISTIC_READ and PESSIMISTIC_WRITE.

# PESSIMISTIC_READ

Using this scenario in a PESSIMISTIC_READ context should result in the following flow:

Step 1: Transaction A fetches the author with an ID of *1* and acquires a shared lock.

Step 2: Transaction B fetches the same author and acquires a shared lock.

Step 3: Transaction B wants to update the author's genre.

Step 4: Transaction B times out since it cannot acquire a lock to modify this row as long as Transaction A is holding a shared lock on it.

Step 5: Transaction B causes a QueryTimeoutException.

Now, let's see how this flow is respected by different databases and dialects.

## MySQL and MySQL5Dialect Dialects (MyISAM)

When running the aforementioned pessimisticReadWrite() via MySQL5Dialect, Hibernate generates the following output (notice the presence of LOCK IN SHARE MODE in the SELECT statements; this is MySQL-specific syntax for shared locks):

```
Starting first transaction ...

-- Transaction A fetches the author with id 1 and acquire a shared lock
SELECT
    author0_.id AS id1_0_0_,
    author0_.age AS age2_0_0_,
    author0_.genre AS genre3_0_0_,
    author0_.name AS name4_0_0_
FROM author author0_
WHERE author0_.id = 1 LOCK IN SHARE MODE

Starting second transaction ...

-- Transaction B fetches the same author and acquire a shared lock
SELECT
    author0_.id AS id1_0_0_,
    author0_.age AS age2_0_0_,
    author0_.genre AS genre3_0_0_,
    author0_.name AS name4_0_0_
FROM author author0_
WHERE author0_.id = 1 LOCK IN SHARE MODE

Commit second transaction ...
```

```
-- Transaction B updates the author's genre successfully
UPDATE author
SET age = 23,
    genre = "Horror",
    name = "Mark Janel"
WHERE id = 1

Resuming first transaction ...
Commit first transaction ...

Done!
```

> Even if the syntax for acquiring shared locks is present (LOCK IN SHARE
> MODE), the MyISAM engine doesn't prevent writes. Therefore, avoid the
> MySQL5Dialect dialect.

## MySQL and MySQL5InnoDBDialect/ MySQL8Dialect Dialects (InnoDB)

When running the aforementioned pessimisticReadWrite() via MySQL5InnoDBDialect or MySQL8Dialect, the result will follow the steps of the scenario. So, using the InnoDB engine applies locks as expected and writes are prevented (while a shared lock is active, InnoDB prevents other transactions from acquiring an exclusive/write lock on this data).

In syntax terms, the MySQL5InnoDBDialect dialect uses LOCK IN SHARE MODE, while the MySQL8Dialect dialect uses FOR SHARE. The following output is specific to MySQL8Dialect:

```
Starting first transaction ...

-- Transaction A fetches the author with id 1 and acquire a shared lock
SELECT
    author0_.id AS id1_0_0_,
    author0_.age AS age2_0_0_,
    author0_.genre AS genre3_0_0_,
    author0_.name AS name4_0_0_
```

```
FROM author author0_
WHERE author0_.id = 1 FOR SHARE
```

Starting second transaction ...

```
-- Transaction B fetches the same author and acquire a shared lock
SELECT
    author0_.id AS id1_0_0_,
    author0_.age AS age2_0_0_,
    author0_.genre AS genre3_0_0_,
    author0_.name AS name4_0_0_
FROM author author0_
WHERE author0_.id = 1 FOR SHARE
```

Commit second transaction ...

```
-- Transaction B wants to update the author's genre
-- Transaction B times out since it cannot acquire a lock for modifying
-- this row as long as transaction A is holding a shared lock on it
UPDATE author
SET age = 23,
    genre = "Horror",
    name = "Mark Janel"
WHERE id = 1

-- Transaction B causes a QueryTimeoutException
-- org.springframework.dao.QueryTimeoutException
-- Caused by: org.hibernate.QueryTimeoutException
```

> Employing the InnoDB engine via MySQL5InnoDBDialect or MySQL8Dialect works as expected.

## PostgreSQL and PostgreSQL95Dialect

In the case of PostgreSQL and `PostgreSQL95Dialect`, the syntax relies on `FOR SHARE` to acquire a shared lock. The following `SELECT` is an example:

```
SELECT
    author0_.id AS id1_0_0_,
    author0_.age AS age2_0_0_,
    author0_.genre AS genre3_0_0_,
    author0_.name AS name4_0_0_
FROM author author0_
WHERE author0_.id = ? FOR SHARE
```

## Other RDBMS

Oracle doesn't support row-level shared locks.

SQL Server acquires shared locks via the `WITH (HOLDLOCK, ROWLOCK)` table hint.

# PESSIMISTIC_WRITE

Creating this scenario in the `PESSIMISTIC_WRITE` context should result in the following flow:

> Step 1: Transaction A fetches the author with an ID of *1* and acquires an exclusive lock.

> Step 2: Transaction B wants to update the genre of an author with an ID of *1* to *Horror*. It attempts to fetch this author and to acquire an exclusive lock.

> Step 3: Transaction B times out since it cannot acquire a lock for modifying this row as long as Transaction A is holding an exclusive lock on it.

> Step 4: Transaction B causes a `QueryTimeoutException`.

Now, let's see how this flow is respected by different databases and dialects.

# MySQL and MySQL5Dialect dialect (MyISAM)

When running the aforementioned pessimisticReadWrite() via MySQL5Dialect,
Hibernate generates the following output. Notice the presence of LOCK IN SHARE MODE
in the SELECT statements. This is MySQL specific syntax for shared locks:

```
Starting first transaction ...

-- Transaction A fetches the author with id 1 and acquire an exclusive lock
SELECT
    author0_.id AS id1_0_0_,
    author0_.age AS age2_0_0_,
    author0_.genre AS genre3_0_0_,
    author0_.name AS name4_0_0_
FROM author author0_
WHERE author0_.id = 1 FOR UPDATE

Starting second transaction ...

-- Transaction B wants to update the genre of author with id 1 to Horror
-- It attempts to fetch this author and to acquire an exclusive lock
SELECT
    author0_.id AS id1_0_0_,
    author0_.age AS age2_0_0_,
    author0_.genre AS genre3_0_0_,
    author0_.name AS name4_0_0_
FROM author author0_
WHERE author0_.id = 1 FOR UPDATE

Commit second transaction ...

-- Transaction B updates the author's genre successfully
UPDATE author
SET age = 23,
    genre = "Horror",
    name = "Mark Janel"
WHERE id = 1
```

```
Resuming first transaction ...
Commit first transaction ...
```

Done!

`--`

> Even if the syntax for acquiring exclusive locks is present (FOR UPDATE), MyISAM engine doesn't actually acquire exclusive locks. Therefore, avoid the `MySQL5Dialect` dialect.

## MySQL and MySQL5InnoDBDialect/ MySQL8Dialect Dialects (InnoDB)

When running the aforementioned `pessimisticReadWrite()` via `MySQL5InnoDBDialect` or `MySQL8Dialect`, the result will follow the steps of this scenario. So, using the InnoDB engine applies locks as expected.

In syntax terms, both dialects use FOR UPDATE. The following output is common to `MySQL5InnoDBDialect` and `MySQL8Dialect`:

```
Starting first transaction ...

-- Transaction A fetches the author with id 1 and acquire an exclusive lock
SELECT
   author0_.id AS id1_0_0_,
   author0_.age AS age2_0_0_,
   author0_.genre AS genre3_0_0_,
   author0_.name AS name4_0_0_
FROM author author0_
WHERE author0_.id = 1 FOR UPDATE

Starting second transaction ...

-- Transaction B wants to update the genre of author with id 1 to Horror
-- It attempts to fetch this author and to acquire an exclusive lock
-- Transaction B times out since it cannot acquire a lock for modifying
-- this row as long as transaction A is holding an exclusive lock on it
```

**SELECT**
    author0_.id **AS** id1_0_0_,
    author0_.age **AS** age2_0_0_,
    author0_.genre **AS** genre3_0_0_,
    author0_.name **AS** name4_0_0_
**FROM** author author0_
**WHERE** author0_.id = 1 **FOR UPDATE**

-- *Transaction B causes a QueryTimeoutException*
-- org.springframework.dao.QueryTimeoutException
-- Caused by: org.hibernate.QueryTimeoutException

> Employing the InnoDB engine via MySQL5InnoDBDialect or MySQL8Dialect
> works as expected.

## PostgreSQL and PostgreSQL95Dialect

In the case of PostgreSQL and PostgreSQL95Dialect, the syntax relies on FOR UPDATE to acquire a shared lock. The following SELECT is an example:

**SELECT**
    author0_.id **AS** id1_0_0_,
    author0_.age **AS** age2_0_0_,
    author0_.genre **AS** genre3_0_0_,
    author0_.name **AS** name4_0_0_
**FROM** author author0_
**WHERE** author0_.id = ? **FOR UPDATE**

## Other RDBMS

Oracle acquires exclusive locks via FOR UPDATE.

SQL Server acquires exclusive locks via the WITH (UPDLOCK, HOLDLOCK, ROWLOCK) table hint.

The complete application is available on GitHub[68].

---

[68]HibernateSpringBootPessimisticLocks

# Item 137: How PESSIMISTIC_WRITE Works with UPDATE/INSERT and DELETE Operations

When we talk about PESSIMISTIC_WRITE, we talk about exclusive locks. Consider the Author entity and the following repository, AuthorRepository:

```
@Repository
public interface AuthorRepository extends JpaRepository<Author, Long> {

    @Override
    @Lock(LockModeType.PESSIMISTIC_WRITE)
    public Optional<Author> findById(Long id);

    @Lock(LockModeType.PESSIMISTIC_WRITE)
    public List<Author> findByAgeBetween(int start, int end);

    @Modifying
    @Query("UPDATE Author SET genre = ?1 WHERE id = ?2")
    public void updateGenre(String genre, long id);
}
```

## Trigger UPDATE

The scenario that we want to use is based on the previous repository and follows these steps:

> Step 1: Transaction A selects the author with an ID of *1* via findById() and acquires an exclusive lock. This transaction will run for 10 seconds.

> Step 2: While Transaction A is running, Transaction B starts after two seconds and calls the updateGenre() method to update the genre of the author fetched by Transaction A. Transaction B times out after 15 seconds.

To see when the UPDATE is triggered, let's use two threads to represent the two transactions via TransactionTemplate:

```
public void pessimisticWriteUpdate() throws InterruptedException {
```

```
Thread tA = new Thread(() -> {
    template.setPropagationBehavior(
        TransactionDefinition.PROPAGATION_REQUIRES_NEW);

    template.execute(new TransactionCallbackWithoutResult() {

        @Override
        protected void doInTransactionWithoutResult(
                            TransactionStatus status) {

            log.info("Starting first transaction ...");

            Author author = authorRepository.findById(1L).
            orElseThrow();

            try {
                log.info("Locking for 10s ...");
                Thread.sleep(10000);
                log.info("Releasing lock ...");
            } catch (InterruptedException ex) {
                Thread.currentThread().interrupt();
            }
        }
    });

    log.info("First transaction committed!");
});

Thread tB = new Thread(() -> {
    template.setPropagationBehavior(
    TransactionDefinition.PROPAGATION_REQUIRES_NEW);
    template.setTimeout(15); // 15 seconds

    template.execute(new TransactionCallbackWithoutResult() {

        @Override
        protected void doInTransactionWithoutResult(
                            TransactionStatus status) {

            log.info("Starting second transaction ...");
```

```
                authorRepository.updateGenre("Horror", 1L);
            }
        });

        log.info("Second transaction committed!");
    });

    tA.start();
    Thread.sleep(2000);
    tB.start();

    tA.join();
    tB.join();
}
```

Calling `pessimisticWriteUpdate()` reveals the following output:

Starting first transaction ...

**SELECT**
  author0_.id **AS** id1_0_0_ ,
  author0_.age **AS** age2_0_0_ ,
  author0_.genre **AS** genre3_0_0_ ,
  author0_.name **AS** name4_0_0_
**FROM** author author0_
**WHERE** author0_.id = 1 **FOR UPDATE**

Locking for 10s ...

Starting second transaction ...

**UPDATE** author
**SET** genre = "Horror"
**WHERE** id = 1

Releasing lock ...

First transaction committed!

Second transaction committed!

Transaction B triggers the update only after Transaction A commits. In other words, Transaction B is blocked until it times out or until Transaction A releases the exclusive lock.

## Trigger DELETE

Further, let's tackle a scenario that attempts to delete a locked row:

> Step 1: Transaction A selects the author with an ID of *1* via findById() and acquires an exclusive lock. This transaction will run for 10 seconds.

> Step 2: While Transaction A is running, Transaction B starts after two seconds and calls the built-in query-method findById()to delete the author fetched by Transaction A. Transaction B times out after 15 seconds.

To see when the DELETE is triggered, let's use two threads to represent the two transactions via TransactionTemplate:

```
public void pessimisticWriteDelete() throws InterruptedException {

    Thread tA = new Thread(() -> {
        template.setPropagationBehavior(
            TransactionDefinition.PROPAGATION_REQUIRES_NEW);

        template.execute(new TransactionCallbackWithoutResult() {

            @Override
            protected void doInTransactionWithoutResult(
                                    TransactionStatus status) {

                log.info("Starting first transaction ...");

                Author author = authorRepository.findById(1L).
                orElseThrow();
```

```
                try {
                    log.info("Locking for 10s ...");
                    Thread.sleep(10000);
                    log.info("Releasing lock ...");
                } catch (InterruptedException ex) {
                    Thread.currentThread().interrupt();
                }
            }
        });

        log.info("First transaction committed!");
    });

    Thread tB = new Thread(() -> {
        template.setPropagationBehavior(
            TransactionDefinition.PROPAGATION_REQUIRES_NEW);
        template.setTimeout(15); // 15 seconds

        template.execute(new TransactionCallbackWithoutResult() {

            @Override
            protected void doInTransactionWithoutResult(
                            TransactionStatus status) {

                log.info("Starting second transaction ...");

                authorRepository.deleteById(1L);
            }
        });

        log.info("Second transaction committed!");
    });

    tA.start();
    Thread.sleep(2000);
    tB.start();

    tA.join();
    tB.join();
}
```

Calling pessimisticWriteDelete() reveals the following output:

```
Starting first transaction ...
```

**SELECT**
    author0_.id **AS** id1_0_0_,
    author0_.age **AS** age2_0_0_,
    author0_.genre **AS** genre3_0_0_,
    author0_.name **AS** name4_0_0_
**FROM** author author0_
**WHERE** author0_.id = 1 **FOR UPDATE**

```
Locking for 10s ...
```

```
Starting second transaction ...
```

**SELECT**
    author0_.id **AS** id1_0_0_,
    author0_.age **AS** age2_0_0_,
    author0_.genre **AS** genre3_0_0_,
    author0_.name **AS** name4_0_0_
**FROM** author author0_
**WHERE** author0_.id = 1

**DELETE FROM** author
**WHERE** id = 1

```
Releasing lock ...
```

```
First transaction committed!
```

```
Second transaction committed!
```

> Transaction B triggers the delete only after Transaction A commits. In other words, Transaction B is blocked until it times out or until Transaction A releases the exclusive lock.

# Trigger INSERT

Typically, even with exclusive locks, INSERT statements are possible (e.g., PostgreSQL). Let's focus on the following scenario:

> Step 1: Transaction A selects all authors whose age is between *40* and *50* via findByAgeBetween() and acquires an exclusive lock. This transaction will run for 10 seconds.

> Step 2: While Transaction A is running, Transaction B starts after two seconds and attempts to insert a new author. Transaction B times out after 15 seconds.

To see when the INSERT is triggered, let's use two threads to represent the two transactions via TransactionTemplate:

```
public void pessimisticWriteInsert(int isolationLevel)
                                    throws InterruptedException {

    Thread tA = new Thread(() -> {
        template.setPropagationBehavior(
            TransactionDefinition.PROPAGATION_REQUIRES_NEW);
        template.setIsolationLevel(isolationLevel);

        template.execute(new TransactionCallbackWithoutResult() {

            @Override
            protected void doInTransactionWithoutResult(
                                    TransactionStatus status) {

                log.info("Starting first transaction ...");

                List<Author> authors
                    = authorRepository.findByAgeBetween(40, 50);

                try {
                    log.info("Locking for 10s ...");
                    Thread.sleep(10000);
                    log.info("Releasing lock ...");
                } catch (InterruptedException ex) {
```

```java
                        Thread.currentThread().interrupt();
                }
            }
        });

        log.info("First transaction committed!");
    });

    Thread tB = new Thread(() -> {
        template.setPropagationBehavior(
            TransactionDefinition.PROPAGATION_REQUIRES_NEW);
        template.setTimeout(15); // 15 seconds

        template.execute(new TransactionCallbackWithoutResult() {

            @Override
            protected void doInTransactionWithoutResult(
                                    TransactionStatus status) {

                log.info("Starting second transaction ...");

                Author author = new Author();
                author.setAge(43);
                author.setName("Joel Bornis");
                author.setGenre("Anthology");

                authorRepository.saveAndFlush(author);
            }
        });

        log.info("Second transaction committed!");
    });

    tA.start();
    Thread.sleep(2000);
    tB.start();

    tA.join();
    tB.join();
}
```

# Trigger INSERT in MySQL with REPEATABLE_READ

As noted, even with exclusive locks, INSERT statements are typically possible (e.g., PostgreSQL). The exception is MySQL, which for the default isolation level, REPEATABLE READ, it can prevent INSERT statements against a range of locked entries.

Let's call the aforementioned `pessimisticWriteInsert()` service-method with a REPEATABLE_READ isolation level (this is the default isolation level in MySQL):

```
pessimisticWriteInsert(TransactionDefinition.ISOLATION_REPEATABLE_READ);
```

The following output reveals the flow:

```
Starting first transaction ...
```

```sql
SELECT
  author0_.id AS id1_0_,
  author0_.age AS age2_0_,
  author0_.genre AS genre3_0_,
  author0_.name AS name4_0_
FROM author author0_
WHERE author0_.age BETWEEN ? AND ? FOR UPDATE
```

```
Locking for 10s ...
```

```
Starting second transaction ...
```

```sql
INSERT INTO author (age, genre, name)
  VALUES (?, ?, ?)
```

```
Releasing lock ...
```

```
First transaction committed!
```

```
Second transaction committed!
```

> Transaction B triggers the insert only after Transaction A commits. In other words, Transaction B is blocked until it times out or until Transaction A releases the exclusive lock.

## Trigger INSERT in MySQL with READ_COMMITTED

Now, let's switch to the READ_COMMITTED isolation level:

```
pessimisticWriteInsert(TransactionDefinition.ISOLATION_READ_COMMITTED);
```

This time, the output is as follows:

```
Starting first transaction ...

SELECT
    author0_.id AS id1_0_,
    author0_.age AS age2_0_,
    author0_.genre AS genre3_0_,
    author0_.name AS name4_0_
FROM author author0_
WHERE author0_.age BETWEEN ? AND ? FOR UPDATE

Locking for 10s ...

Starting second transaction ...

INSERT INTO author (age, genre, name)
    VALUES (?, ?, ?)

Second transaction committed!

Releasing lock ...

First transaction committed!
```

Transaction B triggers the insert even if Transaction A is holding an exclusive lock. In other words, Transaction B is not blocked by the exclusive lock of Transaction A.

The complete application is available on GitHub[69].

---

[69]HibernateSpringBootPessimisticLocksDelInsUpd

# CHAPTER 15

# Inheritance

## Item 138: How to Efficiently Use Single Table Inheritance

The single table inheritance is the default JPA strategy. Conforming to this strategy, all the classes in an inheritance hierarchy are represented via a single table in the database.

Consider the inheritance hierarchy given in Figure 15-1.

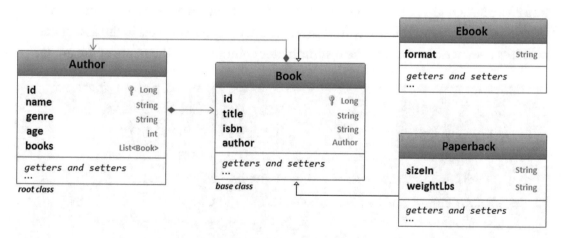

***Figure 15-1.*** *Single table inheritance Domain Model*

Between Author and Book there is a bidirectional lazy @OneToMany association. The Author entity can be seen as the *root class,* since without authors there are no books. The Book entity is the *base class.* To employ the single table inheritance strategy, this class is annotated with @Inheritance or @Inheritance(strategy = InheritanceType. SINGLE_TABLE). The Ebook and Paperback entities extend the Book entity; therefore, they don't need their own @Id.

© Anghel Leonard 2020
A. Leonard, *Spring Boot Persistence Best Practices*, https://doi.org/10.1007/978-1-4842-5626-8_15

The tables that shape this inheritance strategy are shown in Figure 15-2.

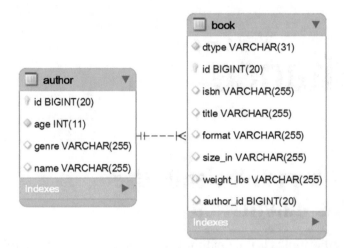

***Figure 15-2.***  *Tables of single table inheritance strategy*

The book table contains columns associated with the Book entity and with the Ebook and Paperback entities. It also contains a column named dtype. This is known as the *discriminator column*. Hibernate uses this column to map result sets to the associated subclass instances. By default, the discriminator column holds the name of the entity.

> If you have to use the SINGLE_TABLE strategy with a legacy database then most probably you will not have a discriminator column and you cannot alter table definitions. In such cases, you can use @DiscriminatorFormula to define a formula (a derived value) as the inheritance discriminator column. Once you are aware of @DiscriminatorFormula, you can easy find examples on the Internet.

The relevant code of the Book base class and its subclasses is listed here:

```
@Entity
@Inheritance(strategy = InheritanceType.SINGLE_TABLE)
public class Book implements Serializable {
    ...
}
```

```
@Entity
public class Ebook extends Book implements Serializable {

    ...
}

@Entity
public class Paperback extends Book implements Serializable {

    ...
}
```

## Persisting Data

It's time to persist some data. The following service-method persists an Author with three books created via the Book, Ebook, and Paperback entities:

```
public void persistAuthorWithBooks() {

    Author author = new Author();
    author.setName("Alicia Tom");
    author.setAge(38);
    author.setGenre("Anthology");

    Book book = new Book();
    book.setIsbn("001-AT");
    book.setTitle("The book of swords");

    Paperback paperback = new Paperback();
    paperback.setIsbn("002-AT");
    paperback.setTitle("The beatles anthology");
    paperback.setSizeIn("7.5 x 1.3 x 9.2");
    paperback.setWeightLbs("2.7");

    Ebook ebook = new Ebook();
    ebook.setIsbn("003-AT");
    ebook.setTitle("Anthology myths");
    ebook.setFormat("kindle");

    author.addBook(book); // use addBook() helper
    author.addBook(paperback);
```

```
    author.addBook(ebook);

    authorRepository.save(author);
}
```

Saving the author instance triggers the following SQL statements:

```
INSERT INTO author (age, genre, name)
  VALUES (?, ?, ?)
Binding:[38, Anthology, Alicia Tom]
```

```
INSERT INTO book (author_id, isbn, title, dtype)
  VALUES (?, ?, ?, 'Book')
Binding:[1, 001-AT, The book of swords]
```

```
INSERT INTO book (author_id, isbn, title, size_in, weight_lbs, dtype)
  VALUES (?, ?, ?, ?, ?, 'Paperback')
Binding:[1, 002-AT, The beatles anthology, 7.5 x 1.3 x 9.2, 2.7]
```

```
INSERT INTO book (author_id, isbn, title, format, dtype)
  VALUES (?, ?, ?, ?, 'Ebook')
Binding:[1, 003-AT, Anthology myths, kindle]
```

The author was saved in the author table, while the books (book, ebook, and paperback) were saved in the book table. So, persisting (writing) data is efficient, since all books have been saved in the same table.

## Queries and Single Table Inheritance

Now, let's check out the efficiency of fetching data. Consider the following BookRepository:

```
@Repository
@Transactional(readOnly = true)
public interface BookRepository extends JpaRepository<Book, Long> {

    @Query("SELECT b FROM Book b WHERE b.author.id = ?1")
    List<Book> fetchBooksByAuthorId(Long authorId);

    Book findByTitle(String title);
}
```

# Fetching the Books by Author Identifier

Let's call fetchBooksByAuthorId():

List<Book> books = bookRepository.fetchBooksByAuthorId(1L);

The triggered SELECT is as follows:

```
SELECT
  book0_.id AS id2_1_,
  book0_.author_id AS author_i8_1_,
  book0_.isbn AS isbn3_1_,
  book0_.title AS title4_1_,
  book0_.format AS format5_1_,
  book0_.size_in AS size_in6_1_,
  book0_.weight_lbs AS weight_l7_1_,
  book0_.dtype AS dtype1_1_
FROM book book0_
WHERE book0_.author_id = ?
```

Inheritance provides support for polymorphic queries. In other words, the fetched result set is correctly mapped to the base class (Book) and subclasses (Ebook and Paperback). Hibernate does this by inspecting the discriminator column of each fetched row.

# Fetching the Books by Title

Further, let's call findByTitle() for each book:

```
Book b1 = bookRepository.findByTitle("The book of swords");     // Book
Book b2 = bookRepository.findByTitle("The beatles anthology"); // Paperback
Book b3 = bookRepository.findByTitle("Anthology myths");        // Ebook
```

The triggered SELECT is the same for all three types of books:

```
SELECT
  book0_.id AS id2_1_,
  book0_.author_id AS author_i8_1_,
  book0_.isbn AS isbn3_1_,
  book0_.title AS title4_1_,
  book0_.format AS format5_1_,
  book0_.size_in AS size_in6_1_,
```

```
book0_.weight_lbs AS weight_l7_1_,
book0_.dtype AS dtype1_1_
FROM book book0_
WHERE book0_.title = ?
```

Fetching b1, b2, and b3 as Book instances doesn't confuse Hibernate. Since b2 is a Paperback, it can be explicitly casted to display the size and weight:

```
Paperback p = (Paperback) b2;
System.out.println(p.getSizeIn());
System.out.println(p.getWeightLbs());
```

Of course, this is not as practical as relying on dedicated repositories of subclasses. Notice that we defined findByTitle() in BookRepository. If we want to use it from EbookRepository or PaperbackRepository then it is not practical to duplicate it (generally speaking, it is not practical to duplicate query-methods in all repositories). In such cases, start by defining the findByTitle() in a @NoRepositoryBean class:

```
@NoRepositoryBean
public interface BookBaseRepository<T extends Book>
                        extends JpaRepository<T, Long> {

    T findByTitle(String title);

    @Query(value="SELECT b FROM #{#entityName} AS b WHERE b.isbn = ?1")
    T fetchByIsbn(String isbn);
}
```

Next, BookRepository, EbookRepository and PaperbackRepository extend BookBaseRepository. This way, findByTitle() and findByIsbn() are available in all repositories that extends the base repository. The complete application is available on GitHub[1].

---

[1]HibernateSpringBootSingleTableRepositoryInheritance

# Fetching the Paperbacks

Consider the Paperback repository listed here:

```
@Repository
@Transactional(readOnly = true)
public interface PaperbackRepository
    extends JpaRepository<Paperback, Long> {

    Paperback findByTitle(String title);
}
```

Now, let's trigger two queries. The first query uses the title that identifies a Book. The second query uses the title that identifies a Paperback:

```
// this is a Book
Paperback p1 = paperbackRepository.findByTitle("The book of swords");

// this is a Paperback
Paperback p2 = paperbackRepository.findByTitle("The beatles anthology");
```

Both queries trigger the same SELECT:

```
SELECT
    paperback0_.id AS id2_1_,
    paperback0_.author_id AS author_i8_1_,
    paperback0_.isbn AS isbn3_1_,
    paperback0_.title AS title4_1_,
    paperback0_.size_in AS size_in6_1_,
    paperback0_.weight_lbs AS weight_l7_1_
FROM book paperback0_
WHERE paperback0_.dtype = 'Paperback'
AND paperback0_.title = ?
```

Notice the WHERE clause. Hibernate has appended a dtype-based condition for fetching only a paperback; therefore, p1 will be null while p2 will be a Paperback instance. That's so cool, right?!

# Fetching the Author and the Associated Books

Consider the following Author repository:

```
@Repository
@Transactional(readOnly = true)
public interface AuthorRepository extends JpaRepository<Author, Long> {

    Author findByName(String name);

    @Query("SELECT a FROM Author a JOIN FETCH a.books b")
    public Author findAuthor();
}
```

Calling findByName() will fetch the author without the associated books:

```
@Transactional(readOnly = true)
public void fetchAuthorAndBooksLazy() {
    Author author = authorRepository.findByName("Alicia Tom");
    List<Book> books = author.getBooks();
}
```

Calling getBooks() triggers a secondary query as expected:

```
-- fetch the author
SELECT
  author0_.id AS id1_0_,
  author0_.age AS age2_0_,
  author0_.genre AS genre3_0_,
  author0_.name AS name4_0_
FROM author author0_
WHERE author0_.name = ?

-- fetch the books via getBooks()
SELECT
  books0_.author_id AS author_i8_1_0_,
  books0_.id AS id2_1_0_,
  books0_.id AS id2_1_1_,
  books0_.author_id AS author_i8_1_1_,
```

```
   books0_.isbn AS isbn3_1_1_,
   books0_.title AS title4_1_1_,
   books0_.format AS format5_1_1_,
   books0_.size_in AS size_in6_1_1_,
   books0_.weight_lbs AS weight_l7_1_1_,
   books0_.dtype AS dtype1_1_1_
FROM book books0_
WHERE books0_.author_id = ?
```

This is exactly the expected behavior.

On the other hand, thanks to JOIN FETCH, calling findAuthor() will fetch the author and the associated books in the same SELECT:

```
@Transactional(readOnly = true)
public void fetchAuthorAndBooksEager() {
    Author author = authorRepository.findAuthor();
}
```

The triggered SELECT relies on INNER JOIN as follows:

```
SELECT
   author0_.id AS id1_0_0_,
   books1_.id AS id2_1_1_,
   author0_.age AS age2_0_0_,
   author0_.genre AS genre3_0_0_,
   author0_.name AS name4_0_0_,
   books1_.author_id AS author_i8_1_1_,
   books1_.isbn AS isbn3_1_1_,
   books1_.title AS title4_1_1_,
   books1_.format AS format5_1_1_,
   books1_.size_in AS size_in6_1_1_,
   books1_.weight_lbs AS weight_l7_1_1_,
   books1_.dtype AS dtype1_1_1_,
   books1_.author_id AS author_i8_1_0__,
   books1_.id AS id2_1_0__
```

```
FROM author author0_
INNER JOIN book books1_
  ON author0_.id = books1_.author_id
```

Nice! Looks like the single table inheritance sustains fast reads and writes.

## Subclasses Attributes Non-Nullability Issue

Specifying non-nullable constraints on the *base class* (Book) is supported and straightforward, as in the following example:

```
public class Book implements Serializable {

    ...
    @Column(nullable=false)
    private String title;

    ...
}
```

Attempting to persist Book will result in the expected exception of type `SQLIntegrityConstraintViolationException: Column 'title' cannot be null`:

```
Book book = new Book();
book.setIsbn("001-AT");
book.setTitle(null);
```

But attempting to add non-nullable constraints on subclasses of Book is not allowed. In other words, is not possible to add `NOT NULL` constraints to columns belonging to Ebook or Paperback. This means that the following Ebook is successfully persisted:

```
Ebook ebook = new Ebook();
ebook.setIsbn("003-AT");
ebook.setTitle("Anthology myths");
ebook.setFormat(null);
```

Obviously, setting the `format` to null defeats the purpose of creating this Ebook. So, creating an Ebook should not accept null for `format`. In the same manner, creating a Paperback should not accept null for `sizeIn` or `weightLbs`.

Nevertheless, there are several solutions for ensuring subclass attributes' non-nullability. First, on Domain Model, rely on `javax.validation.constraints.NotNull` to annotate the corresponding fields, as in the following examples:

```
public class Ebook extends Book implements Serializable {
    ...
    @NotNull
    private String format;
    ...
}

public class Paperback extends Book implements Serializable {
    ...
    @NotNull
    private String sizeIn;
    @NotNull
    private String weightLbs;
    ...
}
```

This time, attempting to persist this ebook will result in an exception of type `javax.validation.ConstraintViolationException`, which mentions that `format` cannot be null.

This solves only half of the problem. There is also the possibility to insert rows with `null` formats via a native query. Blocking such attempts implies a check at the database level.

For MySQL, this can be accomplished via a set of triggers created for the base class (or, in PostgreSQL and other RDBMSs, the `CHECK` constraint). For example, the following triggers act at the database level and disallow `null` formats (in the case of Ebook) and `null` sizes or weights (in the case of Paperback):

Here's the trigger for EBook:

```
CREATE TRIGGER ebook_format_trigger
  BEFORE INSERT ON book
    FOR EACH ROW
```

```
    BEGIN
      IF NEW.DTYPE = 'Ebook' THEN
        IF NEW.format IS NULL THEN
          SIGNAL SQLSTATE '45000'
          SET MESSAGE_TEXT='The format of e-book cannot be null';
        END IF;
      END IF;
    END;
```

Here are the triggers for Paperback:

```
CREATE TRIGGER paperback_weight_trigger
BEFORE INSERT ON book
  FOR EACH ROW
    BEGIN
      IF NEW.DTYPE = 'Paperback' THEN
        IF NEW.weight_lbs IS NULL THEN
          SIGNAL SQLSTATE '45000'
          SET MESSAGE_TEXT='The weight of paperback cannot be null';
        END IF;
      END IF;
    END;

CREATE TRIGGER paperback_size_trigger
  BEFORE INSERT ON book
    FOR EACH ROW
      BEGIN
        IF NEW.DTYPE = 'Paperback' THEN
          IF NEW.size_in IS NULL THEN
            SIGNAL SQLSTATE '45000'
            SET MESSAGE_TEXT='The size of paperback cannot be null';
          END IF;
        END IF;
      END;
```

These triggers should be added to your schema files. Placing them in an SQL file requires you to set the `spring.datasource.separator` in `application. properties`:

```
spring.datasource.separator=^;
```

Then in the SQL file, all ; statements not within the trigger need to be updated with the new separator, as in the following example:

```
CREATE TRIGGER ebook_format_trigger
    ...
    END ^;
```

In the code bundled with this book, the triggers were added to `data-mysql. sql`. It's better to add them to `schema-mysql.sql` or, even better, to SQL files for Flyway or Liquibase. I used this way to allow you to see how Hibernate generates the DDL schema based on the single table inheritance annotations.

---

As a rule of thumb, database triggers are very useful for implementing complex data integrity constraints and rules. Here[2] is an example that backs up this statement.

## Optimize Memory Footprint of the Discriminator Column

Adjusting the size and data types of columns is an important step for optimizing the memory footprint of your databases. The discriminator column is added by the JPA persistence provider and its data type and size is VARCHAR(31). But storing the Paperback name requires at least 9 bytes, while storing the Ebook name requires 4 bytes. Imagine storing 100,000 paperbacks and 500,000 ebooks. Storing the discriminator column indexes will require $100000 * 9 + 500000 * 4 = 2900000$ bytes, which is 2.76MB. But, how about defining the discriminator column as TINYINT(1)? This time, 1 byte is needed, so the computation becomes $100000 * 1 + 500000 * 1 = 600000$ bytes, which is 0.57MB. This is way better!

---

[2]HibernateSpringBootDatabaseTriggers

You can alter the default discriminator column via @DiscriminatorColumn and @DiscriminatorValue. First, use @DiscriminatorColumn to change the type and size of the discriminator column. Second, use the @DiscriminatorValue to assign an integer to each class (these integers should be used further to reference the classes):

```
@Entity
@Inheritance(strategy = InheritanceType.SINGLE_TABLE)
@DiscriminatorColumn(
    discriminatorType = DiscriminatorType.INTEGER,
    columnDefinition = "TINYINT(1)"
)

@DiscriminatorValue("1")
public class Book implements Serializable {

    ...

}

@Entity
@DiscriminatorValue("2")
public class Ebook extends Book implements Serializable {

    ...

}

@Entity
@DiscriminatorValue("3")
public class Paperback extends Book implements Serializable {

    ...

}
```

That's all! The complete application is available on GitHub[3].

---

[3]HibernateSpringBootSingleTableInheritance

Now let's look at some pros and cons of single table inheritance.

Pros:

- Reads and writes are fast

- @ManyToOne, @OneToOne, and @OneToMany are efficient

- The base class attributes may be non-nullable

Cons:

- NOT NULL constraints are not allowed for subclass columns, but, as you saw, there are solutions to this problem.

## Item 139: How to Fetch Certain Subclasses from a SINGLE_TABLE Inheritance Hierarchy

This item uses the Domain Model and knowledge from **Item 138**; therefore, consider getting familiar with that item first.

So, between Author and Book, there is a bidirectional lazy @OneToMany association. The Ebook and Paperback entities extend the Book entity by relying on the SINGLE_TABLE inheritance strategy.

The book table contains columns associated with the Book entity and with the Ebook and Paperback entities. It also contains a column named dtype. This is known as the discriminator column.

You can fetch a certain subclass (e.g., Ebook) via its dedicated repository, as in the following example (here, the query fetches an Ebook by title):

```
@Repository
@Transactional(readOnly = true)
public interface EbookRepository extends JpaRepository<Ebook, Long> {

    Ebook findByTitle(String title);
}
```

```
SELECT
  ebook0_.id AS id2_1_,
  ebook0_.author_id AS author_i8_1_,
  ebook0_.isbn AS isbn3_1_,
  ebook0_.title AS title4_1_,
  ebook0_.size_in AS size_in6_1_,
  ebook0_.weight_lbs AS weight_l7_1_
FROM book ebook0_
WHERE ebook0_.dtype = 'Ebook'
AND ebook0_.title = ?
```

Notice the WHERE clause. Hibernate has appended a dtype based condition for fetching only ebooks.

This is absolutely great, but it doesn't always work like this. For example, consider the following @Query in the EbookRepository:

```
@Repository
@Transactional(readOnly = true)
public interface EbookRepository extends JpaRepository<Ebook, Long> {

    @Query("SELECT b FROM Author a JOIN a.books b WHERE a.name = ?1)
    public Ebook findByAuthorName(String name);
}
```

This time, the triggered SELECT looks as follows:

```
SELECT
  books1_.id AS id2_1_,
  books1_.author_id AS author_i8_1_,
  books1_.isbn AS isbn3_1_,
  books1_.title AS title4_1_,
  books1_.format AS format5_1_,
  books1_.size_in AS size_in6_1_,
  books1_.weight_lbs AS weight_l7_1_,
  books1_.dtype AS dtype1_1_
```

```
FROM author author0_
INNER JOIN book books1_
  ON author0_.id = books1_.author_id
WHERE author0_.name = ?
```

The discriminator column (dtype) was not automatically added to the WHERE clause, so this query will not fetch only Ebook. Obviously, this is not okay! The solution to this problem consists of relying on an explicit TYPE expression, as follows (see the bold query part):

```
@Repository
@Transactional(readOnly = true)
public interface EbookRepository extends JpaRepository<Ebook, Long> {

    @Query("SELECT b FROM Author a JOIN a.books b
            WHERE a.name = ?1 AND TYPE(b) = 'Ebook'")
    public Ebook findByAuthorName(String name);
}
```

This time, the triggered SELECT is as follows:

```
SELECT
  books1_.id AS id2_1_,
  books1_.author_id AS author_i8_1_,
  books1_.isbn AS isbn3_1_,
  books1_.title AS title4_1_,
  books1_.format AS format5_1_,
  books1_.size_in AS size_in6_1_,
  books1_.weight_lbs AS weight_l7_1_,
  books1_.dtype AS dtype1_1_
FROM author author0_
INNER JOIN book books1_
  ON author0_.id = books1_.author_id
WHERE author0_.name = ?
AND books1_.dtype = 'Ebook'
```

Thanks to the TYPE expression, things are getting back on track! How about fetching a Book of type Ebook of an Author? Via the TYPE expression, this kind of query can be written in the BookRepository as follows (the query definition is exactly the same as the previous one, but it is placed in BookRepository and it returns a Book of type Ebook):

```
@Repository
@Transactional(readOnly = true)
public interface BookRepository extends JpaRepository<Book, Long> {

    @Query("SELECT b FROM Author a JOIN a.books b
            WHERE a.name = ?1 AND TYPE(b) = 'Ebook'")
    public Book findByAuthorName(String name);
}
```

The complete application is available on GitHub[4].

# Item 140: How to Efficiently Use Join Table Inheritance

The join table is another JPA inheritance strategy. Conforming to this strategy, all the classes in an inheritance hierarchy are represented via individual tables in the database. Consider the inheritance hierarchy given in Figure 15-3.

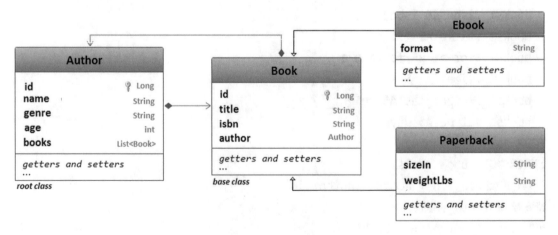

***Figure 15-3.*** *Join table inheritance Domain Model*

---

[4]HibernateSpringBootSpecificSubclassFromInheritance

Between Author and Book, there is a bidirectional-lazy @OneToMany association. The Author entity can be seen as the *root class* since without authors there are no books. The Book entity is the *base class*. To employ the join table inheritance strategy, this class is annotated with @Inheritance(strategy = InheritanceType.JOINED). The Ebook and Paperback entities extend the Book entity; therefore, they don't need their own @Id. The tables that shape this inheritance strategy are shown in Figure 15-4.

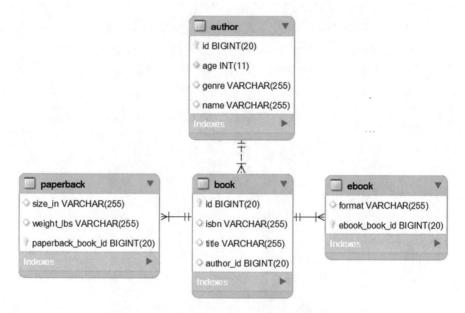

***Figure 15-4.***  *Tables of join table inheritance strategy*

The relevant code of the Book base class and subclasses is listed here:

```
@Entity
@Inheritance(strategy = InheritanceType.JOINED)
public class Book implements Serializable {

    ...
}

@Entity
@PrimaryKeyJoinColumn(name="ebook_book_id")
public class Ebook extends Book implements Serializable {

    ...
}
```

```
@Entity
@PrimaryKeyJoinColumn(name="paperback_book_id")
public class Paperback extends Book implements Serializable {

    ...

}
```

By default, subclass-tables contain a primary key column that acts as a foreign key as well. This foreign key references the *base class* table's primary key. You can customize this foreign key by annotating the subclasses with @PrimaryKeyJoinColumn. For example, the Ebook and Paperback subclasses rely on this annotation to customize the name of the foreign key column:

```
@Entity
@PrimaryKeyJoinColumn(name="ebook_book_id")
public class Ebook extends Book implements Serializable {

    ...

}

@Entity
@PrimaryKeyJoinColumn(name="paperback_book_id")
public class Paperback extends Book implements Serializable {

    ...

}
```

By default, the names of the primary key column of the *base class* and the primary key column of the subclasses are the same.

## Persisting Data

The following service-method persists an Author with three books created via the Book, Ebook, and Paperback entities:

```
public void persistAuthorWithBooks() {

    Author author = new Author();
    author.setName("Alicia Tom");
    author.setAge(38);
    author.setGenre("Anthology");

    Book book = new Book();
    book.setIsbn("001-AT");
    book.setTitle("The book of swords");

    Paperback paperback = new Paperback();
    paperback.setIsbn("002-AT");
    paperback.setTitle("The beatles anthology");
    paperback.setSizeIn("7.5 x 1.3 x 9.2");
    paperback.setWeightLbs("2.7");

    Ebook ebook = new Ebook();
    ebook.setIsbn("003-AT");
    ebook.setTitle("Anthology myths");
    ebook.setFormat("kindle");

    author.addBook(book); // use addBook() helper
    author.addBook(paperback);
    author.addBook(ebook);

    authorRepository.save(author);
}
```

Saving the author instance triggers the following SQL statements:

```
INSERT INTO author (age, genre, name)
  VALUES (?, ?, ?)
Binding:[38, Anthology, Alicia Tom]

INSERT INTO book (author_id, isbn, title)
  VALUES (?, ?, ?)
Binding:[1, 001-AT, The book of swords]

INSERT INTO book (author_id, isbn, title)
  VALUES (?, ?, ?)
```

```
Binding:[1, 002-AT, The beatles anthology]
INSERT INTO paperback (size_in, weight_lbs, paperback_book_id)
  VALUES (?, ?, ?)
Binding:[ 7.5 x 1.3 x 9.2, 2.7, 2]

INSERT INTO book (author_id, isbn, title)
  VALUES (?, ?, ?)
Binding:[1, 003-AT, Anthology myths]
INSERT INTO ebook (format, ebook_book_id)
  VALUES (?, ?)
Binding:[kindle, 3]
```

This time, there are more INSERT statements needed than in the case of single table inheritance strategy (see **Item 138**). Mainly, the data of the *base class* is inserted in the book table, while the data of the Ebook class, respectively the Paperback class, goes in the ebook and paperback tables. The more inserts there are, the more chances of a performance penalty.

## Queries and Join Table Inheritance

Now, let's check out the efficiency of fetching data. Consider the following BookRepository:

```
@Repository
@Transactional(readOnly = true)
public interface BookRepository extends JpaRepository<Book, Long> {

    @Query("SELECT b FROM Book b WHERE b.author.id = ?1")
    List<Book> fetchBooksByAuthorId(Long authorId);

    Book findByTitle(String title);
}
```

## Fetching the Books by Author Identifier

Let's call fetchBooksByAuthorId():

```
List<Book> books = bookRepository.fetchBooksByAuthorId(1L);
```

The triggered SELECT is as follows:

```
SELECT
  book0_.id AS id1_1_,
  book0_.author_id AS author_i4_1_,
  book0_.isbn AS isbn2_1_,
  book0_.title AS title3_1_,
  book0_1_.format AS format1_2_,
  book0_2_.size_in AS size_in1_3_,
  book0_2_.weight_lbs AS weight_l2_3_,
  CASE
    WHEN book0_1_.ebook_book_id IS NOT NULL THEN 1
    WHEN book0_2_.paperback_book_id IS NOT NULL THEN 2
    WHEN book0_.id IS NOT NULL THEN 0
  END AS clazz_
FROM book book0_
LEFT OUTER JOIN ebook book0_1_
  ON book0_.id = book0_1_.ebook_book_id
LEFT OUTER JOIN paperback book0_2_
  ON book0_.id = book0_2_.paperback_book_id
WHERE book0_.author_id = ?
```

There is a single SELECT, but Hibernate must join each subclass table. So, the number of subclass tables dictates the number of joins in polymorphic queries (for $n$ subclasses, there will be $n$ joins). Furthermore, the number of joins influences the query speed and the execution plan efficiency.

## Fetching the Books by Title

Let's call findByTitle() for each book:

```
Book b1 = bookRepository.findByTitle("The book of swords");     // Book
Book b2 = bookRepository.findByTitle("The beatles anthology");  // Paperback
Book b3 = bookRepository.findByTitle("Anthology myths");        // Ebook
```

The triggered SELECT is the same for all three types of books:

```
SELECT
  book0_.id AS id1_1_,
  book0_.author_id AS author_i4_1_,
  book0_.isbn AS isbn2_1_,
  book0_.title AS title3_1_,
  book0_1_.format AS format1_2_,
  book0_2_.size_in AS size_in1_3_,
  book0_2_.weight_lbs AS weight_l2_3_,
  CASE
    WHEN book0_1_.ebook_book_id IS NOT NULL THEN 1
    WHEN book0_2_.paperback_book_id IS NOT NULL THEN 2
    WHEN book0_.id IS NOT NULL THEN 0
  END AS clazz_
FROM book book0_
LEFT OUTER JOIN ebook book0_1_
  ON book0_.id = book0_1_.ebook_book_id
LEFT OUTER JOIN paperback book0_2_
  ON book0_.id = book0_2_.paperback_book_id
WHERE book0_.title = ?
```

Again, there is a single SELECT, but Hibernate must join each subclass table. So, fetching subclasses via the base class repository is not efficient. Let's see what happens with dedicated repositories of the subclasses.

## Fetching the Paperbacks

Consider the Paperback repository listed here:

```
@Repository
@Transactional(readOnly = true)
public interface PaperbackRepository
    extends JpaRepository<Paperback, Long> {

    Paperback findByTitle(String title);
}
```

Now, let's trigger two queries. The first query uses the title that identifies a Book. The second query uses the title that identifies a Paperback:

```
// this is a Book
Paperback p1 = paperbackRepository.findByTitle("The book of swords");

// this is a Paperback
Paperback p2 = paperbackRepository.findByTitle("The beatles anthology");
```

Both queries trigger the same SELECT (p1 will be null, while p2 will fetch a Paperback):

```
SELECT
  paperback0_.paperback_book_id AS id1_1_,
  paperback0_1_.author_id AS author_i4_1_,
  paperback0_1_.isbn AS isbn2_1_,
  paperback0_1_.title AS title3_1_,
  paperback0_.size_in AS size_in1_3_,
  paperback0_.weight_lbs AS weight_l2_3_
FROM paperback paperback0_
INNER JOIN book paperback0_1_
  ON paperback0_.paperback_book_id = paperback0_1_.id
WHERE paperback0_1_.title = ?
```

Fetching subclasses via the dedicated repositories requires a single join with the base class table.

> If it is possible, avoid fetching subclasses via the base class repository. Use subclasses' dedicated repositories. In the first case, the number of subclasses influences the number of joins, while in the second case, there will be a single join between the subclass and the base class tables. In other words, use queries rather than the subclass entities directly.

> Of course, this is not as practical as relying on dedicated repositories of subclasses. Notice that we defined findByTitle() in BookRepository. If we want to use it from EbookRepository or PaperbackRepository

then it is not practical to duplicate it (generally speaking, it is not practical to duplicate query-methods in all repositories). In such cases, start by defining the findByTitle() in a @NoRepositoryBean class:

```
@NoRepositoryBean
public interface BookBaseRepository<T extends Book>
                        extends JpaRepository<T, Long> {

    T findByTitle(String title);

    @Query(value="SELECT b FROM #{#entityName} AS b WHERE b.isbn = ?1")
    T fetchByIsbn(String isbn);

}
```

Next, BookRepository, EbookRepository and PaperbackRepository extend BookBaseRepository. This way, findByTitle() and findByIsbn() are available in all repositories that extends the base repository. The complete application is available on GitHub[5].

## Fetching the Author and the Associated Books

Consider the following Author repository:

```
@Repository
@Transactional(readOnly = true)
public interface AuthorRepository extends JpaRepository<Author, Long> {

    Author findByName(String name);

    @Query("SELECT a FROM Author a JOIN FETCH a.books b")
    public Author findAuthor();
}
```

---

[5]HibernateSpringBootJoinTableRepositoryInheritance

Calling findByName() will fetch the author without the associated books:

```
@Transactional(readOnly = true)
public void fetchAuthorAndBooksLazy() {
    Author author = authorRepository.findByName("Alicia Tom");
    List<Book> books = author.getBooks();
}
```

Calling getBooks() triggers a secondary query:

```
-- fetch the author
SELECT
  author0_.id AS id1_0_,
  author0_.age AS age2_0_,
  author0_.genre AS genre3_0_,
  author0_.name AS name4_0_
FROM author author0_
WHERE author0_.name = ?

-- fetch the books via getBooks()
SELECT
  books0_.author_id AS author_i4_1_0_,
  books0_.id AS id1_1_0_,
  books0_.id AS id1_1_1_,
  books0_.author_id AS author_i4_1_1_,
  books0_.isbn AS isbn2_1_1_,
  books0_.title AS title3_1_1_,
  books0_1_.format AS format1_2_1_,
  books0_2_.size_in AS size_in1_3_1_,
  books0_2_.weight_lbs AS weight_l2_3_1_,
  CASE
    WHEN books0_1_.ebook_book_id IS NOT NULL THEN 1
    WHEN books0_2_.paperback_book_id IS NOT NULL THEN 2
    WHEN books0_.id IS NOT NULL THEN 0
  END AS clazz_1_
FROM book books0_
LEFT OUTER JOIN ebook books0_1_
  ON books0_.id = books0_1_.ebook_book_id
```

```
LEFT OUTER JOIN paperback books0_2_
  ON books0_.id = books0_2_.paperback_book_id
WHERE books0_.author_id = ?
```

The secondary SELECT has the same drawback from earlier. There is a join for each subclass table. So, combining polymorphic queries and deep class hierarchies and/or a large number of subclasses will cause performance penalties.

On the other hand, thanks to JOIN FETCH, calling findAuthor() will fetch the author and the associated books in the same SELECT:

```
@Transactional(readOnly = true)
public void fetchAuthorAndBooksEager() {
    Author author = authorRepository.findAuthor();
}
```

The triggered SELECT is listed here:

```
SELECT
  author0_.id AS id1_0_0_,
  books1_.id AS id1_1_1_,
  author0_.age AS age2_0_0_,
  author0_.genre AS genre3_0_0_,
  author0_.name AS name4_0_0_,
  books1_.author_id AS author_i4_1_1_,
  books1_.isbn AS isbn2_1_1_,
  books1_.title AS title3_1_1_,
  books1_1_.format AS format1_2_1_,
  books1_2_.size_in AS size_in1_3_1_,
  books1_2_.weight_lbs AS weight_l2_3_1_,
  CASE
    WHEN books1_1_.ebook_book_id IS NOT NULL THEN 1
    WHEN books1_2_.paperback_book_id IS NOT NULL THEN 2
    WHEN books1_.id IS NOT NULL THEN 0
  END AS clazz_1_,
  books1_.author_id AS author_i4_1_0__, books1_.id AS id1_1_0__
FROM author author0_
```

```
INNER JOIN book books1_
  ON author0_.id = books1_.author_id
LEFT OUTER JOIN ebook books1_1_
  ON books1_.id = books1_1_.ebook_book_id
LEFT OUTER JOIN paperback books1_2_
  ON books1_.id = books1_2_.paperback_book_id
```

This time, the JPA persistence provider needs three joins. So, for $n$ subclasses there will be $n+1$ joins. This is not efficient.

---

Here are some pros and cons of join table inheritance.

Pros:

- The base class and subclasses attributes may be non-nullable

- As long as there are no polymorphic queries needed, this strategy is proper for a deep class hierarchy and/or a large number of subclasses

Cons:

- Persisting a subclass entity requires two INSERT statements

- Reads are efficient only via dedicated repositories of subclasses (in other words, use queries against the subclass entities directly)

- The database must index the base class and all subclass primary keys

- In the case of polymorphic queries, for $n$ subclasses, Hibernate needs $n$ or $n+1$ joins. This can lead to slow queries and increases the curve of determining the most efficient execution plan

---

The complete application is available on GitHub[6].

---

[6]HibernateSpringBootJoinTableInheritance

# How to Use JPA JOINED Inheritance Strategy and Strategy Design Patterns

First of all, strive to use inheritance strategies such as SINGLE_TABLE, JOINED, or TABLE_ PER_CLASS combined with a software design pattern (e.g., Template, State, Strategy, Visitor, etc.). Teaming up an inheritance strategy with a software design pattern is the best way to exploit a JPA inheritance. To propagate specific properties from a base class to all subclasses, you can use @MappedSuperclass.

The Strategy pattern is a well-known behavioral pattern. In a nutshell, the Strategy pattern allows you to define a group of algorithms, wrap each one in a class, and make them interchangeable.

For example, let's assume that at the end of each day your bookstore delivers the books ordered in that day. For ebooks, you send a download-link by email, while for paperbacks, we send a parcel. Of course, other strategies can be adopted, but let's keep things simple.

You start the development by writing the following interface:

```
public interface Delivery<T extends Book> {

    Class<? extends Book> ofBook();
    void deliver(T book);
}
```

The deliver() method is where the action takes place, while the ofBook() method simply returns the class type of the book that takes advantage of the strategy implementation. You will see immediately why you need this method. For now, let's add the strategies (for brevity, we simulate the deliveries via System.out.println()):

```
@Component
public class PaperbackDeliver implements Delivery<Paperback> {

    @Override
    public void deliver(Paperback book) {
        System.out.println("We've sent you a parcel containing the title "
            + book.getTitle() + " with a size of '" + book.getSizeIn()
            + "' and a weight of " + book.getWeightLbs());
    }
}
```

```
    @Override
    public Class<? extends Book> ofBook() {
        return Paperback.class;
    }
}

@Component
public class EbookDeliver implements Delivery<Ebook> {

    @Override
    public void deliver(Ebook book) {
        System.out.println("You can download the book named '"
            + book.getTitle() + "' from the following link: http://
            bookstore/" + book.getFormat() + "/" + book.getTitle());
    }

    @Override
    public Class<? extends Book> ofBook() {
        return Ebook.class;
    }

}
```

Next, you need a service that uses the strategies. The strategy beans (EbookDeliver and PaperbackDeliver) are automatically injected by Spring as a List<Delivery>. So, the new strategies will be automatically injected in DeliverService. Further, you loop this list and use ofBook() to build a map of strategies. The *key* in this map is the book class type (e.g., Ebook.class and Paperback.class), while the *value* is the strategy itself (the strategy bean instance). This way, you can call the proper deliver() method depending on the book type (ebook or paperback):

```
public interface Deliverable {

    void process();
}

@Service
public class DeliverService implements Deliverable {

    private final BookRepository bookRepository;
    private final List<Delivery> deliverStrategies;
```

```
    private final Map<Class<? extends Book>, Delivery>
        deliverStrategiesMap = new HashMap<>();

    public DeliverService(BookRepository bookRepository,
                            List<Delivery> deliverStrategies) {
        this.bookRepository = bookRepository;
        this.deliverStrategies = deliverStrategies;
    }

    @PostConstruct
    public void init() {
        deliverStrategies.forEach((deliverStrategy) -> {
            deliverStrategiesMap.put(deliverStrategy.ofBook(),
                                                deliverStrategy);
        });
    }

    @Override
    public void process() {

        // we just need some books to deliver
        List<Book> allBooks = bookRepository.findAll();

        for (Book book : allBooks) {
            Delivery deliveryStrategy
                = deliverStrategiesMap.get(book.getClass());
            deliveryStrategy.deliver(book);
        }
    }
}
```

The process() method is responsible for applying the strategy. You loop the books that should be delivered and apply the corresponding strategy. Just for grabbing some books for testing, you can apply a findAll() query.

The complete application is available on GitHub[7]. Moreover, on GitHub[8], you can find another example that uses the Visitor design pattern.

---

[7]HibernateSpringBootJoinedAndStrategy
[8]HibernateSpringBootJoinedAndVisitor

# Item 141: How to Efficiently Use Table-Per-Class Inheritance

The table-per-class is another JPA inheritance strategy. Conforming to this strategy, all the classes in an inheritance hierarchy are represented via individual tables in the database. Each subclass-table stores the columns inherited from the superclass-table (*base class*). Consider the inheritance hierarchy given in Figure 15-5.

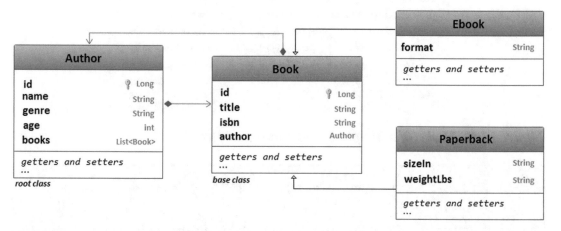

***Figure 15-5.***  *Table-per-class inheritance Domain Model*

Between Author and Book, there is a bidirectional-lazy @OneToMany association. The Author entity can be seen as the *root class* since without authors there are no books. The Book entity is the *base class*. To employ the table-per-class inheritance strategy, this class is annotated with @Inheritance(strategy = InheritanceType.TABLE_PER_CLASS). The Ebook and Paperback entities extend the Book entity, so they don't need their own @Id. The tables that shape this inheritance strategy are shown in Figure 15-6.

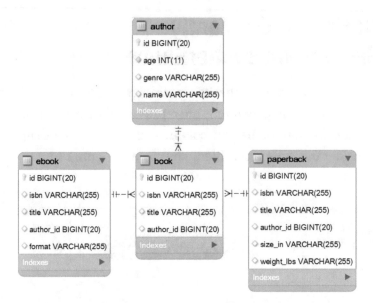

**Figure 15-6.** *Tables of table-per-class inheritance strategy*

Each subclass-table contains a primary key column. To ensure the uniqueness of the primary keys across subclass-tables, the table-per-class strategy cannot rely on the IDENTITY generator. Trying to use the IDENTITY generator results in an exception of type: Cannot use identity column key generation with <union-subclass> mapping.

This is an important drawback for RDBMSs such as MySQL. The IDENTITY is not allowed and SEQUENCE is not supported (MySQL does not support database sequences; therefore the SEQUENCE strategy is not supported). The TABLE generator type doesn't scale well and is much slower than the IDENTITY and SEQUENCE generator types, even for a single database connection. So, you should avoid the combination of MySQL and a table-per-class inheritance strategy.

The relevant code of the Book base class and subclasses is listed here:

```
@Entity
@Inheritance(strategy = InheritanceType.TABLE_PER_CLASS)
public class Book implements Serializable {
    ...
}
```

```
@Entity
public class Ebook extends Book implements Serializable {

    ...
}

@Entity
public class Paperback extends Book implements Serializable {

    ...
}
```

# Persisting Data

The following service-method persists an Author with three books created via the Book, Ebook, and Paperback entities:

```
public void persistAuthorWithBooks() {

    Author author = new Author();
    author.setName("Alicia Tom");
    author.setAge(38);
    author.setGenre("Anthology");

    Book book = new Book();
    book.setIsbn("001-AT");
    book.setTitle("The book of swords");

    Paperback paperback = new Paperback();
    paperback.setIsbn("002-AT");
    paperback.setTitle("The beatles anthology");
    paperback.setSizeIn("7.5 x 1.3 x 9.2");
    paperback.setWeightLbs("2.7");

    Ebook ebook = new Ebook();
    ebook.setIsbn("003-AT");
    ebook.setTitle("Anthology myths");
    ebook.setFormat("kindle");
```

```
    author.addBook(book); // use addBook() helper
    author.addBook(paperback);
    author.addBook(ebook);

    authorRepository.save(author);
}
```

Saving the author instance triggers the following SQL statements:

```
INSERT INTO author (age, genre, name)
  VALUES (?, ?, ?)
Binding:[38, Anthology, Alicia Tom]
```

```
INSERT INTO book (author_id, isbn, title, id)
  VALUES (?, ?, ?, ?)
Binding:[1, 001-AT, The book of swords, 1]
```

```
INSERT INTO paperback (author_id, isbn, title, size_in, weight_lbs, id)
  VALUES (?, ?, ?, ?, ?, ?)
Binding:[1, 002-AT, The beatles anthology, 7.5 x 1.3 x 9.2, 2.7, 2]
```

```
INSERT INTO ebook (author_id, isbn, title, format, id)
  VALUES (?, ?, ?, ?, ?)
Binding:[1, 003-AT, Anthology myths, kindle, 3]
```

Table-per-class triggers a single INSERT per subclass, so it's more efficient than the joined table inheritance strategy.

## Queries and Class-Per-Table Inheritance

Now, let's check out the efficiency of fetching data. Consider the following BookRepository:

```
@Repository
@Transactional(readOnly = true)
public interface BookRepository extends JpaRepository<Book, Long> {

    @Query("SELECT b FROM Book b WHERE b.author.id = ?1")
    List<Book> fetchBooksByAuthorId(Long authorId);

    Book findByTitle(String title);
}
```

# Fetching the Books by Author Identifier

Let's call fetchBooksByAuthorId():

List<Book> books = bookRepository.fetchBooksByAuthorId(1L);

The triggered SELECT is as follows:

```
SELECT
  book0_.id AS id1_1_,
  book0_.author_id AS author_i4_1_,
  book0_.isbn AS isbn2_1_,
  book0_.title AS title3_1_,
  book0_.format AS format1_2_,
  book0_.size_in AS size_in1_3_,
  book0_.weight_lbs AS weight_l2_3_,
  book0_.clazz_ AS clazz_
FROM (SELECT
  id, isbn, title, author_id,
  NULL AS format, NULL AS size_in, NULL AS weight_lbs, 0 AS clazz_
FROM book
UNION
SELECT
  id, isbn, title, author_id, format,
  NULL AS size_in, NULL AS weight_lbs, 1 AS clazz_
FROM ebook
UNION
SELECT
  id, isbn, title, author_id,
  NULL AS format, size_in, weight_lbs, 2 AS clazz_
FROM paperback) book0_
WHERE book0_.author_id = ?
```

In the case of polymorphic queries, Hibernate relies on SQL unions for fetching data from the base class and every subclass table. Obviously, the polymorphic queries decrease in efficiency as more unions are needed.

## Fetching the Books by Title

Let's call findByTitle() for each book:

```
Book b1 = bookRepository.findByTitle("The book of swords");     // Book
Book b2 = bookRepository.findByTitle("The beatles anthology"); // Paperback
Book b3 = bookRepository.findByTitle("Anthology myths");        // Ebook
```

The triggered SELECT is the same for all three types of books:

```
SELECT
  book0_.id AS id1_1_,
  book0_.author_id AS author_i4_1_,
  book0_.isbn AS isbn2_1_,
  book0_.title AS title3_1_,
  book0_.format AS format1_2_,
  book0_.size_in AS size_in1_3_,
  book0_.weight_lbs AS weight_l2_3_,
  book0_.clazz_ AS clazz_
FROM (SELECT
  id, isbn, title, author_id,
  NULL AS format, NULL AS size_in, NULL AS weight_lbs, 0 AS clazz_
FROM book
UNION
SELECT
  id, isbn, title, author_id, format,
  NULL AS size_in, NULL AS weight_lbs, 1 AS clazz_
FROM ebook
UNION
SELECT
  id, isbn, title, author_id,
  NULL AS format, size_in, weight_lbs, 2 AS clazz_
FROM paperback) book0_
WHERE book0_.title = ?
```

Again, Hibernate relies on SQL unions for fetching data from the base class and every subclass table. So, fetching subclass entities via the base class repository is not efficient and it should be avoided.

# Fetching the Paperbacks

Consider the Paperback repository listed here:

```
@Repository
@Transactional(readOnly = true)
public interface PaperbackRepository
    extends JpaRepository<Paperback, Long> {

    Paperback findByTitle(String title);
}
```

Now, let's trigger two queries. The first query uses the title that identifies a Book. The second query uses the title that identifies a Paperback:

```
// this is a Book
Paperback p1 = paperbackRepository.findByTitle("The book of swords");

// this is a Paperback
Paperback p2 = paperbackRepository.findByTitle("The beatles anthology");
```

Both queries trigger the same SELECT (p1 will be null, while p2 will fetch a Paperback):

```
SELECT
  paperback0_.id AS id1_1_,
  paperback0_.author_id AS author_i4_1_,
  paperback0_.isbn AS isbn2_1_,
  paperback0_.title AS title3_1_,
  paperback0_.size_in AS size_in1_3_,
  paperback0_.weight_lbs AS weight_l2_3_
FROM paperback paperback0_
WHERE paperback0_.title = ?
```

Fetching subclasses via the dedicated repositories is efficient.

> If possible, avoid fetching subclasses via the base class repository. It's better to use subclass-dedicated repositories. In the first case, the number of subclasses influences the number of unions, while in the second case, there will be no union. In other words, it's better to use queries against the subclass entities directly.

Of course, this is not as practical as relying on dedicated repositories of subclasses. Notice that we defined `findByTitle()` in BookRepository. If we want to use it from EbookRepository or PaperbackRepository then it is not practical to duplicate it (generally speaking, it is not practical to duplicate query-methods in all repositories). In such cases, start by defining the `findByTitle()` in a @NoRepositoryBean class:

```
@NoRepositoryBean
public interface BookBaseRepository<T extends Book>
                                    extends JpaRepository<T, Long> {

    T findByTitle(String title);

    @Query(value="SELECT b FROM #{#entityName} AS b WHERE b.isbn = ?1")
    T fetchByIsbn(String isbn);
}
```

Next, BookRepository, EbookRepository and PaperbackRepository extend BookBaseRepository. This way, `findByTitle()` and `findByIsbn()` are available in all repositories that extends the base repository. The complete application is available on GitHub[9].

## Fetching the Author and the Associated Books

Consider the following Author repository:

```
@Repository
@Transactional(readOnly = true)
public interface AuthorRepository extends JpaRepository<Author, Long> {

    Author findByName(String name);
```

---

[9]HibernateSpringBootTablePerClassRepositoryInheritance

```
    @Query("SELECT a FROM Author a JOIN FETCH a.books b")
    public Author findAuthor();
}
```

Calling findByName() will fetch the author without the associated books:

```
@Transactional(readOnly = true)
public void fetchAuthorAndBooksLazy() {
    Author author = authorRepository.findByName("Alicia Tom");
    List<Book> books = author.getBooks();
}
```

Calling getBooks() triggers a secondary query:

```
-- fetch the author
SELECT
  author0_.id AS id1_0_,
  author0_.age AS age2_0_,
  author0_.genre AS genre3_0_,
  author0_.name AS name4_0_
FROM author author0_
WHERE author0_.name = ?

-- fetch the books via getBooks()
SELECT
  books0_.author_id AS author_i4_1_0_,
  books0_.id AS id1_1_0_,
  books0_.id AS id1_1_1_,
  books0_.author_id AS author_i4_1_1_,
  books0_.isbn AS isbn2_1_1_,
  books0_.title AS title3_1_1_,
  books0_.format AS format1_2_1_,
  books0_.size_in AS size_in1_3_1_,
  books0_.weight_lbs AS weight_l2_3_1_,
  books0_.clazz_ AS clazz_1_
FROM (SELECT
  id, isbn, title, author_id,
  NULL AS format, NULL AS size_in, NULL AS weight_lbs, 0 AS clazz_
```

```
FROM book
UNION
SELECT
  id, isbn, title, author_id, format,
  NULL AS size_in, NULL AS weight_lbs, 1 AS clazz_
FROM ebook
UNION
SELECT
  id, isbn, title, author_id,
  NULL AS format, size_in, weight_lbs, 2 AS clazz_
FROM paperback) books0_
WHERE books0_.author_id = ?
```

The secondary SELECT has the same drawback from earlier. There is a union for each subclass table. So, deep class hierarchies and/or a large number of subclasses will cause performance penalties.

On the other hand, thanks to JOIN FETCH, calling findAuthor() will fetch the author and the associated books in the same SELECT:

```
@Transactional(readOnly = true)
public void fetchAuthorAndBooksEager() {
    Author author = authorRepository.findAuthor();
}
```

Unfortunately, the triggered SELECT is not efficient, since it needs a union for each subclass ($n$ subclasses result in $n$ unions):

```
SELECT
  author0_.id AS id1_0_0_,
  books1_.id AS id1_1_1_,
  author0_.age AS age2_0_0_,
  author0_.genre AS genre3_0_0_,
  author0_.name AS name4_0_0_,
  books1_.author_id AS author_i4_1_1_,
  books1_.isbn AS isbn2_1_1_,
  books1_.title AS title3_1_1_,
  books1_.format AS format1_2_1_,
```

```
  books1_.size_in AS size_in1_3_1_,
  books1_.weight_lbs AS weight_l2_3_1_,
  books1_.clazz_ AS clazz_1_,
  books1_.author_id AS author_i4_1_0__,
  books1_.id AS id1_1_0__
FROM author author0_
INNER JOIN (SELECT
  id, isbn, title, author_id,
  NULL AS format, NULL AS size_in, NULL AS weight_lbs, 0 AS clazz_
FROM book
UNION
SELECT
  id, isbn, title, author_id, format,
  NULL AS size_in, NULL AS weight_lbs, 1 AS clazz_
FROM ebook
UNION
SELECT
  id, isbn, title, author_id,
  NULL AS format, size_in, weight_lbs, 2 AS clazz_
FROM paperback) books1_
  ON author0_.id = books1_.author_id
```

Now, let's consider some pros and cons of join table inheritance.

Pros:

- Writes are fast since there is one INSERT per subclass

- The base class and subclasses attributes may be non-nullable

Cons:

- The IDENTITY generator cannot be used

- Reads are efficient only via dedicated repositories of subclasses (in other words, it's better to use queries against the subclass entities directly)

> - In the case of polymorphic queries, for *n* subclasses, Hibernate needs *n* unions, which may lead to serious performance penalties

The complete application is available on GitHub[10].

# Item 142: How to Efficiently Use @MappedSuperclass

You already saw @MappedSuperclass at work in **Item 24** and **Item 87**.

The @MappedSuperclass is an entity-level annotation that's useful for shaping an inheritance model similar to the table-per-class strategy but with a *base class* that is not an entity. It's not materialized in a database table. The base class is annotated with @MappedSuperclass and it can be abstract or not. Its subclasses will inherit its attributes and store them in subclass-tables next to their own attributes. Consider the inheritance hierarchy given in Figure 15-7.

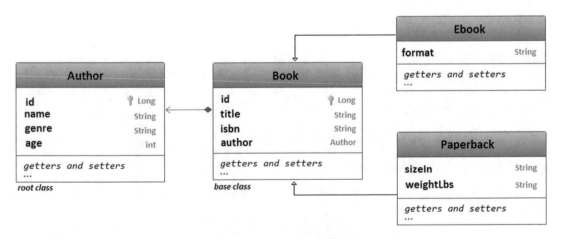

***Figure 15-7.*** *Mapped superclass Domain Model*

---

[10]HibernateSpringBootTablePerClassInheritance

Between Author and Book there is a unidirectional lazy @ManyToOne association. Since Book is not an entity, it doesn't support associations; therefore, the Author entity cannot define a @OneToMany relationship. The Author entity can be seen as the *root class* since without authors there are no books. The Book entity is the non-entity *base class*. The Ebook and Paperback entities extend the Book entity, so they don't need their own @Id. The table relationships are shown in Figure 15-8 (notice that there is no book table).

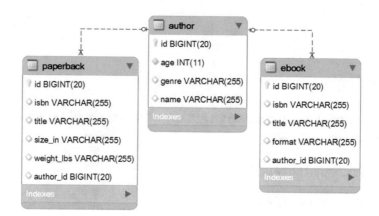

***Figure 15-8.*** *Tables of mapped superclasses*

The relevant code of the Book base class is listed here:

```
@MappedSuperclass
public abstract class Book implements Serializable {

    private static final long serialVersionUID = 1L;

    @Id
    @GeneratedValue(strategy = GenerationType.IDENTITY)
    private Long id;

    private String title;
    private String isbn;

    @ManyToOne(fetch = FetchType.LAZY)
    @JoinColumn(name = "author_id")
    private Author author;

    // getters and setters omitted for brevity
}
```

```
@Entity
public class Ebook extends Book implements Serializable {

    ...

}

@Entity
public class Paperback extends Book implements Serializable {

    ...

}
```

# Persisting Data

The following service-method persists an Author with three books created via the Book, Ebook, and Paperback entities:

```
public void persistAuthorWithBooks() {

    Author author = new Author();
    author.setName("Alicia Tom");
    author.setAge(38);
    author.setGenre("Anthology");

    Paperback paperback = new Paperback();
    paperback.setIsbn("002-AT");
    paperback.setTitle("The beatles anthology");
    paperback.setSizeIn("7.5 x 1.3 x 9.2");
    paperback.setWeightLbs("2.7");
    paperback.setAuthor(author);

    Ebook ebook = new Ebook();
    ebook.setIsbn("003-AT");
    ebook.setTitle("Anthology myths");
    ebook.setFormat("kindle");
    ebook.setAuthor(author);

    authorRepository.save(author);
    paperbackRepository.save(paperback);
    ebookRepository.save(ebook);
}
```

Saving the author, paperback, and ebook instances triggers the following SQL statements:

```
INSERT INTO author (age, genre, name)
  VALUES (?, ?, ?)
Binding:[38, Anthology, Alicia Tom]
```

```
INSERT INTO paperback (author_id, isbn, title, size_in, weight_lbs)
  VALUES (?, ?, ?, ?, ?)
Binding:[1, 002-AT, The beatles anthology, 7.5 x 1.3 x 9.2, 2.7]
```

```
INSERT INTO ebook (author_id, isbn, title, format)
  VALUES (?, ?, ?, ?)
Binding:[1, 003-AT, Anthology myths, kindle]
```

Writes are efficient. There is one INSERT per entity instance.

## Fetching the Paperbacks

Consider the Paperback repository listed here:

```
@Repository
@Transactional(readOnly = true)
public interface PaperbackRepository
    extends JpaRepository<Paperback, Long> {

    Paperback findByTitle(String title);

    @Query("SELECT e FROM Paperback e JOIN FETCH e.author")
    Paperback fetchByAuthorId(Long id);
}
```

Now, let's trigger two queries via findByTitle(). The first query uses the title that identifies a Ebook. The second query uses the title that identifies a Paperback:

```
// this is a Ebook
Paperback p1 = paperbackRepository.findByTitle("Anthology myths");

// this is a Paperback
Paperback p2 = paperbackRepository.findByTitle("The beatles anthology");
```

Both queries trigger the same SELECT (p1 will be null, while p2 will fetch a Paperback):

```
SELECT
  paperback0_.id AS id1_2_,
  paperback0_.author_id AS author_i6_2_,
  paperback0_.isbn AS isbn2_2_,
  paperback0_.title AS title3_2_,
  paperback0_.size_in AS size_in4_2_,
  paperback0_.weight_lbs AS weight_l5_2_
FROM paperback paperback0_
WHERE paperback0_.title = ?
```

This query is quite straightforward and efficient.

How about fetching the author of a paperback? This can be accomplished by calling fetchByAuthorId(). Since this query-method relies on JOIN FETCH, the author is fetched in the same SELECT as the paperback, as follows:

```
SELECT
  paperback0_.id AS id1_2_0_,
  author1_.id AS id1_0_1_,
  paperback0_.author_id AS author_i6_2_0_,
  paperback0_.isbn AS isbn2_2_0_,
  paperback0_.title AS title3_2_0_,
  paperback0_.size_in AS size_in4_2_0_,
  paperback0_.weight_lbs AS weight_l5_2_0_,
  author1_.age AS age2_0_1_,
  author1_.genre AS genre3_0_1_,
  author1_.name AS name4_0_1_
FROM paperback paperback0_
INNER JOIN author author1_
  ON paperback0_.author_id = author1_.id
```

The query uses a single JOIN and it is efficient. Since Author has no associations, there are no getBooks(), getEbooks(), or getPaperbacks().

Now, let's consider some pros and cons of @MappedSuperclass.

Pros:

- Reads and writes are fast
- @MappedSuperclass is the proper alternative to the table-per-class inheritance strategy as long as the *base class* doesn't need to be an entity

Cons:

- Base classes cannot be queried
- Polymorphic queries and associations are not permitted

As a rule of thumb, @MappedSuperclass is a good fit when you want to propagate specific properties from a *base class* to all subclasses, since the object hierarchy visibility remains at the object domain level. Do not use inheritance strategies such as SINGLE_TABLE, JOINED or TABLE_PER_CLASS for accomplishing such tasks. Rely on SINGLE_TABLE, JOINED, or TABLE_PER_CLASS combined with a software design pattern (e.g., Template, State, Strategy, Visitor, etc.). Teaming up an inheritance strategy with a software design pattern is the best choice for exploiting JPA inheritance.

The complete code is available on GitHub[11].

Exactly as in case of SINGLE_TABLE, JOINED or TABLE_PER_CLASS, we can avoid query-methods duplication by creating a base repository that it is extended by concrete repositories. A complete example is available on GitHub[12].

---

[11]HibernateSpringBootMappedSuperclass

[12]HibernateSpringBootMappedSuperclassRepository

# CHAPTER 16

# Types
# and Hibernate Types

## Item 143: How to Deal with Hibernate and Unsupported Types via the Hibernate Types Library

As a rule of thumb, strive to choose the best database column types. Take your time and scroll your database types, since most databases come with specific types that you can use. For example, MySQL's MEDIUMINT UNSIGNED stores an integer in the range of 1 to 99999, PostgreSQL's money type stores a currency amount with a fixed fractional precision, the cidr type holds an IPv4 or IPv6 network specification, and so on. Moreover, strive to use compact types. This will reduce the index memory footprint and allow the database to manipulate larger amounts of data.

Think of a Hibernate type as a *bridge* between a Java type (object or primitive) and an SQL type. Hibernate ORM comes with a built-in set of supported types, but there are also other Java types that Hibernate doesn't support (e.g., java.time.YearMonth introduced in Java 8).

Especially for unsupported types, you can rely on the Hibernate Types Library.

© Anghel Leonard 2020
A. Leonard, *Spring Boot Persistence Best Practices*, https://doi.org/10.1007/978-1-4842-5626-8_16

> The Hibernate Types Library is an open-source project developed by Vlad Mihalcea and is available on GitHub[1]. I strongly recommend you take a few minutes and check out this project. You will love it!

This library provides a suite of extra types and utilities that are not supported by the Hibernate ORM. Among these types, there is java.time.YearMonth. Let's store this type in a database via Hibernate Types. First, add the dependency to the pom.xml file (for Maven):

```
<dependency>
    <groupId>com.vladmihalcea</groupId>
    <artifactId>hibernate-types-52</artifactId>
    <version>2.4.3</version>
</dependency>
```

Further, define an entity named Book. Notice how you map the java.time.YearMonth Java type to Hibernate's YearMonthIntegerType (or YearMonthDateType) type via the @TypeDef annotation:

```
import org.hibernate.annotations.TypeDef;
import com.vladmihalcea.hibernate.type.basic.YearMonthIntegerType;
...
@Entity
@TypeDef(
    typeClass = YearMonthIntegerType.class, // or, YearMonthDateType
    defaultForType = YearMonth.class
)
public class Book implements Serializable {

    private static final long serialVersionUID = 1L;

    @Id
    @GeneratedValue(strategy = GenerationType.IDENTITY)
    private Long id;
```

---

[1]https://github.com/vladmihalcea/hibernate-types

904

```
    private String title;
    private String isbn;
    private YearMonth releaseDate;

    // getters and setters omitted for brevity
}
```

Finally, a service method can help you persist a Book instance in the database:

```
public void newBook() {

    Book book = new Book();

    book.setIsbn("001");
    book.setTitle("Young Boy");
    book.setReleaseDate(YearMonth.now());

    bookRepository.save(book);
}
```

Figure 16-1 reveals the database contents (check the release_date column).

***Figure 16-1.*** *The release_date column*

And a service method for fetching this Book:

```
public void displayBook() {
    Book book = bookRepository.findByTitle("Young Boy");

    System.out.println(book);
}
```

Here is the output:

```
Book{id=1, title=Young Boy, isbn=001, releaseDate=2019-07}
```

The complete code is available on GitHub[2].

---

[2]HibernateSpringBootYearMonth

# Item 144: How to Map CLOBs and BLOBs

Let's look at the Author entity. Among its properties, an author can have an avatar (a photo) and a biography (several pages of text). The avatar can be considered a *binary large object* (BLOB), while the biography can be considered a *character large object* (CLOB). Mapping binary/character large objects is a trade-off between *ease of use* and *performance*.

## Ease of Use (Trade-Off with Performance)

Conforming to JPA specifications, binary large objects can be mapped to byte[ ], whereas character large objects can be mapped to String. Let's see this in code:

```
@Entity
public class Author implements Serializable {

    ...
    @Lob
    private byte[] avatar;

    @Lob
    private String biography;
    ...

    public byte[] getAvatar() {
        return avatar;
    }

    public void setAvatar(byte[] avatar) {
        this.avatar = avatar;
    }

    public String getBiography() {
        return biography;
    }

    public void setBiography(String biography) {
        this.biography = biography;
    }
    ...
}
```

Persisting and fetching avatar and biography can be done easily, as in the following service-methods (assume that findByName() is a query method in the AuthorRepository and the data to be persisted is stored in two local files):

```java
public void newAuthor() throws IOException {

    Author mt = new Author();
    mt.setName("Martin Ticher");
    mt.setAge(43);
    mt.setGenre("Horror");

    mt.setAvatar(Files.readAllBytes(
        new File("avatars/mt_avatar.png").toPath()));
    mt.setBiography(Files.readString(
        new File("biography/mt_bio.txt").toPath()));

    authorRepository.save(mt);
}

public void fetchAuthor() {

    Author author = authorRepository.findByName("Martin Ticher");

    System.out.println("Author bio: "
        + author.getBiography());
    System.out.println("Author avatar: "
        + Arrays.toString(author.getAvatar()));
}
```

> Mapping binary/character large objects to byte[] and String is easy, but it may come with performance penalties. When you fetch binary/character large objects, you are fetching all the information and mapping it to a Java object. This causes performance penalties, especially if the amount of information is very large (e.g., videos, high-definition images, audio, etc.). In such cases, it's better to rely on JDBC's LOB locators java.sql.Clob and java.sql.Blob, as described next.

The complete application is available on GitHub[3].

---

[3]HibernateSpringBootMappingLobToByteString

# Avoiding Performance Penalties (Trade-Off Is Ease of Use)

Mapping binary/character large objects via JDBC's LOB locators `Clob` and `Blob` sustains the JDBC driver optimization, such as streaming the data. Entity mapping is pretty straightforward:

```
@Entity
public class Author implements Serializable {

    ...
    @Lob
    private Blob avatar;

    @Lob
    private Clob biography;
    ...

    public Blob getAvatar() {
        return avatar;
    }

    public void setAvatar(Blob avatar) {
        this.avatar = avatar;
    }

    public Clob getBiography() {
        return biography;
    }

    public void setBiography(Clob biography) {
        this.biography = biography;
    }
    ...
}
```

While entity mapping is quite easy, persisting and fetching binary/character large objects requires Hibernate-specific `BlobProxy` and `ClobProxy` classes and some I/O code. These classes are needed to create `Blob`s and `Clob`s. The following service-methods reveal how to persist and fetch `avatar` and `biography`:

```java
public void newAuthor() throws IOException {

    Author mt = new Author();
    mt.setName("Martin Ticher");
    mt.setAge(43);
    mt.setGenre("Horror");

    mt.setAvatar(BlobProxy.generateProxy(
        Files.readAllBytes(new File("avatars/mt_avatar.png").toPath())));
    mt.setBiography(ClobProxy.generateProxy(
        Files.readString(new File("biography/mt_bio.txt").toPath())));

    authorRepository.save(mt);
}

public void fetchAuthor() throws SQLException, IOException {

    Author author = authorRepository.findByName("Martin Ticher");

    System.out.println("Author bio: "
        + readBiography(author.getBiography()));
    System.out.println("Author avatar: "
        + Arrays.toString(readAvatar(author.getAvatar())));
}

private byte[] readAvatar(Blob avatar) throws SQLException, IOException {

    try (InputStream is = avatar.getBinaryStream()) {

        return is.readAllBytes();
    }
}

private String readBiography(Clob bio) throws SQLException, IOException {

    StringBuilder sb = new StringBuilder();
    try (Reader reader = bio.getCharacterStream()) {

        char[] buffer = new char[2048];
        for (int i = reader.read(buffer); i > 0; i = reader.read(buffer)) {
```

```
        sb.append(buffer, 0, i);
    }
}

return sb.toString();
}
```

The complete application is available on GitHub[4].

> Dealing with binary/character large objects causes performance penalties if they are loaded eagerly and are not used/exploited. For example, loading an `author` doesn't require that `avatar` and `biography` be loaded as well. This information can be loaded on demand via the lazy attribute loading technique presented in **Item 23** and **Item 24**.

> For nationalized character data types (e.g., NCLOB, NCHAR, NVARCHAR, and LONGNVARCHAR), replace @Lob with @Nationalized, as so:
>
> ```
> @Nationalized
> private String biography;
> ```

# Item 145: How to Efficiently Map a Java Enum to a Database

Consider the Author entity and the genre property. This property is represented by a Java enum, as follows:

```
public enum GenreType {

    HORROR, ANTHOLOGY, HISTORY
}
```

Now, let's look at several approaches for mapping this enum to the database.

---

[4]HibernateSpringBootMappingLobToClobAndBlob

# Mapping via EnumType.STRING

A very simple approach consists of using @Enumerated(EnumType.STRING), as follows:

```
@Entity
public class Author implements Serializable {

    @Enumerated(EnumType.STRING)
    private GenreType genre;
    ...
}
```

But how efficient is this approach? In MySQL, the genre column will be a VARCHAR(255). Obviously, this column takes up way more space than necessary. How about now?

```
@Enumerated(EnumType.STRING)
@Column(length = 9)
private GenreType genre;
```

A length of nine bytes is enough to persist the ANTHOLOGY value. This should be okay as long as you don't have millions of records. It is unlikely, but assuming you have 15 million authors, the genre column alone will will need 120+ MB. This is not efficient at all!

# Mapping via EnumType.ORDINAL

To increase efficiency, let's switch from EnumType.STRING to EnumType.ORDINAL:

```
@Enumerated(EnumType.ORDINAL)
private GenreType genre;
```

This time, in MySQL, the genre column will be of type int(11). In MySQL, the INTEGER (or INT) type needs four bytes. It's way better than VARCHAR(9). Most likely, you will not have more than 100 genres, so TINYINT should do the job:

```
@Enumerated(EnumType.ORDINAL)
@Column(columnDefinition = "TINYINT")
private GenreType genre;
```

In MySQL, TINYINT needs only one byte to represent values between -128 and 127. In this case, storing 15 million authors will require 14+ MB.

Even so, TINYINT may be not sufficient in certain scenarios. For a larger range, rely on SMALLINT, which requires two bytes and covers the range between -32768 and 32767. It is unlikely to have an enum with so many values.

> To conclude, it's way more efficient to rely on EnumType.ORDINAL than on EnumType.STRING. Nevertheless, the trade-off is with readability.

The complete application is available on GitHub[5].

## Mapping an Enum to a Custom Representation

By default, using EnumType.ORDINAL will link HORROR to 0, ANTHOLOGY to 1, and HISTORY to 2. But, let's assume that HORROR should be linked to 10, ANTHOLOGY to 20, and HISTORY to 30.

One approach for mapping an enum to a custom representation relies on AttributeConverter. We used an AttributeConverter in **Item 19**, so the following implementation should be déjà vu:

```
public class GenreTypeConverter
            implements AttributeConverter<GenreType, Integer> {

    @Override
    public Integer convertToDatabaseColumn(GenreType attr) {

        if (attr == null) {
            return null;
        }

        switch (attr) {
            case HORROR:
                return 10;
```

---

[5]HibernateSpringBootEnumStringInt

```
            case ANTHOLOGY:
                return 20;
            case HISTORY:
                return 30;
            default:
                throw new IllegalArgumentException("The " + attr
                                            + " not supported.");
        }
    }

    @Override
    public GenreType convertToEntityAttribute(Integer dbData) {

        if (dbData == null) {
            return null;
        }

        switch (dbData) {
            case 10:
                return HORROR;
            case 20:
                return ANTHOLOGY;
            case 30:
                return HISTORY;
            default:
                throw new IllegalArgumentException("The " + dbData
                                            + " not supported.");
        }
    }
}
```

Finally, use @Converter to instruct Hibernate to apply the converter:

```
@Entity
public class Author implements Serializable {
    ...
```

```
@Convert(converter = GenreTypeConverter.class)
@Column(columnDefinition = "TINYINT")
private GenreType genre;
...
}
```

The complete application is available on GitHub[6].

# Mapping an Enum to a Database-Specific Enum Type (PostgreSQL)

PostgreSQL defines an ENUM type that can be used via the CREATE TYPE command, as in the following example:

```
CREATE TYPE genre_info AS ENUM ('HORROR', 'ANTHOLOGY', 'HISTORY')
```

## Writing a Custom Type

Hibernate doesn't support this type (Hibernate can map the enum values to an int or a String, but PostgreSQL expects values as an Object), so mapping a Java enum to PostgreSQL ENUM requires you to implement a custom Hibernate type. Defining this custom Hibernate type means you need to extend the Hibernate EnumType and override the nullSafeSet() method to shape the desired behavior:

```
public class PostgreSQLEnumType extends EnumType {

    @Override
    public void nullSafeSet(PreparedStatement ps, Object obj, int index,
            SharedSessionContractImplementor session)
                throws HibernateException, SQLException {
        if (obj == null) {
            ps.setNull(index, Types.OTHER);
        } else {
            ps.setObject(index, obj.toString(), Types.OTHER);
        }
    }
}
```

---

[6]HibernateSpringBootEnumAttributeConverter

Finally, let's register this type using a @TypeDef annotation and putting it in a package-info.java file:

```
@org.hibernate.annotations.TypeDef(
    name = "genre_enum_type", typeClass = PostgreSQLEnumType.class)

package com.bookstore.type;
```

Now, let's use it:

```
@Entity
public class Author implements Serializable {

    ...
    @Enumerated(EnumType.STRING)
    @Type(type = "genre_enum_type")
    @Column(columnDefinition = "genre_info")
    private GenreType genre;
    ...
}
```

Persisting an author reveals that their genre is of type genre_info, which is a PostgreSQL ENUM, as shown in Figure 16-2.

| id<br>[PK] bigint | age<br>integer | genre<br>genre_info | name<br>character varying (255) |
|---|---|---|---|
| 1 | 34 | HORROR | Maryus Yarn |

***Figure 16-2.***  *PostgreSQL ENUM type*

The complete application is available on GitHub[7].

# Using the Hibernate Types Library

The Hibernate Types Library was introduced in **Item 143**. Fortunately, this library already contains a mapping of a Java enum to a PostgreSQL ENUM type. First, add this library to your application via the following dependency:

---

[7]HibernateSpringBootEnumPostgreSQLCustomType

```
<dependency>
    <groupId>com.vladmihalcea</groupId>
    <artifactId>hibernate-types-52</artifactId>
    <version>2.4.3</version>
</dependency>
```

Then, use the @TypeDef annotation at the entity class-level and @Type at the entity field-level, as follows:

```
@Entity
@TypeDef(
    name = "genre_enum_type",
    typeClass = PostgreSQLEnumType.class
)
public class Author implements Serializable {

    ...

    @Enumerated(EnumType.STRING)
    @Type(type = "genre_enum_type")
    @Column(columnDefinition = "genre_info")
    private GenreType genre;

    ...
}
```

The complete application is available on GitHub[8].

# Item 146: How to Efficiently Map a JSON Java Object to a MySQL JSON Column

> JSON fits very well with non-structured data.

MySQL added JSON types support starting with version 5.7. However, Hibernate Core doesn't provide a JSON Type that works for JSON Java Objects and database JSON columns.

---

[8]HibernateSpringBootEnumPostgreSQLHibernateTypes

Fortunately, the Hibernate Types Library (you should be familiar with this library from **Item 143**) fills this gap and provides two generic JSON types—JsonStringType and JsonBinaryType. In the case of MySQL, from the JDBC perspective, the JSON types should be represented as Strings, so JsonStringType is the proper choice.

Let's use the Author entity and the Book JSON Java Object. The Author entity is listed here:

```
@Entity
@TypeDef(
    name = "json", typeClass = JsonStringType.class
)
public class Author implements Serializable {

    private static final long serialVersionUID = 1L;

    @Id
    @GeneratedValue(strategy = GenerationType.IDENTITY)
    private Long id;

    private String name;
    private String genre;
    private int age;

    @Type(type = "json")
    @Column(columnDefinition = "json")
    private Book book;

    // getters and setters omitted for brevity
}
```

The Book JSON Java Object is listed here (this is not a JPA entity):

```
public class Book implements Serializable {

    private static final long serialVersionUID = 1L;

    private String title;
    private String isbn;
    private int price;

    // getters and setters omitted for brevity
}
```

## Persisting an Author

A service-method can easily persist an author as follows:

```
public void newAuthor() {

    Book book = new Book();
    book.setIsbn("001-JN");
    book.setTitle("A History of Ancient Prague");
    book.setPrice(45);

    Author author = new Author();
    author.setName("Joana Nimar");
    author.setAge(34);
    author.setGenre("History");
    author.setBook(book);

    authorRepository.save(author);
}
```

The INSERT statement is:

```
INSERT INTO author (age, book, genre, name)
    VALUES (34, '{"title":"A History of Ancient Prague",
                "isbn":"001-JN","price":45}', 'History', 'Joana Nimar')
```

The author table is shown in Figure 16-3.

**author**

| id | age | book | genre | name |
|----|-----|------|-------|------|
| 1 | 34 | {"isbn": "001-JN", "price": 45, "title": "A History of Ancient Prague"} | History | Joana Nimar |

*Figure 16-3.* *JSON in MySQL*

## Fetching/Updating the Author

Fetching an author will map the fetched JSON to the Book object. For example, consider the following query:

```
public Author findByName(String name);
```

Calling `findByName()` triggers the following `SELECT` statement:

```
Author author = authorRepository.findByName("Joana Nimar");
```

```
SELECT
  author0_.id AS id1_0_,
  author0_.age AS age2_0_,
  author0_.book AS book3_0_,
  author0_.genre AS genre4_0_,
  author0_.name AS name5_0_
FROM author author0_
WHERE author0_.name = ?
```

Via the fetched author, you can call `getBook().getTitle()`, `getBook().getIsbn()`, or `getBook().getPrice()`. Calling `getBook().setTitle()`, `getBook().setIsbn()`, or `getBook().setPrice()` will trigger JSON updates. This UPDATE looks as follows (`getBook().setPrice(40)`):

```
UPDATE author
SET age = 34,
    book = '{"title":"A History of Ancient Prague",
            "isbn":"001-JN","price":40}',
    genre = 'History',
    name = 'Joana Nimar'
WHERE id = 1
```

# Fetching the Author by Querying the JSON

MySQL provides functions that extract parts of or modifies a JSON document based on the given path expression. One of these functions is `JSON_EXTRACT()`. It gets two arguments: the JSON to query and a path expression. The path syntax relies on a leading $ character to indicate the JSON document, which is optionally followed by successive selectors that indicate certain parts of the document. For more details, review the MySQL documentation[9].

---

[9]https://dev.mysql.com/doc/refman/8.0/en/json.html

Calling JSON_EXTRACT() in the WHERE clause can be done via the JPQL function() or a native query. Via JPQL, it looks like the following example (this finds the author who wrote the book with the given isbn):

```
@Query("SELECT a FROM Author a "
     + "WHERE function('JSON_EXTRACT', a.book, '$.isbn') = ?1")
 public Author findByBookIsbn(String isbn);
```

Or, as a native query:

```
@Query(value = "SELECT a.* FROM author a
                WHERE JSON_EXTRACT(a.book, '$.isbn') = ?1",
       nativeQuery = true)
public Author findByBookIsbnNativeQuery(String isbn);
```

> Calling JSON_EXTRACT() (and other JSON-specific functions such as JSON_SET(), JSON_MERGE_*FOO*(), JSON_OBJECT(), etc.) in the SELECT part of the query can be done via native queries or by registering the function, as shown in **Item 79**.

The complete application is available on GitHub[10].

# Item 147: How to Efficiently Map a JSON Java Object to a PostgreSQL JSON Column

**Item 146** covered the MySQL JSON type. Now, let's focus on PostgreSQL.

PostgreSQL added JSON types support starting with version 9.2. The PostgreSQL JSON types are json and jsonb. PostgreSQL JSON types are represented in binary data format, so you need to use JsonBinaryType (in **Item 146**, we said that the Hibernate Types Library provides two generic JSON types—JsonStringType and JsonBinaryType).

---

[10]HibernateSpringBootJsonToMySQL

Let's use the Author entity and the Book JSON Java Object. The Author entity is listed here:

```
@Entity
@TypeDef(
    name = "jsonb", typeClass = JsonBinaryType.class
)
public class Author implements Serializable {

    private static final long serialVersionUID = 1L;

    @Id
    @GeneratedValue(strategy = GenerationType.IDENTITY)
    private Long id;

    private String name;
    private String genre;
    private int age;

    @Type(type = "jsonb")
    @Column(columnDefinition = "jsonb") // or, json
    private Book book;

    // getters and setters omitted for brevity
}
```

The Book JSON Java Object is listed here (this is not a JPA entity):

```
public class Book implements Serializable {

    private static final long serialVersionUID = 1L;

    private String title;
    private String isbn;
    private int price;

    // getters and setters omitted for brevity
}
```

## Persisting an Author

A service-method can easily persist an author as follows:

```
public void newAuthor() {

    Book book = new Book();
    book.setIsbn("001-JN");
    book.setTitle("A History of Ancient Prague");
    book.setPrice(45);

    Author author = new Author();
    author.setName("Joana Nimar");
    author.setAge(34);
    author.setGenre("History");
    author.setBook(book);

    authorRepository.save(author);
}
```

The INSERT statement is:

```
INSERT INTO author (age, book, genre, name)
    VALUES (34, '{"title":"A History of Ancient Prague",
               "isbn":"001-JN","price":45}', 'History', 'Joana Nimar')
```

The author table is shown in Figure 16-4.

**author**

| id<br>[PK] bigint | age<br>integer | book<br>jsonb | genre<br>character varying (255) | name<br>character varying (255) |
|---|---|---|---|---|
| 1 | 34 | {"isbn":"001-JN","price":45,"title":"A History of Ancient Prague"} | History | Joana Nimar |

*Figure 16-4.  JSON in PostgreSQL*

## Fetching/Updating the Author

Fetching the author will map the fetched JSON to the Book object. For example, consider the following query:

```
public Author findByName(String name);
```

Calling findByName() triggers the following SELECT statement:

```
Author author = authorRepository.findByName("Joana Nimar");
```

```
SELECT
    author0_.id AS id1_0_,
    author0_.age AS age2_0_,
    author0_.book AS book3_0_,
    author0_.genre AS genre4_0_,
    author0_.name AS name5_0_
FROM author author0_
WHERE author0_.name = ?
```

Via the fetched author, you can call getBook().getTitle(), getBook().getIsbn(), or getBook().getPrice(). Calling getBook().setTitle(), getBook().setIsbn(), or getBook().setPrice() will trigger JSON updates. This UPDATE looks as follows (getBook().setPrice(40)):

```
UPDATE author
SET age = 34,
    book = '{"title":"A History of Ancient Prague",
            "isbn":"001-JN","price":40}',
    genre = 'History',
    name = 'Joana Nimar'
WHERE id = 1
```

# Fetching the Author by Querying the JSON

PostgreSQL provides two native operators for querying JSON data (more details are available in the PostgreSQL documentation[11]):

- The -> operator returns a JSON object field by key

- The ->> operator returns a JSON object field by text

---

[11]https://www.postgresql.org/docs/9.4/datatype-json.html

Being native operators, they have to be used in native queries. For example, fetching the author who wrote a book with a given ISBN can be done as follows:

```
@Query(value = "SELECT a.* FROM author a "
            + "WHERE a.book ->> 'isbn' = ?1",
      nativeQuery = true)
public Author findByBookIsbnNativeQuery(String isbn);
```

Sometimes you need to cast the JSON field to the proper data type. For example, to involve the book's price in a comparison, it must be converted to INTEGER, as shown here:

```
@Query(value = "SELECT a.* FROM author a "
            + "WHERE CAST(a.book ->> 'price' AS INTEGER) = ?1",
      nativeQuery = true)
public Author findByBookPriceNativeQueryCast(int price);
```

The complete application is available on GitHub[12].

---

[12]HibernateSpringBootJsonToPostgreSQL

# APPENDIX A

# (Hibernate) JPA Fundamentals

## What Is a Persistence Unit?

Think of a *persistence unit* as a box holding all the needed information to create an
EntityManagerFactory instance (see Figure A-1).

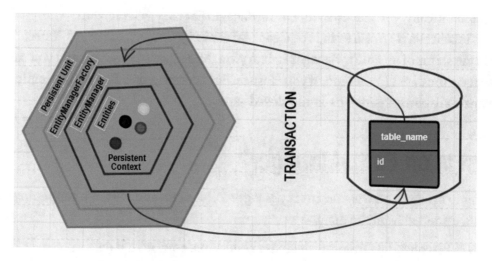

***Figure A-1.*** *Persistence unit*

Among this information are details about the data source (JDBC URL, user, password,
SQL dialect, etc.), the list of entities that will be managed, and other specific properties.
And, of course, the persistence unit transaction type can be *resource-local* (single data
source) or *JTA* (multiple data sources). In Java EE, you can specify all these details in

© Anghel Leonard 2020
A. Leonard, *Spring Boot Persistence Best Practices*, https://doi.org/10.1007/978-1-4842-5626-8

an XML file named `persistence.xml`. In Spring Boot, you can do it via `application.properties` and Spring Boot will handle the creation of persistence unit on your behalf. The `javax.persistence.spi.PersistenceUnitInfo` implementation alternative is for bootstrapping JPA programmatically (in Java EE and Spring). You may also be interested in HHH-13614[1]. You identify a persistence unit by the name that you choose. In the same application, you can have multiple persistence units and identify them each by name; therefore you can connect to different databases from the same application.

# What Is an EntityManagerFactory?

As its name suggests, an `EntityManagerFactory` is a factory capable of creating on-demand `EntityManager` instances.

Basically, you provide the needed information via the persistence unit, and this information is used to create an `EntityManagerFactory` that exposes a method named `createEntityManager()`, which returns a new application-managed `EntityManager` instance at each invocation.

Programmatically, you can open an `EntityManagerFactory` via injection (`@PersistenceUnit`) or via `Persistence#createEntityManagerFactory()`. You can check the status of an `EntityManagerFactory` via the `isOpen()` method, and you can close it via the `close()` method. If you close an `EntityManagerFactory`, all its entity managers are considered to be in the closed state.

# What Is an EntityManager?

In order to understand what an `EntityManager` is, let's talk about what's happening with the data extracted from the database.

- Fetching data from the database results in a copy of that data in memory (usually referred to as the *JDBC result set,* or simply *result set* or *data snapshot*). This zone of memory that holds the fetched data is known and referred to as the *Persistence Context* or the *First Level Cache,* or simply the *Cache.* See Figure A-2.

---

[1]https://hibernate.atlassian.net/browse/HHH-13614

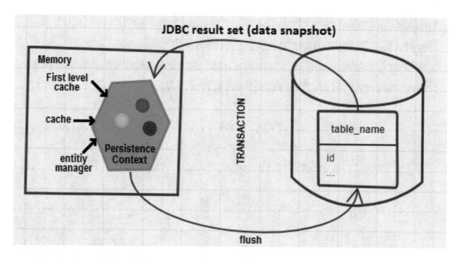

***Figure A-2.*** *Persistence Context*

- After a fetching operation, the fetched *result set* lives outside the
  database, in memory. In applications, you access/manage this *result
  set* via entities (so, via Java objects), and for facilitating this context,
  Hibernate JPA applies specific techniques that transform the fetched
  *result set* to an array of *raw* data (Object[] - *hydrated/loaded state*)
  and to the manageable representation referenced as *managed entities*.

Planning to modify the fetched entity objects is a way to exploit the fact that, besides being a cache for entities, the Persistence Context acts as an entity state transitions buffer and as a transactional *write-behind* cache as well. At flush time, Hibernate is responsible for translating the buffered entities state transitions into Data Manipulation Language (DML) statements that are meant to optimally synchronize the in-memory persistent state with the database.

- One single active Persistence Context should be allocated to
  the currently active database transaction. During the current
  database transaction lifespan, you can manipulate entities via the
  EntityManager methods (verbs/actions) and Hibernate JPA will
  buffer the entities' state transitions. Actions—such as as finding
  objects, persisting or merging them, and removing them from the
  database and so on—are specific to the EntityManager. In a more

simplistic day-to-day chat, there is nothing wrong with saying that the EntityManager instance is the current Persistence Context. As a rule of thumb, avoid using more than one Persistence Context per database physical transaction. See Figure A-3.

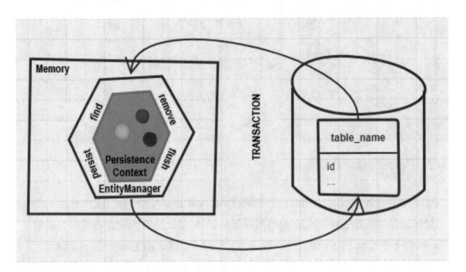

***Figure A-3.*** *Persistence Context operations*

- After you modify the in-memory Persistence Context via entity state management methods (e.g., persist(), remove(), etc.), you expect to see these modifications reflected in the database. This action is known as a *flush*, and it can be automatically or manually (not recommended) triggered multiple times during a transaction lifespan (for details about flushing, consider reading **Appendix H**). We say that, at the flush time, we synchronize the Persistence Context to the underlying database. There are different flushing strategies. The most commonly used method is likely Hibernate JPA: AUTO (the flush is triggered automatically before every query execution—SELECT—and prior to transaction commit) and COMMIT (flushing occurs only prior to transaction commit). Roughly, think of the flush operation as the bunch of SQL statements (DML) that need to be sent to the database in order to propagate your modifications. See Figure A-4.

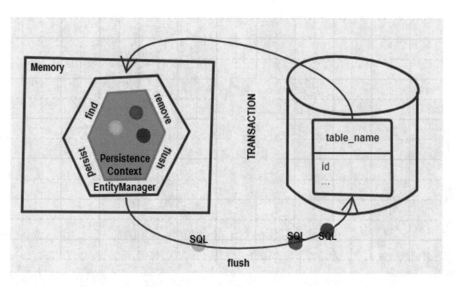

**Figure A-4.** *Persistence Context flush time*

- Once the current transaction completes (by commit or rollback), all objects that were in the Persistence Context are *detached*. Detaching all entities takes place when the EntityManager is cleared via the clear() method or closed via the close() method. Certain entities can be detached by calling a dedicated method named detach() (or evict() in Hibernate ORM). This means that further modifications to these objects will not be reflected in the database. Propagating subsequent changes is possible only after *merging* (via the merge() operation) or *reattaching* the objects (via the Hibernate ORM update(), saveOrUpdate(), or lock() operations) in the context of an active transaction. This is the default behavior of a *transactional-scoped* EntityManager (a.k.a., transactional Persistence Context). There is also the EntityManager that spans across multiple transactions (*extended-scope*), known as the Extended Persistence Context.

Don't conclude that JPA *merging* and Hibernate *reattaching* operations are the same.

JPA *merging* is an operation that loads a new entity object from the database (fetches the latest state of entity from the underlying database) and updates it by copying onto it the internal state of a detached entity. But, before loading a new entity, JPA merging takes into account the current Persistence Context managed entities. In other words, if the current Persistence Context already manages the needed entity, there is no need to load a new one from the database. It simply takes advantage of session-level repeatable reads. Note that this operation will overwrite changes that you have performed on this managed entity during the current session (the attribute values of the detached entity are copied to the managed entity). The `merge()` method returns the newly updated and managed instance.

*Hibernate reattaching* is a Hibernate-specific operation. Mainly, this operation takes places on the detached entity itself. Its purpose is to transition the passed entity object from a *detached* to *managed* (*persistent*) state. Trying to reattach a *transient* entity or an already loaded entity in the current Persistence Context will throw an exception. This operation bypasses the Dirty Checking mechanism and it is materialized in an UPDATE triggered at Persistence Context flush time. Since Hibernate didn't read the latest state of the entity from the underlying database, it cannot perform Dirty Checking. In other words, the UPDATE is triggered all the time, even if the entity and the database are in sync (contain the same values). This can be fixed by annotating the entity with `@SelectBeforeUpdate`. As the name of this annotation suggests, it instructs Hibernate to trigger a `SELECT` to fetch the entity and perform Dirty Checking on it before it generates an UPDATE statement. The `update()` method returns `void`.

Keep in mind that calling `update(obj)` with `@SelectBeforeUpdate` will select only *obj*, while calling `merge(obj)` will select *obj* and all associations with `CascadeType.MERGE`. This means that JPA merging is the proper choice for graphs of entities.

Generally speaking, try to respect the following rules:

- Use JPA `merge()` if you want to copy the detached entity state
- Use Hibernate-specific `update()` for batch processing
- Use JPA `persist()` for persisting an entity

- Upon detaching, objects leave the Persistence Context and continue to live outside of it. This means that JPA will not manage them anymore. They don't get special treatment and are just usual Java objects. For example, calling EntityManager#remove (*detached_ entity*) will throw a meaningful exception. See Figure A-5.

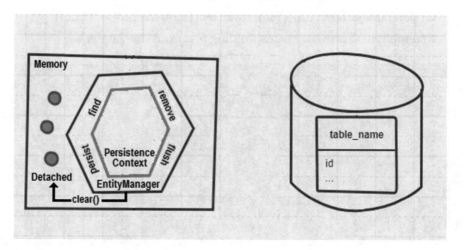

***Figure A-5.*** *Persistence Context with detached entities*

Programmatically, you can open an EntityManager via injection (@PersistenceContext) or via EntityManagerFactory#createEntityManager(). You can check the status of an EntityManager via the isOpen() method, you can clear it via the clear() method, and you can close it via the close() method.

# Entity State Transitions

A JPA entity can be in any of the following states:

- *Transient* (or *New*): A new entity that is totally unknown to the database (at flush time, Hibernate will issue an INSERT statement for it).

- *Managed* (or *Persistent*): The entity has a corresponding row in the database and is currently loaded in the Persistence Context. In read-write mode, at flush time, Hibernate will run the Dirty Checking mechanism for this entity, and, if it detects modifications, it will issue the proper UPDATE statements on your behalf.

- *Detached*: The entity was in the Persistence Context but the Persistence Context was closed or the entity was cleared/evicted (any modifications of a *detached* entity are not propagated automatically to the database).

- *Removed*: The entity was in the Persistence Context and it was marked for deletion (at flush time, Hibernate will issue the proper DELETE statement to delete the corresponding row from the database).

An entity that passes from *transient* to *managed* is translated into an INSERT statement.

An entity that passes from *managed* to *removed* is translated into a DELETE statement.

An entity that is *managed* and modified is handled by Dirty Checking to issue an UPDATE.

Figures A-6 and A-7 represent the entity state transitions in Hibernate JPA and Hibernate Core ORM.

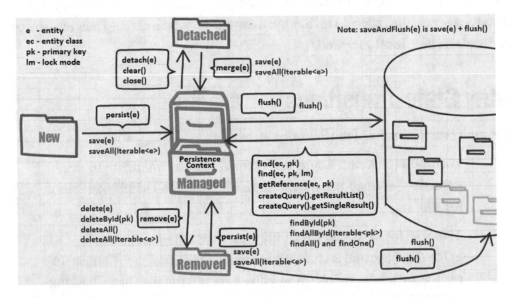

***Figure A-6.*** *Hibernate JPA entity state transitions and Spring Data built-in counterparts*

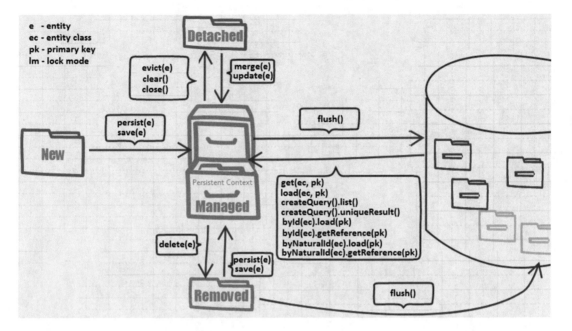

*Figure A-7.* *Hibernate ORM entity state transitions*

# APPENDIX B

# Associations Efficiency

The first chapter of this book covered the best practices for writing efficient associations. As a quick guide, try to follow these rules:

**One-to-One**

- Unidirectional/bidirectional @OneToOne with @MapsId and bidirectional @OneToOne with Bytecode Enhancement is efficient

- Bidirectional @OneToOne without @MapsId and Bytecode Enhancement and bidirectional @OneToOne with Bytecode Enhancement and optional=true is less efficient

**One-to-Many**

- Bidirectional @OneToMany and unidirectional @ManyToOne are efficient

- Bidirectional @OneToMany with @JoinColumn(name = "*foo_id*", insertable = false, updatable = false), unidirectional @OneToMany with Set, @JoinColumn and/or @OrderColumn are less efficient

- Unidirectional @OneToMany with List is quite inefficient

**Many-to-Many**

- Unidirectional/bidirectional @ManyToMany with Set and the alternative (relying on two bidirectional @OneToMany associations) are efficient

- Unidirectional/bidirectional @ManyToMany with @OrderColumn is less efficient

- Unidirectional/bidirectional @ManyToMany with List is quite inefficient

© Anghel Leonard 2020
A. Leonard, *Spring Boot Persistence Best Practices*, https://doi.org/10.1007/978-1-4842-5626-8

# Five SQL Performance Tips That Will Save Your Day

## Using SQL Functions in the WHERE Clause

It's well known that database indexes are meant to increase the performance of SQL queries. An index can turn a slow SQL into a fast SQL and influence the choice of the execution plan.

In order to be used by the database, the existence of an index is necessary, **but** it is not sufficient. In other words, an index is used or ignored depending on how you write the SQL.

For example, consider an index on a table column (e.g., address) to which you apply a SQL function in the WHERE clause. In such a case, the index will not be used! The index cannot be used because the database can't find the corresponding index on *function_name*(address). The index is only on that column.

One potential solution is to create an index on *function_name*(address). This is known as a *function-based* index (see Figure C-1):

```
CREATE INDEX addridx ON address (TRIM(addr));
```

Or, if function-based index is not supported:

```
ALTER TABLE address ADD trim_addr AS TRIM(addr);
CREATE INDEX addridx ON address (trim_addr);
```

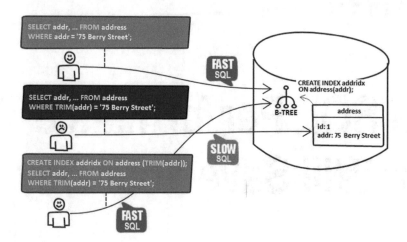

**Figure C-1.** *Function-based index*

# The Index Column Order Matters

A database index can be created on a single column or on multiple columns. In the latter case, the index is known as a *concatenated* index.

The performance of your SQL statements may be adversely affected if you don't take into account the fact that the concatenated index column order has a major impact on index usability.

Figure C-2 depicts the usability of a concatenated index created on two columns. Notice how the concatenated index column order affects the second query:

```
SELECT id, type, engine FROM car WHERE engine = 'V8';
```

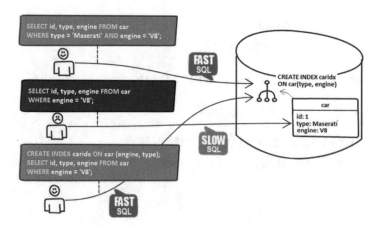

**Figure C-2.** *Concatenated index*

# Primary Key vs. Unique Key

Deciding between primary keys and unique keys is a task that requires you to be aware of the following main differences between them:

- A primary key uniquely identifies a row in a table, whereas a unique key ensures unique values in a column.

- A primary key cannot be NULL, whereas a unique key can be NULL.

- A table supports a single primary key but it supports multiple unique keys.

- By default, a primary key leads to a clustered index, whereas a unique key leads to an unclustered index.

- A primary key can be a composite (combining multiple columns in the same table, including columns that have unique keys), whereas a unique key can be used to make multiple columns unique together (composite unique constraint).

- A primary key cannot be deleted/modified, whereas a unique key can be deleted/modified.

- A primary key is built via a primary key constraint and a unique constraint (the latter is automatically added), whereas a unique key is built via a unique constraint (the unique constraint ensures that there are no duplicate values in that column).

> Commonly, unique indexes come into play when performance is involved. For example, if the database knows that, for a condition of type WHERE a = ?1, there will be only one suitable record, it will prepare an optimized execution plan.

# LIKE vs. Equals (=)

There is a debate about using the LIKE operator versus equals (=).

The LIKE operator is useful for flexible string matching, whereas equals (=) is useful when you don't need wildcards. The positions of wildcards in the LIKE expressions can have a significant impact on choosing the execution plan and on the index range that needs to be scanned. In the case of the LIKE operator, as a rule of thumb, you should put wildcards as late as possible in the pattern matching and try to avoid wildcards on the first position. This can trigger a full table/index scan and, as a consequence, a performance penalty.

Think of LIKE performance and LIKE vs. equals (=) in terms of SARGability, not in terms of comparing the operators. LIKE operator usage is strongly related to index utilization. If there is an index and the search string starts with a wildcard (e.g., LIKE '%abc') or there is no index to sustain SARGable expressions, then the query will read every row in the table (full table scan). Most probably, in this case, LIKE and equals (=) will act the same.

If the LIKE operator starts to represent a significant performance penalty then maybe it's time to consider full-text indexing or full-text search tools (e.g., Hibernate Search, Lucene, Solr, etc.). These tools provide more advanced operators than LIKE.

In Figure C-3, you can see usage of LIKE to search for a maryland string.

**Figure C-3.** *Placing the % wildcard in the LIKE operator*

As a rule of thumb:

- Place wildcards as late as possible and never on the first position
- Try to provide a "consistent" access predicate

## UNION vs. UNION ALL and JOIN Flavors

First, let's take a quick look at UNION vs. UNION ALL:

- UNION removes duplicates (it performs a DISTINCT on the result set), whereas UNION ALL doesn't remove duplicates.

- If you know that all the returned records are unique, then use UNION ALL instead of UNION.

- UNION is much less performant, especially if the number of duplicates is big. On the other hand, transferring more data (duplicates) over the network may be slower than applying DISTINCT and transferring less data.

- UNION sorts the final output, whereas UNION ALL doesn't (for sorting, you need to specify ORDER BY).

Second, let's bring JOIN into the discussion. If JOIN is an alternative to UNION(ALL) then inspect the execution plan and benchmark before deciding. Keep in mind that UNION(ALL) are blocking operators while JOIN is not. Even if they converge to the same result, UNION(ALL) and JOIN have different purposes. UNION(ALL) operators are just for combining the results of two (or more) SELECT statements, whereas JOIN combines data into new columns. Usually, JOIN performs better than UNION, but this is not a rule.

A famous and very inspired[1] representation of how JOIN and UNION work is shown in Figure C-4.

---

[1]https://www.essentialsql.com/what-is-the-difference-between-a-join-and-a-union/

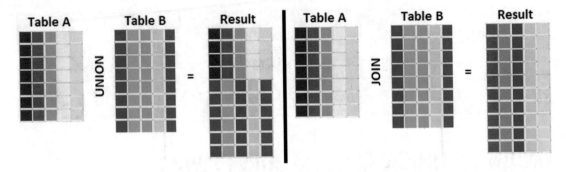

***Figure C-4.*** *UNION vs. JOIN*

In the context of this appendix, I strongly recommend you read this article[2] as well. And, if you have ever wondered how to calculate multiple aggregate functions into a single query,[3] then follow this second link.

---

[2]https://blog.jooq.org/2016/04/25/10-sql-tricks-that-you-didnt-think-were-possible/
[3]https://blog.jooq.org/2017/04/20/how-to-calculate-multiple-aggregate-functions-in-a-single-query/

# How to Create Useful Database Indexes

You can create an index via the SQL CREATE INDEX statement (as you saw in the previous appendix) or programmatically via JPA 2.1 or Hibernate-specific annotations.

## JPA 2.1 @Index

Starting with JPA 2.1, you can easily create indexes via the @Index annotation, as in the following example:

```
import javax.persistence.Column;
import javax.persistence.Entity;
import javax.persistence.Index;
import javax.persistence.Table;

@Entity
@Table(
    name = "author",
    indexes = {
            @Index(
                name = "index_name",
                columnList="name",
                unique = true
                ),
            @Index(
                name = "index_genre",
                columnList="genre",
```

© Anghel Leonard 2020
A. Leonard, *Spring Boot Persistence Best Practices*, https://doi.org/10.1007/978-1-4842-5626-8

```
                        unique = false
                        )
                }
        )
public class Author{

    @Column(name = "name", nullable = false)
    private String name;

    @Column(name = "genre", nullable = false)
    private String genre;
}
```

Or, to define multi-column indexes, follow this example:

```
import javax.persistence.Column;
import javax.persistence.Entity;
import javax.persistence.Index;
import javax.persistence.Table;

@Entity
@Table(
    name = "author",
    indexes = {
                @Index(
                    name = "index_name_genre",
                    columnList="name, genre",
                    unique = true
                    )

                }
        )
public class Author{

    @Column(name = "name", nullable = false)
    private String name;

    @Column(name = "genre", nullable = false)
    private String genre;
}
```

Hibernate ORM provides a deprecated `org.hibernate.annotations.Index`; therefore, you should rely on the JPA 2.1 approach.

Ideally, we create indexes to optimize the performance of our database and SQL queries. We create super-fast data access paths to avoid scanning the table space. But, this is all easier said than done. What is the best set of indexes for your tables? How do you decide when an index is needed? How do you decide if an index is useless? These are hard questions and the answers are tightly coupled to which queries you execute.

Nevertheless, this appendix spells out a developer-dedicated guideline that applies in most cases.

## Don't Guess the Indexes

Over the years I have witnessed this bad practice for creating database indexes. Developers watch the tables (schema), and without knowing how these tables will be accessed, try to guess what the proper indexes should be. This is like trying to guess which queries will be executed. Most of the time, you won't be right.

---

As a rule of thumb, to create the proper set of indexes, try to do the following:

- Get the list of SQL queries to be used

- Estimate the frequency of each SQL query

- Try to score the importance of each SQL query

Having these three coordinates, find the proper set of indexes that results in the highest optimizations and the least number of trade-offs.

---

## Prioritize the Most Used SQL Queries for Indexing

This tip highlights the second bullet from the previous section, "estimate the frequency of each query". The most frequently used SQL queries should have priority for indexing. If the most frequently used SQL queries are optimized, then you're more likely to get optimal application performance.

> As a rule of thumb, create indexes for the most used (heavily exploited) SQL queries and build indexes based on predicates.

## Important SQL Queries Deserve Indexes

When we talk about a query's importance, this primarily concerns the importance of the query for the business and, secondarily, for its users. For example, if a query is run every day for banking transactions or is run by an important user (e.g., the CIO/CDIO), it might deserve its own index. But, if a query is a simple routine or is executed by a clerk, then the existing indexes should provide the proper optimizations. Of course, this is not a rule for determining a query's importance! You have to decide on that in your context.

## Avoid Sorting Operations by Indexing GROUP BY and ORDER BY

Calling SQL clauses such as GROUP BY and ORDER BY may invoke sorting operations. These kinds of operations are typically slow (resource-intensive) and therefore prone to performance penalties (e.g., as ORDER BY does in SQL queries specific to pagination).

> By indexing on the columns specified in GROUP BY and ORDER BY, you can take advantage of optimizations that avoid sorting operations. Since an index provides an ordered representation of the indexed data, it keeps data preordered. Instead of applying sorting operations, the relational database may use the index. Here is an example:
>
> ```
> SELECT
>   *
>   FROM book
> WHERE genre = "History"
>   AND (publication_date, id) < (prev_publication_date, prev_id)
> ORDER BY publication_date DESC, id DESC
> LIMIT 50;
> ```

To optimize this query, you can create an index as follows:

```
CREATE INDEX book_idx ON book (publication_date, id);
```

Or, even better:

```
CREATE INDEX book_idx ON book (genre, publication_date, id);
```

This time, the database uses the index order and doesn't use the explicit sort operation.

# Rely on Indexes for Uniqueness

Most databases require unique indexes for primary keys and unique constraints. These requirements are part of the schema validation. Striving to write your SQL queries around these required indexes results in important benefits.

# Rely on Indexes for Foreign Keys

As the previous step mentions, a primary key constraint requires a unique index. This index is automatically created; therefore, the parent table's side takes advantage of indexing. On the other hand, a foreign key is a column (or a combination of columns) that appears in the child table and is used to define a relationship and ensure integrity of the parent and child tables.

**It is highly recommended that you create an index on each foreign key constraint on the child table.**

While the unique index for the primary key is automatically created, the unique index for the foreign key is the responsibility of the database administrator or the developers. In other words, if the database doesn't automatically create indexes for the foreign keys (e.g., SQL Server), then the indexes should be created manually by the database administrator or by the developers.

Among the benefits of using indexes for foreign keys are the following:

- Calling the indexed foreign key on your SQL JOIN between the child and the parent table columns will result in better performance.

- Reducing the cost of performing UPDATEs and DELETEs that imply cascading (CASCADE) or no action (NO ACTION).

> As a rule of thumb, after schema modifications, consider testing and monitoring your indexes to ensure that current/additional indexes don't negatively impact performance.

## Add Columns for Index-Only Access

Adding columns for *index-only* access is a technique known as *index overloading*. Basically, you create an index containing all the columns needed to satisfy the query. This means that the query will not require data from the table space. Therefore, it requires fewer I/O operations.

> For example, consider the following query:
>
> ```
> SELECT
>   isbn
>   FROM book
> WHERE genre = "History";
> ```
>
> And the following index:
>
> ```
> CREATE INDEX book_idx ON book (genre);
> ```
>
> The index can be used to access columns with a given genre, but the database would need to access the data in the table space to return the isbn. By adding the isbn column to the index, we have:
>
> ```
> CREATE INDEX book_idx ON book (genre, isbn);
> ```
>
> Now, all of the data needed for this query exists in the index and no additional table space operations are needed.

# Avoid Bad Standards

From coding style standards to recommended snippets of code for specific problems, companies love to use standards. Sometimes, among these standards, they sneak *bad* standards in as well. One of the bad standards I have seen says to limit the number of indexes per table to a certain value. This value varies between standards (e.g., 3, 5, 8, etc.), and this is the first sign that should raise your eyebrows that something is wrong here.

> It doesn't matter how many indexes you create per table! What matters is that every index must increase or sustain the performance of your queries and not cause significant issues in the efficiency of data modification. Data modifications (INSERT, UPDATE, and DELETE) require specific operations for maintaining the indexes as well. In a nutshell, database indexes speed the process of retrieval (SELECT), but slow down modifications (INSERT, UPDATE, and DELETE). So, as a rule of thumb, create as many indexes as are needed to support your database queries, as long as you are satisfied with the trade-off between retrieval and data modification.

# APPENDIX E

# SQL Phenomena

The SQL *phenomena* (or anomalies) are:

- *Dirty reads*

- *Non-repeatable reads*

- *Phantom reads*

- *Dirty writes*

- *Read skews*

- *Write skews*

- *Lost updates*

As their names suggest, these phenomena represent a set of data integrity anomalies that may occur when a developer tries to squeeze performance from transaction concurrency by relaxing the SERIALIZABLE isolation level in favor of another transaction isolation level.

> There is always a trade-off between choosing the transaction isolation level and the performance of transaction concurrency.

## Dirty Writes

A *dirty write* is a *lost update*. In a *dirty write* case, a transaction overwrites another concurrent transaction, which means that both transactions are allowed to affect the same row at the same moment. Figure E-1 depicts a scenario that folds in under the *dirty write* umbrella.

951

© Anghel Leonard 2020
A. Leonard, *Spring Boot Persistence Best Practices*, https://doi.org/10.1007/978-1-4842-5626-8

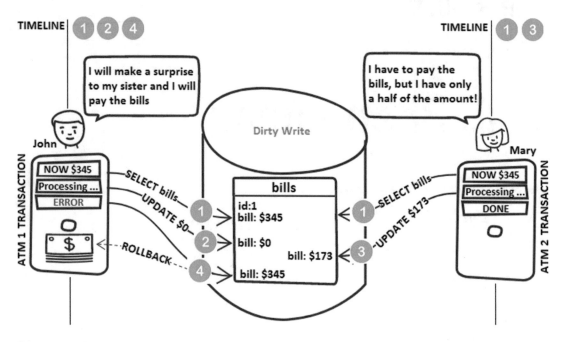

*Figure E-1.* *Dirty write*

**Step 1:** John tries to pay Mary's bills. First, his transaction triggers a SELECT to query the amount owed. Mary tries to pay these bills at the same time. Therefore, she triggers the exact same query and gets the same result as John ($345).

**Step 2:** John's transaction attempts to pay the entire amount owed. Consequently, the amount to pay is updated to $0.

**Step 3:** Mary's transaction is not aware of this update, and it attempts and succeeds to pay half of the amount owed (her transaction commits). The triggered UPDATE sets the amount to pay to $173.

**Step 4:** Unfortunately, John's transaction doesn't manage to commit and it must be rolled back. Therefore, the amount to pay is restored to $345. This means that Mary has just lost $172.

Making business decisions in such a context is very risky. The good news is that, by default, all database systems prevent *dirty writes* (even at the Read Uncommitted isolation level).

# Dirty Reads

A *dirty read* is commonly associated with the Read Uncommitted isolation level. In a *dirty read* case, a transaction reads the uncommitted modifications of another concurrent transaction that rolls back in the end. Figure E-2 depicts a scenario that folds in under the *dirty read* umbrella.

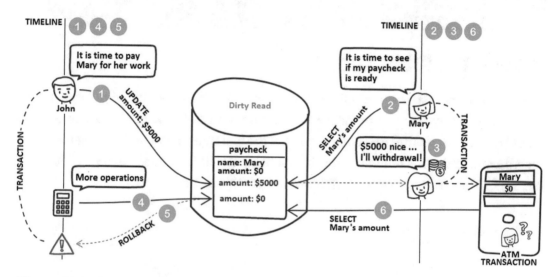

***Figure E-2.***  *Dirty read*

**Step 1:** John tries to pay Mary for her job. His transaction triggers an UPDATE that sets the paycheck amount to $5,000.

**Step 2:** Later, Mary is using her computer to query her paycheck and notices that John has transferred the money. Mary's transaction is committed.

**Step 3:** Mary decides to go to an ATM to withdraw the money.

**Step 4:** Meanwhile, John's transaction is enriched with more queries.

**Step 5:** John's transaction fails and is rolled back. Therefore, Mary's paycheck amount is restored to $0.

**Step 6:** Finally, Mary reaches the ATM and attempts to withdraw her paycheck. Unfortunately, this is not possible since the ATM reveals a paycheck of $0.

As you can see in Figure E-2, making business decisions based on uncommitted values can be very frustrating and can affect data integrity. As a quick solution, you can simply use a higher isolation level. As a rule of thumb, always check the default isolation level of your database system. Most probably, the default will not be Read Uncommitted, but check it anyway since you must be aware of it.

# Non-Repeatable Reads

A *non-repeatable read* is commonly associated with the Read Committed isolation level. A transaction reads some record while a concurrent transaction writes to the same record (a field or column) and commits. Later, the first transaction reads that same record again and gets a different value (the value that reflects the second transaction's changes). Figure E-3 depicts a possible scenario in this context.

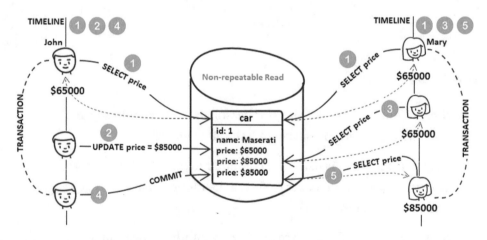

**Figure E-3.** *Non-repeatable reads*

**Step 1:** John's transaction triggers a SELECT and fetches the amount of $65,000. At the same time, Mary's transaction does exactly the same thing.

**Step 2:** John's transaction updates the price from $65,000 to $85,000.

**Step 3:** Mary's transaction reads the price again. The value is still $65,000 (therefore, a *dirty read* is prevented).

**Step 4:** John's transaction commits.

**Step 5:** Mary's transaction reads the price again. This time, she gets a price of $85,000. The price was updated due to John's transaction. This is a *non-repeatable read*.

*Non-repeatable reads* become problematic when the current transaction (e.g., Mary's transaction) makes a business decision based on the first read value. One solution is to set the isolation level as Repeatable Read or Serializable (both of them prevent this anomaly by default). Or, you can keep Read Committed, but acquire shared locks via SELECT FOR SHARE in an explicit way. Moreover, databases that use MVCC (Multi-Version Concurrency Control), which is most of them, prevent *non-repeatable reads* by checking the row version to see if it was modified by a transaction that is concurrent to the current one. If it has been modified, the current transaction can be aborted.

Hibernate guarantees session-level repeatable reads (see **Item 21**). This means that the fetched entities (via direct fetching or entity queries) are cached in the Persistence Context. Subsequent fetches (via direct fetching or entity queries) of the same entities are done from the Persistence Context. Nevertheless, this will not work for conversations that span over several (HTTP) requests. In such cases, a solution will rely on the Extended Persistence Context or, the recommended way, on detached entities (in web applications, the detached entities can be stored in an HTTP session). You also need an application-level concurrency control strategy such as Optimistic Locking to prevent *lost updates* (see **Item 131**).

# Phantom Reads

A *phantom read* is commonly associated with the Repeatable Read isolation level. A transaction reads a range of records (e.g., based on a condition). Meanwhile, a concurrent transaction inserts a new record in the same range of records and commits (e.g., inserts a new record that passes the same condition). Later, the first transaction reads the same range again and it sees the new record. Figure E-4 depicts a possible scenario in this context.

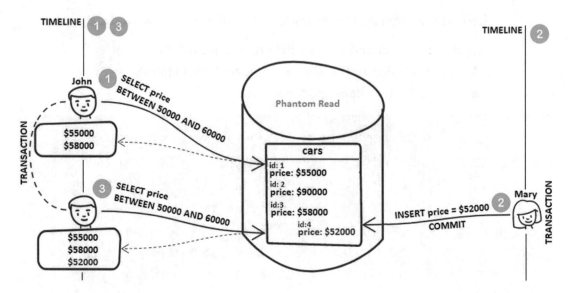

**Figure E-4.**  *Phantom read*

**Step 1:** John fetches car prices between $50,000 and $60,000. He gets two records.

**Step 2:** Mary inserts a new price of $52,000 (so a new record in the price range used by John). Mary's transaction commits.

**Step 3:** John fetches the prices between $50,000 and $60,000 again. This time, he gets three records, including the one inserted by Mary. This is called a *phantom read*.

> This anomaly can be prevented via the SERIALIZABLE isolation level or via MVCC consistent snapshots.

# Read Skews

A *read skew* is an anomaly that involves at least two tables (e.g., car and engine). A transaction reads from the first table (e.g., reads a record from the car table). Further, a concurrent transaction updates the two tables in sync (e.g., updates the car fetched by the first transaction and its corresponding engine). After both tables are updated, the first transaction reads from the second table (e.g., reads the engine corresponding to the car fetched earlier). The first transaction sees an older version of the car record (without being aware of the update) and the latest version of the associated engine. Figure E-5 depicts a possible scenario in this context.

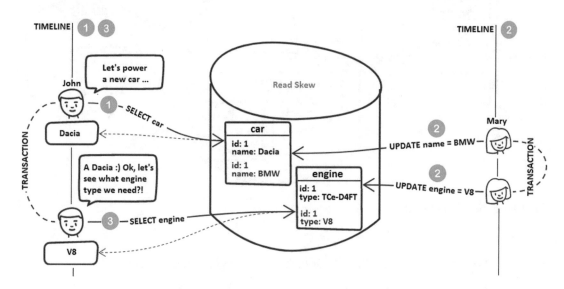

**Figure E-5.** *Read skew*

**Step 1:** John selects the car called Dacia from the car table.

**Step 2:** Mary updates in sync the car and engine tables. Note that Mary's transaction modified the engine corresponding to the Dacia car from TCe-D4FT to V8.

**Step 3:** John selects the engine corresponding to the Dacia car, and he gets V8. This is a *read skew*.

> You can prevent a *read skew* by acquiring shared locks on every read or by MVCC implementation of the Repeatable Read isolation level (or Serializable).

# Write Skews

A *write skew* is an anomaly that involves at least two tables (e.g., car and engine). Both tables should be updated in sync, but a *write skew* allows two concurrent transactions to break this constraint. Let's clarify this via the scenario shown in Figure E-6.

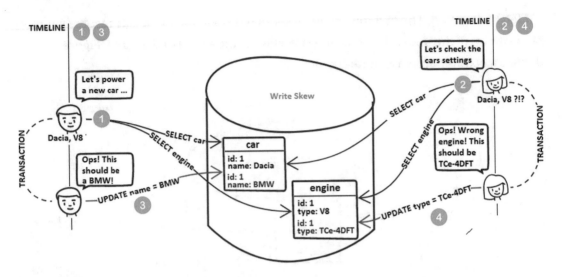

**Figure E-6.**  *Write skew*

**Step 1:** John selects the car Dacia and its associated engine, V8.

**Step 2:** Mary performs the same queries as John and gets the same results (both of them are aware that Dacia and V8 are not a compatible configuration and either the name of the car or the engine type is wrong).

**Step 3:** John decides to update the car name from Dacia to BMW.

**Step 4:** Mary decides to update the engine type from V8 to TCe-4DFT. This is a *write skew*.

> You can prevent *write skews* by acquiring shared locks on every read or by MVCC implementation of the Repeatable Read isolation level (or Serializable).

# Lost Updates

A *lost update* is a popular anomaly that can seriously affect data integrity. A transaction reads a record and uses this information to make business decisions (e.g., decisions that may lead to modification of that record) without being aware that, in the meantime, a concurrent transaction has modified that record and committed. When the first transaction commits, it is totally unaware of the *lost update*. This causes data integrity issues (e.g., inventory can report a negative quantity). Consider the possible scenario shown in Figure E-7.

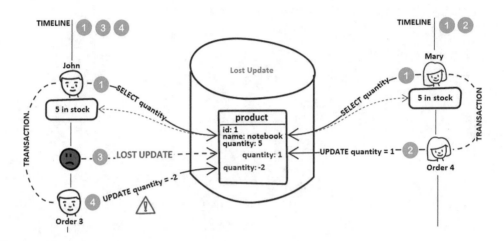

***Figure E-7.*** *Lost update*

**Step 1:** John and Mary fetch the quantity of notebooks (there are five in stock).

**Step 2:** Mary decides to buy four notebooks. Therefore, the quantity is reduced from 5 to 1.

**Step 3:** John's transaction is not aware of Mary's update.

**Step 4:** John decides to buy three notebooks. Therefore, the quantity becomes -2 (by definition, the quantity should be a positive integer).

This anomaly affects Read Committed isolation level and can be avoided by setting the Repeatable Read or Serializable isolation level. For the Repeatable Read isolation level without MVCC, the database uses shared locks to reject other transactions' attempts to modify an already fetched record.

In the presence of MVCC, a concurrent transaction (Transaction B) can perform changes to a record already fetched by a previous transaction (Transaction A). When the previous transaction (Transaction A) attempts to commit its change, the database compares the current value of the record version (which was modified by the concurrent transaction commit (Transaction B)) to the version that it is pushed via Transaction A. If there is a mismatch (which means the Transaction A has stale data), then Transaction A is rolled back by the application. When a record is modified, Hibernate can automatically attach the record version to the corresponding SQL via the application-level Optimistic Locking mechanism.

With long conversations that span over several (HTTP) requests, besides the application-level Optimistic Locking mechanism, you have to keep the old entity snapshots via Extended Persistence Context or, the recommended way, via detached entities (in web applications, they can be stored in the HTTP session).

# APPENDIX F

# Spring Transaction Isolation Level

Transaction isolation level is directly related to transaction ACID properties. As a developer, you can control how the changes to data in a transaction affect concurrent transactions by setting the transaction isolation level to one of its possible values. Moreover, each transaction isolation level closes the gate to a range of *phenomena*. This setting can be accomplished via the @Transactional annotation, isolation element.

## @Transactional(isolation =Isolation.READ_UNCOMMITTED)

|  | MySQL | PostgreSQL | SQL Server | Oracle |
|---|---|---|---|---|
| READ_ UNCOMMITTED | Prevents only *dirty writes* | Not supported | Prevents only *dirty writes* | Not supported |

The READ_UNCOMMITTED isolation level is the most relaxed isolation level. It states that a transaction can read data that is not committed yet. Figure F-1 depicts a possible scenario in this context (notice the *dirty read* phenomena).

A. Leonard, *Spring Boot Persistence Best Practices*, https://doi.org/10.1007/978-1-4842-5626-8

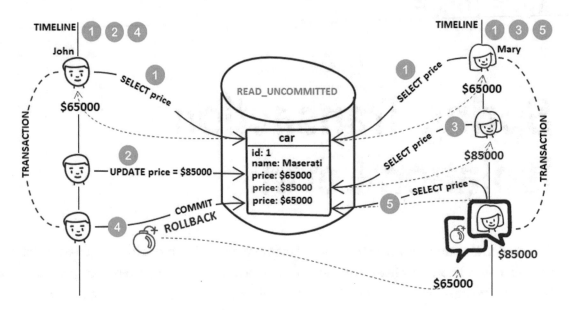

***Figure F-1.*** *Read uncommitted*

**Step 1:** John and Mary select the price of the Maserati in their own transactions.

**Step 2:** John updates the price from $65,000 to $85,000.

**Step 3:** Mary selects the price again as $85,000 (this is caused by Read Uncommitted).

**Step 4:** John commits his transaction but an error occurs and the transaction rolls back. Therefore, the Maserati's price is reset to its initial value, $65,000.

**Step 5:** Mary selects the price again as $65,000, but she already made some important decisions based on the $85,000 price that she saw earlier.

# @Transactional(isolation =Isolation.READ_COMMITTED)

|  | MySQL | PostgreSQL | SQL Server | Oracle |
| --- | --- | --- | --- | --- |
| READ_ COMMITTED | Prevents only *dirty reads* and *dirty writes* | Prevents only *dirty reads* and *dirty writes* | Prevents only *dirty reads* and *dirty writes* | Prevents only *dirty reads* and *dirty writes* |

The READ_COMMITTED isolation level states that a transaction cannot read uncommitted data of other concurrent transactions. It's a common approach to have this isolation level as the default, but note that even if it prevents *dirty write* and *dirty reads*, it still leaves the gate open to many other *phenomena*. Figure F-2 depicts a possible scenario in this context (notice the *non-repeatable read* phenomena).

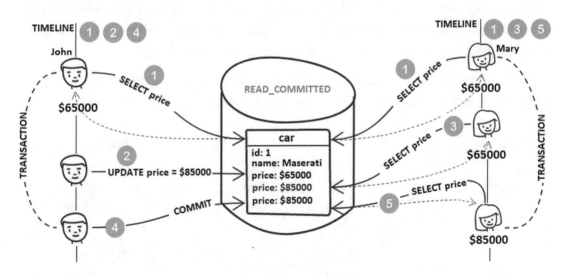

***Figure F-2.*** *Read committed*

**Step 1:** John and Mary select the price of the Maserati in their own transactions.

**Step 2:** John updates the price from $65,000 to $85,000.

**Step 3:** Mary selects the price again as $65,000. Thanks to the read committed isolation level, Mary doesn't see the new price, $85000, since John's transaction was not committed yet.

**Step 4:** John successfully commits his transaction and the price becomes $85,000.

**Step 5:** Mary selects the price again as $85,000 (John's transaction was committed earlier).

# @Transactional(isolation =Isolation.REPEATABLE_READ)

|  | MySQL | PostgreSQL | SQL Server | Oracle |
|---|---|---|---|---|
| REPEATABLE_READ | Still allows *lost updates* and *write skews* | Still allows *write skews* | Still allows *phantom reads* | Not supported |

As its name suggests, the REPEATABLE_READ isolation level states that a transaction reads the same result across multiple reads. For example, a transaction that reads one record from the database multiple times obtains the same result at each read.

Figure F-3 depicts a possible scenario in this context (this is specific to MySQL, which doesn't prevent *lost updates* but does prevent *non-repeatable reads*).

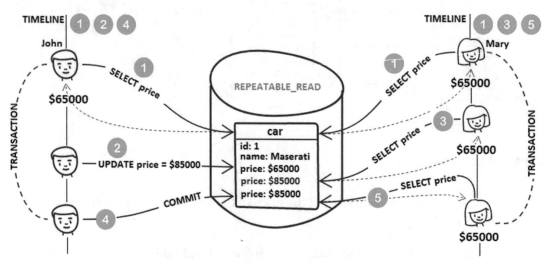

***Figure F-3.*** *Repeatable read*

**Step 1:** John and Mary select the price of the Maserati in their own transactions.

**Step 2:** John updates the price from $65,000 to $85,000 (in MySQL, this is allowed).

**Step 3:** Mary selects the price again as $65,000.

**Step 4:** John successfully commits his transaction and the price becomes $85,000.

**Step 5:** Mary selects the price again as $65,000 (MySQL prevents non-repeatable reads).

# @Transactional(isolation =Isolation.SERIALIZABLE)

|  | MySQL | PostgreSQL | SQL Server | Oracle |
|---|---|---|---|---|
| SERIALIZABLE | Prevents all *phenomena* | Prevents all *phenomena* | Prevents all *phenomena* (MVCC still allows *write skews*) | Still allows *write skews* |

The SERIALIZABLE isolation level is very strict but the trade-off is with performance. It uses locking at all levels, so it's equivalent to a serial execution. Theoretically speaking, SERIALIZABLE should prevent all *phenomena*, but in practice things are not quite so. The details of implementation are specific to each database and some of them are still prone to several *phenomena* (see the previous table mention). Figure F-4 shows serializable in action.

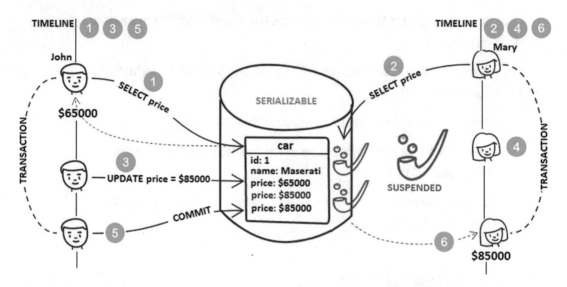

***Figure F-4.*** *Serializable*

**Step 1:** John selects the price of the Maserati in his transaction.

**Step 2:** Mary attempts to select the same record in her transaction but John's transaction has locked this data. So, Mary's transaction is suspended until the lock is released.

**Step 3:** John updates the price to $85,000.

**Step 4:** Mary's transaction is still suspended.

**Step 5:** John's transaction is successfully committed and the lock is released.

**Step 6:** Mary's transaction is resumed and she reads the price as $85,000.

# APPENDIX G

# Spring Transaction Propagation

Spring allows you to control the behavior of logical and physical transactions via transaction propagation mechanisms. There are seven types of transaction propagation mechanisms that you can set in a Spring application via `org.springframework.transaction.annotation.Propagation`.

> By default, the only exceptions that cause a transaction to roll back are the unchecked exceptions (like `RuntimeException`). Nevertheless, you can control this aspect via the `noRollbackFor`, `noRollbackForClassName`, `rollbackFor`, and `rollbackForClassName` elements of `@Transactional`.

## Propagation.REQUIRED

`Propagation.REQUIRED` is the default setting of a `@Transactional` annotation. The `REQUIRED` propagation can be interpreted as follows:

- If there is no existing physical transaction, then the Spring container will create one

- If there is an existing physical transaction then the methods annotated with `REQUIRE` will participate in this physical transaction

- Each method annotated with `REQUIRED` demarcates a logical transaction and these logical transactions participate in the same physical transaction

© Anghel Leonard 2020
A. Leonard, *Spring Boot Persistence Best Practices*, https://doi.org/10.1007/978-1-4842-5626-8

- Each logical transaction has its own scope, but, in case of this propagation mechanism, all these scopes are mapped to the same physical transaction

> Because all the scopes of the logical transactions are mapped to the same physical transaction, when one of these logical transactions is rolled back, all the logical transactions of the current physical transaction are rolled back.

Consider the following two logical transactions (or think of it as one outer logical transaction containing an inner logical transaction):

```java
@Transactional(propagation=Propagation.REQUIRED)
public void insertFirstAuthor() {

    Author author = new Author();
    author.setName("Joana Nimar");

    authorRepository.save(author);

    insertSecondAuthorService.insertSecondAuthor();
}

@Transactional(propagation = Propagation.REQUIRED)
public void insertSecondAuthor() {

    Author author = new Author();
    author.setName("Alicia Tom");

    authorRepository.save(author);

    if(new Random().nextBoolean()) {
        throw new RuntimeException("DummyException: this should cause
            rollback of both inserts!");
    }
}
```

**Step 1:** When the insertFirstAuthor() method is called, there is no physical transaction. Spring creates one for executing the outer logical transaction—this method's code.

**Step 2:** When insertSecondAuthor() is called from the insertFirstAuthor(), there is an existing physical transaction. Therefore, Spring *invites* the inner logical transaction represented by the insertSecondAuthor() method to participate in this physical transaction.

**Step 3:** If the RuntimeException caused randomly at the end of insertSecondAuthor() method is thrown, then Spring will roll back both logical transactions. Therefore, nothing will be inserted in the database.

Figure G-1 depicts how the Propagation.REQUIRED flows (1 - this is the **START** point representing the first method call, insertFirstAuthor(); 2 - this is the second method call, insertSecondAuthor().)

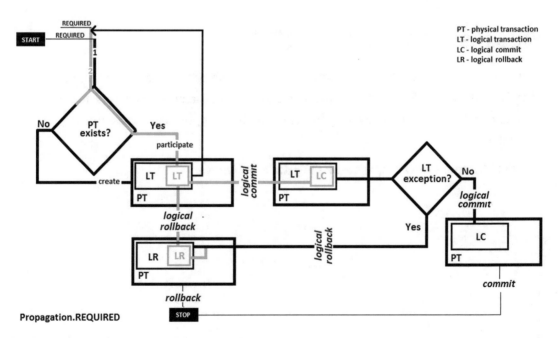

***Figure G-1.*** *Propagation.REQUIRED*

Catching and handling `RuntimeException` in `insertFirstAuthor()` will still roll back the outer logical transaction. This is happening because the inner logical transaction sets the *rollback-only* marker, and, since the scopes of both logical transactions are mapped to the same physical transaction, the outer logical transaction is rolled back as well. Spring will silently roll back both logical transactions and then throw the following exception:

```
org.springframework.transaction.UnexpectedRollbackException:
Transaction silently rolled back because it has been marked as
rollback-only
```

The outer logical transaction needs to receive an `UnexpectedRollbackException` to indicate clearly that a rollback of the inner logical transaction was performed and it should therefore be rolled back as well.

# Propagation.REQUIRES_NEW

`Propagation.REQUIRES_NEW` instructs the Spring container to always create a new physical transaction. Such transactions can also declare their own timeouts, read-only, and isolation level settings and **not inherit** an outer physical transaction's characteristics.

Figure G-2 depicts how `Propagation.REQUIRES_NEW` flows.

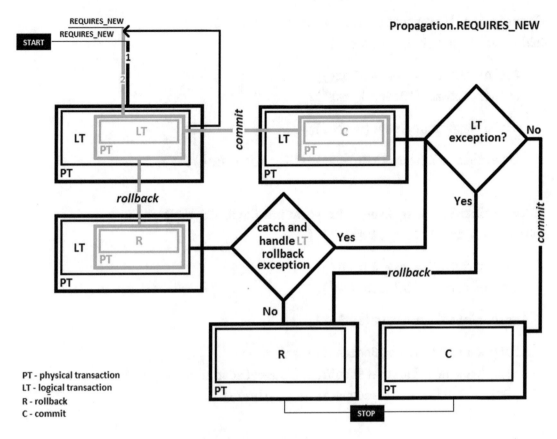

*Figure G-2.*  *Propagation.REQUIRES_NEW*

Pay attention to how you handle this aspect since each physical transaction needs it
own database connection. So, an outer physical transaction will have its own database
connection, while REQUIRES_NEW will create the inner physical transaction and will
bound a new database connection to it. In a synchronous execution, while the inner
physical transaction is running, the outer physical transaction is suspended and its
database connection remains open. After the inner physical transaction commits, the
outer physical transaction is resumed, continuing to run and commit/roll back.

> If the inner physical transaction is rolled back, it may or may not affect the
> outer physical transaction.

971

```
@Transactional(propagation=Propagation.REQUIRED)
public void insertFirstAuthor() {

    Author author = new Author();
    author.setName("Joana Nimar");

    authorRepository.save(author);

    insertSecondAuthorService.insertSecondAuthor();
}

@Transactional(propagation = Propagation.REQUIRES_NEW)
public void insertSecondAuthor() {

    Author author = new Author();
    author.setName("Alicia Tom");

    authorRepository.save(author);

    if(new Random().nextBoolean()) {
        throw new RuntimeException ("DummyException: this should cause
            rollback of second insert only!");
    }
}
```

Step 1: The first physical transaction (outer) is created when you call insertFirstAuthor(), because there is no existing physical transaction.

Step 2: When the insertSecondAuthor() is called from insertFirstAuthor(), Spring will create another physical transaction (inner).

Step 3: If the RuntimeException is thrown, then both physical transactions (the inner first and outer afterwards) are rolled back. This is happening because the exception thrown in insertSecondAuthor() is propagated to the caller, the insertFirstAuthor(), therefore causing rollback of the outer physical transaction as well. If this is not the desired behavior, and you want to roll back only the inner physical transaction without affecting the outer physical transaction, you need to catch and handle the RuntimeException in insertFirstAuthor(), as shown here:

```
@Transactional(propagation = Propagation.REQUIRED)
public void insertFirstAuthor() {
    Author author = new Author();
    author.setName("Joana Nimar");

    authorRepository.save(author);

    try {
        insertSecondAuthorService.insertSecondAuthor();
    } catch (RuntimeException e) {
        System.err.println("Exception: " + e);
    }
}
```

The outer physical transaction commits even if the inner physical transaction is rolled back.

---

If the outer physical transaction is rolled back after the inner physical transaction is committed, the inner physical transaction is not affected.

---

## Propagation.NESTED

NESTED acts like REQUIRED, only it uses *savepoints* between nested invocations. In other words, inner logical transactions may roll back independently of outer logical transactions.

Figure G-3 depicts how Propagation.NESTED flows.

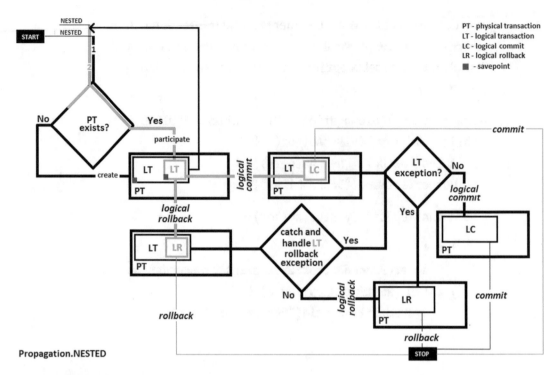

*Figure G-3.*  *Propagation.NESTED*

Trying to use NESTED with Hibernate JPA will result in a Spring exception as follows:

```
NestedTransactionNotSupportedException: JpaDialect does not support
savepoints - check your JPA provider's capabilities
```

This is happening because Hibernate JPA doesn't support nested transactions. The Spring code that causes the exception is:

```
private SavepointManager getSavepointManager() {

    ...

    SavepointManager savepointManager
        = getEntityManagerHolder().getSavepointManager();
    if (savepointManager == null) {
            throw new NestedTransactionNotSupportedException(
                "JpaDialect does not support ...");
    }
```

```
    return savepointManager;
}
```

One solution is to use `JdbcTemplate` or a JPA provider that supports nested transactions.

## Propagation.MANDATORY

`Propagation.MANDATORY` requires an existing physical transaction or will cause an exception, as follows:

```
org.springframework.transaction.IllegalTransactionStateException: No
existing transaction found for transaction marked with propagation
'mandatory'.
```

Figure G-4 depicts how `Propagation.MANDATORY` flows.

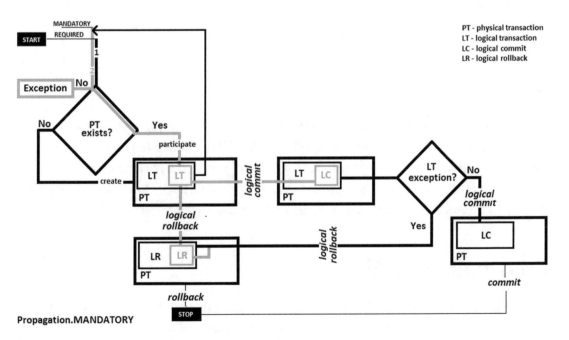

Propagation.MANDATORY

***Figure G-4.*** *Propagation.MANDATORY*

Consider the following code:

```
@Transactional(propagation=Propagation.REQUIRED)
public void insertFirstAuthor() {

    Author author = new Author();
    author.setName("Joana Nimar");

    authorRepository.save(author);

    insertSecondAuthorService.insertSecondAuthor();
}

@Transactional(propagation = Propagation.MANDATORY)
public void insertSecondAuthor() {

    Author author = new Author();
    author.setName("Alicia Tom");

    authorRepository.save(author);

    if (new Random().nextBoolean()) {
        throw new RuntimeException("DummyException: this should
            cause rollback of both inserts!");
    }
}
```

When insertSecondAuthor() is called from insertFirstAuthor(), there is an existing physical transaction (created via Propagation.REQUIRED). Further, the inner logical transaction represented by the insertSecondAuthor() code will participate in this physical transaction. If this inner logical transaction is rolled back, then the outer logical transaction is rolled back as well, exactly as with the case of Propagation.REQUIRED.

# Propagation.NEVER

The Propagation.NEVER states that no physical transaction should exist. If a physical transaction is found, then NEVER will cause an exception as follows:

```
org.springframework.transaction.IllegalTransactionStateException: Existing
transaction found for transaction marked with propagation 'never'
```

Figure G-5 depicts how `Propagation.NEVER` flows.

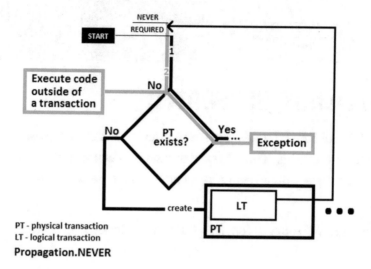

**Propagation.NEVER**

***Figure G-5.*** *Propagation.NEVER*

Check out the following code:

```
@Transactional(propagation = Propagation.NEVER)
public void insertFirstAuthor() {

    Author author = new Author();
    author.setName("Joana Nimar");

    authorRepository.save(author);
}
```

**Step 1:** When `insertFirstAuthor()` is called, Spring searches for an existing physical transaction.

**Step 2:** Since none is available, Spring will not cause an exception and will run this method's code outside of a physical transaction.

**Step 3:** When the code reaches the `save()` method, Spring will open a physical transaction especially for running this call. This happens because `save()` takes advantage of the default `Propagation.REQUIRED`.

> When you call a method annotated with NEVER, you must ensure that no physical transaction is open. The code inside this method can open physical transactions with no problem.

## Propagation.NOT_SUPPORTED

Propagation.NOT_SUPPORTED states that if a physical transaction exists, then it will be suspended before continuing. This physical transaction will be automatically resumed at the end. After this transaction is resumed, it can be rolled back (in case of a failure) or committed.

Figure G-6 depicts how Propagation.NOT_SUPPORTED flows.

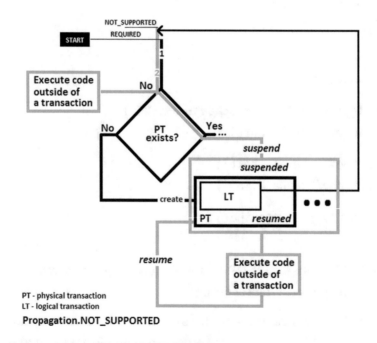

***Figure G-6.***  *Propagation.NOT_SUPPORTED*

Let's see some code:

```
@Transactional(propagation = Propagation.REQUIRED)
public void insertFirstAuthor() {
```

```
    Author author = new Author();
    author.setName("Joana Nimar");

    authorRepository.save(author);

    insertSecondAuthorService.insertSecondAuthor();
}

@Transactional(propagation = Propagation.NOT_SUPPORTED)
public void insertSecondAuthor() {

    Author author = new Author();
    author.setName("Alicia Tom");

    authorRepository.save(author);

    if (new Random().nextBoolean()) {
        throw new RuntimeException("DummyException: this should cause "
            + "rollback of the insert triggered in insertFirstAuthor() !");
    }
}
```

**Step 1:** When insertFirstAuthor() is called, there is no physical transaction available. Therefore, Spring will create a transaction conforming to Propagation.REQUIRED.

**Step 2:** Further, the code triggers an insert (the author Joana Nimar is persisted in the database).

**Step 3:** The insertSecondAuthor() statement is called from insertFirstAuthor(), and Spring must evaluate the presence of Propagation.NOT_SUPPORTED. There is an existing physical transaction; therefore, before continuing, Spring will suspend it.

**Step 4:** The code from insertSecondAuthor() is executed outside of any physical transaction until the flow hits the save() call. By default, this method is under the Propagation.REQUIRED umbrella; therefore, Spring creates a physical transaction, performs the INSERT (for Alicia Tom), and commits this transaction.

**Step 5:** The insertSecondAuthor() remaining code is executed outside of a physical transaction.

**Step 6:** After the `insertSecondAuthor()` code completes, Spring resumes the suspended physical transaction and resumes the execution of the `insertFirstAuthor()` logical transaction where it left off. If the `RuntimeException` was thrown in `insertSecondAuthor()`, then this exception was propagated in `insertFirstAuthor()`, and this logical transaction is rolled back.

---

Even if the transaction is suspended thanks to `Propagation.NOT_ SUPPORTED`, you should still strive to avoid long-running tasks. Note that while the transaction is suspended, the attached database connection is still active, so the pool connection cannot reuse it. In other words, the database connection is active even when its bounded transaction is suspended:

```
...
Suspending current transaction
HikariPool-1 - Pool stats (total=10, active=1, idle=9, waiting=0)
Resuming suspended transaction after completion of inner transaction
```

---

# Propagation.SUPPORTS

`Propagation.SUPPORTS` states that if a physical transaction exists, then it will execute the demarcated method as a logical transaction in the context of this physical transaction. Otherwise, it will execute this method outside of a physical transaction. Let's see some code:

```
@Transactional(propagation = Propagation.REQUIRED)
public void insertFirstAuthor() {

    Author author = new Author();
    author.setName("Joana Nimar");

    authorRepository.save(author);

    insertSecondAuthorService.insertSecondAuthor();
}
```

```
@Transactional(propagation = Propagation.SUPPORTS)
public void insertSecondAuthor() {

    Author author = new Author();
    author.setName("Alicia Tom");

    authorRepository.save(author);

    if (new Random().nextBoolean()) {
        throw new RuntimeException("DummyException: this should cause
            rollback of both inserts!");
    }
}
```

**Step 1:** When insertFirstAuthor() is called, there is no physical transaction available. Therefore, Spring will create a transaction conforming to Propagation.REQUIRED.

**Step 2:** Further, Spring starts the execution of the outer logical transaction represented by the insertFirstAuthor() method and triggers an insert via the save() method (the author Joana Nimar is persisted in the database).

**Step 3:** The insertSecondAuthor() is called from insertFirstAuthor(), and Spring must evaluate the presence of Propagation.SUPPORTS. There is an existing physical transaction. Therefore, the code from insertSecondAuthor() is executed as an inner logical transaction in the context of this physical transaction. If a RuntimeException is thrown, then the inner and the outer logical transactions are rolled back.

Catching and handling the RuntimeException in insertFirstAuthor() will still roll back the outer logical transaction. This is happening because the inner logical transaction sets the *rollback-only* marker and the scopes of both logical transactions are mapped to the same physical transaction.

Figure G-7 depicts how `Propagation.SUPPORTS` flows.

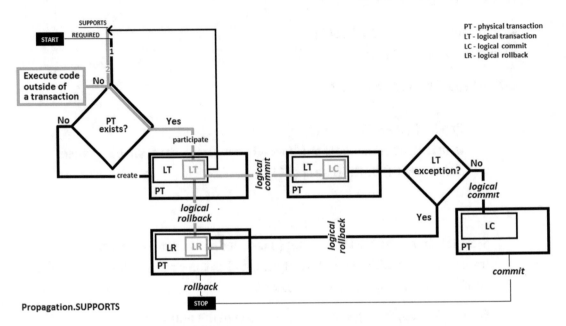

**Figure G-7.** *Propagation.SUPPORTS*

Let's remove `@Transactional(propagation = Propagation.REQUIRED)` from `insertFirstAuthor()` and evaluate the flow again:

> **Step 1:** When `insertFirstAuthor()` is called, there is no physical transaction available, and Spring will not create one because `@Transactional` is missing.

> **Step 2:** The code from `insertFirstAuthor()` starts to be executed outside of a physical transaction until the flow hits the `save()` call. By default, this method is under the `Propagation.REQUIRED` umbrella, so Spring creates a physical transaction, performs the insert (for Joana Nimar), and commits this transaction.

> **Step 3:** When `insertSecondAuthor()` is called from `insertFirstAuthor()`, Spring will need to evaluate the presence of `Propagation.SUPPORTS`. There is no physical transaction present and Spring will not create one conforming to the `Propagation.SUPPORTS` definition.

**Step 4:** Until the flow hits the save() method present in insertSecondAuthor(), the code is executed outside of a physical transaction. By default, save() is under the Propagation. REQUIRED umbrella, so Spring creates a physical transaction, performs the insert (for Alicia Tom), and commits this transaction.

**Step 5:** When RuntimeException is thrown, there is no physical transaction, so nothing is rolled back.

The suite of examples used in this appendix is available on GitHub[1].

---

[1]HibernateSpringBootTransactionPropagation

# Understanding the Flushing Mechanism

*Flushing* is the mechanism of synchronizing the in-memory persistent state (Persistence Context) with the database. During a transaction's lifespan, flushing can occur multiple times and can be done manually (via an explicit call of the `EntityManager#flush()` method or the Hibernate-specific, `Session#flush()`—use this technique only if is absolutely necessary) or automatically. Automatic flush is very convenient since you may forget to explicitly call the `flush()` method (especially before the transaction commits). If the Persistence Context is closed (or cleared) and you forget to flush the pending modifications, these modifications are lost. They will not be available in the database. Moreover, automatic flush comes with cool optimizations.

Besides storing or caching the entities (remember that the Persistence Context is also known as the First Level Cache), the Persistence Context acts as a buffer for entities' state transitions. In other words, the Persistence Context buffers the entities' modifications that you perform via entity state management methods (e.g., `persist()`, `remove()`, etc.) provided by the `EntityManager` API (or, in Hibernate ORM, by the `Session` API).

The Persistence Context acts as a transactional *write-behind* cache. What does this mean? First of all, since the entities' state modifications are buffered, Hibernate can postpone the Persistence Context flush until the last moment. However, at flush time (which can be multiple times during a transaction), Hibernate translates the buffered entities' state transitions into Data Manipulation Language (DML) statements (`INSERT`, `UPDATE`, and `DELETE`), which are meant to synchronize the in-memory persistent state with the database. The operation of copying the entity state into an `INSERT` or `UPDATE` statement is called *dehydration* in Hibernate. Since the pending modifications are delayed until the last moment, Hibernate can determine the minimum number of DML statements needed to synchronize the in-memory Persistence Context with the

985

© Anghel Leonard 2020
A. Leonard, *Spring Boot Persistence Best Practices*, https://doi.org/10.1007/978-1-4842-5626-8

database. **Obviously, by manually forcing flush (by explicitly calling** *flush* **methods), you may diminish the benefits of letting Hibernate decide the best flush plan.** For example, among the benefits of a transactional *write-behind* cache are these:

- JDBC batching is used.

- If an entity is updated more than once, Hibernate still fires only one UPDATE statement.

- If an entity is updated and then deleted, only the DELETE is performed.

# Strict Flush Order of Actions

Until the flush time, Hibernate buffers the entities' modifications (actions) in the Persistence Context—more precisely, in ActionQueue. At flush time, Hibernate empowers a very strict order of processing these actions, as follows:

1.  OrphanRemovalAction

2.  EntityInsertAction and EntityIdentityInsertAction

3.  EntityUpdateAction

4.  CollectionRemoveAction

5.  CollectionUpdateAction

6.  CollectionRecreateAction

7.  EntityDeleteAction

It's very important to be aware of this order. In a nutshell, the DML corresponding to the entities' actions starts with INSERT statements, continues with UPDATE statements, and finishes with DELETE statements. Since this strict order governs the data access layer actions and it was chosen to minimize the chances of constraint violations, you have to pay attention to how you write and interpret your data access layer code. Coding without respect to this strict order may lead to unexpected behaviors and exceptions (e.g., ConstraintViolationException). Whenever you are in such situations, take your time and try to find the correct fix. Almost always, the wrong fix (hack) is to disturb this order by forcing flushes via explicitly calling the *flush* methods. Consider that explicit flush is a *code smell* and should be used only in a handful of cases (e.g., in batching inserts or in bulk operations such as deletes).

## Flush Before Executing a Data Query Language (DQL): SELECT Query

JPA (and Hibernate ORM) empowers a *flush-before-query* strategy in order to maintain the *read-your-own-writes* consistency.

Unless you use a Second Level Cache, DQL SELECT queries are executed against the database, and a query must see the in-memory changes as well. Therefore a prior flush is required. **If this flush is not triggered before the query execution, the query is prone to not read your own writes, which may lead to data inconsistencies**. But, once the flush is triggered, the flushed changes become visible to the query and to the current database transaction. They will become visible to other transactions and Persistence Contexts only after this transaction commits.

## Flush Before Transaction Commits

After the current transaction commits, the Persistence Context is cleared and closed (except when using the Extended Persistence Context).

Once the Persistence Context is cleared and closed, the entities' in-memory changes are lost. In order to prevent this behavior, JPA (and Hibernate ORM) triggers the flush right before the transaction commits. This way, the entities' in-memory changes are propagated to the database and these changes become *durable*.

## Automatic Flush Modes

Flushing before a query execution and before transaction commits is accomplished by JPA (and Hibernate ORM) via automatic flush modes.

The automatic flush mode of the Persistence Context should work as follows:

- Before running a DQL SELECT, JPA JPQL, or Hibernate-specific HQL query

- Before executing a native DQL SELECT query

- Before the transaction commits

JPA defines two flush modes via `javax.persistence.FlushModeType`:

- AUTO: This is the default flush mode that triggers a flush before every query execution (including native queries) and before the transaction commits. This flush mode follows the JPA specification, which says that AUTO should guarantee that all pending changes are visible by any executing query. **This is the default flush mode if we bootstrap Hibernate as the JPA provider in a Spring Boot (Spring) application**.

- COMMIT: Triggers a flush only before the transaction commits.

Hibernate ORM defines four flush modes via `org.hibernate.FlushMode`:

- AUTO: This is the default flushing mode that sits behind a Hibernate-specific optimized flushing mechanism meant to increase the performance of the data access layer. The goal of this optimization is to reduce the number of flushes by using an intelligent algorithm that detects when a flush is mandatory and when it can be avoided. The main target behind this optimization is to perform a flush operation only if the current executed query needs a pending DML, INSERT, UPDATE, or DELETE statement. So, while a flush is triggered before the transaction commits, it may skip the overhead of premature flushes before query execution. This way, the premature flushes are delayed as much as possible. Ideally, it will remain a single flush, the one triggered before the transaction commits, and this flush will propagate all the needed DML statements.

The Hibernate-specific smart AUTO flush mode also has a major shortcoming. It doesn't work for native queries. Even if necessary, it will not trigger a Persistence Context flush when a native query is executed.

Hibernate cannot parse native queries because it understands limited SQL syntax (database vendors support a lot of features exposed via SQL native queries). Therefore, it cannot determine the referenced tables that may require a flush.

This behavior may lead to *read-your-writes* inconsistencies. In such cases, it is advisable to switch to flush mode, ALWAYS, or add a table space synchronization via `org.hibernate.SQLQuery` (until Hibernate 5.2)/`org.hibernate.NativeQuery` (Hibernate 5.3+) dedicated methods (e.g., the `addSynchronizedEntityClass()` method). Consider reading the documentation for details.

**This AUTO flush mode is used automatically only if you are bootstrapping Hibernate natively (e.g., via the Hibernate `SessionFactoryBuilder`, `BootstrapServiceRegistryBuilder`, etc.). If you bootstrap Hibernate as the JPA provider, this flush mode is not used automatically. Therefore, from this perspective, there is no risk of data inconsistency.**

**Using Spring Boot and `spring-boot-starter-data-jpa` as the starter for using Spring Data JPA with Hibernate will rely on JPA's AUTO flush mode, not on the Hibernate-specific AUTO flush mode.**

- ALWAYS: This is like the JPA AUTO mode. It triggers a flush before every query execution (including native queries).

Whenever the Hibernate-specific flush mode AUTO is automatically used (**e.g., if you bootstrap Hibernate natively via the Hibernate `BootstrapServiceRegistryBuilder`, `SessionFactoryBuilder`, etc.**), you should consider the shortcomings described here about this flush mode and native queries. For example, say you bootstrapped Hibernate natively and you have the following code running in a transaction:

```
entityManager.persist(new Book().setTitle("Carrie"));

entityManager.createNativeQuery(
    "SELECT COUNT(*) FROM book").getSingleResult();
```

The flush is delayed until the transaction commits, so the triggered SQL statements are:

```
SELECT COUNT(*) FROM book
INSERT INTO book (title, ...) VALUES ("Carrie", ...);
```

This is a common *read-your-writes* inconsistency scenario. The native SQL query didn't benefit from the prior flush, so it doesn't see the *Carrie* book.

To fix this quickly, you can switch to flush mode ALWAYS for the native query as follows:

```
entityManager.createNativeQuery("SELECT COUNT(*) FROM book")
    .unwrap(org.hibernate.query.Query.class)
    .setHibernateFlushMode(FlushMode.ALWAYS)
    .getSingleResult();
```

This time, the flush takes place before the SQL native query execution. That means the *read-your-writes* inconsistency was eliminated:

```
INSERT INTO book (title, ...) VALUES ("Carrie", ...);
SELECT COUNT(*) FROM book
```

Setting flush mode for all queries in the current `Session` can be done as follows:

```
entityManager.unwrap(Session.class)
    .setHibernateFlushMode(FlushMode.ALWAYS);
```

Or, for all sessions (application-level) via `application.properties`:

```
spring.jpa.properties.org.hibernate.flushMode=ALWAYS
```

Relying on the ALWAYS flush mode guarantees *read-your-writes* consistency. Native queries will take into consideration any pending modifications that were scheduled to be executed at flush time.

As a rule of thumb, do not trade data consistency for application efficiency. In other words, don't permit data inconsistencies just to avoid several premature flushes.

- COMMIT: This is like the JPA COMMIT mode.

- MANUAL: This flush mode disables automatic flushes and requires explicit calls of dedicated *flush* methods.

## Let the Code Talk

First of all, notice that when the flush() method of a repository is called (automatically or manually), Spring Boot calls the EntityManager#flush() behind the scenes. This flush() method is defined in SimpleJpaRepository as follows:

```
// em is the EntityManager
@Transactional
Override
public void flush() {
    em.flush();
}
```

This is the EntityManager provided by Spring Boot via Hibernate JPA. Its implementation simply delegates the call to the underlying Session. Its implementation is available in Hibernate ORM, in AbstractEntityManagerImpl:

```
public void flush() {

    if (!isTransactionInProgress()) {
        throw new TransactionRequiredException(
            "no transaction is in progress");
    }

    try {
        getSession().flush();
    } catch (RuntimeException e) {
        throw convert( e );
    }
}
```

> When you use Hibernate as the JPA provider in a Spring Boot application, flushing operations will synchronize the underlying current Session with the database.

The following examples use Hibernate as the JPA provider configured via application.properties as usual. Let's see how you can set flush modes.

You can determine the current flush mode for the JPA EntityManager as follows:

```
System.out.println(
    "Flush mode, Hibernate JPA (EntityManager#getFlushMode()): "
    + entityManager.getFlushMode());

System.out.println(
    "Flush mode, Hibernate JPA (Session#getFlushMode()): "
    + (entityManager.unwrap(Session.class)).getFlushMode());
```

And you can determine the current flush mode for the Hibernate Session as follows (starting with Hibernate 5.2):

```
System.out.println(
    "Flush mode, Hibernate Session (Session#getHibernateFlushMode()): "
    + (entityManager.unwrap(Session.class)).getHibernateFlushMode());
```

If you run this code in a service-method annotated with @Transactional, the output will be as follows:

```
Flush mode, Hibernate JPA (EntityManager#getFlushMode()): AUTO
Flush mode, Hibernate JPA (Session#getFlushMode()): AUTO
Flush mode, Hibernate Session (Session#getHibernateFlushMode()): AUTO
```

If you run this code in a service-method annotated with @Transactional(readOnly=true), the output will be as follows:

```
Flush mode, Hibernate JPA (EntityManager#getFlushMode()): COMMIT
Flush mode, Hibernate JPA (Session#getFlushMode()): COMMIT
Flush mode, Hibernate Session (Session#getHibernateFlushMode()): MANUAL
```

> Setting @Transactional(readOnly=true) sets the flush mode to MANUAL. For more details on how @Transactional(readOnly=true) works, see **Item 61**.

Setting the flush mode in a Spring Boot application that uses Hibernate JPA can be done globally via application.properties or at the session-level or query-level via dedicated methods. The next sections cover several aspects.

# Global Flush Mode

Setting the flush mode at application-level can be done via the spring.jpa.properties. org.hibernate.flushMode property in application.properties.

- Set flush mode to COMMIT.

The JPA and Hibernate COMMIT flush modes work the same way:

```
spring.jpa.properties.org.hibernate.flushMode=COMMIT
```

In a service-method annotated with @Transactional, the output will be:

```
Flush mode, Hibernate JPA (EntityManager#getFlushMode()): COMMIT
Flush mode, Hibernate JPA (Session#getFlushMode()): COMMIT
Flush mode, Hibernate Session (Session#getHibernateFlushMode()): COMMIT
```

In a service-method annotated with @Transactional(readOnly=true), the output will be:

```
Flush mode, Hibernate JPA (EntityManager#getFlushMode()): COMMIT
Flush mode, Hibernate JPA (Session#getFlushMode()): COMMIT
Flush mode, Hibernate Session (Session#getHibernateFlushMode()): MANUAL
```

Even if you set the COMMIT flush mode explicitly in application. properties, the presence of readOnly=true (which is a signal that the annotated method doesn't contain database write operations) has instructed Spring Boot to switch to the Hibernate-specific, MANUAL flush mode. This means that the setting has no effect in this context. There will be no automatic flush before the transactions commit.

- Set flush mode to ALWAYS.

```
spring.jpa.properties.org.hibernate.flushMode=ALWAYS
```

In a service-method annotated with @Transactional, the output will be:

```
Flush mode, Hibernate JPA (EntityManager#getFlushMode()): AUTO
Flush mode, Hibernate JPA (Session#getFlushMode()): AUTO
Flush mode, Hibernate Session (Session#getHibernateFlushMode()): ALWAYS
```

In a service-method annotated with @Transactional(readOnly=true), the output will be:

```
Flush mode, Hibernate JPA (EntityManager#getFlushMode()): COMMIT
Flush mode, Hibernate JPA (Session#getFlushMode()): COMMIT
Flush mode, Hibernate Session (Session#getHibernateFlushMode()): MANUAL
```

Remember that you need the Hibernate-specific flush mode ALWAYS **only** if you bootstrap Hibernate using the native mechanism and you need to avoid the Hibernate-specific smart AUTO flush. You instruct Hibernate to behave just like setting the JPA `FlushModeType.AUTO` mode (trigger Persistence Context flush prior to any query, including native SQL queries) in order to avoid potential *read-your-writes* inconsistencies.

- Setting the flush mode, MANUAL.

```
spring.jpa.properties.org.hibernate.flushMode=MANUAL
```

In a service-method annotated with @Transactional, the output will be:

```
Flush mode, Hibernate JPA (EntityManager#getFlushMode()): AUTO
Flush mode, Hibernate JPA (Session#getFlushMode()): AUTO
Flush mode, Hibernate Session (Session#getHibernateFlushMode()): AUTO
```

Even if you set the MANUAL flush mode explicitly in `application.properties`, the presence of @Transactional (which is a signal that the annotated method contains database write operations) has instructed Spring Boot to switch to the JPA, AUTO flush mode. This means that the setting has no effect in this context. Pay attention to this aspect, since you may think that there will be no automatic flushing since you disabled it via MANUAL.

In a service-method annotated with @Transactional(readOnly=true), the output will be (so, no automatic flush will take place):

```
Flush mode, Hibernate JPA (EntityManager#getFlushMode()): COMMIT
Flush mode, Hibernate JPA (Session#getFlushMode()): COMMIT
Flush mode, Hibernate Session (Session#getHibernateFlushMode()): MANUAL
```

# Session-Level Flush Mode

You can set a flush mode at session-level—for all queries in the current session—via the EntityManager#setFlushMode(), Session#setFlushMode(), or Session #setHibernateFlushMode() methods. Via EntityManager#setFlushMode() and Session#setFlushMode(), you can set the JPA, FlushModeType.AUTO, or COMMIT flush modes, as in the following example:

```
@Transactional
public void foo() {
    entityManager.setFlushMode(FlushModeType.COMMIT);
    // or
    (entityManager.unwrap(Session.class)).setFlushMode(FlushModeType.COMMIT);
    ...
}
```

Outputs:

```
Flush mode, Hibernate JPA (EntityManager#getFlushMode()): COMMIT
Flush mode, Hibernate JPA (Session#getFlushMode()): COMMIT
Flush mode, Hibernate Session (Session#getHibernateFlushMode()): COMMIT
```

> The same result is obtained for @Transactional(readOnly = true).
> But, since a method annotated with @Transactional(readOnly = true)
> doesn't allow database write operations (causing an SQLException:
> Connection is read-only. Queries leading to data
> modification are not allowed), you don't need flush operations.

To set Hibernate-specific flush modes, such as FlushMode.ALWAYS or MANUAL, you need to rely on Session#setHibernateFlushMode(). It's available starting with Hibernate 5.2. For example, you may want to provide manual flushing in a @Transactional method:

```
@Transactional
public void deleteAuthor() {
```

```
(entityManager.unwrap(Session.class))
    .setHibernateFlushMode(FlushMode.MANUAL);

Author author = authorRepository.findByName("Joana Nimar");

authorRepository.delete(author);

// without explicit call of flush() the author is not deleted
// there is no automatic flush
authorRepository.flush();
}
```

> Pay attention to these types of use cases. While automatic flush is disabled,
> you are responsible for managing flushes manually. Therefore, you are prone
> to forget calling dedicated *flush* methods. Remember to think twice before
> explicitly calling *flush* methods, since this is a *code smell*. This aspect was
> detailed previously in this appendix.

# Query-Level Flush Mode

You can set a flush mode at query-level—therefore only for certain queries in the current
session—via the EntityManager#setFlushMode(), Session#setFlushMode(), or
Session#setHibernateFlushMode() methods. Via EntityManager#setFlushMode() and
Session#setFlushMode() you can set JPA, FlushModeType.AUTO, or COMMIT flush modes,
as in the following example:

```
entityManager.createNativeQuery("DELETE FROM book")
    .setFlushMode(FlushModeType.COMMIT)
    .getSingleResult();

(entityManager.unwrap(Session.class))
    .createNativeQuery("DELETE FROM book")
    .setFlushMode(FlushModeType.COMMIT)
    .getSingleResult();
```

To set session-level Hibernate-specific flush modes, such as FlushMode.ALWAYS or MANUAL, you need to rely on Session#setHibernateFlushMode(). This is available starting with Hibernate 5.2.

```
entityManager.createNativeQuery("SELECT COUNT(*) FROM book")
    .unwrap(org.hibernate.query.Query.class)
    .setHibernateFlushMode(FlushMode.ALWAYS)
    .getSingleResult();

(entityManager.unwrap(Session.class))
    .createNativeQuery("SELECT COUNT(*) FROM book")
    .setHibernateFlushMode(FlushMode.ALWAYS)
    .getSingleResult();
```

Done! Now you know how to deal with flushing tasks.

# APPENDIX I

# Second Level Cache

Besides the non-thread-safe, `Session` bound, Persistence Context (referenced as the First-Level Cache as well), Hibernate ORM comes with a Second Level Cache that is bound to the `SessionFactory` and is thread-safe. Common implementations of the Second Level Cache come from EhCache, Infinispan, Hazelcast, OSCache, and SwarmCache.

Enabling the Second Level Cache can be done in several steps, as follows:

- `hibernate.cache.use_second_level_cache`: true (default)

- `hibernate.cache.provider_class`: Fully-qualified class name of the cache provider

- `hibernate.cache.region.factory_class`: Fully-qualified class name of the `CacheRegionFactory` third-party implementation

- `hibernate.cache.use_reference_entries`. Setting this to true tells Hibernate that, instead of copying entire immutable datasets, Hibernate can now store the reference to the data in the cache. In other words, immutable (`@Immutable`) data objects without any kind of association are not copied into the Second Level Cache. Instead, only references to them are stored

- Point out the entities that should be cached via @Cache: Such as `@Cache(usage = CacheConcurrencyStrategy.READ_WRITE)`

Setting the same synchronization strategy for all entities that should be cached can be done via the `cache.default_cache_concurrency_strategy` configuration property. Further, you can use @Cache to override the synchronization strategy at the entity-level or via @Cacheable (`javax.persistence.Cacheable`).

© Anghel Leonard 2020
A. Leonard, *Spring Boot Persistence Best Practices*, https://doi.org/10.1007/978-1-4842-5626-8

A Second Level Cache stores its entities in a row-level data format. In other words, a Second Level Cache stores its entities in the *hydrated state,* referenced as the *disassembled state.*

You can inspect a cache region via the following method:

```
public void inspectCacheRegion(String region) {
    SecondLevelCacheStatistics stats =
        getSessionFactory().getStatistics()
            .getSecondLevelCacheStatistics(region);

    System.out.println("Region: " + region);            // log region
    System.out.println("Stats: " + stats);              // log stats
    System.out.println("Entries: " + stats.getEntries()); // log entries
}
```

Unwrapping `SessionFactory` via `EntityManager` can be done as follows:

```
EntityManager em;
...
public SessionFactory getSessionFactory() {

    return em.getEntityManagerFactory().unwrap(SessionFactory.class);
}
```

Hibernate's Second Level Cache supports four strategies:

- NONSTRICT_READ_WRITE

- READ_ONLY

- READ_WRITE

- TRANSACTIONAL

# NONSTRICT_READ_WRITE

This strategy is *read-through* and it doesn't use locks. It is useful when data is rarely modified. Its main features are:

- Inserts, updates, and deletes are done via *read-through* strategy

- Updates and deletes remove cache entries from the cache at flush time and after commits

- These actions are valid for entities and collections

# READ_ONLY

This strategy is useful for immutable data. Its main features are:

- Inserting entities is *read-through* if the entity identifier generation strategy is IDENTITY

- Inserting entities is *write-through* if the entity identifier generation strategy is SEQUENCE or TABLE

- Inserting in collections is always *read-through*

- Updating entities/collections is not supported

- Deleting an entity will delete the corresponding cache entries

- Starting with Hibernate 5.1.0, deleting a collection will delete the corresponding CacheEntry, but will not invalidate the CollectionCacheEntry

# READ_WRITE

This strategy uses soft locks to ensure data integrity. It is asynchronous. Moreover, it supports the *write-through* strategy without requiring JTA transactions. Its main features are:

- Inserting entities is *read-through* if the entity identifier generation strategy is IDENTITY

- Inserting entities is *write-through* if the entity identifier generation strategy is SEQUENCE or TABLE

- Inserting in collections is always *read-through*

- Updating entities is *write-through* and follows two steps:

  - At flush time, the cache entry is replaced with a soft lock (this prevents reading uncommitted data)

  - After commit, the soft lock is replaced with the actual value

- Updating a collection requires two steps:

    - At flush time, the cache entry is replaced with a soft lock (this prevents reading uncommitted data)

    - After a commit, you still have a soft lock that will be replaced with the actual value via the *read-through* strategy

- Deleting entities or collections requires two steps:

    - At flush time, the cache entry is replaced with a soft lock (this prevents reading uncommitted data)

    - After a commit, the soft lock is replaced with another lock whose timeout period is further increased (soft locks cannot be rolled back; they have to expire in case of transaction rollback)

# TRANSACTIONAL

This strategy is the proper choice when the data is frequently modified and rolled back. It provides extreme consistency, but is synchronous and requires JTA transactions (e.g., Bitronix). Its main features are:

- Inserting entities is *read-through* if the entity identifier generation strategy is IDENTITY

- Inserting entities is *write-through* if the entity identifier generation strategy is SEQUENCE or TABLE

- Inserting in collections is always *read-through*

- Updating entities or collections follows these steps:

    - At flush time, the entities modifications are performed, while the collections cache regions are invalidated; this is visible only to the current transaction

    - After a commit, the modifications are visible to all transactions (the collections' cache regions remain invalid until read)

- Deleting entities or collections simply removes all the corresponding cache entries

# Query Cache

Besides entities and collections, Hibernate can cache query results. You simply link a search (SELECT) to the returned result.

Enabling query caches can be done via hibernate.cache.use_query_cache=true.

For a query cache, Hibernate uses a *read-through* strategy, so the query is executed and the results are cached in a region named org.hibernate.cache.internal. StandardQueryCache.

For JPQL/HQL, Hibernate uses tablespace changes to orchestrate the invalidation process in order to guarantee strong consistency. Nevertheless, this is not possible with native queries, where Hibernate cannot detect the affected tablespaces. In that case, Hibernate needs to invalidate all entries from the StandardQueryCache region. To avoid this drawback, the native query must explicitly indicate the tablespaces that will be affected via addSynchronizedEntityClass().

> As a rule of thumb, the best results when using query cache can be obtained with immutable entities and entities that are seldom modified.

In a Spring Boot application, you can cache the result of a query via the JPA hint, HINT_ CACHEABLE, as in the following example:

```
@Query("SELECT b FROM Book b WHERE b.price > ?1")
@QueryHints(value = @QueryHint(name = HINT_CACHEABLE, value = "true"))
public List<Book> fetchByPrice(int price);
```

A complete application representing a kickoff with Hibernate and a Second Level Cache using an EhCache provider can be found on GitHub[1].

---

[1]HibernateSpringBootHibernateSLCEhCacheKickoff

Do not confuse Hibernate's Second Level Cache with Spring caching support. Spring caching is enabled via the @EnableCaching annotation and is controlled via a bunch of annotations, such as @Cacheable, @CachePut, @CacheEvict, @CacheConfig, etc. Spring supports from a built-in cache provider that relies on concurrent maps in memory to providers such as EhCache, JCache, Hazelcast, Caffeine, and others. A basic kickoff Spring caching application using EhCache can be found on GitHub[2].

---

[2]HibernateSpringBootSpringCacheEhCacheKickoff

# APPENDIX J

# Tools

At the end of this book, I want to introduce you to several amazing tools.

The first tool, called FlexyPool[1], is used to tune the connection pool parameters for the best performance possible.

The second one is called Hypersistence Optimizer[2] and it automatically detects if you are using JPA and Hibernate properly. As you can see in this article[3] and in this video[4], this tool is very useful for Spring applications as well. A quick setup of this tool starts by adding its Maven dependency:

```
<dependency>
    <groupId>io.hypersistence</groupId>
    <artifactId>hypersistence-optimizer</artifactId>
    <version>${hypersistence-optimizer.version}</version>
</dependency>
```

And, to your integration tests, simply add the following:

```
public void testNoPerformanceIssues() {
    ListEventHandler listEventHandler = new ListEventHandler();

    new HypersistenceOptimizer(
        new JpaConfig(entityManagerFactory())
            .addEventHandler(listEventHandler)
    ).init();

    assertTrue(listEventHandler.getEvents().isEmpty());
}
```

---

[1]https://github.com/vladmihalcea/flexy-pool
[2]https://vladmihalcea.com/hypersistence-optimizer/
[3]https://vladmihalcea.com/spring-petclinic-hypersistence-optimizer/
[4]https://www.youtube.com/watch?reload=9&v=x1nOVct9P2g

© Anghel Leonard 2020
A. Leonard, *Spring Boot Persistence Best Practices*, https://doi.org/10.1007/978-1-4842-5626-8

The third tool is Querydsl[5]. Querydsl is a framework that supports statically type-safe queries via fluent API. Several Spring data modules offer integration with Querydsl via the built-in `QueryDslPredicateExecutor` interface. Feel free to explore this further (a good point to start is with the Spring Data Reference documentation), but not before considering jOOQ as well.

The fourth tool is jOOQ[6]. jOOQ is a Query Builder framework that excels at generating SQL for a wide range of databases (e.g., MySQL, PostgreSQL, Oracle, etc.). Is useful for writing complex and optimized queries, and it supports keyset pagination, streaming, and much more.

The fifth tool is Codota[7]. This tool is available as a plug-in for IntelliJ IDEA, Android Studio, and Eclipse. Its main purpose is to help you use coding via a solid AI. For example, Codota can simplify the usage of the Criteria API.

---

[5]http://www.querydsl.com/
[6]https://www.jooq.org/
[7]https://www.codota.com/

# APPENDIX K

# Hibernate 6

When this book was being written, Hibernate 6 had reached version 6.0.0.Alpha3. Once Hibernate 6 is released, Spring will likely start to add support for it. Therefore, it is advisable to scroll the entire list of goodies (adds, fixes, removes, etc.) available on the Hibernate ORM JIRA page. From this list, I filtered a few things as follows:

- Implement support for the `LIMIT` and `OFFSET` clauses (HHH-11474[1]).

- Split `ResultTransformer` into `TupleTransformer` and `ResultListTransformer` (HHH-11104[2]). It is also in discussion to make the result transformers lambda-friendly (HHH-10581[3]).

- Support for versioned dialect resolution against a pre-configured database name (HHH-13253[4]).

- `ProcedureCall` should implement `AutoCloseable` (HHH-13215[5]).

- Allow for selection of single properties of map key elements (HHH-11668[6]).

- Support constructor expression mixed with other select expressions (HHH-9877[7]).

---

[1]https://hibernate.atlassian.net/browse/HHH-11474
[2]https://hibernate.atlassian.net/browse/HHH-11104
[3]https://hibernate.atlassian.net/browse/HHH-10581
[4]https://hibernate.atlassian.net/browse/HHH-13253
[5]https://hibernate.atlassian.net/browse/HHH-13215
[6]https://hibernate.atlassian.net/browse/HHH-11668
[7]https://hibernate.atlassian.net/browse/HHH-9877

© Anghel Leonard 2020
A. Leonard, *Spring Boot Persistence Best Practices*, https://doi.org/10.1007/978-1-4842-5626-8

- Allow `RevisionTimestamp` to be of type `java.time.LocalDateTime` (HHH-10496[8]).

- Entity joins are not polymorphic (HHH-11437[9]).

**The end!**

---

[8]https://hibernate.atlassian.net/browse/HHH-10496
[9]https://hibernate.atlassian.net/browse/HHH-11437

# Index

## A

Aggregate roots, 119
and() method, 288
AnnotationValueGeneration interface, 580
authorRemove() method, 703
AUTO flush mode, 989
Auto-Generated keys
    Author entity, 479
    getId() method, 480
    JdbcTemplate, 480, 481
    SimpleJdbcInsert, 482

## B

Batch deletes (with associations)
    deleteAllInBatch() method, 336, 343
    deleteAll(Iterable<? extends T>
        entities)
        CascadeType.ALL, 339
        removeBooks() method, 340
        Spring repository, 338
        SQL statements, 339
    deleteAll(Iterable<? extends T>
        entities) method, 344, 345
    deleteInBatch(Iterable<T> entities)
        method, 337, 338, 343, 344
    JDBC URL, 334
    ON DELETE CASCADE, 342
    @OneToMany association, 334
        orphanRemoval, 335

Batching, 297
    deletes
        Author entity, 327
        deleteAllInBatch()
          method, 328
        deleteAll(Iterable<? extends T>
          entities), 331, 332
        delete(T entity) method, 333
        JDBC URL, 326
        Spring Boot, 327
    entities
        BatchExecutor, 319, 321
        CompletableFuture API, 319
        CompletableFuture/JPA, 322
        ExecutorService, 321
    inserts, Spring Boot style
        entities, 300, 301
        implementation (*see* Custom
          implementation)
        saveAll(Iterable<S> entities)
          method, 302, 303
        saveInBatch() method, 307
        testing, 307, 308
Batching updates
    bulk operations
        drawbacks, 324
        Persistence Context, 325
        service-method, 326
        trigger, 324
    JDBC URL, 322

© Anghel Leonard 2020
A. Leonard, *Spring Boot Persistence Best Practices*, https://doi.org/10.1007/978-1-4842-5626-8

# N

# T

Printed in the United States
By Bookmasters